THE ELEGANT AUCTIONEERS

By the same author
THE LIBERATORS

THE ELEGANT

AUCTIONEERS

BY WESLEY TOWNER

Completed by Stephen Varble

HILL & WANG · NEW YORK

A portion of *The Elegant Auctioneers* appeared in the April 1959 issue of *Good Housekeeping* magazine under the title "The Elegant Ones."

1 2 3 4 5 6 7 8 9 10

Publisher's Note

IT WAS SOME FIFTEEN YEARS AGO that Wesley Towner and the publisher approached the late Leslie Hyam of the Parke-Bernet Galleries to ask his cooperation in accomplishing the research for a history of the art auction in America. Hyam did not know Towner, but as a result of that conversation, he agreed to the project and was so impressed by the author that he made available to him, from that time forward until Towner's death in 1968, all the resources of Parke-Bernet.

By Hyam's direction, Towner was given permission to interview not only the galleries' principals but also any of the lesser employees who had information or recollections that could serve the purposes of the book. He was given access to correspondence and records of every kind. Above all, he was made welcome. An immense debt of gratitude is due Miss Mary Vandegrift, Executive Vice-President of the galleries, whose intimate knowledge of obscure sources and people made the way easier. Miss Vandegrift worked tirelessly and made a seemingly impossible task lighter without imposing on the independence of the writer.

Doubtless, had Wesley Towner lived to complete his book, he would have been able properly to acknowledge, in addition to those named above, the very many people who helped him. Besides the staff of the Parke-Bernet Galleries, there were countless libraries, museums, art dealers, and collectors who cooperated in a multitude of ways to trace the many long-forgotten wills, letters, and memoirs of the people who were a significant part of the auction world. It is impossible for the publisher to name all these persons and institutions, but their help did much to make this book.

PUBLISHER'S NOTE

The publisher would like to thank Stephen Varble, who accepted the usually thankless task of completing someone else's work. Wesley Towner had written the great bulk of the book and had done virtually all the research required. Stephen Varble undertook to complete those chapters that bring the book to its conclusion, and in so doing has managed to retain the spirit, the style, and the integrity of what Mr. Towner had done—a difficult challenge indeed.

August, 1970   ARTHUR W. WANG

CONTENTS

CONTENTS

ILLUSTRATIONS

viii

ONE

THE HAMMER AND THE
HEART'S DESIRE

IN THE LATTER PART of the nineteenth century Jules Fleury-Husson, a Parisian writer who signed himself simply Champfleury, published a book entitled *Les Petits Mystères de l'Hôtel des Ventes*. In it he lists sixty helpful hints for collectors addicted to public auctions. Freely translated, a sampling of Champfleury's sardonic counsel reads as follows.

A plain overcoat without furs or trimming is the dress most propitious for making a good strike.

To let yourself be carried away by the tide of bidding is to expect to make your fortune at roulette.

Fortify your nerves by washing in cold water every morning.

Don't irritate your stomach by spicy meals.

A bar of chocolate, or anything sweet, fortifies the system around four o'clock, when the bidding gets hot.

A bottle of smelling salts is indispensable to combat the exhalations of the crowd.

Marriage and collecting, two natural rivals, together make life unbearable. Collectors who marry should abdicate and sell their accumulations.

Every collection that does not offer a panorama ceaselessly renewed palls, like a too faithful wife.

All irrelevant thought has to be sacrificed to the collection. Do not occupy yourself with politics; never go to the theater; forbid yourself to open a book; scorn the pleasures of family; always have ready money in your pocket; arrive each day at the auction rooms at one o'clock, leave at six, return for the evening sales. With this you will have a full life. You will be a perfect collector.

Nearly a hundred years later, and in another country, Champfleury's oblique observations still have a recognizable validity. There are, however, some superficial differences.

At the Parke-Bernet Galleries in New York, which is the *hôtel des ventes* for collectors in America, it is unnecessary for bargain hunters to wear plain clothing. Furs and outfits from the House of Dior are far less conspicuous. As for bringing along a reviving scent, the suggestion is still a good one, though for reasons opposite to those Champfleury had in mind. At painting sales, which often draw a thousand champagne-fed connoisseurs, many of them ladies *en grande toilette,* the odor of Chanel may create a smoglike atmosphere calling for a counterirritant.

The eating and washing habits of modern auction hounds have not been adequately studied. Candy bars are looked upon as the height of vulgarity in the plush halls of the Parke-Bernet, but at jewelry sales the wholesale diamond merchants often chew the butt ends of old cigars; and the late Vitall Benguiat, the bearded rug dealer, used to carry a sausage in his pocket to sustain him in the heat of battle.

Collectors with wives—or husbands—still have domestic problems, but marriage is not frowned upon by modern auctioneers. Substantial profits have been made from sales arising from the exigencies of divorce, an institution that did not flourish conspicuously in the days of Champfleury. There is evidence that collections still pall if not renewed. One café society art lover switched from impressionist painting to Italian primitives and then to the postimpressionists in five years. He had three wives in the same period. If accurate statistics on the wives' fidelity were available, neat correlations could probably be made between the palling of the pictures and the decrease of marital, and increase of extramarital, activity.

It is unlikely that the sacrifice of thought would greatly concern Champfleury in these times. The only known reading matter of the true addict is old auction catalogues. Far from being irrelevant, the publications of the Parke-Bernet Galleries are masterpieces of accuracy and erudition. To digest them thoroughly leaves no time for theater, politics, or any other foolishness.

The Parke-Bernet Galleries today occupy a stately modern building, stretching along a block front on upper Madison Avenue in that section of New York where it is sometimes said the streets are paved with gold. On the white sandstone wall, above the plate glass doors, hangs a mellowing aluminum statue depicting Venus, a torch-bearing lady of alluring chest dimensions, attempting to seduce Manhattan with the wiles of art and culture from overseas. Lusty Manhattan is personified as an earth-bound giant in a semiprone position, half asleep but unmistakably tempted by the charms of the nude goddess hovering overhead.

In 1949, when this million-dollar auction center was erected, an art critic on *The New York Times* expressed some confusion as to

The entrance to the Parke-Bernet Galleries. Above the plate glass doors hangs a mellowing statue of Venus attempting to seduce Manhattan with the wiles of art and culture (PARKE-BERNET GALLERIES).

whether Venus was carrying a torch for art or merely tempting the dazed young man with an overflowing ice cream cone. Another carping observer has remarked that the total effect of the huge ten-ton emblem—which supplants the rakish crimson flag of more plebeian auctions—is faintly suggestive of a misalliance between Dick Tracy and the Statue of Liberty.

Nevertheless, the allegory intended by the sculptor is significant. The art-selling activities of the Parke-Bernet Galleries have certainly stimulated innumerable earth-bound mortals to arise from cultural slumber. Many of them, though by no means all, have been Manhattanites, and the greater part have been giants, at least in a financial sense. It is also true that much of the fuel for what Champfleury used to call "the fire of bidding" has come from overseas, though usually by an indirect route, involving a stopover in the Palladian dwellings of American millionaires. For through the various proud halls occupied by these élite auctioneers and their predecessors for the last three quarters of a century, endless chattels of the wealthy have passed and passed again. Here the Rembrandts of the moguls, and their bedsteads, have been sold, their guns and books and gilded plates, and all those portable treasures of this earth which, portable or no, the dead cannot take with them. Here the forty-two fur coats of Mrs. August Heckscher have been knocked down to the highest bidder, the jewels of Eva Stotesbury, the gold-fitted Rolls-Royce that Edith Rockefeller McCormick drove to the Chicago Opera. Here have ended dreams of grandeur and dynastic hopes—decorations bought for the forty-eight castles Hearst once planned to have, miles of brown canvas from the vanished palaces the robber barons used to build.

Coming in from the somber streets on a winter's afternoon, an uninitiated visitor may well be blinded by the glitter, for there are times when a fair sampling of the wealth of the ages is literally poured into the eleven sumptuous galleries now composing this otherworldly supermarket of the arts. In a single exhibition he may encounter chests and tables carved in the storied days of Chippendale, a Renoir painted by Renoir, jeweled snuffboxes of impregnable nobility, a stained-glass window from a Gothic church. He may marvel at the patina of Chinese bronzes, observe the pictures of Picasso or Juan Gris, fondle glassware from the banquet tables of the Romans. He may try out chairs made for the kings of France or admire the highboys of Philadelphia's triumphant craftsmen. In one illuminated manuscript he may see the life work of a monastery painter. He may covet a necklace fashioned by a Medicean goldsmith, a Romanov's tiara, or sparkling stones that once belonged to Diamond Jim. He may wander among Egyptian statues, amulets, and scarabs, examine medieval arms and armor or Augsburg furniture fashioned out of silver. He may stand before canvases by Rouault, Utrillo, or Toulouse-Lautrec. He may wonder at the sheen of Oriental carpets or be fascinated by a Shakespeare folio. The parade is endless, but this is no conglomerate museum. From the adjoining salesroom floats the crier's ceaseless hollow drone, punctuated by the callers' stentorian responses: "A hundred! Five! A thousand in the rear!" By next week all this will be gone, superseded by a new array.

The parade is endless, for in that dream world where collectors travel, the fire of bidding is kindled not only by the things the great have made. Any thing used or owned or touched by famous persons has had its price; Lillian Russell's golden shoes, her bird cage, and her ruby ring (which turned out to be a fake), the great Caruso's wigs, a chair that Dickens may have sat in, a cup with a potpourri (since evaporated) prepared by Marie Antoinette. Lincoln's ax handle brought $800 in 1951, and Washington's boot box, a few years earlier, considerably more; a lock of Napoleon's hair once made $285; and in 1930, Francis P. Garvan paid $9,800 for an anvil used by Paul Revere.

Posthumous glory, as well as the whims of eccentric collectors, is reflected in auction prices. Once upon a time a Scottish plowman neglected his farm for the joy of making songs. In payment for the best of his work Robert Burns received a shawl for his wife, a picture, and £5 sterling. Wretched and abandoned, he died, in 1796, while trying to negotiate a meager loan to avoid spending his last days in jail. But 145 years later, in the glittering salon of the Parke-Bernet, the bidding ran up to $15,500 for a copy of *The Scots Musical Museum* containing "Auld Lang Syne" in Burns's handwriting. The miseries of Vincent van Gogh would have been immeasurably alleviated if he had been paid the $19,000 his *Portrait of Mlle. Ravoux* fetched in 1939; Edgar Allan Poe could have lived much of his life in peace on the current price of just one copy of *Al Aaraaf, Tamerlane, and Minor Poems*; and the unknown artist who painted *Wall Street in 1820* would doubtless have been pleased to hear the hammer fall at $13,500 on the charming unschooled picture he did not even sign.

History itself is often sold in fragments on the auction block. In 1949 the final draft of the Gettysburg Address fell to Oscar B. Cintas, a Cuban sugar baron, for $54,000. The "Olive Branch" Petition, which might have averted the American Revolution if George III had bothered to read it, made $53,000 for its British owner and now reposes in the New York Public Library. The yellowed slip of paper on which Francis Scott Key scribbled "The Star-Spangled Banner," a deed signed by John Alden on the *Mayflower*, a plaintive letter from John Brown—all things that have their luster from the past—also have their price at the Parke-Bernet, the ghosts along with the gems of vanished ages, countless vestiges of Once Upon a Time, and yesterday, and long ago.

Behind this romantic surface lies a twofold saga; on the one hand, the long dispute over who shall possess the fine things of this earth, and on the other, the even more rigorous controversy over who shall sell them. Since its alliance with Sotheby's of London in August 1964, Parke-Bernet might be considered an almost invincible institution. Annual sales now total close to $100 million. Prior to its alliance with Sotheby's, Parke-Bernet had to brave the perils of a contingent market, the fickle development of American tastes, and the ferocious competition that was necessary to appease the diverse desires of auction hounds with such diligence that the galleries eventually stood alone, the last supermarket of its kind. The Parke-Bernet Galleries, before joining with Sotheby's, encompassed not only the dramatic annals of its own relatively short existence but also those of New York's two great auction houses of the past, the American Art Association and the Anderson Galleries. Once bitter rivals, and then, in 1929, combined, the AAA and the Anderson Galleries are now mere corporate titles listed among the negative assets of the Parke-Bernet.

The formation of the Parke-Bernet Galleries resulted from a secession from the AAA–AG led by Major Hiram H. Parke in 1937. Today, even after the affiliation with the London house, a few of the staff members who accompanied the Major in his rebellion against the mother company still remain active at the galleries, having prosperously survived the dangers of an occupation wherein the dog-eat-dog competition has always been rough and has even, on occasion, been bloody.

Hiram Haney Parke himself was something of a miracle of survival. Unquestionably the most remarkable auctioneer this country has ever known, he outlived most of the men who were bold enough to challenge his supremacy, and also saw a number of them come to bitter ends. Three of the vanquished committed suicide. Some retreated into less precarious lines of work. Others landed in the bankruptcy courts. One notorious pair of tyros succeeded only in involving themselves in a gruesome murder plot. Parke, however, showed no battle scars even at his death on April 1, 1959. He abdicated his throne-like rostrum in early 1950 in favor of younger associates, his three protégés—Leslie A. Hyam, Louis J. Marion, and Mary Vandegrift—who would rule the galleries until the alliance with Sotheby's. But for thirty years the Major managed to preside over most of the great carnivals of public spending staged in the United States, first under the auspices of the American Art Association, then during its ill-starred merger with the Anderson Galleries, and finally with the rebel company named after Otto Bernet and the Major himself.

Bernet, whose name the public invariably mispronounces, with a French ending prompted by the Parisian elegance of the galleries, was in reality a Swiss-German with the stolid traits of a capable burgomaster. His career ran parallel to Parke's, but it was Bernet's fate to conduct the people's auctions, to disperse the endless pictures of grazing sheep and wading cows, the second-class Virgins, saints, and martyrs, the furniture in reproduction, the objects of art unworthy to be labeled *objets d'art*. Meanwhile, Parke sold the masterpieces. The two partners together, appearing in their derby hats at the mansion of some deceased Maecenas whose possessions might be worthy of an auction, called to mind nothing so much as the pastor and the undertaker paying their respectful visits in each other's company. On the marble doorstep the portly Bernet would rub his hands in a gesture combining eagerness and unction, while Parke, handsome and magnificently composed, would assume the superior role of family counselor. Wry observers used to say that Bernet, who was stronger on the homely virtues, would present the flowers while Parke carried the sales contract ready to be signed. A more literal version is that the contract fitted snugly in the pocket of Parke's dark-blue jacket, and on suitable occasions, both partners would arrive with competing bouquets. For there was a certain rivalry between them.

Aside, however, from whatever ludicrous aspects may be inherent in the profession, Major Parke's reputation as the dean of auctioneers was based on solid and eminently respectable achievement. His title, a hangover from a term of service in the Pennsylvania National Guard, was something of a misnomer. Far from having a propensity for military show, the Major, in his later years at any rate, managed to bring to a traditionally suspect calling a judgelike quality seldom achieved by judges. His mercenary incantation was less the empty ranting of a huckster than a form of impartial arbitration, somehow mystically attuned to the special character of the object in the spotlight on the stage. In the presence of worthy spoils and a crowded house, with his ivory hammer poised in a fateful gesture, he was capable of drawing to himself a kind of grandeur not unlike that of the treasure on the block, as if the gleam of mellow wood could rub off on his person, or the glitter of crystal stay reflected in his steel-blue eyes.

One antique dealer, who followed the public sales of two continents for more than forty years, described him as "a historical precedent."

"Few people understand the exquisite artistry of Hiram Parke's performance," he went on to say, "the grace, breeding, and hidden force which molds a pack of rapacious wolves into a pliable audience. And it is all done in such a charming way. With his judicial eye fixed upon them, those cold-faced harpies back down, ashamed of the paltry prices they have come prepared to pay. For how can you steal right in front of the Lord Chief Justice, especially when he has such a good opinion of you?"

The old antique dealer's hard view of auction-goers was from the seller's standpoint. Probably the majority of the Parke-Bernet clients deserved no such sweeping condemnation, but it is true that even the most ruthless bargain hunters responded to the infectious enthusiasm that Parke projected to his public, a high opinion not only of the object on the block but of its potential buyers as well. He increased their self-esteem, and their bids increased accordingly. Collectors in the gay, free-spending twenties took pleasure in telling each other how the Major had induced them to pay twice what they had intended for their Romneys and Corots. Parke became as popular as a matinee idol. Attendance at important sales had to be limited to ticket holders, and even then, there was frequently a stampede.

Withal, the clients of this leviathan among secondhand stores— buyers and sellers, the living and the dead—present a life-size portrait of the tyranny of possessions. Hardly a conspicuous family name identified with big money in America can be found missing from the rosters. For there is an inevitability about the natural flux of possessions that in the end draws the tangible relics of the mighty to such a clearinghouse, as the sea heaves driftwood on the endless shore. Affluent citizens who do not appear as buyers are almost certain to show up on the lists of sellers. Even the miserly Hetty Green made auction history in the end, though during her lifetime she built no palace and spent no money on the folderols that delighted her contemporaries.

Once the richest woman in the world, Wall Street's lady Croesus sometimes wandered homeless from state to state, living in Hoboken rooming houses or boarding with acquaintances in order to avoid paying taxes. On one occasion she climbed a ladder in her wedding dress to fix a hole in the roof of one of her tenant houses, thus saving the half-day's wages she would otherwise have had to pay a carpenter. When Hetty Green died she left an incalculable fortune in a joint trust for her son and daughter, with the hope that, with it, they would perpetuate a dynasty. Her son, Colonel E. H. R. Green, was no black sheep. He had been carefully trained in his mother's Spartan precepts, and he followed them with no apparent deviations. A lonely, thick-necked, round-faced man, he dedicated his life to conserving Hetty's colossal wealth; and when he died, in 1936, he relinquished the fortune practically intact to his sister, Mrs. Sylvia Wilks.

Mrs. Wilks lived on to a ripe old age, spending her time listening to the radio and discussing the baseball scores with elevator boys. However, when she died, in 1951, leaving odd sums of money to people whose names had caught her fancy in the newspapers, it was found that there had been one slight breach in the stark walls of the Green austerity. Among the assets of the family estate were found bureau drawer after bureau drawer overflowing with forgotten jewels, for Hetty's model son, it was disclosed, had had a secret vice.

In moments of unaccountable extravagance the homely moon-faced Colonel had bought diamonds in quantities that would have done credit to a 52nd Street Lothario. Often, in the cold dawn of a winter's morning, he would allow a certain commercial jeweler to ride with him down to Wall Street in a cab. En route, with a minimum of time wasted on conversation, Green would pick out a gaudy trinket from the jewel merchant's hastily assembled stock. Stuffing the necklace or bracelet into his overcoat pocket, he would dream, perhaps, of dangling it in front of some imaginary showgirl in the adventurous evening when the day's pay had been made. Sometimes, if the diamond mood came on him during holidays, he would summon the merchant, with his suitcase, to Palm Beach. But no one ever wore the jewels. In the end, Mrs. Wilks's executors sent them to the Parke-Bernet, where the stones, though stuck in settings that might have been designed by Woolworth's artisans, brought $390,000.

Such stoic simplicity as that of the Green family is a quality rarely linked with the names on the Parke-Bernet rosters. Most of the active clients are marked by a greater flamboyance; for such a market place is, above all else, the mecca of collectors, the Jockey Club of connoisseurs with the gleam of acquisition shining strongly in their eyes.

During the late fifties its glamorous exhibitions were also the haunt of decorators, who were sometimes brash females with modish hats, sometimes handsome young men with Continental manners, and occasionally persons of extravagent ways and indefinite gender who expressed themselves volubly in a kind of New England cockney dialect. The decorators—or experts—were often accompanied by their clients, sleek ladies with jeweled lorgnettes, whose exteriors appeared to have been created with the same dedicated craftsmanship as some of the rarefied objects on display. The clients, in turn, were accompanied by indulgent cavaliers and often also brought dogs—Afghan hounds or well-coiffed poodles, which they frequently addressed in French.

One fortunate canine habitué of the recent past, named Zita, had a platinum collar, set with a solitary emerald, which her master had insured for $3,000. Zita was a regular at Parke-Bernet exhibits and something of a dowager in dog circles of the collecting world. She had her own tiny calling cards, and once a year her master—a man, incidentally, who had risen from the ranks—sent out engraved invitations to her birthday party. Apparently Zita, like many of her human contemporaries of the female sex, looked upon an auction as more fun than a matinee. Naturally she ignored the sign, "No Dogs Allowed in the Salesroom," that insensitive authorities had tacked to a velvet curtain at the entrance to the auditorium.

Suave habitués, however, form only one constellation in the crowd, sometimes two thousand strong, that swarms into a noteworthy Parke-Bernet show on a single day. Less conspicuous are the thrifty shoppers, the studious collectors, the responsible art dealers who have arrived at a place where a kind of lofty honesty pays better than deception. Rubbing elbows with these esteemed gentlemen are the musty keepers of musty antiquity shops, the proprietors of dubious galleries, the shrewd speculators in everything old, or rare, or merely secondhand. They study their catalogues like horse players poring over scratch sheets, making copious notes in the margins with the yellow stubs of old lead pencils. Their eyes, behind heavy dark-rimmed lenses, are swift and sharp in their appraisals, the eyes of men who live by wit and well-seized opportunity. They pretend to be oblivious, or even contemptuous, of their more worldly competitors, but their ears are open, ever alert to pick up a clue as to the wants of some potential client.

Some of them dream of detecting the lost Rembrandt, the painting underneath the painting, the mistake in the catalogue, the Raphael obscured by time and dust and varnish. Others are interested in school pictures (properly catalogued as such) that can be converted into Gilbert Stuarts with a little time and skill. In between are the cunning but not wholly fraudulent tradesmen who buy the large canvases on which Renoir used to make sketches and doodles in his arthritic old age, when he was unable to paint. These, cut up and elegantly framed, are in great demand in circles where a Renoir and a swimming pool are the twin badges of success.

The lowest of these fringe traders bear careful watching. A certain amount of thievery is to be expected, but there are also elaborate tricks. One well-known antiquarian used to have a special talent for making surreptitious pencil marks on the inner surfaces of Chinese porcelains. The marks, indistinguishable from cracks, would reduce the price of K'ang Hsi bowls to almost nothing, and the sly old dealer would bid them in at the auction while his perfectionist rivals held their noses in the air. After soap and water had restored them to their pristine state, his ill-gotten porcelains would bring handsome prices at his highly respected Fifth Avenue shop.

Several years ago it was estimated that an average auction crowd is composed roughly of one-third dealers, one-third collectors, and one-third casuals, or sightseers. Of the total attendance, about one person in ten is actually a bidder. But these statistics are extremely variable. In any case, the line between sightseer and potential buyer cannot be clearly drawn. Strangers or part-time hounds who do not want to be known as collectors often appear to be mere onlookers while bidding on the most expensive lots by some elaborate system of signals or relayed bids. At the other extreme, casual buyers not at all averse to publicity will sometimes breeze into the more illustrious sales and carry off the prize with a flourish for which they are given awed credit in the newspapers.

Billy Rose was known to do this, causing a flare of trumpets in quarters where the activities of serious collectors are seldom reported. Rose was given to decorating the walls of his midtown honky-tonk with contemporary paintings that, if noticed at all, tended to make the yokels titter. An even more sensational contribution to culture for the masses was his permanent exhibit of surreal canvases by Salvador Dali in the lower lounge of the Ziegfeld Theatre. The Dalis may have been successful in stimulating conversation among the patrons of musical shows on their way to the lavatory, but how much they enhanced their owner's reputation as a connoisseur is another question. On the safer side, Rose, turning from the ridiculous to the sublime, whizzed over to the Parke-Bernet in December 1942 and bought Frans Hals's *The Reverend Caspar Sibelius, Preacher at Deventer.* The *Preacher* had once sold for $45,000 at an American Art Association auction. Rose paid $30,000, so it was possible to speak offhandedly of his having got a bargain.

Three years later at the auction of Isabel Van Wie Willys' celebrated collection, the bustling showman solidified his position as a man with a taste for the Dutch masters by bidding $75,000 for Rembrandt's *A Pilgrim at Prayer*. Rose modestly said he paid too much for his Rembrandt. With the air of an old-timer who might have whiled away many a listless evening at picture sales, he magnanimously gave Major Parke credit for mesmerizing him into a spendthrift coma. But the Rembrandt paid off in publicity. According to the tabloid accounts of Rose's marital battles a few years later, it was *A Pilgrim at Prayer* that his wife used to bar the door when she decided not to let him come home again. Reporters obligingly gave the impression that the place was full of Rembrandts, and readers of the *Daily News* clucked their tongues in admiration at such tangible evidence of higher culture along Broadway.

Casual buyers, flushed with excess profits or possessed of a new inheritance, have been known to develop auction fever. Starting with a single picture or piece of bric-a-brac, they may gradually succumb to a virulent disease similar to that of addicts around the gaming tables at Reno or Monte Carlo. And the addiction is frequently as hazardous. There are those who, though ruined by a tyrannical passion for possessions, never miss a sale. There is no longer anything they can buy, but like inveterate gamblers, they return to watch the others play. There are men who have abandoned all human society for incunabula or English porcelains. There are bargain hunters who, lacking human outlets for affection, cram their houses with useless furnishings picked up at random in the sales. There are accumulators who have no place to put the things they buy, but leave them at the galleries for a time (ignoring all the regulations about removal) and then sell them and use the money to buy more. There are soft-gray-eyed elderly ladies, once Gotham heiresses, now penurious, who day after day make the rounds of auction houses, always in white shoes, always toting a huge handbag crammed with lists and photographs of the things they cannot buy. And there are disillusioned gentlemen whose hearts beat faster in the presence of the auctioneer, for whom his endless drone and the hammer's click are like opium or alcohol.

On the other hand, many munificent buyers, having better things to do, never attend the sales, but come only to the exhibits and leave their bids to be executed *in absentia*. Oil barons in Texas and movie lords in Hollywood send their offers by mail or telephone, after poring over illustrated catalogues, as some of their less affluent forebears studied the utilitarian objects pictured by Sears Roebuck and Montgomery Ward.

Among the most whimsical of auction hounds, at least in the prestige-seeking camp, is the habitual underbidder, the man who, like Prufrock, may ". . . swell a progress, start a scene or two," but seldom buys anything. Token bidders occupy a chimerical position somewhere between the nonbuying addict and the big-buying client. They must be wealthy enough to be able actually to buy expensive art. Otherwise no one will take them seriously. A token bidder of prominence can impress more than just the spectators around him, for if he has the courage to stay in the running long enough, he will often be mentioned in the newspapers as having "engaged in a bidding contest with several other collectors, which finally resolved into a duel between [so and so, the buyer] and [so and so, the underbidder]."

Reputations have been built in this way, but the game is fraught with hazard.

Greed and the follies of the self-important are not, however, the only qualities demonstrated in this febrile playground of the wealthy. Casual shoppers, the proudlings, the bargain hunters, and the foolish addicts, the guileful traders, the boastful neophytes and nearly rich pretenders do not fairly epitomize the patrons attracted by such an overwhelming confluence of things. There are collectors of a very different species, for whom auction halls are truly a happy hunting ground. There are the gentlemen in button shoes whose sun sets and rises on ivory miniatures or illuminated manuscripts. There are the gentle antiquarians who follow no fashion and know no reverence for price, the quiet accumulators who, weary of the present, or finding little satisfaction in the uses of this world, seek some greater reality in the tangible relics of the past. Often they do not even pretend to be connoisseurs, but many of them have a flair for the exquisite and fabulous which more stylish collectors sometimes lack. Year in and year out, in these sumptuous galleries, gnarled hands can be seen stroking palace carpets from the empires of the East. Old eyes with the luminosity of youth peer at fine bindings through magnifying glasses. Strange figures wander here and dream, lonely shoppers in the market place of Once Upon a Time. For the past is many things to many people. It is the light in Botticelli's paintings, a golden snuffbox from the glorious days of France, a first edition of *Alice's Adventures Underground*. It is the pallid bust of Pallas and the melancholy Raven's "Nevermore." It is a blue angel of the della Robbias, a letter written by Keats to Fanny Brawne, or the hundred figures carved in a nutshell by a Middle Ages monk.

Of these unsung and unpretentious clients Grandpa Springs was perhaps the most endearing. Eli B. Springs, according to the stories he used to tell, was one of seven brothers, born at Cornucopia Plantation, Hancock County, Georgia. The father of these seven boys was a Confederate officer in the Civil War. When the war was over, he counted up what remained of his fortune and found he had $7,000. In a gesture of Biblical simplicity, he gave each son $1,000 and told him he was on his own. The sons went forth, and in due course, all but one became millionaires. The lone prodigal was provided for in true brotherly fashion by the other six. Eli was one of those with the Midas touch. First he moved north and opened a grocery store

An endearing, unpretentious collector, Eli (Grandpa) Springs bought whatever
he fell in love with. His greatest joy was sitting in his brownstone house—
crowded with porcelains, prints, paintings—admiring his treasures.

in Charlotte, North Carolina. In time, the little business developed
into a wholesale one, and then into the largest grocery firm in the
state. Eli was elected mayor of Charlotte. He became president of
the Atlantic, Tennessee and Ohio Railroad, and later a director of
the Southern Railway. Having exhausted the possibilities of North
Carolina, he moved to New York, where his younger brother Richard was in the cotton brokerage business. Eli became a trader on the
Cotton Exchange and made millions in shrewd speculations. For the
most part, the Springs family money went back into cotton mills, but
with some of his winnings, Eli bought Manhattan real estate. Soon a
large part of West 47th Street belonged to him, and there he lived,
at number 25, surrounded by office buildings and the wholesale
jewelry market. Eli never married. In his narrow brownstone house,
a few steps from the glitter of Times Square, he lived alone with
Nils, his Swedish butler. Nils was something of a genius at his call-

ing: he drove the car, kept the house, watched the bills, and took care of all his master's goods. Of these there gradually came to be an overwhelming number.

The addiction to auctions began around 1918, when Eli Springs was in his middle sixties, at a time when his brother Richard was buying color prints and sets of books in handsome bindings. One day Richard brought Eli into the Anderson Galleries with him. "My brother wants to get a few nice books," Richard said to Tony Bade. (Anthony N. Bade became a mainstay at the Parke-Bernet's book department, but originally he was an Anderson man.) A collection of French memoirs in translation happened to be on exhibition. Bade showed him the volumes. The old man put on his spectacles and stayed all afternoon, lost in the intrigues of courtiers and courtesans of the gallant days of France. It was a period he had always wanted to read about, he said. When he left, his face was glowing with the first symptoms of the auction fever. The next night he came to the sale and bid in not only the French memoirs but many other lots as well—English sporting books, books on fashions, and one on bullbaiting, an unbelievably cruel British pastime that was prohibited by act of Parliament in 1835. For his illustrated text on that gruesome subject he cheerfully paid $1,800.

From that time on, an auction-room friendship developed between Tony Bade and Uncle Eli—Bade called him Uncle Eli, but he came to be affectionately known as Grandpa Springs. As a client, Uncle Eli was made in heaven. In the beginning he bought illustrated books on every subject that happened to interest him. Then came the color prints. With his catalogue in one hand, he would thumb through all the prints on exhibition and check the ones he liked—this one and that one, and the next one and the next. In the end, half of the sale would be checked off. "When are they being sold? . . . I'll be there!" he would call over his shoulder gaily as he hurried off, as likely as not to attend some stern directors' meeting. When the night of the sale came, he would be there, sitting in the front row, right under the rostrum. If Bade was the auctioneer, Springs would just look up at him for as long as he wanted to keep on bidding, which was usually longer than anyone else.

But Bade would not allow him to buy a poor impression of a print or any article that was second-rate. "Wait until a good one comes along," he would say. "There will be other sales." Grandpa Springs appreciated this. He was an infinitely kind old man, but he was no fool, and he was not unaware of the pitfalls for the novice in the collecting world. Bade, whose ingenuous qualities have ingratiated him with far more hard-boiled clients, inevitably became Uncle Eli's boy.

At first, Springs would lie in bed, in an upper room of his old brownstone house, reading his rare editions of obscure books long forgotten by everyone but bibliophiles and scholars. His eyes would sparkle with excitement over color prints of far-off places and other eras. When he acquired Francis Wheatley's thirteen *Cries of London*—one of the two complete sets in this country, for which he paid nearly $10,000—he retired into the English eighteenth century for a week.

"Turnips and carrots, ho!" he would call down to Nils, and chuckle with delight. Or Nils would have to mount the stairs to observe some new-found detail in *Milk Below Maids* or *Hot Spice Gingerbread, Smoking Hot*.

A New Love Song, only ha'penny a piece . . . *Round and Sound, Five Pence a Pound, Duke cherries* . . . *Old Chairs to Mend* . . . *Sweet China Oranges, sweet China* . . . *Do you want any Matches* . . . *Knives, Scissors, and Razors to Grind*—all of them Springs fingered over and over, glowing at the enchanting sounds and colors, and perhaps even the smells, of the London streets of long ago.

The books and prints were only a beginning, however. They were fascinating, but so were a thousand other things. As time went on, Grandpa Springs retired from active business. His main occupation became collecting. But his was no ordinary hoarder's passion. Unlike Hearst, who frequently competed with him at auctions, Springs had no warehouses, no unpacked boxes. He hired no vaults in which to store his spoils. Everything he owned had to be displayed where he could see it and meditate upon it. He had become enamored of the world's pretty things late in life, and perhaps there would not be much time. He had no great pride in his possessions, no belief that their acquisition gave him stature or importance. But gradually a kind of mania enveloped him. He would come into the Anderson Galleries and bid on anything that caught his eye: a full-rigged carved ivory ship under glass, old Dutch drawings, Rowlandson water colors, the continents allegorically represented by porcelain figures. He bought no junk, but as it happened, the most expensive art then being sold held no glamour for him. The ages of the Church, in great favor at the time, were not for Grandpa Springs. In his house there were no Savonarola chairs removed from gloomy monasteries, no Virgins, no Madonnas, not a single tortured saint or beatific angel. But he had an eye for subtle color, and it was fated that he should fall in love with porcelains.

A thousand years of triumphant accomplishment in the transformation of the humble clay were represented in the washbaskets of pottery Nils carted home from the auctions Grandpa Springs attended. Into the cluttered house on 47th Street went superb examples from the ancient Chinese dynasties, single-color vases with a marvelous purity of form, vases that shone like jewels with a plethora of decoration. But Grandpa cherished equally the European imitations of the eighteenth century, the lustrous productions of Meissen, Sèvres, Chelsea, Bow, and Dr. Wall of Worcester. Most of all, perhaps, he loved the delightful French images of court gallants and ladies, no longer imitative, but truly marvels of ceramic art, exuding a gaiety of spirit and a brilliance of color that made their new owner's eyes glisten with delight. For another mood, one that may have been reminiscent of his rural childhood, there were the idealized English rustics, wonderful folk characters portrayed in humorous poses or storytelling groups. Even more than in the prints, Grandpa could see in his variety of porcelain objects a panorama of what to him was beautiful in life. For hours in the evenings he would sit and contemplate his bright toys, feeling their wondrous texture with his aging hands, watching their gala colors refract the yellow light.

Grandpa Springs grew to love an auction as a gambler loves a race. Though his first passion was for the things themselves, it came to the point where the chase was even more important than the prize. Competition with the others thrilled him, for Grandpa was a trader and a gambler in his heart. One time when Frank Crocker was his opponent the bidding ran up to unusually sporting heights, but neither bidder would give in. Crocker, who was no mean trader himself, was sitting directly behind Springs. At a certain point, Crocker leaned forward and tapped Grandpa on the shoulder.

"I'll match you for it," he offered.

A funny little grin spread over Springs's determined face, but he shook his head. "No," he said, "let's fight it out."

Another time, during a sale of George Morland engravings, a girl at the other side of the room was bidding against him. Uncle Eli loved George Morland, but he was nothing if not chivalrous. The rare print on the block—*Morning, or the Higglers Preparing for Market*—went up to $2,600. When Bade knocked it down to Springs, the girl burst into tears. Grandpa called an usher.

"Go over and tell her she can have it," he said. "With my compliments," he added. Then he looked down shyly at his catalogue to see what the next race had to offer.

At one sale of French and English prints, for which the total intake was $25,000, Grandpa's bill was $23,000. All these prints Bade had framed for him in a uniform way, surrounded by black glass mats. Shelves had to be built, glass cupboards for the porcelains installed between the dining room and butler's pantry. Where to put the things became a problem. Every inch of space in the four floors of the narrow house was covered. And still more came in. In the morning, after a sale, when Nils returned from the gallery with his washbasket laden, he would telephone Bade in despair.

"Come down to dinner this evening, please, and figure out where to put the things."

Then, when all the walls were covered, Grandpa fell in love with painting. He had bought paintings before, about seventy in all, but they were mostly the story pictures that had been popular in his youth, genre scenes interesting to Grandpa for their subject matter, but for the most part, inconsequential as works of art. Now, in 1926, the C. K. G. Billings sale came up, one of Major Parke's carnival affairs at the American Art Association. Uncle Eli seldom went to auctions at the American Art, mainly because of his attachment for Tony Bade. The Anderson Galleries, being more intimate and not as showy, was better suited to Grandpa's unpretentious ways. But on one of his daily rambles he dropped in at the American Art to have a look at Billings' pictures.

Cornelius Kingsley Garrison Billings, yachtsman, horse breeder, financier, and builder of skyscrapers, was, like Grandpa Springs, a romantic. Unlike Springs, however, Billings inherited his basic fortune, his father having been one of the manipulators of Chicago's harassed public utilities. With his enormous wealth, C. K. G. founded, among other enterprises, the Union Carbide and Carbon Corporation, financed the Pierre Hotel, and made himself one of the most colorful figures in horse racing. He was part owner of the

Jamaica race track. Lou Dillon, the Harvester, and the great trotter Uhlan were his; and he also had a piece of the famous Kentucky Derby winner Omar Khayyam.

As a site for his stable he bought Fort Tryon of Revolutionary War fame. The stable, when completed, was inaugurated by a dinner party, complete with livery stable horses, held at Sherry's.

Subsequently, Billings bought more land and built a lodge to go with the stable, establishing himself like a feudal lord on what was virtually a huge country estate surrounded by New York City. Finally, he built Fort Tryon Hall, a Louis XIV castle with the Hudson and the Harlem River Speedway for a moat. The castle alone cost $2 million. When it was finished, having at least one other empire of comparable magnificence, on Long Island, Billings sold the whole works to John D. Rockefeller, Jr. Rockefeller gave the park to the city and the castle now houses the Cloisters, the medieval branch of the Metropolitan Museum. But while Billings occupied Fort Tryon Hall its walls were decorated with thirty-one major paintings of the nineteeth-century romantic school.

At the last stage in his peregrinations, when C. K. G. pulled up stakes and went to live in Santa Barbara, he took the thirty-one pictures with him, but when he had established himself in what was euphemistically called a California "bungalow," he felt restricted. Blaming his lack of elbow room on the burden of being surrounded by so many romantic paintings, he trundled them into a chartered railway car, and with a reliable man to keep them company, sent them on the long trek back to New York to be sold at auction.

When Grandpa Springs saw Billings' much-touted pictures hanging in splendor in the great galleries of the American Art Association he hankered to possess a few. It is beside the question whether a responsible critic could be found nowadays to list many of C. K. G.'s romantic pictures as masterpieces. They were masterpieces then. In 1926, Corot and the British landscapists, the Dutch marine artists and cattle painters, had not yet palled upon the chic, if somewhat unsophisticated, crowd of picture fanciers that jammed the auctions. Grandpa Springs was not chic, but he was also no snob. Corot had been the most popular romantic painter ever sponsored by the American public, and Grandpa, too, thought Corot was beautiful. Standing before *Landscape with Lake and Ruin*, the old man was overcome with lyrical emotion. The French countryside enchanted him, and the great peace of Barbizon came over him. Yes, Corot was his dish, and so were Théodore Rousseau, Daubigny, Dupré, and Diaz.

Grandpa Springs was ill the night of the Billings sale and could not attend, which was just as well, perhaps, for the crush was so great at the American Art Association that two persons were injured in the fracas. Every seat was filled, every box crowded; the aisles and doorways were packed to capacity; and two hundred people milled around outside with no chance of getting in. Ordinarily, if he could not have the thrill of competing in person, Grandpa would not buy, but the Billings paintings were irresistible. He commissioned Otto Bernet to bid for him, and the next morning a third of Billings' renowned collection was delivered to the house on 47th Street. There were three Corots—including his famous *La Charrette de Grès,* which cost $27,000—and seven other works besides. Grandpa's bill was $153,300.

Somehow Tony Bade fitted the new acquisitions into spaces on the cluttered walls, though with some misgivings, for never before had Uncle Eli been seriously unfaithful to the Anderson Galleries. What was more, the animosity between the two houses, at that time, was so strong that loyal employees of one establishment would not even walk on the sidewalk in front of the other. The Anderson had no famous Barbizons for sale, however, and Bade, a man of conscience, could not honestly advise Grandpa against buying the latest objects of his heart's desire. He could only hope that such lapses would not become habitual.

But no sooner had the new pictures been hung than a disaster occurred in the Springs household. Nils telephoned Bade one afternoon in panic. "Come down! Come down! Something terrible has happened!"

Bade rushed to 47th Street in a cab. In the house there was the sound of woe, and in the dining room, he found a dreadful turmoil. The newest porcelains had been crowded into the top of the largest cabinet. They were heavy, and the glass shelf had collapsed. Grandpa sat at the table brokenhearted. All his lovely children lay there, murdered, on the floor.

Everything was broken, English, Chinese, French alike; for the top shelf had fallen on the one beneath, the second shelf upon the third, and so on, like a house of cards. The door, forced open by the weight, was swinging on its hinges. On the floor, surrounded by the scrambled porcelain, Nils fished around helplessly, trying to fit to-gether pieces—a Chinese rose, a Chelsea plume, a pair of soft-paste breeches, a Worcester queen with a headless consort, a Sèvres gallipot with a pair of Meissen cherubs for a handle.

Bade went to the telephone and called Miki, a Japanese repairman. "Jump in a taxi and get over here," he said, as if the matter were one of life and death.

Miki giggled when he saw the mess. He was very small, and he giggled irrepressibly, from head to foot. Uncle Eli glared at him, annoyed.

"Give me a washbasket," Miki ordered when he could control his merriment. Nils fetched the basket. Miki shoveled all the pieces into it. "I take. I fix," he said, and grinning happily, he went away.

In the course of time, much time, Miki reappeared. He had done an amazing job. All the pieces had been separated by nationality, and the figures were intact. The cement and glue were barely visible, and all the chips had been restored. A casual observer would not have noticed that there were imperfections. Once more Uncle Eli could sit at dinner and bask in the luster of his porcelains as the lamplight touched upon their many hues and shades. But they were never quite the same, for meanwhile the old man had been to many auctions.

He had filled the shelves temporarily vacated by the porcelains with a variety of treasures: miniature paintings, carvings out of crystal, jade, and coral. He had bought two hundred ivories depicting the vicissitudes of life among the birds and animals, as well as pleas-ing episodes in human history. He had consoled himself with the art of the jeweler, with golden boxes set with semiprecious stones, many watches, many costly bibelots from the reign of Louis XV through the time of Napoleon I. These rococo objects were tremendously expensive, but there were scores of them, for as time went on, Uncle Eli's silent bidding took on a frantic quality, as if he sensed the need to hurry.

Grandpa loved good food, but as health began to fail, he had to forgo many of the pleasures of the flesh. Collecting was his one remaining passion. Nevertheless, every Christmas Eve he had an eggnog party for all his many friends, for his Wall Street cronies, for his nieces and his nephews, for the old men who were dropping off now, one by one. But there were new faces too—a tradesman whose honest ways had caught Grandpa's fancy, an actress in the latest play, a vanquished bidder from the auction sales—and of course, there was Tony Bade.

Grandpa would make the eggnog himself, in a regal Chinese bowl, adding the flavor slowly to bring the final brew to the perfection he remembered from his plantation days. In the last years it was Nils who did the tasting, for Grandpa could no longer drink. He would stand from two o'clock to eight, alternately stirring and ladling for his guests, but he could not touch a drop himself. Surrounded by his treasures from the corners of the earth, Grandpa Springs, in the fading Christmas twilight, took on for his friends some of the wondrous mystery and glow that lives in childhood recollections of festival and peace. His baubles, though, were real, his tinsel carved from quartz and lapis lazuli, his yuletide ornaments fashioned by impassioned artists through many ages of the creativity of man. In the soft light reflected from the crystals, the old gambler and the trader disappeared, transformed by time and fortune into a gallant figure touched by what is beautiful and good.

One day his brother Richard came to visit Tony Bade. "Eli is sick," he said. "He is concerned about his property. He thinks someone may be stealing it. What do you suggest?"

"We have records," Bade told him. "There are bills for everything he has bought."

"Then come down," Richard said, "and make an inventory. I'll arrange about the cost."

Bade, with Charles Retz, another Anderson man, got out the old catalogues and vouchers. With a stenographer, they went down to 47th Street and spent a week. A piece of ambergris was gone, Grandpa told them from the bed he could not leave, an ivory minia-ture, a portrait of the Queen of Greece. But when the week was over, it was found that not a scrap was missing, not a teacup or a snuffbox. Not a golden bird had flown. Nils, the faithful butler, wept with relief, and Grandpa for the moment was convinced. Bade totaled the figures on the sheets. Grandpa's purchases at auction came to a little less than $700,000.

His treasure was intact, but an old man was dying. His nights were spent in hallucinations that he was poor. By day he dreamed that thieves were rampant in his house. Although he was eighty-one years old, his doctors sent him to a hospital for an operation. It was an emergency, they said. But there was no real emergency for Grandpa Springs. Within a few days he was dead.

The house without its master lost its strange reality. It was a bulging warehouse now, of labyrinthian proportions, a museum that had lost its sense. Its riches were overpowering, the problem overwhelming, for the old man had been unspecific in his will. Often he had spoken to Bade about making a division of the things he loved among his heirs. Where to begin was a hard decision, one to be put off and finally avoided. Once or twice he started. His mahogany sideboard should go to his nephew Richard Junior, he wrote in the will disposing of his ordinary wealth. In a last minute codicil, he remembered that he wanted the same nephew to have the portraits of his father and mother. He bequeathed a dozen silver plates and half a dozen saltcellars to a sister in Charlotte. But that was all. There were no doubt unspoken reasons why Grandpa Springs could not divide his life up into lists. Nieces and nephews had their own ways of living, a newer generation would not cherish these treasures as he had done, foolishly perhaps, but in his old man's way. Blood relations though they were, they had not battled for these things at auction; they had not known the thrill of winning, or the separate meaning each pretty bauble had. His death had not been sudden. There was ample time to plan and reason and revise. But it was better, he must have thought, to leave to fate the toys he could no longer keep. For dying, in all its details, was a boring ritual for Grandpa Springs. He knew too well the joy of life.

In the end, there was an auction. Back to the galleries—the American Art–Anderson now, for the two had been combined—went the washbaskets of porcelains, the paintings from Fort Tryon Hall. But there was no great haggling for them now. The bubble of easy money had vanished, and men once as rich as Springs had been selling apples in the street. It was in vain for Major Parke to wheedle, scold, and threaten. His eloquence was lost as he read the distinguished pedigrees of the pictures that had brought an old man so much pleasure. Romance was cheap in 1934. Grandpa's treasures, including the porcelains Miki had so neatly mended, brought a little more than a third of the money they had cost. But even in a better market, the measure of their past worth could never have been decimated into cash.

TWO

MADISON SQUARE

THE AMERICAN ART ASSOCIATION, the older of the two auction galleries now perpetuated by the Parke-Bernet, rose to fame in the Elegant Eighties on the tide of what was presumed to be America's great cultural awakening. The business of amassing fortunes had left a vacuum the new élite were determined to fill as quickly as possible. Robber barons had robbed enough to feel the urge to spend excess profits by some means that would secure their status as lords of creation. Merchant princes and industrial tycoons were building palatial mansions the more forcefully to demonstrate their princeliness—dwellings so lavishly and improbably conceived and furnished that their owners, poorly acclimated to such marmoreal surroundings, sometimes retreated to the servants' quarters to read the stock market reports.

Lesser moguls imitated the greater and richer moguls above them. It was an era of watered stocks and magnificent humbug, a time when snobbery could be a full-time job, when Mrs. Astor, sweating under a load of diamonds as heavy as a hod of coal, received the chosen from a regal dais in her sheep-and-cow-lined drawing room and fed them from golden plates, which, to the disenchantment of a nation of idolators, an iconoclast appraiser listed as only gilt after her demise in 1908. Boston and Philadelphia, once rival centers of the pseudo-aristocracy, struggled to keep up but fell behind. The West was beyond the pale. The South sulked and licked its wounds. The New World Babylon was unquestionably New York. The ropes of pearls, the swans swimming in the middle of banquet tables, the gowns that cost more than a workingman could make in a year, were part of a fabulosity benumbing to the perceptions of ordinary citizens, and yet somehow reassuring as proof of the possible fulfillment of the great American dream.

In the decades following the Civil War, art collecting, the ultimate luxury, proof that a man could afford the utterly inutile, came into vogue with the virulence of an epidemic. Picture galleries became as common as diamond stomachers, connoisseurs as numerous as Wall Street bulls and bears. After the Philadelphia Centennial of 1876 everybody with anything resembling a fortune developed a mania for Meissonier and marble. Where there had been only thrifty storekeepers, art dealers sprang up and prospered. Where there had been only railway shares, now came canvas worth its weight in gold.

What was on the canvas was the prefabricated painting decreed official by the industrial bourgeoisie of nineteenth-century Europe, particularly by the French Académie des Beaux Arts. Railway kings and bankers with no previous disposition to art appreciation divested themselves of hundreds of thousands at a clip for little scenes from the kitchen of life or for huge canvases illustrating storied events in history with a cameralike precision that was looked upon as genius.

If one wished to be in the higher bracket of art lovers, one engaged a dealer-expert—as William H. Vanderbilt had employed Samuel P. Avery to supervise the gathering of the collection said to be "the finest on this continent." A really big collector would go abroad in company with an agent who could introduce him to the French Salon painters. That way the prospective investor could choose his subjects and leave orders. He might even require a few alterations, before the work was done, to bring the end result closer to his own view of what was true to life. With the finished product the patron received a letter that served at once as a certificate of authenticity and an expression of the painter's respectful sentiments. When he had an adequate number of letters and matching pictures installed in his mansion the art lover held receptions and received the plaudits of his business and social peers.

Many of Vanderbilt's pictures were custom painted. The details—the number of armorial banners, the breadth of the staircase, the size of the crowd, how many goblets were on the table, and so on—depended not so much on the whim of the artist as on the pocketbook of the patron. On his estate at Bougival, Jean Léon Gérôme would receive suppliant millionaires from America with a graciousness that ebbed and flowed according to his foreknowledge of their bank accounts. Laden with every honor that could befall a French official painter, Commander of the Legion of Honor, his chest a vivid patchwork of medals from the Salons, Gérôme himself, in his later days, looked like a retired cavalry officer in constant readiness to head one of the triumphal processions he depicted. After he had unlocked his cabinet and shown the bronze and silver trophies of his valorous painting campaigns, he would outline a picture at so many francs per personage, so much for the entourage, so much for each plume in the king's resplendent hat. And it would all come out exactly as he promised.

Jean Louis Ernest Meissonier was even more demanding, for by choice, he would have painted no one but Napoleon. A very small man himself, and passionately devoted to horsemanship, he had long ago achieved a pleasant state of identification with his hero. When moved to produce a masterwork, he strewed his garden with flour to simulate the snow on Napoleon's retreat from Moscow. Sometimes, in the courtyard of his mansion in Poissy, the narcissistic little painter could be observed in the full noonday sun, dressed in the uniform of the Imperial Grenadier Guards, mounted on a saddle attached to a bench before a long mirror, engaged in making a minute study of his own figure, to be grafted later onto the face of the Little Corporal. Nevertheless, when William H. Vanderbilt—who did not care much for Napoleon—laid $40,000 on the table, Meissonier graciously contracted to reproduce a dazzling throng of society folk from the court of Louis XIII, and for a fee of $188,000, the master of soulless painting agreed to concoct for Vanderbilt seven smaller pictures of scrupulous exactitude, recalling the splendor of other knightly eras.

Since there was a certain limitation on the supply, everybody could not readily acquire a Meissonier, a Gérôme, and a Bouguereau, but there were scores of Salon painters almost as popular, and in some cases, even more demanding. Alexandre Cabanel was perhaps the most imperious of all, for he was painter-in-ordinary to numerous budding dynasties. When, in company with Samuel P. Avery, Vanderbilt called on him in his sumptuous studio in the Rue de Vigny the ultrastylish artist received the applicant with a cold smile and a courtly manner, as if he himself might have been the ambassador from the monied world.

Cabanel's beard was tonsured to unreal perfection, his dress unbearably meticulous. He could paint a masterpiece without soiling his coat, he said; and he could afford to be no more than routinely impressed by a lonely, dyspeptic railway magnate reaching for the stars with $200 million in his bank account. At the moment, he was engaged in rendering his fourth portrait of Mr. W. H. Mackay, the gold miner, but he would enter Vanderbilt's name on the waiting list—if Mr. Avery would be so kind as to spell it for him. As soon as the press of business allowed, he would be happy to supply an original composition on some pleasantly remote historic topic; but alas, time flew, and as everyone was aware, not only the gold miners but half the ladies of America were beating at his door to have their charms immortalized by his suave and sympathetic brush.

Fortunately, however, history and archaeology could be had without waiting on the favors of the painters who imagined themselves the contemporary Leonardos. Even a modest mansion could boast a note of classical antiquity in the form of a Lawrence Alma-Tadema, perhaps one of his architectural reconstructions of the Roman baths—with the bathers, if any, modestly draped in splendid togas.

Anyone who had taken the grand tour was almost sure to be in the market for a Félix Ziem. Ziem specialized in scenes of Venice and Constantinople, but he lived in Montmartre, high above the Paris rooftops, in a little castle at the top of a long staircase with the prow of a gilded gondola for a newel post. He seldom descended into the world, for the world came to him. It was his custom to let down a basket for supplies and messages. Often his views of the Grand Canal could be seen floating through the air at the end of a rope before taking the boat for America, where they sold like hot cakes to a public possessing the wealth of Venice but, alas! no gondolas, and only imitation palaces.

War was a specialty with many of the white-haired boys of the Académie, and no fraternity of brush wielders was neater or more scrupulous about including all the bald particulars. Edouard Detaille never tired of acting out in pantomime his own firsthand experiences in the Franco-Prussian war. He had grasped the musket, donned the uniform, and sailed into the fray, he said, alternately shooting at the enemy and sketching the bloody scenes around him. Almost with a twist of the wrist, he could reproduce these exploits for the military-minded client. If the patron was sufficiently wealthy, Detaille would even arrange a preview in the courtyard of his mansion, revealing in advance the horrors he was prepared to paint to taste. He would strew the ground with mannequins to represent the corpses, while living models in uniform and grease paint posed as active combatants. The stirring madness of battle could be reproduced to whatever extent the client wished: the smoke, the roar of guns, the multicolored shells bursting like flowers in the air—and over all, by way of irony, "the blessed light of heaven coming from a smiling sky."

The hesitant client was no doubt gratified to have this rough idea of how the thing would look, but Alphonse Marie de Neuville, whose studio was also crammed with guns, helmets, cannon balls and daggers, could lay claim to an even more theatrical technique. De Neuville was a temperamental fellow. He required his models, a pair of lusty veterans who also doubled as cook and valet, to discharge a running fire of musketry to keep him in the mood while painting battle pieces—an overhead expense that increased the cost along with the verisimilitude.

War was all right in its way, but what the captains of industry really liked was a touch of behind-the-scenes romance. Intimate scenes in the private lives of artists intrigued them: artists with lace at the wrists making love to models between masterpieces, artists in Louis XVI costumes painting saucy courtesans, artists with brush in hand lolling in silken waistcoats on the sumptuous divans of old-time Paris studios.

Bathing, whether in Rome or elsewhere, was a favorite subject: people going to the bath, coming from the bath, or better still, people at the bath, as in Vibert's *Le Bain des Dames* or Bouguereau's *The Bather*.

Pictures about money—with titles such as *The Lucky Lottery Ticket, Love and Avarice,* and *Paying the Rent*—had an irresistible appeal; so did such pithy allegories as Bouguereau's *Hesitating Between Love and Riches*—a study of a maiden caught by doubt in a tableau suggesting that the projector might have stopped at the decisive moment in one of the early silent movies. But most comforting of all was the subject of the humble poor.

Cottages and cottage folk lined the walls of almost every grand ballroom. Stock figures, produced in degrading imitation of the great genre painters of the seventeenth century, posed with enviable placidity in a modulated paradise where *The Battle of Life* (a title often used) was really all in fun. It was a discreet world, where the skies were dependably blue or gray, where people cried without suffering, and where, though the motto was Keep Smiling, no one ever really laughed. Old men fed the cat; babies gurgled in their high chairs; fishermen gossiped beside the fire; thankful peasant families bowed their heads in prayer before the porridge bowl.

Enchanted as they were by the fabled contentment of the poor, the giants of metropolitan finance were almost equally drawn to the idylls of the gentle herd. Rosa Bonheur—of whom a cynic once remarked, "She hugged the taxidermist too closely all her life and loafed too little by the way"—did a land-office business in horses, fighting bulls, hounds, and even friendly lions, but she had a number of stiff competitors when it came to sheep and cattle.

Anton Mauve could turn out a fine, healthy flock—with dog and shepherd or without. He also sometimes painted cows, but the champion exponent of bovine charm was Emile van Marcke. Van Marcke lived on a farm in Normandy, where he raised fat, pampered herds solely to function as models for the stream of canvases that flowed from his unimpassioned brush like printed fabrics from a mill. His cows never ventured forth in inclement weather, their serenity was never interrupted by any discomfort greater than a poetic dewfall. He painted them, one of his admirers wrote, "as lost in endless content, gravely chewing the cud of comfort, standing hoof-deep in lush grasses under the quietude of wide-spreading heavens."

Inspired by this great upsurge of negotiable culture, a young auctioneer named Thomas Kirby came over from Philadelphia to New York in 1876 to try his hand at selling art. In 1858—according to his later recollections—when Thomas Ellis Kirby was twelve years old, he had "cried and begged" to go to work for M. Thomas & Sons, Philadelphia auctioneers. Moses Thomas was a stern old Quaker, penurious, but reputed to possess the cardinal virtues conspicuous for their absence in other followers of the trade. He had taken to the rostrum a half century earlier to get rid of a mountainous overstock of Dr. Johnson's *Dictionary* (which he had been foolhardy enough to publish in a four-volume edition), and stayed to form the largest auction and commission house in Philadelphia. Moved by the would-be Dickensian hero's entreaties, he gave the boy a job, but no salary—because he was so young and had the added disadvantage of being small for his age. The hours were from eight in the morning to ten o'clock at night. After a few months, the old man called young Kirby into his office. "Tommy," he said, "I like the way thou hath served me. From now on thy salary will be doubled."

Despite this unprofitable beginning, Kirby stayed thirteen years, learning to appraise everything from grandfather clocks to stocks and bonds and "genuine oil paintings." In 1871, still somewhat undersize, he emerged from the Thomas firm a full-fledged auctioneer, formed

Thomas E. Kirby at seventy-five. In 1883, at thirty-seven, he headed the AAA and, for decades, dominated the auction scene in America.

a partnership, which promptly failed, and spent another five years in Philadelphia crying miscellaneous sales for Thomas Birch & Son. But the commodity in which Thomas Kirby saw the greatest future was art. He had an instinct for expensive things, and the dazzling Philadelphia Centennial convinced him more than ever that he was wasting his talents hawking books, real estate, and secondhand farm machinery.

Kirby was thirty when he came to New York with his wife and two children. He opened his first art auction room in Clinton Hall, on Astor Place at 8th Street, and while waiting for picture galleries to disperse, took a job crying book sales for George A. Leavitt & Company. He had had eighteen years of what amounted to apprenticeship, and in his heart there was a boundless lust for fame and fortune.

He could hardly have chosen a more unpromising means to either. With the exception of book auctioneers—those jocular nineteenth-century littérateurs, whose integrity was avouched by the low price and high cerebral content of their wares—auctioneers were carnival showmen schooled in artifice, blood brothers to the fairground pitchman and at least cousins to the salesman of gold bricks.

Out on the plains many an itinerant "Colonel" was conducting vendues to trap the foolish. Colonel J. P. Gutelius, "the converted auctioneer," cried sales, according to his own testimony, "for twenty-two years without Christ and ten in the service of the Master." Self-styled one of the wickedest men who ever lived in Oklahoma, he was happily "converted" one rainy night by a comet seen through a black umbrella. Thereafter Gutelius combined selling and soul saving, practicing both from the same platform. When bids were slow, he would roll his eyes to heaven and roar, "O Lord, if I could only turn this sale into a revival!" Apparently that was what he often did, for in his book *High Lights on Auctioneering,* he claimed to have won nearly two thousand souls to Christ—though, he added succinctly, "only Eternity will tell."

Gutelius boasted that he could sell things utterly unsaleable in the ordinary course of business: oil paintings, rusty farm machinery, blind horses, Japanese table covers. The best method, he said, was to love children, be kind to mothers, and entertain the multitude. The last he accomplished with free lunch and a Wild West show boasting six cowboys and an outlaw horse known to have killed a number of men.

Above all, he "loved the light in the faces of the crowd." After his conversion, he opened all auctions with a prayer, asking for grace, wisdom, and the physical power to conduct a clean sale.

The effect on the multitude was wonderful, he said. Standing on a wagon end covered with a red blanket, wearing a white shirt and a cowboy hat, using a spring bell for a hammer, he performed in what must have been a grand manner. "O, we'll never say good-bye in Heaven," he would sing out at the top of his lungs as a crippled horse was being led to the block. Sometimes he employed two Negro shouters to render "The Holy City" for background effect, but more often he managed the whole show himself:

Thirtika, makita five, makita five. . . . O let's take the glory road, Folks! I got the five, makita six. . . . Six! Thank you, Lord, for the blessings of the day. The six . . . the seven . . . and the lady makes it eight! Thank you, Mother. I'll ask Him to give you a double portion of grace. Nine . . . nine. . . . There's the nine! I'll put you down on my prayer list, Brother! Now let's hear the forty! O come angel band and bear me to my home! Makita fortika, Lord! Fortika . . . fortika . . . fortika . . .

Gutelius' book—over which he said he "prayed that God would bless the name of same"—was addressed to readers having a compulsion to go into the selling racket. The most succinct advice he had to give, even after his conversion, was to "put in a few real good ones so nobody can say you're selling only the cheap ones." This, and keep talking—entertain the multitude.

The metropolitan contemporaries of Gutelius—though most of them could entertain the multitude without recourse to religion—were bound by no sterner code of ethics. Throughout the first three quarters of the century memorials, petitions, and reports were written, in strong language, condemning auction rooms as academies of trick and chicanery. The New York Anti-auction Committee issued a flood of pamphlets on "this painful subject," adopting as its standard themes "death, dissipation and bankruptcy," all of which were said to be embodied in "the ruinous tendency of auctioneering." Back in the early days the committee came up with some arresting bits of information. "It is found," one of the pamphlets stated,

that the evils which afflict commerce and palsy enterprise have been produced not by the downfall of Napoleon's empire, but by thirty-six auctioneers residing in the city of New York. Their zeal has ripened into crime, their genius into profligacy, shedding lustre upon error. Speculation, deprived of its accustomed opportunities for adventure, now shows itself in sales at auction, which are fashionable machines of polite and licensed swindling, producing all the pernicious effects of gambling.

By the third quarter of the century the committee had grown more realistic, if no more resigned:

It will be in vain for the government to trust to the virtue of the people to resist the allurements held out to tempt them into the arms of some one of the numerous and increasing progeny of auction-marts. Already the respectable classes congregate by the hundreds before the knights of the hammer. Here they change into a sort of Ishmaelites. Bad passions ascend and they are unfit for the society of other men. . . . There is little doubt that auctioneering will, unless returned to the hell which commissioned it, root out in the end every seed of intellectual polish from the mind and change us back to rank Barbarians.

There was a grain of truth in the Anti-auction Committee's jeremiads. Once or twice at painting sales the respectable classes had assumed the guise of Ishmaelites. As far back as 1863 a collection of pictures imported by John Wolfe, a semiprofessional connoisseur with numerous rich relatives, had brought $114,000—a sum never before achieved and not to be surpassed for thirteen years.

In 1876—the year of Thomas Kirby's migration from Philadelphia—the private collection of John Taylor Johnston came to the auction block. Johnston had been one of New York's pioneer art lovers. The Metropolitan Museum was in part his inspiration, and he was its first president. He had built the first marble house in New York, at the southwest corner of 8th Street and Fifth Avenue. Above the stable in the rear he maintained a picture gallery which was open to the public one day a week. When "by reason of the misfortunes of the owner," the gallery's contents had to be sold, the auction was held under the direction of Samuel P. Avery, William .H. Vanderbilt's adviser, and the most influential art dealer in New York.

So eagerly did the respectable classes congregate that they filled Chickering Hall, the plush new eighteen-hundred-seat concert auditorium opened the year before on Fifth Avenue at the northwest corner of 18th Street. The auction was conducted by Robert Somerville, a knight of the hammer who normally held forth at 74 University Place. Titans came from all over the country to bid for what *The Art Journal* called "the most important private collection of Artworks in the United States." James Gordon Bennett paid $11,500 for

Meissonier's *Soldiers at Cards*. Alfred Pell of Boston bought Turner's *The Slave Ship* for $10,000. There was cheering for Niagara Falls, as depicted by F. E. Church; W. W. Corcoran of Washington got the huge watery canvas for $12,500. The total for 323 lots came to $327,792.

This was the kind of auction Thomas Kirby had in mind. But misfortune did not strike men like John Taylor Johnston every day. For five years Kirby struggled along crying Leavitt's book sales and occasionally a nondescript art sale on his own. Then, in 1881, he found, as he said, "a capitalist."

James F. Sutton, Kirby's capitalist, was a son-in-law of R. H. Macy, proprietor of the one-price dry goods bazaar down on 14th Street. Macy's son-in-law leaned to the more aesthetic side of trade. He was a retailer of "the finest Chinese and Japanese art objects and curios," supplied by a trader named R. Austin Robertson, who traveled in the Orient. But Sutton had a diversity of interests. Like Kirby, he held the conviction that there was money to be made in art, particularly in American art—which, so far as he could see, was just about as good as the imported.

In 1880 Sutton had gone into partnership with an art dealer named Rufus E. Moore. Moore and Sutton, with Sutton as capitalist, took over a gallery at 6 East 23rd Street, on the south side of Madison Square. The white-faced, irregular-shaped studio building, owned by William Kurtz, a prosperous photographer, was the last word in luxury. The Moore and Sutton salesroom—which they named the American Art Gallery—was small (46 by 36 feet), but easily the most sumptuous commercial art gallery in New York. Sutton leased some extra rooms and broke through a wall into the adjoining building at the corner of Broadway and 23rd Street, later to become the Bartholdi Hotel, rendezvous of the sporting set from Madison Square Garden. In those rooms Moore and Sutton displayed the Oriental objects imported by Austin Robertson, while in the main gallery they endeavored to persuade the rich to decorate their walls with canvases by native painters.

They were not overrun with customers. All of Sutton's enterprises tended to accumulate overstocks, and with a view to disposing of what otherwise could not be sold, Sutton and the Oriental trader Robertson supplied the capital for the firm of Thomas E. Kirby & Company at 845 Broadway. Kirby conducted ear-splitting auctions on behalf of the overstocks, but for the most part, his eloquence was lost on sly traders who stood around with their hats on and refused to allow themselves to be bid up by the house. Autumn landscapes and Ming porcelains "hundreds of years old" were sometimes knocked down to legitimate bidders, but just as often they were bought in and put back on display at the American Art Gallery. Moore and Sutton failed to prosper, and in the fall of 1882 Kirby was given the job of liquidating the partnership altogether. A reporter, writing in *The Art Amateur* for December 1882, described the sale in the tone commonly inspired by such events:

> The auction of the American pictures and Oriental bric-a-brac, lately in the American Art Galleries, belonging to the dissolved firm of Moore and Sutton, afforded unusual opportunities for the judicious buyer. I noticed Mr. Moore himself at Kirby's, securing scores of valuable objects, sometimes at considerably less than half of what they cost. Several paintings, which had been sold more than once before at much better prices without leaving the auction rooms, this time went in earnest at prices which, out of regard for the feelings of the artists, I refrain from quoting.

The breaking up of Moore and Sutton was a fortuitous event for Thomas E. Kirby. Sutton was stuck with the lease on the Madison Square premises and Robertson, who had just returned heavy laden from the Orient, was stuck with a plethora of Ming vases. They needed a man of Kirby's stripe, and they offered to take him into partnership with them. But Sutton had had his fill of flimsy enterprise. He was willing to provide the capital for a resuscitated American Art Gallery, but if Kirby wanted to run it, he would have to give up auctioneering.

Kirby wanted very much to run it. He, too, was tired of flimsy enterprise, and fancied himself in the role of impresario. With the years, he had acquired a dogmatic air and an abundance of swagger. His complexion was ruddy. His eyes were dark, almost black, and mercilessly sharp. His pointed beard, then called an imperial, after the Emperor Louis Napoleon, gave him the look of a small, waspish field marshal. In repose, with his wing collar, his cutaway and striped trousers, he might have been taken for a lecturer on bugs or interesting fossils, or even, possibly, for what he imagined himself to be—an art expert. But Kirby was seldom in repose. In the rostrum he had the voice of a ringmaster, and out of it he was a fierce little man super-charged with egomania.

And so, with the air of an old trouper taking leave of a fond public, Kirby announced to whomever it may have concerned that he was retiring from the auction hall forever. He was only thirty-seven at the time, but he was weary, he said. In fact, only the year before, he had been compelled to visit Europe to recover his health. The luxury and stability of Madison Square would be a salubrious change for a well-scarred veteran of the red flag and the ivory hammer.

Madison Square today has the air of a blighted neighborhood left to stagnate in the midst of a city whose god is change. A merchandising center for gift-shoppe novelties occupies the space where once stood the epicurean Brunswick Hotel. Quick lunch counters have long since replaced Delmonico's, the Saint James, and the Albemarle. The glassy nudity of Bouguereau's 12-by-8-foot *Nymphs and Satyr* above the Hoffman House bar has titillated no young blade or old roué for almost sixty years. Canfield's gambling house, Amen Corner, the old Fifth Avenue Hotel with its Republicans and once-astonishing verti-cal railway—these and a hundred other wonders have given way to cut-rate clothing stores and manufactories of plastic novelties.

The labyrinthine time-grayed buildings that once housed the American Art Gallery escaped change until several years ago. They were destroyed as a result of a fire that took place on October 17, 1966, and today 6 East 23rd Street is the site of a parking lot. Now, every quarter of an hour, the leaden bells in the tower of a life insurance building bong out their doleful admonition—time is pass-ing . . . time is passing—disturbing the pigeons and the dreams of the uninsured in the grubby, half-forgotten park. It is a superfluous warning in a corner of the city where time has already passed. Flora M'Flimsey of Madison Square ("a hundred dresses and nothing to wear") has lived uptown these half a hundred years.

But in 1883 Madison Square, more than any other spot in the United States, was the focal point of cosmopolitan society. Here, Broadway and Fifth Avenue met and crossed, literally and figura-tively. The Flatiron Building, which was to convert the district into one of mundane commerce, had not yet been built; nor had Madison Square Garden, which was to bring with it the circus and the masses, and even worse, the scandalous murder of Stanford White, its architect. Stretching to the south on Broadway were the fashionable stores of the Ladies' Mile. To the north, on Fifth Avenue, were the houses of the solid wealthy. At 34th Street stood the pallid marble palace built by A. T. Stewart, and across the way, where the Empire State Building now stands, the sober, brown extravagances of the Astor family. Higher up on Fifth Avenue the new châteaux of the Vanderbilts were beginning to appear. But the city above 59th Street was mainly inhabited by citizens more interested in groceries than art. Far to the north, the ground where the Parke-Bernet stands today was the site of charming country houses surrounded by linden and magnolia trees. Goats roamed the empty lots in herds. Madison Avenue so far uptown was not even paved. The golden streets were all down Kirby's way.

From the wide bow windows of 6 East 23rd Street the reformed auctioneer could look out on the new Farragut Statue by Augustus Saint-Gaudens on its handsome base by Stanford White, or at the celebrated new triangular horse trough erected by Miss Olivia Egleston Phelps Stokes; but also—and what was probably more appealing—he could peer through leafless winter trees at the gray stone mansion of Catharine Lorillard Wolfe, the Lady Bountiful of Madison Square (so-called for her benevolence to newsboys, churches, horses, artists, drunkards, and others worthy or unfortunate), whose lofty walls contained a patchwork of "modern paintings" said to be "the finest on this continent." Or, closer still to his new stand, Kirby could rest his glance on the home of the famous lawyer S. L. M. Barlow at 1 Madison Avenue, with its art treasures and library of American historical documents said to be "the finest in this country." Albeit these superlatives were lightly given, nowhere in a city that was mostly brown and ugly was there a vista of urbanity and wealth to compare with the one the eye could sweep from the Barlow mansion on the east to the luminous hotel façades that formed a three-block stretch of Paris on the west. The south side of the square, where trade had crept discreetly in, was afflicted with the brownstone blight, but one oasis stood out—the white stone building with its exquisite French portico leading to the premises over which the hawk-eyed, bombastic Thomas Kirby came to preside.

Stimulated by such green pastures, Kirby took over the American Art Gallery with a zest remarkable for a man of delicate constitution.

The first step was to erase the stigma of failure left by the old firm of Moore and Sutton. The more dubious Chinese objects were relegated to a back parlor; the main gallery was lavishly redecorated and hung with the works of unappreciated artists; and overnight—with due pronouncements of principle and platform—what had been a place of common trade was reconstituted as an association "for the Encouragement and Promotion of American Art."

In almost any other social climate the effort to encourage and promote a few nondescript American pictures would have passed unnoticed. But Kirby had an extraordinary instinct for the pulsebeat of the times. Never before had New York known such a blossoming of culture as in the year 1883. It was the year the Metropolitan Opera opened, with boxes sufficient to accommodate such opulent music lovers as J. Pierpont Morgan, the Rockefellers, Vanderbilts, Goulds, Huntingtons, and Whitneys, previously banned as *nouveaux riches* by the hereditary members of the old Academy of Music. It was the year when American craftsmanship received unprecedented recognition by the appointment of Messrs. Tiffany and Company of Union Square as imperial and royal jewelers to Queen Victoria, the Emperor of Russia, the Sultan of Turkey, and numerous other regal mainstays of the jewelry business. It was the year when the opening of the Brooklyn Bridge was all but overshadowed by Mrs. William K. Vanderbilt's Corinthian costume ball, designed to obliterate Mrs. Astor and her old-fashioned sheep-and-cow-lined drawing room socially and open Mrs. William K.'s new $3-million palace, copied from not one but two Renaissance châteaux.

Richard Morris Hunt's setting for the social onslaught of the overweight and overwhelmingly aggressive Mrs. Vanderbilt (formerly Miss Alva Smith of Mobile, Alabama, and subsequently Mrs. O. H. P. Belmont, mistress of far grander and more expensive palaces) was described in *Harper's Bazaar* as "one of the most gorgeous houses of modern times," with a staircase "wide enough for a troop of cavalry to ride up," and an alabaster bathtub. For the great ball traditionally credited with ushering in the age of elegance 140 dressmakers were said to have worked day and night for five weeks. Mrs. William K. herself appeared as a Venetian princess after a painting by Cabanel, with live doves flitting about her head. Mrs. Cornelius Vanderbilt came as the electric light, an effect achieved by the liberal use of diamonds and white satin. Richard Morris Hunt, architect of the castle, came disguised as Cimabue, "the father of Italian painting." Possibly few of the guests were familiar with the legend of Cimabue's discovery of Giotto as a shepherd boy of ten in the pastures of Vespignano drawing the figure of a lamb with coal on a slate. But Hunt's fancy dress excursion into the more obscure reaches of Renaissance lore was no idle gesture. It was intended, as the papers faithfully reported, to epitomize the burgeoning of cultural awareness, the death of provincialism and the birth of enlightenment among the new élite.

Also reported in connection with the historic Vanderbilt housewarming was the rumor "so disagreeable, even so frightful . . . that the communists meant to attack the house and sack it, with its immeasurable wealth of jewelry, bric-a-brac, silver and gold and *objets d'art*." Nothing happened, however. Later in the year Mrs. W. K. appeared with all her jewelry intact at the reception given by her father-in-law, William H. Vanderbilt, to show off his one hundred new French paintings. Unhappily, she was overshadowed on that occasion by Mrs. Chauncey Depew, who wore a petticoat of red satin caught up with real birds of red and black plumage.

All this had nothing much to do with American art. According to customs collection figures for the previous year, paintings to the value of $2,853,535 had been purchased in Europe and brought to this country. "These plain, business-like figures," *Frank Leslie's Illustrated Newspaper* observed, "confirm the statement now frequently heard that art is being more generally recognized as our wealth increases." This was true, but it was also a fact that many people hated to see all that good money go out of the country. Playing on their sentiments, the proprietors of the new American Art Association put up signs warning visitors that since no foreign artist had more than two hands, many of those imported pictures must perforce be fake. Nobody paid any attention to the signs, but Kirby had surmised correctly that the time was ripe for artistic enterprise furbelowed with national conscience. Caught in the great upsurge of culture, the respectable classes liked to meet and show enthusiasm for the finer things. There was no more respectable cause than native art, and no more agreeable atmosphere in which to espouse it than the sumptuously refurbished galleries on Madison Square.

The Art Amateur, which only a few months earlier had written so disparagingly of the Moore and Sutton auction, now called the Art

Association's first exhibition the most notable event of the season, confining its critical remarks to a passing statement that in one of the pictures "some cows in the foreground were too badly drawn even for use in a landscape." On the whole, the press was favorable, though it was usual to make some complaint about the cattle. After viewing a later exhibition, the *Tribune* reporter wrote, "When Mr. Carleton Wiggins announces that his study of a cow was painted in an hour's time, who would be unkind enough to wish that the hour had been otherwise employed?"

The defects in the cows notwithstanding, art lovers now came in carriages and paid twenty-five cents admission to see the same sort of pictures that they had declined to view for nothing in the Moore and Sutton gallery. Opera hats and canes (which had to be left at the desk) were as prevalent as the sheep in the landscapes on the walls. The galleries rustled with watered silk and glowed with satin merveilleux. Brocade dolmans and sealskin sacques swished in lovely configurations. Clubs held meetings to listen to art-appreciation speakers and served tea in the gaslight filtered through "aesthetic yellow sunflower shades." Nobody wanted to buy any pictures of badly drawn livestock signed by unknown artists, but everyone was willing to contribute an occasional quarter to the upkeep of such a pleasant place.

Encouraged by this response, the association broke down the walls into the building to the rear and annexed four more splendid rooms with skylights. The proprietors, in an effusion of civic beneficence, expressed the hope that the public "would find in the enlarged galleries a pleasant place of resort where American art could at last, after long waiting, be sure of a welcome and be seen with all the advantages of space and light hitherto reserved for the works of foreigners." They had spared no expense, they said. Warming, lighting, and ventilation were of the finest. The gas reflectors, the fireplaces, the ornamental carving, the ironwork at the main entrance, had cost a fortune. The Wilton carpets had been provided by Messrs. Sloane. What they sincerely had at heart, the generous entrepreneurs reiterated, was that native artists would take full advantage of this, their first opportunity of placing their canvases, hot off the easel as it were, before the American picture-loving and picture-buying public.

The struggling artists cooperated to the best of their ability. For the second grand opening, the halls were decked with flowers, the walls plastered with canvases depicting farm animals in every conceivable pose. *Two Friends*, a study of sheep by Miss Olive E. Cheritree of 6 Avenue Montaigne, Paris, France (but nonetheless an American) was priced at $350. *Who Loves Me Follows* by Henry Bacon—some pigs pursuing a girl with a pail of swill—was hopefully tagged at $800. Titles more descriptive of the human situation were equally seductive: James Symington's *The Girl I Left Behind Me, You Must Eat, Widowed!, A Hot Bargain, The Aunt's Visit, The Capricious Model.* The flowers, everyone said, were beautiful.

Charles A. Dana's *Sun*, the newspaper from which most of the élite found out what to think about art, ignored the pictures but said the new rooms were "far more commodious, elegant and appropriate" than those of almost any similar institution in London.

Kirby was an inspired promoter. He instituted prize fund exhibitions and contrived to get some of the richest men in the country not only to pay for the prizes but to judge the merits of the entries as well. "Prominent connoisseurs, amateurs and art institutions" from Boston, Philadelphia, Washington, and Baltimore expressed their zeal for the encouragement of painters of native beef and pork in prizes of $2,000 and $2,500 each. Wealthy citizens of Chicago, Milwaukee, and Louisville joined with such princely New Yorkers as B. Altman, Andrew Carnegie, Jay Gould, and Collis P. Huntington in contributing to the onward march of art in America. With such golden names and tidy sums to dangle, Kirby induced hundreds of American painters "in this country and abroad" to whip up canvases for his salons. Some of the local connoisseurs formed the habit of dropping in at the association on their way to and from Wall Street, to look over the pictures and, as Kirby said, "to talk art." Sleek rows of ladies and gentlemen in evening dress gathered to listen to speechmakers give out the prizes. But what to do with the winning pictures was a problem. They were presented to ungrateful museums, where, it was found, they were hung over doorways until strong protests "brought them down where they belonged."

The advancement of American art turned out, in the end, to be mainly the advancement of George Inness.

Inness—then sixty-eight years old and, in Kirby's words, "a born artistic genius"—had for several years enjoyed the patronage of Thomas B. Clarke, a rich manufacturer of collars and cuffs and a pioneer collector of American pictures (and of just about everything else). Clarke had bought thirty-five Inness landscapes. He had also persuaded George I. Seney, art-loving president of the Metropolitan Bank, to lay in a batch. Clarke and Seney were two of Kirby's prize fund cronies. Being well-supplied with Innesses themselves, they were of the opinion that the time had come for Inness to seek a wider public. With a view to relieving him of "all business anxiety," they talked the born artistic genius into putting himself under the management of the American Art Association.

Kirby planned a George Inness loan exhibition, and in the meantime, set out to tame the wild-haired painter and put him on a paying basis. Inness, preoccupied with the things of the spirit, pretended to be sublimely indifferent to money. At the time, he was either a Methodist or a Swedenborgian, or both, a socialist, and a partisan of the single tax—a confusion of convictions that Kirby held responsible for his alternate moods of exaltation and depression. Moreover Inness hated picture dealers. But for a while he cooperated.

Kirby, on the other hand, held some convictions of his own. One of them was that Inness worked too long on his pictures. His solution to this problem was to take them wet off the easel at a moment when the painter was distracted by metaphysical speculation. *Grey, Lowering Day*, for instance—a picture Kirby sold for $10,150 at a Thomas B. Clarke auction in 1899, five years after Inness' death—was spirited away before Inness was anywhere near through with it. "If we had left it on the easel an hour more, it would have been spoiled," Kirby said.

The speed-up system notwithstanding, Kirby was a stickler for accuracy. On the morning of the day the loan exhibition was to open, he was striding about the gallery making a final inspection of the pictures, which had been hung during the night. Suddenly he stopped in front of one of the largest, a landscape with figures.

"Rose, come here!" he cried. (Rose Lorenz, a Kirby employee later to become the power behind the rostrum, was then serving her apprenticeship in art appreciation.) "Rose, look at that painting!"

"That's a great painting," Rose said.

"But count the fingers on the right hand!"

"Why, Mr. Kirby, there are six fingers on the right hand!"

"Where's Randolph?" Kirby demanded. "Send for him. Tell him to get Inness. Quick, before it's time to open the doors."

John B. Randolph, connoisseur, friend of artists, adviser to collectors, and hanger-on at the galleries, had been up all night arguing with Inness over the hanging of the pictures. He shared with the artist a predilection for whisky at breakfast time; hence in this emergency he was the man to be called into action. He would know where to find Inness. But, first, Randolph had to be found.

Boys were dispatched by Rose Lorenz to comb the saloons. At last Randolph was located, and he in turn found Inness. Inness came in, looking as formidable as possible, his long hair ruffled and a metaphysical gleam in his eye.

"Look at that picture," Kirby said.

"Wonderful picture," said Inness, gazing at the canvas with the freakish hand. "Best I ever did."

"But that figure," Kirby pointed out fretfully. "Six fingers on the right hand. Count them, Mr. Inness."

Inness counted. "Give me my palette," he ordered.

The bleary artist had just finished painting out the extra finger when the doors opened for the special preview for "prominent connoisseurs." Kirby heaved a sigh of relief. Surely, he reasoned, a six-fingered hand would have drawn even more scathing criticism than those ill-shaped cows people were always complaining about.

The loan exhibition was a success. "Not to know Mr. George Inness," the *Tribune* reporter said, "argues oneself to be a benighted Philistine as regards our native art." Two hundred anti-Philistines crowded the galleries daily, and for the first time, the Art Association had the glory of showing a winner.

But in the long run, efforts to convert the Inness born artistic genius into cash were not particularly rewarding. An incident told in Kirby's own words illustrates the touching, if fruitless, relationship between the artist and his managers:

Our Prize Fund Exhibition was then just about forming. My partner suggested, "Inness, you should paint a picture for the Prize Fund Exhibition. There are prizes of $2,500 to be awarded. You will certainly get one. You are the greatest landscape painter."

He said, "I will."

I can see Mr. Inness now, coming in with a canvas and taking it into the private office. "There is my picture for the Prize Fund Exhibition."

I looked at it and Mr. Sutton looked at it. He said, "Inness, that doesn't do you credit."

"What!" Inness said.

"No, you can paint better than that, a great deal better than that."

"Well, what's the matter with it?"

"Well," Mr. Sutton said, "there is something. I don't know. . . . Kirby, what is the matter with it?"

I said, "I don't know, exactly, Mr. Inness, but there is something in the composition there. It is a little out of drawing."

"I know what it is. It is that tree in the center. It cuts it in half."

"I don't know whether it does or not. . . ."

Just then Mr. George I. Seney, the banker, came into the office. Inness said to Mr. Seney, "You are the man I want to see. What is the matter with this picture?"

He said, "I don't know, but it is not up to your mark."

"I know there is something wrong with it," Inness said. "There is something wrong with it."

At that time we had given over to the Devoe Company a part of our Gallery so as to supply the art students in the neighborhood with paints and brushes. Mr. Inness rushed out to the Devoe branch, bought a palette, colors, oils and brushes and he rushed back into the office and said, "I will fix that."

Mr. Seney said, "I cannot wait until you fix it, but I am coming uptown in the afternoon and I will stop in and look at it."

We left Mr. Inness in the office by himself, and in about a couple of hours he came out with beads of perspiration all over his forehead and face, and said, "I've got it all right now, Sutton. Come in and look at it."

We went in to look at it. I said, "We won't express an opinion until Mr. Seney comes."

Mr. Seney came, in the afternoon, and we all agreed that the picture was worse than it originally was.

Inness said, "I believe you are right." He again rushed out and he got turpentine and rags and new paint and tried again, but the picture was not included in the Prize Fund Exhibition.

"That," said Kirby, "was the nature of Mr. Inness all the way through."

At the end of two years American art was just about where it had been before Kirby and Sutton took it in hand. The Oriental trade, too, was something less than satisfactory. Upper-bracket dealers had begun to teach their upper-bracket clients that how a thing looked was less important than whether it was real or not. Kirby, who knew the value of an honest reputation, had at times felt called upon to warn such influential customers as Charles A. Dana, publisher of the *Sun*, against some of the Chinese porcelains on display in the oval room of the now ultrafashionable Art Association. On one occasion, when Dana fell for an especially gaudy sage-colored vase, Kirby said, "Confidentially, I wouldn't buy that if I were you, Mr. Dana."

"Oh, but it's lovely, lovely," Dana purred. An ardent connoisseur of porcelains, and no man to be crossed, he had it wrapped and started to walk out with it under his arm.

Kirby followed him to the door. "When you get home, Mr. Dana," he said, "put it in your bathtub with water and leave it there overnight."

The next morning, Dana returned, carrying a sad white-livered jug under his arm. "You were right, Kirby," he admitted ruefully. "The color has all come off."

Kirby was uneasy. "This gimcrack stuff won't go," he said to his partners. The Art Association had corralled the rich. The galleries were exquisite. But the Wilton carpets, the lighting, and the warming notwithstanding, the fact remained that there was nothing much to sell.

Sutton would find something, he said. Since the customers were so reluctant to buy American, he would go to Europe and find some other kind of art. But in the meantime the financial panic of 1885 brought with it personal misfortune that was to shape the entire future of the AAA.

George I. Seney, at the very moment when he was puzzling over what was wrong with the Inness prize fund picture, had been teetering on the edge of an abyss. A few weeks later he fell over. The "conservative and respectable" president of the Metropolitan Bank had been using the bank's resources for reckless railroad financing. Within two or three years he had stacked up a personal fortune of $9 million. The railways were bankrupt; when the panic came, the stocks fell and the bank had to close its doors. To escape prosecution, Seney turned over to the receivers all his possessions, including his mansion in Brooklyn and his art collection. By winter 1885 a dour creditors' committee was looking for a way to convert 285 paintings into cash. Seney suggested that they let the American Art Association hold an auction.

Sutton and Robertson were reluctant to turn the high-toned, if profitless, gallery into an auction hall. Kirby, on the other hand, wanted nothing so much as to put the fire into the bidders once more. Surrounded by so much money itching to be spent, the retired auctioneer was like an old fire horse pawing the ground at the smell of smoke and the sound of the bell.

Moreover, the Seney art was highly marketable. There were some American pictures, but all the stylish French and German names were there: the Salon painters; the geniuses of Düsseldorf and Munich; the Men of 1830—sometimes called the Barbizons—just now coming into such vogue. The cottage folk were all present: women churning, gathering, and picking; washerwomen by the score. The landscapes were all there: all the livestock and the battles, the poultry yards and Spanish pharmacies, people going to and returning from the ball, Turkish ladies, Arab hunters, people fishing, tending sheep, making out the bill of fare. Who could have resisted such a gallery? It was decided that the Art Association could with dignity *manage* the sale.

The word *manage* was the key to all that followed, though the idea was not original with Kirby. Samuel P. Avery, arbiter of taste and lordliest of artmongers, had "managed" auctions—not only the precedent-setting Johnston sale nine years before but others, where the take was only in five figures. With the billing "Under the direction of Samuel P. Avery," the auctioneer became a secondary figure and hence presumably less shady. Now that the American Art Association had acquired a quasi-institutional character, with some of the country's richest moguls listed as its prize fund sponsors, it too could represent itself as "Managers." True, its working partner chanced to be an auctioneer, but that was all to the good. Had he not been an exception to the breed, would he be impresario of a splendrous gallery on Madison Square, giving out prizes for the encouragement of art?

It was more than a question of language. In Kirby's mind, and in his propaganda, the difference between management and ordinary auctioneering was the justification for his return to the hucksters' ranks. Far from converting itself into anything so tawdry as an auction house, the association would lend its "long experience in art matters," and "the handsomest and best-adapted galleries in the country, if not in the world," to the public sale of "collections of special importance." There were not many precedents in the United States for the sale of collections of special importance. The Johnston was almost the only one. But on his trip abroad, which was primarily for the purpose of regaining his declining health, Kirby had not been too preoccupied with his physical well-being to make a study of the famous London auction houses. He had observed, among other things, the reason for the proverbial English paradox that when one sells at auction one sells cheaply but when one buys one pays dearly.

English auction houses, by tradition and by design, catered then almost exclusively to the trade. Sales of famous art collections sometimes drew the curious as spectators, but private buyers were excluded from the bidding by custom. If they wanted to buy, they placed their bids through dealers, who had entree to the sales and charged 5 or 10 per cent commission on the purchase price.

The rooms had the atmosphere of a catchall for derelict possessions. Things were sold just as they came from the consignor—often dirty and in disrepair. The lots were numbered and just put around. Mediocrities were not readily distinguishable from things of value. Catalogues, unless interpreted by an expert, gave little clue as to which was which. Oil paintings had the dust and grime of years thick upon the glass that preserved the brush strokes of a master or blurred the hand of copyist or forger. The sales had an air of cut-and-dried professionalism. Porters in green baize aprons held up chairs by one leg or hoisted portraits that may or may not have been painted by Reynolds above the bidders' heads. The auctioneer wore the formal dress of a stockbroker and, in contrast to his surroundings, was a man of similar dignity and consequence. The porters, it was said, did not even wash their necks. The dealers who did the bidding sat around a big table or stood near it, subdued, expressionless, and tense, like the seasoned players in a gambling house. They were firmly organized in the Ring.

The Ring, or Knockout, system—which still prevails at auctions where the bidding is predominantly by the trade—is an age-old conspiracy to control auction prices and keep the "privates"—the dealers' word for nonprofessional bidders—from getting anything of value at less than the going retail price. The dealers in a particular category of art property form a syndicate and agree not to bid against one another. When one member of the combine bids, the others—however much they may want to buy the lot—refrain from running up the price. After the public sale, the Ring holds its own auction, and the members bid on the lots obtained among themselves. If an item is of no interest to other members of the combine, the original bidder may pay for it and keep it. When two or more dealers in the Ring compete for it, the difference between its knockdown price in the public sale and the amount it brings in the Ring auction goes into the profits of the syndicate. An object of exceptional value may remain the joint property of the syndicate members until one of the dealers finds a customer for it and submits a bid acceptable to the others. The gravy is then portioned out among the members as usual.

There are many variations and vicissitudes in the operations of the syndicates. Occasionally a rival combine will invade the auction rooms and bid against the regulars with the object of gaining membership in the established gang. Strong and unpleasant measures may have to be taken to restore monopoly. Sometimes syndicates operate within the syndicate, in which case two or more members form a conspiracy not to compete against each other in the Ring auctions. If the Ring-within-the-Ring succeeds in obtaining objects below their market value, its members may hold a third auction to divide the spoils.

For instance, a Chelsea soup tureen may bring £100 in a London auction. If the porcelain syndicate is composed of ten dealers and the soup tureen brings £1,000 in the Ring auction, each of the ten members gets £90 profit. But the £1,000 may have been paid by three dealers united in a Knockout of their own. The soup tureen brings, say, £4,000 in the subsequent auction among the three. Regardless of which dealer buys the tureen, each of the three comes out with an additional £1,000 profit. Moreover, a syndicate member, whether the mere circumstance that a Chelsea soup tureen has come up at auction nets him £90 or £1,090, would be unlikely to pay taxes on his ill-gotten gains, since the operations of the Ring are illegal in England, and in any case, undercover.

In any event, the "privates" are not to be tolerated at Ring-controlled auctions. A functionary, who used to be given the colorful title King of the Knockout, is delegated to take over the casual intruder who imagines he can buy advantageously for his own account at auction. If, for instance, a gentleman fancies a Georgian silver coffee-pot and attempts to bid for it against the silver Ring, the King of the Knockout will run him up to about the retail value of the coffeepot—or higher, if the gentleman appears to be well heeled and stubborn—and let him have it. The intruder goes home with his prize—for which he may have paid more than it would have cost in a Bond

Street silver shop—pondering on the fact that in the published reports of auction sales similar coffeepots had frequently fallen for the price of crockery.

Now and then the King of the Knockout may get stuck with the piece he is bidding up. In that event, the Ring sells it in the backstairs auction as usual. The difference between what it brings and what it cost in the public sale is absorbed by the syndicate as a business expense.

Obviously the Ring cannot exert any such rigid control over art works that are well known or significant enough to incite collector competition on a broad scale. In prosperous times, when the quality dealers' pockets are stuffed with bidding orders, it is from the large floating supply of secondary art works that the Ring contrives to reap its profits. But through the years the effect of the various dealer combines operating in the auction room has often been to divert much of the real value of every kind of property sold to its own account.

As a defense against the Ring, English auction houses operate on a system of reserve prices. The consignor is permitted by law to put a secret reserve, or "upset," price on each lot to be sold. When the bidding fails to reach the upset price, the auctioneer knocks the lot down to himself, and the would-be seller pays only a reduced commission. Thus the bidder is placed in the position of playing a kind of game of blindman's buff with the auctioneer, who alone is supposed to know what the reserve price is.

French auctions, in contrast to the subdued, dealer-dominated ones in London, were tumultuous affairs in Kirby's time, as they are today. The auctioning of personal property is a time-honored business of immense proportions. Every afternoon for nine months of the year the galaxy of simultaneous auctions in the huge, barnlike Hôtel Drouot—which was opened in the eighteen-fifties—affords an army of bargain hunters the opportunity to make a "good strike." Everything is sold, from three-wheeled baby carriages to the finest Louis XV furniture. The crowd stands; the noise is like Black Friday on the Stock Exchange; the air unbreathable. The Ring, or Black Band, as it was picturesquely called in the nineteenth century, is said to operate, but not to the exclusion of the private buyer. Although French auctions can be a maze of intricacy to the uninitiated, the auctioneer functions under strict government control. A syndicate of experts passes on the authenticity of art works to be sold. If, at a later date, the auction buyer can prove the attribution wrong, he may demand reimbursement from a fund maintained for that purpose. The expert in charge of the sale also places a minimum valuation on each lot—the French version of the English upset price, except that it is not secret. And whether in the raucous Hôtel Drouot or in the plush art galleries where great picture sales are sometimes held, the expert stands beside the auctioneer, prepared to announce the appraised value of each item offered, and if need be, open the bidding at that figure.

Nothing would have distressed Thomas Kirby more than an expert standing up there monitoring his performance. He had not, in fact, been much taken with Europe and its auctions. On the other hand, no one knew better than Kirby the practices of America's freebooting auctioneers.

After almost every art sale the press bristled with sarcastic comment: "Was there ever . . . a worse mock auction than the recent Carroll affair conducted by the new firm of Ortgies & Co., successors to Kirby & Co. at 845 Broadway . . . ?" or "The usual mystery as to the identity of certain purchasers of pictures was not lacking at the recent Runkle sale at Chickering Hall."

Secret reserve prices, though not sanctioned by law, certainly prevailed at New York auctions. What was worse, if the auctioneer did not actually own the property he sold, he mixed in derelict objects of his own in order to cash in on the good will emanating from a real consignor's name. Moreover, the consignor—if consignor there was— could hardly be said to be in a better position than the bidder faced with all those unidentified competitors. Most auctioneers were shoe-string operators; they delayed payment interminably, juggled the accounts, and sometimes absconded with the funds altogether.

During his retirement from the rostrum Kirby had been mulling over the trouble with auctions, and he had come up with some cardinal principles to herald the Art Association's entrance into the field of management. What he proposed to establish, with the Seney sale as a springboard, was a free and unrestricted auction commission market with the private buyer as its main support. In the language of his manifesto this was to be accomplished by "selling without reserve, restriction or protection, never permitting additions to sales of private or estates' collections, prominently advertising and displaying real ownership, making final payment within thirty days from the date of sale."

These are in essence the principles under which the Parke-Bernet Galleries functioned for many years. If they do not sound particularly cardinal now, they did in 1885. "There is a distinction," a further declaration read, "between a public sale held under the auspices of the American Art Association, where the buyer knows what he is bidding on, whom he is competing against and what he will get if he becomes the purchaser, and the regular auction sale where the prospective buyer does not know whether he is bidding against the owner or his agent and, if a successful bidder, may not get what he was bidding on."

But reform was not to come from moral precepts alone. Nowhere in the world was there a precedent for the kind of art sales Kirby saw rising from the "unsurpassed facilities" of the new association on Madison Square. For elegance, no less than ethics, was the means to his objective—elegance, luxury, and snob appeal. In the effulgent rays of the Art Association's sunflower-shaded lamps, he would raise art auctions from the mire of humbug to the realm of stylish culture. He proposed to make auction-going a social event.

The rich would come, as they would come to give out prizes for the encouragement of native painters. The dealers, he knew, would come. The Ring was not unknown in New York, but with the titans of finance as their opponents, the sly art traders would walk off with little to their credit. There would be "friendly rivalry and bitter competition," with Mr. Thomas E. Kirby the guileless and impartial arbiter.

With these pronouncements, "Mr. George I. Seney's collection of Modern Paintings" was booked for a three-night auction at Chickering Hall "under the management of The American Art Association." A catalogue was printed with all the artists' names spelled correctly (in contrast to the lordly Mr. Avery's deplorable orthography); the signs warning patrons that imported paintings were likely to be fake disappeared from the association's walls; and a fortnight's exhibition, day and evening, was advertised at the Madison Square galleries, with an admission charge of $1, to keep the riffraff out.

But all was not smooth sailing. As *Town Topics*, the weekly tipsheet of the monied classes, stated, "The securing of the sale by the American Art Association caused deep chagrin among certain dealers and auctioneers who were desirous of managing it." Chagrin was not the word for it. Auctioneers and picture dealers were goaded into active combat. Cardinal principles indeed—reform, promotion, and encouragement! Of what? Of Thomas E. Kirby and nothing else! New-fangled auctions indeed! The little man with the schoolmaster's goatee was a pious fraud, a crackpot out to ruin the picture trade and the auction business as well. Any man on Broadway knew a picture sale had to be manipulated. If 285 highly desirable paintings were to be auctioned off in Chickering Hall without any restriction or reserve, with nobody to puff the bids or boost the sale, the art market would be irremediably depressed.

Moreover, these were panic times. Bargains would roll down the aisles. The poor Seney creditors would be rooked out of the few good cents they might have realized on a bad dollar. Old-fashioned auc-tioneers clenched their black umbrellas and alternately shook with rage and trembled with pity for the bereft depositors of the Metropolitan Bank. So wrung with pity were they for the Seney creditors that Kirby's jealous rivals called upon the creditors' committee with admonitions and gratuitous advice.

The committee called upon Kirby. There was a panic on . . . the chairman said.

"Wall Street panic be damned, sir!" snapped Kirby.

What about the bargains in the aisles? Was it true that the pictures would be sold no matter what they brought?

Had he not made that clear? Everything would go, said Kirby.

Then the committee requested that the sale be canceled, or at least postponed.

Kirby would not hear of it. Did the honorable creditors presume, he inquired, that the passion for Jules Breton was suspended by a drop in railway shares?

The creditors had never heard of Jules Breton.

But surely the committee had heard of human nature. It was the same, Kirby remarked, the whole world over. Precisely because of the panic, the public would come to Chickering Hall expecting to get the greatest bargains in the world. And once men of real wealth were assembled there in competition, the timid creditors would see what miracles could happen.

The creditors fingered their silk hats. Times were bad down-town. . . .

Times were bad everywhere, said Kirby. But did the creditors imagine that he planned to sell Seney's art to the middle classes, or to the working people? Surely it was unnecessary to remind the committee that rich men often thrived on hard times. No, he would not postpone the sale now, after it had been advertised throughout the country, and even abroad, after his office had been flooded with requests for catalogues, and the pictures all but hung upon the association's walls. The committee tried to force the issue. But in the end it departed, silenced if not convinced.

The washerwomen and painted cattle were lovingly put on display. The rooms were perfumed by flowers and manned by stalwart Negro guards with floss-silk gloves and courtly manners to improve the tone for the distinguished trade. More than ever before, the galleries rustled with satin and echoed with the voices of enraptured connoisseurs.

Kirby's enemies were not through however. Among the opposing forces was Samuel P. Avery, the logical manager for such a fine sale. Avery was American promoter for the rustic artist Jules Breton, and—the creditors' ignorance notwithstanding—Breton was the coming thing in painters. He turned out moody scenes of life in French hamlets, nostalgic pictures recalling the lost innocence of youth and the dubious charms of thatched roofs and evil-smelling cowyards. He was also a poet. Many of his paintings were accompanied by rhapsodic verses explaining in detail what was already abundantly clear.

Among Seney's paintings was a Jules Breton, with poem, called *Evening in the Hamlet of Finistère*. Avery had bought the picture in the Salon of 1882. It was so beautiful that it was beyond criticism, some reviewers of the Salon said. It had everything: the squalid huts in a gloomy village street faintly illuminated by the sunset afterglow, the gossiping women in long dark dresses and sabots, the stray cats, the gray farm animals, the crescent moon, and a lovelorn couple leaning against the cowyard wall. By way of sales talk, Avery had printed a 109-page book of critical panegyric translated from the French, and Seney had bought the picture from his gallery.

In Kirby's opinion *Evening in the Hamlet* was a fine picture but a little dark. To correct this, he placed it, for the exhibition, high up, near the skylight, where, weather permitting, a stream of filtered sunlight supplemented the artist's palette with a rich golden glow. Kirby was proud of his day-is-dying-in-the-west effect, but when Avery saw it he was bitterly offended. He looked upon the sunset aura as a presumptuous gilding of the lily, as libel and restraint of trade.

On the day after the grand opening of the exhibition the creditors' committee appeared again in Kirby's office, bearing a formal written demand from Avery that *Evening in the Hamlet* be taken out of the blazing sun and brought down to a reasonable height. Breton was a valuable property, his stock was ever going up, and the cheap tricks of an auctioneer were about to ruin the sale of a masterpiece, Avery said.

The creditors' committee knew enough to tremble at the name of the veteran dealer Avery. They twisted their silk hats. But Kirby was a stubborn man. "I cannot conscientiously change it," he told the chairman. "I think I have done right and to the benefit of the picture, and I think that I can convince you I have not made an error. Come upstairs with me."

The Seney creditors cared not a jot for art, but when they saw the crowd beneath the picture they could think of no argument in support of Avery's plaint, for the rapt expression was inescapable on the faces tilted back to gaze at Breton's turgid canvas glowing like a stained-glass window in the orange rays of the setting sun.

"There is the result of my hanging," Kirby said triumphantly. "Just wait for the sale."

In those ebullient days the press cared passionately about everything. At one time in the Art Association's early years there were twenty-three daily newspapers in New York, and most of them held strong opinions on artistic matters. After the exhibition opened, the papers were filled with articles about Seney and his "omniverous propensity in the matter of pictures." The *Tribune* said that Seney nobly exemplified the "present taste for modern French art," but criticized him for acquiring "more pictures than he could properly house or enjoy." The *Times* writer loved the Meissoniers, Daubignys, and Rousseaus, but was pleased to find that there were indifferent pictures too. This showed, he said, that Seney was "not so much bent on buying costly and convertible painting as pleasing himself—the only self-respecting way of owning pictures." All was going well until the *Evening Post* raised the ugly question of authenticity.

The *Post* was crochety about all matters cultural. At the time, it was waging a campaign against Luigi Palma di Cesnola and the

Cyprian antiquities he had "palmed off" on the Metropolitan Museum, but it had space for Seney and the Art Association as well. Doubtless from ulterior motives—"professional jealousy" because the *Tribune* had printed so many favorable columns, said *Town Topics*— the *Post* writer called Seney's *Washing Clothes* by A. G. Decamps a "flimsy forgery," damned his Cabanel *Brother and Sister*, his Turner, a Gérôme water color, and relegated six examples by the Men of 1830 to the limbo of forgery.

The *Post* was no sooner on the streets than crowds gathered before the condemned pictures, whispering. Kirby was enraged. Ten rotten apples could make the whole barrel suspect. He saw the plot against him thickening. He saw rows of empty seats in Chickering Hall, his enemies triumphant, a gloomy future for the cardinal principles of auctioneering.

He went to the dealers who had sold Seney the ten pictures. Some of the targets of the *Post*'s malediction appeared to have been hastily chosen. The Gérôme had come from M. Knoedler; the Cabanel and Turner from Avery. Avery had papers tending to prove that those two, at least, were all right. Avery also had papers hinting that the Decamps was probably a Decamps. The other seven pictures remained in doubt, though on their behalf, Kirby gathered a stack of quickly written testimonials from experts at least as expert as the expert on the *Post*. But how was the public to be convinced?

Kirby was a man of action. Fiery with temper, he stalked into the *Post* building, threw down a sheaf of papers, and demanded a retraction. The *Post* did not print retractions. That was no news to Kirby, but thereupon he played his best possible card. Ten days before the first night of the auction the American Art Association brought suit against the *Post*, asking $25,000 in damages for malicious libel.

It made no difference whether the pictures were right or wrong. Courtroom proceedings could not possibly begin before the sale. But meanwhile every newspaper but the *Post* headlined the impending lawsuit. Some, no doubt in a flank attack against the *Evening Post*— for rivalry ran high among the papers—went so far as to defend the suspect pictures. "Nothing is gained by reckless talk of this kind," said the *Times*, which went on to suggest that "the critic was hasty." Chauvinism came to the fore. "Nobody supposes that the dealers on this side who sold Mr. Seney the pictures are to blame; the culprits, if they exist, are the French and English plagiarists."

Seldom had plot, if plot there was, backfired so magnificently. The publicity brought visitors to the galleries in droves. On the first night of the auction the Art Association jubilantly called for police reserves to hold back the sightseers from Chickering Hall so that "wealthy patrons of the arts" could get in with their tickets.

As Kirby had predicted, Wall Street was there, titans of finance with bald heads and stiff high collars, men with side whiskers and chin whiskers and opulent dark mustaches. The eighteen hundred seats were filled, and people were standing in the aisles. The dealers were all present, the skeptics and the bargain hunters, even a few ladies, in ribboned toques and feathered turbans. The clergy was represented by Henry Ward Beecher, the sporty Brooklyn dominie, in company with his friend "Deacon" S. V. White, "the smiling King of Lackawanna." Jay Gould regretted that he could not attend in person, but sent his private connoisseur, who sat in the front row of the balcony with orders to bid on all the humble poor. William T. Walters of Baltimore was there; John G. Johnson of Philadelphia; and Daniel W. Powers, whose art gallery was "the pride of Rochester" (New York). It contained copies of old masters said to surpass the originals in freshness and beauty of coloring, a marble *Venus at the Bath* that weighed a ton, and a mechanical prodigy called an orchestrion that weighed eight tons and was said to "possess a musical skill no human performer could equal."

On stage in the concert hall, confronting the vista of red plush and black broadcloth, Kirby in his tailcoat and wing collar, behind the pedestal wont to hold the conductor's score, could have been an importunate maestro niggling a choir of hirsute choristers. His stance was stiff and formal, legs straight, heels together, torso bent slightly forward. His slender ivory hammer, extending from his outstretched arm like a baton, beat the air with crisp authority. Negro stalwarts in Second Empire livery placed the pictures one by one on a crimson-draped easel. Flooded by the limelight from the trough above, each canvas had its moment in the golden glow that had done such wonders for *Evening in the Hamlet*. They were not all masterworks. The maestro did not begin with kettledrums and trumpet flares. But along about No. 9, a fishing priest by some artist long forgotten, the tempo and emotion quickened. The bidders stirred, the baton swung. By twenty-fives and fifties *Fishing Priest* made $1,200. It was worth twice the money, the maestro tearfully declared.

Now badgering, now bullying, now coaxing, he gradually increased the tension and suspense. His hammer was his tyrant's sword, his scepter—the symbol of the potency he craved. He could wring a dollar, or five, or ten, where none had been forthcoming. He had to, for he had staked his all on this, his first big-time performance.

He could be humdrum, acid, fiery; he could pause and make a little joke. He could roll off a description of a soft Daubigny landscape. In this one you could feel the wind in the willows; in that one you could feel the breath of cattle. Up and up the price would go— and it was "worth it, every cent!" He would lower his voice an octave for Anne Boleyn decapitated—it was a gem of a picture, "and don't you forget it!" He would whisper, and he would shout art appreciation in a hell-fire roar. He would dwell with rapture on "a little gem of beauty"; he would pass over pictures as if they were not there. When the libeled pictures stood upon the red-draped easel he was nonchalant, aloof. But there were bidders for them, libel or no libel. The Smiling King of Lackawanna paid $1,075 for a woodsy Diaz that had displeased the *Post*—as much as a good Diaz sometimes brought in ordinary auction sales.

The evening wore on. The tension mounted. The Negro stalwarts, their white gloves gleaming in the limelight, brought out *Romeo and Juliet* by Professor Carl Becker of Berlin. A small black-whiskered man stood up and clapped his hands.

It was the largest picture in the sale—6 feet by 6 and some over, "worth seven thousand if it was worth a cent." The immortal lovers in Friar Laurence's cell! Four square yards of Shakespeare tragedy. It was worth $8,000! Two thousand a yard would be no more than fair.

The bidding ran to $3,500. The little man with the black beard sat on the edge of his seat. Nervously he offered another $25.

There was silence from the other bidders. "You may let it go, but you'll regret it!" Kirby shouted at them.

The little man clutched his derby with both hands. He half rose and looked around. There was apprehension in his eyes.

"Opportunity knocks but once, sir!" Kirby warned the underbidder. "Going . . . going. . . ." Perspiration glistened on the little man's forehead. "Gone!"

The little man with the black whiskers smiled benignly when he was declared the winner. No, he would not give his name to reporters. But the four square yards of Shakespeare, he said proudly, would occupy a place of honor in his parlor.

Each night had its moments of excitement. The maestro with his second wind grew more imperious, more importunate. He had to win the game. My dear idiots, his tone implied, when bids were slow for Meissonier's *The Smoker*. Had no one heard that Meissonier was the modern Leonardo? Had all these people dwelt in darkness? Had they no eyes, no ears? They could let it go but they would regret it!

The same went for Defregger's *Ankunft zum Ball*—a gem if Kirby ever saw one. Did the niggardly patrons expect him to knock it down for a mere $10,000? Could they not see by the catalogue that this *Going to the Ball* had taken a gold medal in Vienna? Were they—all two thousand of them—conspiring to commit a joint crime against the very name of art? No, heaven be praised! There was a man in the second row who would pay $500 more. Ten thousand five hundred! Now the eleven . . . the eleven. . . .

He was ringmaster, critic, teacher. There was humbug in his manner, no doubt a touch of larceny in his soul. But in a way he was sincere. He had a lust for these things.

On the third night, four lots before the end, when Kirby's voice was hoarse and he was fairly exhausted, the Second Empire boys brought out *Evening in the Hamlet*. Transferred to the beam of limelight on the stage it caused an unprecedented furor. The audience applauded; the bids were like champagne corks simultaneously popping all over the hall.

"Why you haven't begun yet!" Kirby rasped when the price had risen by quick hundreds to $18,000.

Evening in the Hamlet fell at $18,200—the highest recorded price a picture had ever brought at public sale. It was Kirby's triumph, his vindication and his crown of glory. Four decades later, with an infinity of auction records behind him, he was still talking about his "mascot picture," *Evening in the Hamlet of Finistère*.

The buyer was a young man no one there had ever seen before. After the sale the dealers and reporters clustered around him. His name was John L. Mitchell, he said. No, he had had no idea the picture would cost so much. His father had seen it at the exhibition and sent him to the sale to buy it. A well-known dealer called him aside. Wouldn't his father be upset when he heard the price? The dealer might be able to help the young fellow out. He would take the picture off his hands—and give him a few hundred dollars profit. It happened that he had a client. . . . The young man was tempted, but he shook his head. His father had been very definite. He thought he had just better go along home and take *Evening in the Hamlet* with him.

When all was added up, the Seney sale brought $405,821, a staggering sum for those days, far surpassing any previous auction total in the United States. The newspapers smiled on the event. "Sales of private collections," *The New York Times* commented, "form excellent and healthful means of spreading the love of pictures." The New York *Sun* for April 3, 1885, said it "was the largest, the best managed, and the most interesting sale that has been known in New York and the successful issue which attended it reflects no little credit upon the AAA in whose charge Mr. Seney placed it."

The libel suit against the *Evening Post* was dropped. Since the ten pictures had brought about as much as they would have brought anyhow, Kirby said, it would be hard to prove any damages. Privately he remarked that but for the necessity to save face, he would have given away those ten pictures in return for the publicity that had helped to swell the crowd in Chickering Hall.

Picture dealers hastened to make up to the fiery little man who had been catapulted overnight to the front rank of art auctioneers. The great sale had strengthened, rather than weakened, the art market, they admitted. Collectors swarmed into the Madison Square galleries to offer their congratulations. Finding Mr. George I. Seney lounging there, some of the new owners of his pictures offered their condolences on the loss of such a great collection. But they could have saved their breath. Within a year the fallen banker was again gratifying his "omnivorous propensity for pictures." It seemed that in turning over his property to the creditors, he had kept out a large block of worthless railway stock, which later turned out to be highly salvageable. Just two years after the auction, *Town Topics,* in writing of Seney's nice gifts to the Metropolitan Museum, was lyrical with admiration for such a speedy comeback: "A few years ago Mr. Seney was a ruined man, with little but his self-respect and the friends his generosity had made to sustain him. Today he is again among the millionaires and his princely charities and large generosities are larger and more princely than ever. . . . Mere financial ruin cannot contain such men. Sensible as they are of an obligation to humanity, they never find humanity remiss in its duty to them."

Of more immediate concern to the managers of the American Art Association was the next step forward in its suddenly enlivened career. Sutton was still reluctant to think of his cultural association as a firm of auctioneers.

"Managers," said Kirby.

In any case, one swallow did not make a summer. Where was the next Collection of Special Importance to come from?

It would come, said Kirby. Death or disaster, God forbid, would be sure to strike some wealthy connoisseur of art.

All the same, Sutton would look around for something to encourage and promote. Since the customers were so reluctant to buy American, he would see what he could find on his next trip abroad. There were the impressionists, for example. They were beginning to make quite a stir in the French art world.

He was reminded that they were lunatics and incompetents, according to reports from Paris. The same effect could be had by tying a brush to a donkey's tail.

Maybe so. But the great art dealer Durand-Ruel had staked a fortune on them. Sutton thought he would take a look at the impressionist exhibition when he got to Paris, and maybe have a talk with Durand-Ruel. Those crazy paintings might be something to promote in New York. They would make a sensation at any rate.

Sutton's French finds were not shown until the next spring. Meanwhile, the partners decided to remodel once more. A grand staircase was added, and a new gallery in the Moorish taste. Opinion was unanimous that "nothing like these handsome rooms" had ever been seen in the United States. At the grand opening in the fall—the third in a little over two years—the American pictures shown were slighted or ignored, as usual; but as for the place, it was so enlarged and luxurious, the Brooklyn *Eagle* said, that no gallery on this continent could compare with it.

THREE

TWO WIDOWS AND THE
BLOOM OF THE PEACH

IN KIRBY'S RECKONING the best auction prospect on the horizon was the A. T. Stewart collection, celebrated during Stewart's lifetime, but for years unseen by any amateur of art. Now, the long, murky gallery gathered dust while old Mrs. Stewart, wearing a brown wig and laden with jewels, flitted aimlessly among the marble statues like a ghostly cocotte in a neoclassic purgatory. For nearly a decade the vast white palace at the northwest corner of Fifth Avenue and 34th Street had been little more than a regal prison for the vain and friendless widow, ailing in body and abandoned to the caprices of dotage, but nonetheless reputed to be the richest woman in America. In this glaring monument to a merchant prince's greed, with its lofty pillars approached by thirty marble steps, no art receptions any longer disturbed the mortuary calm, no Sunday evening guests yawned among the dreary pictures and the bric-a-brac. The only important visitor left to come was death; and even now expectant heirs were flocking like buzzards over the millions that would somehow be divided.

It was sad, very sad, Judge Henry Hilton remarked, but Mrs. Stewart was growing weaker day by day. As warden of the ebbing Stewart dynasty, Hilton had already profited enormously, but after the passing of the widow, even greater plunder would be possible. If anything should happen to poor old Mrs. Stewart, the contents of the palace would be liquidated promptly. The thrifty ex-Tammany judge rubbed his moist hands together like a man overburdened with the sadness of the world and wistfully inquired for Kirby's lowest terms.

The Stewart saga was a sordid one even for an era of ruthless fortune building. Cold and calculating in and out of trade, esteemed in no social circle more exalted than the Tweed Ring, which ran City Hall, Alexander Turney Stewart had lived and died the world's most successful merchant. Born in County Antrim, Ireland, he had come to New York around 1820, a bantam, tight-lipped seventeen-year-old trader with reddish hair, effeminate ways, and shrewd, saucerlike blue eyes. Three thousand dollars invested in Irish laces brought him enough profit to open a store on Broadway in 1823. Success followed success and by 1846 he had prospered enough to build a block-long marble dry-goods palace facing City Hall Park, at the northeast corner of Broadway and Chambers Street, an architectural wonder of its day, with a façade of fluted marble columns and a great dome rising 80 feet above the street.

As wholesale merchant and proprietor of New York's first department store, Stewart was a cruel and exacting master. Hours were from seven to seven; a huge lantern hung from the dome to light early morning and late evening shoppers. Key employees were rival merchants he had forced out of business. His wage policy was scandalous even for his time. Discipline was so strict that a clerk could lose his job for wasting a piece of string. A new man could owe his whole month's wages in fines for infractions of the rules. But the Stewart genius for merchandising paid enormous dividends, and by the eighteen-sixties he was one of the three wealthiest men in the country.

He became, next to William B. Astor, the largest landholder in New York. In 1862, following the northward trend of retail trade, he opened the Great Iron Store on Broadway between 9th and 10th Streets—the building later occupied by Wanamaker's. He owned nine factories in Europe, which supplied his wholesale and retail business with dry goods manufactured at the lowest possible wages. He built the Grand Union Hotel at Saratoga Springs and embellished it with the longest veranda in the world, an acre of white marble, twelve acres of carpet, and a patriotic allegory said to be the largest painting ever seen on this side of the Atlantic.

Stewart had commissioned *The Genius of America* in 1870 from Adolphe Yvon of Paris to glorify the east wall of the picture gallery in his Fifth Avenue mansion, facing Rosa Bonheur's *The Horse Fair*, which occupied 17 feet at the opposite end. But Yvon had been so carried away either by his own genius or that of his subject that he made the canvas 5 feet wider than the Stewart gallery. Twenty-two feet high by 35 feet long, it had to be relegated to the ballroom of the Grand Union Hotel and a shorter replica whipped up for the palace.

Yvon charged $100,000 for his labor, and well he may have, for—to list but a fraction of the picture's official inventory—it encompassed the States of the Union personified by beautiful maidens, Minerva and the Republic hand in hand on a triumphal car drawn by lions, a statue of the Father of the Country, a noble river quenching the torch of war while the spirits of the immortal founders ascended from the

A. T. Stewart, collector and New York merchant prince (BETTMANN ARCHIVE).

vapors, fruits and flowers of the Republic, implements of manufacture, grateful and loving citizens bringing wreaths of laurel, the winged messengers of eternal Fame, Indians regarding the scene with admiration and amazement, the colored race rejoicing in its liberation, the rising sun, vessels of many nations bearing emigrants to the land of freedom, where Industry, Enterprise, et cetera, were united in a glorious vista of equality, wealth, and assured social position.

Social position was the thing Stewart could never be assured of, and so, toward the end of his life, he took to raising edifices of a pseudo-philanthropic nature. At 2 Park Avenue he started to build a non-profit hotel for workingwomen of good character, a very nice-looking place with red pillars, palm gardens, and 502 sleeping rooms warranted impregnable to males or frivolity of any other sort. Out on Long Island he bought ten thousand acres of sandy wasteland on the Hempstead plain and began the creation of Garden City, an ideal community with himself as landlord, mayor, and sole owner of

A. T. Stewart's residence on the corner of Fifth Avenue and 34th Street (BETT-MANN ARCHIVE), with an interior view of Stewart's private art gallery (BROWN BROTHERS). At the far end of the room is Rosa Bonheur's *The Horse Fair*.

absolutely everything, the whole to be surmounted by the Gothic spire of a Stewart memorial cathedral containing in its lower regions a marble crypt for the burial of his mortal remains. These grandiose projects Stewart never saw completed. At the time of his death in 1876 the culminating vanity of his yardstick soul (as the newspapers acridly referred to it) was the neo-Florentine palazzo on Fifth Avenue, finished in 1868 and for a time regarded as the most ostentatious dwelling in America.

It took seven years to build the grand stairways, to construct the floors entirely of Carrara marble, to paint the Brigaldi frescoes on the ceilings and weave the carpets to reflect their identical patterns underfoot. The vast entrance hall was lined with marble statues—life-size water nymphs and fishergirls presided over by Thomas Crawford's giant *Demosthenes,* towering 8 feet above his pedestal and keeping a stern forensic eye on *Zenobia in Chains* across the way. Between *Zenobia* and *Nydia, the Blind Girl of Pompeii* stood a 12-foot clock, indicating the time, the day of the week, the temperature and atmospheric pressure, the changes of the moon, and sundry other matters. The grand drawing room, too, had its quota of clocks and statues, interspersed with 7-foot Sèvres vases and quantities of gilded furniture upholstered in pale yellow satin. But these and all the other colossal chambers were only a prelude to the picture gallery.

Fifty feet high, 30 feet wide, and 75 feet long, that windowless gaslit vault contained two more rows of Carrara marble maidens, some on revolving pedestals—maidens posing with wreaths, weaving garlands, or merely standing on tiptoe hugging modest draperies. Every inch of the four walls was concealed by paintings ingeniously fitted together from floor to ceiling, like the pieces of a giant puzzle. Not a crevice showed between the gilded frames. Pictures standing on the floor leaned against the lowest pictures on the walls. Two rows of easels ran the length of the gallery, parallel to the marble maidens. There were no facilities for contemplation; no space remained for chair or bench; there was barely room to walk.

Many of the pictures would not have borne much contemplation. In the days before the merchant prince's net income soared to $4 million a year he had bought artistic yard goods indiscriminately, picking up mill ends at auction or anecdotal daubs from the Dusseldorf gallery on Broadway. Later on he bought *The Horse Fair,* from William P. Wright of Weehawken, and the original of Hiram

Powers' *The Greek Slave,* widely copied and hailed in mid-nineteenth-century America as the greatest work of sculpture ever chiseled.

In Paris Stewart placed orders with the most expensive artists, invariably demanding the largest canvases they could concoct. In return, Meissonier demanded $60,000 for creating *Friedland, 1807.* But then, his expenses were heavy. The more precisely to depict the galloping war horses, he built a tramway to speed him and his easel alongside model chargers whipped into a simulated battle frenzy. In consequence, the 8-foot canvas starring Napoleon with a cast of impeccably dressed cuirassiers crying out for the joy of dying on behalf of their beloved captain turned out so well that Meissonier could not bring himself to part with it until a few weeks before Stewart's death. For so long a time it had been the "life and joy" of his studio, the imperial painter wrote. Only the knowledge that Stewart, with his enlightened love of art, was to possess it had dulled the pain of final separation. "Be good enough to receive it as a friend," Meissonier implored, "one of those who, by intimate acquaintance, is loved more and more."

The letter itself was a masterpiece, particularly the last paragraph: "Now, dear sir, let me close by offering you my portrait. I have had the pleasure of painting it for you myself. With it you will always be enabled to recall how much I am, Your devoted E. Meissonier."

Stewart put the battle of Friedland in his bathroom, where, for the remaining six weeks of his life, he could cultivate its intimate acquaintance from his gold-encrusted tub. Each day "the grand painting developed additional beauty," he dutifully replied to its creator; he would always cherish the letter and the little water color portrait as coming "from my dear friend Meissonier."

The old storekeeper wanted to make a grand impression. But on whom? On the public that had enriched him but certainly would never enter his art gallery? On the seven thousand employees who lived in abject poverty, fearful that some whim of an arrogant master would deprive their children of tomorrow's watered soup? Stewart had no children. His wife was a silly, good-natured creature, poor in intellectual resources and desperately lonely. She could not have told a Bierstadt from a Bouguereau. Except on those gloomy Sunday evenings attended by uncouth politicians or satellites who dared not stay away, no disciples came to soil the yellow satin chairs or envy their owner's profuse display of outsize works of art.

In all the world, the solitary merchant prince possessed but a single friend and confidant. Shyster, sycophant, and sometime henchman of Boss Tweed, Judge Henry Hilton—an overgrown, full-faced creature with the general air of a Saint Bernard—was the only man that Stewart loved and trusted. They were constant companions. What Stewart had Hilton also had, only smaller: a marble house next door on 34th Street; a smaller drawing room, with smaller yellow chairs, smaller frescoes by Brigaldi, with smaller rugs to match; a smaller picture gallery, with smaller paintings by Meissonier. Like the pilot fish and the shark, the two men were seldom seen apart, and before Stewart died, he appointed Hilton coexecutor and manager of all the widow's vast estates, leaving him $1 million as his fee.

With the million, Hilton forthwith purchased from himself, as agent, business interests of the Stewart empire having a market value of many times the sums his right hand demanded of his left. On every side, the property confided to his care went to swift decay or landed in his pocket through strange transactions that set the world of commerce buzzing. Mrs. Stewart did not care. Millions remained. As nominal executrix, she refused to muddle her giddy head with figures. Nor did Hilton care to trouble her with details of accounting. The hinges of his knees were well oiled. He knew from long experience how to flatter the vain old widow who would rather have lost nine tenths of her fortune than found a new wrinkle in her face.

One unfinished project the Widow Stewart carried to completion: the Cathedral of the Incarnation at Garden City. She had promised the dry-goods king a Gothic cathedral as his last resting place, and nothing could sway her from her vow. The thirteenth-century spire rose majestically heavenward; 200 feet below, the best stonecutters available labored over the Carrara marble crypt for the regal interment of herself and her late husband. The slender spire, the elaborate and rich interior, most critics thought, justified the widow's pious Protestant-Episcopal extravagance. The bishop of the diocese was grateful. Mrs. Stewart's cathedral, though oddly situated for parishioners, on the barren Hempstead plain, was well worth the expenditure of a fortune, even if its grandest feature was the mortuary chapel underneath.

As a temporary measure, Stewart's body had been placed in the churchyard of St. Mark's-in-the-Bouwerie. There, for a time, the deceased merchant prince presumably rested in peace. But on a starless November night in 1878 the sleep of the dead was rudely interrupted. Grave robbers snatched the Stewart corpse from the vault at 11th Street and Second Avenue, made off with it, and held it for ransom.

Though handicapped by a shortage of dependable copy, newspapers treated this ghoulish impiety as the crime of the century. There was some feeling that the thieves had been guided by poetic justice in their choice of quarry. A popular versemaker who called himself TAD expressed these irreverent sentiments in a hastily composed epic called "A. T. Stewart's Dream." Canto I begins:

> At last to slumbers sweet he has resigned
> The drowsy remnant of his scheming mind;
> His trading embryo ghost essays to glide
> Through regions weird! on Luna's hither side.
> On thy blest plains, "pale empress of the skies,"
> Rapt visions greet his avaricious eyes!

In the dream that follows, the ghost merchant is treated to a long montage of his alleged misdeeds and shady associations. Then the poet, for his concluding lines, returns to the terrestrial plain and the matter immediately at hand:

> And tears less fraught with grief were never shed,
> Than those which fall around the dying bed
> Of him, who through this life's uncertain span,
> Has used his wealth to crush his fellow-man.
> Stewart had bagged his last of earthly pelf,
> Thieves forced his tomb! And he got bagged himself!

The grave robbers set $200,000 as a fair ransom for the purloined corpse. Judge Hilton, taking the high moral position that it would be encouraging crime to compound a felony, was not inclined to pay. A number of go-betweens told conflicting stories of attempts to redeem the body at bargain rates. Twenty-five thousand dollars, it seems, was all Hilton could bring himself to offer for his benefactor's remains.

Mrs. Stewart had no moral position and no such thrifty instincts as the Judge. Her dilemma could hardly have been more embarrassing. The cathedral crypt was coming along nicely, but she was without the wherewithal to fill it. Moreover, she was possessed of ancient superstitions about the inadvisability of allowing the dead to prowl about unburied. For months she consulted spiritualists and wrung her hands in consternation. Then one day the news leaked out from her palace that the corpse had been recovered and stored in Brooklyn to await the completion of its princely sepulcher.

The thieves read these glad tidings in the papers and were bitterly offended. Taking a high moral position of their own, they sent a $100 bill as a retainer to a lawyer-politician named Patrick H. Jones and followed it with various credentials by way of proving that Stewart still resided with them. Packages arrived from Montreal and Boston containing screwheads from the coffin, a piece of velvet torn from the lining, and eventually, the coffin plate itself. Hilton admitted that he had deceived the widow with the fiction that the corpse had been found, in order to restore her peace of mind.

Informed of the hoax, Mrs. Stewart bypassed Hilton and undertook to treat with the go-between Jones herself. A body was said to have been recovered. According to a watchman at the unfinished cathedral, two men arrived one night with a bundle that was later buried under 14 feet of cement. Four sentries were thereafter posted at the crypt. The ghouls, however, continued their activities, even to the point of offering the Stewart corpse for sale on the open market—to P. T. Barnum and other likely customers. Questioned some time later about the reinterment, Judge Hilton shrugged. The body that reposed in Garden City, he said privately, would be "a good enough Stewart till the Resurrection."

Nobody ever found out what became of the real Stewart, but the widow was at least partially satisfied with the cathedral burial. She returned to the care of her face and decked herself once more in the gaudy clothes she loved.

In her lofty corner bedroom the tiny, withering heiress sat before her mirrors, fascinated by her wigs and philters, her elixirs, and her alchemistic pastes and powders. Where, she would ask her French maid, in a small, pathetic voice, where, oh, where was the fountain of youth? In which country, in which bottle? Would a million buy an ounce of its enchanted water? She would pay two, or three, or six— provided it were guaranteed. Somewhere she had read—though it was years since she had opened the book, or any other for that matter—of a balm, a magic recipe. . . . Had she read about it, or had someone told her? Her memory was failing . . . but it was not important. . . . No doubt the chemist was a fraud like all the others.

The French maid smiled and tried another wig. She was young and pretty, this new French maid. But she, too, would turn out to be a fraud. She would steal a pair of earrings and run off with the coachman. But who cared? Who wanted to go joggling over cobblestones? It did nothing for the figure. As for the constitution, that was a nonexistent thing invented by the doctors . . . and doctors were the biggest frauds of all. The widow would hate to lose her handsome coachman . . . but it was of no importance. . . . Perhaps, in the end, the girl would only take the earrings.

They would not need to steal if only they would show a little warmth. The widow had fortunes to dispense at random . . . if only someone in her icy world could conjure up a shred of admiration for a lonely woman haunted by so many specters, by all the unmade friends of all the empty years that had somehow slipped away, by the faces of phantom children, by the ghost of a husband who had cared less for her than for muslins and Meissoniers. But they all smiled alike— Judge Hilton and the servants, the impatient relatives who paid duty calls at her palace. How strange it was that money should turn the very statues of the hallway into parasites and frauds. Had the French maid noticed that Demosthenes had a way of bowing as she passed? Only yesterday he had smiled a sickly smile. . . . Unless, of course, she had mistaken him for the sentry. It was possible. There were so many sentries, posted by Judge Hilton. Sentries in the hallways, sentries on the roof and in the streets. They were there to guard against kidnapers. A foolish precaution, when she was not even dead.

Through the long day, the mistress of the palace catered to her terrifying vanity. But at dusk she emerged, wraithlike, into the gaslit marble halls. Wearing her giddy brown wig, laced into her décolleté ball dress, she descended the grand staircase with a queenly but uncertain step. In the gilded drawing room, lighted by a pair of torches 10 feet high, she held court to the empty whitewood chairs. Her own rouged specter greeted her from the colossal mirrors between the windows looking on Fifth Avenue, where Hilton's grim detective measured off the hours with his lugubrious, heavy step. From their pedestals, *Purity* and *Little Nell* mocked her presence with their chiseled beatific faces. Her laughter was answered by no rippling laughter. Her wineglass clinked alone in a toast directed to herself.

In the garish banquet hall, she sat at the foot of the empty dining table, flashing her imperial jewels before the butler and the footman. The servants made respectful conversation while she tasted sauces.

Sometimes, when the long dinner was over, if her glass had been filled too often, her rouge would be smeared, her tiara tilted a little to one side as she left the table. But no matter, for now began the long and horrifying night.

Through the sepulchral halls she floated, a tiny wineglass in her feeble hand, meeting her own ghastly shadow in every passing mirror. Sometimes, the lurking servants would report, she might start the evening on a merry note by receiving an imaginary guest or two in the shut-up parlors that were clammy from disuse. In the reception room she might sit in the small, low rocker by the window facing Mrs. Astor's place across the street and pour her friends a cordial from the Baccarat decanter. Here, with an amiable unreal caller, she might discuss her jewels for half an hour or so. But more often, haunted by unspecific fears, she would wander restlessly from room to room, turning up the gaslights suddenly, laughing at the portrait of the Czar of Russia or the ghostly statues she surprised. In the tomb-like picture gallery, she wove her way among the dancing girls and easels. *The Greek Slave* and *Eve Tempted* stared vacuously at nothing while she scolded at their wan and bloodless nudity. Proserpine and Sappho mocked her from their pedestals as she giggled at the falseness of their stone emotions. From the wall, Fortuny's *The Serpent Charmer* made her shudder; Gérôme's *The Gladiators* sent cold chills up and down her spine. And over all, the shade of Stewart hovered, sinister, accusing, vengeful at the slipshod management of his return to dust. By day she had her creams and treatments, but in her idle hours she knew no respite from her inturned thoughts until at last a streak of daylight came, and exhausted by the night's frustrations, in her gala dress she fell asleep.

The Great Iron Store was in receivership by 1882. But the failure of A. T. Stewart & Company held less significance for the self-infatuated widow than the failure of her newest beauty aid. The nonprofit workingwomen's hotel opened with house rules modeled after the women's penitentiary; the shopgirls stuck to their hall bedrooms, and number 2 Park Avenue was reconstituted as a luxury hotel. The sands of Garden City were voracious fortune eaters. The Saratoga hotel was a white elephant in Hilton's hands. But the moonstruck lady remained oblivious. In 1885, though she was in her eighties, she sent forth the rumor that she was about to make her entrance into society. The gates of her palace, after nine years' disuse, would swing on their rusty hinges, and Sleeping Beauty would receive the homage of the great. Society writers sneered. "Her family was very poor," an especially snobbish one remarked, "and did not aspire to social preferment in any way."

The octogenarian debutante was saved by fate from this crowning folly. She fell sick and took to her bed instead. The fraudulent doctors replaced the fraudulent practitioners of alchemy. The brown wigs stared in hideous mockery from the wooden blocks on her dressing table.

But Mrs. Stewart, though pitifully moribund without the props of vanity, lived on a few months longer; and meanwhile an unexpected bonanza showed up in Kirby's own front yard.

Across Madison Square, at 7 East 26th Street, directly opposite the American Art Association, was the unpalatial home of Mary Jane Morgan, an heiress of a very different caliber, though scarcely less anomalous. Mrs. Morgan was a modest, quiet, unassuming lady, people said, if they noticed her at all, the commonplace widow of Charles Morgan, the commonplace, if commercially gifted, steamship man. But that was before Mary Jane's secret life, or some small part of it, was suddenly revealed.

One of eight children born to Francis Sexton, a once prosperous merchant in the East India packet trade, Mary Jane Morgan began her life in the lambrequined and tasseled atmosphere of a middle-class home in Dey Street, not far from the lower tip of Manhattan Island. She was given an unusually thorough education for a girl in the first half of the nineteenth century. Her studies began at Miss Hallet's School for Young Ladies, where only French was spoken; from there she moved on to the Reverend Mr. Porter's boarding school at Lawrenceville; but the big adventure of her youth was St. Ann's Hall, a fancy institution of higher learning in Flushing, Long Island. St. Ann's was a far cry from the puerile seminaries then ordinarily provided for feminine enlightenment. It had a gymnasium with a great variety of alluring calisthenic paraphernalia, a hippodrome 900 feet in circumference for equestrian exercises, and archery grounds extensive enough to train a whole bevy of female Robin Hoods. Above all, it had the Reverend Doctor Frederick Schroeder, a veritable god of culture and virility.

Schroeder had spent some time in Europe absorbing a cosmopolitan refinement that he was apparently successful in imparting to his young ladies, along with the more warlike subjects for which the school was noted. His usual lecture topics were the fine arts and the nuances of urban life in places far removed from Flushing, but he was also given to preaching on the "Intellectual and Moral Resources of Horticulture," a subject that seems to have greatly impressed young Mary Jane. It is probable that under the spell of the good Doctor Schroeder her extraordinary dreams of glory began to form; at any rate, it is reasonable to suppose in the happy, cloistered days of St. Ann's the seeds were planted that later burgeoned into her inordinate fondness for art, clergymen, and esoteric flora.

An eager, studious girl, a little on the buxom side, Mary Jane must certainly have been one of the Reverend's favorite pupils, for when her father failed in business and she was faced with removal from the school, Schroeder kept her on as a part-time instructor. She was seventeen at the time. Later, when the Reverend Doctor opened a branch establishment in Greenwich Village, Mary Jane became a full-fledged teacher of French and mathematics.

Here, one of her students was the daughter of Charles Morgan, a widower who owned a fleet of coastwise sailing vessels. Morgan himself was almost illiterate, but he had a profound respect for book learning. So profoundly was he taken by young Mary Jane's erudition in two of the subjects basic to the steamship business that he paid court to her, and in June of 1852, they were married. Morgan was fifty-seven and Mary Jane was a blooming girl in her twenties, considerably younger than the oldest of his two sons and two grown daughters.

Charles Morgan was a Connecticut Yankee of Welsh descent, with an all-absorbing passion for commerce. In 1809, at the age of fourteen, he had sailed across Long Island Sound and down the East River to Peck Slip, where he found work as a grocery clerk. By the literal hoarding of pennies, he saved enough to start importing fruit. With the profits from his bananas and pineapples, he eventually acquired a ship, and then a line of freighters to New Orleans, Galveston, and the West Indies. In the eighteen-thirties, when Texas was struggling with Mexico for her independence, at a time when Galveston consisted of but one house, nine of the Morgan vessels were lost in rapid succession by shipwreck in the shallow Texas harbors. Although his ships were uninsured, he built others and persevered in the Texas trade with the zest of a bulldog pioneer. But it was not until after his marriage to Mary Jane that he established the Morgan Line and built the splendid fleet of mail steamers that made him the foremost shipowner in the United States.

At fifty-seven Morgan was by no means an unprepossessing bridegroom. Though gouty and showing some symptoms of wear and tear, he was a handsome man, vigorous, and still infected by a youthful, almost demoniacal urge to achieve the ultimate in one-man power. He was clean shaven, with straight white hair, rather long at the sides. His face was square, his mouth very wide, and in his eyes there was a shy, inarticulate expression. When he was not engaged in the "War of the Three Commodores" (with Vanderbilt and George Law), he had a lovable way of smiling in humility and self-depreciation, for he was painfully conscious of his lack of education. This lack Mary Jane remedied as best she could for twenty-six years.

Serenely and competently, Mistress Morgan—as the old man always called her—managed to put on paper the thoughts the steamship magnate could not express in any but the crudest terms. She was his only partner. Though in his lifetime Morgan built and operated 110 ships, sail and steam, he held no directors' meetings. There were no stockholders but himself. He did not believe in lawyers, and he had little faith in banks. His office consisted of one room, containing a safe and an old bookkeeper named Rintoul, whose accounts Mary Jane, with her handy knowledge of arithmetic, could check and double check. In Morgan's bedroom there was another safe. What was in it no one ever told, for only Mary Jane was privy to its contents. In the winter Morgan divided his time between New York and New Orleans, where large transactions were sometimes negotiated in French, with Mistress Morgan as interpreter, but if for any reason Mary Jane could not accompany him, the old man would not travel, however urgent the business at hand.

In celebration of their marriage Morgan built the house on Madison Square, a high-stooped brownstone exactly like the home of every other solid tradesman. It was a good house, but Morgan, for all his millions, had no mind for frippery and no money for extravagance. In the parlor there was a rosewood suite of eleven pieces, with mauve silk-plush upholstery. There was a rosewood grand pianoforte on which Mary Jane, in the early years, sometimes played a little Chopin in the evenings. On the rosewood table stood a solid-silver mechanical steamboat with music box attachment, but there were no fine paintings on the walls, no gleaming porcelains in the cabinets. The intellectual and moral resources of horticulture were explored only through a few hardy shrubs in the back yard, and one small greenhouse for sprouting petunias and geraniums. It was not exactly a parsimonious life, but it was hardly stimulating for a rich man's wife forced to stifle in her childless bosom the craving to surround herself with art and beauty.

As time went on, Mary Jane found herself surrounded, instead, by a crowd of jealous rivals and a flock of stepgrandchildren with a keen eye for her aging husband's moneybags. Morgan's two daughters turned out to fulfill his fondest hopes. One married the proprietor of the ironworks that supplied the hulls for ships. The husband of the other was the agent for the Morgan Line in New Orleans. But the two sons Morgan had counted on to perpetuate the steamship dynasty died of tuberculosis, leaving wives and children for the old man to support. The house was frequently besieged by mercenary daughters-in-law accompanied by their offspring, sometimes accusing Mary Jane of wielding undue influence, sometimes beseeching her to help gain access to the millions she herself was not free to spend.

There were grandsons who developed tuberculosis or bad characters. One, in particular, pilfered $8,000 from the steamship line's receipts and contributed it to the support of a "frail woman." There were scenes of wrath, with Mary Jane as mediator, for she was the only one who could soften the old man's uncompromising heart. There were endless family dinners, with unfavored relatives attempting to undermine the favored, for Morgan was a clannish man, and the clan never disobeyed a summons.

In the later years the house was almost always filled with woe and talk of money. No social circle gathered in the Morgan parlor except the Morgan family—the sons-in-law who were the old man's lieutenants in his battle for control of the Texas harbor, the indigent relatives who were scarcely able to contain their greed. The square piano was closed and locked; the music box was silent. No fashionable carriages drove up with a flourish to the unlighted doorway at number 7. No laughter floated from the shuttered windows in the soft spring evenings when the sap was rising in the trees and ordinary people went strolling beneath the gas lamps in Madison Square. In the rosewood parlor after tea, if there were no relatives present, Mary Jane would read aloud to Morgan from *The Commercial*

Advertiser, or humor him with a two-handed game of bezique. At ten o'clock they went upstairs. The old man went to bed then, in the windowless middle room, beside his safe; and in the silence of the night Mistress Morgan's private life began. For, like Mrs. Stewart, she was afflicted with insomnia.

On the shelves of her sitting room facing Madison Square, Mary Jane had every issue of *The Art Journal* published since her wedding day in 1852. The snobbish neighbors, who knew her only as a genial, unpretentious lady who, they said, "occupied a menial position in her rich husband's life," could not have imagined that she was familiar with every artist's work that appeared in the London art magazine, of whose very existence her self-appointed betters were fully unaware. There was no one but an indiscreet servant to tell of the twenty-six years of wakeful nights when the seemingly complacent Mrs. Morgan thumbed and marked and thumbed again the pages reproducing pictures by Corot, Millet, Daubigny, and Diaz. In the morning, when the small gas flame had been extinguished, her textbook on the care of orchids was back on the shelf; her French monographs on porcelains were safely tucked away in drawers. Gone from her watery eyes was the afterglow of dreams remembered from St. Ann's school, banished for the daylight hours the image of the Reverend Doctor Schroeder, long since dead but living still in the wistful fancies of a restless lady's middle years.

Charles Morgan was determined not to die, for his work was not yet finished; but by 1878 it was clear that in this matter he would be overruled. He was eighty-three and tortured by an abundance of diseases, but the steamship empire he envisioned was by no means safe from competition. Recently he had bought the railway lines in Texas and Louisiana in order to secure a transportation monopoly in the Gulf of Mexico. Now time threatened to run out before he could consolidate these gains. In desperation, though it was against his principles, he went to New Orleans and formed a corporation to insure that all his holdings would remain together in case the inevitable should happen. When this business had been accomplished, Mary Jane brought him home, where, in spite of his iron resistance, he collapsed upon his bed.

Horrendous was the deathbed scene that followed, lasting through the month of April and a little into May. The dying man had made no will, being unable to bear either the thought of death or the sight of a lawyer. But now the future of the Morgan properties obsessed him. If he could not enter the hereafter in company with his many ships, he wanted to know that they would continue sailing on this planet. He had meant to copy the will of old Cornelius Vanderbilt, who had succumbed the year before, leaving the bulk of his fortune to his eldest son, William H., in order to keep the dynasty intact. "There will be hell to pay," the mean old Commodore had predicted. But even with the aid of his pet clairvoyants, he could not have foreseen that his body would be dismembered, the condition of its component parts disputed in the law courts, all its organs measured and discussed. (Significantly, the heart was found to be abnormally small.) "The whole world is watching to see whether that will can be broken!" the Reverend Mr. Talmadge cried in an impassioned sermon at the Brooklyn Tabernacle. "Don't any of you be guilty of constructing your own will," Brooklyn's Isaiah adjured the rich men of a town in uproar. "Above all, pray to God for help in disposing of your property. Let your children share and share alike. Give something for the blind and lame and ignorant!"

Forewarned was forearmed. Charles Morgan would put his faith in no written testament. There was nothing left to do but give away the shares of Morgan's Louisiana and Texas Railroad and Steamship Company before he died.

But to whom should he give the demesne he cherished more than life itself? To Mary Jane, for one; for, as he had often said, she had helped him make his fortune. After days of tortured indecision, the others he chose were his two daughters, whose husbands understood the precarious aspects of monopoly, and a grandson who thus far had remained aloof from sporting women.

A lawyer, presumably less perfidious than any in New York, was summoned from New Orleans. Rintoul, the old bookkeeper, was called in with his pen and ink and a packet of blank stock certificates. The chosen daughter from New Orleans arrived and was rushed to the bedside in a swift carriage from the Morgan Line dock. Rintoul was instructed to write, while in the darkened airless room, singly and in unison, the four recipients were required to swear that never would they sell a share, that the Morgan fleet would sail the seas unto eternity. They swore; but when Rintoul had written, the old man could not bear to sign. He had no real intention of dying after all. The favored ones were disbanded and recalled another day . . . another, and another. Eventually, with a wasted, trembling hand, the signatures were affixed. The servants stood around as witnesses. The ink blurred a little with portentous tears.

But the certificates were not distributed. Instead, they were entrusted to Mary Jane, who put them in the safe beside the bed so that the dying man could tear them up when he recovered. In the last analysis there was no one Morgan really trusted but the faithful Mary Jane.

Next came the disposition of the millions not included in the corporation. It was Morgan's theory that if his cash fortune was distributed among his natural heirs, those unfavored by shares in the corporation would have no legal ground for challenging his deathbed gifts to the chosen four. Accordingly, he signed a little will, written by Rintoul to save a lawyer's fee. In this paper he said, "I appoint my wife, Mistress Mary Jane Morgan, to be my Executrix. All my property, real and personal, is hereby given, devised and bequeathed as provided by the laws of the State of New York in cases of intestacy."

With these worldly matters finished, Morgan turned to the preservation of his soul. The Reverend Doctor Conkling, pastor of the Rutgers Presbyterian Church, was called in for consultation. He advised baptism. The clan was summoned, this time in its entirety, and the solemn ceremony was enacted by a flickering gas jet in the darkened room. A single event, however, though conducted in the presence of so many witnesses, did not satisfy the Reverend Conkling. A few days later messengers were dispatched into the streets to round up the clan once more and bid them, on an hour's notice, to attend a confirmation service.

And so it went, until the deathbed scene had been prolonged beyond the limits of its drama. When Mary Jane collapsed from lack of sleep, a son-in-law took over; then the other son-in-law; then Mary Jane again. The favored waited to be summoned; the unfavored called at the front door and were turned away. The lawyer whose advice was never taken waited in the parlor. The doctor of physic was on constant call. The Reverend Doctor Conkling seldom left the house.

At last the inevitable seemed possible even to Charles Morgan. "I'll come back to see you," he promised Mary Jane. She smiled and took his hand. Soon after that he died.

Mary Jane distributed the stock certificates and divided the remaining spoils according to law, retaining one-third as her widow's portion. Her neat arithmetic was unassailable; but, ironically, the old man's attempts to control the destiny of his fleet turned out to be futile. Mary Jane and the other three, who had sworn so valiantly in the darkened room, cared not a farthing for monopolies. They sold the steamship empire to the Southern Pacific for $7,500,000. The unfavored heirs bitterly contested Morgan's act in giving, but not giving, the corporation to the favored four. Though they lost the case in the end, the most expensive lawyers in the country endeavored for eight years to prove that, since the stock certificates had never left the safe in Morgan's room, the transfer had not been legal.

From all these lawsuits Mary Jane remained sublimely aloof. Her conscience was clear, for under the laws of intestacy, if she had never produced the stock certificates from the bedroom safe, she would have received a third of the corporation instead of the fourth that Morgan gave her. But Mary Jane had lived long enough with the sordid preoccupation of money valued only for itself. The disgruntled relatives were banished from her parlor, the years of bookkeeping and boredom erased as by the flourish of a magic wand. Though the details of her small, dull life were laid bare by many witnesses, she gave no testimony. She did not go to court. She went shopping instead.

From her chrysalis she emerged, and while the other heirs were wrangling, quietly and methodically pursued her heart's desire. On almost any afternoon the proud inhabitants of Madison Square could have seen her coming from her doorway, a large woman in her middle fifties, unpretentious and correct as always, but no longer absorbed with mundane cares. If the day was fine, there would be no carriage waiting. Perhaps she would stand for a moment on the sandstone doorstep, adjusting a glove or tightening the grosgrain strings of her bonnet. Then, lifting the folds of her stylish skirts only enough to show the toes of her sleek French shoes, she would descend the steps and set off across the park with firm and matronly precision. People who chanced to pass remembered later that they saw, or thought they saw, a profligate glow exuding from her genial, undistinguished face; for the rich Mrs. Morgan, her reticule filled with $1,000 bills, was off on one of her daily shopping sprees.

At the other side of the square, in the shadow of the American Art Gallery, she might hesitate a moment at the junction of Broadway and Fifth Avenue, for there were two main routes she could take, and both of them had strong appeal. The Broadway fork would lead her through the Ladies' Mile, with its tremendously expensive shops and lines of carriages with footmen in anachronistic livery waiting while their ladies chose silks from the Orient or the latest luxuries from France. Such vanity shopping was mere routine for Mary Jane, but in that direction, too, were the porcelain dealers and the cabinetmakers. Down that way was the salon of the decorator who was helping her dream up a bathroom that, he said, would surpass the Pompeiian elegance of Mrs. Vanderbilt's.

If her trend was down Broadway, she was almost certain to end at Tiffany's in Union Square, a shop that eventually became her second home. It was Tiffany's that cast for her in silver and gold the curious sculptures that now began to fill her hallway—small statues and plaques from the drawings she had made in the midnight silence of her married years: a herd of buffalo, for example, pursued by a group of mounted Indians with golden lassos in the air. It was Tiffany's that made her a pair of Roman candelabra, of sterling silver, 5 feet 8 inches high, for $40,000; that furnished the designs for her cameo flint glass service and sent the molds overseas, where the 226 pieces were made to order by Webb of London. Tiffany's men did all her errands and sold her $1 million worth of diamonds; and yet their store was not her first choice as a destination. The left fork was not her favorite way.

It was down Fifth Avenue she loved to go, for there the picture dealers lay. It was seldom that Mr. Knoedler would not have something new for her, a Corot landscape or two or three Millets, an Italian scene by Fortuny, or an Arab horseman by Eugène Fromentin. Once seated in Knoedler's parlor, she would take off her gloves and rest her pinched feet on a charming footstool fetched by a respectful attendant who seemed to understand that French shoes always hurt. Mr. Knoedler would sit beside her while two porters displayed the newest paintings one by one. The poorest pictures were brought in first, for Mary Jane had an instinct for quality which it gave her pleasure to display. No, she would say, compressing her lips and shaking her head in instant rejection, that was not a first-class example of Alma-Tadema's work. Mr. Knoedler would agree. He had only wanted her to see the things he had. But the next one! Ah, here was a different story altogether.

A joy that old Charles Morgan had never seen would come into his widow's face as she walked over to examine the details of the brushwork. *Roman Lady Feeding Fish* it was called? A pleasant subject, pleasantly painted. How much did Mr. Knoedler want for it?

Mr. Knoedler was adept at playing the little scene that always followed. Seven thousand, he would suggest, a note of question coloring his tone. Both of them knew that he was bluffing. Mary Jane cared not in the least whether she paid $5,000 or $10,000, but she could not let the gentlemanly dealers look upon her as a fool. Would he take $4,000? the lady would inquire, charmingly if not convincingly. Impossible, but $6,000 he might consider. After a few minutes of the most congenial kind of bargaining, they would agree on $5,000, the original price marked on the back in Mr. Knoedler's code.

With that settled, the attendants would be summoned to bring the next examples—Aubert's *Love Quenching His Thirst*, perhaps, or *Cow and Calf* by Rosa Bonheur. The same program of acceptance and rejection, of bargaining and agreement, would follow the showing of each canvas, until Mr. Knoedler had revealed to his appreciative client all the newest importations he had set aside, he said, especially for her. Opening her reticule, Mary Jane would then count out the necessary thousands and prepare to take her leave. He fondly hoped that Mrs. Morgan would find the time to pay a call next week, Mr. Knoedler would say. There should be some fine Barbizons coming over on the next French boat.

Yes, indeed, she would be back next week, if not before. Smiling graciously, she would bid Mr. Knoedler a fond good day and continue down the avenue, her long skirts trailing in the flagstone dust, her face flushed with the excitement of the chase.

A few blocks down she would pay a call on Mr. Cottier and perhaps invest in a van Marcke cattle scene or a new work by Professor Ludwig Knaus. From Cottier's she might continue down as far as 14th Street, the southern boundary of her peregrinations. There, she would spend an hour or so with Mr. Avery, who possibly would have a new Jules Breton or a Bouguereau Madonna she would want to snap up before William Vanderbilt got his clutches on it. If Avery's stock had been replenished since her last visit, she might spend $50,000 or $100,000 before wending her way slowly back uptown again.

There would probably not be time then to pay a call on Mr. Christian Herter, who was working on a bedroom suite the like of which even Mrs. Astor had not yet commanded, or visit any of her favorite horticulturalists. But tomorrow was another day. Mr. Schaus, a picture dealer of whom she was inordinately fond, would probably come to tea, at any rate. Schaus might have a new Rousseau for her, or better still, another glimpse of the forest of Fontainebleau by Narcisse Virgile Diaz de la Peña to make her afternoon complete. And so, her reticule considerably slimmer than when she had set out, Mary Jane would return to Madison Square, to the house that was ostensibly a somber bourgeois brownstone but in reality a place rapidly undergoing a transformation so magical and secret that it might have been the lair of a modern Ali Baba with a retinue of picture-loving thieves.

No one knew what she was doing. It was known, of course, that she possessed some pictures, but the art writers who described every Etruscan bronze and Munkácsy daub belonging to Catharine Lorillard Wolfe remained in ignorance of the far more significant collection of Mrs. Morgan, a stone's throw across the square. The awed society reporters who wrote of Mrs. Astor's latest diamond sunburst as breathlessly as if another sun had actually risen on Manhattan Island knew nothing of the shopping orgies of Mary Jane. The picture dealers and porcelain sellers gladly kept her secret. Tiffany's was as silent as the grave. Mrs. Morgan never went into society, never appeared in public laden with her $1 million worth of jewels. She was on no visiting lists. No one ever asked her to a ball. No stylish ladies ever stopped to leave a card. She was a peculiar woman, hermitlike and timid, her few acquaintances said. Even her relatives had no idea that, within five years of Charles Morgan's death, his once drab house had come to harbor what was to be described as "the choicest collection of contemporary paintings in the world."

That she had spruced up the place was all too obvious to William Moir when he came to inquire after the comforts of his "poor, weak sister-in-law." Moir, the husband of Mary Jane's sister Emily, was a

Scotsman and a jeweler, a man of sterling character, but an unctuous bore. On his brotherly calls, while waiting in vain to be asked advice about the careful conservation of the millions Mary Jane had so fortunately inherited, he might share the rosewood parlor with the lustrous Peachbloom Vase. Pretty little bottle, he would remark. It was, he supposed, no more than a foible in the Chinese taste, something his poor sister-in-law might have picked up in the crockery department of a Broadway store. He could not know that locked in a cabinet behind his back were portfolios containing etchings that had cost $100,000. He kept a jewelry store, but he had no knowledge of the diamonds upstairs in old Charles Morgan's safe. The paintings on the walls, he was aware, represented a nerve-racking extravagance. But he was a beaver of a businessman with not much eye for art. If he sat facing *The Cardinal's Menu* one week and *The Frugal Meal* the next, he would scarcely notice the difference. In any case, he never dreamed that Mary Jane could, if she chose, change the pictures in her parlor as often as a jewel merchant changed his shirt. Even Mary Jane's sisters could not guess that all the walls of all the upstairs rooms were honeycombed with secret drawers and closets. Almost no one was aware that the top floor of the house contained a gallery of pictures the like of which the Metropolitan Museum did not then possess.

One innovation, however, Mary Jane could not conceal. Gone from the back yard were the commonplace ailanthus trees, the little greenhouse with its geraniums and petunias, the shrubs that hardly ever flowered. In their place, Mary Jane erected huge glasshouses filled with orchids. Winter, summer, spring, or fall, she could now partake of the intellectual and moral resources of horticulture. On her humid, tropical forest, blazing with the richest and most subtle colors, she spent $300,000, about half for the rarest South American plants, and the remainder on their cultivation.

Mary Jane's relatives saw no great harm in the orchids. The flowers were undeniably beautiful, and the watchful William Moir had no way of knowing that she sometimes spent $1,500 for a single plant. Moir, however, took a dim view of her attachment for the Reverend Doctor Conkling, for, it seemed, the Reverend remained in constant attendance at the 26th Street house long after old Charles Morgan was beyond the need of clerical ministrations.

The Reverend Doctor Nathaniel W. Conkling, later to be known in headlines as "Lucky Pastor Conkling," or "The Clergyman Who Enjoyed the Friendship of Widow Morgan," had started his career as a Philadelphia preacher. His style was strongly imitative of the Reverend Mr. Talmadge, the celebrated whiplash of Brooklyn sinners; but eccentricity paid less handsomely in Philadelphia, and Conkling's wife prevailed upon him to move to New York. There, she imagined, his talents would be better appreciated, and there, she hoped, a rich husband could be found for her eldest daughter, a winsome creature of whose accomplishments both Mrs. Conkling and the Reverend were exceedingly proud. Conkling received a call to take over Rutgers Presbyterian Church on Madison Avenue; his oratory increased the flock enough to warrant building a new and grander church; and for a time it looked as if his wife's hunch had been a good one. But no sooner had the new church opened than the Conkling star began to wane. By 1878, when the Reverend was summoned to Charles Morgan's bedside, no considerable flock was crowding the Rutgers pews. Moreover, no desirable suitor had yet presented himself at the Conklings' modest door. By 1881 over-expansion had run the church into the ground, and the Reverend Conkling was called upon to leave the pastorate. But never was unemployed preacher less concerned about the wolf at the door. For by now the Reverend Doctor's friendship with Mary Jane was paying handsome dividends.

Now the once somber dining table of the Morgan house became a forum for scintillating conversation. Amid talk of horticulture, painting, or the history of Chinese art, punctuated by the Conkling daughter's well-timed peals of silvery laughter, Mary Jane assumed at last the role projected for her thirty years before, in the days of St. Ann's school. Her diamonds glittered like so many little suns and planets surrounded by their satellites of emeralds and rubies. Her Royal Vienna china depicting Biblical subjects, her eighteenth-century Sèvres with medallions of court beauties, her Minton, Royal Worcester, Dresden, Copeland, and Crown Derby, multihued and glowing in the white flames of the forty tapers burning in the $40,000 candelabra, the delicate sterling, the rarest of laces, the vintage wines poured by soundless maids into the cameo flint glasses—all this and more was none too good for the Reverend Conkling and his family.

"He got a million dollars from her first and last," William Moir blubbered ruefully to the press, when finally his sister-in-law's profligacy was unmasked. Moir was given to exaggeration, but this time his accounting was probably not far off. For $52,500 Mary Jane bought the Lucky Parson a fine house on East 34th Street, in a region that harbored numberless potential suitors for his daughter's lily hand; $45,000 more was spent for furniture and decorations. She paid his living expenses and bought elaborate wardrobes for the women of his household. She sent him on a holiday to the Pacific coast, with his whole brood, including two other children in addition to the daughter waiting to be plucked. She was said to have made a will leaving her estate to her Reverend friend; as an advance, she gave him $600,000 in government bonds. "The story goes," the horrified *Tribune* later reported, "that he took these bonds away from her house in a cab and went to Europe." When Mary Jane died, in July 1885, he had not returned.

She died without ever seeing the bathroom to rival Alva Vanderbilt's, without ever sleeping in the bed to outrank Mrs. Astor's. By the spring of 1885 her progress through the arts was practically complete, but it had been so rapid that there had not been time to arrange the setting properly. In May she had some of her pictures and more valuable objects packed by Tiffany's and sent to storage. Then she left the house in charge of workmen and went to Saratoga to take the waters. There she died quite suddenly of Bright's disease.

Speedily the revelations came. William Moir was, of course, Johnny on the spot. Reporters were welcomed to the house. A lady writer fell into raptures over the new bedroom furniture—solid rosewood, inlaid with brass (or was it gold?) and four kinds of mother-of-pearl. The bathroom, too, shed posthumous glory on its designer. Mrs. Vanderbilt, lolling in her alabaster makeshift, was privileged to read about the porcelain tub lined with onyx, the waterspout set in a panel of Siena marble carved with dolphins, the basin and ewers of "solid silver." Additional dolphins formed a letter M in the mosaic floor; the wainscot was of San Domingo mahogany, the panels of "exquisite Indian carving." The stained-glass window, "in rich but subdued tones," represented Cupid at a fountain. But, alas! this visionary chamber, like the tower of Babel, never saw completion.

Moir took over manfully. The will in favor of the Reverend Conkling was, like the Reverend himself, nowhere to be found. The servants who had witnessed its execution conceded that it must have been destroyed. The surrogate ruled that Mrs. Morgan had died intestate. Letters of administration were granted to Moir and his wife, Emily, as representatives of the lady's next of kin. Mrs. Moir somewhat precipitously announced to the press that her late sister's personal property was worth $250,000. Upon reading this, one of Mary Jane's picture dealers said she had spent $700,000 in his gallery alone. Mr. Moir said Mrs. Moir was not to be relied upon. Like Mary Jane, she had "temporary fits of dementia."

At this point Kirby walked across the square and offered to make an inventory. They would be delighted, the Moirs said. The auctioneer made a trip to the warehouse, and Mrs. Moir's appraisal was roughly increased by from $2 million to $4 million. Among 240 paintings, Kirby had discovered Millet's *The Spinner*, "well-known through etchings." Jules Breton's *Communicants* was very famous, Kirby said, "and he has written a poem to go with it." The lady had Count Kleczkowski's famous porcelains. . . . Kirby's superlatives flowed as freely as the saliva from William Moir's gaping mouth. "My poor sister-in-law," Moir wailed. "She was the prey of any quantity of sharps."

Kirby could do nothing about the Lucky Pastor Conkling—the cruelest thorn in Moir's unhappy flesh—but he could be enormously helpful in converting the spendthrift lady's art back into cash. By no conceivable means other than public auction could such an estate be settled. Happily the Seney sale existed as a precedent! In relief and gratitude Moir put the whole confusing mess into Kirby's hands.

Given a free rein, the gascon little auctioneer seized the opportunity to stage a drama of superspectacle extravagance. His most striking innovation was the Mary Jane Morgan catalogue, a 305-page quarto volume that so far surpassed any cynosure of art collecting previously published in the United States that it not only launched the business at hand but synthesized Kirby's whole new concept of the élite auction. Printed on heavy rag paper, with twenty-nine etchings and twenty-four photographs tipped in, bound in pristine white boards with rich gold lettering, this weighty tome cost $40,000 to produce. It contained biographical notes on 116 artists favored by Mary Jane, interspersed with vignettes of their countenances; "the famous Peach-bloom Vase" was shown full-page, tinted, in photogravure; and the whole, "compiled by Thomas E. Kirby," described 2,628 lots from Mrs. Morgan's unbelievable collection. It was a book to rest in splendor on the tables of the proudest salons. There was, of course, an ordinary catalogue, without illustrations, for ordinary customers, the de luxe edition being limited to five hundred numbered copies. The price was $10, but if mere money could have bought such a book, its propaganda value would have been lost. Except for a few copies sent to other cities, the entire edition was delivered by hand, with the compliments of the American Art Association, to the front doors of the most exclusive mansions in New York.

The exhibition opened February 12, 1886. Every foot of space in the Art Association's eleven galleries was required to display the pictures and decorative objects Mary Jane had somehow crammed into her house across the square. Even so, the mother-of-pearl furniture, and everything else that could not be classified strictly as art, was excluded from the catalogue and left to be disposed of at a later series of house sales. The jewels, too, were absent. Mr. and Mrs. Moir had deposited them with a trust company as bond for their services as administrators. The orchid plants were sold at a florists' auction in Horticultural Hall. But with the exception of these things, Mistress Morgan's monumental possessions were displayed in their entirety before the eyes of a public agape with curiosity.

There was a feeling in the press that everyone had been cheated, including Mary Jane herself. Art, in that feverish era, was a social asset, collecting the province of the socially elect or, inevitably, of such interlopers as A. T. Stewart. Culture was a commendable thing, but what would a woman who never entertained want of it? Furthermore, there were rules about collecting that this Mrs. Nobody had flagrantly ignored. Where were the letters from the Salon artists, the custom-painted pictures, the gleanings from the grand tour in company with a courier-connoisseur? The whimsical Mrs. Morgan had simply gone down the street and bought what was there. By all the regulations, her collection should have revealed the crotchets of a quaint and foolish woman. But it did not. If her taste had been more advanced, it would have created no sensation; but, inconceivably, she had what the moguls had, only more and better. And somehow she had rudely put them in their place.

"Money sticks out all over the collection," *Town Topics* reported, with more snobbery than erudition. "The collections are dealers' ones and in no way reflect credit on the lady who made them. A person of comparatively limited education and little or no art taste, she bought pictures and art objects of all kinds at fabulous prices, simply because she had a hobby for spending her money in this way. . . . It seems somewhat strange that in so young a country such collections as these of modern art, rivalling any offered for sale in recent years abroad, could have been gotten together."

"It is daringly asserted that dealers have thrown in their own stock," one observer wrote, dragging up the old charge against art auctions by way of minimizing the fabulosity of Mary Jane's accumulation. In rebuttal, Kirby simply displayed the receipted bills Mary Jane had kept as meticulously as she had formerly preserved Charles Morgan's secret papers. To this the undaunted detractor replied, "Poor lady, how she was fleeced!"

But by the second week of the exhibition even *Town Topics* conceded that everyone went to see the pictures—"the gay young beauty . . . the dude." Strange blunders were made, the ultrasophisticated editor sneered. Millet was confused with Millais, he observed, without noticing that Mary Jane had no pictures by Millais. "But," he concluded witheringly, "it is the fashion to at least affect to be artistic and so the fashionable world betakes itself to the Morgan Collection."

Fashionable or unfashionable, the citizenry did indeed betake itself to the American Art Association's galleries. Every afternoon carriages blocked the progress of the horsecars on 23rd Street; visitors overflowed into the square. During the three weeks of the exhibition 100,000 people came to see Mary Jane's dreams of glory waiting for the hammer of the auctioneer.

In the face of such enthusiasm, most of the newspapers refrained from belittling the pictures. The *Tribune* ignored Mary Jane's art in favor of her unaccountable relations with the Reverend Doctor Conkling. The *Times* chose to titillate its readers with the scandal of the Peachbloom Vase.

What eventually developed into the most whimsical controversy of the decade began innocently enough with a sentence in an art magazine. Shortly after Mary Jane's death, William Moir, voluble as always, and imbued with his more or less permanent state of incredulity, had conducted a writer from *The Art Amateur* on a tour of his late sister-in-law's closets. Lest the reporter should be insufficiently impressed with the phenomena before his eyes, Moir followed him about with a sheaf of receipted bills, thumping at the astronomical sums with a vigorous forefinger the better to substantiate in black and white the facts and figures he himself could barely comprehend. The result was that the writer, after eulogizing Mrs. Morgan's boundless enthusiasm and almost bottomless purse, mentioned that "among the most costly pieces of what is known as solid color [porcelain], the most precious is the little vase of 'Peach Blow' for which Mrs. Morgan is reported to have paid $15,000."

Kirby himself, in extolling the collection a few weeks later, fanned the flame by casually mentioning to reporters a peachblow vase 15 inches high, which cost $15,000 and was "said to be worth it." He added that Mrs. Morgan had bought the thing at the American Art Association.

The only accurate information in Kirby's offhand remark was the statement that the item had been bought in his own establishment. As every newspaper reader subsequently came to know, the Peachbloom Vase had cost only $12,000 and was not 15, but 8 inches high, a fact tending to make it twice as expensive, since there was only half as much of it. But even Kirby's plug would probably have passed as no more than another tribute to the Widow Morgan's extravagance if Charles A. Dana had not taken up the banner.

Dana's friendship for the American Art Association had been firmly cemented by Kirby's refusal to let him buy the sage-colored vase that lost its charms in a tub of water. Though his enthusiasms sometimes ran away with him, the *Sun*'s learned editor was a man with an abundance of intellectual and artistic interests. He was a student of many languages, a theosophist, a believer in pantheistic evolution and the doctrine of reincarnation. He was an admirer of tapestry and paintings and the Brahmanic scriptures, a grower of mushrooms and gloxinias. He had a passion for Chinese porcelain. Now in his sixties, he had accumulated enough profits from his newspaper to be able to indulge his expensive tastes. The three drawing rooms of the beautiful house he had recently built on Madison Avenue were gold and gray and ruby plush; in one of them there was an ebony cabinet containing a peachblow vase. It was only natural that Dana should have considered it news that Mary Jane Morgan, unbeknown to anyone, had possessed the rarest Chinese porcelains in the city. Out of what was undoubtedly a sincere wish to bring the *Sun*'s readers a smattering of information on a subject close to his heart, Dana had one of his writers prepare a piece on her collection. In referring to the Peachbloom Vase, the writer, or perhaps Dana himself, stated that "there is not now enough inventive genius or knowledge in the world to duplicate it or any piece of the same porcelain."

This simple tribute to a lost art of the mysterious East was incendiary to *The New York Times*. Concern for social justice and Chinese history, worries about the spendthrift ways of the upstart Mary Jane and about treachery at the American Art Association, scorn for the *Sun*'s lofty cultural awareness, antitheosophy, and anxiety about a number of other loosely related subjects converged in a maelstrom of indignation in the editorial rooms of the rival newspaper. Alarums and excursions first appeared in the news items. Then, three days before the auction was scheduled to begin, the *Times* department of culture mustered what information it could and produced an all-out attack against Dana and the Peachbloom Vase. Under the title "Booming Peach-blooms," the *Times* editorial declared in part:

From a depth of knowledge which enables him to correct the Chinese concerning their own ceramics, and from a power theosophical which permits him to learn in visions all about a "porcelain that has not been described by any Chinese writer," some brazen person labors to prove in the New York Sun that the so-called peach-blow vases in the Morgan collection are as rare and valuable as the public is asked to believe. The public does not own peach-blow vases, and is in no hurry to, but it sympathizes with those who, owning one or two, therefore seek, with an effrontery truly amusing, to boom their peach-blooms as they boom a stock in Wall Street. It can afford to laugh at a parade of learning which begins with such an untenable statement as this: "For nearly one thousand years, of which we have historical knowledge, and probably for a much longer period, the Chinese have made fine porcelains."

Ordinary students of Eastern questions who do not evolve the past of China in the Hindu fashion by steadfast contemplation of the navel . . . are unable to find any evidence of the existence of Chinese porcelain a thousand years old. Faience, glass, stone ware, can be accepted with some certainty, but there is no proof that till some time after the Mongol dynasty, A.D. 1260–1367, such a thing as porcelain was known. Six centuries is the furthest stretch and the difference between six and ten is material.

. . . It [the Peachbloom Vase] may be worth fifteen thousand dollars but it is in the nature of a monster or other spectacular object and is regarded with open mouth by the public solely because it cost the price of a New York house.

The assumptions in this jaunty editorial were almost wholly fallacious, for the *Times*, in those days, was ill equipped to joust with the intellectual *Sun*. Dana's information, whether derived from contemplation of the navel or not, was far more accurate. The evolution of true porcelain from kaolinic pottery is believed to have occurred in the interval between A.D. 220 and A.D. 618. At any rate, porcelain of extraordinary beauty was manufactured in large quantities during the Tang dynasty (618–906). The gaping public, however, knew nothing of such historical facts and cared less. Those who had previously neglected to view the treasure heaped up by Mrs. Morgan hastened to do so. To the utter horror of the *Times*, it was reported that at closing hour one evening, when attendants were locking things up for the night, an open-mouthed old lady lingered at the case that held the now famous peachblow monster.

"I want you to do me a favor," she said. "I want you to let me kiss that vase before you put it away." The attendant did so, and the lady went off happy.

In reply to such foolishness, the antipeachblow faction had a number of trump cards to play, but the game had only just got started when the Mary Jane Morgan painting sale began. For a few days the colossal matter of the Peachbloom Vase was overshadowed by the news from Kirby's rostrum.

On Wednesday, March 3, 1886, the doors of Chickering Hall opened at 6:45 in the evening for the first session of the sale that was to stand until 1910 as the most important art auction ever held in this country. But long before six o'clock, in the words of a contemporary observer, "Fifth Avenue was like Calvé night at the opera." Prospective buyers had traveled from all parts of the country. Some had even come from Europe to attempt to redeem the works of famous modern painters from the land of barbarism and upstart millionaires. Not a titan or a mogul was unrepresented; not a dealer was absent; not a struggling museum but had its hopeful bidder in the packed auditorium. The result, as Kirby described it, was "a battle by the Napoleons of Finance."

Never was the judgment of a poor lady who had been fleeced vindicated with so much drama. Incredibly—or so it seemed to the shamefaced art reporters—the follies of Mrs. Morgan turned out to be the fancies of F. O. Matthiessen and James A. Garland; of Rothschilds who had journeyed all the way from Paris; of Sir Donald Smith, who had recently driven home the last spike of the Canadian transcontinental railway; of William T. Walters of Baltimore, John G. Johnson of Philadelphia, and the numerous other men who represented the hierarchy of collecting in 1886.

Jehan Georges Vibert's *The Missionary's Story*, for which Mary Jane had given Knoedler the shocking sum of $12,500, fell to Collis P. Huntington for $25,500. (It now hangs in the Metropolitan Museum as *The Missionary's Adventures*.) H. O. Havemeyer bid twice what Mary Jane had paid for Decamps' *The Walk to Emmaus*. But, just as in the Seney sale, the star of the show was the peasant-painter Jules Breton. His *Communicants* (complete with poem) went to Sir Donald Smith for $45,500, double what Mary Jane had paid for it, and almost $27,000 more than the record price of Kirby's mascot picture, *Evening in the Hamlet of Finistère*.

In her devil-may-care extravagance Mary Jane had bought sixty canvases by the Barbizon painters, a school still looked upon as a dubious investment in modernity by many of her contemporaries. Her seventeen works by the late one-legged Narcisse Virgile Diaz de la Peña sold for over $50,000. Her eleven figure pieces by Millet ranged from $650 for a charming, if miniscule, *Woman in Kitchen* (4½ by 3 inches) to $14,000 for *The Spinner*. Among her eight Corots was the huge *Wood Gatherers*, for which the Corcoran Gallery of Washington contributed $15,000. A nephew, Thomas Newcomb of Brooklyn, who was one of the heirs to Mary Jane's fortune, paid $14,000 for a silvery view of Lake Nemi. This Corot landscape (which had cost Mary Jane $16,500) stayed in the Newcomb family for twenty-six years. In 1912, when Kirby sold it again, the *Lake Nemi* which had hung in the foolish Mrs. Morgan's stair well went to Cyrus H. McCormick of Chicago at $85,000, a record price at that time for a Corot at auction.

But if twenty-six years and the boom in Corot were to prove that Mary Jane knew a blue-chip picture when she saw one, there was even stronger evidence that her prescience as a collector was developing at the time of her demise. Sandwiched in among the standard works of her era were small but vibrant paintings by Constable and Delacroix.

There was not much bidding for them in 1886. A Constable landscape brought $3,350. Knoedler bought her finest Delacroix, *Tiger and Serpent*, at $4,450. In the last year of her life the lady "who had bought with so little knowledge" had acquired two pictures from A. P. Ryder, the greatly gifted recluse who lived on dreams and bread crusts in a debris-cluttered tenement not far from Madison Square. It is not unlikely that the unpredictable Mrs. Morgan felt a genuine affinity for those richly colored visions to be acclaimed long years after as works of such significance in the history of modern art. Kirby's bidders could only sniff at such deviations among the crackpots and eccentrics. One of Ryder's pictures sold for $225, the other for $375.

There were few such paltry prices. Nondescript academic pictures were carried along by the stylish ones. If the bidding lagged, the dealers, Knoedler, Avery, Schaus, and Cottier, made an absurdity of the claim that they had taken advantage of a rich widow's naïveté by buying back the pictures they had sold her for about what she had paid for them. But this was seldom necessary. Not only Thomas Newcomb but the rest of Mary Jane's heirs, spurred by the tumult and the shouting, and perhaps jubilant in the knowledge that her fortune was by no means lost, bid in the lots which threatened to go cheaply. Even Mrs. Moir, no doubt in the throes of dementia, bought a few nice paintings, which were later sold at a handsome profit.

When, on the third night, Kirby let his hammer fall on the last of the Morgan pictures, only a husk remained of what was beginning to be called his "famous stentorian voice." The total for the 240 paintings was $885,800. One of the newspapers, which only a week before had depicted Mary Jane as a ridiculous figure, now conceded that her picture sale was "the most important affair of its kind ever known and the most cleverly conducted."

But Kirby had no time to bask in the success of the initial skirmishes. Nine days of the auction remained. Moreover, in the very next session, three days hence, the fate of the monstrous Peachbloom Vase would have to be settled. Once more, as in the case of Seney's slandered pictures, the infant reputation of the American Art Association was endangered; and again, some bold action on Kirby's part seemed to be in order. But what? To withdraw the controversial bottle from the sale would be a cowardly escape. To drop the foolish thing and break it would be even more suspicious. A lawsuit was out of the question, for the vase had not been directly libeled. The *Times* had said Charles A. Dana was a fool and that there were no porcelains a thousand years old, but nobody had ever suggested that the Peach-bloom Vase was ancient. It was catalogued as of the "Kang-he period, 1661–1722," a designation carelessly spelled but clearly intended to indicate the time of the Emperor K'ang Hsi. So far, no one had suggested that the bottle might have been made in Brooklyn, but if someone had, it would have been difficult to prove otherwise, for there were no porcelain scholars in America whose word could have been taken as authoritative. And yet, by some method, suspicions of double-dealing had to be allayed.

The solution Kirby and Sutton worked out appears to have been spiced with the wisdom of Solomon. So long as the vase was genuine, it was priceless. The essence of the scandal, then, was the mere fact that Mrs. Morgan had paid the price of a house for an 8-inch bottle. To this there was only one dignified reply. The Peachbloom Vase would have to be resold for the price of not one, but two New York houses.

The sale, of course, would have to be legitimate. Obviously the vase could not be bid in by the house, or by any of Mary Jane's heirs. For Charles A. Dana to so much as raise his hand would be interpreted as a gesture of self-defense. An anonymous buyer would be immediately suspected of collusion. Only one type of purchaser would do. He had to be a man of wealth, a porcelain lover by reputation, and above suspicion as a conspirator.

William T. Walters was a gentleman who superbly fitted this description. Walters had been a big buyer at the painting sale. He had, in his Baltimore museum, the best collection of Chinese porcelains in the country. In his cabinets there were many specimens of the K'ang Hsi period, but alas no peachblow. What could be more natural than that Walters should covet Mary Jane's expensive vase? Apparently he did.

On the Monday afternoon following the closing session of the picture sales, Kirby, never more businesslike and self-composed, mounted the rostrum to continue the auction of Mary Jane's possessions. The main room of the Madison Square galleries was crowded to the rafters, but for once Kirby seemed unaware of the throb of expectation in his audience. He was, if anything, a little better-natured than usual, but his voice was strangely humdrum as he plowed through the first ninety-nine lots. If he noticed the rustle of anticipation as the Peachblow Vase was brought in, covered with a cloth of gold, he showed no sign.

"Series of Chinese Porcelains," he read from the catalogue. " 'Peach Blow' or 'Crushed Strawberry' color."

One attendant placed the precious object in the center of the block. The other removed the gold cloth with a respectful flourish. There were murmurs from the audience, but no one started any applause. Kirby barely glanced at the tiny, pale, red-pink object.

" 'Number three forty-one,' " he read from the catalogue in a monotone. " 'Vase of graceful ovoid shape, with slender neck, slightly spreading at top, perfection in form, color and texture. Height, exclusive of carved stand, eight inches, diameter three inches. Mark of the Kang-he period, 1661–1722. The above from the private collection of I Wang-ye, a Mandarin Prince, has a world-wide reputation as being the finest specimen of its class in existence.' What am I offered?"

Even the *Times* could make nothing spectacular of the unheated contest that followed. Kirby let his hammer fall with no intimation that he was adding insult to injury. The price was $18,000—to William T. Walters, the noted connoisseur of Baltimore.

"Bidding against Walters for some time," the *Times* observer wrote, "was a tall, gaunt, rather countrified looking man of thirty whom no one seemed to know and who told inquirers they might as well call him Mr. Ferguson as anything else." Actually, Walters was not present at the sale. Sutton did the bidding on his behalf. The reporter, for want of more dramatic material, had to fill out his dispatch with a narrative of Charles A. Dana's battle with two other theosophs over what the *Times* was pleased to call "a Buddhist communion service."

But the antipeachblow crowd was by no means silenced. Within a week, ammunition had been gathered for a devastating new attack, and by the time Kirby had finished selling Mary Jane's major possessions, the town was rollicking with the quaint particulars of her original purchase of the now-$18,000 bottle. According to the alleged confession of a shamelessly disloyal salesman, Mrs. Morgan had paid a casual visit to the American Art Association one afternoon while on one of her shopping tours. She saw the vase, liked it, and asked the price. The clerk looked at the code, misread $2,000 for $12,000, and the lady bought it.

Whether true or not, this story was a source of boundless delight to everyone but Dana, Mr. W. T. Walters, and the American Art Association. It was a cruel task, one commentator sympathized, to have to protect a peachblow vase to the tune of thousands when you knew yourself that it was not worth hundreds. And to have the foolish tattle of a mendacious employee upset the whole sacrifice by telling brazen untruths about it which cannot be supported!

In the weeks that followed the *Times* grew sillier and sillier, the *Sun* angrier and angrier. The *Times* editors were not greatly inspired by the salesman's alleged confession. But by the latter part of March they had dug up a Man Who Knew.

He was a gentleman recently arrived from China, they said. Though nameless, he was possessed of social position, official position, probity, veracity, and a collection of porcelains. He would tell, it was promised, a well-kept secret surrounding the *pièce de résistance* of Mary Jane Morgan's porcelain collection. He had seen the notorious vase in Peking, and his statements, in the opinion of his interviewers, would be astonishing.

Under the headline "Not Even a Peachblow," the revelations of this anonymous gentleman occupied front-page space comparable to that ordinarily reserved for war and pestilence. According to the Man Who Knew, Mr. Austin Robertson, agent for the American Art Association, had bought the $12-15-18,000 vase in 1884 from a Pekingese curio dealer for 250 Mexican silver dollars. Previously it had been declined by several others, including the Man Who Knew himself, for one-half the amount.

But that was not all. Columns of further revelations ensued, all no doubt made with probity and veracity, but at the same time, flavored with a certain inconsistency.

The peachblow family of porcelain, said the Man Who Knew, was entirely unknown to collectors in China. The craze for it here would cause amusement there, for the peachblow family did not exist except in the fertile brains of American dealers and collectors. This was proved, he said, by the low price Robertson had paid for the peach-bloom vase in question.

On the other hand, the Chinese dealer had boasted about getting

Mary Jane Morgan's famed Peachbloom Vase, height eight inches (WALTERS ART GALLERY).

such a high price for his peachblow vase, since it was by no means the most perfect of its (nonexistent) kind. A number of annoying spots near the base were off-color. They were green, of all things!

In any event, Mary Jane's vase was not genuine peachblow at all, as peachblow (though entirely unknown) was understood in China. It was crushed strawberry. Kirby had catalogued it as either or both, but the descriptions in the Morgan catalogue, said the Man, were absolute rubbish. He happened to know that Mrs. Morgan's vase was never in the collection of the Mandarin Prince I Wang-Ye. How did he know? Because there were no Mandarin princes. A Mandarin prince did not become a prince except in art catalogues.

All the same, the Prince of Ye (who was not a prince) did have a very famous collection. He was formerly in favor with the reigning family and therefore very rich, but after the emperor died he received the white silken cord. When the Prince of Ye consequently was no more, his collection was scattered, though not the Peachbloom Vase, for he did not have it.

There was a great deal more in the same vein, but the highest scorn of the Man Who Knew was naturally reserved for Charles A. Dana. In an article called "The Bloom of the Peach," Dana had remarked loftily: "Yet for our aspiring contemporaries, greedy of learning which they are not able unaided to attain, we will here add the fact that these objects are of the genuine *ou-tsai-khi* and that they were made at King-Te-Chin about the latter part of the seventeenth century for the imperial delectation alone."

Simple rubbish, said the Man Who Knew. King-Te-Chin existed and so did *ou-tsai-khi*, but the date of manufacture was impossible. Furthermore, if it were not for annoying Mr. Dana, which of course no gentleman of probity would dream of doing, the Man Who Knew would have written him to ask what *ou-tsai-khi* meant. It meant, in case some dim-witted reader did not know, simply "porcelain decorated in color." How, then, could the Peachblow Vase be *ou-tsai-khi*, since it was monochrome—except for those green spots—and not decorated at all?

The Man Who Knew shot his bolt all in one issue, but two days later, having allowed Dana twenty-four hours for rebuttal, the *Times* printed another editorial. This one was entitled "The Red Jug," since technically the Peachbloom Vase no longer existed.

"What a pity," the *Times* editor lamented, "that an excellent kind-hearted elderly gentleman should get into a towering passion about a miserable red jug! . . . Though well aware of the prominent part which the editor of the Sun has taken in the peachblow vase swindle, we have paid no particular attention to him, his performance being of slight consequence in comparison with the work of carefully collecting and truthfully setting forth the facts in the history of the vase which the American Art Association bought in Pekin for $200 and sold to Mrs. Morgan for $12,000."

The barbs continued to fly back and forth, while the circulation of both papers increased. After skipping a day, the *Times* again deplored Dana's bad humor: "It is a thousand pities that he should not share in the town's innocent merriment over the peachbloom vase. His is the only scowling face. The applewomen adorn their stands with choice *ou-tsai-khi;* the scalpers throw in peachbloom vases with their cut-rate tickets and every fancy goods store on Sixth Avenue has them on its bargain counter."

This was not a wholly exaggerated summary of the pass things had come to. In the window of a shop near the Fifth Avenue Hotel a small bottle of crushed strawberry color stood on a wooden block. Leaning against the block was a sign:

PEACHBLOW VASE—price, $15,000
(Less Will Be Taken)

Judge Hilton, in a waggish mood, bought a supply at ninety cents apiece. He was "thoroughly tired of hearing so much about peachblow vases," he said. Whenever Mrs. Morgan's miniscule bottle was mentioned in his presence he would snort, "Humph! Peachblows! Why, I'll give you one."

Editorial comment appeared all over the country as the two papers wrangled. Friends and enemies of the Peachbloom Vase divided into bitterly partisan camps, the preponderance of strength being on the side of the enemy. *The Art Amateur,* which had started the whole affair by drooling with admiration for Mrs. Morgan's extravagance, now reversed its position and remarked, "It is certainly curious that no one of the numerous French writers on Oriental porcelain from Jacquemart to Gonse tells us of the rarity of this interesting product of the potter."

Probably the most elaborate effort inspired by the controversy was a narrative poem thirty-two stanzas long, printed by the *Times* and recited by humorists at many an evening party. Modeled after "The Ancient Mariner" and entitled "The Rime of a Peachblow Vase," this cynical parody starts:

> It is an ancient connoisseur
> And he stoppeth one of three,
> And saith "Now hearken while I tell
> A tale of Ou-T'sai-Khi."

> "Now, by Our Lady," whispers one,
> "He hath a gruesome gaze."
> "Oh hark!" quoth he, "and list to me.
> I tell of a peachblow vase.

> "In the Yang-Khi time, some ages back
> My tale it doth begin,
> When spring was fair in the flowery land
> And the town of King-Te-Chin . . ."

The peachblow Coleridge goes on to relate one of the many current variations on the origins of the controversial bottle. He tells of how the vase, when baked, was a disappointment to its maker, who had been trying to produce the deep *sang de boeuf* color. Disgusted, the potter throws the thing into the sea, but it is found by a fisherman, who takes it home and uses it. From the fisherman's shanty it passes into a shopkeeper's hands, and eventually is bought by Robertson. In the final two stanzas the poet neatly sums up the scandal:

> Across the ocean to dealers in notions
> The little red jug then crossed;
> And they sold it off at a slight advance
> Of fifty times the cost!

> And so it chanced that this red jug
> Of diminutive dimensions
> Will always be a fruitful source
> Of very grave dissensions.

While all this was going on, poor old Mrs. A. T. Stewart gave up the ghost. As soon as she had been laid to rest in the cathedral crypt, beside whatever companion her ransom money had provided for the interval preceding Judgment Day, Judge Hilton put all her chattels up for sale. In a thrifty operation, which *Town Topics* called "stripping the carcass," he even announced a sale of her clothing at the Fifth Avenue palace. But then, *Town Topics* sniffed, "the annals of the Stewarts have been chiefly characterized by the superiority of dollars to decency."

Kirby took no part in the redistribution of the lady's gowns and wigs and silken underwear, but on behalf of the Stewart art he produced a catalogue even more costly and magnificent than Mary Jane's—in three sizes: atlas folio for the very rich, folio for the wealthy, and quarto for the well-to-do. The enormous pictures, their dust removed, their frames regilded, were placed on exhibition at the American Art Association with some twelve hundred other Stewart items. The colossal statues, due to their weight, had to be left in the palace, to be seen by appointment. This was just as well, perhaps, for by now Anthony Comstock, on behalf of the Almighty, had declared the ideal figure an indecent spectacle. On one occasion, *The Greek Slave* in replica appeared at a sculpture fest in Cincinnati draped in a calico blouse and a pair of ankle-length Canton flannel drawers.

Curiosity or the love of art, to say nothing of the Stewart notoriety, brought the carriage trade to Madison Square day and evening for a month. When at last, on March 23, 1887, the crowd proceeded to Chickering Hall for the first round of the ten-session auction, Kirby seems to have been in better form than ever. A reporter known as The Sport reviewed his opening night performance as follows:

At 7 o'clock last evening, Chickering Hall began to display unwonted evidences of life, at 7:30, a pack of carriages began to accumulate in the Avenue and across the streets. At 8 o'clock most of the wealth and fashion of New York was gathered in the auditorium upstairs.

There was so much wealth and fashion there, indeed, that good taste and critical judgment could not squeeze in at the doors in any numbers. But admission was by card, and as good taste and critical judgment do not buy many pictures at the AAA, the lack of favor shown them in the invitations may be accounted for.

The great knocking out contest between Mr. Thomas E. Kirby and the Stewart collection of pictures began promptly as advertised. The match opened by the appearance on the stage of the Art Association's champion in the person of a middle-aged, sandy-complexioned gentleman, with the general air and style in manner of the floor walker in a 6th Avenue dry goods bazar. His eminently respectable appearance evoked quite a little murmur of applause, in acknowledgment of which he bowed in excellent imitation of Sol Russell as the Hungry Boy who is fond of goose and onions.

This gentleman made the usual preliminary statements of the terms of the match. So ingenious was his invention and so copious his disrespect for the rules of grammar as formulated in the text books, that his address passed for Oriental with some of the less cultured members of the audience, and several suggestions passed from mouth to mouth as to its being in the Peachblow dialect, an idiom in familiar use among the pugilistic fraternity of Pekin.

The voice of the speaker proved that he was in excellent training. It echoed from wall to wall in rebounding roars, suggestive of a dynamite blast on the Harlem rockeries, with a chorus composed of the deafening crash of timber and stone and the screams of the eagles and ravens in Central Park, aroused from their repose by the explosion. This symphonic effect so wrought upon the nerves of an elderly lady in the audience that she fainted and had to be sent home at once, a misadventure which cast quite a cloud on the performance, as she was reported to be as rich as the late Mary Jane Morgan and nearly as foolish.

Two extremely Ethiopian attendants, with extremely flabby white gloves on, put a picture on the easel and the entertainment began in earnest.

The Association champion attacked art with the fury and science of Mr. Sullivan of Boston, and he scored a knock out in every round. The victims were borne to the rear, one by one, completely exhausted. The scornful energy with which their redoubtable foeman assailed their titles and the names of their creators at times savored of malignity, and there were several instances when the interference of the police was looked for.

It was to be noted, by the way, that whenever art received a particularly savage and merciless facer, as in the case where a picture was described as a "perfect gem of genius, and a bargain at any price, and don't you forget it," and again when the audience was adjured to "look at them three cows," the applause was most rapturous and prolonged. While the statement that a particularly gruesome and unpleasant pictorial puzzle was "worth all you could pay for it and TWYST as much more to boot," brought down the house and nearly brought down the roof.

After some seventy odd rounds had been fought, the bets were averaging a great deal more in favor of the pictures than they were worth, though a great deal under the rates at which Mr. Stewart had trained them, and most of the plaster having been shaken from the dome, the first night's match was announced to be over, in favor of the champion. The match will continue nightly for the rest of this next week. Desperate fighting is anticipated tonight and bloody work is promised for tomorrow.

In the course of the bloody work that followed, Cornelius Vanderbilt paid $53,000 for *The Horse Fair* and sent it off as a surprise package to the Metropolitan Museum, where it was long considered one of the artistic highlights of New York. In later years the monumental canvas was consigned to oblivion in the warehouse, but in 1954 it was restored to a place of honor, and now museum wayfarers of a new generation are to be seen standing before Rosa Bonheur's *chef d'oeuvre* with about the same degree of awe and wonder as that expressed by their great-grandfathers.

Some of the other pictures brought high prices, but even a myopic millionaire could see that most of Stewart's art works were far inferior to Mary Jane's. His 7-foot vases held no charms comparable to those of Mrs. Morgan's 8-inch bottle. Hilton, who was an indefatigable bidder on everything, got the gaudiest of them at $2,900 the pair. (They had cost Stewart $20,000.) The heroic marble statues, including *The Greek Slave,* brought $965 each. The versatile hall clock joined the prodigious orchestrion in the Powers Art Gallery of Rochester at $2,550.

The big moment came on the third night, when *Friedland, 1807,* with the letter and Meissonier's souvenir portrait of himself thrown in, fell at $66,000. The buyer was Judge Hilton, and he, too, consigned his purchase to the Metropolitan Museum. He could well afford it, for to the greedy Judge the addlepated Mrs. Stewart had bequeathed the bulk of what remained of the Stewart fortune—about $9 million in cash and many parcels of real estate, including the Fifth Avenue palace.

He moved in, with the towering Sèvres vases, a preponderance of the ghostly statues, and twenty-seven clocks, which he kept precisely regulated to strike the hours in unison throughout the marble halls. Four years later he moved out and rented the place to the Manhattan Club for ten years at $37,000 a year. In 1901, when Hilton was dead, the vast white palace, which no chronicler had doubted would stand forever, was summarily torn down. In a grim apostrophe to the Stewart saga, its marble was salvaged by a tombstone manufacturer.

Friedland, 1807 still hangs in the Metropolitan Museum, with a plaque attesting to Henry Hilton's cultural largess. The price was right, its value would increase with time, Meissonier had written in his self-appreciative letter. No prediction could have been less accurate, but as the snide Judge Hilton's bid for immortality, the 8-foot canvas has proved more durable than most of Stewart's architectural extravagances.

The Park Avenue Hotel, without benefit of working girls or chastity, lasted until 1947. The fabulous Grand Union, long a Saratoga derelict, has succumbed to the wreckers. The Great Iron Store survived as part of Wanamaker's until 1952. Four years later, while in the process of demolition, its iron frame melted in the most stubborn and mysterious fire New York had seen in twenty years.

One Stewart edifice on Manhattan Island remains—the marble dry-goods palace facing City Hall Park, minus its dome and most of its Corinthian columns, its glories long forgotten as the world's first great department store, its façade embellished with neon signs and other twentieth-century gauderies. And out among the smokestacks and split levels of suburbia the Cathedral of the Incarnation looms. Pigeons roost among its pinnacles and parapets, while the eerie cenotaph below provokes recurrent waves of speculation as to who lies buried there.

The imperial collection on which the merchant Croesus had lavished an inestimable fortune brought $565,568 at auction. "Like everything else connected with the Stewart estate, the art sale will remain with us as a monumental memory of humbug, ignorance and fraud," *Town Topics* churlishly observed. This was an exaggeration. The tribute paid for Meissonier and Rosa Bonheur—the highest prices any pictures had ever brought at auction—would alone have given the event a place in the annals of great sales. But it was true that the championship contest Kirby had envisioned turned out to be something of an anticlimax. Only a few days before the Stewart exhibition opened, Mary Jane's grand total was announced.

By then her last chair and bedspread had been dispersed, her many snuff bottles, the thousand tinkling wineglasses, the Sèvres plates that had held the guinea fowl served to the Reverend Pastor Conkling. Gone was the mother-of-pearl bedroom set, the cameo flint glass service, for which Tiffany's still retained the molds. Nothing remained but cobwebs and empty cupboards, their doors swinging open into hollow rooms—these and the unfinished dolphins, and a disgruntled stained-glass Cupid gazing with distraction into space. Already there were broken panes in the greenhouse above the carriage house. Now, in spring, the ragweed and the chickweed were sprouting in place of last year's orchids. Already a legend was growing up in place of Mary Jane; for her possessions, minus the diamonds and the orchids, had sold for $1,205,153—with the exception of the Hamilton Palace sale of 1882 in London, the highest auction total that had ever been recorded anywhere in the world.

The Peachbloom Vase scandal died, slowly, of its own absurdity. William T. Walters, a gentleman of stern propriety, who thought it vulgar to discuss the price of art, remained wholly aloof while the scribblers ranted and citizens of Baltimore clamored to see his notorious $18,000 purchase. They clamored in vain, for while Mr. Walters' private museum was sometimes opened to the public, he was so infuriated by the publicity that he withdrew the vase from exhibition. This led to the rumor that Walters had not been the buyer after all, and tales of further, darker machinations on the part of the American Art Association.

Never again was the Peachbloom Vase seen in William T. Walters' lifetime or that of his son, Henry Walters, who died in 1931. So offended were the Walters' sensibilities by the furor over the tiny object's cost that from that time on, both father and son destroyed all records of prices paid for art works in their Baltimore museum. But the Peachbloom Vase exists—No. 49.155 among the four thousand pieces of Chinese porcelain in that vast collection. The Walters Art Gallery became a public museum in 1931, and on occasion nowadays the vulgar and curious may freely gaze upon Mrs. Morgan's much-maligned bottle, shedding—in the words of the museum catalogue—"the delicate play of color of a ripening peach splashed with apple green."

It was not until the turn of the century that the English-reading public could readily avail itself of books confirming the accuracy of the *Sun*'s information, if not the authenticity of the vase itself. By then Charles A. Dana was dead, or at best, reincarnated. In 1898, Kirby sold the peachblow vase in Dana's collection for $3,600, an average price but no longer significant. For in the space of twelve years even the dullest art reporter had come to understand what Mary Jane, in her solitary studies, had probably observed for herself. When one can afford to go shopping for the past, as any truly obsessed collector knows, the difference between $2,000 and $12,000 becomes irrelevant. Both prices are expensive; both are cheap.

Certainly the Peachbloom story diminished confidence in the porcelains Austin Robertson sent over from the Orient for private sale, but this was of small concern to Thomas Kirby. He had never wanted to keep a china store. The aspersions on the Red Jug made him angry, but the headlines made him famous. The Seney and the Stewart sales helped establish an institution that was to endure, with its original title, for almost fifty years, but it was Mary Jane herself who gave the galleries on Madison Square an aura of legendary drama that made the AAA name a household word.

"They ought to erect a monument!" one observer wrote when Mary Jane's grand total was announced. And in a sense they did. It was an auction house.

FOUR

THE TITANS IN THE
MARKET PLACE

As long as James F. Sutton remained an active partner the AAA played a dual role in the art market. Kirby's Million-Dollar Voice—as the papers had begun to call it—in no way stifled Sutton's impulse to encourage and promote. In Paris he had found the impressionists' champion Paul Durand-Ruel receptive to the idea of trying their hard-to-sell pictures on New York. Durand-Ruel assembled 289 paintings; Sutton induced the customs collector to let them into the country under bond without exacting the 30 per cent duty on whatever hypothetical value they may have had; and on April 10, 1886, with echoes of Mary Jane's Lot No. 2,628 still vibrant in the halls, "The Impressionists of Paris" burst upon the baffled clients of the AAA.

The catalogue—to look at its yellowed pages now—was a poor thing for a document of such relevance in the archives of collecting. The painters were identified by their last names only, as if they were ephemeral beings worth no more than a modicum of printer's ink. The titles of the pictures were shortened, crudely translated, expurgated, revised. There were no sizes given. Some of Manet's paintings were listed as Monets. The town of Pontoise, glorified by Pissarro, was spelled "Poutoise." Berthe Morisot was unidentified as to sex, and to add to the confusion, rechristened "Morizot." There were no birth dates or places, no schools or biographical data. There were no honors from the Salons listed in that wan, unprepossessing pamphlet, no ribbons, prizes, laurels, no mention of the Legion of Honor. But in the galleries there were the pictures Durand-Ruel predicted would one day become a century's glory.

There were no fewer than forty paintings by Monet: the Seine at Argenteuil, the Seine at Giverny, scenes at Etretat and Pourville, *Le Jardin de Monet à Vetheuil*, the famous *Bordighera* now in the Louvre. There were thirteen important pictures by Manet: *Fifre de la Garde*, *Le Buveur d'Absinthe*, *On the Balcony*, now also in the Louvre. There were twenty-three harbor scenes by Boudin, thirty-nine paintings by Pissarro, fifteen by Sisley, eight by Berthe Morisot. There were thirty oils and pastels by Degas: the effervescent dancers, the jockeys, café singers, milliners, the *Ballet de Robert le Diable* now in the Metropolitan Museum. There were thirty-five Renoirs:

his portrait of Wagner; the two portraits of Jeanne Samary, both now in the Pushkin Museum at Moscow. The halls were radiant with Renoir's outdoor crowds in mauve and blue and yellow costumes, the joyous fetes and festivals painted with sonorous red, rococo boldness. There were pictures by the younger artists who came to be called postimpressionist—six by twenty-three-year-old Paul Signac, three by Georges Seurat. Almost unimaginable, certainly overwhelming, was the light-drowned, color-drenched panorama that greeted the bustled and bewhiskered patrons on their labyrinthine progress from Gallery A through Gallery E.

As anyone could have predicted, press comment in New York was borrowed largely from the jaundiced view of the French Academy. Under the headline "Gallery of Colored Nightmares," *The Commercial Advertiser* called the exhibit a collection of monstrosities that would not be tolerated in a well-regulated barbershop. The *Times*, still convulsed with merriment over the Peachbloom Vase, dismissed this latest folly of the AAA with a rhetorical question and a shrug: "The three hundred oil and pastel pictures by the Impressionists of Paris belong to the category of Art for Art's sake, which rouses more mirth than a desire to possess it. . . . Coming suddenly upon the crude colors and disdain of drawing, which are the traits positive and negative in the works of Renoir and Pissarro, one is likely to catch the breath with surprise. Is this Art?"

The artists, all so different, were dismissed en masse, as were the paintings, whether technically impressionist or not. None of the wretches could draw, not Degas, not Manet. No one noticed the precision in the twenty-three pictures, big and little, by Boudin, "the ships so accurately rigged," as Monet once wrote, "the skies and water so exact." No one stopped in wonder before Monet's coruscating field of red poppies, or Renoir's *Le Déjeuner à Bougival*—"his masterpiece," Durand-Ruel declared, "which sooner or later will be found in the Louvre." No critic noticed Renoir's portrait of Durand-Ruel's winsome teen-age daughters, which was to soar to $255,000 in the Thelma Chrysler Foy sale in 1959. Nowhere in that mindless avalanche of scorn was there a hint that anyone had paused in Gallery C before 68 square feet of canvas listed in the cryptic catalogue:

SEURAT
112. Island Grande Jatte.

In 1891, when Seurat died of a fever at the age of thirty-two, *Sunday Afternoon on the Island of La Grande Jatte*—to give his pointillist masterwork the full title the AAA did not bother to print— was sold in Paris for $200. Frederick Clay Bartlett, who gave it to the Art Institute of Chicago, paid $24,000 for it in 1924. In 1931 a French syndicate raised $450,000 in an unsuccessful effort to redeem the picture for the Louvre. There is no sum of money, however great, that can buy *La Grande Jatte* now; but in 1886 at the AAA the three huge pictures by Seurat were beneath contempt.

Only the New York *Daily Tribune* had a friendly word for the "bizarre and original works" that left the old guard wheezing with sophisticated laughter. One of its editorial writers, while observing that "these men [have] evidently no moral nor literary mission" and "[are] not given to the painting of serious subjects," confessed to having been drawn a little to those "unconventional water parties at Bougival" and "bathers basking in the sunlight." On the subject of "the lurid warnings uttered by the molders of artistic opinion" he wrote: "Those who have the most to do with such conservative investments as the works of Bouguereau, Cabanel, Meissonier and Gerome have imparted the information that the paintings of the 'Impressionists' partake of the character of a 'crazy quilt,' being only distinguished by such eccentricities as blue grass, violently green skies and water with the coloring of a rainbow. In short that they are absolutely worthless. We do not find them so." Manet and Degas, the *Tribune* man surmised, might well represent an interesting movement in "foreign art," and it was his considered opinion that Americans should not wait to learn of it from history.

The *Tribune*'s advice was not widely taken. So violent was the opposition to the "monumental humbuggery" at the AAA that the impressionists remained on view there for only a month. While imparting the information that the pictures were worthless, the dealers having the most to do with conservative investments in Bouguereau at the same time raised a cry that the custom house was being hoodwinked on a Peachblow Vase basis. Bringing all those subversive paintings into the country under bond was a shrewd trade trick, they said. The bonding privilege was intended for public institutions devoted to cultural advancement. The AAA, for all its high-sounding propaganda, was backed by R. H. Macy's son-in-law. Was it not therefore in reality the picture-dealing branch of Macy's? A very pretty and safe speculation it was indeed for Macy's, disguised as The American Association for the Promotion and Encouragement of Art, to import cargoes of expensive art works free of duty until they were actually sold. A campaign was waged to have the paintings taxed. The port collector found that he could cooperate by demanding his full pound of flesh.

Neither Durand-Ruel nor the AAA cared to pay a fortune in duties on 289 presumably unmarketable pictures. But the scheme to send The Impressionists of Paris back where they came from failed. The paintings were removed to the National Academy of Design, a bona fide citadel of culture two blocks east on 23rd Street. There they remained on view, as the opposition grumbled, "until the last possible customer had been worked."

The customers worked were not as numerous as the enemy supposed. Art buyers came to scoff, but during the month's exhibition on Madison Square only five remained to pay: William Loring Andrews, William H. Fuller, Cyrus J. Lawrence, A. W. Kingman, and H. O. Havemeyer. Together they bought fifteen pictures—by Monet, Renoir, Sisley, and Pissarro—for a total of $17,150.

As far as the AAA was concerned this country's first impressionist exhibition was a noble failure, but within a year Durand-Ruel had returned to pursue what he called with some bravado "a success so well begun." A branch of the Durand-Ruel Gallery was opened at 297 Fifth Avenue. Shuttling the pictures back and forth across the ocean, Paul Durand-Ruel and his sons, Georges and Joseph, undertook to create a taste for the artists still ridiculed in Europe. Among the able propagandists in this proselytizing venture was Mary Cassatt, some of whose works Durand-Ruel brought back from France on his return trip in 1887. Mary Cassatt's reputation as America's foremost woman artist was still barely in the making, but she had wealth, social position, and the gift of persuasion. It was she who induced Mrs. Potter Palmer to try the new art on Chicago. Mary Cassatt's lifelong friend Mrs. H. O. Havemeyer was perhaps an early convert. As a schoolgirl in Paris, back in 1873, she had saved a hundred dollars to buy a Degas pastel; as a lady of boundless resources, Mrs. Havemeyer—to quote *The New York Times* in a more amiable frame of mind—"came close to being the ideal toward which all collectors should aspire." But that reversal of *Times* opinion came in another century, on the occasion of Mrs. Havemeyer's death, in 1929, and the bequest of her great collection, including some of the pictures that had aroused such mirth at the AAA in 1886, to the Metropolitan Museum.

The beginnings were slow, but a nucleus of distinguished American torchbearers for impressionist painting developed: E. F. Milliken and a few others in New York, George N. Tyner of Holyoke, Massachusetts, Alfred A. Pope of Cleveland. As early as 1889 two important works of Manet, *Woman with a Parrot* and *Boy with a Sword,* were hanging in the Metropolitan Museum, the gift of Erwin Davis. James F. Sutton himself became one of the most ardent patrons of Monet. He covered the walls of his home with scenes of Bennecourt and Giverny and piled up an overstock of Monets at the galleries in Madison Square. As long as the AAA continued in the retail porcelain and picture business, one of the rooms containing things for private sale was hung with the works of Degas and the impressionists. Thus, while French critics were still railing against the "talented incompetents" and connoisseurs abroad were tittering over the naïveté of American *arrivistes,* a wealth of pictures now considered priceless slipped across the Atlantic to join the cultural assets of the United States.

Meanwhile, the investors in Bouguereau and Gérôme continued to grow in both number and fervor. When a Very Valuable Collection fell into Kirby's hands for redistribution, the galleries resembled a vast storybook framed and varnished and hung upon the walls. If the deceased (or ruined) had been rich enough to patronize the more lavish specialists in the pomp and splendor of times past, the rooms would gleam with yellow paint. Golden vessels, plumed hats, and ermine capes dramatized the ups and downs of kings, the homage of princes, the adventures of knights and magnificoes. Court ladies with ideal countenances posed like wax dolls among a smothering array of jeweled garments. Heroic receptions were held on the staircase at Versailles. Banquet tables, at which every plate was priceless and meticulously rendered, were lined with regal figures as stiff and unconvincing as actors chosen only to fit the costumes and enhance the grandeur of the stage set. It was a lovely world, with the finest people arriving at the château and departing from it, but it was not art.

In view of the demand, it was only natural that when works by the white-haired boys of the Salons appeared in Kirby's auctions the bidding would run high. At the James H. Stebbins sale in 1889 a Meissonier smaller than a penny post card (*The Stirrup Cup*, 3½ by 4¾ inches) brought $7,100. For exactly the same sum, in an auction held by the Fifth Avenue branch of Durand-Ruel to raise money for the customs collector, the buyer of that undersize post card could have possessed—if he had so chosen—five large Renoirs, two Degas pastels of the races, four landscapes by Sisley, two large pictures by Pissarro, and a round dozen harbor scenes by Boudin. At that same Stebbins sale, in 1889, Collis P. Huntington spent $26,300 for *The Game Lost*, a Meissonier that comprised less than a square foot of seventeenth-century barracks-room atmosphere, and another $26,300 —a mystical sum, no doubt, for Huntington was very superstitious— on Gérôme's *Moliere Breakfasting with Louis XIV at Versailles.*

These were the conservative investments of 1889. Alas, when *Moliere Breakfasting* turned up in one of the Hearst sales at the Parke-Bernet in 1939 it brought $1,400.

If the collection to go under Kirby's hammer was at all well rounded, one did not need to dwell too long on history or war's romance. There were eleven galleries, and one could turn the page by merely walking through the door. The peace-loving could, if they chose, bypass the gory battlefields of de Neuville and Detaille. In the next room the browsing client might find himself among the Arabs of Eugène Fromentin or Adolph Schreyer, for the titans were uncommonly fond of a good story coming out of Africa. Numberless were the scenes of Asia Minor and Algeria that crossed the ocean to broaden the horizons of the stay-at-homes on Fifth Avenue: Arabs fighting, resting, and retreating; Arab horsemen hunting, camping, galloping; Arabs attending the bazaar, crossing fords, or plucking thorns from their callused feet. In this department, too, one might still encounter the anecdotal canvases of Gérôme, for his beat extended from the château of the Loire to the coffeehouses of Cairo, and he was renowned not only for the adventures of the Louis' but for the doings of the pashas as well, and the eccentricities of carpet sellers, sword dancers, and beggars loafing around the mosque.

Invariably the shower of the $1,000 bills would be precipitated by such titles as *Young Mother* or *Young Brother, The Little Pilferers, Sweet Charity,* or *The Road to Ruin.* Above all else, the Alger boys' nostalgia for the pasture kept the Million-Dollar Voice perpetually exultant. By 1891, when Emile van Marcke was dead, his least distinguished herd of painted cattle was worth far more than a comparable number of live animals in any farmer's barn. Sheep had an easily predicted value: one sheep, $1,000; two sheep, $2,000; and so on to the limits of the fold. The barnyard craze brought Anton Mauve, who had once tried to teach his cousin Vincent van Gogh to earn a living painting pictures, a posthumous glory in the auctions that it would take van Gogh death and forty years to achieve. In 1905, when the "Art Treasures Collected by Thomas E. Waggaman," a bankrupt picture fancier of Washington, D.C., were liquidated at the AAA, Mauve's *Sheep Coming Out of the Forest* brought $40,500. A few years earlier Waggaman had paid $2,000 for it.

In the long run, however, the laurels for both sheep and cattle went to the Barbizon painter Constant Troyon. Nothing, not even a Rembrandt, was more coveted than those lazy droves and flocks lolling in the summer pasture, the red cows and the white cows, the cows going to market, drinking, or being milked, the mellow sunsets and the hayracks, the interminable migrations of sheep with faithful dogs that crossed and recrossed the Troyon canvases. Although Durand-Ruel offered the gratuitous counsel that Boudin had often painted the scenery and only the livestock were added by Troyon, the barnyard addicts were unmoved. In 1896, when a large Boudin could be had for less than $500, Troyon's *Return to the Farm* (which boasted only two cows, with one and a half sheep in the background) brought $24,500. Eleven years later Kirby sold *Return to the Farm* again—this time for $65,000.

As the reverence for art expanded, the ensign of taste became the seven golden men of Barbizon: Corot, Troyon, Théodore Rousseau, Daubigny, Diaz, Dupré, and Millet. Every scrap of canvas the so-called Men of 1830 had ever touched was seized upon and sold, along with many a picture that they had never touched at all. Good, bad, or blatantly forged, a Corot of some kind—preferably a large landscape with pool and silvery birches—was standard equipment in any household with serious pretensions to luxury or fashion. Ironically, the small figure pieces that have earned Corot his niche among the immortals were scorned. At a time when Charles H. Senff could buy *Woman Reading* (now in the Metropolitan Museum) for a mere $4,000, impoverished painters were employed on a sweatshop basis to produce sufficient glimpses of Lake Nemi and the Ville d'Avray to meet the inexorable demand. By the turn of the century the saying was current that during his long life in art Corot had produced eight thousand canvases, thirty thousand of which were in America. No other painter appeared so often at the AAA, or with more gratifying results. In 1903 *Orpheus and Eurydice* fell to Emerson McMillan for $21,500. Later, when Kirby sold the same picture for McMillan, it brought $75,200. Then, in 1912, Cyrus H. McCormick bid a new high for a Corot at auction—$85,000 for the *Lake Nemi* that had once belonged to Mary Jane Morgan.

But while Corot and Troyon provoked the greatest furor at the auctions, it was Jean François Millet who inspired the Art Association's most spirited adventure in enlightenment.

Until almost the end of Millet's life his stark heroes of the soil were unwanted and unsung. Often the bison-bearded painter and his nine children almost literally starved to death in their dismal three-room cottage at Barbizon. Once, in want of bread, Millet sold five of his best paintings for the equivalent of $15. In later years Durand-Ruel paid him liberally for his pictures and made a great effort to promote them, but they were only beginning to be appreciated when Millet died in 1875. The Hermit of Barbizon did not live to see his zenith, but after he was dead his countrymen began to look upon him and the peasants he had painted as a nation's glory.

All of Millet's pictures were in demand, but none was so eagerly coveted as *The Angelus,* a small canvas showing two figures against a twilit sky, a young man and a young woman surrounded by the symbols of their never-ending toil, their heads bowed and their hands folded in simple piety. Behind them is a long field, and in the distance, the spire of a church. It is a picture that treads the knife-edge between sentiment and sentimentality; but in the eighties it was thought by many people to be Millet's masterpiece. You could hear the bell, they said, and feel the rustle of the whispered prayer.

The Angelus was owned by a French collector named Secretan, who fell on evil days with the crash of a copper syndicate he controlled. In 1889 it was announced that his pictures would be dispersed at public sale. For months the Paris press was filled with tributes to the magnificence of the Secretan treasure. It comprised, every writer agreed, one of the most splendid gatherings of rare and precious objects ever brought together by a single person, a veritable galaxy of witnesses to the glory of French art. A monumental catalogue was prepared. Volumes of criticism were written. Patriotism waxed hot, and a movement was started to force the French government to buy the collection outright. When this failed, the auction was scheduled for July 1889 and the pictures were placed on exhibition at the Galerie Sédelmeyer.

In the modern contingent, *The Angelus* received the place of honor. It stood apart, on an easel in the center of a great hall hung with works of all the contest winners of the nineteenth century—an eloquent testimonial, everyone said, to one of the great artists of all time, whose genius had gone so long unrecognized. For weeks Frenchmen and foreigners alike stood spellbound before Millet's devout peasants. Receptions and assemblies were held in their honor. Spectators wept and a number of ladies of high position swooned. Pilgrimages were arranged, and the common people—or at least the middle classes—traveled from outlying districts to worship humbly, cap in hand, as before a shrine.

As the fervor mounted, a shout went up that *The Angelus* was a national monument, and many voices rose to decry the awful possibility that at the auction this priceless heritage of French culture might fall into the hands of foreigners. A movement was started to persuade the government—if it could not afford the entire collection—to buy at least this picture. Petitions were signed and patriotic speeches were made from the Arc de Triomphe to the Bastille. Whereupon, spurred by all the shouting, Kirby and Sutton decided to buy the picture.

No sooner had Sutton embarked for France to attend the sale than the trustees of the Corcoran Gallery in Washington, hearing some echoes of the clamor, began to wonder if *The Angelus* was not something they ought to have. William W. Corcoran had recently died, leaving the gallery a pile of money which was already burning holes in the trustees' pockets. Since time was of the essence, a director of the Corcoran, with a suitable entourage, was dispatched posthaste in Sutton's wake. The Corcoran boys' boat was slow, however, and in order to reach Paris in time for the auction, they had to engage a special train from Le Havre—an extravagance never before encountered in the experience of French railway officials.

With the aid of a death-defying engineer the Washington contingent arrived at the Galerie Sédelmeyer in midafternoon, breathless and sweltering in the July heat—only to be confronted by another hurdle. In the street a small riot was in progress. When the doors of the gallery had been opened to general admission, people who had been waiting in the street since dawn found that the hall was already filled. The privileged of the art world, along with the counts and viscounts, the *nouveaux riches,* and worst of all, the foreigners, had been admitted by a private entrance. A roar of protest filled the air. The deprived crowd refused to leave, for no people more dearly loves an auction than the French. Fists were doubled and fusillades of angry words were hurled. Liberty, equality, and the inalienable rights of the curious became hopelessly confused; and just at the moment when the Corcoran boys arrived, the *Angelus*-worshipers were threatening to take the auction hall by storm.

The valiant little band from Washington turned pale, but screwing up their courage, they dashed into the fray—amid cries of *"Cochons!"* and other epithets, which they fortunately did not understand. Aided by a cordon of police, they beat a path to the door with their ministerial walking sticks and entered the hall shaken but undaunted, their silk hats bashed, their coattails battered, looking for all the world like the Marx Brothers on a diplomatic mission.

They were in the nick of time. Before they had a chance to inspect their wounds, their interpreter was translating the tense words of M. Paul Chevallier, the auctioneer: "We will now sell *The Angelus* by Millet. What am I bid?"

From the rear, above the humming voices, a jester called, "One hundred thousand francs!"

Now it was the turn of the crowd inside to threaten riot. Derisive shouts and hisses filled the hall. Millet and the honor of all France had been insulted by such a puny bid. The two government experts in charge of the sale stepped forward and proclaimed in unison that the upset price was 300,000 francs. Anger turned to mass approval when that sum was bid simultaneously from two sides of the house. As soon as he could catch his breath, the bidder for the Corcoran Gallery raised the ante 100,000. Georges Petit, bidding for the French Minister of Fine Arts, upped him fifty thousand. And then Sutton's bidder, I. Montaignac, rose to his feet. In superb pear-shaped tones, Montaignac called a half million francs on behalf of the American Art Association of New York.

M. Petit countered with another thousand. Montaignac raised, and M. Petit raised again. In the bedlam that now prevailed, the dauntless Corcoran boys lost their resolution. They looked at the bone of contention on the block, and turned to look at one another. The picture was very small. By rapid calculation, 500,000 francs came to $100,000; and that, the director muttered, was certainly not hay. The trustees had sent the delegation off in haste, with no clear idea of what it was they were to buy. The bid was now 503,000, in favor of the French government. The boys from Washington hesitated long enough to go into a huddle, and at the very moment of their indecision, Chevallier was crying, in a voice that made the windows rattle, "Once! Twice! . . ."

"Five hundred four thousand!" Montaignac shouted on behalf of Sutton. But the applause had already begun, and Chevallier either did not hear or pretended not to. "Sold to the Republic of France!" he declared, with a triumphant blow of his ivory mallet.

A clamor arose that Alfred Trumbull, in his eyewitness account, called indescribable. Montaignac plowed his way to the front and angrily protested the ignoring of his bid. Partisan Frenchmen, exuberant over the government's victory, shouted him down, but others cried that an injustice had been done. The audience divided itself into two hostile camps. Impassioned speeches were made for both sides simultaneously; and when it appeared that blood was certain to be shed—more than likely his own—Chevallier rescinded his decision and put the picture back on the block.

The deputy for the Minister of Fine Arts covered Montaignac's raise. Montaignac raised again. The Corcoran boys, having regained their composure, jumped back into the fight, but soon lost their courage in the face of the dogged bidding of Sutton's man. Thousand by thousand the price rose, until it was clear that the American Art Association would conquer.

But now a spontaneous demonstration erupted. In a frenzy of patriotism, the sons of France rose as a man and demanded that the picture be bought for the Louvre at any price. Fervid voices shouted subscriptions of 10,000 francs, 20,000, and even 100,000. Spurred by this mass support, the Minister of Fine Arts himself took over the bidding, and when the price stood at 553,000 francs, Sutton, seeing that he was up against a torrent of national feeling, called off his dogs. Montaignac shrugged his shoulders, and for the second time that afternoon, *The Angelus* was knocked down to the Republic of France.

A scene of acclamation followed that raised the Minister of Fine

Arts momentarily to the status of a conquering hero. The auction addicts kissed him, wrung his hand, wept upon his breast, and some of them attempted to carry him through the streets on their shoulders. But the mob, in the way of mobs, turned out to be fickle. Newspapers opposed to the government cried out against the Minister's extravagance. Millet was well enough, they said, but like the pathetic figures he had painted, the people were in need of bread. Artistic circles predicted that the Senate would not dare to appropriate the money to pay for the picture. The impulsive subscribers disappeared, and within twenty-four hours it began to look as if the Minister of Fine Arts had been left to hold the bag.

Brimming with sympathy, Sutton called upon him and offered to take *The Angelus* off his hands at the price for which it had fallen, plus expenses. The Minister tentatively accepted the offer and signed a little contract agreeing that, if the Senate had not appropriated the money within a fortnight, Sutton could have the picture. The ink was not yet dry when the Corcoran boys, having also heard of the Minister's difficulties, rushed around with a similar offer. But they were late, as usual. When a fortnight had elapsed, *The Angelus* became the property of the American Art Association.

Now that they had the famous picture, Kirby and Sutton were in a quandary over what to do with it. One hundred and fifteen thousand dollars was a lot of money for a work of art in 1889. Since there was no immediate purchaser on the horizon, they put the painting out at interest, so to speak, by exhibiting it first in New York, then in other cities throughout the country. Thousands of people came to see it, paid a modest fee, and bought a copy of Alfred Trumbull's pamphlet *The Life, Labors and Vicissitudes of Millet*. But though they could all hear the bell, few Americans were overwhelmed, and there is no known case of any lady's having swooned.

As Kirby said, many people, taking the price into consideration, expected the picture to be the size of a barn door. One afternoon, while it was on exhibit in New York, a prominent Wall Street man called him on the new-fangled telephone. "Kirby," he said, "I've made a bet on the size of *The Angelus* and I want you to settle it. I say the size printed in the catalogue is a mistake. Instead of twenty-one by twenty-five inches I've wagered a champagne dinner that the thing must be twenty-one by twenty-five feet."

"Well, you lose," Kirby snapped, and peremptorily rang off.

A few months passed and the American Art Association received a cabled bid from a M. Chauchard in Paris, offering to pay $150,000 for the picture. But Kirby hated to see it go. *The Angelus* had become an international pawn, and the little auctioneer had a streak of national pride of his own. The AAA was growing rich enough out of its amazing procession of auction sales; it did not need to make a profit on Millet's masterpiece. Kirby convinced Sutton that it would be an act of public benefaction to sell *The Angelus* to some American museum for a fraction of M. Chauchard's offer; and to demonstrate his sincerity, he pledged a contribution from his own pocket to any institution that would undertake to buy the picture. Sutton first offered it to Henry G. Marquand, then president of the Metropolitan Museum, but Marquand refused it. Thereupon Kirby went to Washington to interview the presumably frustrated director of the Corcoran Gallery.

"Kirby," the director said, "as you know, we were sent to Paris by the trustees to buy the picture, and on our return without it, we were not received with open arms. In fact, we were scolded for not making a greater fight for it. Well, then you placed the painting on exhibition, and some of our enthusiastic trustees went to New York to see it. On their return to Washington, they said to us, 'We have seen *The Angelus* and we want to say that if you had bought that little bit of a painting for anything like the price it sold for, we would have resigned as trustees.'"

Kirby returned from Washington and shipped *The Angelus* to M. Chauchard in Paris. In the end, it came into the possession of the Republic of France without the expenditure of a sou, for M. Chauchard, upon his death, willed it to the Louvre.

For a few more years Sutton attempted to make the AAA the contemporary art center it had set out to be. In 1889, in another burst of promotional zeal, he brought to Madison Square the works of Vasili Vereshchagin. A gloomier Russian would have been hard to find, but Sutton, in an excess of promotional ardor, imported not only his pictures but Vereshchagin as well, with all his props and furniture.

Sutton's man of sorrows called himself "a disciple of progress and realism." In Paris he had occupied a studio as remarkable for its display of useful objects made from human bones as for the fact that it revolved with the sun, so that no shadow ever fell on the canvas being executed. There he painted pictures of tombs. Mainly they were tombs of Old Testament notables—Abraham, Isaac, Joseph, Samuel, Jacob—all shadowless, if understandably overgrown with weeds. The authenticity of the tombs was indisputable, Vereshchagin said, for he had made sketches of them while traveling in Palestine for the purpose of "observing life." In his spare time he had painted the conquest of India "by the brave and enterprising British," also without shadows; but he was a devout Russian patriot, and the call to arms was always luring him from his easel. Having himself "killed many a poor fellow creature in different wars," he had "thought the matter over," he said, and thenceforth concentrated less on tombs and more on their prospective occupants: those dying on the battlefield, preferably in heaps, or for variety, "scenes of individual killing"— fellow creatures being shot, beheaded, crucified, hanged, or "speedily and humanely" blown up by British guns.

The illustrated catalogue dwelt at some length on these matters and included a grim little parable to go with each picture. "Owing to the great size of some of the paintings," it also conveyed the artist's suggestion that they be viewed from as great a distance as possible. No one took the hint. When his life's work, along with the stark souvenirs of his travels, had been assembled at the AAA, there were those, including General Sherman, who proclaimed Vereshchagin "the greatest painter of the horrors of war that ever lived." Squads of cadets from West Point came down to admire how "real soldiers" died—not, their battle-hardened officers pointed out, face down, as slipshod painters imagined, but face up, as realism's disciple depicted them.

Vereshchagin might have made a lot of money for the AAA, but he was temperamental. "Like all geniuses," Kirby said, "he was very erratic, a queer type of man." His person, including a long, crinkly beard, straggling down over his bosom in two obscene points, was inexplicably attractive to female clients. The attraction was not mutual. Though the wives of clean-shaven millionaires implored him to paint their portraits and offered to pay any price he might ask, he steadfastly refused. They had moles, he said, and they were ugly. What was more, he declined to "observe life" at fashionable dinners, even at receptions given by prominent generals and their presumably nevus-marked ladies.

"Notwithstanding these terrific handicaps to popularity," Kirby reported, "his exhibitions were a great success." Thousands of people came and shuddered. But just when the patriot painter could have become a "fashionable pet," he once more felt the call to Russian arms, and departed. Kirby auctioned off his paintings and impedimenta—caskets, intruments of torture, soup bowls made of human skulls, the root of a tree from beneath the Temple of Jerusalem, all those mangled upturned faces—for $84,300. A few years later Vereshchagin witnessed the explosion of the battleship *Petropavlovsk* in the harbor of Port Arthur. It would have made a rip-roaring picture, but unhappily Vereshchagin exploded with it.

There were other exhibitions, most of them on the more cheerful side: the paintings of Raffaelli and Cazin, a memorable loan show of Barye's bronzes, the first public showing of Rodin's sculpture in America. But the auctions drove the retail trade, first, into the background, and then out of the picture altogether. By 1892 Austin Robertson was dead and the last of his troublesome porcelains had been sold. Three years later James F. Sutton withdrew from active participation, retaining his financial interest but leaving Kirby and his Million-Dollar Voice in sole command. The AAA became wholly an auction house, a one-man institution autocratically built and autocratically conducted by Thomas E. Kirby. For more than twenty years no other auctioneer was allowed in the rostrum. One factotum, and one only, Kirby allowed himself: Miss Rose H. Lorenz.

With stars in her eyes and darns in her stockings, Rose Lorenz had charmed Kirby into giving her a job at his first New York auction hall back in the early 1880's. Among people who knew her in after years as a despotic old maid, crabbed but able, the impression persists that as the fourteen-year-old breadwinner of a poor German family she was a winsome, straggly creature with two long braids of tawny hair, a Broadway innocent rescued from the garish company of common hucksters by luck and pluck and the warm heart of Thomas E. Kirby. This touching portrait has probably been heightened by the passage of time, but Rose's success story was nonetheless remarkable.

Her first job at the newly formed AAA was to hand out catalogues and charm the customers, a task she accomplished with such aplomb that, as Kirby said, "many prominent amateurs and connoisseurs took much interest in her welfare, often instructing her as to what was desirable and what was not." Before many years had passed, the roles

Miss Rose Lorenz. In Kirby's time she ran the auctions with a tyrant's hand (BROWN BROTHERS).

were reversed. Happy then was the fledgling amateur rich enough to induce the queenly Miss Lorenz to take an interest in *his* welfare, for to the considerable portion of the public which looked upon the AAA as the seat of higher culture, Rose herself had become the symbol and epitome of taste.

Behind the scenes Kirby and Rose Lorenz were the ultimate experts, the designers, publicists, solicitors, appraisers, and chief cataloguers. For the first thirty years there were no stenographers, no files, no confidential clerks. When letters had to be written, Kirby wrote in longhand, or Rose wrote. But there was very little writing to be done. Kirby's word was better than the bond of any ordinary auctioneer. He kept notes of transactions involving fortunes on slips of paper in his waistcoat pocket, or Rose kept the details in her head. The price of art was recorded with flawless penmanship in portentous tomes under Rose's eagle eye. Bookkeeping, like the cataloguing, was done according to her whim. Though as the fortunes of the AAA increased, there were many employees, no authority was ever delegated to an underling. Kirby and Lorenz trusted no one and shared no scrap of glory.

As virtual manager of the galleries, the lady was a Prussian disciplinarian. Though her own wardrobe was comparable to that of Mrs. James Brown Potter, the women under her command were required to wear plain black from head to toe. Sex, in Rose's view, was a synonym for inefficiency, and best concealed as much as possible before the slapdash gentlemen who frequented the AAA. Male employees were allowed a certain leeway, but if a girl flirted with a wealthy client, or even with a fellow employee, she was summarily dismissed. Striding through the galleries, ominously tapping her stick, the lady tyrant issued orders as if the fate of nations depended upon their precise fulfillment. But the obeisance Rose demanded was not to herself. Commands and dispensations alike were in the name of the omnipotent and cantankerous Mr. Kirby. Whether Mr. Kirby threatened or forgave, passed a general order or had a case of nerves, his lieutenant relayed his mood with imperial and Teutonic emphasis. "Miss Potsdam," an unintimidated member of the male staff called her—an epithet that hurt her feelings, for beneath her awesome exterior she had a craving to be liked.

It was a craving mainly satisfied by the ever-faithful Mr. Kirby. When, in commemoration of the twentieth anniversary of the founding of the AAA, "her firm" publicly presented her with a $20,000 purse it was a mere token of esteem, the newspapers surmised. No one ever saw her pay check, but it was rumored that she was the most highly paid woman in the United States.

Munificent as they were, Rose's rewards were justified, at least in Kirby's view. Among other things, she was—to use his phrase—"a world-renowned expert in the decorative arts." In particular, she was said to have a world-renowned clairvoyance in the matter of Chinese porcelains. Indubitably, Rose knew a nice vase when she saw one, but there were busybodies who said that, world renown or not, she would have had to break her crystal ball and retire from Oriental prognostication if some untimely fate had deprived the AAA of the services of Thomas P. Clarke.

Tom Clarke—not to be confused with Clark the Senator (who was Rose's best client) or with Thomas B. Clarke, the art-loving collar-and-cuffs man—was a heavy-set, laconic Negro, whose job it was to unpack the porcelains, check, and number them. It happened that Tom not only loved the rare porcelains he unpacked but was endowed with a mystical affinity for them that, under more favorable circumstances, might have sent experts from Jacquemart to Gonse looking to their laurels. As it was, old hands around the gallery used to smile at the subtle comedy that took place whenever a porcelain collection came into the back room.

The world-renowned Kirby and the world-renowned Lorenz would stand behind a long table, with the mute, inglorious Tom forming the butt end of the trio. His head lowered, a trancelike concentration in his deep, melancholy eyes, Tom would lift each piece and wipe away the dust with his marvelously sensitive hands. Simulating a passion for tidiness, he would study the almost inscrutable signs of the great factories fired into the glaze, the symbols of ancient gods, the flowers and dragons of old celestial empires. With the slow deliberation of a scholar, he would compare the mark of the potter with the product of his labor, separating the real from the false, the Ming from the Han and from the Chien Lung and the Tang. If an object was plainly spurious, he would lift his eyes and place it on the table with an indignant grunt; but when a piece was "right," he would mutter its identification softly, like a harmless eccentric given to talking to himself, and pass it on to the omniscient Miss Lorenz. Rose, in her turn, would gaze at it and feel its texture for a decent interval. Then, in ringing tones of authority, she would place the kiss of approval on Tom Clarke's mumbled attribution. Kirby would second the motion, and together they would solemnly predict its value in the forthcoming auction.

Kirby was by no means unappreciative of Tom Clarke's subtle and (in view of the riotous trade in things Chinese) important contribution to the fame and fortune of the AAA. The relative accuracy of the porcelain catalogues brought high praise to Rose Lorenz, which she acknowledged with many a graceful bow. But Tom had compensations of his own. At the auctions he stood at the door of the salesroom in a resplendent uniform and assigned the seats, for he was no less a master of protocol than of porcelains. In a speech in 1922 Kirby testified that Tom Clarke had handled every object of art that had passed through the AAA since 1892, without injuring a single piece; and Tom was as proud as if Kirby had acclaimed him the expert that a limited circle of porcelain connoisseurs knew him to be. In his will Kirby left him $1,000, a gesture that brought Tom happiness out of all proportion to the value of the money. For Tom Clarke (whose son, incidentally, is now a full book cataloguer at the Parke-Bernet) was of a rare, contented breed. He asked nothing better than to live with porcelains and bask in the great man's affection and respect.

Rose's claims as a porcelain expert may have had their ludicrous aspects, but no one seriously disparaged Kirby's dictum that she was "an acknowledged genius in the arrangement of objects of art." With her corps of assistants, she would normally devote two frenzied weeks to assembling a major exhibit, a ghastly fortnight during which she spent money like a drunken sailor and gave full vent to her volatile artistic temperament.

For a really important sale, the pedestals would have to be re-covered, the walls relined with fabrics, the pictures all but hung on golden nails. Perched on a ladder, with a perfectionist gleam in her eye, Rose herself would drape the plush and damask, while the page boys stood about and held the pins. Then, wielding her yardstick like a regimental madam, she would direct and redirect the hanging and the lighting, the placement of the porcelains, the grouping of the ensemble. When at last, at some unholy hour of the night, one of the eleven galleries appeared sufficiently resplendent, she would allow her many assistants a few hours respite between dawn and the next day's labor. Exhausted, Rose herself would go home and go to bed.

But it was in bed that she got her best ideas. Within a few hours she was back, stick in hand, directing the dismantling of all that had been accomplished the night before. As often as not, then, everything would be moved, the drapes unpinned and pinned again, the pictures rearranged, the brackish ones relighted or given the *Evening in the Hamlet* treatment, up close to the skylight. The man-hours spent in hunting for her yardstick—a prop she was perpetually losing—would have been prohibitive at union wages. Her bill for flowers at an opening was sometimes $1,500. It was small wonder that the results were not infrequently spectacular.

When the final, frantic touches had been made, with the Negro porters in their white gloves standing about like Second Empire courtiers, the doors would open and Rose herself, marvelously coiffed and gowned, would receive the clients like a woman of society on her afternoon at home. Moving through the galleries with an imperial dignity that sometimes made the courtiers titter, she would bow to the great and frown on the vulgar, proffering her advice to the famous, and sometimes, reluctantly, to the infamous.

For mingled with the élite, there was a certain element of riffraff, some of which warranted Rose's indulgence. Diamond Jim Brady would drop in for a breather after cooking up a million-dollar deal at the Hoffman House, or pause for spiritual regeneration on his way to Dorland's restaurant, a sporting folks' rendezvous adjacent to the AAA that was said to have the largest and most aphrodisiac oysters in the world.

Diamond Jim, with his jeweled underwear and his $1,500 umbrella, was the antithesis of all that Rose admired in an auction hound. But he was a natty spender. In consequence of which, when America's number one vulgarian appeared in the galleries, his gluttonous person aglitter with one of his thirty sets of jewels, Rose would even, on occasion, risk her stays to bend and pat his dog, a pampered beast which in its declining years viewed her exhibitions through a pair of rose-colored glasses set with diamonds said to have cost $6,500. On the artistic side, Diamond Jim acquired the requisite cattle for his walls, and cattle-painted dinner plates as well. The embellishments of his iniquitous bachelor dens included countless undraped representations of the feminine anatomy in paint and statuary, by whose hand fashioned, Diamond Jim never much cared. Works of Delacroix and even Rodin could be discerned among the

Turkish corners, the tiger skins, and the loving cups inscribed "For He's a Jolly Good Fellow," the jeweled pool tables, and the costly items Rose bid in for him by Gérôme and Bouguereau.

To be sure, there were those who made so bold as to say that the priestess of the auctions was a phony and a harridan. Certainly she was not above selling choice pieces out of the consignments under the table, so to speak. In a time when a fruitful introduction to an art-happy *arriviste* was worth from 2 to 20 per cent, she did a land-office business recommending dealers' stocks to bewildered shoppers who relied upon her world-renowned clairvoyance. It was even said that, as proxy bidder for a raft of clients, she was a sordid politician who would "get it for you cheap if you paid her." But those who uttered such derogatory sentiments were, for the most part, artmongers not in her favor. It was true that a dealer on bad terms with Rose Lorenz was *persona non grata* at the AAA, but most of her circle found it possible to please her. Stanford White designed her New York house; others contributed to the beautifying of her estate at Sound Beach, Connecticut; the King of Belgium decorated her with the Palm of Silver; Vitall Benguiat, the Oriental rug peddler, gave her a string of Oriental pearls.

Her jealous rivals notwithstanding, at the evening sales, in her chinchilla and her pearls—or on lesser occasions, with a mink scarf slung over a gown of wine-colored velvet—she might have been taken by a stranger for the most spendthrift heiress present. For not infrequently, when all her bidding commissions had been assembled, Rose herself turned out to be the most abundant buyer of the things she had appraised and catalogued and so meticulously displayed. Sometimes half the lots would fall to her under a variety of monikers: "Stanley" for Morgan, "Chelsea" for Hearst, "Carlos" for Huntington; and above all "Chester" for Senator Clark the Copper King of Montana.

William A. Clark made his first appearance at the AAA in 1891, when he dropped in unannounced and bought a picture called *Weary Wayfarers* by Jean Charles Cazin for $3,150. Kirby told the bid callers not to demand a deposit from the important-looking gentleman, for whereas he was a total stranger, he had "the appearance of responsibility." It was the beginning of a beautiful friendship.

In his early twenties Clark, a Pennsylvania farm boy, had crossed the Western plains, driving the ox team that was his only capital. He had been one of the first to reach Bannack, Montana, upon the discovery of gold there in 1862. Now, in the nineties—in the throes of his metamorphosis from a wild-haired little jackal to a spidery, dapper *élégant*—he was the richest man west of the Mississippi, one of "the hundred men who own America," and one whose name was inordinately tinged by association with bribery, corruption, and scandal.

Having acquired—in addition to gold mines—copper mines, smelters, wireworks, coffee, tea, tobacco, sugar, and rubber plantations, as well as newspapers to sing his praises in Montana, he was ready to take up art, politics, and architecture. He was, moreover, uncommonly thrifty for a man whose income for a single year was reported to be $10 million. In garnering his art collection, he discovered at the outset that dealers had a tendency to wish to make a profit, a character defect he looked upon with about the same disfavor as the demands of his miners for a wage of $2 a day. Auction rooms appealed to him as places where profiteering would be at a minimum, but whenever he attended sales in person, he took care to conceal his participation from greedy consignors who might recognize him and be tempted to run up the prices. Kirby was given to understand that so long as Clark was willing to bid, he would hold his lapel with his right hand. Old-timers remember that two or three quick bids were usually called for him while his hand was on the way down.

As a further precaution against being cheated, Clark studied French and went abroad to see what this painting business was all about. The results of his investigations were this way and that. In the modern line he decided to put his biggest bets on Corot, Cazin, and Monticelli, but this trio gradually expanded to include a number of flashier artists. Among them was Mariano Fortuny, one-time leader of the Roman-Spanish colony, a swashbuckling, guitar-strumming clique of painters who enjoyed what they called "the franchise of the rich," along with the scorn of most of the serious artists of their time. It was at the Fortuny sale in 1898 that the Copper King most vividly displayed his new-found aesthetic passions.

To the palace-ridden, the charmed life of the dashing Spanish painters was a wellspring of vicarious adventure. A contemporary writer said of one of the lesser members of the school, "With a few cigarettes and his guitar, he might start this evening for a tour of the world." In reality, however, most of the *caballero* painters' touring consisted of following their patrons from Rome to Paris to New York, for while the main subjects of their pictures were masked balls, snake charmers, and unemployed Arabs sitting in the sun, they also had a deft hand with society ladies' profiles. All in all, it was an exhausting life, and one that had driven Fortuny to his grave in 1874, at the tender age of thirty-six.

By 1898 most up-to-date collectors had a few Fortunys, but there were those who had to confess, with downcast eyes, that they had none at all. This was due in part to the untimely death of the painter—a circumstance tending simultaneously to reduce production and increase the demand—but also to the niggardly fact that a former New Yorker named William H. Stewart had attempted to corner the market. Now that Stewart's demise and the exigencies of the auction block were about to equalize the distribution, art lovers heretofore deprived looked forward to making up an embarrassing deficiency.

The deceased Mr. Stewart had made a fortune early in life in the West Indies trade. Thereupon he had moved to Paris to patronize the arts. For more than three decades his house on the Avenue d'Iena had been a rendezvous for American merchants on the grand tour, and when Stewart died, his heirs, mindful of his prestige back home, bundled up his pictures, along with some of his Japanese lacquered furniture, and shipped them over to Kirby for a gala auction.

If the panting of the newspapers and art journals can be taken as a guide, the captains of industry must have been dancing in the streets as the boat slid into the harbor. The late Mr. Stewart, said the *Sun*, had had "a very clear idea of what was art," and the public, which had heard little but Millet and Barbizon for twenty years, would profit no end by tripping off to the AAA to view a very different school of painting. Other critics hailed the auction as the greatest redistribution of culture that had ever taken place in America.

Of all the Fortunys in the de luxe Stewart catalogue (which cost $25), the one most coveted was *The Choice of a Model*. As the *Sun* pointed out, this supersumptuous picture had "always been held in the highest esteem by the public, if not by artists." It contained everything: rich draperies, fine metalwork, choice marbles, and all the exotic furniture and crockery that possibly could be crammed into a nineteenth-century conception of an eighteenth-century apartment. In this fruity Roman setting (it took the cataloguer a whole page to list the inventory and get down to the gist of the matter), a group of male connoisseurs are assembled "to criticize a nude female model who is posing before them in an attitude of studied grace," a ritual indicating "to what an extent the study of art was at this period indulged in as a fashionable accomplishment."

Kirby's latter-day connoisseurs sighed in ecstasy as *The Choice of a Model* was placed before them on the block; and none more ecstatically than George J. Gould, who was then in the process of equipping his Fifth Avenue mansion with the most fashionable art obtainable. In a fast getaway that drew a spontaneous burst of applause, Gould shouted an initial offer of $30,000. Most of the Fortuny lovers were left at the post, but coming down the stretch, Clark bent forward in his front-row seat and clung to both lapels like a devil-may-care jockey determined to bring in a winner. Gould was finally outdistanced, and to long and loud applause, the prize fell to Clark at $42,000. Seldom, if ever, had the thrifty Copper King paid so much for a picture, but then, seldom had a painter given so much for the money.

To keep *The Choice of a Model* company, Clark bought a number of Stewart's other Fortunys. But once he had the gem of the collection, he was careful not to push the prices beyond reason, and most of his opponents were allowed to share in the bounty at comparatively modest rates. Harry Payne Whitney got *The Court of Justice—Alhambra* for $13,000. Henry Walters took an *Arab Fantasia* at $12,000. Collis P. Huntington, who was never very fussy, contented himself with *Breakfast in the Old Convent Yard* at $6,900. Stanford White, H. C. Frick, Adolph Lewisohn, and Samuel Untermyer picked up the crumbs, and generally speaking, the wider distribution of Fortuny and his circle was equitably carried out among America's budding connoisseurs—for a total of a little more than $400,000.

Budding, however, was scarcely the word for William A. Clark. He was determined to burgeon. At the time of the Stewart sale, he was engaged in commanding a palatial mansion that was to be palatial to a hitherto undreamed-of degree. Although there were later complications, his original instructions to his architects had the virtue of extreme simplicity. They were given carte blanche to equal any of the fine houses on Fifth Avenue; and when completed the Copper King's abode at the northeast corner of Fifth Avenue and 77th Street was to contain "the finest art collection on this continent."

While a battery of draftsmen pondered over how to outdo Mrs.

Astor, William C. Whitney, and the Vanderbilts, Clark himself set about acquiring a title to match the splendor of his castle. In 1899, despite his predisposition to economy, he spent an estimated $5 million getting himself elected Senator from Montana. He was forced to resign, however, with tears in his eyes, when an investigating committee uncovered so much fraud and bribery that he was declared not duly and legally elected. Two years later he had himself a little more duly and slightly more legally elected, and that time the office stuck. At the end of one term, he gave up the job, but not the title, which was what he had paid all the money for in the first place, and for the rest of his life—he lived to be eighty-six—he was known in both society and trade simply and grandly as "Senator Clark."

After he acquired his title, Clark decided that it was beneath his dignity to be seen in an auction room. Rose Lorenz became his secret agent, his go-between, and in effect, his aide-de-camp in embellishing the mansion that came to be known as "Clark's folly." He would come to the darkened galleries after hours and pick out what he wanted; Rose would then either sell it to him by "private treaty" or bid for him in the sales. Since only a fraction of the requisite grandeur was available at auction, Rose often had to look elsewhere for supplies—to the dealers, in fact, who could not have sold the suspicious Senator a doge's footstool by the direct approach. One way or another, Rose managed to furnish much of Clark's palatial acreage with what he imagined to be bargains.

Senator Clark's endeavor to prove that he was as good as anybody turned out to be a twelve-year project with a well-nigh indescribable result. The New York *American* called the house "the nearest to an imperial palace up to date in this hemisphere." Another newspaper said it would have been an appropriate residence for the late P. T. Barnum. *The Architectural Record* thought the steeple invited speculation as to what sort of meeting place was there and remarked that a certified check to the amount of the stone carving hung on the outer wall would have served every artistic purpose attained by the carving itself. At a later date, when time had consecrated the monstrous pile as "a peerless piece of ludicrous solemnity," Robert Littell wrote in *The New Republic:*

The coldness, the stoniness, the marbleness of the halls and staircases grope timidly toward what the twenty-one bathrooms alone achieve.

There are 130 rooms in this house, thirty of them for servants. The kitchens wind and angle up, from the deep dungeons, to the dining room as narrowly and darkly as if they were the ammunition vaults of an obsolete battleship. Hundreds, thousands of feet below ground, a clammily magnificent swimming pool echoes to our hushed voices. Here, in the underworld, are endless cellars, recesses, cubby holes, lanes, in sinister glazed white tile. A fabulous pit, black and full of wheels: the elevator power room. Another pit, crawling with white, worm-like pipes: the furnace which burned seventeen tons of coal a day and required four tons merely to get going. But these viscera are not supposed to be seen; it may be doubted if the Senator ever saw them himself. So let's go back to the naked alleys of stone and Circassian walnut; to the self-supporting staircase, to the ceiling from Sherwood Forest, to the mineral beauties from the two quarries, marble and granite, which the Senator bought outright, for the building of this house; to walnut, sandalwood and satinwood and natural American oak; to the carved · maple, innumerable wainscotings and panelings, exquisite and expensive, forlorn and dull; to the banquet room and the music room and the breakfast room and the petit salon. . . .

When at last the place was declared habitable, the great bronze doors were thrown open one afternoon a week for those who wished to behold the Senator at home in the midst of his treasure. A pipe organ that would have cluttered St. Patrick's Cathedral played mood music. Canaries sang in 9-foot bird cages of tortoise shell, jade, and carved ivory. A large part of the Book of Genesis was depicted on the sofa pillows. Famous paintings in the Louvre were reproduced in the lace medallions of the banquet cloths. There were yards, perhaps miles, of brocades, tapestries, and velvet, wagonloads of majolica and Hispano-Moresque pottery, enough gold paint to gild the domes of many state capitols.

"Art, like everything else," Clark used to say in his ex-Senatorial capacity, "is best and sanest in America." He even expressed his zeal for enterprise by buying works of the late George Inness and the Hudson River school. But on his afternoons, having led the curious through his four galleries of Fortunys, Raffaellis, Corots, Cazins, and Barbizons, the Senator would choose as a background for his aureate person those nut-brown, glass-protected pictures catalogued as Old Masters—the trade name for varnish-mellowed canvases that looked like heirlooms and appeared to have weathered a minimum of two centuries. For long before the effulgent Senator's stonecutters had completed the setting for his apotheosis the art of the past had become as basic as Corot in the palazzi of America's comic-opera nobility.

Kirby's first large-scale effort to disperse the art of the centuries had been something less than gratifying. In 1889, S. Montgomery Roosevelt imported and consigned to the AAA a collection of Old Masters purported to be worth $1 million. S. Montgomery Roosevelt was, among other things, a portrait painter, a gentleman cowboy, a fencing expert, and a cousin of Theodore Roosevelt, though perhaps, in the long run, his chief claim to fame was a dinner of roast baby lion he once served to fellow members of the American Association of Portrait Painters. A very nice poem was written about it, and the members declared that never again would they be satisfied with roast ostrich or crocodile steak. In the case of the million-dollar collection, S. Montgomery was functioning as a shoestring art dealer, another of his part-time occupations. The Old Masters did not belong to him. He was merely their agent. The pictures were the property of a Spanish nobleman who signed himself as follows. "His Highness, Don Pedro Alicàntara de Borbon y Borbon, First Duque de Durcal, a grandee of Spain of the Grand Cross of Charles III, member of the Society of the Maestrante of Seville, and of the Spanish Geographical Society, etc., etc., etc."

The Duque, a young dandy of twenty-seven, crossed the ocean with his Old Masters to see that everything went off all right. Kirby, with unaccustomed restraint, issued a lukewarm catalogue containing a two-page description of the Duque's relatives but very little solid information about the pictures. Heirlooms, the Duque said they were, inherited from his father, who had got them from any number of royal families, all of whom—not to mention the late Pope—had thought the world of the old man. Kirby added—with no great conviction— that since so large a representation of Spanish, Dutch, Flemish, and Italian art had never been seen in America before, he supposed the public could not fail to be agog. A four-day sale was scheduled and the pictures were put on exhibition.

This time the *Tribune* took up the cudgels. In all modesty, that newspaper's art man said, there was really no expert in this country whose word could be taken as final on adorations, entombments, crucifixions, and martyrdoms. But he felt that, somehow, the individual powers of the great masters were missing. Take, for instance, that florid head assigned to Rembrandt, or that beat-up painting ascribed to van der Weyden. Antiques they were, undoubtedly, but it did seem strange that neither they nor the titles of the pictures shown with them were listed anywhere in the *catalogues raisonnés* of the great painters' works. The expression on the faces of those cherubs by Murillo was beatific enough; but if Murillo cherubs they were, surely they were an example of his heavier manner. With disconcerting thoroughness, the *Tribune* man demolished the Duque's heirlooms one by one, and then, as a final blow, came up with an old book describing the family collection that had really belonged to His Serene Highness, the Duque's father, in his palmy days. "The collection as offered to us," the critic remarked with lofty understatement, "does not appear identical with the collection bequeathed by Don Sebastian to his heirs."

The young Duque's Spanish blood was mightily aroused. He jumped on his horse and galloped over to the *Tribune* office, prepared to fling down his glove in defense of his honor. Failing to find a pedigreed gentleman to fling it in front of, he cooled off and said he would guarantee every picture with his royal signature. When the papers questioned the value of such certificates, however noble the hand that wrote them, the Duque sulked and demanded that upset prices be put on what he considered his more important "examples."

Kirby took a good look at the pictures and decided to keep out of the controversy, but he refused to allow the Duque's upset prices to remain secret. Before the bemused little crowd that came to Chickering Hall for four gloomy sessions, as each Titian, Velásquez, or El Greco came to the block, he announced what the Duque would take for it. The fiasco was sensational. As Kirby had warned His Highness, American buyers would not tolerate upset prices, even if their tongues were—and they were not—hanging out for Virgins and entombments. There was not a single bid for any of the pictures on which the Duque had dictated the minimum. Three paintings were sold. A Mrs. Drexel squandered $1,000 on *The Infant Saviour Extracting a Thorn*, labeled Murillo; Henry Walters paid the same amount for a Dürer; a third client was willing to gamble $80 on something called *Christ at the Gates of Hell;* and a number of drawings were sold for negligible sums. The Duque de Durcal picked up his small change, loaded his heirlooms back on the boat, and departed, muttering Spanish curses on Kirby's rich barbarians. In Paris the pictures were again put up at auction, and the *Tribune* was pleased to report that the million-dollar collection, between the New York and Paris sales, brought a grand total of $38,796.

The Duque's indignation notwithstanding, American indifference to the art of the past could hardly be measured by the failure to palm off some unlikely daubs on an auction public whose naïveté was not quite as fantastic as many Europeans imagined. By 1889 John G. Johnson of Philadelphia was already gathering the Italian primitives that now hang in the Philadelphia Museum. In Boston, Mrs. Jack Gardner was beginning to acquire some very beautiful Renaissance pictures, and by the mid-nineties, she was to conceive the notion of transplanting a little corner of Venice to New England, to serve, first, as a temple for her earthly shenanigans, and later, as an immutable public monument to her especially lush immortal soul. J. P. Morgan, having decided to buy everything in the world, employed a network of agents to go about it in a rational manner. In 1895 Kirby checked off a milestone when Van Dyck's *Marchese de Spinola and Her Little Daughter* fell to a Morgan bidder for a record $50,000. The following year a Rembrandt painted by Rembrandt brought $18,600, only $7,000 less than a tenebrous view of the Barbizon woods by Théodore Rousseau. In 1902 a Titian in the E. F. Milliken sale made $42,000; and a few weeks later, when Kirby sold F. O. Matthiessen's collection, *The Holy Family with Saint Francis*, labeled Rubens, soared to $50,000 and tied the Van Dyck record.

The buyer of *The Holy Family* was listed as George P. Blow, but during the sale an aureate gentleman called James Henry (Silent) Smith had taken a fancy to the picture. When Kirby descended from the rostrum, Smith asked him to negotiate its purchase from the successful bidder. This Kirby did—at heaven only knows what advance—for James Henry (Silent) Smith had just inherited $56 million from a miserly old uncle in London.

Up to the time of this singular event Silent Smith, a torpescent Wall Street broker with rimless pince-nez, balding head, and wilting black mustaches, had lived a modest bachelor's life in the simplest kind of apartment, with only one picture on the wall: a portrait of his rich old Uncle George. (Uncle George was a dour Scotsman who had come to this country fortune hunting in 1834, made his pile in the Midwest, and retired to London, where for forty years he lived on a budget of $200 a month.) But it was not as a pendant to his nice old relative's portrait that James Henry wanted *The Holy Family with Saint Francis*. He presented it, with a beneficent flourish, to the Metropolitan Museum, where it is now catalogued "Workshop of Rubens."

Workshop or not, in 1902 the gift of *The Holy Family* served to trumpet lucky James Henry's meteoric flash in the purlieus of the socially élite. Before his windfall, he had spent most of his leisure time reading. The dusty chairs of his apartment were stacked with good books that had overflowed from his many shelves. "The seclusion of poverty is a blessing," he used to say. It was one of his few known utterances. But now, already, he was practicing with Mrs. Stuyvesant Fish, Mrs. John Jacob Astor, and Mrs. Cornelius Vanderbilt for his first cotillion at Sherry's.

In 1904, when William C. Whitney died, Silent Smith bought the newly remodeled Whitney mansion at Fifth Avenue and 67th Street, with its Stanford White decor and champagne-flowing fountains; he took over its staff, which, it was said, could serve a hundred guests on golden plates at an hour's notice, and undertook to supplement its splendor with Gainsboroughs and dubious Old Masters. In this setting—called "as near an approach to a Venetian or Florentine palace . . . as is possible to obtain"—he gave entertainments at which Caruso sang and young blades got drunk and threw cigarette butts on the Isfahans. In company with the blades, the Silent One—as *Town Topics* called him—learned to drive four-in-hand. He built a country place at Tuxedo Park, commissioned Anthony J. Drexel's yacht, and went on trips with Mr. and Mrs. William Rhinelander Stewart.

Alas, the high life very shortly did James Henry in. In 1906 Mrs. Stewart got a divorce and took it into her head to marry him. The Silent One rented an estate in Scotland for the ceremony. Guests were summoned as for a feudal joining of the clans. The local gentry lighted fires on the tops of hills and played bagpipes. These glorious nuptials over, the happy couple boarded the Drexel yacht for a wedding tour around the world in company with the Duke and Duchess of Manchester and other notables. But by the time the honeymoon party had progressed as far as Kyoto, Japan, the $56-million bridegroom was dead.

Rubens, Van Dyck, Murillo, Titian, and "examples" (quasi or otherwise) bearing other noble attributions were beginning to make records at the AAA, but the season 1902–3 was also a banner one for the decorative arts. In 1902 Henry G. Marquand, who had begun life as a silversmith and made millions in Wall Street speculations, departed this earth, "full of years and honors"—as the *Tribune* put it—"and left to the City of New York the inspiring example of a blameless and fruitful life." He also left a good many more tangible items.

In 1889 Marquand had presented to the Metropolitan Museum a collection of fifty-three pictures that would have been the envy of any gallery in the world. Among them were three Van Dycks, three Frans Hals, Rembrandt's *Man with a Beard,* a Turner, and above all Vermeer's *Young Woman with a Water Jug.* Through his extraordinary benefactions, of which the fifty-three pictures were only the beginning, Marquand became president of the museum, and remained in that office, an imposing gentleman in sideburns and frock coat, until the end of his days. But even after his generosity to the Metropolitan, there were enough choice objects left in the Marquand mansion to bring nearly three quarters of a million dollars at the AAA.

"He bought like an Italian prince of the Renaissance," Russell Sturgis wrote in a sonorous introduction to the Marquand catalogue. "For him who longed for European wealth and the abundance of sensations, and who hardly expected to find them in America, Henry Gurdon Marquand's house was a comforting place to visit . . . differing in nothing . . . except in the more moderate size of the apartments . . . from the palace interiors which we dream of as existing in the great times of creative art." Comforting perhaps, but even Sturgis had to admit that it was a marvel of confusion and profusion.

The great hall was shrouded in tapestries and cloth of gold. Spanish tiles in massive frames adorned the stairways and corridors. Rembrandt, Constable, and Raimundo de Madrazo played hide-and-seek behind Greek vases and terra-cotta statues. Van Dyck noblemen and dubious English portraits consorted with Persian ceramics, enameled retables, and Italian cassoni. Beakers, pots, and bottles made a forest of iridescence and translucence. The mansion was French Renaissance in principle, but mongrel in practice. There were Moorish rooms crammed with Hispano-Moresque platters. There were Greco-Roman marbles, Limoges enamels, and multicolored seas of Chinese porcelains. There was a famed Japanese room with walls covered with watered silk embroidered to order in Japan. There were chambers of quebracho wood polished to look like ivory, salons with lacquered panels, parlors of purple silk containing bronzes and Italian embroideries. There were rooms wholly lined with Persian tiles. There were stained-glass windows, vast areas of mosaic, miles of friezes, and acres of carving. Paintings by Théodore Rousseau and Alma-Tadema mingled with Renaissance ironwork, with reproductions of Imperial Russian gold and silver trophies, and surrounded the beautiful della Robbia altar piece now in the museum.

On the Marquand floors were Oriental rugs, the first of any importance to be sold at auction in the United States. One of them, a Royal Persian animal rug, about 12 feet long by 6 feet wide, was described by John Kimberly Mumford, a writer and expert on antique rugs, as "probably as near perfection as the woolen carpet of the East has come, or will ever come." On a dark green, almost black, background a medallion of Isfahan red formed a central figure interwoven with traceries of delicate pink surmounted by an arabesque of branches in silver thread. Amid a wilderness of moss-green creepers, leaves, tendrils, lotus flowers, and stems of deep orange edged in red, the miniature animals of the Moslem allegories frolicked—deer, gazelles, sheep, goats, lions, leopards; over all, four hawklike birds of prey hovered with an air of impending doom; and in the borders of rich golden-yellow were couplets from the poetry of Saadi woven in a beautiful calligraphy.

Some four centuries before the Animal Rug found its way to Kirby's auction block it had been a gift from the Emperor of the Persians to the Sultan of Turkey. Now, its pedigree, if not its beauty, made it an item to be coveted by J. P. Morgan. Perfection in the woolen carpet was, however, at that time less a fetish with Pierpontifex Maximus than with Vitall (the Pasha) Benguiat, who had recently appointed himself torchbearer for Oriental carpets in this country. Doggedly, the brash, debt-ridden, and all but insolvent rug peddler bid against the impregnable wealth of Morgan. Pierpontifex retreated, and at $38,000—a price that in 1902 was worth clamorous headlines in the papers—Vitall (the Pasha) became the possessor of a speculative strip of carpet that was to grow threadbare as a subject of dispute in the course of his long and contentious career in the shadow of the AAA.

All this, one stern economist wrote, when the results of the Marquand sale were printed in the papers, was a far cry from the thrifty habits of our forefathers. Politicians in Washington were horrified when they read about the number of imported objects. Congress would have to impose a higher tariff, they said, in order to protect American artists. Nonsense, Ernest Knaufft replied in the *Review of Reviews*, the Messrs. Morgan, Vanderbilt, and hundreds of others were performing the salutary function of educating public taste. "It will be seen from this educational point of view," the *Review* argued, "that though the Marquand sale was simply the auctioning of the household effects of a private citizen, it had a national significance, for sooner or later every one of the two thousand articles disposed of may become an object-lesson for American art workers."

The anxiety of the Congress notwithstanding, American art was doing as well as could be expected, and in some instances, better than the judgment of posterity has warranted. This was due in part to the missionary spirit of Thomas B. Clarke, the collar-and-cuffs manufacturer who had delivered Inness into the hands of the AAA back in the dreamy, idealistic days of the beginnings on Madison Square. By 1891, when Clarke was forty-two, he had made so many collars and cuffs and sold them for so much money that he saw no reason to make any more. Forsaking common trade, he became a full-time connoisseur, and by way of justifying the enormity of his collecting, set himself up as a kind of gentleman art dealer.

Thomas B. Clarke collected everything. Moreover, it became his mission in life to encourage others to do the same. He was as eager to publicize the ninth-century potters of the Euphrates valley as the lyrical, soul-searching paintings of Albert Ryder. All pictures, Clarke said, were not necessarily pictures in paint. Specialists in the fields he so blithely invaded sometimes remarked that he was an ignorant bore, but others considered the Clarke name synonymous with art. His energy and avidity, they said, was "one of the wonders of the world's metropolis."

Clarke's cultural activities were carried on in a mansion he called Art House, a title everyone admired for its simplicity. Art House was a plush shopping center, impractical and elegant, if a little cluttered; for Clarke was not in the thing for profit. He was more of a booster than a tradesman. Above all, he was a joiner. He belonged to country clubs and dry-goods associations, fine arts societies and anticorruption committees. He decked the Century Club and the Union League Club with ancestral portraits that the members, in their warm, deep-cushioned chairs, endeavored to resemble. And inevitably, he had a following, if not among the élite, at least among the rich.

Out of all this busyness—which continued until his death in 1931—one clearly defined specialty emerged. Clarke was the champion gatherer of American pictures. Young artists were the object of his philanthropy; painters of standing often sold him their best work; obscure and neglected geniuses could sometimes persuade him to discover them. As with his other collections, when the number of American canvases got out of hand, he held an auction at the AAA. In later years these January clearances were often routine trade affairs, but the Clarke auction of 1899 was a trail-blazing event. For the first time a panoramic selection of contemporary American art was put to the test of public sale, with the result that the red barn, the wide plains, and the hills of home were established as dignified commodities in the collecting world.

The Inness called *Grey, Lowering Day* that had made its debut at the American Art Association fifteen years earlier, when an Inness was worth from $50 to $500, made the highest price: $10,150. But two Winslow Homers brought between $4,000 and $5,000 each. George Fuller's *A Romany Girl* sold for $4,100; Homer Martin's *Adirondack Scenery* made $5,500; and D. W. Tryon, J. Francis Murphy, and George de Forest Brush passed the $2,000 mark. The total for the sale was $235,000, a sum that set a great many picture buyers wondering if American art might not be a long-term investment worth looking into.

After the 1899 sale Clarke more or less abandoned living American artists for the dead. It became his main pursuit—and the most rewarding of his many activities—to collect original American historical portraits. For more than thirty years he ransacked the parlors and garrets of the country, adding and subtracting, weeding out, and selling his mistakes at auction. The time came when even Clarke's rejections—a Gilbert Stuart copy or a questionable Rembrandt Peale —would bring $10,000 or $20,000 at the AAA, but in the beginning, few of the élite followed his example in searching for the past on native ground. Some ghosts were needed to inhabit the pseudo-antique castles, but plain American ancestors did not come into vogue until after the emotional upheaval of the First World War. Like their splendid, primordial architecture, the colonists' art and artifacts, and even their portraits, had to be lost and found again before they could become chic and expensive as collectors' items.

Some ghosts were needed to inhabit the castles, for with the resurrection of so much anachronistic splendor, the Alger boys had grown self-conscious about having no distinguished origins of their own. The architecture of the Medici was all very well, since the Medici had been so very rich, but no one wanted Italian ancestors. Men of large affairs were willing to come home and sit in Spanish choir stalls to read the closing Wall Street prices, or plan the latest merger in rooms decorated with Moorish tiles; but no one wished to bolster up his social position by claiming the Spaniards or the blackamoors as kin-folk. No one, that is, except Boston's Mrs. Gardner, who somehow got the notion that she was a throwback to Queen Isabella. There were those who favored the French as dream progenitors—Mrs. Pembroke Jones, for instance, or Mrs. William Salomon, women especially equipped by intellect and temperament to escape the Puritan aversion to the frivolous art of the French court painters. But in less effervescent circles the loadstone of snobbery was Anglomania, mingled with a concomitant respect for Prussian arrogance. For all practical purposes, British ancestors were the thing.

And so, into the palazzi came the English landed gentry. Beside the lowing cattle of Barbizon hung the silken gown, the powdered wig, the Gainsborough. The privileged classes of the English eighteenth century emigrated to America in every quality and condition, mainly in large sizes. They came by the dozen and by the hundred, the lord of the manor and the lady, singly and in pairs. Admirals came that were stern and disapproving; generals and country squires; families of model children, including the dog; windblown girls with wholesome English faces; titled ladies with buttermilk complexions. The English big six—Gainsborough, Hoppner, Lawrence, Raeburn, Romney, Reynolds—were easy to appreciate, but their most backward pupils were almost equally in demand. It was not the painting, but the aristocratic bearing, the sumptuous clothing, the long, thin, aristocratic noses, the lace cuffs and royal decorations, the refinement and the solid self-contentment, that gave the Alger boys the feeling that they were entertaining the very sum and substance of society.

Art in this sense was a genuine extension of the social ideals of the time, for dynastic hopes ran high on the shores of the great democracy. Some of the robber barons' heirs were content to marry their sons and daughters to other great American fortunes, but many looked to the European nobility as a means of buying a long past and what promised to be an even longer future. Heiresses prowled the court circles of England and the Continent shopping for titles. Through the shameless machinations of the titaness Alva Vanderbilt (later Mrs. O. H. P. Belmont) whose ball in 1883 had ushered in the neo-Babylonian era, her daughter Consuelo unwillingly became the Duchess of Marlborough and mistress of Blenheim Palace, a privilege said to have cost the William K. Vanderbilt estate some $10 million. Mary Leiter captured the Marquess Curzon of Kedleston; at a million-dollar wedding in St. Thomas' Church, William C. Whitney's daughter Pauline married Sir Almeric Hugh Paget; May Goelet became the Duchess of Roxburghe; Clara Huntington brought a multimillion-dollar dowry to Prince von Hatzfield-Wildenburg. The intercontinental mating progressed to the point where spoilsport patriots called for preventive legislation to stem the flow of so much money out of the country.

Sometimes when a girl made a sensational match, the common people, no less than the wealthy, would be agog. In 1895 when Anna Gould married the singularly unmanly Count Boni de Castellane, otherwise known as France's Powder Puff, cordons of police were required to keep the crowds moving in the sleet and snow outside the Gould mansion on Fifth Avenue. A thousand East Side schoolchildren partook of Gould largess in the form of sandwiches and ice cream and practiced for a week raising three cheers to the red, white, and blue and "the Countess de Castellane."

To many heirs of plain, industrious Americans the dream of noble birth became an obsession. Sanctimonious old John Wanamaker had started in the clothing business as a barker. His father was a brickmaker, and John Wanamaker's idea of higher culture was the Bethany Sunday School or the Y.M.C.A. But his son, Rodman, self-styled patron of the arts and a devotee of Kirby's rostrum, displayed the Wanamaker coat of arms above his mantelpiece. Larz Anderson, who was American ambassador to Japan in 1912 and 1913, had the walls of his Washington house painted with murals depicting the military exploits of his or his wife's ancestors in the Revolutionary War, but for his own full-length portrait as ambassador, Anderson wore knee breeches and other finery copied after the diplomatic uniform of the Court of St. James. Genealogists of the period charged $500 to trace "noble ancestors" for those who wished to join the Order of the Crown. If they were foolish enough not to turn up any, the client invariably refused to pay.

This rampant social climbing had a profound effect on the art sales. Dealers with a sixth sense understood that the English portraits fitted the prevailing spiritual attitude like a glove. They sold what was easiest to sell, with the result that by the time the problem of authenticity came to outweigh other considerations, all the highest prices were paid for a school of painting that—in the words of the Parke-Bernet's Leslie Hyam—occupies ten pages out of six hundred in any competent history of art.

In Kirby's day, however, the authenticity of the pictures was a lesser problem than the authenticity of the $1,000 bills that paid for them. The public sales afforded anyone and everyone a simple means of acquiring an aristocratic scheme of decoration. If people wished to live in a fool's paradise of somber Raeburns and bastard Romneys, Kirby did not feel called upon to discourage them. He boasted that of the 1,595 Barbizon pictures he sold at auction, only eight were questioned; but when it came to the older paintings, he threw up his hands with disarming nonchalance. It was impossible, he said, to determine who had painted what. Experts could seldom be persuaded to agree. The simplest procedure was to catalogue the pictures in accordance with the most grandiose suppositions of the consignor.

These suppositions sometimes reached the point of colossal foolishness. It was the notion, for instance, of William H. Fuller, a wallpaper manufacturer of Binghamton, New York, that he could sell *The Blue Boy* for a small fortune to some purblind bidder at the AAA. Fuller did not actually own *The Blue Boy*—either the celebrated one over in Grosvenor House or the one he wished to sell. He had got the picture on consignment from a London dealer who agreed to take $6,500 for it in the event that Fuller could unload it in the auction of his "Very Notable Private Collection."

The project was complicated by the general awareness that the Duke of Westminster also had *The Blue Boy*. But were there not two of almost everything? It was a known fact that Rosa Bonheur had painted *The Horse Fair* four times. There were two of Millet's *The Sower*—one in Boston, the other in the Vanderbilt collection—and who was to say that one was more *The Sower* than the other? Whenever Meissonier had been lucky with a picture, he had duplicated it as often as the traffic would bear. There was even a second version of the $66,000 *Friedland, 1807* that Judge Hilton had so kindly presented to the Metropolitan. Who, then, was to say that Gainsborough had not run off a second view of Master Buttall?

Nevertheless, the Duke of Westminster's *Blue Boy* was a formidable rival. To be on the safe side, Fuller placed an upset price of $30,000 on his version and wrote a pamphlet defending it. The rhetoric of the pamphlet, like its subject, was enveloped in the soft, mellow tone of old satin, but it cast no light on the duality of Master Buttall except to suggest that if Gainsborough had not made a habit of painting Blue Boys, Hoppner might have painted this one. That was a tactical error. The one thing Kirby's clients could not abide was ambiguity. If the catalogue said Gainsborough, it was Gainsborough they expected to buy, not Hoppner. Nobody would bid $30,000. The picture was withdrawn, and Fuller proposed to return it to his coconspirator in London. Nobody wanted to keep on paying the anomalous *Blue Boy*'s passage back and forth across the ocean, however, and after some haggling, a notorious dealer named Theron Blakeslee bought the picture for $5,000 and sold it to George A. Hearn for $6,000.

Hearn would buy anything. He was proprietor of the huge department store his father had established a generation earlier on 14th Street in New York, and he was widely known as a fine example of that dying breed the merchant prince. A beauty lover of Gargantuan indiscrimination, he was a pushover for what advanced connoisseurs used to call "Sir Joshua and His Circle," albeit what he gathered emanated mainly from the Circle. He was also a "friend to American art," particularly to the Hudson River school, whose members were all safely dead and beyond the need of friendship. The papers were frequently filled with paeans to the Merchant Prince's generosity to museums, especially to the long-suffering Metropolitan, which he stocked, like a Pharaoh's dream boat, with the best of his worldly impedimenta, tagged with donor's plaques and recorded in de luxe illustrated volumes in preparation for his journey through immortality. His house was crammed with everything that went by the name of art; his store, behind the aerial display of union suits and Mother Hubbards, was a labyrinthine mixture of dry goods and museum culture. It was pleasant, he thought, for a belabored housewife pawing among the eiderdowns and pillow slips to look up and catch a glimpse of *Tobias and the Angel* labeled Rembrandt or *Esther and King Ahasuerus* attributed to Van Dyck. And the lady was unlikely to carp if neither of them conformed too closely to the standards of the Masters. Nothing could have been better situated than *The Blue Boy* in the silken breeches department—in those days when the image of Little Lord Fauntleroy was strong in every shopping mother's heart.

Hearn died in 1913, and four years later *The Blue Boy* again showed up at the AAA, amid a residual agglomeration of Hearn pictures and art objects which brought three quarters of a million dollars. The supernumerary Master Buttall by this time had become an object of misplaced affection on the part of the Hearn heirs. They bid it up to $38,000, got stuck with it, and put it in a storage warehouse, where it remained until 1932. Then, feeling the pinch of the Great Depression, they once more consigned it to the auction hall. Meanwhile Sir Joseph Duveen had transferred the Grosvenor House *Blue Boy* to the Huntington Library of San Marino, California, at a price of $620,000. Nevertheless, at that bleak Hearn aftermath, when even a pedigreed Turner fell with a thud at $4,000, the poor man's *Blue Boy* turned out still to be worth $8,500.

Not only *The Blue Boy* but hundreds of other Hearn items came from Theron J. Blakeslee, the artmonger responsible, more than any other single man, for defacing the walls of upper-class America with those grotesquely lackluster paintings that symbolized a cultural empathy with England and the Continent. Blakeslee had come to New York from Boston in 1885 to get in on the ground floor of the movement to annex the artistic social security of someone else's past. He was credited with bringing the first Romney to this country, but whether or not he brought the first, he brought enough to supply every Anglophile in the country whose snobbery was stronger than his aesthetic vision.

Blakeslee was a cripple, but his zest for traffic in Old Masters and Painted Ladies—as the female English portraits came to be called— would have taxed the strength of an Olympic champion. Even if a successful man in need of art decided to favor one of Blakeslee's competitors among picture vendors of the moderate price range, the walls of his parlor would still have that tawdry costume-party look. For Blakeslee was wholesaler as well as retailer, and moreover, the importers of what were known as "Blakeslee pictures" freely interchanged their stocks. Often one of the dealers of the Blakeslee stripe would be called upon to assemble a package job of gilt and canvas to dignify the premises of a man who had just struck a bonanza. The price would be, say, a quarter of a million dollars. Then the experts would pass a rapid succession of miracles. Brass plaques would be fitted to imposing frames, and a collection would flower overnight that would have been worth millions if the engraver's words could have been credited.

Probably some of Blakeslee's prevarications were less the result of willful deception than of ignorance and wishful thinking. A perennial bidder at Kirby's auctions, he would often buy expensive pictures— occasionally even one that may have been genuine—along with the worst artistic driftwood. But it was as a seller that Fifth Avenue's busiest art dealer was most in evidence at the AAA, for despite the magnitude of his operations, he was always in need of money.

The Blakeslee auctions, and those of other galleries "forced to reduce their stocks of Very Valuable Paintings" contained the most extraordinary items: a portrait of Shakespeare by Richard Burbage, an 11-foot likeness of Fanny Kemble by Lawrence, family portraits from ancestral halls that existed nowhere but in the plaquemakers' imaginations. In the catalogues no particular distinction was drawn between the British big six and the large and once flourishing schools of mediocre painters who had imitated them. Any attractive picture of a woman in the style of 1815 was called a Sir Thomas Lawrence. A Lawrence that was clearly not a Lawrence would not fetch the $10,000 or $20,000 that a more discriminating clientele would pay for a Lawrence that may have been a Lawrence. But the power of the printed word was strong. A portrait described as a Reynolds or a Lawrence would sell for perhaps $2,500, whereas the identical picture catalogued as a genuine Harlow or Philips was worth one fifth of that.

Moreover, between the obvious copy and the wholly genuine, there were limitless degrees of partial authenticity. Like Van Dyck, Sir Joshua Reynolds had sometimes painted only part of his portraits, usually the head, leaving the mass of detail to his pupils. Genuineness, therefore, became a question of percentages. Was the head equal to, or greater than, the costume? When was a Reynolds not a Reynolds? At what point in the anatomy was the decision to be made?

Gainsborough, on the other hand, had found the dress more interesting than the face. For £20 an eighteenth-century lady yearning to be immortalized by the master got a poorish pupil. For £2,000, provided she had the patience to wait her turn, she could have Gainsborough himself. In the middle range, the master would correct the student's work, put a few nice touches to the draperies, and sometimes add his name to the result with the casual flourish of a man of affairs signing a paper written by his secretary. A signature, then, was worth very little, even if genuine; and as everyone knew, many of the best paintings had never been signed at all. Often the pictures that did not sell in one clearance auction would come up in the next under different artists' names, sometimes in round frames, sometimes in square, frequently with improvements in the composition.

A dealer named Eugene Fischoff was a great man for improving pictures that were hard to sell. Fischoff supplied many an ancestor-hungry customer with time-mellowed portraits by the family Vanloo, a long line of painters that flourished in France from the seventeenth century to the last half of the eighteenth. In the course of so much time the Vanloos had painted many well-dressed but unattractive sitters. Since none of Fischoff's clients wished to acquire ugly ancestors, he would take a genuine portrait of a knobby old woman, leave the costume and draperies alone, and substitute a pretty face. Was the picture still a Vanloo or not? No one liked to say precisely.

In time, the trade in hallucinatory old masters ran afoul of the cult of authenticity promulgated by such quality dealers as Joseph Duveen. With the coming of an era when it was said that there were art buyers who would frame the certificate and put the picture in the vault, prestidigitators in the class with Fischoff and Blakeslee were prone to take their profits and either retire or invest in less chancy merchandise. But Blakeslee himself continued to exploit the gullible for twenty-nine years. Then, one snowy March afternoon at dusk, the bubble of his chimerical art world burst. In the midst of a conference with his lawyer and a representative of his European creditors Blakeslee complained of a headache and hobbled to a small room at the rear of his crimson velvet gallery. On a wall behind a couch hung an enormous *Adoration of the Magi*, a Rubens that ostensibly had been sold in the most recent Blakeslee auction for $13,000 but in reality had been bought in by a confederate. The art dealer lay down on the couch before the *Adoration* and, surrounded by all those leering Painted Ladies, put a pistol to his aching head and pulled the trigger.

Blakeslee's suicide had loud reverberations in the flimsier purlieus of the market place and revealed a miasma of self-deception on the part of his clients. A mess of pictures one customer had bought for $240,000 still remained in the Blakeslee storerooms. The mansion they were to embellish had not yet been built. As for the paintings in the Blakeslee showrooms, the first appraisers of his incredibly tangled estate reported that they were worth $900,000. But a forced sale was inevitable, and when Kirby had disposed of everything in the Blakeslee Galleries, including the crimson velvet and the extra brass plaques, the proceeds amounted to about $260,000, minus the expenses of a long and dispirited series of auctions.

Blakeslee's old customers were conspicuous by their absence. Even the cut-rate dealers shied away from the last, lugubrious rites of the man who had often been their wholesaler. The catalogue, true to the bitter end, read like a guidebook to the British Museum, and the bidders, most of whom were strangers to the Kirby congregation, carried off some rare bargains: Lawrences for $100, Murillos for $200, Romneys for $400, Van Dycks and Titians at $1,000 each. A portrait of Anne of Austria, appraised at $10,000, went to Charles A. Platt, architect of pseudo-royal villas, for $700. Other pictures fell as low as $4 and $5.

"Alas poor Blakeslee!" *Art News* wrote. "What a diverting carnival of somersaulting values stands in the record by thy name!" Alas poor Blakeslee indeed, and alas poor Blakeslee's clients. Many a maggoty pleasure dome lost its charm overnight; many a vain ancestral hall turned into a rogue's gallery of strumpets and impostors.

While dealers of varying shades of aesthetic conscience—from the unimpeachable Knoedler and Duveen to Blakeslee and his species—

were bedizening the walls with pictures, there were others who strewed the floors with Oriental rugs and draped the mansions with rich brocades and sumptuous embroideries. In particular there was Vitall (the Pasha) Benguiat.

The Pasha was an epic figure in the pageant of the auctions. His affinity for warp and weft was said to border on omniscience. His prowess as a scavenger kept the AAA perennially arrayed with the carpets of the sultans, the gold-threaded robes of shahs and priests and maharajas, the centuries-old fabrics of Italy and Spain. To a well-informed witness of the early Benguiat ventures he was "far and away the leading dealer in the line of art goods in which he dealt." To Rose Lorenz and Kirby he was almost a son.

The Pasha—the title was nonofficial and both flattering and de-risive of his seriocomic Levantine swagger—was, to say the least, an impressive person to meet, a creature curiously compounded of greed and taste, vulgarity and caprice. He was not much more than five feet tall. Viewed head-on, his expansive stomach loomed, a mogul's extrusion of dark, meticulously tailored opulence. His posture from the rear was somehow reminiscent of a strolling military pigeon as he stalked among his carpets, straight, stiff shouldered, and erect, his hands crossed palms outward at the base of his uncompromising spine. Across the immensity of his vest stretched an ancient gold-wrought chain leading to a diamond-crusted watchcase embellished by a bloody scimitar of rubies. The watch—a gift from the Sultan of Turkey, or was it the Shah of Persia?—chimed the quarter hours (when it was in repair), a dulcet intermezzo to his conversation, like the low bell of a distant temple intruding on the brassy accents of bazaars and caravan-saries.

In his youth, said the Pasha—for modesty was no part of his social charm—he had been the handsomest man in the world. Now, in his early forties, his face—"It was a face like a face on a coin," one of his nephews said—bore an arresting likeness to the classic bearded countenance of Edward VII. His beard, trimmed precisely like King Edward's, owed its matchless sheen, the Pasha said, to the practice of eating shad roe, a between-meals snack that came dried and sealed in wax and in the lexicon of Benguiat superstitions accounted as well for his perdurable manly vigor. His skin derived its silken glow from the regular, and immoderate, consumption of dates. His eyes, prophetic, dream-beguiled, but shrewd, were veiled in Eastern mystery and

Vitall (the Pasha) Benguiat. The Pasha (with his "Magic Carpets") was an epic figure in the pageant of the auctions.

also—when prices were running high—illumined with the bonhomie of the Grands Boulevards. His talk was seasoned with homilies and parables that in his twisted English had the sound of timeless wisdom mingled with the salty adages of trade: "A thousand camels for a cent—where is the cent?" he would roar at an intransigent bargainer; "It is hammering iron with water," would be his comment on an inauspicious project.

Neatness was his passion; gluttony, next to vanity, was his besetting sin. Bowls of olives washed down with champagne and Scotch comprised his favorite appetizer. Caviar he consumed from five-pound jars. At the auctions he would sometimes withdraw a Turkish sausage from his pocket and munch upon it to sustain him in the heat of battle.

The women and the bottles were his refuge and his weakness. In Paris, in the capitals of Europe, surrounded by the twittering impromptu harem he employed to keep his spirits up, he might have been taken for the bawdy, fat, free-spending satrap of some backward Asian province. But in the shadowy, exotic world of carpet merchants he was without a peer. "Everybody loved the Pasha," a contemporary purveyor to the palaces recalled warmly. "It was impossible to imagine that he would cheat you." And in truth, of all the rivals the Pasha counted as thorns in his side, few ever denied his sixth sense for quality or accused him of dishonesty in trade.

There were, in all, five Benguiat brothers, all carpet sellers, all bearded and omniscient. Smyrna had cradled them. Alexandria had conditioned them. According to Ephraim, the eldest and most lugubriously hirsute of the brothers, the family origins went back to Spain in the eleventh century, if not directly to the pages of Genesis and Exodus. Spanish Hebrew was their language, the ritual of a dreamlike Sephardic isolation the only formal education any of them ever had. One by one they had come out of the Levant—Ephraim first, then David, Vitall, Leopold, and Benjamin—to seek their fortunes, first in London, then throughout the Western world. In later times Vitall said that he had supported the whole family since the age of twelve—a libel hotly contested in the internecine lawsuits that preoccupied the Benguiats through their middle years.

But if not the lone breadwinner, Vitall was beyond doubt the prodigy of the family; and this in the face of handicaps that might have crushed a less bodacious antiquary. His views of art history were based on hearsay. There was no European language he could adequately read or write. Even when his transactions came to involve millions, his checkbook stubs were kept in Spanish Hebrew. As a young man in England, the Pasha used to say, he had wanted to study. But he found it hard to stay awake in the hushed libraries that might have thrown the light of scholarship on the rugs and textiles he intuitively adored. He filled his pockets with crisp crackers. The sound of munching, he thought, would keep him from dozing. But the night mists of London were always luring him to revelry and remorse, and the crackers notwithstanding, book knowledge advanced at an imperceptible rate. Soon he abandoned it altogether, and took to the road with a pack on his back.

In Spain he bought the rugs from churches, the cloths from the high altars, the vestments entrusted to the care of the venal-minded clergy. From Italy he brought back master fabrics from the great looms of the Renaissance, Persian rugs unloaded on the quays of Genoa and Venice in the sixteenth and seventeenth centuries, the prayer rugs of Ghiordes, Kulah, Ladik, Melas, woven for the glory of Islam but preserved for the most part in Italian sacristies. Into his trunks went the banners and regalia that had framed the pageant of the Moors, the kings, the grandees, and the effulgent Church of Rome, the silks and velvets and embroideries handed down from heir to impoverished heir. Selling some to buy others, he stalked through palaces and villas, flea markets, temples, and bazaars, bargaining, bribing, conniving, offering new rugs for old, a few francs or lira or pesetas for tattered remnants that could be restored by an artful Turk in his employ. With his profits, he undertook the canvassing of original sources—that vast area stretching roughly from the Aegean Sea to the mountains of Tibet, which had spawned the classic carpets of the fifteenth to the eighteenth centuries. He consorted with miscreants and smugglers; he learned the dialects of trade, the ways of the itinerant peddler, the pawnbroker, the fence; he mingled with furtive men in coffeehouses—men with jewels in their pockets and carpets in their saddle packs. He wandered through all the galleries and byways of the world, until little was foreign to him from Egypt to the sub-Arctic, from the East of mystery to the western boundaries of Europe.

The London shops of the Egyptian-Spanish-Turkish brothers flourished. Queen Victoria herself was said to have ventured into the velvet twilight of the premises—which also served as gypsy cantonment for an indeterminate number of Benguiats—to sit in dalliance over fine old laces and hold colloquy on the intricacies of Eastern weaving. A visitor of far more consequence to the Benguiat future was Stanford White, architect of palaces, looking for anything that was movable and old. After White's death various Benguiats claimed to have served as his adviser in the furnishing of American mansions. In any event, Ephraim, Benjamin, and Vitall came to the United States —Ephraim first, for in his role as eldest brother (he piously recollected in the law courts some years later) he had quarreled with Vitall over the question of keeping the shop open on Saturday. David remained in London; Leopold established himself in Paris as Vitall's partner (though he always said no gentleman ever worked) and retained a permanent one-quarter interest in the operations of V. & L. Benguiat. Vitall crossed the ocean in 1898, a bona fide accomplice of Stanford White; and from White, it was but a step to a broader outlet for his cargo at the AAA.

He had found the floors in a deplorable state. In the nineties there were a few connoisseurs of Persian carpets—Morgan, Charles T. Yerkes, Henry G. Marquand; but the average rich American's conception of an Oriental rug was a travesty on a noble craft. The country swarmed with Armenian traders whose chief commodity was the ugly Turkish "dining-room carpet" so prevalent in Victorian England. At auction Kirby was selling "palace pieces" for about $100—rugs that the clients were advised "should never be thrown underfoot, but panelled upon the walls of living rooms of distinguished houses, by daily ministry teaching and toning the taste." Vitall set about to disabuse them of this notion.

Kirby, repentant of past follies, undertook the distribution of the Pasha's treasure. With Rose Lorenz' genius for arrangement, the contents of the Pasha's boxes brought the centuries of grand display to Madison Square. The halls would glow with subtle color; Rose Lorenz would glow with cultural enlightenment; and Vitall, his hands upraised in messianic ecstasy, would discourse to the ignorant on the virtues of his time-consecrated wares. The first Benguiat auction, in February 1901, composed of "Textiles of the 15th–18th Centuries," brought almost $100,000 and added, Kirby said, a new category to the roster of the priceless.

Thereafter almost all the Pasha's business was done through the American Art Association. He kept no shop; he had no use for pen and ink, certificate, or pedigree. "I tell you, dear, all this is badly done," he wrote his educated nephew Mordecai, at a time when Mordecai proposed to boom the rugs in Newport by means of an elaborate, if highly ungrammatical, brochure:

I tell you, dear . . . you people think it is understood that all your earnings goes for paper and ink as the orators. I have told you the day you do not see any more paper and ink, that is the day your eyes will be opened. I have told you to throw into the sea all the books and all the announcements. Only keep track of me and who owes you and to whom you owe, eat well and sleep well and keep cool in all your doings. All what people relate and all what they do don't take notice. All this is peanuts.

Unorthodox though his business methods were, the Pasha labored doggedly at teaching and toning the taste of the titans. Once a year, and sometimes twice, he held an auction of "sumptuous textiles and art in needlework, Renaissance embroideries, magnificent brocades, velvets, tapestries, exceedingly fine old laces." And in his own words he "prospered mightily."

For all that, his dreamy eyes were fixed upon the future. Never in Kirby's time would he risk his best rugs at public sale. They were sold by private treaty, with Kirby or Rose Lorenz as arbiter. Or they were stashed away in the Pasha's boxes. The Animal Rug, for instance— which he boosted to $38,000 in the Marquand auction, by way of demonstrating that it was at least as good as a Corot or Sir Joshua— went into his "private collection," along with many another vintage treasure, against the day when a strip of Persian carpet would be worth the price of a New York mansion.

He had prospered mightily, but he never had any money, for he always bought far more than he sold. Kirby was his banker, his guarantor, his creditor. If Frick or Senator Clark paid a bill in six figures, Vitall never saw the cash. He would long since have drawn the sum, and more, from the AAA to finance his rapturous, increasingly expensive shopping tours. "You say there is no money—it is our usual disgrace," he sadly wrote his nephew Mordecai while bargaining for the spoils of a Visconti, the silver of an old Spanish family, the carpets of a royal house in Portugal. He was insatiable, and he was prodigal. Moreover, he was prone to misadventure.

There was the matter of the Ascoli cope.

Perhaps to Mr. J. Pierpont Morgan, possibly even to Vitall Benguiat, the historic capelike vestment presented to the cathedral of Ascoli by Nicholas IV, who ascended the papal throne in 1288, was just another item in a sea of plunder. But to the citizens of Ascoli, if not to the whole Italian nation, it was the very bread and joy of life—once it had disappeared.

It was, if newspaper descriptions of the time can be trusted, not only historic but gorgeous. Its material was brocade formed by gold threads worked into a kind of canvas. Against this aureate background, attenuated by six centuries of cathedral must, were nineteen embroidered medallions representing the Virgin, the Child, the head of Christ, the crucifixion of St. Peter, and sundry figures of early popes. It had once had pearls scattered over it, but these had been removed to pay a war tax levied by Napoleon. Even without the pearls, it was much admired when exhibited at London as "the property of a well-known American collector." Astonishment was great, the international press reported, when the director of an Italian art gallery recognized it as the purloined treasure of Ascoli.

The well-known American collector, identified as J. P. Morgan, was asked where he got it. Morgan was evasive. He said he thought it might have come from Paris—an answer Vitall must have applauded for its vagueness. "Little talk and much hearing" was a maxim he often quoted and one of the few precepts he held in common with international bankers.

Back in Ascoli, however, a number of clues turned up. The cope had not been stolen, the *carabinieri* revealed, with a nice feeling for the nuances of malfeasance, but—oh, heinous crime!—*sold* by its custodians. Five priests and a photographer were arrested. The photographer, whose name was Rocchiggiani, was found to have taken a picture of the cope. He had also made a mysterious trip to Egypt. (Could it have been to one of those coffeehouses the Pasha was known to frequent?) A large sum of money was found in Rocchiggiani's atelier, although he had been very poor while the cope still languished in the cathedral. Now Rocchiggiani languished in jail. More arrests were imminent, a bulletin from Ascoli promised. Swift and awful justice was predicted for all parties to the sacrilege—as soon as a full confession had been extorted from the wretched photographer.

A few days later, the parties, wherever they were, no doubt breathed a collective sigh of relief. For Rocchiggiani cut short his confession by hanging himself on a bar in his cell.

Meanwhile all Italy, it seemed, was praying for the cope's return. On the secular front, the Italian embassy in London took the direct approach and asked Morgan to give it back. Morgan's representative said he was not in a position to discuss the matter. A public subscription was opened in Italy to *buy* it back, and while officials were debating how much money to offer, newspapers on both sides of the Atlantic reviewed the ethics of the situation.

The cope was very likely *opus Anglicum* to start with, a British pundit wrote, and who was to say it had not been stolen from England before being given to Ascoli? All the same, a spokesman for

Italy replied, the stealing of art objects ought not to be encouraged. No, a London paper agreed, but "on the other hand, it is pointed out that if every famous art object which has at one time or another been stolen were returned to its original possessor, the museums of Europe and America would lose a great number of their chief treasures." *The New York Times,* which had at first supposed the bone of contention to be "a picture by the late C. W. Cope, R.A., the English painter," pulled itself together and remarked that Nicholas IV had been no great shakes as a pope anyhow. Had he not ordered Roger Bacon to prison and obtained the papal throne owing to his zeal in repressing the first faint stirrings of science?

Moreover, said the *Times,* carrying editorial pun making to the limits of *non sequitur,* the disputed object "must have been under the magical care of Fata Morgana, sister of King Arthur and pupil of Merlin." For in the midst of the palaver, Morgan, with his happy faculty for turning greed to glory, suddenly returned the cope as a gift to the Italian government.

Oh, joy! Oh, magnanimous benefaction! Official Italy could barely contain itself at the fortune that had descended upon an erstwhile bereft nation. "Ascoli Adopts Morgan" international headlines blazoned. By acclamation, he was made an honorary citizen; his bust was ordered to be placed in the City Palace with a marble tablet; *Te Deums* were sung; and one of Ascoli's principal streets was forthwith renamed Via Morgana. In recognition of Italy's gratitude, King Victor Emmanuel conferred upon the American banker the Grand Cordon of St. Maurice and St. Lazarus. This, the *Times* observed, made Morgan a cousin of His Majesty. It was announced that the Italian government would have a gold medal struck in commemoration of the affair. Artists were commissioned to prepare sketches, and when the winner had been chosen, Morgan journeyed to Italy on his yacht, *Corsair,* to pass on the design. On one side was the Ascoli church, with the Roman Forum in the background. A nude youth personified Art; a female figure, History. On the other side was the head of the benefactor with his coat of arms. Mr. Morgan approved.

The *Corsair* moved on through the Mediterranean in triumphal progress. A hitch occurred at Taormina, where a meddlesome detective boarded the yacht and demanded, the Cordon of Saints notwithstanding, that the buyer of the cope testify as to the circumstances of its acquisition. The banker's awesome person swelled with indignation. What! After returning the thing without even asking for reimbursement! The detective was told that the cousin of His Majesty remembered nothing.

In dudgeon, the benefactor traveled on to Rome, where everything possible was done to atone for the annoyance at Taormina. Foreign Minister Tittoli thanked him. The King summoned him to a private audience. The Papal Secretary of State entertained him in the Borgia apartment. The Pope conducted him in person through the Vatican galleries. And with that, the pique of Morgan was presumably assuaged.

No more was heard from the *carabinieri*, nor of the five allegedly perfidious priests. To be sure, a really meddlesome detective, picking up a copy of *Art News* for February 25, 1905, could have read, at the end of an item about "the indefatigable Mr. Vitall Benguiat's" current auction of priests' robes and other venerable paraphernalia: "Mr. Benguiat was the artistic purveyor who found and sold the Ascoli cope to Mr. J. Pierpont Morgan."

But the reticence of Morgan precluded further repercussions. The King's new cousin traveled on to Florence, where he bought a small sixteenth-century drinking cup for $81,375. The scandal and the glory subsided; and Vitall, though no longer *persona grata* as artistic purveyor to the House of Morgan, continued unmolested on his journey through the centuries.

Vitall Benguiat's spadework on behalf of the titans revealed on occasion what might be called an excess of indefatigability, but even the threatened vengeance of the *carabinieri* was as peanuts to the Pasha compared to the long-drawn family feud of Benguiat against Benguiat. For some of the Benguiats had prospered, and some had not, but none had prospered as mightily as Vitall, and all were unbearably contentious.

Ephraim, when he came to America, had first tried Boston, then the 1893 World's Columbian Exposition in Chicago, then San Francisco. In all these places, the citizens were able to contain their enthusiasm for Turkish carpets, Egyptian mummy cloths, and the hand-me-down wardrobes of sultans' harems. But in San Francisco Ephraim acquired one inestimable patron: Mrs. Phoebe A. Hearst, mother of William Randolph, and like her son, a pushover for almost any kind of negotiable refinement. Mrs. Hearst, to her lasting sorrow, loaned

Ephraim $85,000 to install himself and his antiquities in a grand pavilion at the Louisiana Purchase Exposition of 1904; and for a fleeting summer on the fairgrounds at Saint Louis, opposite the Palace of Forestry, Fish, and Game, a murky enterprise came into being called the Benguiat Palace of Ancient Art.

An "Art Portfolio" (price $1, though Ephraim's name was misspelled on the cover) described the contents and importuned fairgoers to gaze in wonder on "rare works of every art." So rare and numerous were the carpets, embroideries, and Passover dishes that "a million dollars probably would not buy them," the rhapsodic guidebook hinted. Visitors willing to squander the admission charge could see the "Original Historical Damascus Palace" (a palace within a palace, as it were), which Ephraim had salvaged from the Turkish pavilion when the Chicago fair was dismantled. And among the shadows of "the tout ensemble" intrepid fairgoers could behold "the Collector" himself, or at least that part of him which was visible beyond the dark expanse of his long, untrammeled beard—a man all eyes and nose and forehead—as he reclined among the divans, looking into "the mosaic fountain, which had reflected the smiles of Syrian women 600 years [ago]." Not many did. The sheriff was the most frequent visitor. Only after Vitall had come to the rescue with $10,000 would the Saint Louis authorities release the Collector and his rare works (including such treasures on loan from the Pasha as the $38,000 Animal Rug) from the clutches of the unpaid builder of the Benguiat Palace of Ancient Art.

He had hooked himself on it, as Vitall was wont to say of his brother's follies. But in the Benguiat family there was nothing like adversity to fan the flame of brotherly love. Vitall, then forty-four, had begun to think of dying. His health was poor. There were his weaknesses—"the chippies and the booze." He had no wife, no child. He had a misery in the foot; and in his heart there was a longing for something he called *adahert*, a Benguiat word meaning, roughly, harmony.

The animosity among the Benguiats was chronic and incurable, but in this resurgence of tribal feeling, the Pasha was moved to invite Ephraim and his educated son Mordecai to share a loft with him, for business purposes, above the Knickerbocker Trust Company in New York. Mordecai, who was then twenty-nine and splendidly versed in the three R's, would busy himself with the paper work and thereby absorb some of his uncle's indefinable talents, with a view to becoming "a second Vitall." It occurred to Ephraim, he recalled later, that it would be well to have some sort of formal agreement about all this. But Vitall was shy of pen and paper. "Why, what is the use of a writing between us?" he allegedly replied. "We will make one pot for ourselves, and it will all belong eventually to Mordecai."

With the new arrangement, reform entered into almost every phase of Vitall's life. "Let me tell you that I have given up smoking and drinking," he wrote Mordecai from London, "it was time to, otherwise I would suffer pains continuously." Joint living quarters were rented, with the Pasha's portrait above the mantel, the better to savor the joys of communal existence. "Tell Ephraim," Vitall wrote Mordecai from Paris, "to prepare the flat as nice as he can for us to feel happy in it—and no more cafés! I may bring a female cook with me." The other brothers were drawn into the fold. Benjamin was urged to give up smoking and otherwise reform. David and Leopold were invited to join in the fraternal solidarity from their outposts abroad. In short, as a tongue-in-cheek witness observed, "Peace having spread her dovelike wings," the quarrelsome Benguiats presumably were "sitting every night with their arms around each other's necks."

For a time, a brief time even as such things go, *adahert* reigned in the Knickerbocker loft. The Pasha plied the ocean on the great ships of the French Line with the windy pomp of a floor-level Duveen, while Mordecai endeavored to learn the art of doing business with no visible finances. At one end of the long L-shaped, dimly-lighted loft, Ephraim sat like a brooding Arab among his Turkish carpets and the dismantled pieces of the Damascus Palace. At the other, Vitall parlayed all his winnings into a lair of Renaissance and Persian splendor. The main obstacle to harmony, as the Pasha put it later, was that H. Ephraim Benguiat & Son had "no business, no clientele, no prospects, and debts exceeding $100,000."

A carping tone crept into the notes to Mordecai: "I beseech you not to borrow money of everybody. . . . I beseech you to take notice of everything so that when I get there there should be nothing forgotten because I like it this way, everything clean and in shape."

Reform, too, had its inevitable setbacks: "In London I did nothing because I fell ill with the foot and I could not work and that John made me get mad with a booze."

The Pasha's tyranny and the treasure in his hoards increased, until Mordecai, despairing of his future as a second Vitall, conceived a simpler way of sharing his uncle's redoubtable prosperity. Fratricidal disputes arose; *adahert,* a sentiment irreconcilable with greed, fled the loft; and the smoldering farrago of Benguiat grievances was cast upon the law courts of New York.

The immediate issue in the barrage of litigation known as Benguiat versus Benguiat was whether or not Ephraim and Mordecai had been partners of the Pasha, as they claimed, in the buying, selling, and stockpiling of rugs and textiles valued in one bill of particulars at $1,520,428. But as time went on, the original complaint expanded into a tangle of cross-suits and countersuits and tributary actions of such baffling complexity that the judges and the lawyers, the ordinary juries and the sheriffs' juries, and possibly even the Benguiats themselves, could not have told offhand who was the victim, who the accuser, and what the appeal was from.

Into the Chambers Street courthouse, like an animated gallery of litigious Biblical portraits, came the wily, hirsute Benguiats, their testimony and their affidavits prolix with memories from boyhood days in Alexandria and Smyrna up through the global machinations of their middle years. David from London was hostile, the Pasha said. Benjamin, once a partner, but now a rival in New York, was a thorn in his side and out to ruin him altogether. Ephraim, with his long hair and beard and large, mournful eyes, sat martyred and sanctimonious in his dual role of injured party and keeper of the patriarchal keys.

"Mordecai is capricious," said one of Vitall's lawyers, and as time went on, Mordecai—an impudent caricature of his father, except for a small clearing between the two long, drooping swirls of his handlebar mustaches—became arrogant, too, and flippant in his linguistic advantage over his uncles; for Mordecai alone, of all the Benguiats, could read everything—the cash book, the ledgers, the briefs, complaints, demurrers, the court summonses, and the ancient Oriental characters in which his uncles communicated with each other. Looking at his oppressors, father and son, Vitall would remark acridly, "The apple does not fall far from the tree."

At first, Leopold (though utterly useless to him in the business, the Pasha said) lent his ponderous presence to the proceedings as co-defendant, by virtue of his quarter interest in the firm of V. & L. Benguiat. But in time, Leo returned to Paris, and the lawyers sent questions to him there, trusting to French advocates, interpreters, and notaries to get such answers as they could. To his ambushed codefendant, holding the fort alone through months that lengthened into years, Leo's depositions—which came typed in purple ink, with little or no margin, heavy with large gold seals and the ancient, awesome terminology of the law—though lagging a month or two behind the relevant crises of the trials, were a comfort and a reassurance. This although of all the sentiments attributed to Leopold, the most pertinent appears to have been that Vitall should have had his head held under water for twenty-four hours for ever having involved himself with Ephraim and Mordecai.

The wisdom of this observation became more and more apparent with the unfolding of that many-volumed saga of brother against brother. Dark and sinister were the deeds recounted: how Mordecai, taking advantage of the Pasha's limited proficiency in the circumlocutions of business English, had obtained his signature on papers designed to bring about his ruin; how the thieving nephew Mordecai, using an old power of attorney left over from the days of *adahert*, had drawn large sums of money from the Pasha's evanescent bank accounts. In as many versions as there were witnesses, it was told how Mrs. Hearst, in a move to collect the $85,000 she had loaned Ephraim, had all but paralyzed the carpet trade by getting out a warrant of attachment on the contents of the Knickerbocker loft; how Ephraim and Mordecai, in a scheme to outwit Mrs. Hearst, had hauled away their carpets under cloak of night; how Vitall, in a scheme to outwit Ephraim and Mordecai, had made off with his choice items on a Saturday, when Ephraim's piety forbade his faction to be present in the loft; how Mordecai, in connivance with his thorny Uncle Benjamin, had kidnaped the $38,000 Animal Rug— pawn of pawns in so many Benguiat altercations—and held it as hostage throughout the preliminary skirmishes in the battle of the carpets.

Endless was the jumble of contested articles, so hard for ordinary men to visualize, so varied, so valuable—to the Benguiats if to no one else: the Royal Portuguese carriage, the Gothic velvet umbrella, the Mexican saddle, the silver Hebrew lamp for seven days of the week, the collection of old fringes consisting of 458 pieces. Marvelous was the testimony about plots and counterplots, replete with biographical irrelevancies.

Long and motley was the supporting cast of characters. Almost as capricious as the Benguiats themselves were the employees, who through the years had drifted away and back again, switching loyalties from one Benguiat to another: Abraham Eisner, the tailor, who made repairs—or was that word strong enough?—on the ancient, delicate fabrics; John Pearce, who was always getting the Pasha "mad with a booze" and swearing never to touch another drop; Paul Allo— "disgruntled Allo," one of the lawyers called him—whose wages as rug expert, cleaner, and restorer were never fully paid, a circumstance that had moved him to wander off now and then to try his hand at such mundane occupations as the chicken-raising business in France.

Brilliant and kaleidoscopic was the display of legal talent, for the Benguiats were always switching from one law firm to another; and the lawyers, as the family feud became a perennial feature of the New York courts, often deserted the Benguiats midstream. "It is me who knows what it is, lawyers," Vitall had written Mordecai prophetically, at a time when Benjamin was suing a Mrs. Caswell over the alienation of certain wealthy art buyers' affections. It was a knowledge that was to be improved to the point of satiety. Often rage would sweep the Pasha's countenance as he faced some new and ever more expensive opposing counsel retained with funds advanced in the days of *adahert* to save Ephraim and his family from the rigors of the almshouse. But never had warring Benguiat listened with such fear and trembling as on the day it was announced in court that Max D. Steuer had interested himself in the case of Ephraim and Mordecai.

Everyone who could read a newspaper—and even the Benguiats who could not—knew the name of Max D. Steuer. Had he not, with his diabolical genius, defended the most disreputable of causes, set thieves and rascals free, twisted the very words in the mouths of witnesses so that the innocent became the guilty, the victim the transgressor? He always won; and, it was already being said, he charged $1,000 for every day he went into court. Surely, Vitall must have consoled himself, this was only another of Mordecai's caprices.

But in a matter of days, there in court beside Ephraim and Mordecai, though solitary and aloof even from them, his clients, was Steuer— the most dreadful mischance that could befall a litigant, wrong or right.

Currently Vitall had assumed the role of plaintiff in a damage suit for $143,950.99. Out of a well of bitterness he had supplied his lawyer, Charles W. Gould, with a list of grievances against Ephraim and Mordecai, starting with the Animal Rug and working backward and forward to include Luna Benguiat's $500 wedding dress, Ephraim's trouble with the sheriff in Saint Louis, Mordecai's pejorative letters to the customers, and other salient memorabilia, in all of which the Pasha was victim and hero.

Lawyer Gould filed the damage suit, and when the answer came back, it bore the Steuer stamp. It conceded nothing, and it forgot nothing, not even the unpleasant matter of the Taranto collection back in the pre-American years, not the smallest chore performed by Mordecai as he was practicing to become a second Vitall, not a noonday meal brought to the Pasha in the Knickerbocker loft. In it Ephraim became a sage, Mordecai a genius—and industrious beyond all ordinary limits of human endeavor. The item of labor alone, as estimated by Steuer, came to $600,000. With the $480,000 claimed as Ephraim's share in the Taranto collection—not one of its fifty-eight rugs nor even a scrap of embroidery was overlooked—the Pasha found himself the outraged defendant in a countersuit for $1,080,000.

"Surely I shall be ruined altogether," Vitall must have cried out, as he had so often done in lesser courtroom crises. But in all the stories printed and told of Steuer's invincibility there is no mention anywhere of the case of Benguiat versus Benguiat. For Steuer lost the case.

Steuer lost the case, but he was a man who hated defeat, and the ignominy must have rankled; for three years—and several Benguiat lawsuits—later he again appeared against the Pasha, and this time the story was different. Miraculously Paul Allo—disgruntled Allo—had amassed sufficient funds to retain the now even more famous and more expensive lawyer. Allo sued the Pasha for $8,091 in back wages and broken promises, and got it all with interest. It was a small case for Steuer, but one that offered an irresistible opportunity to explore the arcane mysteries of the antiquary's nether world. Not for Boo Boo

Hoff, nor Bridgie Webber, nor even, years later, in the Harry Daugherty case did Steuer give of himself more freely than he gave for Allo, the rug cleaner, the chicken raiser, the drifter.

The crafty, swarthy little legal strategist brought no brief case into the courtroom of Judge Goff as the trial began. Instead, he carried, for all to see, a moth-eaten, badly raveling, faded rug. This object, he announced, his client, Allo, would restore to wholeness and beauty before the eyes of judge and jury so that they might estimate his real worth in this nefarious business. The exhibition was discouraged by the court, but hardly less effective was the recital through which Steuer led the willing Allo. It was a story rich in details of how old rugs could be made to look like new or new rugs like old, a story fascinating to all the listeners, except a sprinkling of antiquaries who had come downtown to see the show.

Allo told how pumice stone, used patiently and expertly—sometimes for an hour on a square inch of rug—could add hundreds of years and thousands of dollars to the final result, how crude rugs could be dipped in saffron to relieve the harshness of the colors. He told about the inks and acids, lemon juice, hot irons, grease, and wax used to give a temporary sheen to lackluster palace pieces. From this the testimony went on to specific rugs: the Polonaise carpet bought in Paris for 80 francs and sold here by Vitall for $12,000; the Indian rug that cost £50, and after $400 worth of "repairs," sold for $15,000.

"It's impossible! You could tell it a mile away!" Vitall cried out in helpless fury. But his words went unheeded as Steuer built his case point by point into a resounding triumph for disaffection and the underdog.

For five long, pettifogging years the Benguiats wrangled over whose rugs were whose, who had lied and who had stolen, and who owed whom $1 million; and in the end, no one had won much of anything, except Allo and the lawyers. Safely back in Room 2-L-4 of the Manhattan Storage Company warehouse were the Animal Rug and its companion wonders—some of which years hence, in the Roaring Twenties, were to take the center of the stage again as glittering pawns in the complex fortunes of the AAA.

And while with one hand the indefatigable Pasha was engaged in the alleged high jinks culminating in that marathon of barratry, with the other—as Kirby testified in court—he had done $1 million worth of business at the American Art Association. With Rose Lorenz as

Stanford White. He dominated architecture and decor until his murder by Harry Thaw in the café on the roof of Madison Square Garden in 1906 (BROWN BROTHERS).

intermediary, he had rustled up for Senator Clark a thousand yards of old red velvet, a smothering array of Isfahans and other palace carpets. He had hung the curtains in the Whitney mansion and draped its salons and grand ballrooms with priestly gear and seventeenth-century altar frontals. The halls of Frick and Morgan, Walters, Widener, Schiff, and Havemeyer coruscated with Benguiat rugs and ducal crowns in ancient purple. And though the Pasha's thirty-year role in the auction saga had only just got under way, he had contributed an engorgement of timeworn splendor to the pageantry of *La Belle Epoque*.

Indubitably the master hand in the adornment of that rhapsodic era was Stanford White's. His tall, lank figure, his lowering eyes and forward-bent shoulders, his bushy brows and luxuriantly bushy mustaches were everywhere familiar where worldliness and opulence prevailed. His flaming red hair was like a talisman of taste and splendor. His skill and knowledge were a Baedeker to orgiastic spending.

Under the aegis of the firm McKim, Mead and White, architectural marvels sprang up along the Eastern seaboard, from the Boston Public Library to the University of Virginia. Stately mansions, shingled villas, and Georgian-inspired houses of the colonial revival rose in Mamaroneck and Southampton; in Cornwall, Pennsylvania; in Richfield Springs, New York; on the Rhode Island coast at Bristol. In Newport, tall chimneys and graceful archways, long piazzas and rambling interiors, stone bridges, massive cupolas, and whimsical towers enthroned the social tyranny. The Casino (commissioned by James Gordon Bennett in pique at his expulsion from Newport's Reading Room for having ridden a horse up the stoop thereof) still bears the pastoral Victorian mark of Stanford White's Tudor-inspired gables, a pastiche of pillars, latticework, and Chinese ornamentation. But latticework and shingles were not for the likes of Mrs. Hermann Oelrichs. Rosecliff, the castle White built for her on a Newport promontory, drew its inspiration from the Grand Trianon at Versailles. For the prevailing mood was antiquarian and royal.

McKim, Mead and White's re-creation of the Renaissance façade at the Chicago exposition of 1893 was dazzling—and responsible, it was said, for the success of the fair. And in New York the master builders to the new social oligarchy, with White the most ebullient member of the trio, undertook to transform a wilderness of brownstone and dry-goods boxes into a likeness of Italy in the fifteenth and sixteenth centuries, a feat that—as the *Tribune* wrote on the sinister occasion of White's murder—in its scale and rapidity suggested Caesar's conversion of Rome from a city of brick to a city of marble.

Apart from the princely residences and monumental structures Stanford White dreamed up conjointly with his colleagues, it was his personal inspiration to erect a triumphal Roman arch in Washington Square to commemorate the inauguration of the first President of the great democracy. He installed the Baptists in a replica of the bell tower of San Giorgio in Velabro; he turned the Palazzo del Consiglio of Verona into a newspaper office, the Palazzo Vendramini of Venice into Tiffany's new store. Above all, he transplanted the Giralda tower of Seville to overlook Madison Square and top the pleasure palace that was his most flamboyant gift to a burgeoning metropolis.

To a generation, rich and poor, Madison Square Garden epitomized the very pulsebeat of New York, its lust and gaieties, its carouse and pageant. Under one vast roof, a city's throngs assembled, its high life and its low life—in an intimate theater that would have been an ornament to Paris, in the great amphitheater for the fights, the circus, and the horse show. There were cabarets and roof gardens, swimming pools and concert halls. There was even provision for the AAA's big spectacles—an assembly hall especially arranged for auctions, where Kirby occasionally held sales in the nineties. A congeries of many borrowed splendors, the block-square Garden was to multitudes who perhaps knew the name of no other architect the master stroke of its creator. The classic arches of its exterior arcades were reminiscent of the Rue de Rivoli. Its misty Moorish cupolas were visions dreamlike and exotic in the half-light of the evening. Atop the saffron, ancient-looking tower Saint-Gaudens' gold Diana stood out against the night sky, her huntress' arrow pointed to the heavens, her pagan nudity the scourge of moralists, her luminous slim figure revered alike by ruffian and aesthete, the only goddess New York ever had.

The buildings Stanford White designed, wholly or in part, would have occupied a leisurely architect to the ripe old age White never saw, but his resurrection of the past was no less manifest in the field of decoration. Great mansions were built to house art collections, but the search for movable reliquiae was often less a deliberate pursuit than an attempt to justify the settings provided by the architects.

In the beginning, the externals of the styles had been diligently copied: the Louis XIII foyer, the Gothic dining room, the eighteenth-century boudoir, the Henry II salon. The colors were brash; the newly gilded furniture symbolized gold, and perhaps, by a long stretch of the imagination, stocks and bonds, but it glittered and refused to glow; angels and cherubim that had been meaningful in the ages that created them were not the same reincarnated in the prosaic world of the great industrial expansion. The trouble was that the ideas that had animated these splendors of old could never be resuscitated by the modern plagiarist. What was needed, Stanford White decided, was to incorporate some original elements in the décor. In this way, the sham atmosphere could be corrected, the basic falsity concealed, the missing poetry and romance gratuitously supplied; and under White's leadership, the movement got under way to strip the bedchambers of the Renaissance and install their contents in the palazzi of America.

It was his notion to put Mrs. Stuyvesant Fish to sleep in a Gothic bed and hang her blood-red dining room with Venetian paintings showing the tortures of the early Christian martyrs at the hands of a pagan mob. On behalf of William C. Whitney—in the mansion that was to redound to the glory of James Henry (Silent) Smith almost as soon as it was finished—White assembled under one roof a veritable patchwork of European castles. The stained-glass windows were resurrected from the seventeenth-century château of the Vicomte Sauze in the south of France. The one hundred gilded coffers of the Renaissance ceiling in the main hall were imported from Florence. The cavernlike fireplace, in which an entire tree could be consumed at one firing, came from a château at Aigues-Mortes. The door from the main hall to the dining room had once been in the chapel of the Château de la Bastie d'Urffe on the Loire. The dining room ceiling came from a palace in Genoa. The columns and arches of the conservatory had once stood in a Roman garden; the statue of Dionysus was dredged from the Tiber; the well curb came from Padua. The paneling of the grand ballroom had originally formed a salon in the château of Phébus d'Albret, Baron de Foix. The musicians' gallery came from an old Italian town hall.

"He scoured Europe," the *Tribune*'s eulogy of the world's busiest architect said, "to lay at the feet of his rich and not always cultivated patrons the spoils of palaces and auction rooms and made himself the master of artistic revels in sumptuous decoration."

He was also given to nighttime revels among the not always cultivated patrons of New York's fleshpots—a weakness that led to his untidy demise, provoked the lustiest courtroom divulgations the country had ever known, and incidentally provided Kirby with an auction that was one of the outstanding social events of the 1907 season.

At five minutes to eleven on the night of June 25, 1906, Stanford White sauntered into the café on the roof of Madison Square Garden, where the opening performance of a revue called *Mamzelle Champagne* was in progress. There were about a thousand people present. On the stage the members of an act called The Big Six were singing and dancing. White sat at a table and cupped his chin in his hand as he listened to the music. Behind some shrubbery at the side of the stage stood Pittsburgh's demoniacal playboy, Harry K. Thaw. Thaw was currently, and unhappily, married to Evelyn Nesbit, an artists' model and chorus girl who had been one of White's entourage of teen-age beauties. As soon as White was comfortably settled, Thaw, pale faced but outwardly calm, his velvet coat collar turned up in the manner of a stage desperado, emerged from the shrubbery and walked down the aisle. At White's table he stopped, pulled a Colt .32 revolver from a leather holster, and shot the fifty-three-year-old architect through the head. He fired two additional rounds for good measure, then walked away and handed the gun to a fireman on duty. Two members of The Big Six promptly left off singing and fainted. In the moment of stillness before the general panic, the handsome murderer addressed the audience in a loud, even voice: "That ——— ——— ——— ——— ——— will never go out with another woman," the press (which censored five words) quoted him as saying. "He ruined my life"; or, "He ruined my wife"—his horrified public never could agree on the initial consonant of the final word.

A dozen female patrons who had withstood the crack of the revolver shots fainted at the sound of Thaw's profanity. Several actresses gracefully followed suit. The orchestra struck up a brassy tune and valiantly played on while ladies not given to fainting screamed at the top of their lungs and men shouted, "Catch the man!" As Thaw strolled unmolested to the elevator, Evelyn Nesbit, weeping as magnificently as Duse, rose from her table and kissed him.

"Oh, Harry! Oh, Harry!" she cried.

The killer went down in the elevator, leaving the roof garden in a pandemonium that resolved itself toward dawn into the prelude to the most prolonged gossip fest the sporting world had enjoyed since Edward S. Stokes killed Jim Fisk over a woman back in 1872.

"It looks bad for Harry," a lawyer in a stovepipe hat remarked, "but I have no doubt that the insanity plea will clear him."

Thaw was picked up and taken to the Tenderloin police station, where he said he was a student named John Smith, and in the next breath, gave a patrolman $10 to cable Andrew Carnegie the information that he, Thaw, was in trouble. Locked in the Tombs and deprived of morphine and liquor, he spent a few restless days smoking cigars, drinking ice water, and sleeping in his evening clothes, until his valet appeared with pajamas and a more suitable wardrobe. The

Tombs doctor reported that the murderer showed "symptoms of emotional insanity and some symptoms of incipient paresis." But the most lurid stories in the newspapers concerned the alleged immorality of the murderee.

Every plainclothesman of the West 30th Street police station was detailed to listen to beguiling anecdotes of Stanford White's career as a man about town. The captain himself, in an abundance of zeal, left his desk to conduct what he called a private investigation among the habitués of the more expensive nightclubs. Chorus girls purged their gaudy souls in an orgy of confession. Barflies, Tenderloin cabmen, and professional muckrakers rose to momentary fame as defamatory witnesses. Thaw's lawyers employed four detective agencies to dig up scandal about the late fun-loving architect, and everybody who collaborated got free publicity. Although the results were somewhat disappointing when examined months later in the cold light of Thaw's first trial, Stanford White's character was effectively blackened, for meanwhile every scrap of irresponsible gossip had been printed and reprinted in the papers. It was in vain for an occasional showgirl to praise the dead man's reputation. White was being shamefully maligned, the district attorney protested. "While he enjoyed the society of beautiful young women and was almost a spendthrift with them, he was not the roué and libertine that many have said." But Thaw's wealth carried the day. His expensive lawyers labored indefatigably, and it was somehow established that the great architect's subumbilical exploits justified his slaughter.

In all, Thaw had four trials. At the first one all the noted alienists in the United States and several from abroad were employed to testify that the murderer was a victim of paranoia—although there were diagnosticians on the side lines who preferred the term "dementia Americana." At the second trial Thaw was found not guilty, declared to be suffering from "inherited insanity," and committed to Matteawan State Hospital. Five years later, after attempts to bribe his way out had been widely publicized, he managed to escape the New York institution and flee to Canada. Captured, he put up a spirited fight and hurled a number of bottles at immigration officials; but the Canadian police escorted him back across the border. He was arrested by a sheriff in Concord, New Hampshire; whereupon a special commission was appointed to rule him sane. Two more expensive trials followed, with the result that in 1915 he was acquitted and freed. Two years later he was indicted for horsewhipping a schoolboy in whom he had "taken a special interest"; but he escaped prosecution by fleeing to Philadelphia and nonfatally cutting his throat. He was again declared insane, committed to an asylum for seven years, and released in 1924. There were further escapades and attempts to gain the spotlight in various parts of the country. The most elaborate nonviolent effort was staged in 1940, when the aging assassin opened an aristocratic old mansion in Philadelphia and invited members of society to pay him their respects. But the party was no great success. In 1947 he died of coronary thrombosis, in Miami Beach, at the comfortable old age of seventy-six.

It was while the lawyers were interviewing prostitutes in preparation for Harry Thaw's initial courtroom frolic that the AAA undertook to sell the remnants of his far-famed victim's days and ways. "Society Flocks to White Auction" headlines screamed; and indeed, not only society but everyone who wished to see society in action betook himself to Stanford White's mansion in Gramercy Park, where his household goods were sold *in situ*. In guidebooks White's house had been listed as "one of the most magnificently decorated in the city." Now it was a tourist's dream of sentiment and sensation.

It was spring when the sales began, Eastertide of 1907, and things were stirring on the fashion front. Hats three quarters of a yard in diameter, trimmed with plumes and birds, lent a touch of pageantry to the crowd that thronged the square. Skirts of mauve and muted mustard color swept the ground in graceful trains. Mandarin coats added a vaguely Oriental touch. Automobiles and carriages filled the tributary streets. Rival organ grinders played *I Pagliacci* in competition with *Il Trovatore*, and their monkeys doffed their caps with twice the usual respect. Sightseers perched on the spiked fences of Gramercy Park; photographers climbed the trees to get a better view; and fashion writers ran out of adjectives before the first day's sale had properly begun.

Only the most exclusive trade was actually admitted to the house. Members of the curious élite who passed Rose Lorenz' entrance requirements had been given tickets made out in their own names. Even John D. Rockefeller, Jr., and William Randolph Hearst were required to identify themselves to the cordon of police that guarded the banded and scrolled front door surmounted by two huge-winged angels in imminent flight for celestial regions.

Inside, the place was bedlam. Kirby was dwarfed and all but lost among the crowd that followed him like salt-starved sheep from room to room. The size of the hats made the signaled bid impractical, and only the strong-voiced could be heard above the babel.

At the outset Mrs. Payne Whitney clashed with Mrs. Stuyvesant Fish over an Oriental cooky jar. Mrs. Whitney prevailed, and having tasted blood, went on to buy all the Chinese jugs in sight. Mrs. Fish sulked. David Belasco frowned at David Warfield when Warfield took two identical reproductions of the same Roman statue at $40 each. Hearst and Belasco tangled over an immense sixteenth-century celestial globe, with Hearst the winner at $500. Belasco consoled himself with the Moorish tiles embedded in the walls of the picture gallery. White had bought a whole mosque to get them, Kirby said; but Belasco got them for $190.

A nice ceiling depicting the court beauties of Louis XIV fell to Elsie de Wolfe for $800. The price was considered low. A gentleman in striped pants remarked that the hussies made him nervous hovering around up there. In the drawing room, however, Hearst paid $8,000 for a ceiling with personages identified as "Angels Bringing Tidings of Christ's Birth." Cornelius Vanderbilt bought the Benguiat carpet underfoot for $1,400, and Charles A. Platt took the Benguiat velvet from the walls at $1,125. Though threadbare, Kirby said, the velvet was a "rare commodity."

A Mr. Damesbury kept bidding on everything, without success. Finally he got an early German harp for $95 and a Russian sledge seat for $50. After that he went to sleep, and snored while Kirby sold the sixteenth-century chair beneath him.

Almost everybody got a rubber plant. The crowd laughed when Colonel Colt of the rubber trust bought a small one for $6, but there were more than enough to go around. Rubber plants grew up the stair wells and obscured the lions rampant on the newel posts. Aspidistras infringed upon the stained-glass windows, twined in among the suits of armor, and tangled with the stuffed Mongolian tigers and the trumpets of the cherubim that hung from the fringes of the painted heavens by their toes. Those who did not care for such virile foliage could pay a little more and have a potted palm.

Professor Bashford Dean, curator of arms at the Metropolitan Museum (and of fish at the Museum of Natural History), gave $240 for a repoussé suit of demiarmor in fine condition, consisting of burgonet with hinged ear flaps, plastron, and mitten gauntlets. It was a handy outfit for a stray knight who could use it, and to make it even more alluring, Kirby threw in a gruesome Japanese mask with the helmet. As time went on, Professor Dean went hog wild and laid in enough arms and armor to start a small Crusade. But the conservative bidders snapped up a weapon now and then as well. John Wanamaker got a hunting sword for $4 and Theodore Offerman armed himself with a seventeenth-century rapier for $6.

After the Easter season there was a spring and summer recess. Then, four days after the end of Thaw's November trial, the sales began again. A few of the spring bidders were missing, for meanwhile panic had struck the financial world. Deposed bank presidents were cutting their throats with razors and Wall Street brokers were furtively driving up to pawnshops with diamonds in little chamois bags. But the select crowd was on hand in Gramercy Park as before.

Mrs. Payne Whitney was more incorrigible than ever, grabbing everything from an old Chinese shawl to a plaster cast of Venus and two convent chairs (at $20 the pair). R. W. De Forest bought a lion's collar at $45, though he confessed to having no lion, and Mrs. Hermann Oelrichs was almost equally determined to have it. She consoled herself with a priest's collar trimmed with silver galloon. Cass Gilbert paid $8 for seventeen old Chinese rain hats—far below cost, Kirby said. Mrs. Joseph Pulitzer took a pair of mounted crocodiles for $5, and E. G. Stillman got a Dutch warming pan without a lid for $12—at a moment when the greedy Mrs. Whitney wasn't looking.

In the long run, Hearst and John D. Rockefeller, Jr., were perhaps the bitterest opponents, spatting like schoolboys over everything in sight. Hearst got most of the stained-glass windows, and enough Venetian weather vanes to supply San Simeon; but Rockefeller refused to be outbid on the Spanish oil jars. They divided the Renaissance doorways and sarcophagi, and came out about even on the Caen stone well curbs, acquiring about a dozen or so each. Hearst paid the highest price—$320 for the only one capable of drawing water, a medieval contraption complete with windlass and a leaky bucket.

A good time was had by all, and after many vivid sessions, the last of the broken Roman columns had been distributed among the palace dwellers whose taste Stanford White had molded out of his relentless seeking of the past. The auction, from Kirby's standpoint, was perhaps more redolent of social comedy than of artistic éclat, but it was a foreshadowing of events to come. Not only was the great architect the pioneer history teacher of the wealthy, he was the father of the decorating profession, the progenitor of the antique trade. Antiquaries who had crossed the ocean under his patronage set up shop and flourished. Their cousins came, too, with cassoni and credenzas by the boatload. Their number increased, until it seemed that there could be no fusty shopkeeper in all Italy or Spain who had not packed at least a suitcase of relics to contribute to America's Medicean frame of mind; and within ten or fifteen years, most of them were holding auctions at the AAA.

FIVE

ART AND THE
HIGH LIFE

THE TRADE SALES, the Painted Ladies, the old Chinese rain hats, and the maladjusted *Blue Boys* never greatly diminished Kirby's reputation as the aristocrat of auctioneers. Large prices and distinguished consignors were what stuck in the public mind. When one of the giants of finance died possessed of authentic spoils, the misnamed school pictures and the indiscretions of accumulators were quickly forgotten. Then the hall would be charged with excitement, applause would interrupt the bidding, and Kirby's incantations would take on an indefinable mystique. These events were not infrequent. Many were the deceased titans who contributed their worldly goods to keep the polish bright on Kirby's name. But the most titanic of all was Charles T. Yerkes.

Actually, when Charles Tyson Yerkes died at the Waldorf-Astoria on December 29, 1905, a colossal auction sale was the last thing anyone expected. The streetcar pirate's forty-five-year romp with art, love, and finance had often made three-column headlines. In Chicago, in the nineties, whole pages of the newspapers had sometimes been devoted to pictures of his mistresses and to the alleged abuses of his traction empire. During the last years of his life, when he was attempting to take over the London underground, the monied world had marveled at his boldness; rival art collectors had snickered at his greed; scandalmongers had thrived on his amoral proclivities.

In spite of this almost constant stream of disapproval, Yerkes had longed for social recognition and financial standing as one of the great lords of creation. He had achieved neither during his lifetime, but his last will and testament was a veritable insurance policy for immortality. He left his Fifth Avenue mansion, with its "priceless" art collection, in trust to the citizens of New York. His widow was to continue to revel in the palace and its splendors for the remainder of her life, but then it was to be incorporated as the Yerkes Galleries, with a large endowment to assure its upkeep through eternity. There might be some delay, in view of the fact that the sultry, alcoholic Mrs. Yerkes was only forty-nine; but art lovers blessed with longevity could hope one day to stroll among the nude bacchantes and gaze with rapture at the Mad King Ludwig's bed.

For those who did not care for art there was to be a great hospital in the Bronx, free to everyone unable to pay, without regard for race, creed, or color. The ailing citizenry might have to wait a little for this too. Half of the Yerkes wealth was to be used for its maintenance, but only after it was no longer needed for the maintenance of Mrs. Yerkes. Nevertheless, arithmeticians pointed out that with the fortune estimated at $15 million, the Yerkes hospital would eventually be richer than any the city then could boast.

There were other bequests of a philanthropic and affectionate nature. Yerkes' son and daughter by his first marriage were modestly provided for, and so were old friends, servants, and the Yerkes Observatory out in Wisconsin. But the high moral character of the document was achieved by the fact that only one of the notorious roué's "wards" was mentioned. Ethel Link Yerkes was given $100,000 in trust, but since she was a granddaughter of Yerkes' half brother she could pass as a blood relation without disturbing the idyllic tenor of the whole. The newspapers, having already predicted a wife-and-mistress battle of major proportions, were frankly too disappointed to take proper cognizance of Yerkes' philanthropy. The whole thing was "an astonishing tribute of affection to his wife, Mary Adelaide Yerkes," the New York *American* said. "Despite years of bitter separation, a post-mortem shower of gold is poured upon the widow."

And indeed, it was a lovely will, if only there had been a fortune to go with it.

Yerkes' storm-tossed voyage on the dark, pirate waters of nineteenth-century finance had begun back in pre–Civil War Philadelphia. The son of middle-class Quaker parents, the future titan was a handsome lad, strong physically and stridently masculine, with hypnotic shallow-set dark eyes that were deceptively frank and a face that was an intriguing mask of sensuality. Even when he was a raw youth, his charm and his instinct for speculative finance won him the confidence of the mighty Drexels and other seasoned plutocrats of the Quaker hierarchy. At the age of twenty-four he had his own banking and brokerage house. Before he was thirty he had a decorous wife and two children, a fortune that would have satisfied an average man, and a noticeable tendency to wander from the stuffy confines of monogamy. At thirty-five he was in the penitentiary.

In connivance with the city treasurer, Yerkes had been gambling on the stock exchange with the city's funds when, in 1871, Mrs. O'Leary's inconsiderate cow, a thousand miles away, had the bad grace to set Chicago on fire. As the great fire burned unchecked, and insurance companies closed their doors in the face of losses they could never meet, financial panic swept the nation. Yerkes' airy brokerage house failed, leaving the citizens of Philadelphia poorer by half a million dollars.

Doubtless the forces of justice that sentenced the swashbuckling young stockbroker to two years and nine months in prison on a charge of technical embezzlement imagined that repentance would be a natural consequence of punishment. At least they may have expected that the chastened financier would take up some other line of business upon his release. But if so, they reckoned without Yerkes' steely mind and pirate heart. While nursing the profound resentment that was to fester in his bosom all his life, he spent his time in jail methodically plotting his revenge. After much humiliation, wealth alone would not suffice. Now he was determined to have the power and the glory too. In his dank and rat-infested cell he was dreaming the dreams of a maharaja, and outside, in the prison courtyard, he was growing flowers.

For beauty was a necessary part of his existence. His home, before the debacle, had been furnished with what he judged to be artistic things, with marquetry and bird's-eye maple furniture, with Brussels tapestries, and a sky-blue-pink triangular piano. He had begun to collect bronzes, bric-a-brac, and figurines. His parlor had exuded the murky green-brown twilight of landscapes by William Hart, his brother James, and other members of the National Academy. There had been singing birds in cages and a conservatory of potted plants—the forerunner of those vast indoor gardens he was one day to bequeath to posterity.

All these "artistic appointments" had been dispersed at a sordid public sale that no crystal-gazer could have seen as the distant portent of an auction that would one day surpass all others in the liquidation of fallen pride and tarnished splendor. But no matter. There would be many mansions in the future.

The first Mrs. Yerkes, while limp with the shame reflected upon

Charles T. Yerkes and Mara Yerkes (BROWN BROTHERS).

the children and herself, remained superbly loyal. Between visits to the prison with baskets of cakes, she trudged from lawyers to officials and back again to other lawyers. Night and day she worked for a commutation of her husband's sentence, and it was largely through her efforts that within seven months Yerkes walked out of jail with a pardon.

In a year he had his fortune back, with interest. In September 1873 the giant financier Jay Cooke, who had reached for the Northern

Pacific Railroad and missed, declared himself bankrupt. Once again panic swept the nation. When the holocaust subsided, the field was strewn with ruined bankers, but Yerkes had a profit of $1 million. With his winnings, he proceeded to take over the horsecar lines of Philadelphia, for in his prison meditations he had settled on street railway transportation as the business closest to the corruption of cities, and therefore likely to provide the quickest and the surest profits.

With the return of his fortune Yerkes permitted himself the luxury of falling in love.

Widely varying anecdotes have been told of his first encounter with the beautiful seventeen-year-old girl who was to share for a long season the pirate splendors of his life, and share so handsomely in his final testament. A writer for *Cosmopolitan,* in 1935, had Yerkes traveling to Chicago in a private car hitched to a train that was delayed at Cairo, Illinois. A "graceful girl with a perfect figure and a bewitching smile" appeared, carrying a box lunch for a brother employed as telegrapher at the railway station. In this version Yerkes got out to send a telegram and fell desperately in love on the spot.

The figure and the smile are authentic, at any rate. Mara's abundant dark brown hair, her large, innocent gray-green eyes, her full red lips, and fresh-blown animal charms would have made a touching picture against the drab background of the Cairo railway station of 1873. But the story smacks of Mara's own invention. In later years, when she had long abandoned all distinction between reality and fiction, she sometimes liked to see herself as at heart a simple country girl. Poking with her long-handled parasol among the espaliered fruit growing under skylights in the Yerkes palace, she would sigh and say that if she had ever had to earn her living, she could have done it growing pears. No such calamity ever befell either Mara or the fruit-growing industry. It is, in fact, the toting of the lunch box that spoils the Cairo story, for on one point, all Mara's biographers agree: she was the helpless type.

Her full name was Mary Adelaide Moore, and in real life she was the daughter of a chemist employed by Powers and Weightman in Philadelphia. She had many sisters and brothers (one of the boys could easily have learned the Morse code and wandered off to Cairo), but Mary Adelaide appears to have been chosen as a winner both by fortune and her mother. Schoolwork Mrs. Moore looked upon with strong disfavor. Bending over books made the shoulders round, she said. As a growing child, Mary Adelaide was required to wear what she called her harness. Every night her mother would strap her into shoulder braces before sending her to bed. "They cut me and hurt me," she recalled in later years. But if she cried herself to sleep, she had to do it silently. Tears, her mother said, made wrinkles. This was a maxim Mara never forgot. In the heyday of her grandeur she returned to Philadelphia in a devastating jet-black outfit, as chief mourner at her father's funeral. How well she bore up under her affliction, an old acquaintance remarked within her hearing. "I have schooled myself against tears," Mara said for local publication. "You know tears make wrinkles, and I have a perfect horror of wrinkles. No, you will not see me cry."

The braces appear to have been a successful antidote both to education and faulty posture. When Mary Adelaide graduated from her mother's charm school, she was an instantaneous success. It was said that she had some idea of going on the stage. Nothing much seems to have come of it. But for a time, at least, the niche she found for herself was no doubt compensation for the unheard wolf calls of the masses.

Forsaking almost all others, Yerkes entertained her in his secret bachelor quarters, renamed her Mara, bought her dresses of purple velvet, marabou, and cloth of gold. Now, from the saturnalian ease of his side-street satin couches, the uncaged larcener could divide his contemplation between the real and the ideal, allowing his gaze to wander from the Venus of Philadelphia to the classic models of his new-bought art works. His taste was improving, the decorators said. For his seraglio they sold him pithy anecdotes and pictures conforming to the Paris schoolmen's recipe for ideal beauty. The fastidious artmongers taught him what he already knew—that the rich Quakers, with their polished sea shells and rose-scattering cupids, did not know how to live. He made friends with the harbingers of new fashions; and with the coming of the great Centennial Exposition, they, and he, discovered the enchantment of bygone times and foreign cultures. He bought ivories and bogus Chinese porcelains, altar cloths and church embroideries, the locks and keys to bastions and harems. He developed a mania for old clocks. His teachers impressed him with the timeless elegance of Chippendale and Sheraton and advised him to ignore all native arts and crafts. The canvas of his life was widening, but in its gaudy texture there were blots.

Yerkes' love affairs were public knowledge. Main Line bankers did business with the man they knew to be a prodigy, but they did not invite him to their houses. Jail, the Drexels and the Wideners might eventually condone. It could happen to anyone. But philandering was another matter. The castoff Mrs. Yerkes was a towering symbol of ingratitude. The gorgeous, wayward Mara, so in love with Yerkes and with life, was a subject for discussion behind ostrich fans. Mara did not care. It was a world well lost, for she was brave and only in her twenties. But Yerkes saw that a maharaja's life was ill-suited to Victorian Philadelphia. He committed the final act of social degradation by compelling the tear-strained Mrs. Yerkes to divorce him, gave the Quakers back their horsecars—at a price—and departed, with Mara, for the Middle West.

Nothing could have been more exhilarating to a man of Yerkes' stripe than the Chicago he invaded in the Golden Eighties, no climate better suited to the realization of his streetcar dream. The Chicago rebuilt since the fire was a city of heroic sights and sounds, a strident, moving, changing, lustily magnificent city, not yet grown, in no way disillusioned with its triumphal march on progress. It was the campsite of a hundred nationalities, of husky workers, virile, sinewy, and roistering. It was a city of builders, railway men, traders, butchers, manufacturers, adventurers. It was a medley of palaces and shanties, a place of tent shows and opera companies, of velvet trailing in the mud. For those who cared to listen to its singing heart, there was in Chicago, then as now, a strange wild poetry, to be heard nowhere else in America, a rhythm and a life hunger as indefinable as song itself. But Yerkes had not chosen Chicago for its poetry. What attracted him was the magnificent corruption of its city government.

On his reconnaissance trips he had watched the brightly painted horsecars swirling gaily through the streets; he had listened to the tintinnabulation of the horse bells, watched the tired, snorting horses, their shoes making yellow sparks as they stepped high over uneven cobblestones, while in his pyrotechnic mind he had formed a plan to take over the sprawling city's transportation system. He had studied the political system under which franchises creating vast monopolies could be handed out as gifts. He had made a chart of ward and district leaders, with each man's price marked beside his name. This and much more he had accomplished before he moved to Chicago, and when he came, he came as no common adventurer, but as a man with the golden key to city hall. He had the backing of Eastern capital. The Chicago bankers were impressed; the boodle aldermen—as the recipients of Yerkes' munificent graft came to be called—fell in line like soldiers; and the conquest of the horsecars proceeded like a well-planned military operation.

Now and then a setback threatened. When rival financiers realized what the cyclonic newcomer from the East was doing, they dug up the details of his Philadelphia past and gave the story to the papers. Yerkes heard about it through his spies. He was worried, but his methods in a crisis were direct, his vocabulary superbly taut. With a revolver in his pocket, he took his own version of his biography around to the editors and threatened to shoot on sight "any rat who prints irresponsible statements."

For a time the newspapers were reticent. The boodle aldermen, unhampered by adverse publicity, continued to do their work. Step by step, year by year, the great fishnet expanded. The details were handled by lawyers, and much of the laborious intrigue was managed by stooges, but only Yerkes fully understood the maze of engineering and finance designed to make him the sole master of Chicago's transportation, and meanwhile, line his pockets with colossal wealth.

The social side was not as easy. At first Yerkes stayed behind the scenes as much as possible, but by 1887 he was beginning to be a public figure. He was fifty years old, and Mara, now the second Mrs. Yerkes, was a little over thirty. For his own part, Yerkes had no great desire to edge his way into provincial society. He could wait until he had $100 million and let the privileged classes claim him on a national scale. But Mara craved attention. Having been an outcast in Philadelphia, she devoutly wished to be a great lady in Chicago. Yerkes was sympathetic, if never very optimistic. He built a fine house at 3201 Michigan Avenue, less with the hope, perhaps, of getting Mrs. Potter Palmer to enter it than as a repository for his works of art. For by now he was becoming an omniverous collector.

With Mara, he began to spend his summers abroad. As a tourist, the traction magnate's bacchanalian queen, with her twenty-six-button gloves, her lavender scarves, her ropes of pearls, her brown hair done in a brown chignon, her brown velvet gowns set off by hunks of Oriental topaz, was a grand success. At the Grand Hotels of all the countries, the Chicago pilgrims met grand dukes and duchesses with something to sell, rich South Americans, English barons with social proclivities, Greek bankers with propositions, hand-kissing Hungarians with old masters in their satchels.

In Brussels, Amsterdam, Paris, London, The Hague, Yerkes bought no end of pictures. He got a Clouet that had belonged to Horace Walpole—which of the three Clouets had painted it he did not inquire. What did it matter? It had hung, they said, in Strawberry Hill before that dream of glory ended in the auctions. He bought four Brueghels before he learned that there were seven Flemish painters by the name of Brueghel who had painted with irreconcilable degrees of skill. The Countess de Bearn sold him a David, which turned out to be by the Flemish primitive Gerard David, not by the great French classicist that everyone admired. (That was, perhaps, an error on the credit side.) But thanks to the more respectable European dealers, Yerkes brought back to Chicago some of the best Dutch paintings that had come to America: four by Frans Hals, one of them a masterpiece; two Jan Steens; four Rembrandts, all of them reasonably Rembrandtesque.

In the nineteenth-century category Yerkes paid enormous sums for aphoristic paintings by Ludwig Knaus and Joseph Israels. He bought sheep and scenery by Jacque, Daubigny, and Diaz. He acquired a Meissonier, of course; and a hideous Gérôme. Detaille assembled on commission a heroic piece called *The Escort of the Emperor*. The Bouguereau "painted to order" for the Chicago house was called *Invading Cupid's Realm* and would have been better situated in a brothel. And yet, fairly early in his collecting years Yerkes got three leafy Corots that were better than most of those acquired by his contemporaries. He bought Millet's *The Pig Killers* and—because Mara thought it was romantic—Jean Charles Cazin's *Moonlight at Midnight*.

Mara had little eye for art, but she, too, had a hand in forming the Chicago gallery. Her favorite painter was a Belgian dandy named Jan van Beers. Van Beers entertained visiting Americans in an epicene Paris studio filled with women's clothes and Japanese fetishes, not to mention the skeleton of a uhlan with plants growing out of the eyes. In the days when Mara was happily commuting between Paris and

Chicago, he was "sacrificing his activity," as he put it, to painting women, "whether duchess or shopgirl . . . and particularly their elaborate toilettes." He never failed to mention that the beautiful Mrs. James Brown Potter, whose toilette could compete with that of any woman in America, was the model for more than one of his studies of "Directoire *grandes dames*." Mara admired van Beers for the photographic quality of his work—and well she may have, for he often painted Mrs. James Brown Potter right over her photograph. Before the first visit of Mr. and Mrs. Yerkes, van Beers's studio contained an overstock of three hundred small landscapes. "But one fine day," said the artist, in the tone of a storekeeper who had just conducted a successful fire sale, "Mr. C. T. Yerkes, the American collector, saw those landscapes, was captivated, and snatched them from me."

Mrs. Yerkes, however, was chiefly given to snatching van Beers's studies of pensive maidens lolling about in situations entitled *Idleness, Indolence, Leisure, A Tale of Love*, or simply *Summer Evening*. To Chicago went a whole gallery of the well-dressed lovelorn, along with a portrait of the actress Ada Rehan impersonating Lady Teazle in a salmon-pink costume with lace cascading from the sleeves, her right hand grasping at a parasol, her wrist arched at a comic angle of coyness that Mara considered the essence of refinement and seriously endeavored to imitate for the rest of her stylish days.

Inevitably Mara supplanted Mrs. Brown Potter as a subject for van Beers's poetic brush. The result was called *A Smile* when it was shown in London and *In the Garden* when it was exhibited at the World's Columbian Exposition of 1893. A London art reporter who saw the Yerkes collection at the Chicago Exposition wrote as follows:

M. Jan van Beers is rightfully a favorite painter of Mr. Yerkes because he depicted so charmingly the "Portrait of Mrs. Yerkes" seated on a rustic bench in a park by the side of a quiet lake and enshrined, so to say, by a circle of gigantic trees, whose darkness and wealth of color set off the bright robes of Madame. She—a happy smile illumines her face—turns on the bench as if to welcome someone coming towards her, while, stirred by the approaching footsteps, her quaint black poodle, "Diamond"—a very Moustache among his kind—jumps to his legs and wags his beribboned tail.

It was a picture that the second Mrs. Yerkes was to cherish in days to come as the glorious souvenir of her happy time.

For, alas! Mara's bright robes and illumined face failed to captivate the butchers' wives of Chicago. Her fish-scale sequins and lime-colored velvet togas, her strident sensuality, her trailing plumes and outrageous feathers were intriguing to their golden husbands, but the social climbers of the Middle West were themselves too insecure to accept a bird of paradise within their midst. By the dictates of Eastern snobbery, many of Chicago's industrial queens were still looked upon as frontier wives; and by the dictates on which they passed on Yerkes, he remained an adventurer, his wife a lurid doll, whose tinsel soon began to tarnish.

Poor Mara! All she asked was admiration, and soon, very soon, even Yerkes denied her that.

She must have known that he would be unfaithful, that there would be bachelor apartments in Chicago as there had been in Philadelphia. But even the least illusioned of titans' wives could not have been prepared for the large-scale disenchantment of the second Mrs. Yerkes. There were stenographers and actresses, and young girls being trained for the stage (at least one of them became a famous star). There were girls who wished to play the violin, girls who wished only to wear golden gowns. There were those who yearned for diamond bracelets, those who already had them and yearned only for immoderate affection. There were wives of other titans, wives of bohemians whose husbands lived on Yerkes pensions. Doubtless some of his branch establishments remained secret, but there were no fewer than six cities—from Portland, Oregon, to Dresden, Germany— where Yerkes' gown and slippers could be laid out concurrently at a moment's notice. There were mother-and-daughter ensembles that were indescribably sordid, and comic arrangements reminiscent of Molière's *School for Wives;* for often, while beguiling the mother, Yerkes would educate the budding daughter in a selected private school. There were households where brothers, mothers, grandmothers, and even cousins lived on the Yerkes stipend to the youngest or the comeliest, for his generosity was overwhelming, his chivalry unprecedented since the decline of knighthood and the old French court. To this day, in the faded Victorian hotels of two or three large cities, elderly ladies with blue-white hair and mannered voices can be found living out their feathered autumn on a nest egg stemming from Chicago's streetcars.

The pruriencies of Yerkes' life were not, of course, disclosed all at once. For Mara the revelation was gradual. At first, she forgave, or pretended not to notice. Then came the scenes. Inevitably, she played the gamut: clawing rage, threats, recriminations, even the tears her mother had forbidden so expressly. Often, if not always, Yerkes was repentant. He would promise to reform—and move his bachelor quarters to another address. In summer they would go to Europe, buy pictures, order gowns in Paris, drink tea with stylish Londoners less austere than Chicago's fledgling aristocracy. And for a season, Yerkes would be kind. But in the winter he would be gone again. In retaliation Mara tried the lower fringe of night society, cavorting indiscriminately with Chicago's café sports and good-time Charlies. But her heart was never in it. For all her seeming lust, the second Mrs. Yerkes was fated to love one man, bitterly, until the end.

She took to drink, moving restlessly from chair to chair in the evening, in the silent house she had pictured as the setting for her social triumphs, watching clocks—there were so many clocks—pretending to the servants that she was not listening for footsteps. She took to driving through the snow in her carriage, urging the coachman to drive faster to no destination—faster, faster, faster; a soapstone at her feet, a flask of whisky concealed within her cloak, her hands cupped at the frosty window, she peered through the gaslit shadows, spying, hoping to catch a glimpse of Charley departing from some midnight rendezvous. Too often she was rewarded.

Meanwhile, Yerkes' fortune was rising to its greatest heights, and with it, his unpopularity. He had conceived the downtown Loop and opened the La Salle Street tunnel under the Chicago River. He had embedded almost every means of coming and going in an impenetrable corporate jungle fed by watered stocks and perpetually in the throes of reorganization. He had built long, flat, lonely miles of railway track and replaced forty-eight horsecar lines with cable cars. But the passengers were brimming with ingratitude.

When asked why travel in Chicago was such a wretched ordeal, he replied, "It is the straphangers that pay the dividends." When asked his recipe for success, or How Can a Young Man Get Ahead in Business? he grinned and answered with a gemlike homily: "Buy old junk," he said, "fix it up a little, and unload upon other fellows." When asked whether he preferred blondes, brunettes, or redheads, he grinned again and rubbed his raffish hands: "God bless them all," he said.

His power was a growing source of rancor to his rivals. He was a hungry ogre, they said, who would swallow up the whole city if something was not done to stop him. Coalitions were formed with the single object of precipitating Yerkes' downfall, but for a long time he was able to forestall their plots. Once, when the opposing forces, led by Philip D. Armour, were sure they had him cornered, he turned the tables and forced them to close the stock exchange in order to prevent the ruin of the banks. These victories—and they were frequent—only served to consolidate the anti-Yerkes movement. The battle lines were drawn for a fight that knew no principle except the lust for power, and on Yerkes' side, his obsessive dream of glory.

It is a way with troubled people to think that they will be happier in another place. Mara was no exception. In the early nineties, when Yerkes began to talk of a palatial mansion on Fifth Avenue with the best, Mara no doubt saw it as another chapter in the Cinderella fantasy that sustained the perpetual childhood of her life. Long before the architects had finished, the palace had become the symbol of new hope, the solace for her lost illusion, her one great consolation prize. Love, she might no longer have, but she would forever be a princess. As for Yerkes, he chose New York perhaps from snobbery, perhaps sensing that all his worlds were temporary and that the least temporary might be one where he was not responsible for the discomforts of the straphangers. At any rate the mansion rose, at 864 Fifth Avenue, a congeries of many splendors, "built by Charles T. Yerkes for his wife," the New York papers said.

The $5-million dwelling expanded by stages, as land was added to the south and east, but from the first, it was a place to house a queen. Eventually it occupied more ground than any other palace on Fifth Avenue, and called for more superlatives. A Winter Garden, as it was called, sprawled L-shaped through the center of the plot, forming a vast inner courtyard covered by skylights and surrounded by a balcony with thirty-two white marble columns. The walls were of bark, the floors of black-and-white marble, the shrubs profuse, and to all appearances, poisonous. One of them, a huge air plant—a particularly obscene travesty on nature—had leaves on a level with the balcony and roots hanging not only to the floor below but hauled together in bunches and tied with cords, like portieres. The fountains were simulated springs trickling from various heights over moss-grown rocks into brackish rivulets forming many little woodland pools. It was a sinister, ever-blooming Eden inhabited by cockatoos and toucans doomed to a dull bird heaven where the worms were served on platters and no leaf was allowed to fall.

Off the balcony there was a second conservatory, called the Italian Palm Room or Vatican Garden. Its glass floor formed the skylight of one of the picture galleries. Its glass roof was set in copper beams. Here exotic fruits grew on wires and trellises. Doves cooed among the busts of Roman emperors. Hundreds of singing birds flitted in the branches of the palm trees and splashed in the great marble fountain. It was a place where Mara often strolled with her Lady Teazle parasol. Her friends called her the Lady of the Vatican, she said.

Immense plate-glass windows separated the Winter Garden from the great hall of Siena marble—windows fitted with weights and chains so that they could be lowered to the basement, creating one vast expanse fit for the kind of ball they have in fairy tales.

Seemingly endless were the changing moods confronting the wanderer in this labyrinthine château. There were halls of mirrors, halls of marble, halls of story-painted panels dwelling on the pleasures of the flesh. There were great vaulted ceilings, timberwork ceilings, columns of green marble topped by men in armor supporting crowning friezes. There was a Louis XV room, an East Indian room, a Japanese room, an Empire room transported from France with its *boiserie* and furnishings intact. The bedrooms were lined with green damask, mahogany, and onyx. There was a golden bed that had belonged to the King of Belgium and was said to have cost $80,000. The Mad King Ludwig's bed was cheaper but in some ways grander. Not counting the green velvet steps that led to the dais, it was 12 feet high. At its head, huge male torsos made of bronze finished to look like gold stood guard over a sleeping enamel goddess of night. At the foot, violet ebony cupids supported green draperies disclosing a nymph couchant personifying morning. The whole was surmounted by a dome of ebony and ormolu and shrouded in bolts of green silk damask with gold lace trimming.

The two long picture galleries were simple and uncluttered, but the third, and largest, gallery—on the Fifth Avenue side, with an entrance from the street—boasted a marble staircase to outdo all other marble staircases. Here were the sculptures—groups by Rodin and figures by Houdon, mingled, alas! with a ghostly community of 8-foot maidens en route to the bath. But the chief glory of the marble gallery, of the mansion itself, was the display of Oriental rugs.

Yerkes' fascination with textiles had begun in his early Chicago days. He was the first American collector, with the exception of Henry G. Marquand, to become seriously interested in the art of the rug, and the first to set for himself the goal of assembling an adequate representation of its surviving archetypal models. "It was the product of its marvelous noontime that he was determined to garner," John Kimberly Mumford wrote, "and so deep was his conviction that the weavings of the Orient were among the master fruits of human expression . . . that he never ceased, so long as health remained, from search for the best examples."

Perhaps it increased Yerkes' sense of power to realize that more man-hours than it took to build his entire palace had been consumed in tying the knots in a few square feet of carpet that he could buy by merely scribbling his name. Perhaps he really had a deep and genuine passion for the unique beauty of an art that even then had declined almost to extinction. Whatever the motive, the result was that Yerkes brought together the most remarkable group of sixteenth- and seventeenth-century Oriental rugs that has ever been assembled in private hands. No Oriental prince, it has been said, is likely ever to have possessed a collection comparable to the thirty carpets that came to shed their luster in the soft translucence of the marble gallery.

While Yerkes was building his palace in New York, serious trouble was brewing in Chicago. He had dreamed up a transportation monopoly that would produce the $100 million he coveted, but in order to carry out his program of expansion, he needed long extensions of his franchises. The term he had in mind was a hundred years, but if that should appear too grasping to the boodle aldermen, he intimated that he would compromise on fifty. Either period sounded like eternity to his rivals. Unable to block him behind the scenes, they had decided to attack him through the press. A crusade for civic virtue had been started in Chicago, and temporarily at least, Yerkes' enemies became its most ardent supporters. Reformers and anticorruption societies joined the down-with-Yerkes movement without stopping to realize that they were merely aiding a rival power group. Clergymen censured, along with the sins of Gomorrah, the system of urban travel, and held Yerkes responsible for both. The straphangers were delighted that so many pillars of society were concerned with their aching feet. Within a relatively short time, whether by fair means or foul, every important newspaper in Chicago had been enlisted in the anti-Yerkes cause.

As the campaign against him gained momentum, Yerkes realized that he had been rash in neglecting to buy himself a façade of public benefaction, as most of Chicago's fortune builders had been careful to do. Forthwith he set out to remedy the situation. Currently the most effective means to favorable publicity was to bestow something upon Chicago's new university. Assuming a newborn veneration for higher learning, Yerkes inquired of the trustees what they would like in the way of a gift.

The trustees consulted with the educators and came back with a modest request. If it would not be too expensive, they said, the astronomy department could use a telescope. Good, said Yerkes, he would buy the University of Chicago the biggest telescope in the world. The officials made some inquiries and came back shaking their heads. It would cost a lot of money, they said, to have the largest telescope in the world, but they could do with a smaller one, if Mr. Yerkes could see his way . . .

Yerkes' reply was terse: "I want to give the university the biggest telescope in the world! Have it made, and send me the bills. I'll pay them."

A site was selected in Wisconsin; the lens was ground; and the Yerkes Observatory was built with all possible dispatch. The bills came to $400,000.

But Yerkes had taken up philanthropy too late. It would have done no good if he had built an entire university. In 1897, as the time approached for the board of aldermen to vote on his extended franchises, the newspapers had whipped themselves into a cacophony of circulation-boosting wrath. Revolutions, one paper said, were caused by just such rapacity. Anarchy would result, another predicted, if Yerkes was not stopped from stealing the resources of the people. The alternative clamor was for public ownership of transportation facilities, a magical solution that every straphanger was led to believe would bring instant surcease of his many sorrows. Street meetings were held; bonfires were lit; rabble-rousers shouted Yerkes' name in derision to the skies. On the night of the voting, there were torch-light parades; the city hall was surrounded by a mob armed with guns and nooses; the boodle aldermen were threatened with expeditious lynching, and they were frightened. Yerkes had promised them $1 million in bribes, but with hoarse and trembling voices, they voted down his proposals.

The resources of the people were stolen anyhow, of course. As soon as the smoke had cleared, the newspapers were able to convince their readers that public ownership would not be such a good idea after all. What was known as "the Chicago traction tangle" followed. For half a century rival power groups were to fight over Yerkes' streetcar empire, while new generations of straphangers contributed reluctantly to the profits of politer millionaires. After two years of futile struggle, Yerkes was convinced that he was beaten. He traded his controlling shares for bonds and abandoned his dream of empire in Chicago.

Once more Yerkes was an Ishmael, albeit one who was inordinately well heeled. With $15 or $20 million in his pocket, he took his leave of Chicago, personally escorting his paintings from the Michigan Avenue house to the sumptuous galleries he had prepared for them in New York. He had the seats removed from Pullmans and laid the canvases face up in rows upon the floors. Thus, like an exiled king departing, he said farewell to the roistering city he had won and lost, the only animate passenger on that string of parlor cars attached to a lonely night express. On the garish station platform, the trainman signaled with his lantern. The couplings clanged and clanked. Some-where a whistle screeched. Yerkes, sixty-two years old, gray, no longer handsome, his eyes almost flush with the surrounding flesh, so as to give his whole face a flat and sinister expression, stared dispas-sionately from a window as the train began to move. The trainman (could he have remembered that while buying aldermen and art, Yerkes had been considerate of his street railway employees?), seeing no one else to do it, raised his lantern in a parting gesture. In New York a caravan of wagons met the train, and with Yerkes in the lead, drove the pictures in a long procession to the mansion, a mansion designed as a museum but in service as a nightclub, where the drinks were always on the house.

For Mara, as the wings of the palace were gradually completed, had determined to banish sadness from her life. Though she always kept the Chicago house as a refuge, her playground was Fifth Avenue. She surrounded herself with a rollicking crowd—hucksters, con men, gag men; actors, gamblers, and showgirls; millionaire authors of successful plays. Some of them poured champagne in her birdbaths, borrowed her jewels, slithered down her marble banisters; but most of them admired her for her beauty and adored her for her wealth. She no longer dreamed of breaking into society. In New York the *arrivistes* far outnumbered the élite. They were also more amusing. It no longer mattered if the sporty William C. Whitney, who bought a hundred golden dinner plates and threatened to outdo her palace with a grander one on the corner to the north, did not choose to drop in. He would soon drop dead, that Whitney; but meanwhile, every time he imported a hunk of Italian architecture, Yerkes would call his architects and build another annex. Though Whitney was far richer, Mrs. Yerkes was as rich as God, as she freely said. Moreover, she had the smug assurance of a beautiful woman who has been wronged.

In her vaulted dining room she gave celebrated midnight dinners. She developed gay idiosyncrasies, such as discharging all her servants once every twenty-four hours. She turned into a fitful player of all the meretricious roles her childish imagination could conjure. She was everyone and she was no one. She had a thousand pairs of shoes, a thousand pairs of gloves, dresses no one ever counted. Though she was approaching forty-five, she said she was thirty-two, and looked it. Though she had never cared for art, she acquired a fondness for the female portraits in the Yerkes gallery. She made herself up to look like them. She was a different woman every evening, in all respects except her abandoned and pathetic soul.

Among the pictures Mara now admired were the Roman ladies of Lawrence Alma-Tadema. With her wealth of dark brown hair, her rounded cheeks and classic mouth, it was not difficult to resemble those pagan beauties leaning pensively on fountains—especially since she had the fountains. She had only to order her *coiffeurs* to tumble her hair as they might have tumbled it for Caesar's wife, and add a laurel wreath. Her *couturières* would fashion Grecian robes or flowing togas, with the wondrous plumpness of her bosom surreptitiously accentuated. Her male guests would gasp as she sat gazing languidly into a pool of the Vatican Garden, a white bird sitting on her shoulder, or passed, with a long kerchief as a prop, among the thirty-two

Ionic columns of her inner court, pausing now and then to lean her Latin head against the marble whiteness of a nude bacchante.

Alma-Tadema was a mood, of course—an indoor mood, it might be said. He was only one of many artists Mara now began to study. Van Beers's lovelorn duchesses were a constant source of inspiration, but Mara's oval face with no distinctive features, her long lashes, her gray-green eyes and humorless expression were also suited to the fresh-blown maidens of the less sophisticated anecdotal painters. When under their influence, she would wear no jewels; her hair would take on girlish puffs or ripples. She would affect tulle bows at her wrists, bows of many gossamer hues, "that looked like gorgeous butterflies," a woman admirer recorded. She had millions of these bows and streamers, Mara said. She preferred them to her pearls and bracelets, for she was, after all, a simple person and a patron of the weaver's art. One had only to look at her palace to know that. The Gobelins, for instance. She herself had bought them, she would say, from the Princess of Saigon, who was selling out. Anna Gould had got the tiara. Mara, being simpler, had preferred the tapestries.

But the French court painters, though they had abhorred simplicity, also appealed to her. She liked their "beauty types," as she called them. Often she would transform her face and hair to match the Louis XIV miniatures in Yerkes' collection, or emulate the figures in *The Garden Party* by Watteau. Then she would try to be soft, wilting, stately, and imperious all at once. And if she was reasonably sober, she might succeed.

These were transformations seen in Mara's midnight hours, within the precincts of the palace. When she went into the world, her costumes were more complicated. For public appearances, she favored the portraits of the English school, milky women whose clothes were easily adapted to the current fashions. She would spend hours in the galleries, with her whisky glass, her seamstresses and milliners, remodeling herself into something resembling Reynolds' *Lady O'Brien*, or one of the Painted Ladies Blakeslee had pawned off on Yerkes. She had no specific response to whatever art the pictures may have represented. She was a woman poring over fashion plates. The important thing was the number of ostrich feathers in the hat, the satin drape of the superb, if unauthenticated, Gainsborough dress. She would torture herself with whalebone stays and wasp-waist innovations, though her figure was that of a goddess from the start. (How thankful she was, now, that her mother had made her cry herself to sleep in that cruel harness.) And when at last the operations were completed, she would venture forth resplendent, her parasol extended with that special ripple of the wrist bespeaking drunken elegance. The papers printed her picture frequently: Mrs. Charles T. Yerkes at the horse show in very low décolletage, Mrs. Yerkes at the Waldorf in a hat with eighty-seven plumes. Her deportment, sad to relate, was sometimes less chic than her garments. Once, at a performance of *The School for Scandal*, she rose grandly in her box and accused the Lady Teazle on the stage of fraudulent impersonation. That was not the real Lady Teazle, Mara objected thickly. "She's wearing yellow!" In the original, Lady Teazle dressed in pink. If the audience didn't believe her, they could come on up to the house and see.

It is not recorded whether the public accepted Mara's beguiling invitation, but there was seldom any lack of patronage at the Yerkes supper club. Only when the hilarity threatened to end and her "host of friends," as the papers called them, began to dwindle would the elaborate Mrs. Yerkes descend to maudlin introspection. Then, in the clammy dawn, tipsily piloting a visitor through the skylit picture galleries, she would indulge in the extravagant confidences of the inebriate, borrowing little homespun platitudes from the dime novels she occasionally read. "If one has felt the pangs of heart hunger," she would philosophize, "instead of choosing for his gallery a Bouguereau, a Rubens, or a Romney, he will choose a simple little picture of life, painted by himself, in which the word happiness is unmistakably spelled out."

More often, the dawn would bring on salty bursts of morose defiance. Charley Yerkes loved her, she would state with the categorical belligerence of a barfly no one dares to contradict. "Charley Yerkes loves me!" she would cry to the last three or four night creatures who had not yet slipped out into the breaking day. Hunched in the oval of the great piano, her elbows propped on the gaudy *vernis Martin* cover, she would expatiate ad infinitum on her single woebegotten theme. Her whisky voice would rise and fall to the drumming of the newest honky-tonk pianist, or disheveled with the long night's merriment, propped on a couch before the great hood of the Norman fireplace, she would go on and on, with burrlike repetition: "No matter what they say, Charley Yerkes loves me!" Her filmy handkerchief would flutter to her eyes. Her voice would strain and break. Oh, she knew about the others, but Charley Yerkes loved her all the same. "And don't you forget it!" she would threaten the last guest who could be kept to listen. But Charley Yerkes would be absent, and when at last the night's charade was ended, there would be scenes of greater violence.

Sometimes then, to the despair of her secretaries and her servants, she would stalk the palace, heaving her bosom like an overzealous actress lost in the woes of Grecian tragedy, flashing scorn and hatred from her big round suffering eyes, shrieking curses on the elfin creature she called "the Grigsby woman."

For there was another Yerkes mansion in New York, inhabited by Miss Emilie Grigsby, her golden harp, her jade wine cups, and her singing birds. You could even see a gable of Miss Emilie's high gray pile of stone from the upper chambers of the palace. The sight of it, even the thought of it, was enough to send poor Mara into storms of rage. No, Charley Yerkes did not love *her!* Multiple infidelities Mara could endure, but Miss Emilie Grigsby she could not.

Yerkes called Miss Emilie his ward; the Boston *Evening Transcript*, in an excess of delicacy, once referred to her as his adopted daughter; but by whatever title, Miss Emilie Busby Grigsby was a striking addition to the decade when New York most profusely flowered. Fiction writers were warned that they would have to step up their imaginations to create stories "that would equal the facts in the life of the ward of the streetcar magnate." Princes and potentates showered her with gifts from such distant regions as Egypt and Japan. Edward VII gave her an embroidered footstool. Henry James and George Meredith were fond of her. François Coppée, the renowned French poet, gave her the andirons from his library. Pope Leo XIII was said to have given her a lock of his hair.

As a child Miss Emilie was educated in a convent, at Yerkes' expense; and never—not even when he bought Turner's *Rockets and Blue Lights*—did the spendthrift titan make a more dazzling investment. When she emerged, in the full blow of adolescence, bedewed with modesty and religious ecstasy, the effect was almost otherworldly. Her marvelous red-gold hair would have defied the brush of Titian, a number of admirers said; no angel of the golden ages had been depicted with such purity of alabaster skin; the ever-changing sea itself could not aspire to the azure softness of her languid eyes; nor could the sorrows of the Muses describe the peculiarly mournful expression beneath their heavy lids. There were others who said she was proud and cold, like a diamond in disposition, but most of those who saw her were inarticulate with wonder. They simply said she was a poem.

Miss Emilie's origins were checkered. Although veracity was not one of her strong points, it was reliably established that she was born in old Kentucky of a distinguished, if somewhat seedy, family. One of her ancestors was Carter Braxton, a signer of the Declaration of Independence. Miss Emilie's brother, who lived with her in New York, was called Braxton in his honor. Her maternal grandfather, who also shared Yerkes' bounty, was called Governor Robinson— governor of where, no one seemed to know. Her widowed mother, alas, was Mrs. Susan Grigsby of Cincinnati, whose red-plush citadel of illicit frolic was widely known to traveling men, including Charley Yerkes, until the Cincinnati police forced her to close her doors in 1897.

Upon Miss Emilie's departure from the convent, the good nuns, apprehensive for the future of the dream child they had reared, told her the nature of the family enterprise in Ohio. It was her cross to bear, they said, and implored her to convert her mother. This Miss Emilie did. The former Sue Grigsby of Cincinnati became a devout Catholic and made pilgrimages to Rome, where she sought and obtained the blessing of the Pope.

Miss Emilie fortified her own position with a papal plenary indulgence granted to her and her heirs to the third generation. This impressive document used to hang next to a marble bust of Madame du Barry in Miss Grigsby's purple damask bedroom, attached to an autographed portrait of His Holiness. Beneath the portrait was a golden locket said to contain the strand of papal hair. But mainly, Miss Emilie used the broadening advantages of travel to further her life's ambition, for she was possessed of one all-absorbing passion: despite manifestly insurmountable handicaps, she was determined to carve herself a career in high society.

After the Chicago fiasco, Yerkes paused in New York only long enough to supervise the hanging of his pictures. Then he moved the center of his financial operations to England, where he undertook to expand the London underground railways into what he envisioned as "the greatest system of urban transportation in the world." In the attempt to raise the money for so vast an enterprise, he traveled between London and New York with the bustling air of an ordinary man commuting between home and office. Both Mara and Miss Emilie followed him, though fortunately for decorum on the high seas, never on the same boat. Miss Emilie traveled with twenty trunks of dresses. Her clothes were inventoried in a book, which her maid brought to her each morning while she selected the costumes of the day. The extent of Mara's impedimenta no one bothered to record.

In London Yerkes established his young "ward" in a suite near Berkeley Square, where she gave stately dinners for the investors. When she appeared at a party in a clinging white satin robe, with a sapphire at her neck an inch and a half square, the monied world professed with one accord never to have set eyes on a creature so ravishing. In the summer she took a house at Maidenhead on the Thames. There she wore flowing muslins and ropes of pearls and danced on the lawn for the aristocratic neighbors. From Mayfair to the Riviera, Miss Emilie became known almost overnight as the Kentucky Beauty. It was reported that a Prince Windischgratz of Hungary was engaged to marry her, likewise Prince Deldrago of Italy. But these rumors were denied by her maternal grandfather, who handled press relations, while the repentant Madame Grigsby, schooled as she was in business, managed finances. Though Miss Emilie's costumes often symbolized the purity of bridehood, she was in the market for no earthly husband. She was merely taking a last look around this world, she said, before retiring for the rest of her life into a convent.

Wonderful and expensive was Miss Emilie's inspection of the follies of England and the Continent, marvelous were her arrivals and departures, starborne her adventures with royalty and genius. Her beauty and her sables, her whitewashed pedigree, and her mythical Southern fortune opened doors that Yerkes could never have entered except as her guardian. She looked like a thoroughbred and behaved like an empress; and when, amid the festivities of a yachting party, or while languishing at an ancestral board after the long day's hunt, she would talk with tragic earnestness of her ultimate retirement from the giddy world, a shadow would cross the faces of the most intrepid merrymakers. Once, it was said, Edward himself heaved a royal sigh. Yerkes would "wear a worried look," a close observer noted, and "stroke her shapely white hand comfortingly."

In Paris Miss Grigsby of Kentucky stayed in the Prince of Wales suite at the Bristol, the most elaborately furnished hotel apartment in all Europe. Between sittings for her many portraits, and listening to marriage proposals from unemployed royalty, she did a mite of shopping. Browsing on the Rue de Rivoli with shipboard acquaintances—women with a toehold in New York's social stratosphere—she would pay $700 for a snuffbox and laugh if one of them suggested that it was a lot of money. The amorphous Southern fortune diminished in the presence of her compatriots; but, Miss Emilie said, she had inherited $50,000 from a horse-loving aunt in Kentucky.

In the line of food, the metaphysical Miss Grigsby partook mainly of truffles and nectar. Once, in January, she saw strawberries in a Paris restaurant. They were 300 francs a box. "Very well, my man," Miss Emilie said, with what her companion described as the contemptuous smile of a queen who scorns to count the cost of anything, "just bundle up all you have. I'll take them with me in my carriage." There were six boxes, or a total of $360 worth.

Paris and London were amusing, but it was the home ground Miss Grigsby most urgently desired to conquer. Whether, as she said, she was proud to be an American, or whether, with the true instincts of an adventuress, she was drawn to the *champs de bataille* most fraught with danger—whatever the reason, it was in New York that she put forth her noblest efforts.

While her great house was building, she gave "little affairs," as the society pages called them, at the suite in the Grenoble whither Mrs. Grigsby had taken refuge from the Cincinnati vice squad. It was said that the most prominent people attended. She took a season box at the opera and blinded the spectators on even Tuesdays with her wide dog collar of blue-white diamonds, her red-gold hair cascading over an ermine cape that alone would have consumed the bequest of the horse-loving Kentucky aunt. Matrons on the outer ramparts of society "took her up" without bothering to check her references. "She was the most beautiful woman I ever saw," said Mrs. Dunlap Hopkins, a Whitney-sponsored dowager who acted as her chaperone in 1901. Mrs. Spencer Trask invited her to Saratoga, where she danced for a season among the rose gardens of Yaddo, gazed at her own reflection in its limpid pools, flitted nymphlike through the giant forests, and deftly parried the lovesick advances of many a financier's young son.

At Old Point Comfort, Virginia, she met Captain Richmond Pearson Hobson, the handsome hero of the *Merrimac* exploit at Santiago. As the *Independent* described Hobson's day in the sun, then in its noontime blaze, he went "prancing and dancing over the country, ringed with lovelocks," while thousands swarmed lyceums and opera houses "to see and hear the man who scuttled a coal-ship and was supposed to cultivate kissing bees." Miss Grigsby of Kentucky went dancing and prancing with him and cultivated a large part of the navy's officer personnel along the way. Matchmaking reporters had it, inevitably, that the Southland Venus and Apollo were engaged. This, too, was denied—by all hands, as it turned out in the end.

There were other preliminary skirmishes, but the poesy of Miss Emilie's life is somehow inseparable from the poetry of her house.

Miss Emilie Grigsby was nineteen in 1898, when Yerkes bought for her that quaint rectangular sacrarium extending 100 feet 5 inches on the west side of Park Avenue northward from the corner of East 67th Street. Designed originally as a block of flats, it rose five stories high, turreted and gabled, like the façade of a cold, gray English castle, by far the most conspicuous building on a street of breweries and stables. Remodeled into a private dwelling, it was staggering in its height and width; but it was only 20 feet deep. One had only to walk around the corner to realize that Miss Emilie's mansion, like Miss Emilie herself, was all front, with but little substance. Nor was Park Avenue, in those days, any plum of a location. While Mara could gaze at the loveliness of Central Park from the windows of her marble gallery, Miss Emilie had to endure the smoke and cinders of the New York Central trains belching from black holes outside her mauve and velvety salons. But Miss Grigsby's place was not precisely back street either, for she was in love with art, and she managed to do nicely with what she had.

The entrance was imposing. Two broad flights of steps led to a glass-and-iron-covered vestibule jutting out upon the sidewalk—impudently, some people said—as if in anticipation of many carriages drawn up in holiday formation, many decorous figures in tall hats and trailing cloaks milling in the torchlit blaze before Miss Grigsby's tall cathedral doors.

Inside, you knew immediately that this was no vulgar house of Vanderbilt or Gould. There was, rather, a churchly atmosphere in Miss Emilie's center hall, a waft of incense in the air, the soft prismatic twilight of jeweled lamps from an old Italian altar, the time-worn glow of Persian rugs and old church vestments. Some of the rugs had poetic queries woven into their designs, which read, Miss Grigsby had been told: "What says the lark to the rose in the garden?" and "Why weary of life when everything around you is beautiful?" The translations were most certainly incorrect, improvised no doubt by Vitall Benguiat to suit the temper of his client. But no matter. The rugs were beautiful at any rate. One, a Persian silk hunting carpet, was composed of warring figures symbolizing the eternal struggle between Good and Evil. It was the one Miss Grigsby cherished the most.

But the walls and ceilings were scarcely less inspiring than the floors. Callers susceptible to Miss Grigsby's charms were intrigued not only by her many portraits, but by a familiar figure that kept reappearing everywhere. For Miss Emilie had had herself incorporated in all her mural decorations—in the panels depicting scenes from Wagner's operas, in the heavenly population that floated, blissful and abundant, above the many splendors of her drawing room. (Was it that Miss Grigsby looked like an angel or the angels like Miss Grigsby, visitors would argue sotto voce, while gazing at the gold-lined fleece and blueness of her painted heavens.) A mere glance at that Regency drawing room, an anonymous reporter wrote, after taking the guided tour for the benefit of the *Tribune*'s subscribers, "and you begin to appreciate more fully than, perhaps, you have ever done before, how wealthy Miss Grigsby really is." But a mere glance would not satisfy, the *Tribune* man went on to say, and perhaps it is only fair to record a few of his impressions verbatim:

. . . You revel in the soft luxury of purplish maroon and orange. You marvel at the exquisite fitness of things that should present to your charmed vision, just at this time in your life, the first view of a great golden harp.

Surely no harp ever seemed more in keeping with its surroundings. It is silent, of course, but imagination makes easy the haunting sweetness it would be possible for an artist to extract from those golden strings. Ah! Well a day.

There are many cabinets here, each filled with the works of artists of China, Italy, Germany and France. Ancient Greece has sent a sample of her opalescent blown glass. There is a gold bracelet from Tibet, pounded by hand.

ART AND THE HIGH LIFE

There are golden boxes evolved by some deceased mechanician. He belonged to the court of Louis XVI. The boxes contain little singing birds. You set the birds to sing at a certain time. They will not disappoint you. You touch the button, they do not rest. The cover of the box flies open and the golden bird flutters its wings, swings its head and produces song. . . .

Venus without a head, a flask from some tomb in Corinth, a fragment of a torso in bronze, are also present. Each makes its own appeal. Shall we look at another cabinet? If you are interested in Chinese jades, you will not hang back. See their reds and purples and greens. . . .

Oriental ivories grip your attention and jewelled watches, all telling the time of day with an impractical variety of results, are set in the midst of amethyst crystals or concealed in brooches.

. . . Someone tells you there is moonstone jewelry of Lalique close by, but you cannot digest it—you ask the way to somewhere else.

The dining room—ah! It is the heart of any home, you murmur softly to yourself. You cross the hall. You get that feeling again as of being in a cathedral. "From the Monastery Nuremberg," someone whispers. You do not know whether the monastery furnished the chairs or the silverware. Perhaps it was the tapestries. It is all good, so no matter.

Old English silver, the Gladstone tea caddy, old blue China with a lovely little flower in the middle of each plate; twenty-four jewelled plates—count them, twenty-four—from the collection of the Comtesse de Fernandina of Paris.

The color scheme is crushed grape, the draperies are maroon, the carpets, in a way, are a purplish hue. There are so many instruments arranged on each side of the plates at table that one involuntarily thinks of a dentist's layout. And then one moves on. But not until one learns that the oak in the room is Flemish, the great tapestries from Flanders, the cabinets filled with Dresden and Royal Vienna plates. . . .

There are five stories to the house. Suppose we climb at least one flight of stairs. In Miss Grigsby's bedroom you note immediately a marble group, life size, over in the shadow of an alcove. It is "The Temptation of the Vestal Virgin by Cupid," the conception of A. Rossetti, a modern sculptor of Rome.

Another visitor, a woman, says to her friend, also a woman, "I wonder if the statue is meant for Miss Grigsby."

"How silly," her friend replies. "Don't you see it is the Blessed Mary?"

Mme. Du Barry smiles from across the room, a warm though marble smile. You walk upon Persian rugs. In a corner stands a fan case, containing perhaps forty fans. There are flirtation fans, with two little windows in the sticks; wedding fans, French marriage fans—all the work of masters in the fan-making art. Indeed dreams should be sweet when dreamed here.

The library! Will you linger a little in the library?

The room is lighted by cathedral lamps of silvered bronze from the palace of Cardinal Serafino Vanatelli. There are a great many pieces of ecclesiastical silver from church treasuries in this room, including an ostensorium, the vessel in which the priest elevates the host during mass. Numerous church embroideries are used by Miss Grigsby as panels or table covers. On the library table you see an old velvet cloak worn by a knight of the Golden Fleece.

There is a motto over the mantel, "God is in Heaven and all is well." The chairs are from old Spanish originals. . . . There are nine servants in the house to try to keep everything dusted.

We had almost forgotten to look at the books in the library. There are complete sets of first editions, fine collections of standard authors and modern poets in fine bindings—6,000 volumes in all.

The room is 16th Century while most of the books are 19th Century and to this extent at least the library and its contents fail to match. But the color scheme is perfectly lovely. . . .

It was hopeless to try to give an adequate description of Miss Emilie's plush surroundings. When her goods and chattels eventually fell into the hands of the auctioneer it took 427 pages merely to list them. Moreover, the guided tour did not include all the noteworthy attractions of her mansion. With its nether and supernal regions, its eccentricities increased, and so did—as a prowler from the New York *American* observed—its "romantic possibilities."

At the third story, the grand staircase abruptly ended, and with it, apparently, all means of access to the floors above. Secret elevators ran behind unobtrusive panels in passageways and closets—small pitch-dark elevators, reserved, it was said, for the use of Miss Grigsby's inner circle. A passenger making his first ascent to the grand salon at the top of the house reported that it was a trek fraught with mystery-story sensations, which increased, rather than diminished, when at the end of the shaft the panel slid back, revealing the room where "Miss Grigsby delighted to entertain her friends."

The grand salon ran, to all appearances, the entire 100-foot width of the building. Architecturally it resembled the attic of a farmhouse. The walls sloped in. Solid oak beams protruded at intervals of about 10 feet. Its fireplace was reminiscent of that in an old Dutch kitchen. But its "gorgeous appointments"—as the *American* once described them—were far from kitchenlike. Looking down at nightmarish angles, due to the inward sloping of the walls, were trophies of the hunt, including a moose head with antlers spreading 67 inches and said, like the Roman missal in Miss Grigsby's music room, to be "the largest in the world." Fur rugs with ferocious heads lay about the floor, bears, tigers, cheetahs, leopards, and wolves overlapping one another so as to give the impression of a recent massacre of a considerable representation of the animal kingdom. Swords, firearms, cutlasses, and daggers swung from the protruding beams. Men in armor stood about in awful array. Between the moose head and the battle axes, the slanting walls were plastered with paintings of a strangely incongruous refinement: Alfred Stevens' *Waiting* (which had once been a joy to Mara), Anders Zorn's *The Bather*, a Pissarro, a Sisley, and an excellent Monet. Miss Emilie herself was present in a water color that the auctioneers, in good time, described as follows: "Through a garden of lillies and azaleas, backed by a wall of greenery, a tall and willowy young woman in floating gray drapery walks as in a dream. Her head is raised in ecstasy."

Ecstasy was perhaps the word for the grand salon. Gilded throne chairs comprised the seating arrangements, and one end of the room was bounded by the gilded pipes of a tremendous organ. Saturnalian indeed must have been the evenings when its roaring diapason made the sabers rattle, when its celestial trumpets whined, and Miss Grigsby in her veils danced among the fallen beasts.

Though bizarre, the grand salon itself was nothing to start the tongues of gossips wagging. There was, however, a small door concealed behind the organ pipes; and inevitably, a busybody thin enough to squeeze around the console found and opened it. On the other side was a bare white cubicle containing a narrow white iron bed, a prie-dieu, and in a niche the figure of a saint. Miss Emilie's cell might have passed as a commendable aid to the mortification of her proud spirit but for a single remaining item of furniture, which was far from standard for the life of contemplation. A long white-framed cheval glass stood beside the bed.

Various explanations for the whitewashed cell emanated from 660 Park Avenue. In escorting visitors on the guided tour, Miss Emilie would sometimes bypass her purple brocade boudoir with the bed that had belonged to a prince of India (the Bluegrass region had never possessed anything like it, the *Tribune* reporter said) and show the humble little room to visitors as her own. At other times she said the cell was a convenience for the nuns from the convent where she was educated, who always stayed at her Park Avenue mansion when passing through New York. A spokesman—probably the Governor—said that Miss Grigsby maintained her nun's cell "as a retreat into which she could retire for rest and quiet as the gaiety of worldly life palled on her." But neither Miss Emilie nor any of her spokesmen would discuss the concealed elevator shaft running from this room of mystery to a place behind secret panels in the basement floor—"a vast apartment," as one informer described it, "containing everything to appeal to the senses."

Society blushed and gasped when eventually the story got around that the pious Miss Grigsby's lovely house was honeycombed with such unconventional arrangements, but even before her architectural aberrations were revealed, Miss Grigsby of Kentucky had encountered rough going on the primrose path.

One of her earliest misadventures was with the navy. Through the osculatory hero of the *Merrimac,* Admiral Charles D. Sigsbee, commander of the ill-starred *Maine,* had joined Miss Emilie's seafaring cortege. Like the nuns, the Admiral had a way of passing through New York. On one of his visits he invited Hobson, Miss Emilie, and the dowager Mrs. Grigsby to dinner at the Waldorf-Astoria. They were a gala party, the ladies superbly gowned, the gentlemen in full nautical regalia, their breasts a patchwork of battle decorations; but it was as if the Furies had chosen that very night to descend. An old horse trainer, who had been a client of Sue Grigsby's place in Cincinnati, showed up at the Waldorf very drunk, rushed to the table, and greeted the bejeweled Mrs. Grigsby with all the effusions of old home week. Never was old acquaintance more delighted to meet old acquaintance or happier to find one so laden with the fruits of repentance. There was some dreadful mistake, Mrs. Grigsby protested shrilly, as the naval heroes rose to defend the honor of their ladies; but before the Waldorf sentries could eject him, the horse trainer had amply demonstrated his validity.

The time had come for Miss Emilie to prove her mettle. She could do without the navy. (Questioned by reporters, the hero of the *Merrimac* said, "Oh, yes, I knew her. I met her at Old Point Comfort. She was quite popular at the Point.") But she could not afford to let the navy win. She had made a brave beginning, and a proper one for an adventuress. She had gone to the bad, and she had done it magnificently. Her brazen house, her twenty trunks, the lovely fabric of her invention, her defiance of morality and marriage (the very bulwarks of feminine respectability) all were in the grand tradition. The stage was set; the costumes, the billboards, and the lights were ready; above all, the supporting cast: kings, counselors, admirals, and generals; distinguished men of letters; shahs, khedives, maharajas; crown princes and popular heroes; even the Pope of Rome. The first act of her classic comedy had gone very well, but somehow the rest of the script got lost. The witty and seductive Madame du Barry, across from the Vestal Virgin in that purple brocade boudoir, may well have turned her warm smile to a withering grimace, for when du Barry would have laughed and played her grandest scene, Grigsby sniveled and made a desperate stab at keeping up appearances.

Yerkes' agents bought a foolish apology from the horse trainer, who, when sober, was induced to state that he had been mistaken after all. Miss Grigsby's household bogged down in a welter of silly lies that would have discredited the imagination of a shopgirl. Miss Emilie called Yerkes her uncle in America and her guardian in England, but if cornered, she would confide with dull humility that he was her illegitimate father. The servants at 660 Park Avenue called him Mr. Grigsby. Braxton, Miss Emilie's brother, called him Uncle Charley. Yerkes himself favored the vagueness of the ward relationship, but at least once he greeted reporters in the dim light of Miss Emilie's altar lamps disguised as "Captain F. B. Grigsby, late of Roosevelt's Rough Riders," who may or may not have been Miss Emilie's father, but who, at any rate, had been dead for years.

Alas, Miss Emilie became a victim of her own delusions. When she had no choice but to proclaim herself a Queen of Babylon, she continued to storm the fortress of respectability. And when at last she reached its most impregnable defenses, she came up against her nemesis.

On a wintry transatlantic crossing on the *Kronprinz Wilhelm* Miss Grigsby's regal suite, whether by design or accident, was next to that of Mrs. James P. Kernochan. The second day out, Miss Emilie met Mrs. Kernochan, and Mrs. Kernochan introduced her to Mrs. Stuyvesant Fish. Mrs. Fish was renowned for her pioneering efforts to improve upon the tedium of society, but in the entire membership of the Four Hundred there was none truer to its most conservative tenets than the formidable Mrs. Kernochan. Society reporters, observing her at a ball in deep red satin with a spreading lace ruff, had compared her to "some mighty dame at the Elizabethan court." Her "rhinitic dust," as *Town Topics* once called it, had blinded many an upstart crow decked in peacock's feathers. Her imperial tongue was likened to the serpent's hiss, her disapproval to the lion's roar. "Nevertheless," a historian for the *World* recorded, "in the skillful hands of Emilie Grigsby, this accomplished woman of the world was as clay." The progressive Mrs. Fish was no more than putty. Before the ship had docked at Plymouth she had invited Miss Grigsby of Kentucky to Newport for the following summer. It was the proudest hour of her life, Miss Emilie said.

In Paris Mrs. Fish gave a dinner at the Ritz in honor of her new-found protégée. Mrs. Kernochan declined to go quite so far without certified credentials, but she did attend the dinner—an act of depravity that all but ruined her reputation for austerity. Miss Emilie reciprocated by inviting her Newport chums to a "strawberry lunching" in the Bristol's Prince of Wales suite at midnight.

Charmed by the setting no less than by the cost of the victuals, the ladies sent to the home base for the particulars of a conspicuous, if hitherto uncharted, fortune. Upon their return to New York, agents met them at the boat with Miss Emilie's dossier. A Cincinnati police captain had been more than pleased to recount the lusty saga of Sue Grigsby's past. A Kentucky aunt had been found, both wealthy and deceased. She had married at sixty and had three race horses named for her. But Miss Emilie had inherited no money from this aunt. It had taken no more than rudimentary detective work to establish Charley Yerkes as the sole source of Miss Emilie's prosperity. Mrs. Fish canceled the invitation to Newport before leaving the dock. Mrs. Kernochan, eyewitnesses said, was "almost prostrated." The charmed circle laughed uproariously—not primarily at Miss Emilie, but at the imperial dowager and her unthinkable faux pas.

Ripples of hilarity echoed from drawing room to drawing room, until there was no one left who did not "know." The son of a downtown merchant, who had imagined himself a candidate for Miss Grigsby's lily hand in marriage, impetuously attempted suicide. Mrs. Trask considered having the rose gardens of Yaddo fumigated. Mrs. Dunlap Hopkins uttered the word "audacious" with a pursed-mouth eloquence that almost sprained her jaw. Miss Emilie sulked.

"I don't think anyone ever visited her after that," a society woman said two or three years later. "Everyone knew. She was pointed out at the opera, but no one ever went to her box."

Miss Grigsby of Kentucky continued to sail the ocean, but not at the captain's table. Her Park Avenue house received no stylish visitors. Strange tales were told of its concealed elevators and secret panels. Fathers walking with their sons on Sunday afternoons would circle round the block to avoid answering questions. Patrician mothers professed a discreet ignorance when their daughters inquired who the lady was who so grandly lived there. For a decade Miss Emilie's tall gray English castle was known as the House of Mystery.

The Herculean London underground effort was not only Yerkes' last attempt to enter the topmost ranks of financiers, it was to be an aspect of his monument as well, for by now, he had begun to think of dying. It was his fondest dream that the tubes and tunnels of the largest city in the world should eternally demonstrate to the citizens of Chicago the error of their ways. But if his own works should fail, he was determined to ride to glory on his rugs and pictures. With an almost pathetic eagerness, he bought the most expensive art that came his way. He ordered a fine Greek tomb to be erected in Green-Wood Cemetery, with two bronze caskets, one for Mara, the other for himself. For posterity was to think of him as respectable and touchingly monogamous.

To that end, there were surface reconciliations with Mara. In Paris, in 1901, they had their portraits made, in large dimensions, for the benefit of future generations that were to wander through the Yerkes gallery. The artist, Jean Joseph Benjamin Constant, then in the last year of his life, had started with Moors and slave girls and graduated to Jay Gould and Queen Victoria. He was expensive. Mara, leaning on her Lady Teazle parasol, turned out very busty—she might have been mistaken for Sadie Thompson in a later day—but there were those who admired the picture greatly and said it was an exact reproduction of a Gainsborough.

Meticulous as were his preparations for nirvana, however, Yerkes did not permit them to interfere with the realities of corporeal existence. In Charles Street, hard by Miss Emilie's London suite, lived Miss Gladys Unger. Gladys was even younger than Miss Emilie, and her house was described as "crammed with the most exquisite works of art." She wrote plays and gave teas to Bohemia. Miss Ethel Link

Yerkes, on the other hand, played the violin and lived, appropriately enough, in Dresden.

Ethel's father had been a good enough provider when he was a high roller in the Tenderloin, but he had disappeared when a judge issued a bench warrant for his arrest. After Clarence Yerkes' disappearance, Mrs. Clarence had induced an aged trust magnate to take Miss Ethel on as his "ward." The trust magnate had established mother and daughter in an obscure apartment on West 63rd Street, but he had been a poor provider, and Mrs. Clarence had quarreled with him. In order to make ends meet, she had been reduced to putting her daughter on the stage in a female minstrel show. But as luck would have it, a well-timed appeal to Charley Yerkes on the grounds of a somewhat watery consanguinity had saved Miss Ethel from the breadwinner's ordeal.

Miss Ethel was younger than Gladys, and according to some authorities, even prettier than Miss Emilie. It was said that she was far and away Yerkes' favorite during the last year of his life.

It was a life, as fate would have it, that was due to end before the London venture quite came off. Given time, Yerkes might have eased out of the role of freebooter into that of transportation prince. In the beginning J. P. Morgan had challenged his right to invade the British traction field. By 1902 Morgan had been defeated, and Yerkes became a major power in international finance. But London was more difficult to conquer than Chicago. Without the boodle aldermen, there were endless complications and delays. Even with the money and the franchise, a subway took a while to dig. London could wait, but Charles T. Yerkes was growing old. Moreover, he was ill. When he learned that he had an incurable disease, he returned to New York and took a suite at the Waldorf-Astoria. Though he still talked with zest of building the great electric subways, he never again left his room.

Miss Emilie Grigsby was in constant attendance at his bedside, a circumstance which made it difficult for Mara to observe the formalities of reconciliation. Once, when Yerkes was reported to be dying, Mrs. Yerkes paid a stately call and found Miss Emilie in the room. "What right have you here?" Mara demanded in a feline roar.

"Mr. Yerkes has requested me to remain with him, and I don't propose to leave him at this critical hour," the languishing Miss Emilie replied.

"We'll see about that," said Mara. She swooped down on Miss Grigsby and escorted her from the sickroom with the deftness of a panther. Guests of the hotel reported that the row in the corridor was deafening. Ostrich feathers flew, but Miss Emilie was no match for Mara. She was within a twist of being strangled with her infamous rope of pearls when the Waldorf reserves arrived, weighed the merits of the case, and sided with the bonds of matrimony. Miss Emilie was evicted.

She was back the following morning; but Mara came no more until, in the last hour, she was induced to form a family tableau with the first Mrs. Yerkes' son and daughter, for the benefit of the press. Thus, with one eye on the camera, Charles T. Yerkes died, on December 29, 1905. He was sixty-eight years old.

By the following night the body was lying in state at the palatial mansion. In the south wing the scaffolding still remained from the last picture gallery, which had barely been completed. On the coffin there was a wreath of orchids, placed there by Mrs. Yerkes. There were no other flowers. The servants were instructed to admit no female mourners. The *Sun* reported that the mansion was in a state of siege. Over at 660 Park Avenue Miss Grigsby's butler told inquirers that there was no one home. Dark green shades were drawn in the House of Mystery, on all the windows except one looking west, up 67th Street to Fifth Avenue. The night before the burial, Mara attended a New Year's Eve party at the Café Martin.

New York had seldom witnessed a more forsaken funeral, the *World* reported. Detectives guarded both entrances against unwelcome guests. Only one showed up—Clarence Yerkes, the father of Miss Ethel. Though a fugitive from the New York police, he had disguised himself as a farmer in order to attend the services. Reporters described him as a nervous little man with soft brown eyes, a long straggling mustache, and clothing of unmistakably rural cut. He said he was a Quaker and presented a card that read "Charles T. Yerkes, Grain and Oats, Johnstown, Pa." But the detectives would not let him in.

There were only four coaches in the procession to Brooklyn. The sky was overcast, and a bleak wind swept the graves of Green-Wood Cemetery. Mara, the *World* reported, "halted at the open door of the mausoleum, refusing to enter. Rigidly she stood while the officiating minister offered prayer. Only once and but for an instant did

Mrs. Yerkes betray emotion. As the prayer ended, her tall figure swayed forward. A spasm of grief seemed to convulse her. With one hand she pressed a handkerchief to her eyes and with the other clutched the arm of the woman beside her for support."

Barred from the mansion, the unwelcome Quaker had rushed to the cemetery. "I am only a poor relation, you know," he explained to the gatekeeper. He then got lost among the wind-swept graves and failed to find the Greek tomb until long after the funeral cortege had departed.

The end was the beginning. For a few days after the reading of the beautiful will, everyone was happy. Newspapers searched their files for kind things to say about the city's great benefactor. Art journals took photographs of such pictures as Troyon's *Normandy Ox* and a Blakeslee Van Dyck called *Wolfgang, Duke of Nieubourg*, the better to show the citizens how fortunate they would be when one day they came into possession of the Yerkes mansion. Miss Ethel Yerkes arrived from Dresden on the first boat. The New York *Press* described her as "blithely exuberant, like a young girl returning from college"—in a Paris hat and Russian sables. "Oh, Uncle was just the finest, greatest-hearted man in the world!" she told reporters as she tripped down the gangplank and hurried off to the trust company where the Yerkes assets were deposited. The storm clouds did not appear until Miss Emilie Grigsby, after a decent interval, raised her curtains and tripped off to the Yerkes depository herself. Though unmentioned in the will, she had, it seems, accumulated a few choice bits of paper in those sessions at the Waldorf. One was a check for $250,000. Another was a certificate for 47,000 shares in the London underground. Like old Charles Morgan, Yerkes felt there was always the chance that he might recover. He had not recorded the transfer. But Miss Grigsby's lawyers assured her it was valid.

Jubilantly the papers abandoned the search for laudatory material on Yerkes and concentrated on Miss Emilie's success story. Mathematicians promptly diminished their estimates of the curative powers of the Yerkes hospital. Mara went into what her doctors called a nervous collapse, but was eminently cheered by the zeal of the press in depicting the whimsy of Miss Emilie's life. After all, the London subways were nothing but unfinished tunnels. Mara had the palace and uncounted millions at her disposal. With her finger in the philanthropic pie, she might yet achieve the long-coveted status of great lady; while the Grigsby woman, her subways notwithstanding, had become the target of moralists and the laughingstock not only of society but of everybody who could read. Though Mara was recovering from an illness, the *Herald* was able to state by the sixteenth of January that Mrs. Yerkes graciously saw reporters.

She would build the hospital at once, she said. Not only the hospital but a convalescent home as well. It must be on high land, she mused, with sun parlors and baths of all kinds, lots of trees and gardens. . . . "There will be little boats so that the patients will be able to go out on the water. . . . They will be absolutely free from care." No, she would never marry, Mrs. Yerkes confided to the *Herald*. She would devote her life to charitable endeavor.

The New York *American* was skeptical about the little boats and inquired of Mara's lawyer if it was true that the hospital was to be built at once. "I know nothing about it," the lawyer said. "But it may be so; you can never tell what Mrs. Yerkes will do from one day to another; you would be aware of that if you knew her."

Two weeks later the Widow Yerkes was married to Wilson Mizner.

If Mara had screened her entire roster of palace revelers, it is doubtful if she could have turned up a less comforting bridegroom than Wilson Mizner. To list but a few of his matrimonial disadvantages, he was a dope fiend, a confidence man, a thief, a cardsharp, a blackmailer, an exploiter of crooked prize fighters and prostitutes, a parasite on society in general and the criminal classes in particular. His education had begun on the Barbary Coast of San Francisco and continued in Nome, Alaska, where, according to his own testimony, he was something of a boulevardier among the scoundrels and sporting ladies of the gold rush. Now, at the age of twenty-nine, an abnormally tall young bruiser with a huge head, spindly legs, and knuckles that he said had been permanently deformed by knocking down dames in the Klondike, he had descended upon New York with a tall hat, green spats, an Inverness cape, and the highest Celluloid collars Broadway had ever seen.

Later in life Mizner achieved a vaunted reputation as a wit, and even professional standing as nonwriting collaborator on a play or two dealing with the life of crime. More recently, and posthumously, he has shared the fame of his architect brother, Addison, in a number of biographies, notably Alva Johnston's *The Legendary Mizners*. But until the headlines accompanying his marriage to Mara, Wilson Mizner was unsung. In moments of hilarious self-deprecation he boasted that his principal occupation was fleecing suckers. Thus far no victim had come his way with the lush potentialities of the lonely, alcoholic, forty-nine-year-old Mrs. Yerkes.

For three days after her marriage Mara appeared to be unaware of the event. Questioned by reporters over the telephone she said, "Mizner, Mizner . . . ? I don't know Mizner." Meanwhile, the exuberant bridegroom, from headquarters in the Hotel Astor, was bombarding the newspapers with signed press releases declaring that he had wed the rich Mrs. Yerkes "with bell, book and candle," and that he was now lord of the Yerkes manor. Louis Owsley, coexecutor of the as yet uncounted fortune, said it was incredible. Mrs. Yerkes' doctor said she was suffering from nervousness but positively was not married to Mizner.

At the bridegroom's direction, however, the press located the Reverend Andrew Gillies, a Methodist Episcopal clergyman. The Reverend Gillies confessed to having performed the ceremony and hotly denied that Mrs. Yerkes had not been in her right mind at the time. He had been recommended for the job, the parson said, by one of Mrs. Yerkes' secretaries, who happened to be a member of his congregation, and a more idyllic little wedding he had never had the pleasure of conducting.

By prearrangement with Mizner, he had gone to the palace the night of January 30. Overwhelmed by the glamour of his surroundings, he had been escorted through the marble gallery to the grand drawing room. After some delay, Mrs. Yerkes had appeared, wearing a black glitter gown and a large picture hat of black lace and plumes. She was in high spirits, he said, "and her well-preserved face beamed with delight." There had been a number of witnesses. Though no one had given Mrs. Yerkes away, the handsome young bridegroom had been accompanied by stalwart ushers. The parson had asked no questions beyond the ones in the book. To those, he said, Mrs. Yerkes had responded in a clear, firm, joyous voice heard distinctly over the large room.

After the ceremony there had been light refreshments, consisting of fruit, ice cream, and cake, but not a drop to drink. Then the parson had departed, and so, almost at his heels, had the bridegroom and his ushers, leaving the bride to her own devices. The Reverend Gillies, upon reflection, did think that a little odd, but he swore that the bonds he had tied were legal beyond question.

Confronted by the parson's evidence, Mrs. Yerkes said she had never set eyes on the man. On the morning of February 2, however, Mizner corralled a group of reporters, employed a string of horse-drawn taxicabs, and led the ribald procession uptown in Yerkes' electric automobile—on which the gold monogram "C. T. Y." had already been replaced by "W. M." A butler ushered the reporters into the Japanese salon. After keeping them waiting half an hour, Mizner rejoined them.

"Mrs. Mizner has not been well," he said, "and is not dressed for receiving. For that reason, she can appear only on the balcony in the inner court, but from there she will say a few words."

Leading the little band into the Winter Garden, he faced the balcony, waved his arms joyfully, and summoned the bride with an endearing cry described as somewhere between a Swiss yodel and the mating call of a large, ungainly bird. The *American* spelled it "Oo-ee! Oo-ee!"

Mara appeared on cue, wearing a rose-colored silk wrapper, her hair dressed carelessly, and evidently in haste. The representative of the *American*, surprised to find her so beautiful, was inevitably reminded of Juliet as she leaned against a marble column and smiled down charmingly from a height of about twenty feet.

"Is that you?" the bridegroom crooned.

"Yes, dear, I am here."

Mara then confessed the marriage and denied the report that she had given Mizner $1 million as a wedding present. Mizner wryly corroborated the latter statement.

"My husband never expressed a wish that I would not marry again," Mara continued, "but he did elicit from me a promise that I would lie beside him in the mausoleum over there." She waved her hand in the general direction of Brooklyn and dabbed her eyes with a long, filmy handkerchief. She then urged the reporters not to say she was eighty and withdrew.

Later in the day, the management of the Hotel Astor having decided that its reputation could no longer stand the strain of harboring him, the notorious bridegroom moved bag and baggage into the Yerkes mansion. At five P.M. he granted another interview. Mrs.

Yerkes-Mizner by then was sleeping. Mizner showed reporters through the art galleries and tried the Mad King Ludwig's bed for size. "This has got Nome skinned to a finish," he said.

The marriage lasted fifteen days. Thanks to the precautions of Louis Owsley and the trust company in employing detectives to guard the contents of the palace, the Mizner take consisted mainly of Yerkes' personal jewelry. It was damned embarrassing, the bridegroom said, to be frisked by a couple of Pinkertons every time you left your own house. He was also irked by Mara's niggardly attitude toward what he looked upon as community assets. She flatly refused to sign checks. These indignities, aggravated by the growing rumor that when Miss Grigsby's subways had been deducted, there might be no huge checks to sign, tried the bridegroom's patience beyond endurance. On Saint Valentine's Day, after a cyclonic dispute over the size of his allowance, Mizner departed with two suitcases and the Yerkes auto. Mrs. Yerkes-Mizner went into a nervous collapse and had the telephones disconnected.

Ten days later, Louis Owsley presided over a conference with the bride and groom in the library of the palace. Reluctantly, Mizner agreed to a pay-off of $20,000. He pleaded for more, claiming that his professional standing as a shakedown artist would be damaged if it got around that he had accepted such a paltry sum. But Owsley, who had been Yerkes' financial secretary, was a tough man when it came to bargaining. After two hours, Mizner emerged from the palace, looking haggard. He had abandoned all hope of a reconciliation, he told reporters sadly.

The following night Mrs. Yerkes-Mizner, superbly gowned, bared her soul to Viola A. Rodgers of the New York *American*. Miss Rodgers, ensconced in the Vatican Garden, dutifully and masterfully recorded the situation as of the moment.

"The man was after my money," Mara confided bitterly, a cobwebby handkerchief fluttering to her big round eyes. "Will he get it? Never!" Mizner had come to her when she was looking at life through tears, she said. He had read to her from books and sung sad songs to her. How could she know that all his tenderness and spontaneity had been planned the day before? How could she know he sought her only for her money?

The magnificent fountain, Miss Rodgers reported, plashed a musical accompaniment to Mrs. Mizner's words, and bright-hued birds fluttered and twittered among the ferns and palm trees, but love had gone out of the marble window. She had lost all faith in humanity, the mistress of the palace said. She had forsaken the outside world forever. Her solitary remaining friend was a small bulldog, whose shadow Miss Rodgers observed thrown against a marble dado. Save only for the brindle bulldog, named Bully, whose collars always matched her gowns, nothing remained to the disillusioned bride but the memory of a shattered dream.

"I am Mrs. Yerkes," she said sadly, as her eyelids drooped in the mellow light from the candelabra. "I am even Mrs. Charles T. Yerkes, if you will. But from this day forth and forevermore I will never be called Mrs. Wilson Mizner. Never!"

Miss Rodgers herself was very nearly moved to tears at the sight of the beautiful woman, her voice breaking as she reiterated that Charley Yerkes had loved her. Say what they would about the Grigsby woman, had Charley Yerkes not made her swear under oath that she would be buried in Green-Wood Cemetery beside him? What better proof of his devotion could anyone desire? "There I shall be laid away when I am free, as he is," Mrs. Charles T. Yerkes said, sighing heavily and not a little smugly.

As for Mizner, he besieged her to take him back. "He pleads and implores, but I will never yield!"

The next night there was a grand reconciliation. "We had a little quarrel, it is true," said Mara at a dinner she gave in Mizner's honor at the New Netherland Hotel, "but I now know that, but for him, I might have been put in a position where the roof could have been sold over my head."

This sudden reversal was motivated not so much by a reassessment of the bridegroom's virtues as by the bride's transcendent rage at Louis Owsley. In the will, Yerkes had appointed Mara and Owsley coexecutors, but after the wedding, Owsley had persuaded the court, without much difficulty, that it would be a stroke of wisdom to cut off both Mr. and Mrs. Mizner from handling any part of the estate. To add insult to injury, Owsley had hinted to the press that Mrs. Yerkes-Mizner was no more eager to erect a hospital than she was to build a doghouse.

These aspersions upon her competence and philanthropy had driven Mara to seek refuge in both Mizner and the bottle. She summoned the bridegroom to the palace, and together they worked themselves into a fighting mood. There were a great many complications that neither of them understood, but one thing Mara knew: under the dower laws of Illinois, where the will was to be probated, she could retain the palace as her home, will or no will, and receive one third of the estate outright. The post-mortem shower of gold Yerkes had theoretically bestowed upon her was contingent upon her surrendering these rights. Her counterweapon against the archvillainy of Louis Owsley was to refuse to do so. Moreover, the one thing in all the world Mara wanted was the palace. Reporters at the New Netherland Hotel were thrilled to hear that Mrs. Mizner had decided to contest the beautiful will, and that her new husband, armed with the sword of Cromwell from the Yerkes museum, would henceforth be her lord protector. "All I have is his if he wishes," she said, as she looked lovingly into Mizner's big blue eyes.

The reconciliation was short lived. Mara went back to her old habit of not signing checks, and Mizner forgot his role of lord protector and grew violent. In later years his reputation as a raconteur was based to a large extent upon his rollicking experiences as Mrs. Yerkes' husband; but the sordid truth was that, upon his final exit, he beat poor Mara up and tossed her over the balustrade of the marble gallery. When she recovered from her injuries she went into hiding in the old Chicago house, fearing—not without reason—that Mizner would return to poison her or do her further bodily damage. After a few months she got a divorce and resumed the legal right to call herself Mrs. Charles T. Yerkes. Mizner, after one or two attempts to break down the Chicago doors, became preoccupied with running a bawdy hotel in Times Square and lost interest in the Yerkes fortune. Fifth Avenue lacked gameness and romance, he said. Mara returned to New York and settled down to an almost total preoccupation with whisky and finance. For the post-mortem shower of gold was rapidly turning into a cruel mirage.

After threatening a lawsuit, Miss Emilie received her 47,000 subway shares—or substantially their equivalent—and blithely sailed away on another lap of her brief terrestrial passage. Thus the Grigsby woman, after all, as Mara bitterly lamented, managed to enjoy her fortune freely and in peace, while she, Mrs. Charles T. Yerkes, was left to get what she could by aid of the courts of law. Though according to the official appraisal $12 million remained, what she got was precious little.

To Mara, Owsley was the worst of the vultures. She filed numerous bills objecting to his actions, but the judges always ruled against her. She sued for his removal as executor, but though her testimony was eloquent, the courts gave her nothing but sympathy. It was hinted that the Yerkes school of finance had trained its minions far too well, that his pirate methods had been turned against him by a kind of divine justice in the end. But so complicated were the machinations by which the great fortune melted away that it is doubtful if any one person, least of all Mara, ever fully understood them. By a system of magic that only an unraveling of the Chicago traction tangle could explain, the street railway bonds were reduced to a fraction of their value. Other assets had a similar fate. But even the money that was left was consumed by an army of creditors and lawyers.

The city of New York made a feeble effort to secure its phantom benefactions, but soon abandoned the fight as not worth its cost in legal fees. All thought of the hospital and museum was abandoned. Receiverships and foreclosures followed one another in blinding succession. And Mara, who had never been quite sure of the multiplication table, was completely overwhelmed.

Four years she cowered in the mansion, dreading the moment when the last vestige of her lifelong search for glory would be taken from her. Now the songbirds no longer twittered in the indoor gardens. Had she given them away, as she said, or merely opened the marble window? The fountains no longer gurgled; the taxes and the water bills were unpaid. The vaulted dining room was dark, the supper club disbanded; the great chandeliers were never lighted. In her upstairs apartment the mistress of the palace barricaded herself against collectors and process servers. Her face grew puffy, her figure broad and middle aged. She seldom left the house except to go to court, heavily veiled, with a lawyer to protect her from photographers. Surrounded by a multitude of advisers, she would sit on the edge of her bed, dressed in an Empire negligee, playing with her jewels—the famous cabochon ruby, the famous Brunswick diamond—slipping them in and out of their chamois bags, crying out suddenly, not without reason, that this one or that one had been stolen (an emerald brooch had somehow got into the sewing basket of her companion. A topaz ring was nowhere to be found). She hired a motley crew of lawyers, who sued and collected nothing and eventually sued Mara herself. She hired Evangeline Adams to predict the future, which was black.

When at length, in January 1910, one of the London underground railway companies obtained a judgment for $800,000 Yerkes had pledged as a stock subscription, there was nothing left but the palace and the art collection. The United States district court appointed a receiver, and the mansion and its contents passed into his custody. With Mara in her upstairs rooms, detectives patrolled the great halls below, guarding the silver spoons, the Rembrandts, the very chairs that had become a bone of international contention. Low-browed, shabby men with greasy caps walked beneath the palms and leaned against the marble dancing girls, watching the servants and each other, while the receiver's agents listed the Yerkes chattels on sheets of yellow paper.

And then one day bills were posted for the auction of the real estate. The fateful steps of Thomas Kirby were heard in the halls downstairs. The three hundred paintings were removed to the American Art Association's galleries on Madison Square. The thirty rugs were taken from the marble walls and floors; and Rose Lorenz invaded Mara's palace with her yardstick and her cataloguers to prepare the remaining thirteen hundred items for a three-day auction on the premises.

Under a settlement agreement, Mara was promised a share of the auction proceeds. Nonetheless, she was loathe to go. She leased a house on upper Madison Avenue, but Owsley and the receiver would allow her nothing splendid to put in it. Household goods she was entitled to, but what were goods and what was art no one really knew. They let her have some of the van Beers pictures: *Lady Teazle,* the little landscapes, her smiling portrait from that Paris summer twenty years ago. They let her take the broken sets of glassware, a bed or two, some flat silver engraved with her initials and the Yerkes coat of arms. When her inquisitors were not looking she took some other things she liked—an 11-foot marble statue entitled *Vanity;* the miniatures of Mary Stuart and Madame Pompadour; one singing bird in a golden box, the counterpart of many in Miss Emilie's collection. They were things of little value, but Owsley accused her of stealing them and sued for their recovery.

The time drew near for the auction, and still she would not go. Her new house, she said, was no fit place for living. Her servants had had no time to make it ready. Rose Lorenz was not unsympathetic, but the exhibition had to start on schedule. Already Rose's men were building a green velvet platform in the marble gallery for the sale of the sculpture and bric-a-brac. At last, three days before the first session of the picture sale, Mara was persuaded to go to a hotel. On an April Saturday night she departed.

She wore her sables and her jewels, as if to hide her breaking heart, a feathered hat, a trailing gown. The guards tipped their greasy caps as she descended the marble staircase, followed by her retinue of servants. Rose Lorenz silenced the hammers of her workmen with a movement of her yardstick. There was a swish of silk, no other sound. There was a ripple of the wrist, a head held high, as high perhaps as Marie Antoinette's when she left Versailles. If the auction boys had thought to see her cry, they were unacquainted with her habits. The bronze doors swung open. A stranger walking in the April evening (it was the warmest April ever known) would have said she was going to the opera, except for the sixty trunks piled on wagons in the street. She turned and looked a moment at the brownstone portico. Then she climbed into her motor, and with her sixty trunks of dresses, drove off to the Plaza Hotel.

When the Yerkes rugs and pictures went on exhibition at the AAA, the press, no longer under obligation to relish the feast of culture that was to have contributed to the uplift of the masses, took a superior attitude. The canvases, some writers said, were blackish; the rugs were worn and threadbare; and since nothing fails like failure, Yerkes was accused of lacking "individual judgment."

The American Art Association published two huge illustrated catalogues—one for the pictures, to be sold at Mendelssohn Hall; one for the rugs, tapestries, sculptures, and "rich and costly furniture and embellishments." The rugs were pictured in color and carefully described by John Kimberly Mumford, but in the case of the paintings the descriptions were merely copied from those in Yerkes' files. *Town Topics,* in attempting to reconcile the propaganda with the pictures, "smiled and groaned," and waxing chummy with its many readers, reminded them that "You and I, dear skeptic . . . know that the making of a pedigree is a fine art." The Barbizon canvases "reasserted the virtues of the Men of 1830," *Town Topics'* ultra-sophisticated amateur confided, but if you knew Rembrandt and Hals (and what reader of *Town Topics* did not?), you would be sparing in praise of the *Rabbi* attributed to the former and the *Old Woman* that would do no credit to the latter.

It is true that the pictures, if they had remained together, would have made a dreary showing. But many of the Yerkes paintings were good; and whereas the people writing in the papers knew little about art, the Duveens and Knoedlers and Seligmanns knew a very great deal.

All the quality dealers had clients eager to acquire the best of Yerkes' canvases, for the era of the golden water faucets had arrived, and the demand for concomitant authenticity in art far exceeded the supply. The Duveen Brothers, especially, were anxious to distribute certain of the Yerkes pictures among the disciples they were educating to be connoisseurs. To that end, at the eleventh hour, the Duveens approached Owsley with a blanket offer of $1,250,000 for the contents of the mansion intact. With profits of perhaps $400,000 hovering in the balance, Kirby was understandably distressed.

Only recently he had lost what might have been the greatest sale in the history of the AAA. After James Henry (Silent) Smith's ill-fated honeymoon the Whitney mansion with its Stanford White embellishments passed to a nephew who worried about its upkeep for two or three years and then commissioned the AAA to sell it, lock, stock, and barrel. Kirby had published a rare catalogue matching, if not surpassing, the radiance of its subject. But the book was so beautiful that it backfired. When Harry Payne Whitney read the glowing tribute to his father's bank account he impulsively bought back the old homestead for $3 million—as a sentimental gesture, he said—and the prodigious Mrs. Harry Payne (Gertrude Vanderbilt) Whitney moved in, with heaven only knew how many trunks, just as the wretched Mrs. Yerkes was moving out of her rival palace across the street.

Now a second fiasco threatened. Owsley and eight or nine of the creditors' lawyers—not one of whom knew a van Beers from a Watteau—were all for accepting the Duveen offer. Kirby remonstrated that the pictures alone would bring incomparably more at auction. "Can you guarantee it?" a traction expert demanded. No, Kirby could not. There were no precedents for such a sale. But the art trade stood on the threshold of historic times. Millionaires were crying for Rembrandts as babies cried for mothers' milk. Some of them knew what they were buying, and some did not. In an auction the good pictures would carry the bad, and all would take the glory road together.

All the same, it seemed to the lawyers that the Duveens had offered a fair price. Nonsense, Kirby said. There was no such thing as a fair price from a picture dealer. Though predicated on the most delicate expressions of man's soul, the art trade was, if anything, more cutthroat than the streetcar business. If the Duveens had offered a million and a quarter, they already knew where they could sell the cream of the collection for two and a quarter. But, after all, the market was limited, and those same clients would be in the front rows at the auction.

After a few tense sessions, Kirby won Owsley over, and the lawyers went away, their palms still itching for their respective cuts in this last windfall of the Yerkes fortune. But three days later, the lawyers were back. This time they had a top secret offer of $750,000 for only thirty of the pictures. "Which thirty?" Kirby snapped.

Owsley and the lawyers had sworn not to tell.

"Who offered it?"

That was the deepest part of the secret. The AAA could continue with its auction, but the lawyers demanded that the secret buyer first be allowed to withdraw his selections.

Kirby saw himself as another victim of the four-year crow feast over the dwindling Yerkes riches. With the jewels missing from the crown, the splendid picture auction would be no more sensational than T. J. Blakeslee's annual clearance. He telephoned the receiver and demanded authority to place a public announcement in the next day's papers guaranteeing that everything in the mansion would be included in the sale. He had no faith in this appeal, for on the face of it, a dealer wishing to snag the chief remaining assets of the Yerkes estate would have been unbelievably remiss not to have made his proposition worthwhile to the one man with the legal right to sell them. But the receiver was strangely affable. "Just you hold the wire a minute," he told Kirby.

After a moment, he returned. "Mr. Auctioneer," he said, "I have read the order of the United States district court, and it states explicitly that this collection is to be sold at *public* sale. . . . Go ahead!"

* * *

It was a stifling hot night April 5, 1910, when the first group of pictures went on sale. Ironically, the news of the day centered on the Yerkes Observatory. The sky watchers endowed with the largest telescope in the world had announced that Halley's comet was rising and might "surprise us by an unusual development." Some apprehension was caused by a rumor that the comet's tail contained poison and "might end the human race." But the audience that gathered in Mendelssohn Hall appeared sublimely indifferent to such forebodings.

Pair by pair, the comic opera lords and ladies of that short-lived epoch that was to fade into oblivion with the coming war made their stately progress down the center aisle—the Alger boys grown gray, the second-generation wealthy, the victims of a high sophistication measured by the pedigree of the English butler and the degree of authenticity in one's Corot. White shirt fronts and Romney dresses were banked up to the back wall of the auditorium—ladies in evening wraps of marabou and chiffon, ladies in hobble skirts restricting their steps to a snail's pace, long-waisted ladies with boas made of songbirds' feathers, heavy ladies drooping with chenille tassles, their feet pinched into long, slender shoes with Louis XV wooden heels. There were ladies with hats like cart wheels, ladies iridescent with the plumage of the barnyard, wearing turbans trimmed with roosters' heads or hats with pheasants' tails floating out behind.

Mrs. Harry Payne (Gertrude Vanderbilt) Whitney looked like an eel, a critic of the new skintight fashions reported. There were Olympian gentlemen with side whiskers and big financial voices. There was an exuberance of salon diction, a potpourri of perfumes, the adjusting of lorgnettes, a tiara here and there with a long chignon of curls drooping from the rear. There were Goulds, Goelets, Millses, and Fishes; Armours from Chicago; Wideners from Philadelphia. There were old competitors of Yerkes who ordinarily did not "go for art," the winners, as it were, gathered before the chips of the loser, the dog assembled to consume the dog.

Conspicuous as they were, the members of this showy pageant did not comprise the backbone of the bidding element. It would be the dealer-experts who would make or break the sale. Scattered through the hall were not only the moguls of the American picture trade but many Europeans as well. London and Paris were of course represented, but there were also men in dark, wrinkled suits, with arrogant, inscrutable faces, who had traveled from The Hague, Cologne, Brussels, Berlin, Munich, and other fountainheads of mellow culture to buy back at wholesale prices the pictures they had sold to Yerkes in a less inflated market. It was because of these men that Kirby began the opening session in a bitter and cantankerous mood.

Only the night before, he had been told that the foreign dealers had organized a combine, in accordance with the shady European custom, to introduce the Knockout system at the Yerkes sale. Vows not to bid against one another had been taken by both foreign and native dealers, Kirby's informants told him; and Kirby knew that if the Ring were to operate successfully, his most spectacular auction could turn into a spectacular fiasco, perhaps even—in the face of the offers that had been rejected—into the destruction of the AAA.

Half suspecting a serious plot to wreck his long sovereignty over the élite public sales, Kirby worked himself into an acid state of mind and made a bold decision. If there appeared to be no competition among the professionals, he would stop the sale and expose the Knockout system once and for all before the astonished public. He knew the names of some of the dealers who had joined the Ring. He would point an accusing finger at them and charge them with interfering with the sale of property consigned to him by a United States district court. Then he would descend from the rostrum in a blaze of righteousness and ethics.

The future of picture selling in America might conceivably have been different if all this had taken place, but it did not. Though Kirby entered the rostrum seething with premeditated vituperation, no sooner had the first picture been sold than he began to smile. Lot No. 1 was a wretched 4¼-by-12-inch van Beers, entitled *Return, Sweet Bird,* that had been generously appraised at $25. It fell to a society woman for $1,025.

A few minutes later Joseph Israels' *The Frugal Meal* went to Knoedler for $19,500, after the customary heated contest. When Alma-Tadema's *Spring* fell to the Chicago dealer Henry Reinhardt for $22,600 Kirby was convinced that the dreaded Ring was inoperative.

Most of the pictures catalogued for the first night's session were the old academic staples that had been the height of fashion when Yerkes was stocking his Chicago gallery. But so varied and devil-may-care was the audience that even the artists scorned by the Barbizon disciples of 1910 found eager bidders. In the rear of the hall sat the smaller millionaire, accompanied by his wife and family, the son stuffed unwillingly into a tuxedo for an evening of enforced culture, the daughter diaphanous in gauze and dewy eyed with art appreciation. Many were the whispered consultations among these little families, many the moments of flurried indecision. They were hoping for a Corot, of course, to glamorize the dining room; but the Corots would not be coming up until the second evening, and meanwhile, if something fairly chic—a "Fagot Gatherers" for instance, or a "Peasants Merrymaking"—should go for a mere few thousand, papa might be tempted. A papa somewhere in the hall was tempted to go $10,000 for a Professor Ludwig Knaus. An army colonel, wearing all his medals, paid a like sum for the 7-foot painted-to-order Bouguereau of a bare-bosomed wench fending off seven sexy pubescent male angels.

The prices were not all high. Meissonier's stock, for instance, appeared to have at long last declined. *The Reconnaissance,* which had cost Yerkes $13,500, would budge no higher than $5,300. Sir Edward Burne-Jones of the Pre-Raphaelite Brotherhood also showed a marked decline. *The Princess Led to the Dragon,* which had cost Yerkes $12,500 in 1901, went to Captain Joseph Raphael De Lamar (after a mild struggle with Mrs. George Bliss, who got *The Princess Chained to the Tree*) for $2,050.

Win, lose, or draw, Captain De Lamar—dubbed by the newspapers "the American Count of Monte Cristo"—was a client after the auctioneer's own heart. He had begun life as a Dutch sailor. Later he had gone West, picking up a million here and a million there in the two-gun wilderness of Idaho and Colorado. Now, with his pile—some said $20 million, some said $40 million—he maintained two famous yachts, homes in Paris, Glen Cove, and the West, and principally, the huge granite fortress (later the headquarters of the National Democratic Club) he built on the northeast corner of Madison Avenue and 37th Street, across from J. P. Morgan's brownstone mansion. There, in the roseate glow of stained-glass windows, surrounded by the milk-white marble maidens from A. T. Stewart's palace, the taciturn, unsociable Captain played the organ and accumulated things of beauty. He was no connoisseur, *Art News* once explained loftily, not having had the opportunity in his early years to study and acquire taste. But taste or not, the Captain was no penny pincher; and it was thanks in large part to his impromptu boosting that Kirby was able to observe that the members of the Ring were looking glum. He girded his loins for the second session and predicted that the Barbizon and English pictures would prove his contention that the great art boom was on.

They did indeed. "No such art sale ever took place in America," the front page story in the *Sun* began, the morning after the second session. "Records fell about Mr. Kirby like glasses swept from a table, and he went on talking as if nothing had happened. . . . The dollars seemed to be rolling along the floor and from the gallery of the hall like water flowing from a Croton tap."

At the start, Howard McCormick broke the existing Corot record by bidding $52,100 for *Morning*. But McCormick remained a hero for only a moment. As soon as the applause died down, Henry J. Duveen nobly demonstrated his lack of sympathy with the Ring by calling $80,500 for Corot's *The Fisherman*, followed by $60,500 for Troyon's *Going to Market*. Scott and Fowles, bidding for their prize stable of Barbizon clients, paid $30,100 for *Gathering Fagots* by Diaz, $26,100 for Théodore Rousseau's *Paysage du Berry*, and $44,100 for Millet's *The Pig Killers*.

But all this was only a prelude to the avalanche of rolling dollars incited by Joseph Mallord William Turner in the last half of the evening.

When *Rockets and Blue Lights* came to the block, only the honor students among the connoisseurs applauded. It was known that Yerkes had paid about $78,000 for the picture and had kept it in his London office as a prestige factor, to impress the monied lords of Britain. But on exhibition at the AAA, Turner's misty ships and sprays of vivid color had moved no one to ecstatic contemplation. Sententious critics looking for the "meaning" in such a costly picture had called it "incomprehensible but nonetheless impressive." For despite Turner's solid reputation in England, there was no overwhelming craze for him in America—until the price of *Rockets* placed him, as the *Times* put it, "among the kings of the auction room."

Kirby started the bidding at $50,000. The spectators leaned forward in their seats, and according to one observer, not a feather stirred, not a substantial breath was drawn, until the dreamlike seascape (subsequently to hang in the Charles M. Schwab mansion on

Riverside Drive) had fallen to Duveen at $129,000, far and away the highest price—for the moment at least—a picture had ever brought at public sale in the United States.

"Well, for one thing," an underbidder said, wiping the perspiration from his brow as he left the hall, "this will stop the old fellows from talking about the Mary Jane Morgan sale."

Mary Jane had held the heavyweight auction title for twenty-four years, but the Yerkes receipts had already surpassed the total for her paintings, and half of Yerkes' pictures remained to be sold.

Turner held his championship not twenty-four years, but twenty-four hours. For the following evening was Old Masters night. Fear of being poisoned by Halley's comet had given way to the more immediate dread of Eugene V. Debs, who had chosen April 7 to inflame the multitude at Cooper Union; but the champagne set gathered before Kirby's rostrum in full regalia, as before.

Rembrandt, as exemplified in the Yerkes gallery, did not achieve the lofty status of either Turner or Corot. Nevertheless, the *Portrait of a Rabbi* chosen by *Town Topics* as a target of its ill-considered cynicism went to Ambrose Monell for $51,400. The second object of *Town Topics'* scorn, Frans Hals's *Portrait of a Woman*, not only made the highest price of the Yerkes sale but held the record for seventeen years as the most costly painting to pass through an American auction hall.

The New York Times, in commenting on the wonder of it all, said:

The dear old Dutch woman whose portrait Frans Hals painted more than 400 years ago [the date 1635, but the *Times's* art department was understandably befuddled that morning] could never have dreamed, if her practical soul was given to anything in the nature of visions, of ever being worth, in any form, so very many thousand dollars. She was the calmest looking person in the hall last night and when the curtains were drawn aside and she was revealed sitting quietly in her big chair, a wide ruff around her plump throat, a close cap encircling her placid face, one hand at her waist as she sat primly for her portrait, the other at her side, clasping her Bible . . . there was enthusiastic applause.

The Hals had cost Yerkes $35,000 in Paris in 1893. Now all the dealers helped the dear old woman on her marvelous levitation. As she passed the high-water mark of Turner's *Rockets*, amid cheering from the fans, the contest settled down to Knoedler and Duveen.

Knoedler got her for $137,000. He was bidding for H. C. Frick, and the plain old woman now reposes among the aristocrats of the Frick mansion—for all to see and enjoy in perpetuity, as Yerkes had intended.

A few of the better pictures and many of the grim brown canvases with brass plaques bearing illustrious names went back to Europe with the arrogant gentlemen in wrinkled suits. But Kirby and his spendthrift audience saw to it that they did not go too cheaply. When the dealer-experts balked at poor quality or lack of pedigree, some rash art lover would almost always jump into the fray. Although the *Evening Sun* bluntly stated that "the by ordinary standards well-to-do were made unpleasantly familiar with the limitations of their income," in reality there was something for everyone and someone who wanted everything.

The 7-foot-tall *Wolfgang, Duke of Nieubourg,* for instance, that had inspired a good deal of awed comment from art writers who imagined, with Yerkes, that it was a masterpiece by Van Dyck, failed to impress the experts of 1910. Nobody knew how many tens of thousands Yerkes had paid Blakeslee for it, but it fell to Mrs. J. W. N. Cardeza for $2,500. Mrs. Cardeza was also moved to pay $6,200 for a little "Raphael" called *The Holy Family and the Sparrow.* With the Raphaels fairly well guarded in the museums of Europe, and the Van Dycks among the most expensive paintings in the world, Mrs. Cardeza could be said to have equipped her parlor grandly, with a minimum of outlay.

Almost inevitably Harry Payne Whitney and the incorrigible Mrs. Gertrude (nee Vanderbilt) contributed a moment of hilarity. The sporty Whitneys had taken a fancy to the Venetian scenes by Guardi. The first two were Guardis of considerable insignificance, but the couple who could have, bought the whole Yerkes collection without unbalancing their yearly budget sat in the front row haggling over the little panels shamelessly at $50 and $25 advances. When the two panels fell to Whitney at $1,250 each, close observers noted a twinkle in old Henry Duveen's eye as he glanced down his nose at the bargain-hunting multimillionaires. A somewhat larger panel came up, depicting the Grand Canal. Duveen let the haggling go on for a little and then casually raised the bid $500. Whitney cautiously threw in another $50. Duveen raised $500 again, and again, until the *Grand Canal,* in striking contrast to its companion pieces, had soared to

$17,000. Then, defending his honor with a lordly flourish, Whitney jumped to $20,000. Duveen, simulating despair at such incontestable munificence, shook his head and Kirby let the hammer fall. Whitney stood up in his place. "You made me pay for that," he said, wagging his finger roguishly at Duveen as the audience burst into laughter.

Some of the historic rugs in the unique collection, the scattering of which is still lamented by textile scholars, did not fare as well as even the mediocre pictures. In his introduction to the weighty catalogue that is now a rare book in reference libraries John Kimberly Mumford wrote:

Having enjoyed to a flattering degree the confidence of Mr. Yerkes with regard to this collection, the writer is by way of knowing, as most people cannot know, the sincerity and fine unselfishness which prompted the making of it; wherefore, incomplete as it is, it stands, to me, a memorial more eloquent than bronze. That circumstances have decreed its dissolution is more than regrettable, and I cannot let pass the final opportunity to pay to the man who made it, and to the spirit which impelled him, the tribute of admiration and esteem.

The tribute paid in cold cash was less effusive. Seligmann & Company bid $33,000 for the 40-foot Persian state carpet that had given the floor of the marble gallery its glow of imperial magnificence. Of the three carpets that had been trodden for four centuries by the bare feet of Shiite devotees in the Sufi mosque of Ardebil, one went to the Metropolitan Museum for $15,200, the second went to Duveen Brothers for $35,500, and the third—as distinguished, in Mumford's view, as the famous Ardebil rug in the South Kensington Museum— fell to Captain De Lamar at $27,000. But some of the significant documents of weaving went for $4,000 and $5,000. The combined total for the thirty rugs—a few of which went into the cache of Vitall (the Pasha) to await a further toning of the taste—was only $281,950, a fraction of what Yerkes had paid for them.

The rug prices, however, caused no lull in the mounting excitement. On the fourth, and last, night of the picture sale, after sending a "Botticelli" on its way for $1,550, Kirby paused to observe a milestone. "The returns from this sale," he announced, "have now reached the two-million-dollar mark. And I can tell it by a two-million-dollar smile on the face of the executor."

Owsley's smile was actually a sheepish grin. The thirty pictures he had wanted to sell for $750,000 had brought the tidy sum of $1,308,000.

"Happy, happy auctioneer!" exclaimed a *Globe* editorial writer in a piece entitled "New York's Art Supremacy." "Happy, happy buyers! When in Phidian Athens were such prices paid for combinations of pigment and canvas, or in Medicean Florence or in Venice of the doges or in Milan of the Visconti!"

There remained to be sold the mansion itself and its "costly furniture and embellishments." With Rose Lorenz acting as hostess, the crowd gathered on three successive days for what amounted to a looting expedition. It was the only call the élite ever made.

Mrs. Cornelius Vanderbilt got ten marble vases for $400. Mrs. Hermann Oelrichs paid slightly more for an ormolu candelabrum. Mrs. Harry Payne (Gertrude Vanderbilt) Whitney, in the headgear of an East Indian coolie, went up to $750 for a Louis XV carved and gilded thing that defied description. E. H. Litchfield of Brooklyn got the sword of Cromwell for $1,500. Hearst got a knife and fork for $25.

Captain De Lamar had the best time of all and came away most heavily laden. Among his many gleanings were seven marble statues, the poetic Chartran ceiling from the music room, and the Mad King's bed. Some people said Yerkes had paid $40,000 for the bed; some said $30,000; some $25,000; and some $10,000. The Captain got it for $1,400, perhaps because Rose Lorenz had been impelled to admit that it was not really the Mad King's bed after all, but one just like it. The golden bed of the King of Belgium had disappeared. Perhaps that, too, was a phantom.

The sacking of the Yerkes palace revealed some shockingly low prices, notably in the marble gallery. A *Bacchante* by Falconet for which Yerkes had paid $32,500 fell to Samuel Untermyer for $2,000. A hilarious bronze *Bacchante* by Frederick W. MacMonnies, the other cast of which had been banished from the Boston Public Library as immoral, brought $8,000 from an emancipated Bostonian who announced his intention of loaning it to the Boston Museum. The female figure, alone, Kirby's art lovers could tolerate, but when it came to amorous undraped couples in marble, they blushed and sat on their hands. The two superb groups by Rodin, *Cupid and Psyche* and *Orpheus and Eurydice,* went at bargain-basement prices. Thomas

Fortune Ryan bought them both—one for $1,800, the other for $2,000—and gave them to the Metropolitan Museum.

The work of sculpture that brought the highest price was Houdon's life-size bronze *Diana*, the famous work that had inspired the Saint-Gaudens statue atop Madison Square Garden. Houdon had made three casts of his *Diana*—originally executed for Catherine II and refused by the Salon of 1781 because, said the jury, a huntress, however chaste in expression, had to wear a little something, lest she be taken for a handmaiden of Venus. One of the Houdon *Dianas* was in the Louvre; another in the museum at Tours; and the third, Yerkes had bought for $70,000. At the auction Duveen Brothers took the Yerkes cast for $51,000.

At noon on the first day of the house sale, a real estate auctioneer attempted to sell the palace and its annexes. The offering was unique in that never before had a Fifth Avenue mansion been placed under the hammer with an upset price of $1,400,000—the minimum bid specified by the receiver. About a hundred men gathered in the marble gallery to watch the sport, but purchaser there was none. The upset price was removed and the property was sold for $1,239,000. Fifteen years later Thomas Fortune Ryan, who in 1908 had a house constructed that occupied the adjoining site, tore the Yerkes mansion down and used the ground to enlarge his flower garden.

When nothing was left, not even the sinister air plant from the balcony of the Winter Garden, Kirby announced his total: $2,207,-866.10. This, added to the price of the real estate, was enough to pay the lawyers and the creditors, with some left over for Mara. Nothing remained to perpetuate the Yerkes name but the largest telescope in the world (out in Wisconsin the stargazers announced that Halley's comet appeared to be disintegrating as it moved off toward the sun) and the Greek mausoleum over in Brooklyn. People said for a time that Mara, her plumes crushed under yards of gossamer veils, would drive up and down outside the palace, staring at its windows, boarded up, waiting for the wrecker. It may have been her ghost they saw, for exactly a year after her eviction, Mara died—of pneumonia and a broken heart. She was laid away in the seamless bronze casket beside Charley Yerkes, but even there, she was threatened with eviction. Two years later Green-Wood Cemetery was suing Louis Owsley for the $15,000 Yerkes' beautiful will had provided for the maintenance of his tomb.

SIX

BIBLIOMANIA

KIRBY TOOK PAINS to preserve a vainglorious autocracy within his own doors, but it was inevitable that competition should arise from without, for there were those who looked with longing eyes at the proud activities of the AAA. Many were the stripling auction houses that rose and fell. On the average, about a thousand purporting to dispense some kind of art could be found in operation throughout the country in any given year. Kirby's old employers, M. Thomas & Sons, continued to hold estate sales in Philadelphia until the firm was absorbed by Samuel T. Freeman in 1908. Freeman's, now the oldest auction company in the United States, often sold the trappings of local aristocrats, but art auctions in Philadelphia were unlikely to have a national significance. The Samuel T. Freeman Company, then as now, derived its prosperity more from machinery and real estate than from pictures and peachbloom vases. Sales of minor importance were held in Boston and Chicago, and occasionally in New York a second-string auctioneer would boast a consignment associated with opulence of the second class. But the inroads were small. Until the head-on attack of the Anderson Auction Company, rarely did a lesser house obtain a sale that Kirby had not already rejected.

It was the rise of bibliomania that first threatened the sovereignty of the AAA. Not that the titans took up reading, but as the great culture hunt gained momentum, many colossi of the financial world began to look upon a collection of expensive books as a banner of prestige almost as rewarding as the indispensable gallery of Barbizons.

Kirby had conducted book sales whenever the consignor's name was prominent enough to add luster to the AAA. Early in the Madison Square pageant, the auction of Henry Ward Beecher's library had given the élite an opportunity to acquire a well-bound tract or two on the cardinal virtues as selected by the scandal-tarnished sage of Brooklyn. In 1889 S. L. M. Barlow died of apoplexy following the swindling of his law firm by a clerk who had taken too literally the example set by its lordly clients. The decorations of Barlow's famous mansion on Madison Square, though said to be "the richest in

America," made a modest showing in the cold light of the auction hall. But his library was superb. It contained many of the most· valuable American historical books and manuscripts extant: Livingston's correspondence (more than a thousand original letters, bound in eight volumes); the Chalmers papers (twenty-one volumes of manuscript on Canada and the Colonies); *The Log Book of Paul Jones: A True Copie of the Court Booke of the Governor and Society of the Massachusetts Bay in New England,* which sold for $6,500. The total for the 2,780 lots was a little more than $85,000, a sum the newspapers of 1890 considered excessive. Thirty-three years later Kirby remarked that the Barlow collection would have brought at least $1 million in the postwar Americana market.

Following the Barlow auction, Kirby held a profit-taking sale of "rare Oriental porcelains and jades, Japanese swords and lacquers, and very valuable books and manuscripts gathered by the well-known amateur General Brayton Ives." Well known Ives certainly was. A pint-size Yankee Civil War general, with a mean and military set of side whiskers, he is remembered to this day as the most pompous champion of enlightenment who ever strutted through the auction halls. He haunted the AAA constantly until his demise in 1914, buying, selling, and commanding; but so ulcerous was his personality that the time came when no one who had ever known him, not even the dealers, would add fire to the heated contest over anything he wished to sell. (In the end, Yale was Ives's only friend. He left most of his million-dollar fortune to his old alma mater, cutting off his wife and daughter without a penny, for their "unfilial and harsh conduct," which, he said, had caused him great sorrow.) In 1891, however, the Ives boycott was not yet widespread. Among his crystal balls and peachbloom rouge boxes he had a Gutenberg Bible with seventeen pages missing. Kirby sold it for $14,800—then the highest price a book had brought in an American auction.

After that, literary sales dwindled off at the AAA until 1900, when Kirby sold the effects of Augustin Daly, including the huge library of stage history the renowned producer had gathered through his long theatrical career. Daly's books, prints, manuscripts, and autographs brought $166,000, the record total for a book sale held in the United States. On more than one account, the event was a milestone; for it was at the Daly auction that a cyclonic young man named George D.

Smith opened his campaign to persuade a bauble-hungry public that books were no longer books, but bibelots, and priceless.

G. D. Smith's name is still spoken in awed accents by traders old enough to have witnessed his grandstand performances at the auctions. He was a beefy, bald-headed man, with a thick dark mustache and an abundance of that manly swagger commonly associated with clubhouses and caucus rooms. In 1900 he was thirty and hell-bent on establishing himself as kingpin promoter of two princely sports: horse racing and the gathering of literary rarities. With a view to deliberately manipulating the book market like a Wall Street "situation," he bought nearly a third of Augustin Daly's library, grandly pushing the bids to unprecedented levels. Far from resenting Smith's bullish tactics, the conservative shopkeepers threw their caps in the air and welcomed the inflated value of their stocks. And well they may have rejoiced. In the first two decades of the new century G. D. Smith was to glamorize the idea of book collecting to a point where the most unlettered millionaire was loath to die without a library in his testament.

The messianic book salesman had adopted the auctions as his propaganda medium, but he was not fond of Kirby; and Kirby, for his part, was no more than tolerant of books. During the next ten years it was the soaring price of art that kept the AAA in a state of perpetual celebration; and as it turned out, G. D. Smith's more spectacular performances took place at the Anderson.

When John Anderson, Jr., opened a small book auction house on West 30th Street in February 1900, it is unlikely that Kirby even noticed, much less looked upon him as a competitor. Nevertheless, it was the dawn of a great new century, one that culture vendors believed would see the splendor of the titans surpass anything ever known in Europe; and John Anderson, as well as the next man, was full of proclamations. If the right kind of auction service was provided, he declared, book collectors in this country would soon outnumber those of any other time or nation. But while his pronouncements had the familiar ring of those Kirby had made fifteen years earlier, John Anderson's beginnings were far more modest. His first establishment was a gaunt room patterned after Sotheby's in London. The auctioneer—a man named George D. Morse, imported from

Boston—droned the traditional patter at a long table, with the bidders seated to his right and left like poker players intent upon a deadly game. Appropriately enough, it was a bookish atmosphere, but hardly one to lure the high life and the carriage trade.

Three years later Anderson invested $9,000 in the good will of Bangs and Company, the oldest book auction house in New York. With his new prestige, he moved to more commodious quarters and changed the Anderson Galleries to a more high-sounding title—the Anderson Auction Company. But the free spenders were still able to suppress their glee. For in truth, though his name was to echo through the lore of public sales for almost forty years, John Anderson himself was not the man to set the auction world on fire.

He was a dreamer—he called himself a "knowist"—a forager endlessly prowling after the neglected masterpiece that was to make his fortune. Anderson was forty-five when he established his auction gallery. He had been trading in old books and prints all his life; but, he said, he had only bought books because they were cheaper than pictures. Whenever he had money he went on a treasure hunt to Europe, and it was on one of his foraging expeditions in England that he turned up his most significant contribution to the auctions—not a picture or a library, but a young man named Arthur Swann.

Swann, more than a half century later, recalled the circumstances under which he allowed himself to be discovered, as he recalled just about everything else of moment to his dedicated calling.

It was in the summer of 1901 that a gentleman came to browse in Captain William Jaggard's bookshop in Liverpool, where Swann was employed. He was looking for Shakespeareana, the gentleman said, in an unmistakable Yankee accent. (He was not, of course. He was about to board the steamer home, and hoping to pick up a last-minute print or drawing for twopence in a place so little given to art as Liverpool.) Young Swann, on the other hand, was looking for a job.

"Are you in the trade?" Swann asked, while displaying Captain Jaggard's stock of works pertaining to the Bard.

"Not exactly in the trade, no. I have been a print seller all my life. My name is John Anderson."

They talked for an hour or so. Swann, then in his middle twenties, was an up-and-coming young man. He was short and trim, doubtless with the tendency (so marked in later years) to bound a little, like a hard rubber ball barely capable of restraint. His conversation, though touched with worldly wisdom, would not have been without a glint of humor. Cockney overtones, which he never wholly lost, may have given his words a musical and charming twist. Anderson would not have failed to notice the puckish smile that enlivened his honest English face.

The afternoon was young and drowsy. There was no need for the young book clerk to leave out any of the details of his own small life—of how at the age of thirteen he had gone to work in the bookshop of James Miles in his native Leeds, of how he had worked for eleven years at a salary of five bob a week with hours from eight-thirty in the morning to seven at night, of how he had made the tea and polished the brass and swept the floor and kept the thieves away from the front, where the books were displayed in open racks on the street. And sandwiched in between his mild adventures was a demonstration of the veritable encyclopedia of bibliographical knowledge that had got him the job of manager in Captain Jaggard's shop.

But Swann was dissatisfied in his present job. Reading was no passion of the citizens of Liverpool, and book collectors were almost as scarce as fanciers of shrunken heads. He disliked the place intensely, and as it happened, he had been thinking of moving on. "If I ever went to New York," he asked somewhere toward the end of his narrative, "would I be able to find a job?"

Anderson looked at him a moment. "It would be nice," he said, "if you could be ready to leave at four this afternoon."

Swann did not, of course, walk out on Captain Jaggard so precipitously, but in the weeks that followed, he speculated on the wisdom of pulling up stakes and journeying into what he thought of as the colonial unknown. While he was ruminating, a bookseller from India came into the shop—also looking for Shakespeareana, he said. The gentleman from India was even more drawn to the wonder boy of Liverpool than John Anderson had been. Moreover, his offer of employment had the virtue of tangibility. Anderson had been vague and pleasant, promising little beyond a kind of fatherly sponsorship. India perhaps needed an accomplished bibliographer less than the gentleman imagined; and yet, America was not a wholly enticing goal. In Swann's bookish head there were familiar images of saucer-eyed clerks arriving in the land of milk and honey with their worldly goods tied in kerchiefs on the ends of sticks, only to sleep on counters and labor fourteen hours a day for bare subsistence.

All the same, the bleakness of Liverpool hovered like a pall. One night after choir practice, walking home through the somber streets, listening to the foghorns moaning in the great commercial harbor, talking to himself for want of better company, the restless book clerk came to grips with indecision. "Well," he remembered saying, "well, Arthur, I think you will go somewhere. In fact, Arthur, you are going either to America or to India. Which shall it be?"

In the circle of yellow light under the next gas lamp he stopped and flipped a coin. "Heads, New York; India, tails," he said to his shadow sternly as the penny jangled on the pavement. It came up heads. Swann walked briskly to his lodgings and spent the night writing a long letter to John Anderson, Jr.

Months passed before Anderson replied. The mail had been delayed, he said. Moreover, the letter he was now writing must not be looked upon as a guarantee of employment or as an inducement to cross the ocean. Such baiting promises, having gone so often unfulfilled, were now forbidden by the immigration authorities. Nevertheless, Anderson's admiration for the Swann talents, far from diminishing, had grown in retrospect. If he should decide to make the journey, unbaited and uninduced, Anderson would be glad to receive him as a guest. He must, of course, pay his own passage—the law was explicit on that point too—and he must have £7.10 in his possession to avoid becoming a public charge.

Swann read what he could between the lines, and decided to take the plunge. With seven and ten concealed on his person and the rest of his fortune invested in a one-way passage, he finally set out for America in the summer of 1902.

Upon his arrival, Mr. and Mrs. Anderson treated him like a son. Ensconced in their spare bedroom, he spent a few weeks getting his bearings, perceiving with his own eyes the evidence of New York's monstrous wealth, observing the clang and bustle that was changing Manhattan Island into a giant fantasy of tall buildings and Renaissance palazzi. On his walks, he would pause to watch the stonecutters—immigrants from Europe with centuries of craftsmanship behind their strong arms and grimy faces—as they turned the far reaches of Fifth Avenue into a solid mass of spurious antiquity. Mushroom castles though they might be, the new palaces were indicative of a hunger for gracious living. Not one of them but had a library that would need filling! New York appealed to Swann immensely. He saw at a glance that the rich parishioners could, if they would, buy no end of antique books.

In the fall Swann was made assistant cataloguer under Edward Turnbull, a bibliographer who had been making Anderson's auction catalogues since the beginning in 1900. There was plenty of work to be done; especially after Bangs and Company was absorbed. On the whole, they were successful, if dull and attended mainly by the shopkeepers. For the next few years the Anderson Auction Company did well enough in a routine kind of way, but something was lacking. When all was said and done, the auction business was, in Swann's view, only a little more stimulating than the bookstore he had left behind in Liverpool.

What was wanting, Swann believed, was glamour—if not in the rostrum, at least in the surroundings, and above all, in the catalogues. He was quick to see that one of the secrets of Kirby's success was the de luxe art catalogue. But in those days book catalogues were cryptic lists written mainly for the trade. If the propaganda could be made sufficiently enticing, Arthur Swann was certain that many of the private buyers who swarmed the AAA to wrangle over a few brown trees on a canvas could be tempted by the more enduring charms of books.

On the other hand, John Anderson's notion of the right kind of auction house was a place for "knowists" like himself. Swann belabored him with his ideas for needling the book trade, and eventually, as Swann put it, "turning American book auctions into open-house parties." Anderson listened, with one ear at least. As a beginning, he consented to issue larger catalogues, with here and there an artful phrase. But Swann was discontent with halfway measures. He continued to harp on his main theme—"how best to create the desire to own"—until at last, in 1907, after five years of angling for the job, he was made chief cataloguer.

It looked then as if Swann was on the road to transforming John Anderson's lackluster conclaves into a veritable orgy of open-house parties; but Anderson, for all his high pronouncements, was no doughty man of trade. He was losing interest in the book sales. Within a few months he sold the Anderson Auction Company and went back to the quest for undiscovered pictures.

The business John Anderson sold at the age of fifty-three would probably have made his fortune, but Anderson was no man to take the direct approach to wealth. Like a barkeep given to drink, he was happier on the other side of the rail; and there he stayed, in the limbo of the obsessed collector, until he died, in 1941, at the age of eighty-six. His name first reappears in auction annals in 1916, eight years after he sold his gallery, when he consigned to Kirby his "Important Collection of Paintings by the Great Masters" and picked up the tab for a plush sale at the Hotel Plaza. With the money he received for the Anderson Auction Company, he had gone to Europe and bought an unholy mess of stuff, his notion being that pictures painted by the masters not only did not look like pictures by the masters but were likely to turn up in the most unlikely places.

It had always been his ambition, the voluble "knowist" wrote in an introduction to the AAA catalogue, "to possess at least one good, authentic picture by one of the acknowledged great painters of the world." Now, having enjoyed "the inestimable privilege of travel" his cup verily ranneth over. He had a Rembrandt, a Raphael, a Hubert van Eyck, no less; not to mention eighty-four other pictures "by the old and modern masters." But, he warned, "great paintings, by great masters, do not grow on trees or bushes, to be plucked by the casual passer-by." His introductory sermon was studded with maxims for collectors wishing to emulate his "high ideals." All of his advice was fascinating, but it could be pretty well summed up in a single sentence. Pay no attention to signatures, he urged, or to the lack of them. The pigment may have faded.

The result was one of the silliest auctions Kirby ever conducted. A few quaint customers, looking very seedy in the gilded ballroom of the Plaza, bid up to $85 for "examples" christened with the most resounding names. A "Velásquez" Anderson called *Portrait of a Happy Spanish Beggar* even soared to $200. A water color actually signed "J. M. W. Turner" brought the highest price—$510.

It was fitting that the laurels of the sale, withered though they were, should have been carried off by Turner. In the ensuing years Turner-hunting became John Anderson's main occupation, his total passion, a lust that passed the bounds of reason into monomania. It was, of course, the "unknown Turner" that Anderson sought. He had no use for Turners that anyone could tell were Turners, for of the unknown variety there was, in his opinion, an unlimited supply.

This view was supported to some extent by vagaries known to have existed in the prolific English painter's life. Unmarried, and attached to no one but his father, who was a barber, Turner had partially lost his bearings after the death of the old man in 1830. Sometimes he would imagine himself a sea captain and desert his fine Queen Anne Street house to hide for a time in obscure lodgings along the Thames. Sometimes he would wander back to the scenes of his youth—to the old seaport of Margate, where, in a blue seagoing coat he would regale the children of the neighborhood with made-up tales of his adventures on the sailing ships he loved to paint. But, all the while, Turner was making pictures. In the seventy-six years of his life he produced a mountain of oils, water colors, and drawings, to say nothing of numberless plates for etchings, mezzotints, and engravings. A tremendously popular artist, he amassed a fortune of £140,-000, which, upon his death in 1851, he left to found a charity for the "maintenance and support of male decayed artists, being born in England, and of English parents only; and of lawful issue." All his leftover art he bequeathed to the British nation: some 282 paintings and more than nineteen thousand drawings. The decayed artists never saw any of the cash. (Most of it went to lawyers, for Turner's language was crude, his will a masterpiece of loopholes.) But the National Gallery got the pictures and there they had always remained, well out of the reach of John Anderson, Jr.

The unknown Turners came from no sources that might have had Turners for sale, but from old English houses where Turner may have slept, from flea markets, from obscure shopkeepers blissfully unaware that their stocks were rife with forgotten works by the master. Though to produce the incredible number of signed pictures preserved in England and elsewhere throughout the world, Turner would have had to average more than one finished piece every day of his life, John Anderson was convinced that there was still another Turner, if not on every bush, at least behind it. The old artist had been a very queer man, his latter-day admirer invariably pointed out, and there was no way of knowing what he did with his hypothetical leisure. On the premise that it was dedicated to a kind of frenzied mass production, Anderson, in his scroungings, gathered an estimated ten thousand unsigned water colors and drawings, all of which he was convinced were the work of Joseph Mallord William Turner.

As time went on, however, Anderson decided that his unsigned

Turners were signed after all. To prove it he wrote a book called *The Unknown Turner* and published it in a handsome folio edition at his own expense. Secretive and eccentric, Turner had been inclined to put his worst foot forward, Anderson said in his book. Being so eccentric, he had delighted in signing his name and then covering it up. He had loved to mystify people, and though a poor speller, he had been addicted to microscopic handwriting. Somewhere, on every unknown Turner, some kind of signature could be found: on a sail, a hat, a spade, in the eye of a bird or the wick of a candle, in the wings of a butterfly, on the leg of a cow. A good strong lens was needed to detect those microscopic scratches, and even so, they were written in symbols that the ordinary person could not comprehend. Though many witnesses peered through many microscopes, only John Anderson could see those cabalistic signatures.

It took Anderson twenty-five years to gather his Turners. Meanwhile, to provide the wherewithal for his search, he kept a book and print shop on Madison Square, downstairs in the building occupied by the AAA. Some of his clients had their lamp shades covered with Turners; others had their doors papered with them. But the bulk of the unknown Turners were deposited for safekeeping in a vault of the Brooklyn Trust Company; and there, like a miser poring over the coupons on his bonds—while the gallery that bore his name was growing into the second most important auction house in the country—John Anderson would sit with his magnifying glass, surrounded by his ten thousand sheets of paper.

By a coincidence that would probably be meaningful to a fortune-teller, the name of the man to whom John Anderson sold his auction company was Turner. A tall, pleasant, one-armed veteran of the Civil War, Major Emory S. Turner was no more than superficially informed on the subject of rare books, but he was a forthright businessman. He retained Swann as his technical expert, and though without the money to carry them out, listened sympathetically to those visionary schemes for promoting bookish house parties. For the Anderson star was on the rise. No sooner had the new regime taken over than a small bonanza appeared by way of the stock market crash of 1907 and the timely misfortunes of a Mr. Poor.

Henry W. Poor—whose name was kept alive for years on *Poor's Railroad Manual* and is still seen on financial textbooks—was second-generation wealthy and correspondingly proud. He was a Harvard man, a music lover, an art lover, a book lover, a snob. He had a house in Tuxedo Park, two houses in Gramercy Park. His art treasures had been provided by Stanford White, who, needless to say, had been "commissioned to search Europe for them." His library (of unread books) was reported to have "hardly an equal in the country." But it was with his left hand that Mr. Poor indulged in all these high-brow recreations. With his right, he manipulated securities in leather and rice, grabbing, it was said, a cool $5 million from his paper work in those commodities alone. When he attempted to hatch up a sugar empire, however, he missed the mark. All his papier-mâché corporations came tumbling about his head. Gone with the foul wind of the 1907 panic were his house in Tuxedo Park, his houses in Gramercy Park, his *Railroad Manual* profits, and the gleanings of the late, lamented Stanford White. Every last rubber plant and statue was seized by creditors and bailiffs—and eventually sold by Kirby at the AAA.

The ruined Mr. Poor's sole recourse from suicide or work was his library, and Major Turner was happy to cooperate in salvaging that. Stealthily, by night, before the sheriff quite knew what was happening, the Anderson men moved to a warehouse the fallen culture hound's first edition of the *Imitation of Christ*, along with some six thousand other rare books. There, Arthur Swann prepared a catalogue almost as sumptuous as he would have wished. It was composed of five bound volumes, with many plates and facsimiles interspersed with 750 pages of seductive description.

By the time the catalogue had been printed, the depression of 1908 had set in. Major Turner was beginning to wonder who would buy the books that were to keep the wolf from devouring Mr. Poor, when George D. Smith came stomping into the Anderson.

"I've got a new one," Smith said. "His name is Mr. Jones. I'm bringing him down to see the books."

In the eight years since his blustering appearance at the Augustin Daly sale, G. D. Smith had not been idle. Though it was said that his knowledge of letters was something less than dazzling, his blunt, unsubtle ways were a joy to men who would not have listened to a scholar for ten seconds. Though not a reading man himself, he had a genius for inspiring citizens with excess profits to spend them on the preservation of the printed word. "When the rulers of kingdoms today have crumbled into the dust and their names are forgotten by the people," he would declaim with the fervor of an apocalyptic prophet, "the memory of a maker of a great collection will be a household word in the mouths of thousands. This is the real road to fame!"

Many took to the road, with G. D. Smith in the lead and setting the tolls, but none so munificent as the "new one," Mr. Jones—alias Henry E. Huntington.

In 1908 H. E. Huntington was fifty-eight years old. He had recently sold his West Coast trolley cars to the Harriman combine for $50 million, but he still retained control of numerous shipbuilding companies and railways. He had not yet married Mrs. Arabella D. Y. Huntington, the widow of his rich uncle Collis P. That combined *coup d'amour* and *coup d'état* took place in 1913, representing a stroke of management worthy of old C. P. himself, in that by joining the two main heirs in the bonds of autumn matrimony, it added the limitless to the limitless. Nor had H. E., in 1908, as yet enrolled as a full-time student of the Duveens, for art, at least in its advanced stages, was more in Arabella's line. But Henry was greatly drawn to the books. At the moment, he belonged wholly, if somewhat tentatively, to G. D. Smith.

A bulky, handsome man, nervous about being cheated, naïvely imagining that if Smith introduced him as Mr. Jones, he would be traveling incognito, the "new one" came in the dead of night to the back room of the Anderson. He had a great, bushy mustache and perhaps the shrewdest eyes ever set in a gray old titan's head. Wearing his plug hat, his wing collar, and his big pearl stickpin, he passed quickly among the rows of books, with Swann's delightful catalogue in his hand. "Get me that—that—that," he said, in his vigorous, peremptory manner, tapping the volumes quickly with his forefinger. A minimum of effort was wasted on deliberation, but by the time Swann said good night to Mr. Jones, things were looking up for both the Anderson and the bankrupt Mr. Poor. G. D. Smith had virtually unlimited bids for all the best books in the auction.

The Poor sale ran along for nearly five months, and thanks to Uncle Henry—as the Anderson employees began to call the old gentleman who had decided to form the greatest private library in the world—it turned out to be the most profitable book auction that had yet been held in the United States.

Henry E. Huntington, American railway executive and book collector (BROWN BROTHERS).

Sometimes Uncle Henry would appear unheralded behind the scenes. "Do you think Smith is running up the prices on me—working in with the auctioneer?" he would ask one of the boys in the back room.

The boys, of course, knew nothing of whatever complex machinations Smith might be using to increase the value of Poor's treasure. But they grew fond of the modest titan who, in the presence of workingmen, always tried to give the impression that he was just an ordinary businessman whose luck was running high.

"Good day today, son," he would pretend to boast, jingling a pocketful of those $20 gold pieces that used to be given out as directors' fees. "My spending money," he would explain. Sometimes he would pause long enough to give the young men a word of friendly advice on how to get ahead. "The habit of saving paves the road to wealth," he would tell them. "Save a little every week, and when you get an increase of wages or salary, continue to live within the former limits and *save* the increase." The boys listened to the jangling of gold in Uncle Henry's trousers and made commendable resolves.

Huntington bought nearly a third of the library, and then, when the spoils of Poor had finally been exhausted, an event occurred that was of far more importance to the book-collecting world than the fall of Mr. Poor, more productive than the panic even—which had caused the possessions of so many small-time losers to flow into the big-time winners' vaults. It was the death of Robert Hoe.

In an ordinary brownstone house at 11 East 36th Street, across Madison Avenue from the Villa Medici J. Pierpont Morgan had caused McKim, Mead and White to build to house his books, Robert Hoe had somewhat less ostentatiously gathered the largest private library in the country. Only a few months before Hoe's death, at the age of seventy, in 1909, Morgan had permitted a reporter to publish in the London *Times* the "First Authorized Description" of that "most carefully, jealously guarded treasure-house in the world." The writer, an Englishman and bibliophile of sorts, had gone hog wild with superlatives. Morgan himself was called a genius. His palace, let alone its thirty shelves of Bibles, its manuscripts, its jeweled volumes in glass cases (". . . how they were ever allowed to leave the United Kingdom is incomprehensible!") compared favorably, the breathless reporter said, with the extravagances of Lorenzo—nay, with the wonders of the Forbidden City in Peking. The bronze doors of Morgan were "as fine in workmanship as those of the Baptistry at Florence"; his steel vault contained, one of the headlines ran, "The Most Wonderful of All Collections by the Most Wonderful Collector, Perhaps, of Any Time."

Nevertheless, across the street, in Hoe's dowdy brownstone, a collection existed, not as rich perhaps in jeweled bindings, but more extensive in its categories and more overwhelming by the sheer number of its rarities.

A pauper compared to Morgan (he had only $8 million when he died), Robert Hoe was also a far simpler man—though not as simple as he would have had the public believe. In 1886 he had succeeded his uncle Richard Hoe as head of the printing press factories the first Robert Hoe had established in New York and London at the beginning of the century. Richard Hoe, of the second generation, had invented the rotary press that produced the miracle of the modern newspaper. The third-generation Robert Hoe, in his turn, increased the speed of the presses, perfected the rotary art press, and developed the color presses that, among other things, added the comics to the Sunday supplements. But for a nineteenth-century titan of industry, Robert Hoe's official biography was short. As secretive as Morgan, and twice as conventional, he would talk fluently on almost any subject but himself. When asked for biographical details, he would point to the new double sextuple press and say, "There is the book of my life. It is all written there."

It was not quite all written there. Even as a boy, Hoe had been fascinated as much by the golden fruits of the presses as by the mechanical fantasy of their operations. As an apprentice in his uncle's factory, a boy with no more than a common school education, he had gone hungry to buy books with his lunch money. In later years, as his fortune increased along with the speed of the presses, the nine rooms of Hoe's house on 36th Street became a cluttered arsenal of the history of bookmaking. From basement to attic, volumes were packed like sardines, two deep in bookcases piled upon bookcases. Here, long before they were expensive jewels in the auction rooms, Hoe gathered the books that had belonged to kings. Here, to take a volume down at random, was the Roman Missal, a manuscript on vellum presented June 2, 1420, to Henry V of England by Charles VI of France on the occasion of Henry's marriage to the French king's daughter, Catherine of Valois. Somewhere in the labyrinth of that bulging house were more than 250 such manuscripts, the life toil of many nameless monks—dazzling books, illuminated in colors brighter than on any canvas, embellished with the miniatures of many golden-haloed saints.

Reverently stored somewhere in those rows of locked bookcases were more than 150 incunabula: the first printed editions of Homer and Euclid, the first book printed in Greek, a copy of the original edition of *Roman de la Rose,* two copies of the Gutenberg Bible. Here, if he could find it, the colossus of the presses could feast his eyes on the fourth book printed at Venice—St. Augustine's *City of God,* a folio richly illuminated in gold and printed on vellum by the brothers John and Wendelin of Speyer. Somewhere, behind some other books, were no less than twelve volumes from the press of Nicolas Jenson, who was sent by Charles VII to Mainz to learn the art of printing from Gutenberg. Here were four examples of William Caxton,

England's first printer, among them Sir Thomas Malory's *Le Morte d'Arthur*, dated 1484, and the first edition of the *Canterbury Tales* that was printed in Westminster Abbey during 1477 and 1478.

A mere list of Hoe's books written by English authors before the year 1700 filled six closely printed volumes. The four folios of Shakespeare were there, of course, and no less than fifteen quartos, including the famous *Hamlet* of 1611. In an upper room, where not even the housekeeper was allowed to dust, Hoe could caress the mosaic bindings by Nicolas and Clovis Eve, by Padeloup and Derome, bindings in morocco and Levant of every hue and color, embroidered bindings, bindings made from tortoise shell or inlaid with emeralds and gold. He could finger a book of poems bound for Henry II, or peruse a history of Italy in a magnificent cover made for the bibliophile king Henry III. He could fondle—though it was hard to read—*La Lyre de Jeune Apollon*, bound in 1657 for the Archbishop of Paris. In another mood, he could read a page or two from Queen Elizabeth's *Private Book of Christian Prayer and Meditation*, dated 1569. In still a farther room were the sixteenth-century bindings, glowing with heraldic badges, made for that other great book lover Jean Grolier de Servières, in whose memory Hoe, with eight other bibliophiles, founded the Grolier Club in 1884. And if, perchance, his mind should wander to the pleasure

> That valleys, groves, hills and fields
> Woods or steepy mountain yields,

he could choose among fifty different editions of *The Compleat Angler*.

Among his sixteen thousand books, if ever they had been put in order, Hoe could follow the course of American history, choosing for a start the letters of Columbus, printed in 1493, and continuing with one of the four existing copies of the letter of Amerigo Vespucci printed in Paris in 1503 or 1504. He could look for the first printed reference in English to the discovery of America in his first edition of *The Ship of Fools* by Sebastian Brant, a folio published in London in 1509. Though the language was foreign and the subject matter dry, he could glance at the first book printed in the Western Hemisphere, a theological treatise published in Mexico City, probably in 1539, a hundred years before the Bay Psalm Book. Surfeited by the excellencies and oddities of printing, he could climb another flight and unlock cupboards stacked with modern manuscripts—those of Washington Irving, for example, or long, interesting letters grease-stained by the midnight candle of Edgar Allan Poe.

But the chances are Robert Hoe seldom found time to rummage through those lowering ebony cupboards. His cache of rarities not-withstanding, he was no moldy bookworm and perhaps in no proper sense a bookworm at all. He collected rare cattle, of all things, with almost as much enthusiasm as books, and kept them on model farms in Westchester County, New York. In the house on 36th Street he raised a sprawling brood of children, and there, too, as if the place were not already bursting at the seams, he delved immoderately into the subject of art.

Weaving her way through four and a half centuries of printing, Mrs. Hoe (who, incidentally, was an heiress in her own right) could set her table with German silver of the fifteenth century. She could tell the time of day, albeit with no great accuracy, by any number of old French clocks. A small, sweet-faced, simple-hearted woman, she dwelt among medieval reliquaries, Hispano-Moresque porcelains, Li-moges enamels, the busts of many famous personages. She could feast her eyes on the Painted Ladies, on Daubigny or Gérôme, on works of the Flemish and Italian primitives. But it is unlikely that she did, or that she ever so much as opened one of those fascinating relics of literary history. She preferred to read the daily paper. None of her fortune went for folderols, but in her ninety-eight years she crossed the Atlantic 154 times, for she was as restless as a flitting bird. Gentle, and perhaps a little overwhelmed by her husband's lordliness, she occupied herself—when not on the high seas—with charitable enter-prises; and sometimes she would give a reception with music in whatever space she could clear among those formidable bookcases locked and double-locked like so many Bluebeard's closets.

All in all, the dynastic Hoes lived a decorous life in the grand tradition of industrial suzerainty—stern, secretive, and as far as any-one knew, rigidly righteous. It was not until two years after Robert Hoe had been buried, with a mournful coterie of bibliophiles standing at respectful attention, that an errant English lady, discreetly unre-membered in the will, made a grab for a piece of the Hoe fortune and added a human touch to the sparse biography of the deceased. Then, in 1911, the scandal-printing papers flowed from the giant presses with deliciously indelicate stories. In London, it seems, there had been a secret passage leading from the house next door to the formal residence where Mrs. Hoe had so long given the British version of those charitable teas. The regrettable Mrs. Brown, who lived beyond the sliding panel, publicly confessed to such carryings on as would have done credit to Casanova, let alone the bookish, aged Mr. Hoe. "Door Ever Locked When Mr. Hoe Was With Mrs. Brown" the speedy presses of the *World* revealed in black headlines, and Mrs. Brown, who also had a number of other aliases, even transported a pair of fulsome cockney servant girls to New York to testify how, behind those locked doors, Hoe had customarily taken his bath and then ceremoniously prepared a perfumed tub for Mrs. Brown.

But by 1911, when all this distressing information began to appear, the high-minded papers were more properly concerned with the historic auction of Hoe's books.

In his will Hoe had written, "I specifically authorize my Executors to sell at auction either in this country or in Europe all my furniture, personal property, works of art and library, especially authorizing them as to my books to take expert advice and sell the same either in London, Paris or New York as they shall deem most advantageous to my estate." The millions and the great Hoe factories were left in seven equal parts to Hoe's six surviving children and a grandchild, but no one of the seven heirs received a book. The money would be theirs. If they liked his treasures well enough, they could bid for them at auction.

Naturally, Hoe's executors were besieged by the criers of London, Paris, and New York, and naturally, Kirby assumed that the job of putting Hoe's things back into circulation would be his. The usual "private interests" offered $1,250,000 for the contents of the house outright—books, pictures, bibelots, and all. They were summarily turned down. For Hoe, in his still wisdom, had left his posthumous affairs in the hands of men both incorruptible and able.

One of the two lawyers he had named to settle his estate was Phineas P. Chew, whose brother, Beverly Chew, is still remembered as "the most knowledgeable book collector this country has ever had." Beverly Chew was a lovable old gentleman without an enemy in the world, a man in every way beyond reproach. He was neither wealthy nor competitive, nor did he have any commercial ax to grind, and because his advice was free, he was looked upon as a kind of ambassador without portfolio throughout the inner circle of biblio-philes. Having long been Hoe's close friend, he knew the quality of Hoe's treasure as no one else was capable of knowing it. Clearly the expert advice the executors were enjoined to take would come from him. When, therefore, the conservative Mr. Chew hazarded a guess that the library alone in that creaking house was worth between a million dollars and a million and a half, the book world and the rich world began to be agog.

In the natural course of events, the art sale was entrusted to Kirby. But the executors continued to deliberate about the books. English bibliopoles offered the opinion that no great library could be sold to advantage in America, the land of insubstantial culture. London, by long tradition, was the world center of the trade in antique literature, with Paris a close second. The few important book sales that had been held in the United States had not attracted many European bookmen as bidders.

The unruffled executors listened, but they also understood that they lived in changing times. Morgan had been for years the greedi-est book buyer in the world, and while he had duplicates of many of Hoe's prizes, there were many he did not have. G. D. Smith and his "new one" had clearly set out to rival Morgan's Forbidden City on 36th Street; and while Morgan had bought most of his books in London and Paris, Huntington had never yet set foot in Europe. After many weighty conferences, the executors decided to take a chance on America's millionaires and hold the auction in New York. The London booksellers pursed their lips and predicted bargain day.

The next question to be settled was the auspices under which the sale should be held. The AAA was the obvious choice, but Major Turner, with the successful Poor sale to bolster his prestige, presented strong arguments in favor of the Anderson. Swann, who looked upon the Hoe treasure as the opportunity of a lifetime, stuffed Turner's head daily with fresh statistics and other verbal ammunition with which to bombard the executors. But as the deliberations continued, it was clear that Kirby, with his glamour and his long record of respon-sibility, was about to win. The eleventh hour came. Major Turner, aware that he was about to fail, appealed to Swann to think up a last-minute approach—any manner of new persuasion that might swing the balance in the Anderson's favor.

Swann racked his brain until, out of the far recesses of his memory, the shadow of an idea came. Somewhere, in some English journal—when, he did not know—he had seen an article criticizing the AAA for its absurd conduct of a book sale. It was a long time ago, and whether or not the piece had been of real significance he could not now recall. Probably he had not even read it. And yet, the Hoe executors were counting heavily on the foreign bidders. A blistering review of Kirby's shortcomings as a literary auctioneer, coming from England, where the élite public took such matters seriously, might well influence the decision. But how to find a half-forgotten article by some antiquarian bookman whose name he did not even know?

All night Swann lay awake, going over the names of English literary journals and the names of those carping little men who contributed to them. The morning came, and no one of them had rung a bell. When the public library opened, he was waiting on the steps. The number of Englishmen who had written on the subject of rare books comprised an appalling percentage of the population, but there was one, named William Roberts, who appeared to have a sharp tongue and a low opinion of American auctions.

Back at the gallery, Swann relayed his vague findings to Major Turner. It was a long chance, but would Turner pay for a cable to this man Roberts on the chance that he had been the one to damn Thomas Kirby? Major Turner hated to spend money, but he was grasping at straws. The cable was sent, with the answer hopefully prepaid. Within two hours, the return message came. "It was I," Mr. Roberts replied, "in *The Athenaeum*, March 24, 1900."

In no time, Swann had a transcript. And what a delightful piece it was! The subject was no minor book sale, but the great Augustin Daly auction, which Kirby listed among his historic victories. Roberts had not attended the sale. His article—and it was many pages long—dealt exclusively with the catalogue, the subject nearest to Swann's heart.

"Beyond excellence of paper and typography," Mr. Roberts had begun,

it is difficult to say much in favour of the sale catalogue of the late Mr. Augustin Daly's library. . . . The whole transaction appears to have been carried out with precipitation and with a fine disregard of the interests of the Daly estate. . . . Those who know anything at all about these matters do not need to be told that London is an infinitely better market for such a collection than New York. The books and autographs, for one thing, would have been adequately catalogued; the catalogue as it now stands would be a credit to a third-rate provincial auctioneer.

Mr. Roberts was no mean authority, and from this juicy start, he had gone on to expose the bibliographical naïveté of the AAA almost lot by lot. It seems that nothing had been right; and the venerable *Athenaeum* was a journal that delighted in pinpointing errors. "The late Mr. Daly," Roberts said, "was a princely collector, and a fitting memorial of his singular good luck and excellent judgement would have been of the highest permanent value. . . . His library . . . in its somewhat special way is possibly the finest of its kind ever formed."

Clearly, anyone with the patience to wade through all that tedious documentation would have got the impression that Kirby had thrown the whole kit and caboodle to the dogs. This was not precisely fair. Whether the catalogue was right or wrong, the AAA had sold Daly's books and papers for at least twice the money they would have brought in an auction dominated by the London book ring. But Mr. Roberts and Arthur Swann, no less than the Hoe executors, were sticklers for precision.

Before another day had passed, Major Turner had delivered this sobering document to the lawyers. What transpired at the subsequent deliberations Swann was never privileged to know, but within a fortnight the Hoe book sale had been awarded to the Anderson Auction Company.

Kirby was outraged. It was the first time in twenty-five years he had felt the blow of competition. As if to flaunt the incontestable superiority of the AAA, he and Rose Lorenz prepared a four-volume de luxe folio catalogue glorifying Hoe's household decorations as if they had been imported straight from the Louvre. But the long art sale, which ran from February 15 to March 3, 1911, was a pale second to the Yerkes extravaganza of the year before. Hoe had put his best efforts into his library. A Rembrandt called *Young Girl Holding Out a Medal on a Chain* fetched $70,500, but there were no other sensational prices. The total for 4,801 lots was $604,607.

Meanwhile, the Anderson Auction Company was preparing for the book sale with maddening exuberance. New capital was put into the firm by William K. Bixby of Saint Louis, who was himself an indefatigable collector of manuscripts. With Bixby's contribution, Major

Turner moved the gallery to a vacant mansion, formerly the residence of Clarence M. Hyde, at Madison Avenue and 40th Street. Though a temporary shelter, the Hyde mansion was a place in the sun easily comparable to the American Art Association's galleries on Madison Square, and a perfect setting for those open-house parties Swann had longed to give.

The Hoe catalogue that took shape in Swann's imagination was to be not only as precise as William Roberts and *The Athenaeum* could have wished, it was to stand as a monument to the integrity of the Anderson, to the avidity of the deceased Mr. Hoe, and above all, to the bibliographical talents of its maker. To that end, Swann moved into the book-jammed house on 36th Street and began the prodigious task of sorting that mine of literary treasure, weeding out its duplicates and its not inconsiderable lode of censorable pornography (sold to G. D. Smith under the table), and describing the remainder in eight encyclopedic volumes, which record 14,588 rare items.

Somehow the work was accomplished in record time, partly because Swann's assistants were an up-and-coming crew. Among them was Arthur Wyler, whose backstairs anecdotes of the old Anderson would fill volumes. John J. Gaffney was there, a lean and taciturn bookworm who served the auctions for more than half a century as cataloguer of English literature. The wagon that hauled the books was driven by R. Milton Mitchill and loaded by his son R. Milton Mitchill, Jr., who was to make his mark in auction history as the ill-starred president of the American Art Association–Anderson Galleries. But the most book-struck of all was Anthony N. Bade, a bean-pole-slender recruit from the tenement wilderness of New York's upper East Side, whose salary was then $4 a week.

A dream-beguiled lad roaming the streets after school in search of some clue to a better world, Tony Bade had often stood with his nose pressed against the window of a secondhand bookshop kept by Emory F. Hanaburg on East 106th Street, on the fringes of the Harlem slums. There were no fine books in the tenement where Tony lived with his mother, and it seemed to him that Mr. Hanaburg's shop must certainly contain all the secrets of the universe. He came back again and again to stare longingly into those windows. One day Mr. Hanaburg noticed him and came out. "Can I show you something, boy?" he asked.

"Gosh, no, mister. I'm just looking. I haven't any money."

"Come on in anyhow," Hanaburg said. He led the patched, self-conscious Tony into the shop and showed him all his rarest books.

After that Tony Bade had his secret refuge. Emory Hanaburg, who worked part time as an expert at the Anderson, was a renegade scholar doomed to obscurity by a misplaced affection for the bottle. A man of infinite kindness, he continued to befriend the fragile-looking lad with the lean face and wistful smile and eager, penetrating eyes. It was not often that a youth in Hanaburg's locality was willing to spend endless hours poring over old books. He taught Tony what he could, and when, at seventeen, it was clear that the boy would have to forgo his dream of studying architecture and go to work, he sent him to the Anderson to get a job.

Now, tremulous with wonder at this intimate contact with the greatest private library in the country, Hanaburg's protégé found himself in the rare situation of being able to leaf through not one, but two Gutenberg Bibles. Modest as he was, no such wild thought occurred to him as that, in time to come, he would stand before the moguls of bookdom and sell not only a Gutenberg Bible but substantially all the other literary treasures that were to pass through the New York auction halls over a period of more than thirty years. Certainly it would not have entered the mind of the frail youth so recently recruited from the dense anonymity of New York's tenements that the press would one day refer to him as the Anthony Eden of auctioneers—even if there had been an Anthony Eden then to symbolize the refinements of discourse from the rostrum.

But for all the bookselling adventures the future was to bring forth, neither Swann nor any member of his crew was ever to forget the overwhelming evidence of the collector's spirit in the labyrinth of Hoe's disheveled brownstone. On the morning of the first day's labor, Mrs. Hoe appeared at the foot of the staircase.

"What are you doing, boys?" she asked.

"Packing up, ma'am," Arthur Wyler said.

The charitable old lady was depressed by the prospect of so much labor. "Why don't you just get a lot of potato sacks," she suggested in a kindly, helpful way.

The catalogue, to Swann's lifelong sorrow, did not turn out to be as splendid as he had envisioned. With a view to getting the great sale under way, Major Turner required that Hoe's library be divided into four parts and catalogued in four separate alphabets, with the four two-volume sections published at intervals as they were completed. This, Swann thought, diminished the impact that a single alphabetical listing would have made. Moreover, in the interest of economy, Major Turner limited the number of illustrations and even imposed a degree of reticence on Swann's annotations and descriptions. Nevertheless, the eight closely printed volumes, comprising 1,691 pages and a mine of historical information, represent to this day one of the most fascinating bibliographical documents extant.

Major Turner may have been miserly about the catalogue, but he was not stingy with the publicity. When all the preparations had been· made, bibliophiles in every corner of the Western Hemisphere were aware that New York was to have an auction the like of which the book world had not seen before and perhaps would never see again. By April 1911, when the exhibition opened, European bookmen were craning their necks at New York's skyscrapers, vowing not to bid against one another, and bragging that all the important books would go back across the ocean.

Never before had booksellers from abroad traveled to America for a sale. They were a cocky lot, but Swann and Turner smiled when spies translated their muttered comments in the salons of the Hyde mansion. For night after night, when Madame Theophile Bélin of Paris and the pompous Dr. Ludwig Baer of Frankfort had departed, Uncle Henry Huntington would arrive by the servants' entrance. G. D. Smith had recently bought him $1 million worth of Americana from the collection of E. Dwight Church of Brooklyn, and Beverly Chew was about to sell him his library of English authors for half a million; but Huntington had barely begun on his monument at San Marino, California. "Get that . . . get that . . . that and that," he would snap at Smith as he browsed among the shelves, jangling the gold coins in his pocket. And before many nights had passed, there was an "H" on at least every other page of Smith's catalogue.

The sale began the afternoon of April 24, 1911. For seventy-nine sessions the bookly gentlemen gathered in the little theater atop the old Hyde mansion. Each separate joust was memorable, but none was more festive than the first night meeting, when Hoe's vellum copy of the Gutenberg Bible appeared upon the block.

At the time of the Hoe sale about 457 years had passed since the 42-

line Bible is presumed to have left the press at Mainz. In 1911 even the meticulous Mr. Roberts would not have quibbled with Swann's description of it as the first printed book. It had held that title for more than a century and a half, despite the fact that the oldest known printed book was made in China from wood blocks in the year corresponding to A.D. 868, plus the certainty that the Chinese were printing from movable type four centuries before the principle was independently discovered in Europe. The Constance Missal (one of the four copies known to exist was purchased by the Morgan Library in 1954) was thought for a while to be the oldest European typographical book. The Missal is a crude experimental work once believed to have been turned out by Johann Gutenberg a few years before the completion of the Bible. But nowadays it is generally accepted that it was printed sometime after the Gutenberg Bible.

It is also not certain that the so-called Gutenberg Bible was printed by Gutenberg, although he emerges through the centuries as in all likelihood the inventor of the first practical printing type.

But these and other qualifying footnotes to the traditional claims for the Bible printed at Mainz cannot alter its imponderable significance. The 42-line Bible, heralding the great humanist movement that was to sweep away the darkness of the Middle Ages and open the door to the development of modern civilization, stood in the fifteenth century—and it stands today—as the first concrete proof of the tangible reality of the art of artificial writing. Add to its symbolic stature the beauty and perfection of its pages—evidence that a craft so long in coming burst full-blown upon Europe somewhere between 1454 and 1456—and the Gutenberg Bible, with or without its status as the first of first editions, looms less as a bookman's curiosity than as the initial dazzling ray of a man-made sun. It is truly one of the wonders of the world.

Scholars have estimated that the edition of the Bible printed at Mainz consisted of from 150 to 180 paper copies (of which thirty-four have survived) and perhaps thirty on vellum, twelve of which are still extant. In 1911 there were seven copies in the United States, five on paper, two on vellum.

The first Gutenberg Bible to come to this country, the one now in the New York Public Library, was bought for James Lenox by his London agent in 1847. The cost was £500, or $2,500, and the opinion was freely expressed that Mr. Lenox had taken leave of his senses to pay such a "mad price" for a book. In fact, Mr. Lenox agreed. Only after much reflection and a great deal of angry correspondence did he consent to pay for it and clear it through the customs.

The second Gutenberg Bible to come to America, also a paper copy, was the one Kirby sold for General Brayton Ives in 1891. It had been bought in England in 1872 for George Brinley of Hartford, Connecticut. At the Brinley auction in 1881 it sold for $8,000, to a New York lawyer who in turn sold it to Brayton Ives for $10,000. The dealer who bid it in for $14,800 at the AAA in 1891 sold it to James Ellsworth of Chicago, at a profit of about 100 per cent, and Ellsworth still owned it in 1911. Up to the time of the Hoe sale, this was the only copy that had appeared at an American auction.

In addition to the Ellsworth and Lenox Bibles there was, and still is, a paper copy in an almost perfect state of preservation at the General Theological Seminary in New York, the gift of the seminary's onetime dean, The Very Reverend Dr. Eugene Augustus Hoffman.

All four of the remaining Gutenberg Bibles in America were the property of J. P. Morgan and the Hoe estate. Each collection had one paper copy and one vellum.

Described as "the handsomest and most richly decorated Gutenberg Bible in existence," Hoe's vellum copy was indeed a thing of beauty. Except for two missing pages, which had been replaced in facsimile, its 641 unnumbered leaves could not have been more fresh and crisp the day they left the press at Mainz. Its Latin words, in black, stately type, modeled on the handwriting of the period, were as clear as the latest headlines from the great Hoe presses. In addition, Hoe's copy was adorned with exquisitely painted capital letters and illuminated miniature initials. Many pages had marginal decorations —birds, flowers, fruit, monkeys, grotesques—and there were running titles of the sacred books in blue and red. The two huge folio volumes, the Old Testament and the New, were bound in the original oak boards covered with pigskin, sealed with eight metal clasps and studded with twenty ornamental bosses.

It would have been hard indeed to imagine a more distinguished treasure submitted to the cold reality of the auction block; though, to be sure, this one had appeared before. Fourteen years earlier it had been knocked down to Bernard Quaritch in a London auction room for the sterling equivalent of $20,000—less, certainly, than Kirby was getting at the time for a flock of Troyon sheep, but then the highest price a Gutenberg Bible had ever brought at auction and the second highest bid ever made for a printed book. (The world's record stood, in 1911, at $24,750, the price paid by Quaritch in 1884 for the Mainz Psalter now in the Morgan Library.) Robert Hoe had paid Quaritch $25,000 for his Bible; and now Bernard Alfred Quaritch, the son of the man who had sold it to Hoe, was sitting in the front row at the Anderson, bent, everyone imagined, on toting the famous book back home again.

The warming-up session of the sale, in the afternoon, had been conducted by Daniel R. Kennedy, Major Turner's regular auctioneer. But for the evening meet, Sidney Hodgson of London had been imported to assist the local talent. Hodgson, with his cultured British accents, was only one of the subtle touches of refinement planned to make Kirby's bluff performances at the AAA look like whooping vaudeville shows. In the serene Hyde mansion every detail of the stage managing was in keeping with the dignity and quality of the objects to be sold. All the chairs in the small brown velvet hall were assigned by ticket. There was no room for the clacque that came to cheer Kirby and admire the heavy spenders at the AAA.

There was, nevertheless, a touch of bright plumage here and there, and now and then a note of frivolity. In the preliminary bouts, the inexorable Mrs. Harry Payne (Gertrude Vanderbilt) Whitney got a copy of *Psyche; or Love's Mysteries* for $25. Mrs. William K. Vanderbilt, on the other hand, scorned both love and rarity in favor of an impulse to improve her mind. She got *The British Classics* in twenty-four gigantic tomes for $185. But the society ladies lapsed into silence when G. D. Smith casually bid $12,000 for a book on hawking and heraldry written by the prioress of an English nunnery in the latter part of the fifteenth century. For, in truth, the lady auction hounds were beyond their depth in that sober, businesslike assembly.

Affecting a pose so blasé that he appeared to be half asleep, Bernard Quaritch—known in England as the King of Booksellers— was unquestionably the most impressive of the foreign visitors. Quaritch was J. P. Morgan's London agent, and also, buyer for the British Museum; this juxtaposition of clients saved him the embarrassment of bidding against himself, for Morgan's Anglomania was of such severity that he instructed all his deputies never to compete with the British Empire. Though he did not represent Morgan in New York, Quaritch fairly exuded an aura of opulence, for it was understood that his regal pockets were stuffed with buying orders for half the lordly book collectors of England.

In the front row, at a decent interval from the King of Booksellers, sat G. D. Smith, with Huntington beside him—Smith puffing on a big cigar, Uncle Henry in full evening dress. A little to the rear was the Philadelphia contingent: two generations of Wideners (Joseph and Harry) and the dealers Charles Sessler and A. S. W. Rosenbach. Walter M. Hill of Chicago was on hand to defend the Armour and McCormick interests. Henry C. Folger was there, of course, and Walter T. Wallace. The local dealers occupied strategic blocks of seats—James F. Drake, Smith's friendly rival in the campaign to spread the virus bibliomania; the solid old firm of Scribner's; the Messrs. Dodd and Livingston, for whom Smith and Drake had once worked as clerks.

The Continental buyers, appalled by the formality of the arrangements, found their reserved seats scattered throughout the house, a tactical device on Major Turner's part to make it easier to control the expected machinations of the Ring.

Hoe's family had come to see the fun: his children and his grandchildren, the bewildered widow with her hands primly folded, as for an evensong devotion. Even the law-happy Mrs. Brown lurked somewhere in the nether regions of the theater. Anthony Comstock was there, watching like a bird dog to see that such purchases as Mrs. Whitney's contained nothing that would contribute to her delinquency. In the rear, General Brayton Ives stalked up and down, puffing out his windy chest as if for an army parade, and near him, John Anderson, Jr., basked in the renown that had descended upon his name by proxy.

Every big library, public or private, had its sage and sober envoy. All but the Morgan, which had Miss Belle da Costa Greene. No one—certainly not Rose Lorenz, for all her airs—could cast the spell over an auction room that emanated from "Belle of the Books," as *Time* magazine christened Morgan's incomparable librarian many years later, in 1949. By then, of course, B. G., as she was more commonly known, had grown old in the flesh, if not in spirit; but in 1911 she was an easy match for any glamour girl in New York—and she had brains as well. Where she came from no one knew. Some said Portugal; some Virginia; some said the Creole section of New Orleans. Junius Morgan, a nephew of J. P., found her at Princeton,

Belle da Costa Greene ("Belle of the Books"), friend of J. Pierpont Morgan and librarian of the Morgan Library (BETTMANN ARCHIVE).

and Pierpont the Magnificent put her in charge of his library and empowered her to dip into his coffers as her judgment dictated for the purchase of books and manuscripts.

As a bibliographer and expert on the history of literature, Belle Greene had few peers. As a woman, she had a wild, gay humor that was about as incongruous to Morgan's austere marble palace as the antics of a stripteaser would have been in St. Patrick's Cathedral. Her position was unique, her devotion to her library fanatical, and yet none of the dreadful pomp of Morgan ever rubbed off on her person. She was slim, gray-eyed, vivacious—a black-haired beauty, the reporters used to say. In truth, all her features slanted in strange directions, and nothing about her seemed to go together in the accepted fashion; but if she was not really beautiful, she made many people think she was.

"Ah, the grandeur I have played around with," Belle would sometimes sigh, languidly throwing back her carelessly coiffed head, one arm extended, with a cigarette in a long holder between her drooping fingers. But she kept the particulars of her own life a mystery, and she had no intimate biographer. The nearest substitute for a full-sized word picture of that small lady bustling in brocade among the Morgan corridors is contained in a volume called *Studies in Art and Literature for Belle da Costa Greene,* edited by Miss Dorothy Miner of the Walters Art Gallery and published by Princeton University Press in 1954. That beautiful book was intended to be presented to B. G. as a tribute from the world her long-time presence had so enriched. (Unfortunately Belle died before the book was printed.) In the foreword Miss Miner wrote:

. . . A biography of Belle Greene would be a fascinating and colorful account with a fabulous array of personalities, settings and incidents. It would move against a backdrop of princely palaces and international playgrounds, austere libraries and remote cloisters, of academic meetings and the world of society. The account would be tense with the excitement of the auction room. It would unveil endless hours of study and the lonely agony preceding great decisions. It would be full of triumphs and fairy-tale successes, gaiety and humor, irony, sorrow, bravado and courage. Stories would be told of her loyalty and of her sense of fun, her crushing forthrightness of speech and her surpassing generosity. Through the pages would parade fabulous objects of art and history—paintings, sculptures, books and manuscripts, and other things whose beauty made them immortal. . . . Above all it would be a tale crowded with people—people of every kind and station—some known to all the world by reason of power or accomplishment, some the most obscure of students.

One of the many memorable things about Belle Greene was this astonishing capacity for people. It was inexhaustible—not in the sense of being tireless— but of being infinite. She was always ready to acquire new friends, young friends; and yet her oldest friendships never lost their vitality. These did not merely endure, they flourished, were kept tingling even through long separations of time and space. Those whom she had not seen for several decades felt that they had just talked with her yesterday. There was maintained a bombardment of fresh and buoyant letters, of brief notes and queries, cryptic jokes, of press clippings, books—a breezy conversation over years of time.

And yet . . . B. G. was far from all-inclusive in her enjoyment of people. She was as critical of human beings as of works of art. She could not tolerate mediocrity in either, for it bored her. For pretense and pompous fraud, whether in an object or a person, she had only swift scorn.

Needless to say, Belle Greene was the focal point in that first night audience that gathered to redeem Hoe's treasure. Already, at the afternoon session, newspapermen had recorded her every reaction to the first of the books, her smallest frown along with the least of her vivacious gestures. At one point, she had tangled with G. D. Smith for a lot that Smith drove to five figures. "Gosh! Whew!" the scholarly lady had exclaimed in a husky sotto voce, vehemently shaking the one pert feather sticking straight up from her odd-shaped hat when the auctioneer implored her to raise her bid once more. The book had gone to Smith—an unchivalrous oaf, one sensitive reporter felt. For Miss Greene, momentarily at least, had seemed despondent—an observation that appeared in headlines along with the writer's candid opinion that the prices were too high.

By the after-dinner session, however, B. G. had regained her composure sufficiently to put on a sweeping gown of watered silk. She could hardly be expected to bid on the Gutenberg Bible, since she already had in her custody two sevenths of the local hoard. But she was there—and smiling, the susceptible reporter was relieved to note.

A hum went through the audience as the two great oak-bound folios were placed upon the block, but irrelevant noises were quickly silenced by G. D. Smith, whose bidding signal was a wink. The first offer, winked by Smith, was $10,000. The English auctioneer called it briskly. Would someone care to give $11,000? Almost all the big money promptly made an honorary thrust or two. At $21,000 there were ohs and ahs from spectators aware that the world's auction record for a Bible had been passed. But the auctioneer refused to pause, and G. D. Smith went on winking nervously, as if a mote had stuck in his right eye. Quaritch stayed in up to $30,000, and abruptly stopped. From then on, it was a duel between Joseph Widener and Smith as Uncle Henry's spokesman.

In the forty thousands Huntington turned pale. "Too much money. Nothing doing," he whispered hoarsely to Smith.

"Leave me alone," Smith rasped. "If you don't want it, I'll buy it myself."

At $50,000 even Widener shook his head. Hodgson let his hammer fall.

"Who's the buyer?" voices in the audience cried. "Who's the buyer, Mr. Auctioneer?"

Smith turned questioningly to Huntington. There was a second's hesitation, but Uncle Henry nodded a quavering assent. G. D. spoke to the auctioneer, and Hodgson announced with elaborate courtesy that it was Mr. Henry E. Huntington of California who had just succeeded Mr. Pierpont Morgan as the owner of the world's most expensive book. There were cheers and shrill hosannas. Uncle Henry rose and took a bow. Miss Greene tried not to look despondent.

The rest was by no means anticlimax. Many sessions of the seemingly interminable auction were almost equally spirited. There was, for instance, the afternoon Belle Greene, bidding against Smith, paid $42,800 for *Le Morte d'Arthur*. The 426-year-old Caxton folio had once sold at an English auction for 2s 6d, but it was the only perfect copy known, and Miss Greene said after her victory that it was the one item in the Hoe library she had decided Mr. Morgan could not live without. (Even with it, he only lived two years.) If it had been necessary, B. G. added, possibly with a tinge of regret, she would have gone beyond the price Huntington paid for the Bible, thus restoring Morgan to his former estate as book-world Spendthrift Number One. But Huntington was absent that afternoon, and Smith, bidding for his own account, had grown unaccountably fainthearted. At his signal of retreat, Belle's victory evoked tumultuous applause, and an impromptu intermission followed while her more ardent admirers rushed forward to wring her hand.

Quaritch bought Hoe's paper copy of the Gutenberg Bible for $27,500, but few of the other important items went back across the ocean. "It is possible for one or two persons to influence a sale," the King of Booksellers said, with a wry glance at Smith and Huntington, when a reporter asked if he looked upon the unprecedented prices as a trend. "Books that ordinarily can be had for a few shillings have been selling here for ten or fifteen dollars. Some of the prices seem absurdly high."

"Your prices are as tall as your buildings," little Madame Bélin of Paris remarked, after being driven to pay $4,900 for the 1485 first Flemish edition of *The Consolation of Philosophy*. Soon after that she returned, with empty pockets, to France.

Dr. Ludwig Baer of Frankfort became so incensed at the heavy spenders that he tried to start a scandal. G. D. Smith had paid $2,600 for Guicciardini's *Historia di Italia* from the library of Henry III of France. Bound in red morocco by Nicolas Eve, with a full-length portrait of King Henry in a mosaic of colored leather on the center panel, the Guicciardini was one of the handsomest of books, so handsome that Swann had had the cover reproduced in color as the frontispiece to Volume I of the Hoe catalogue. But Dr. Baer was unimpressed. He told the newspapers that the sixteenth-century binding was a forgery. Also, said the king of German bibliophiles, the twenty-one half-page miniatures in the fifteenth-century Ovid manuscript that had belonged to Anne of Brittany were a clever nineteenth-century hoax. (Smith had paid $10,000 for that.) Dr. Baer would not for the world injure a confrere, he said. His only interest was in scientific truth. Nonsense, said G. D. Smith, and at a press conference of his own, he outlined the frustrated plan of the European dealers to redeem Hoe's books at a fraction of their market value. Beverly Chew and a number of other distinguished experts politely called Dr. Baer a liar; and after a time he, too, embarked upon a transatlantic liner.

The absence of the disgruntled Europeans was hardly noticed. As the sale went into the second year the contest for the rarest items was chiefly among Quaritch, Smith, and Belle Greene. But occasionally a gem would fall to one of the other book tycoons. The night *Helyas, Knight of the Swanne* came up, the intrepid Miss Greene carried the banner for a while and then decided that both she and Morgan could live without it. *Helyas, Knight of the Swanne,* the first English version of *Lohengrin,* was printed in 1512 by Wynkyn de Worde in his shop "in Flete Strete at the sygne of the Sonne." Everybody seemed to have a client for *Lohengrin* with such romantic trimmings and unfamiliar spelling, but as the price advanced as if on wings, first

Quaritch dropped out, then Rosenbach. B. G. shrugged her comely shoulders, and finally even Smith said, "No more." Walter Hill of Chicago triumphed at $21,000. There was a round of applause for Chicago, and the valiant Mr. Hill took a bow. Whether he was bidding for meatman or reaper he declined to say, but twenty years later *Helyas* came to light again in the effects of Mrs. Edith Rockefeller McCormick.

Occasionally one of the Hoe heirs would join the struggle. The granddaughter, Miss Thirza Benson, who inherited one seventh of the fortune and a corresponding portion of the old gentleman's enthusiasms, paid $24,000 for a fifteenth-century manuscript with 107 full-page miniatures painted for Anne de Beaujeu, daughter of Louis XI. Hoe had paid $1,155 for it in 1886.

Hoe's son Arthur was underbidder on the paper copy of the Gutenberg Bible; he was moved—no doubt by sentiment—to pay $850 to get a copy of *Lecture on Bookbinding as a Fine Art* delivered by his father before the Grolier Club in 1885; and when the Pembroke *Hours* came up, Arthur Hoe moved full force into the fray.

Of all the Hoe treasures none was more dazzling to the eye than that famous fifteenth-century manuscript. It consisted of 231 parchment leaves depicting the hours of the Virgin in miniature paintings, with scrolls, borders, and exquisite lettering, all in the richest and most brilliant colors, the whole illuminated with the purest gold. Sir William Herbert, Earl of Pembroke (*c.* 1423–*c.* 1469) had been the original owner and his grandson Sir William Herbert, Earl of Pembroke (1506–1570), the second owner. Now, in what an awestruck reporter called the Bloodless Battle of the Auctions, the winner of the magnificent book was Arthur Hoe, for a sale price of $33,000.

In reality the buyer (*in absentia*) of the Pembroke *Hours* was Cortlandt Field Bishop, the globe-trotting collector who was a few years hence to own the auction halls themselves, but when a scion of the Hoe family was named as high bidder, the audience indulged in prolonged applause. There was, however, one deflated old man present, whose hands struck together with a passive, unenthusiastic sound. The long-faced guest was General Brayton Ives. Albeit the strutting little General had once been vice president of the Stock Exchange, and boasted of omniscience in the finances of collecting as well, he had misjudged the treasure market right and left. Not only had he sold his Gutenberg Bible too soon, he had frittered away the Pembroke *Hours* as well.

It had cost Ives $12,000 for the privilege of briefly owning the beautiful old manuscript, but at his sale in 1891 Kirby had knocked it down to Robert Hoe for $5,900. Wherefore the seventy-year-old General could count his losses, real and theoretical, at some $27,100. These were bitter lessons in the pitfalls of speculation, but inveterate gambler that he was, Ives could not stay away from the auction room. Throughout the seventy-nine sessions the puffed-out little man could be seen, his Civil War medals dangling from his waistcoat—a seedy jockey, someone said, hanging on the fringes of the paddock, watching the new horses run—bidding, perhaps for old time's sake, on the books that Hoe had once bought from him, watching them fall at ten, twenty, and even forty times the prices Kirby had sold them for in 1891.

On and on the great sale went, until even the reporters were surfeited with the glamour of Belle Greene, with the British regality of Quaritch, with the impudence and imprudence of roughriding Smith. "His oriflamme is the wink," the *Times* man wrote of the bold G. D. after a particularly deadly passage of arms somewhere in the middle of part two of the sale. "The wrinkles over his right eye are appraised at a thousand dollars each. . . . He spurs always into the thickest of the fray. His crest may be seen waving in the field whenever bidder to bidder answers and the auctioneer invites rivals to the parley."

On and on, for over a year and a half, the money flowed like manna, and month by month the fame of the Anderson Auction Company grew. Wars threatened, banks defaulted, fires and earthquakes rocked the outside world, while from his tower in the old Hyde mansion Dan Kennedy called the bids and the congregation responded like devotees of ritual assembled in a cloister. Major Turner, his empty coat sleeve dangling, paced up and down the aisles, while at his table near the rostrum, Swann wrote the prices with a consciousness that he was recording history of a kind. Disaster overtook one golden buyer midway through the sale. Harry Elkins Widener went down on the *Titanic* the very day the trumpets sounded for part three. But while the papers were describing the horrors of the shipwreck, the bids went on as always—only faster for a time, as if the beating of wings had drawn a little closer. The seat reserved for young Widener was taken by another, not as rich perhaps, but a squireling who would do to swell an offer now and then. Part four ran through the autumn, and by Thanksgiving 1912 the bottom of the barrel was ready to be scraped.

All existing records had been broken. Whether for individual books, libraries, or special categories such as manuscripts or autographs, there was no precedent in any time or place. When at last the total was announced—$1,932,056.60—it exceeded by one third the combined receipts for the four most valuable libraries ever sold in England. The total of the Hoe sale was not surpassed by any book auction held in the United States until the Streeter sale, which took place between October 1966 and October 1969, with a sales total of $3,104,982.50.

Almost as astonishing as the final figure was the bill presented to G. D. Smith. Either for Huntington or on his own account, Smith had bought more than half the Hoe library in terms of money, or nearly $1 million worth of books.

There were gasps and murmurs from the book world and the auction world. The English traders, stunned and openly resentful, said no good would come of this vulgar demonstration of American exorbitance. Americans grinned, and French and German dealers hurried to New York to open branch establishments. Whatever the future might bring forth, the die was cast. Rare books were no longer the inspiration of scholars, the substance of libraries, the solace of crusty bibliophiles; they were the toys of moguls as well. They were, as Swann had dreamed of making them, as valuable as pictures. As G. D. Smith had set out to make them, they were the building stones of monuments, not only for Morgan, Folger, Huntington, but for their inevitable followers, for the big fish and the little fish who did not wish to die and be forgotten, for the book lover rich enough to gaze at a Latin text he could not read, for the book hater who never opened any book at all.

SEVEN

THE PALE HORSEMAN AND
THE MILLION-DOLLAR VOICE

THE IMPUDENCE of the Anderson Auction Company in depriving Kirby of the Hoe book sale was compounded by a triumphal entrance into the art-selling field. In the fall of 1911 Miss Emilie Grigsby returned from one of her cosmic jaunts in a bridge-burning mood. Impulsively, on a gray November afternoon, she walked out of her Park Avenue house, handed the key to Major Turner, and told him to dispose of all her panoplied possessions: her golden harp, the late King Edward's footstool, her singing birds and jade wine cups, even the two little navy flags Captain Richmond Pearson Hobson had given her in the first blush of their romance. Only one choice item Miss Emilie reserved to go with her to London, where she said she would take up her permanent abode: her portrait by Anders Zorn. She would take her picture and her nine servants with her, she told reporters, and spend her summers on the Thames, her winters on the Riviera, and thus avoid crossing the ocean. She no longer cared for the ocean. Moreover, she said, people were nicer to her in England.

Miss Emilie fled to Canada to avoid the sight of her toppling citadel, and by mid-December news of her retreat began to appear in the papers. "House of Mystery Will Pour Forth Its Treasures for All to See—and Buy," the *Tribune* gaily informed its readers. "Miss Emilie Busby Grigsby's art collection is going to be sold at auction . . . for although in this house her feet can rest upon carpets of crushed grape, her eyes can rest upon the works of old masters, Miss Grigsby seems to be restless."

The almost foolishly shallow house was ill-adapted for a sale on the premises, but before Miss Emilie's things were removed to the Anderson, the three lower floors were thrown open to everyone who cared to see the far-famed Grigsby spoils in their natural setting. Curiosity got the better of the ladies who had declined to call on Miss Emilie in her palmy days. Some of them came in veils or otherwise disguised, but they came; and the velvety salons buzzed with such feminine vociferations as "the most unbelievable," "the most marvelous," "the most dazzling," "the most incredible . . ."

Another landmark was on the wane, the *Tribune* reporter sighed when the preview was over: ". . . in a few days it will be no more. Its outer shell will be with us, 'tis true. But its heart is even now being removed in vans. Somehow vans seem such an unpoetical means by which to erase this kind of landmark."

And apropos of Miss Emilie's history, her *Tribune* biographer remarked: "At first her chief possession was marvelous red-gold hair, obviously natural and as luxuriant as her complexion was alabaster. Now if the auctioneer is not too conservative—and no auctioneer has been arrested yet for that offense—he will probably be put to it for words to describe Miss Grigsby's other possessions—the ones he is going to sell."

There was no need for hyperbole on the part of the Anderson auctioneers. The pace of the two-week sale was set the very first night by the stirring battle of the jade wine cups. They were mutton-fat jade, and their actual value, a dealer in Oriental knickknacks said, was no more than $150. But a lady with a certain spiritual affinity to Miss Emilie Grigsby had decided that nothing would so augment the refinements of her way of life as those five jade cups on a carved Ming tray. At the exhibition, when Arthur Swann had unlocked the cabinet and allowed her to feel their ambrosial texture, she had instructed him to buy them for her at any cost. Being a woman of mystery herself, she would not attend the auction in person; and her name was to remain as secret as that of the well-known pillar of society who paid her bills.

Nowadays unlimited bids are never accepted by auction personnel, but the Anderson was a little slapdash about such matters, and when the wine cups came up, Swann proceeded to fulfill his commission. He was opposed, however, by a mysterious bidder who said his name was M. Mustin and identified himself as agent for a wealthy collector, whose name he had sworn never to divulge.

The price of the wine cups soared, first by the hundred, then by the thousand. Two, three, four, five, six thousand passed, and still neither Swann nor his opponent showed any sign of relenting. At length, when Mustin bid $6,700, Major Turner stepped to the rostrum and called a halt. It was quite apparent, he said, that something had gone wrong. The matter would have to be settled by arbitration in his office after the sale, for pleasant as the sound of the bidding was, he feared that neither of the secret agents' principals would stand for such rhapsodic extravagance.

A few collectors whispered "Folly!" but the rest of the audience cheered. General Brayton Ives remarked that $1,000 would have been enough. The General did not, of course, know the tangled state of affairs that was revealed behind the closed doors of Major Turner's office later in the evening. The lady, it seems, in browsing through the 427 pages of Miss Emilie's catalogue, had become enamored of a whole galaxy of baubles from the House of Mystery. So carried away had she been that she forgot all about Swann and employed the pseudonymous M. Mustin to represent her carte blanche at the sale. She saw that the bill was paid—through Mustin—and perhaps never knew that she had instigated the proverbial heated contest against herself, nor that for $6,700 she could have bought enough jade wine cups to equip a chain of restaurants.

Seldom had even Thomas Kirby opened a sale with such resounding publicity. Night after night the brown velvet hall of the Hyde mansion was crowded to the rafters, and though the morally and socially circumspect declined to be seen in the act of haggling over Miss Emilie's bric-a-brac, their agents kept the prices soaring. The Accarissi tea set, with the initials EBG magnificently inscribed on all its pieces, brought $1,600 from a woman in disguise. A "Mrs. Rouss" paid $300 for twelve Vienna plates. A "Mrs. Carlton," very active in a vividly befeathered hat, garnered a hoard of semiprecious gaudery, including a watch enclosed in a crystal cross at $850. A woman who paid cash and refused to divulge her name even to the Anderson bookkeeper went up to $1,050 for a Minton mantel garniture. Swann, bidding for a shy male client, procured the necklace given to Miss Emilie by a khedive of Egypt, at $760.

A man with the unlikely name of N. Snead got a brackish Painted Lady for $435. *A Garden of Dreams,* depicting Miss Emilie with head thrown back in ecstasy, fell to a gentleman *in absentia* for $635. (Sentimental rather than intrinsic value must have moved the collector, one of the newspapers observed.) But no one, not even Mr. Snead, wanted the murals depicting Miss Emilie cavorting among the Rhine Maidens and the Valkyrie. She had placed a reserve of $2,500 on them, and they remained unsold.

The bidders were not all incognito. Bernard Baruch was bold enough to buy a Louis XV cabinet without subterfuge. Captain De Lamar's old eyes glittered at the sight of Miss Emilie's singing birds and jeweled caskets. Under pressure from the secret agents, he was driven to pay $800 for a gold box set with emeralds and aquamarines, but he got one of the singing birds at $400. Its voice was silent. The key had been lost.

Weber and Fields were there together. Leon Schinasi, who had inherited and multiplied a tobacco fortune, raised his hand frequently, to no avail. David Belasco and David Warfield sat side by side at the afternoon sessions. Warfield got a pair of orphreys, a silver reliquary, and enough similar equipment to start a little chapel of his own. During the day the two priestly gentlemen of the theater refrained from bidding against one another, but in the evenings, when Warfield went off to play in *The Return of Peter Grimm,* Belasco slyly gathered items sacred and profane: priest's robes and cassapancas, prie-dieus and teapots with the covers missing, a pair of buttons that had belonged to George IV for $9, Miss Emilie's 6-foot effigy of *Justice* for $900.

Justice, as represented in the House of Mystery, was a fearful Amazonian figure, her upper regions clad in armor, the lower draped in red Verona marble. She wore a helmet crested by a dragon, gripped a sword in her right hand, scales in her left, and loomed grandly from a crimson velvet pedestal embroidered with many coats of arms. Possibly she was overpriced at $900. A dozen years later, when the shifting tides of fortune brought to the auction block some of the clutter resulting from what Stark Young once called Belascosity, she was worth only $85.

Sentiment indeed ran high at Miss Emilie's grand removal sale, but there were bargains now and then. The late King Edward's footstool brought the ignominious sum of $36—and that from a secondhand man. Captain Hobson's naval flags moved no one to vicarious romance. They sold for $9 and $11 each. François Coppée's andirons zoomed to $610, but Oliver Cromwell's blackjack tankard brought only about a quarter of the sum it was to fetch in 1947 with the name of the House of Morgan added to its pedigree. A "Mrs. Richards" got Miss Emilie's opera glasses, memories included, for $21. A "Mrs. Thomas" snapped up the high prie-dieu from Miss Grigsby's purple bedroom; knights, Virgin and Child, cut purple velvet and all, it went for only $80. The great golden harp was sold to George Tilyou, of Coney Island fame—at $400, alas!

Of the six thousand books in Miss Grigsby's hall of learning, few were rare enough to bring high prices, but many of them bore touching inscriptions from old acquaintances, at least one of whom had grown uncommonly stuffy with the years. William Loring Andrews, honorary librarian of the Metropolitan Museum, issued an indignant press release complaining that the Anderson had catalogued fifteen limited editions of his authorship as if—perish the thought!—they were presentation copies to Miss Grigsby. "I don't know the woman," the venerable (he was commonly referred to as the venerable) Mr. Andrews stated unequivocally for the record. Nevertheless, such absorbing works as *A Prospect of the Colleges in Cambridge in New England* contained the telltale words "To Miss Grigsby" on the flyleaves. In some there were little poems written especially for Miss Emilie, and no fewer than seven of the fifteen books were unmistakably inscribed, the newspapers were duty bound to report, "From the author to Miss Grigsby."

"Trivial," said Major Turner, when queried on the "mix-up," and he declined to fret about the self-righteous Mr. Andrews' consternation. When the fifteen recondite books came to the block, they brought over $400. Scribner's was the buyer, but no one doubted that the bookstore was acting as proxy for a blushing Mr. Andrews blackmailed into a face-saving investment in his own works.

It was in such devious ways that Miss Emilie could be said to have had the last laugh, and even a modicum of revenge. When all her goods and chattels were sold, nearly $200,000 had been added to her nest egg, a sum that was estimated to be double, perhaps triple, what the same articles would have brought if they had never been contained in the House of Mystery. "And now, in a short time," the *Tribune* reporter wrote in a tone of lingering farewell, "she says she is going to leave us for good."

Ironically, before the echoes of Miss Emilie's gala at the Anderson had died out, it fell to the AAA to disperse the dregs of Mara's phantasmagoric years. After viewing the late Mrs. Yerkes' possessions arrayed in Madison Square, the *Sun* reporter wrote: "Altogether a thoroughly gratifying exhibition, the sale of which will surely result in more than one battle of the pocketbooks, but then Mr. Kirby dearly loves such battles."

But the remnants of Mara's giddy life attracted no secretive, impassioned bidders. Most of the crippled splendor she had salvaged from the palace went to secondhand men at pitifully low prices: her mountainous heaps of glasses—champagne glasses, hock glasses, goblets, whisky, sauterne, and claret glasses; her liqueur bottles, carafes, pitchers, beakers, flagons, tankards, decanters; her table china, reduced to broken sets at those celebrated midnight dinners; her flat silver with the Yerkes coat of arms (how many teaspoons turned out to be missing!); the old silver toys Charley Yerkes had bought for her in Philadelphia (a horse and wagon, a horse and sleigh, a miniature royal carriage drawn by six high-stepping silver horses); her high-back tortoise-shell comb; her scarves of rose-point lace; the lovelorn ladies of Jan van Beers; all those many, many clocks and watches.

It was the kind of sale Captain De Lamar most thoroughly enjoyed. He bought the silver-threaded rugs, a golden casket, a golden windmill, a golden watch or two. He united Mara's one singing bird with its mute companion from Miss Emilie's collection. He bought the Greek gods carved in ivory, the bronze nymphs, fisherboys, and satyrs, and—for $575—the marble statue of *Vanity* towering 11 feet 5 inches overall.

David Warfield and David Belasco came as usual. Warfield bought the old church vestments, a clock, a snuffbox, a pair of red silk portieres trimmed with gold galloon. Belasco got the three hundred landscapes by van Beers, mounted on twelve enormous swivel panels attached to a circular shaft and topped by a wrought-iron electrolier—for $960 the lot. Frank A. Vanderlip took the forty miniatures of French court beauties. Louis Owsley—a man of callous sentiment—refurbished his bedroom with Mara's chairs, mirrors, tables, with her *fleur-de-pêche* dressers, her escritoires and screens, even with her high-post double bed, complete with dais and canopy of yellow watered silk.

It was as if the curtain had been raised on intimacies more properly concealed; and when at length the last chapter of poor Mara's tale of woe was closed, her disputed estate received about $45,000 for the odds and ends of her bravura life. Comparison with Miss Emilie's jubilee at the Anderson was inevitable, and with the closing of the Yerkes saga, it was clear that the battle of the pocketbooks was no longer a monopoly of the AAA.

The myth had been dispelled that only the Kirby mystique could produce a gala auction, but there was no suggestion of idleness at the Madison Square galleries. On the contrary, the mortality rate among the titans kept the Million-Dollar Voice rising to an ever higher pitch. In February 1913, paintings, books, and art objects from the estate of the cotton goods manufacturer M. C. D. Borden brought $1,406,974. There were some famous paintings and resounding prices. Rembrandt's *Lucretia Stabbing Herself* (now in the National Gallery) sold for $130,000; Turner's *East Cowes Castle* for $105,-000; Romney's *The Willett Children* for $100,000; Daumier's *The Third-Class Carriage* (now in the Metropolitan Museum) for $40,000.

But even with such new laurels to compensate for the loss of monopoly, all was not well on Madison Square.

Kirby's health was failing. Now in his middle sixties, the peppery, magnetic little man with the silver-rimmed spectacles, the snow-white beard and snow-white head, was in a state bordering on collapse. He was a little deaf. His hands were often bandaged, for he suffered from a nervous complaint diagnosed as eczema. His doctors told him that he would have to retire, employ competent assistance, or die. The employment of competent assistance meant the delegation of authority, a prospect almost as gloomy as the other two. But there was a fourth alternative, and that was to take his son, Gustavus, into the AAA as partner.

G. T. Kirby had not intended to follow his father in the auction business. He was a lawyer, a former Columbia athlete, a gay dog with the ladies, a promoter and a speculator, with a civic-minded interest in amateur sports. In 1906 he had married Wilhelmine Claflin, the adopted daughter of the merchant prince John Claflin. The wedding contract, it was said, contained a clause forbidding the bridegroom ever to become an auctioneer.

Nevertheless, G. T. was something of a chip off the old block. He was proud of the world-famous institution his father had created. He also knew that as a one-man show it was doomed to vanish when at last that Million-Dollar Voice was silenced; and so, in 1912, when he was approaching forty, G. T. thrust his dapper, blunt-spoken presence upon the AAA, never as an auctioneer, but first as a general partner, and then, upon the death of James F. Sutton in 1915, as half owner and equal partner with his father.

Under pretext of relieving the elder Kirby of some of the pressures that were destroying his health, G. T. reorganized the Art Association somewhat on the lines of modern business, with stenographers, bookkeepers, files, and a system of record keeping less precarious than his father's pockets, not to say less ephemeral than Rose Lorenz' memory. And also, having a deep-seated revulsion for his father's female deputy, he contrived to assemble a supporting cast that would be able to carry on when at last the Kirby-Lorenz autocracy should come to an end.

Irked by the Hoe book sale and its exasperating total, G. T. Kirby demanded the founder of the Anderson Auction Company tell him who, in his opinion, was "the best man in this country or abroad to take over the book department of the AAA."

"Arthur Swann," John Anderson replied.

It was unnecessary to invade the enemy camp to obtain Swann's services. Not only had he been something less than jubilant over Major Turner's restrictions, but as the sale wore on, some of the methods used to promote exorbitance had seemed to Swann too roughshod for bibliophilistic house parties.

"Queer tales were told," Gelett Burgess wrote in *Collier's,* "of orders filled by dealers with silent partners who ran up prices under the very noses of their clients." No open scandal had developed, but when at last the Hoe sale was over, Swann decided, without even bothering to flip a coin, that his conscience would no longer permit him to lend his talents to the Anderson. He resigned, and Mrs. Swann—for by now he was a married man—predicted gloomily that they would end in the bread line. But Swann was confident that the rare-book trade could not afford to allow a walking encyclopedia to go unemployed. He whisked the apprehensive Mrs. Swann off to Atlantic City for a holiday, and when they returned, G. D. Smith was waiting.

Over a lunch that was far from bread-line fare, Smith proposed that if Swann would lend his talents to the education of Henry E. Huntington and similar undertakings, he could name his own salary and in addition receive 5 per cent of Smith's annual profits.

"It took real courage to refuse that offer," the dean of book auctions remembered forty years later. But Smith's race-tout tactics were not for the ingenuous, book-bedazzled clerk from Liverpool. When G. T. Kirby offered one-third the salary Smith would have paid, Swann accepted.

Going to work for the AAA would do him no good, said G. D. Smith, for never would he, Smith, darken Thomas Kirby's door again—never would he buy so much as a pamphlet from that unctuous old man who frowned like a haloed little godkin on dealers who puffed sales. It was a threat Swann knew Smith would not carry out, for in his dreams he saw himself supplying the one missing spoke in the golden wheel of the AAA. Once more he envisioned those beautiful book catalogues, similar to the art folio editions on which Rose Lorenz sometimes spent $40,000. G. D. Smith might stay away if he chose. With the Kirby money and prestige, the desire to own would be so wildly stimulated that his bustling presence would not even be missed.

Not all the lieutenants who were to figure in the future of the auctions were recruited by G. T. Otto Bernet, a Swiss-German, had started work in the galleries in 1896 at the traditional age of fourteen. A beaming, good-natured boy of cherubic dimensions, he was at first set to polishing and running errands. So assiduously did he polish, and so swiftly did he run, that Kirby himself could not fail to notice. Rose Lorenz was placed in charge of his preliminary education, and later Kirby added some finishing touches of his own, for Little Otto (the affectionate prefix applied to personality rather than circumference), undeterred by any natural aptitude for the profession, was dead set on becoming an auctioneer.

He was a demon for self-improvement. By day he endured the terrors of Rose's yardstick; by night he took courses in oratory and art appreciation. Often in the evening, if the afternoon's auction had been particularly inspiring, he would go into the darkened salesroom, climb into the rostrum, and re-enact Kirby's whole long-winded performance, item by item. Boldly then, with only the echoes and the night watchman for response, he would rehearse the harsh cries of persuasion in all their timeworn variations, making hollow jokes to the unlaughing chairs, regaling the absent buyers with cajolery and threats.

"Why you haven't begun yet!" he would bellow at the stingy shadows. "Ten, I have—a mere ten thousand! Do I hear eleven? 'Leven . . . 'leven . . . 'leven. . . . *E*leven, says the lady in the rear! Now, gentlemen, let's hear the twelve! . . ." And so on, and on, until the chairs at length relented and the last imaginary thousand had been extracted from the empty hall.

Naturally it was Otto's dream that Kirby would one day meet with some temporary disaster on the eve of a great dispersal. This, Kirby had no intention of doing, but he did recognize the expediency of having an understudy. When Otto had been practicing to the empty chairs for ten years, he got the chance to try out his art—in the last lap of the Stanford White sale.

His debut took place in a warehouse, and the lots consisted mainly of sarcophagi. Mrs. Payne Whitney, by then abundantly supplied, appears to have been absent, but Rockefeller and Hearst were on hand as usual. Otto, unperturbed by the opulence of his first flesh-and-blood audience, kept his composure and even improved a little on the gaiety of previous Stanford White sessions.

"Not too large for your apartment," he called out blithely as the little band of millionaires gathered before a carved and festooned sepulcher.

"Put them in the kitchen and make the cook happy," Otto suggested merrily, when bidding was slow for a pair of lions rampant supporting the shield of some forgotten prince. Mrs. Joseph Pulitzer took them at $22.50 the pair, but whether or not it was the bliss of her cook she had in mind no one bothered to record.

As luck would have it, Thomas Jefferson Coolidge of Newton Center, Massachusetts, showed up in the form of a dark horse with a voracious appetite for marble sarcophagi. Hearst and Rockefeller were pressed to the limit, and when all the tombs had been sold, Otto was found to have added $8,416 to the Stanford White total. Rose Lorenz patted him on the back, and from then on, whether Kirby was sick or not, Otto was allowed to sell the stale ends of many of the big collections.

A folksy, jovial man full of good cheer and Pickwickian amenities, O. B. (thus he came to be called as his corpulence and air of consequence expanded) earned the respect and even the affection of the monied crowd he used to call "the swells." But for all the doggedness of his efforts, Bernet's pedestrian hawking was never more than a strained reflection of the brilliance of the star. Therein, perhaps, lay his supreme merit as understudy to the proud old auctioneer. But when it came to choosing a man to inherit the mantle of his father in the rostrum, G. T. Kirby's mind went back to Philadelphia, where he had become acquainted with a tall, dark, handsome auctioneer named Hiram Haney Parke.

Parke's origins were no less humble than Bernet's, and yet, while

O. B. remained on the far side of the tracks, Parke possessed an indefinable quality that called to mind the word "gentleman." He was born in West Philadelphia, in 1873, one of the seven children of a rural dry-goods salesman. "You see, I had good parents," the Major would say in looking back on his success story from the vantage point of eighty some years. "They gave me a good start in life."

It was a start, fond recollections notwithstanding, that a present-day youth might look upon as something less than adequate. Most of the elder Parke's energies were devoted to making ends meet and keeping a roof above his seven offspring. There was no money for high school education. After young Hiram had spent a few desultory years in grammar school, he was put to work on the drummer's wagon with his father. The customers were general-store-keepers in outlying districts, reached by long, tiresome journeys over rutted dirt roads. "They would buy one week and pay the next," the seller of crown jewels and Rembrandts recollected with that wry, half-querulous expression that so often used to eke an extra thousand out of the lady in the second row.

By that time the family had moved to Strafford, Pennsylvania, a suburban town near Philadelphia, with its quota of wealthy homes and fine stables. Some of the Strafford families took a liking to the tall, soft-spoken, blue-eyed charmer. Young Hiram learned to ride to hounds; he made his way into well-to-do circles, and not unnaturally, developed a liking for people with property—a liking that was to grow into a profound respect for people with property to sell. Traveling in dry goods was not for him, but Strafford was a pleasant place, and young Parke had no immediate plans for setting the world on fire. It was not until he was twenty-one that he left home and went to work for Garber and Birch, general auctioneers, on Arch Street in Philadelphia.

Parke's position at the house of Garber and Birch was that of record keeper, the traditional observation post of apprentice auctioneers. He had been sitting beside the rostrum recording prices and listening to a stream of roistering, nasal patter for some two years when Paul Garber asked him, one day, if he would like to cry a sale. Garber had acquired a job lot of nondescript, or "staircase," pictures, and having little concern for their fate, decided to let the boy see what he could do. The pictures may have been worthless from the standpoint of aesthetics, but as Parke began to study them, their hidden charms developed, and perhaps even magnified a little. With less noise and more eloquence than the Garber and Birch clients were accustomed to, he managed to communicate the results of his homework to the half-hearted beauty lovers who assembled for the auction. The staircase pictures sold for the price of front parlor pictures, and the handsome young record keeper was led to believe that he had found his métier.

Art, however, was no staple of the Garber and Birch auction rooms. At best, it was a comparatively unprofitable side line, and soon Parke was given a chance to try his hand in the more expensive categories, such as work horses, home furnishings, farm machinery, and second-hand baby carriages. It developed that his enthusiasms were highly volatile. As the occasion demanded, he was able to simulate the same admiration for a live cow as for a painted one; and not infrequently, the cow fanciers found themselves sharing the earnest young man's opinion. But Parke had no real affection for livestock, cookstoves, plowshares, and the like. After practicing the art of sorcery on Garber and Birch's clients for about four years, he went to work for the much larger house of Samuel T. Freeman.

The Samuel T. Freeman Company conducted a continuous mass dispersal of just about everything, movable or stationary—from the kilns of a brickyard to the nymphs of Bouguereau. There were three floors at the huge galleries where the less unwieldy chattels were sold, and the sales got better as the floors went higher. The regular Monday morning auction in the basement might consist of old churns, three-legged chairs, ironing boards, and lame sewing machines. Tuesday and Wednesday, four-legged and sometimes quite beautiful furniture was sold one flight up; and at the end of the week, books and art property were distributed to the luxury trade upstairs. Since there were many auctioneers on Freeman's staff, it took Parke some time to work up to the rarefied level, but occasionally he would get a chance at the paintings and marble statues. Then his fine, clear, cultivated voice would rise to a pitch that might have put many a golden-tongued Hamlet of the day to shame.

The story used to be told in Philadelphia that once, on a wager, before a particularly gullible audience, Parke had run up the price of an ordinary $20 gold piece to an even $100; but such pitchmen's stunts were unrelated to the qualities G. T. Kirby saw in the candidate for his father's office. By the time he was ready to leave Freeman's,

Parke had less the air of a cheap-Jack barker than of a provincial squire thrown by chance among the *brusqueries* of metropolitan commerce. He had married and become the father of a son. From a term of service in the National Guard he had acquired the rank of major, and a vaguely deferential title that stuck to him for the rest of his life. Few people knew him well, but those who thought they did would have described him as a reserved, unobtrusive man in a not too respectable business, approaching middle age with no more exciting prospects ahead than to tend his suburban garden, go on an occasional fishing trip, and with the years, advance a little in the hierarchy of Freeman's auctioneer-appraisers.

Possibly if his marriage had been a happy one, that might have been the Major's fate. But it was not. In Atlantic City he had met a lady he wished to make the second Mrs. Parke. By way of luring him to New York, G. T. Kirby agreed to advance the expenses of a divorce, and when Parke left Freeman's he left the first half of his life—including his first wife and son—behind. His second marriage was a model of compatibility, and with his altered status, the obscure Philadelphia crier began to eye the golden hammer.

G. T. Kirby knew better than to disturb the peace of the Madison Square galleries by bringing his handsome protégé directly into the fold. Instead, he set Parke up in a subsidiary gallery fed by the overflow from estates liquidated by the AAA—the trivia deemed unworthy of the Million-Dollar Voice. And so, with Kirby capital, and the promise of the Kirby rejects, the Hiram H. Parke Gallery opened in an old chair factory on Broadway within shouting distance of Madison Square.

The overflow from the AAA was not Parke's only source of revenue. "It was a great new time," he recalled. "All the big department stores were moving uptown from the Ladies' Mile." G. T. Kirby's father-in-law, John Claflin, had an interest in many of the stores, and with G. T.'s influence, Parke got the job of selling their discarded fixtures and warehouse accumulations—the outmoded electric domes and old showcases, the unstylish cuspidors and the brass bedsteads that are now considered antiques, old cash registers, lace curtains, trusses, lambrequins, gloves and shopworn ostrich feathers.

Needless to say, the art sales comprised of Kirby rejects were something less than the mecca of connoisseurs; but Otto Bernet and William W. Seaman—who now made the general appraisals for

Kirby—sometimes threw remarkable items Parke's way: a clock, for instance, "made originally for Queen Isabella of Spain, to replace a newel post in the Palais Bourbon." Splendrous indeed was Isabella's timekeeping newel post, as extolled in the literature of the Parke Gallery. It had panels of lapis lazuli, 8-foot columns made of bloodstone, and the whole was surmounted by an enormous globe with four clock faces. Moreover, one read (by way of anticlimax), the thing had taken so long to gild and embellish that the Queen, after waiting ten years, had died before it was delivered.

Leafing on in that particular catalogue, one came to a "Remarkable Sleigh Robe made from the breasts of penguins." This, Parke discreetly revealed, had been given to "a well-known New Yorker by a Russian Prince." It was, he added, in slight need of repair.

Mingled with such unique attractions were many pictures, some of which Kirby himself had sold once or twice before, in his less choosy days—many barnyards, homely kitchens, woods in autumn leaf; many brooks, meadows, rising mountains and lowering seas; auburn-haired ladies; terriers and other dogs; skiffs, dories, and other craft. Pale young women described as "spirituelle" were perhaps the dominant subject, but there were portraits of Napoleon too, and many cottage madonnas washing linen in the river, milking, fishing, churning with a dreamy look, or clutching roses to their bosoms, surrounded more often than not by a few fowl to "enliven the grass plot in front of the abode."

Occasionally the terrible wrath of Thomas E. Kirby would descend upon Bernet and Seaman for sending a picture to Parke that turned out to belong in the Highly Valuable classification. At a sale in 1916 Parke got $6,500 for some 400 square feet of canvas entitled *Benjamin Franklin before the Privy Council, House of Parliament, London, 1773*. It was said that a New York club had a vacant wall to cover.

In the same auction, Parke sold a picture called *Departure of the Fishing Boats* for a price that tended to strain diplomatic relations. No one had heard of the painter of those teary women on the shore waving farewell to the stalwart men Parke identified as "husband, lover and son who perchance may never return," but the pathos of the story carried the day. With an apt word here and there from the admiring auctioneer, the bidding rose like the wailing of the banshees, to $6,000.

People with something to sell began to approach Parke without first being rejected by the Million-Dollar Voice. One of them, a woman of slipshod conscience, tried to lead him into a parlous adventure in high places. The lady, who lived in Boston—and in Parke's reminiscence remained discreetly nameless—had sold some of her possessions to advantage at the Parke Gallery. Then, in 1917, with the country about to go to war, she asked Parke to come to Boston on a matter pertaining to a chief of state. In her hotel room she showed him some two hundred highly unstatesmanlike letters, accompanied by pictures, written to her by Woodrow Wilson. She wished to sell her treasure trove, she said, either at auction or by private treaty. Parke took the letters back to New York, read them, and could not help agreeing that they would make a timely and unique collector's haul. But he refused to be a party to their sale. The lady was persistent. She came to New York, reclaimed her holograph intimacies, and hung around the Parke Gallery, regaling newspapermen with hints of the scoop her ribbon-tied bundle could offer. Secret Service men closed in upon the gallery. They interviewed Parke repeatedly and found—as reporters were to find in later years—that he was the most reticent auctioneer alive. President Wilson summoned Parke to Washington. Secret Service men shadowed him throughout the journey. At the White House, Senators and members of the war cabinet were waiting to see the President. Parke was ushered in ahead of them. Wilson asked him if he still had the letters. Parke said no, he had given them back. That was all, except that forty years later Parke, who had a low opinion of Democrats, recalled that the President had not even paid the expenses of his trip.

Some time after his pithy interview at the White House Parke met Wilson's friend and wartime minister Bernard Baruch on the lawn of a Saratoga hotel. Baruch said, "You're the man that had those Wilson letters."

"Yes," said Parke.

"Well," said Baruch, "I have them now." The lady, it seems, had found a buyer after all.

While G. T. Kirby was thus fortifying the AAA against the inevitable, a series of countermoves took place at the Anderson Auction Company. In 1915 Major Turner retired; the finances of the corporation were expanded, with John B. Stetson, the hatter's son, as the largest investor; the name was changed back to its original form—The Anderson Galleries; and Mitchell Kennerley made his entrance into the auction field as president of the new company.

Though not handicapped with previous experience in the auction business, Mitchell Kennerley came to the Anderson with an enviable reputation as a littérateur. For a decade he had been one of the most colorful figures in American publishing—"unquestionably the first *modern* publisher in the country," Christopher Morley once wrote in a tribute "to the genius of the Kennerley imprint." He was a *bon vivant*, a cock of the intellectual walk, a man of the boulevards, with a silver-topped walking stick and a respectful following in both book-reading and book-collecting circles. Above all, he was a vigorous showman. To many of the newer connoisseurs, who sensed that vast changes in taste and atmosphere would result from the European war, he was a "charming fellow" who, it was predicted, would bring to the redistribution of things artistic and literary a modish effervescence a world apart from the pious pretensions that had enchanted the large, ignorant, and wealthy public of the gold-brick era on Madison Square.

Like his contemporaries at the AAA, Mitchell Kennerley had started at the bottom of the ladder, but there the similarity in backgrounds ended. He was born in 1878 in Burslem, England, and began his working life as an office boy in London amid the *fin de siècle* exuberance of John Lane's Bodley Head publishing company. The Bodley Head was a brilliant school, not only in the art of fine bookmaking but in the appreciation of good writing as well—a rebel environment seasoned with what may have been an overdose of the swagger and precocity of London's literary nineties. Young Kennerley took to the intellectual high life of Vigo Street with such uncommon zest that by the time he was eighteen, he was sent to the United States as John Lane's representative. After acting as salesman-ambassador of Bodley Head books for about four years, he became business manager of *Smart Set*. Within a few months he was editing a monthly magazine of literature called *The Reader*, and by 1906 he had entered the ranks as a book publisher.

Kennerley's list of authors, many of whom had never before appeared in print, comprised a sweeping representation of the new-flowering talent of the time. It included, to pick a few names at random, Frank Harris, Walter Lippmann, Joseph Hergesheimer,

Upton Sinclair, Leonard Merrick, Edgar Saltus, Vachel Lindsay, D. H. Lawrence, Edna St. Vincent Millay. There were many others, altogether an impressive parade of witnesses to Mitchell Kennerley's instinct for what he sometimes called "the fledgling geniuses." The table of contents of *The Forum*, published by Kennerley from 1910 to about 1915, reads now like an oracle of the future literary scene. The Little Book Shop Around the Corner, which he conducted as an adjunct to his publishing house, became the rendezvous of a discriminating avant-garde; and in the prewar decade, when the manufacture of reading matter could still reflect the personal taste of a gifted publisher, the name of Kennerley became a bold and meaningful symbol in both London and New York.

His authors were grateful for a hearing; and if Miss Millay, for instance, even in the early twenties, when a first edition of her *Renascence* was worth $40 at auction, could complain that from one year to the next she received no royalties from her original publisher, she at least had the satisfaction of seeing de luxe editions of her poems beautifully printed in Goudy type on handmade paper. Moreover, for what it was worth, she had had the experience of being feted by a man of whirlwind cleverness—a homely, virile tiger of a man that women with money, talent, or intellectual disposition (from Miss Emilie Grigsby at one end of the scale to Miss Belle da Costa Greene at the other) found irresistibly attractive until the haze of candlelight and dinners at the Plaza drifted off into the aftermath of cold reality and hardheaded financiers like Miss Grigsby sought the judgment of the courts in the matter of broken promises to pay.

Profits on the fledgling geniuses being slow, Kennerley occasionally printed popular fiction, and as it happened, one of the mediocre novels he published brought him wider renown than all his many worthwhile contributions to letters. In 1913 Anthony Comstock descended upon the Little Book Shop Around the Corner and directed Kennerley's arrest for corrupting the public morals with a story called *Hagar Revelly* by Daniel Carson Goodwin. The tyranny of Comstock had gone virtually unchallenged for forty years, but this time he had chosen a bulldog adversary. Kennerley might have paid his fine, as other Comstock victims had done, but he chose to fight for a principle that, to quote *Publishers' Weekly* in an issue thirty-seven years later, "made every American publisher his debtor."

Judge Learned Hand, in federal district court, ordered a showdown trial by jury, saying that he was doubtful "if we are even today so lukewarm in our interest in letters or serious discussion as to be content to reduce our treatment of sex to the standard of a child's library." Eminent poets, novelists, publishers, and suffragists turned Kennerley's case into a stirring protest against the evils of arbitrary censorship. The judge in criminal court was blatantly sympathetic to Comstock, and in a charge to the jury that the *Times* called "acute and masterful," all but demanded a speedy conviction. When the jury nevertheless returned a verdict of not guilty, the celebrities in the courtroom held an impromptu reception that made headlines across the country and raised Mitchell Kennerley to the status of a knight in armor in the never-ending battle for the freedom of the press.

With these not inconsiderable claims to distinction, Kennerley, at the age of thirty-seven, took over the Anderson with a view to making it the hub of culture selling in America. He ceased to publish magazines and kept only a remnant of his list of authors, mainly the poets and a few prose writers whose works lent themselves to limited editions with beautiful typography. For it was the *feel* of books that evoked the most ardent sentiments in Mitchell Kennerley. He loved beautiful books, and especially, old books, friendly secondhand copies of books with other people's names and bookplates in them. He liked the sense of old words set in old type, the feel of old paper foxed and faded with age, pages that, as he put it, could be dusted off and fondled back to renewed life and service. "Without books, God is silent," he used to quote. And yet, in another side of his nature, Mitchell Kennerley had the soul of a pirate tradesman. The auctions, by hook or crook, were to pay his debts and make his fortune, for with his champagne tastes and epicurean snobbery, he was perpetually in need of money.

He made a bold start, which was due in some measure to the fortunes of war. The Anderson company had led a nomadic existence, moving from pillar to post with a frequency that gave it an almost fly-by-night reputation. The Hyde mansion had been an excellent setting for the Hoe sale, but it was no more permanent than the half-dozen other addresses had been. Now, though hampered by lack of abundant capital, Kennerley was determined to find a location that could be established as a landmark in the public mind. At Park Avenue and 59th Street stood a large and florid Renaissance-style building that had been occupied by a Kaiser-worshiping brotherhood called the

Arion Society. With the entry of the United States into the war, the Arion Society ceased to function on Park Avenue, and Mitchell Kennerley was able to obtain a long-term lease on their meetinghouse at an annual rental of only $28,000. By the fall of 1917, with the excess space sublet as studios and offices, the Anderson Galleries were ensconced in a setting described as "the largest in the United States devoted to the public sale of art and literary collections." The windfall at 489 Park Avenue included a handsome salesroom on the ground floor, with about three hundred dark-red cushion seats. In other parts of the building, Kennerley ripped out the bowling alleys and athletic equipment that had contributed to the *Kultur* of the Arion Society and turned the space into bookrooms and rooms for art. The fourth floor became a suite of beautiful skylit picture galleries. There, having no large consignments of Very Valuable Paintings with which to beguile the wealthy, Kennerley inaugurated a program of exhibitions that brought the patrons of contemporary art flocking to the Anderson as Sutton's program of enlightenment had brought the smart set of another day to Madison Square.

The introductory show was a benefit for soldiers blinded in the war. It not only served a worthy cause but also introduced the handsome new galleries to fashionable society. After the armistice, Kennerley installed a vigorous impresario named Walter Grant as director of exhibitions. Grant knew his way around the art world, and at a time when there was no Modern Museum in New York, his openings packed the house at $2 a head. The immensely popular show of Sir William Orpen's war paintings was a sensation in Kennerley's fourth-floor galleries, and like many of the other Anderson exhibitions, toured the museums of the country. One-man shows were held for Gari Melchers, Joseph Pennell, Augustus John, Georgia O'Keeffe, John Marin, Frank Salisbury, Archipenko, Boutet de Monvel, and innumerable other painters, sculptors, and illustrators. Exhibitions of every conceivable nature kept the Anderson name almost constantly in the papers—the annual Salons of America, exhibits of photographs by Alfred Stieglitz and Arnold Genthe, prize-winning displays of sculpture made of soap, demonstrations of many phases of industrial design, newsmaking expositions of the modern art of various European countries, and most significant of all perhaps, the exhibitions of the New Society of Artists headed by Pennell, Bellows, Luks, Melchers, and Speicher.

Walter Grant's fourth-floor activities were incidental to the real business of the Anderson, but their fame brought a rush of consignors and an exuberant clientele to the auctions. As the Kennerley regime gained momentum, treasure hunters who had been only dimly aware of the AAA began to flock to the galleries so fortunately situated in the heart of the area that then contained the greatest concentration of wealth in the country. Sales were held on a practically continuous basis—sometimes morning, afternoon, and evening—literary sales and sales of fine furnishings, curios, antiques, and numberless categories of so-called "art property." Week in and week out, the rooms were filled with fascinating things—etchings, engravings, water colors; rugs, prints, embroideries; bronzes, snuff bottles, and carvings; French furniture, old English silver; beautiful jades, laces, and necklaces; Egyptian antiquities, Canton enamels; Spanish textiles, Etruscan vases, Greek and Roman marbles; old stringed instruments from Italy and Vienna; playbills, maps, and broadsides; carved ivories and crystals; Persian potteries, porcelains of Staffordshire, Lowestoft, Wedgwood, Minton; and with the growing vogue for early American things, hooked rugs, pewter, American glass, and colonial household relics. Sometimes the rooms would have a nostalgia like that of an old attic on a rainy day. Almost always in that labyrinth of cozy halls a visitor could pore over other people's heirlooms, other people's family treasure, the small things that had made the fabric of other people's lives; and this perhaps is the real enchantment of the auctions, whether on Park Avenue or in some country dooryard.

Paintings were never Mitchell Kennerley's forte, but in the field of prints the Anderson made auction history. One of the first big sales captured from the AAA was the Frederick R. Halsey collection, a galaxy of the centuries in engraving, mezzotints, color prints, and etching that was in some respects unexcelled in any public or private print room in the world. There were 8,275 lots, all told, and so as not to glut the market, Kennerley made thirteen separate catalogues, spreading the sales over a period of more than two years, from November 1916 to February 1919. During that time a whole new cult of print fanciers developed in this country. (It was the exhibition of Halsey's French eighteenth-century color prints that first gathered Uncle Eli Springs to the fold.) The picture-book romance of olden times, spread out chapter by chapter on the walls of the Anderson, had the fascination of a to-be-continued story, and some of Halsey's scarce impressions began to sell for more than first-rate paintings of their corresponding epochs. One of the prints, *L'Aveu Difficile* by Janinet after an eighteenth-century subject by Lavreince, brought $11,000; and when the returns were finally all in, the Anderson had reaped a harvest of over $400,000, a success attributed by commentators to what used to be called "the unparalleled showmanship of Mitchell Kennerley."

For a number of years—until Anthony Bade got his license in 1923—all the important sales at the Anderson were conducted by Frederick A. Chapman, a relaxed, good-humored auctioneer who owed nothing to the Kirby tradition. Chapman sat on a high stool beside the red-curtained stage, flanked by two or three assistants, and presided over the heated contests with the wit and spontaneity of an indulgent master of ceremonies who feels the responsibility for entertaining the customers while relieving them of their cash. He had drifted into the profession by chance back in 1912, when the Anderson Auction Company undertook to sell his father's collection. The auctioneer had done a slapdash job, and young Chapman, a Brooklyn playboy with no previous inclination to join the ranks of the workers, remarked that he supposed even he could do better. Major Turner invited him to try it, and thereafter Chapman found himself the victim of a steady job.

Under Kennerley's regime, Chapman would sometimes give as many as seven of his ingratiating performances a week, but unlike the average run of auctioneers, he took no part in the backstage ramifications of the business. As a result, his conduct in the rostrum had an air of detachment and impartiality that was especially appealing to the Anderson clientele. For it was sometimes suspected that the antique dealers who had sprung up like mushrooms with the change in social climate brought about by the war had a sinister foothold at the Anderson both as buyers and sellers. With Chapman in the rostrum, the sporting crowd felt that they were somehow protected against the swindlers from Third Avenue, Naples, Peking, Constantinople, and all the other breeding places of shoddy antiquarians. Veteran buyers wrote letters to the editor about the incorruptibility of Freddie Chapman; and he contributed in no small measure to what A. Edward Newton, in *The Amenities of Book-Collecting*, called, "that atmosphere of good-humor and good-fellowship which Mitchell Kennerley tries so successfully to disseminate, and which is so important in the auction-room."

Good humored and no doubt incorruptible Chapman was, but he also had the knack of extracting the last possible dollar from an impulsive, not too well-informed crowd that acquired the habit of bidding for the objects of heart's desire less in accordance with established values than with the fluctuations of the stock market. Milton Mitchill, Jr.—who was in charge of finances at the Anderson—would open the *Sun* in the late afternoon and predict the results of the evening's sale with almost unfailing accuracy. "No money tonight," he would grumble if stocks were down, but if the market was up, he would chuckle and say, "Good sale tonight. The boys will be here."

The boys Milton Mitchill referred to were the new Park Avenue set, with villas in Florida, large brokerage accounts, and large apartments that needed only some vestiges of old wealth and artistic accumulation to erase the barrenness of sudden acquisition. But they were only one element of the public that beat a path to Kennerley's Park Avenue galleries. In addition to the dealers and the inveterate collectors who had always been the backbone of the auctions, there were casual bidders who, drawn by the Anderson's reputation as the pleasantest little theater in town, wandered in to look, and sometimes stayed to spend with a delightful spirit of abandon.

There was an old lady who lived in the Spanish Flats, a string of architectural anachronisms intended to duplicate the charms of old Madrid in the neighborhood of West 59th Street. She strolled in one night with her satchel, and as it turned out, with a gleam in her eye for a little crystal clock fashioned in the form of a baseball. It was a novelty, worth perhaps $50 or $100, but the market was up that night, and the baseball that was a clock, or the clock that was a baseball, had also taken the fancy of a sporty gent with a pocketful of new money. The old lady got it—for $4,500—paid for it then and there in large crumpled bills, stuck it tenderly into her satchel, and trotted off, her thirst for curios presumably quenched; for she never reappeared.

One afternoon a furniture sale was scheduled, a routine sale of gaudy reproductions deriving vaguely from the gilded splendors of the Louis'. Long before the appointed hour, a little man came in, took a seat in the empty theater beside a window, opened his paper, and turning to the second section, immersed himself in the real estate and financial news. He was an eyesore, Arthur Wyler recalled, unkempt, uncreased, and unshaven, resembling more a client of the soup kitchens than of that pretty red-cushioned meeting hall. "Go over and talk to him," Kennerley told Wyler. "See if you can get rid of him."

The man was glad to talk. His name, let us say, was Mr. Zatkins. He was waiting for his wife, he said, and confidentially, he was what you might call well heeled. Perhaps the young man had heard of a certain chain of orange-drink stands occupying strategic corners around the city? Well, Mr. Zatkins was the owner of them, or one of the owners. But it was not the watered orange juice that had delivered Mr. Zatkins into the clutches of the Anderson, he hastened to explain. "Oranges, that's not our business. It's the corners," he confided in a whisper. "We find a nice corner, see? We take a lease on it. We open an orange-drink stand. What happens? Somebody comes along and wants to put up a skyscraper. He needs the corner, don't he? So what happens, he pays us twenty thousand for our lease. We find another corner. What happens? Another man comes along and wants to put up a skyscraper. He needs the corner too. . . . Oranges, bah!" Mr. Zatkins repeated with a positively derisive accent. "It's the leases, not the oranges!"

From the leases, not from the insufferable oranges, Mr. Zatkins had bought a place in Westchester, and now his wife wanted some finery to go with it. Him, he cared nothing for such foolishness. He would as soon sit on an orange crate to read his paper. But women craved nice things, so they had come to the sale.

The wife arrived. She was a large woman with a shelflike front and a warm, kind, bewildered face. The auction began, and they bought everything: gilt piano, gilded bed with Venus rising from a gilded sea shell, gilt chairs, tables, mirrors, pictures, candelabra. It was a beautiful auction, Wyler recalled, and the most beautiful part of it was the enraptured smile on Mrs. Zatkins' face as bit by bit her new-found splendor fell before her dreaming eyes.

The Zatkinses went away and came no more. But many others stopped by for a touch of finery and formed the Anderson habit. John Gellatly, a very small man with a very large bank account, used to come every day. In the social swirl, Gellatly was noted for his meticulous attention to dress, but he always appeared at the galleries in the same brown suit. One day when his valet came to tote away the

Gellatly purchases, Arthur Wyler asked about the suit: "How do you ever press it if he always has it on?"

"Oh," said the valet, "he has two hundred of those suits, all just alike."

Originally Gellatly and his rich wife had made a life work of buying pictures by American artists. Then, in 1913, Mrs. Gellatly died, leaving $42,707 to her horse and about $1 million to her dapper husband. The horse managed nicely on his share, but in the postwar real estate boom, Mr. Gellatly increased his million to five. (Among Mrs. Gellatly's assets was a half interest in the Holland House property on Fifth Avenue, and inevitably a man came along who wanted to build a skyscraper.) From then on, as the *Times* put it, there was color in Gellatly's life; circumspectly the reporter added that Gellatly's very "weaknesses were lovable."

With his $5 million, Gellatly made himself the beau ideal of artists, art dealers, and auctioneers. He did not haggle with fortune, one of his friends remarked. He threw out most of the two hundred pictures Mrs. Gellatly had favored and bought better ones by the same painters. He delighted in paying higher prices for contemporary native art than anyone had ever paid before. Soon he was buying old masters to go with his American pictures. At the Anderson his fancy ran to wrought-iron locks, Arabic glass, old jewelry, baptismal fonts, Gothic sculpture, East Indian objects, Chinese antiquities, the ancient art of Syria, Egypt, Greece, and Rome, bowls that looked as if they had been made by Cellini, and whatever else happened to come along. Within ten years, except for a few stray dollars, the entire $5 million had been spent.

Thereupon, after weeding out the "overplus," Gellatly offered his collection to the Smithsonian Institution. It was gratefully accepted by an act of Congress in 1929. But the color refused to fade from the happy-go-lucky Mr. Gellatly's life. A year later, the small elderly dude—then seventy-seven and as renowned for his ironic humor as for his wardrobe—took to wife an adventurous lady from Georgia forty-three years his junior. The lady from the South was unaware that he had already given his art to the government, and she was enormously offended when she discovered that the bridegroom was all but penniless. The colorful Mr. Gellatly, she said, gave her $450 to cover her traveling expenses to New York and permitted her to rent a two-room apartment on East 57th Street. But that was all. He himself lived in a hotel and spent his time having his portrait painted by one of the grateful American artists he had patronized with princely, if misplaced, enthusiasm.

Within a short time the 57th Street landlord was suing for the Georgia lady's rent. Her no-good husband had impoverished himself, she told the judge, "in order to pose as a philanthropist." Gellatly smilingly admitted that he was unable to pay $660 in arrears and denied responsibility for the lady's upkeep anyhow. She had deserted him, he said. A year later he died, and the second Mrs. Gellatly even had to borrow the money to defray his funeral expenses, she said. Subsequently she appealed to the Smithsonian Institution to give back the art collection, on the ground that she had been royally duped. But the Congress took a light view of her petition, if indeed it took any view at all. The Gellatly purchases—sixteen hundred of them at any rate—remain in Washington, a fairly respectable, not to say expensive, component of what is now called the National Collection of Fine Arts.

Anderson addicts with Gellatly's charm were rare, but there was no dearth of clients who refused to haggle with fortune. Hearst customarily beat a path between the Anderson and the AAA and sometimes even stopped off at the smaller auction halls, at least one of which used to get up sales of Spanish antiquities wholly for his benefit, with elderly character actors posing as the underbidders. At considerably less overhead expense, the Spanish importers could have sold him those old church pews and altar cloths direct, but then Hearst would have been certain that he was being cheated.

As it was, he always suspected that the auctioneers were running him up. Once, at the Anderson, Hearst was bidding on an old Italian table. As Chapman rapidly called the bids he kept his eyes fixed only on the *sine qua non* of Italian table buyers, who was standing in the rear signaling his offers by poking an attendant in the ribs. When the price had risen to $7,500 Hearst muttered audibly, "I think I'll let the auctioneer keep this thing."

"Eight thousand," Chapman called, but Hearst sealed his lips with an obstinate smirk.

"Remember, it's against you," Chapman said, smiling, and still looking in Hearst's direction. "The bid is eight thousand dollars. . . . Fair warning . . ."

Hearst smiled, too, and shook his head, though, to be sure, it was a lovely table, pockmarked with time, rifled by termites, and perforated with many delightful wormholes.

"Sold!" cried Chapman with a triumphant smirk of his own. "To the gentleman in the third row."

Hearst strolled grandly down the aisle to confirm the fact that his opponent was nonexistent. There, in the third row, sat H. F. du Pont, a long-time rival and unquestionably a bona fide contestant. The self-satisfied expression faded from Hearst's face, and never again did he try to outwit the incorruptible Chapman.

For archaic decorations in general, the AAA was Hearst's prime hunting ground, and for a long time Otto Bernet was the auction room entrepreneur he trusted more than any other. But when it came to literature, Hearst had a warm spot for the Anderson. He seldom attended the book sales in person, but often late at night, when the galleries were dark and young Tony Bade would be in the back room working on the catalogues under a green-shaded light, he would hear a brisk footfall on the stairs. Hearst's figure would loom in the doorway from among the shadows. First, he would assure himself that there were no dealers lurking in the place; then he would come and perch on Bade's desk and leaf through the catalogues of the coming sales.

"I'll turn on the lights, Mr. Hearst," Bade would offer.

"No, no, don't let anyone know I'm here."

Hearst did not want to see the books, but he would point to numbers in the catalogues. "I have that. . . . I don't have that. . . . Get me this one, that one, and that if it doesn't go too high." He liked simple things, books that were easy to read—Dickens, for example, and other nineteenth-century writers of high moral tone. Sometimes he would buy duplicates of rare editions he already had— for the intellectual, and perhaps the moral, advancement of Miss Marion Davies; but Hearst knew very well what was in his libraries, as, with his extraordinary memory, he knew all his possessions, until they reached the point where no man could have retained a list of them in his head. Bade would bid for him in the sales, using his own discretion about when to stop and when to fight to the finish. After losing a few rare items to G. D. Smith, he learned that when Hearst said to get a thing he meant it, regardless of cost or his dread of being cheated.

Often the prices would soar to nerve-racking heights. For with all its busyness in so many fields, it was the Anderson's leadership in books and prints that kept it from being a second-string auction house by comparison with the AAA.

The seneschals of bookdom came to Kennerley's Park Avenue galleries as to a club. Belle da Costa Greene would be there, electrifying the rooms with her husky voice and her mercurial wit. B. G.'s majesty had, if possible, increased since J. Pierpont the first had died, leaving her the lifetime job of molding a rich man's greed into one of the great libraries of the world. But she continued to wear the dignity of her office lightly. In the sacred halls of Morgan she would sometimes greet an astonished visitor with a Gutenberg Bible balanced on her head. "Where the hell's the *City of God*," she would demand of an assistant in an irreverent tone that would have given a turn to old St. Augustine—to say nothing of old J. P. In the book halls of the Anderson, B. G.'s presence was a benign example, like the presence of a celebrated name as decoy on a list of sponsors. It was said that her influence had put Mitchell Kennerley in charge of the reconstituted Anderson Galleries. Whether or not she was also responsible for turning a stream of monumental literature in Kennerley's direction to be sold, politicos of the book scene agreed that Belle Greene was "a factor in the growth of the Anderson."

At the sales, Belle's friend the blandly self-important Abraham Simon Wolf Rosenbach would be very much in evidence, plugging away at his antic reputation with brash bidding that B. G. would sometimes cut short in a hoarse stage whisper: "Abie, shut up. Don't you know I want that?" And Abie would shut up.

In G. D. Smith's time Dr. R.—as "Abie" or "Rosy" came to be known to his gaping world-wide public—was still comparatively small fry in the rare book world, and still a little self-conscious about the scholarly approach to trade. Then in his early forties, plump, still bearing traces of his cherubic youth, but with a pince-nez to go with the title "Doctor," he combined a Buddha-like sagacity with a tendency to strut like Falstaff. The large-scale maneuvers that were to crown him "the Napoleon of bibliophiles" were still in the future, but to the Philadelphia bookworms who did not care if he added one zero or two to the prices on the flyleaves of the books and manuscripts he secured for their vaults he could quote rabinnical wisdom or Rabelaisian ribaldries, as the occasion demanded. Poetic passages in the classical languages rolled from his tongue as neatly as did quotations in five figures—a touch of showmanship that gave his clients the impression that they were acquiring the priceless pearls of understanding along with the almost priceless tomes of antique literature.

Privately Dr. R. liked to say that he owed his flair for trade to the fact that his grandmother had kept a successful house of ill repute—a pleasantry of self-deprecation not then as overindulged as the wags later made it. But pleasantries and the alleged commercial strain in his blood aside, Dr. R. could more accurately have attributed his rise to the power of advertising. When the publicity value of a lot was high, Chapman's genial incantations would sometimes be accompanied by an assenting movement of Dr. R.'s head that had the measured rhythm of a metronome. Nevertheless, as long as the undoctored G. D. Smith was alive, neither Dr. R. nor any of the other gnostic literary practitioners could budge him from his blustering eminence. When the treasure was newsworthy, it was Smith's name, and frequently Huntington's munificence, that made the headlines almost every time. When it was not, and especially when the bookmen were bidding for their own accounts, they were a ritual-loving cabal, childishly addicted to the secret signal, the almost invisible bid.

One would wag an ear, if he had the talent; another a foot, a pair of spectacles, a pencil. One would look over his glasses with a shrewd expression; another would put his finger circumspectly to his nose. A lifted eyebrow could mean thousands. A crossed leg could signify retreat. It was a long time before G. D. Smith discovered that his vigorous wink was a far from wily means of converse with the auctioneer. As he grew older, the muscles around his eye achieved a strange coordination with the beefy flesh on the back of his neck. He always sat in the front row, and every signal directed to the rostrum was relayed to his competitors in the rear by a reflex action in the bulge above his collar.

James F. Drake, round-faced, jovial, but also one of the shrewdest of commercial bibliophiles, bought many of the first editions in which he specialized by wagging his thumb. In one tense session he wagged Walter M. Hill of Chicago out of the price of a New York house while sitting with his arm affectionately draped around Hill's shoulder. Hill, suspecting foul play, demanded to know who was bidding against him. "I can't tell you, Mr. Hill," said the auctioneer, while

Drake, innocently smiling, continued to wag his thumb within an inch of Hill's ear.

Drake was known for his bookly aphorisms. "Opened with a dull thumb," he would say, if the pages of a rare volume had been carelessly separated by its first owner—a remark that passed into the language of the trade along with other phrases originated by the jolly pundit of the literary stock exchange. Drake worked along with Smith in promoting the great book boom, and he was the only one of the cabal that Smith looked upon as anything less than a mortal enemy. Sometimes, when the contest threatened to get out of hand, Drake would leave off wiggling his thumb and call out his bid in a merry, booming voice. Whereupon, if G. D. was his opponent, he would close his winking eye and let Drake have the lot. For Smith felt about James F. Drake the way Morgan had felt about the British Empire—he was too virtuous to argue with.

On the whole, the bookmen were a merry crowd; but there was one among them who cared not for the robust humor of Dr. R. or the subtle wit of James F. Drake, and especially not for the antics of the drinking members of the cabal, who often broke the spell at the Anderson with irrelevant banter. The unsmiling bidder was Gabriel Wells, a learned, waspy little man who wore the same two or three wing collars almost all his life and subsisted mainly on tea and biscuits. Wells made no jokes and barely nodded to his more flippant adversaries. And by attending strictly to business, he became one of the richest booksellers in the world.

A Hungarian by birth, Wells had arrived in Boston in 1891, a thirty-year-old scholar, penniless, versed in eight modern languages, no one of which was English. He sought refuge at Harvard, became a protégé of William James, and spent some time at the university, first as a special student, then as a tutor in German and psychology.

But profound as his intellectual resources were, Wells found it more fascinating to sell the sources of knowledge *in toto* than to attempt to impart the great books' contents to Harvard's undergraduates. He began by quietly cornering the market in *Stoddard's Lectures*, a many-volumed parlor ornament normally obtainable in installments by subscription. He bought all the sets and odd volumes that came on the market, had them rebound, and resold them to dealers at a tidy profit. With his winnings, he moved to New York and tried the same method with other subscription sets and the many "great books" series designed to provide the wisdom of the ages in one fell swoop.

Haunting the auctions, and working like a mole from his dingy furnished room, he gradually obtained so many near monopolies that dealers in standard literary wares found themselves climbing the stairs to Wells's book-stacked lodgings to bargain for their own specialties. When he outgrew his furnished room he took an office on East 23rd Street, and there he progressed into the realm of the more nearly priceless: first editions and elaborate bindings, color plates and sporting books, French and English literature, incunabula and manuscripts, and above all, American historical documents. For although Wells, to all appearances, might have been resurrected by some miracle from among the *outré* characters of his favorite author, Balzac, he had become a full-blown American with a fanatical devotion to the romance and history of his adopted country.

Gabriel Wells was no specialist, however. He spent five months of each year in Europe, gathering up the treasures that in his scholastic days had seemed as inaccessible as the moon. Over the years (he lived to be eighty-five and died in 1946), no fewer than thirty copies of the Shakespeare first folio passed through his hands, and he is said to have unearthed more Balzac material than any other Balzac student who has ever lived. One summer, in London, he bought a Gutenberg Bible, a bargain copy with fifty pages missing. He disseverated it—the word was his, for Wells's English was richly nonconventional—bound the leaves separately, and sold them, sometimes for as much as $1,000 each. Thus Wells made a far greater profit on his incomplete Bible than any book speculator could ever hope to make on a near-perfect copy.

With the multiplicity of his activities, Wells outgrew his 23rd Street office and moved to a better one, opposite the public library. Still later, he joined the northward trek to 57th Street. But he declined to spend any money on seductive atmosphere. He refused even to list his wares in a catalogue. "Let other dealers catalogue their books," he used to say. "I sell mine."

His penury was legendary. Though his bank account might contain $1 million, his restaurants were cafeterias. If he took a business associate to dinner, he ordered toasted muffins. If he went to a bibliophiles' convention, he licked the banquet platter clean and left the waiters ten cents as a tip. His books were his wives, his mistresses, his children. And yet he was capable of extraordinary philanthropy. When Balzac's house in Passy was about to be destroyed, he quietly wrote a check for the sum needed to preserve it as a national monument. He made many gifts to the libraries of England, France, and Hungary, and above all, he formed a habit of tithing his rarest acquisitions to the institutions of the country that had made him wealthy. Many significant documents on the early history of the New York region were deposited almost surreptitiously by Gabriel Wells in the New York Public Library. The Library of Congress shared his bounty, and so did many universities. But when he gave a check to charity he would sometimes neglect to sign it. He preferred to remain anonymous, he said.

The greatest excitement in Wells's life was an auction sale. Even when the stakes were modest, his blood pressure would mount like the color in the pink rose of a novelty barometer. If his face turned beet red when a book was placed upon the block, the auctioneer would know that he was prepared to bid high; and even with Rosenbach, Smith, and Drake opposing him, there were times when Wells could not be vanquished. For though he scoffed at the practice of making extravagant gestures for publicity, his clients were among the wealthiest of the builders of monuments in books. One of them was Henry C. Folger.

"If you knew what Folger didn't have, you could make a pile of money," a nostalgic brief-case dealer recalled. "Wells and Folger, they would buy any old thing, no matter what it was, so long as it had something to do with Shakespeare." An Anderson employee who liked to do a little trading on the side once picked up a bolt of chintz in a mill-end store for $7.50. It was ordinary chintz, though old and long since out of print, but it had Shakespeare's picture in a repeat about every 18 inches. "Ah," said the Anderson young man to himself, "Shakespeare on cloth! This is surely something Folger hasn't got." There was, of course, too much of it. A bolt of anything belied the necessary condition for rarity. So the young man cut off a piece. He framed it neatly and put it in a sale that Gabriel Wells would be sure to attend. Sure enough, the little square of Shakespeare chintz started at $50 and fell to Wells at $275. The young man, now living in retirement on his country acres, still has the rest of the bolt.

The Shakespeare chintz was no exceptional stroke of fortune. Novelties, relics, and memorabilia, always a side-show attraction of the auctions, achieved a new vogue as a concomitant of fashionable book collecting. When one of the lesser auction houses announced that it would raffle off the charming shoe-form bathtub in which Charlotte Corday stabbed Marat, some of the newspapers gave the event as much space as they would have given a change in ownership of the Hope diamond. Portable desks used by Dickens were in great demand, and pens used by Lincoln to sign the Emancipation Proclamation were worth $1,200. The supply of both was fairly good. A diligent scout dug up a handkerchief with Alexander Hamilton's picture on it, put it in a sale at the Anderson and got $375 for it; an inkwell containing the seal of Thomas Jefferson, for which the consignor had paid $2.50 in a rummage shop, did almost as well; and a locket said to contain a wisp of Jefferson's hair did even better—but only after its contents had been supplemented by Charles Retz, an Anderson employee. There were only two paltry hairs to start with, and while the cataloguer was examining them, a gust of wind blew one out of the window. Retz, nothing daunted, snipped off a lock of his own and contributed it. He liked to think, as time went on, that, somewhere, some Jefferson admirer might still be cherishing that wisp, for with the years, his head grew almost completely bald.

In those days of wonderful naïveté, the most incorrigible vendor of heirlooms was a gentleman named W. Lanier Washington. No other Washington-relic seller could compete with him, for according to the blurbs in his catalogues, he was "a direct descendant of two of George Washington's brothers, and the hereditary representative of General Washington in the Society of the Cincinnati," et cetera, et cetera. All of W. Lanier's relics had been handed down from five family sources, he avowed, and it was of course with reluctance that he offered them at public sale. His first auction, at the Anderson in 1917, had a lot of nice things that the patriots, one of whom was Hearst, snapped up with due avidity: shoe buckles, sword buckles, whist counters, wineglasses, and snuffboxes; a button from a coat worn by Washington while President; a receipt for the return of a slave who had run away from one of Washington's relatives. There were fragments of gowns worn by Martha Washington, things said to have been worn by Washington's mother, a pair of pants said to have been worn by

Washington himself. One of the most expensive items was a pair of Sheffield candlesticks "used by General Washington on his desk at Mt. Vernon." G. D. Smith bought them for several hundred dollars.

Intoxicated by the success of his initial venture, the great-great-great-grandson of a brother of George Washington subsequently showed up at the Anderson with a carload of ancestral trivia. It was possible, of course, that the Father of Our Country had had a mania for Sheffield candlesticks, but as Anthony Bade put it, "The question arose, where is Lanier Washington getting all this stuff?" Enough was enough for Mitchell Kennerley. He showed the wellborn Mr. Washington the door. Thereupon Mr. Washington took refuge at the AAA, where he held two more sales, composed of 931 separate items. Under pressure from the Million-Dollar Voice (and with a little help from Hearst), coat buttons brought $125 apiece; pink sea shells, said to have been bought by Washington from a needy sailor, made $210 each; shoe buckles went as high as $370.

The relic business was booming for W. Lanier Washington, but he was still not satisfied. Though claiming hereditary membership in the loftiest branches of patrician America, he was not above peddling his heirlooms from door to door. On the afternoon of March 4, 1920, he paid a historic call on G. D. Smith. Unaware that Smith had bought the first consignment of silver-plated candlesticks at the Anderson, he proposed to sell him another pair. A furious argument arose over the probable number of candles required to light the great Father's desk at Mount Vernon; and in the course of it, G. D. Smith dropped dead.

George David Smith was fifty years old and barely in his prime when he so abruptly departed this earth, leaving the mad book world and Uncle Henry Huntington in charge of Dr. Rosenbach, with the maggoty Gabriel Wells his bravest adversary. Less than three months before his death, Smith, having wholly smashed the Ring that had once kept book prices down in London, had broken all records at Sotheby's auction rooms and stirred up some little international havoc by paying $75,000 on behalf of Huntington for a tiny volume that weighed just two ounces and measured 2 by 3 inches in height and width. This literary speck, as *The New York Times* referred to it, was the fourth quarto edition of Shakespeare's *Venus and Adonis* bound with *The Passionate Pilgrim*. If Smith had lived through the twenties, the golden madness of that era might have been even madder and more golden, but as it was, Dr. R. made himself chief toll collector on the book-built road to fame.

The flow of chattels at the Anderson Galleries eventually reached the high-water mark, with twenty-two separate auctions held in the course of twelve consecutive days—book sales, dealer sales of lack-luster antiquities, sales bordering on the freak or monomaniacal. But frivolity was no patent of the Anderson. Probably the most bizarre redistribution Kirby ever undertook was that of the pleasure dome of Miss Susan Minns of Boston.

Miss Minns's singular passion, which shè pursued for seventy years, was for things relating to death. Beginning at the age of fourteen, through youth, maturity, and her declining years, her jet black skirts swirling at her jet black heels, her jet black hat pulled squarely over her relentless brow, Miss Susan Minns of Boston had chased death from country to country—death personified in books, manuscripts, curios, engravings, death rampaging through scenes of pestilence, war, famine, conflagration, fever, consumption, and despair, death exemplified in a thousand ways, magic formulas for averting it, recipes and devices for courting it. She was eighty-four at the time of the sale. Which of the magic formulas she used to prolong her life was never disclosed, but she managed to stave off a head-on encounter with her grim objective until 1938 when she was in her ninety-ninth year.

Miss Susan Minns was very rich. She lived alone in an old-fashioned house in Boston, where, if visitors came, she told them of the "enjoyment of life" she had received through her world-wide search for things intended to cause the beholder to shudder—skeletons, death's heads, coffin worms, buzzards, mummies, poison cups, and all recorded processes of "passing from nature to immortality." If prevailed upon to lay the cards, she could take her choice of many lugubrious decks. The nicest one, to Miss Susan's taste, had been painted on ivory by a somber artist of the fifteenth century. The queen of hearts danced enthusiastically with a skeleton. The knave of diamonds had a death mask grimacing over his shoulder. If her guests were disinclined to fortunetelling or an evening of whist in the company of such cheerless figures, Miss Minns could read to them from a Latin book on the art of dying printed in 1560, for she was a woman of scholarly attainment. (She was fond of worms. In her eighties she published a learned volume on the habits of the silkworm.) Or perchance, in the fringe-shaded lamplight of Miss Minns's parlors, a visitor might care to browse through a thousand or so prints and paintings descriptive of the *danse macabre*—scenes from the sixteenth century onward, many of them inspired by grim times when the plague was raging over Europe.

Macabre indeed was Miss Susan's gallery. Death and his victims engaged in fantastic exercises. Figures tortured by the worst diseases, often draped with leeches as a prophylactic measure, whooped it up with the violent acrobatics and jumping dances recommended as a cure by their physicians. These pictures, Miss Minns said, gave her a mite of pleasure; but she was also devoted to her coins and medals. Invidious bits of gold and silver they were, some minted, some hand engraved, portraying Death in many of his traditional postures: Death as a pale horseman riding among monumental tombs; Death with his scythe, cutting twigs from a tree hung with the Hamburg arms; Death as a hand emerging from a cloud with a terrible sword; Death with the symbolic hourglass. Other medallions dealt with the subject more obliquely. One pastoral scene inscribed on a silver plate showed some funereal cherubs burying a fellow cherub. Many simply depicted prostrate forms, commemorated loss of life in great disasters, or celebrated, as Miss Susan gleefully pointed out, "the death of princess and great ones."

Nothing delighted Miss Minns more on a rainy Boston afternoon than to peruse a work called *London's Dreadful Visitation,* a collection of all the bills of mortality for the year 1664, which had been a particularly nasty one for public health in England. The cover of this handsome necrology was pitch black, imprinted with three coats of arms interspersed with skeletons and other death emblems in spectral white. It was possibly her most impressive book, if a little repetitious in the reading.

When the names of London's sometime casualties began to pall, Miss Minns could turn to Holbein's *Dances of Death through the Various Stages of Human Life,* wherein "the capriciousness of that Tyrant" was exhibited in forty-six copperplates, or for a really juicy feast, she could take down from her shelves an illuminated manuscript of the thirteenth century having for its subject a lurid report of a Burgundian execution, illustrated with miniature paintings on pages profusely bordered with skulls and bones.

Surfeited with medieval torture, while sipping her tea from one of her several poison cups (the brew was no doubt spiked with one of those death-preventing formulas), Miss Minns could turn again to her not so Merrie England for more relaxing fare. In the twilight hour she might leaf through a solemn tome by John Weaver, dated 1631, with the title *Ancient Funeral Monuments within the United Monarchie of Great Britain, Ireland and the Islands Adjacent; with the Dissolved Monasteries therein Contained; Their Founders and What Eminent Persons Have Been in the Same Interred.*

Miss Minns was of a philanthropic nature, and after selling some other things at the AAA, she was persuaded to scatter her reminders of the brevity of human life among the Stygian collectors of a younger generation. But after Arthur Swann had made what was certainly the gloomiest catalogue in his archives, somebody told Miss Minns that the University of Louvain had had a gallery similar to hers until, alas! its buildings were destroyed in the war of 1914. Unable to bear the thought of the Belgian scholars' deprivation, she gave $12,500 to the Committee for the Restoration of Louvain to use to purchase some of the items in her auction. Nicholas Murray Butler, the committee's chairman, thanked her kindly and dispatched an emissary to Kirby's salesroom. Thus Miss Minns herself turned out to be the chief buyer of her own collection—a fortunate circumstance for the success of the sale, for Kirby's clients were not greatly drawn to the subject. The total was less than $18,000. Dr. R. paid the highest price—$1,025 for an old edition of *The Consolation of Philosophy,* a work that appealed to Miss Minns mainly because it was written in a sixth-century dungeon while its author was awaiting execution.

The bookmen, Rosenbach, Wells, Drake, Hill, and the others, came to the AAA as they came to the Anderson, but never in Kirby's time with "that spirit of good humor and good fellowship" that was said to prevail under Mitchell Kennerley's management. But if book meets at the AAA were something less than the "open-house parties" Swann had hoped to make them, the time-mellowed galleries on 23rd Street, and the show that had been passing there for so many years, grew more and more rhapsodic with the ever-rising price of art. When the collections could boast the requisite splendor, the rustle of silk was as loud as ever it had been before war had put an end to *La Belle Epoque* in Europe. The gentlemen's hats were not as high, perhaps, but in many cases the eyes of the gentlemen beneath them glittered with memories of heated contests won or lost. There were those at almost any sale who could recall the scandal of the Peach-bloom Vase. Only now, no one, not even *The New York Times*, blinked an eye when an incense burner fashioned in the fifteenth century by Il Riccio of Padua brought $66,000.

The bronze incense burner that turned to gold was the *rara avis* in the 1916 sale of "Art Treasures and Antiquities from the famous Davanzati Palace" of Florence. Famous indeed, to connoisseurs of such matters, was the ancient seigneurial dwelling, part medieval, part Renaissance, which the Italian antiquary Elia Volpi had brought back to life in the old Via di Porta Rossa, to evoke—in the language of its pamphleteers—"the vanity and poetry, the luxury and wealth, of Florence in the ages of its merchant princes." Animated, it was said, by the noblest of enthusiasms, Professore Commendatore Volpi had spent a fortune and years of dedicated labor on the resurrection of that "superb page in the history of Florentine architecture." The magnificent façade of the fortress-palace, the great court with its columns, its alcoves and elliptical-arched doorways, the grand staircase, the ceilings of gilt wood with armorial bearings, the Gothic and fifteenth-century chimney pieces—all had been relieved of centuries of profanations and restored to the harmony and grace of ages past. Entire frescoes had been uncovered; the somber, time-tinted apartments had been restocked with furniture and art works of the fourteenth to the seventeenth centuries, the rich and noble chambers equipped by Professor Volpi with everything from primitives on the walls to fifteenth-century linen towels beside the Renaissance hand basins. "We can enter this home and participate in its daily doings, share its life," *Les Arts* of Paris wrote in a Davanzati Palace number of August 1911. "It is a miracle or is it a dream?"

It was, in fact, a store. From the Davanzati Palace, Professor Volpi had sold such ardent collectors as Hearst and Thomas Fortune Ryan, Widener and Isabella Stewart Gardner many of their lustered works of Renaissance and Gothic origin. Morgan and B. Altman had been cherished customers before death removed them both from the collecting scene in 1913. Mortality and the hazards of war having curtailed the trek of visitors to Florence, Volpi—in the fall of 1915— packed up a boatload of Davanzati Palace furnishings, together with items from the Villa Pia, another of his restorations, and embarked for New York.

The cultural import of his mission was not immediately appreciated. Upon his arrival in New York harbor, the elderly and eminent Professor, who spoke no English, was thrust into captivity on Ellis Island on a morals charge stemming from his relations with his secretary and traveling companion, Signora Morosini. After the press had fully exploited the professor's alleged unchastity, the Italian ambassador obtained his release, and Volpi, presumably wearing the badge of infamy, attempted to sell his collection to New York dealers. A year passed, and the best offer he had received for his 1,215 items *in toto* was $500,000. Disgruntled and discouraged, he was about to accept it when Kirby persuaded him that he could do better at auction.

And, to be sure, he did. The heated contest raged for a week and brought in $938,947. Il Riccio's $66,000 incense burner, which Duveen bought for Joseph Widener, was not the only indication of the mounting Renaissance fever. H. C. Frick got a Tuscan walnut table for $11,100. Thomas Fortune Ryan took a Florentine carved-walnut bench at $8,000. A painted wood bust of a Florentine maiden "a-sparkle with the *joie de vivre*" brought $17,900. Mrs. Payne Whitney got a table presumably designed by Giorgio Vasari for $4,500. Carl Hamilton, an insomniac, got a fifteenth-century bed at $6,600. Joseph Duveen and Joseph Brummer, Arnold Seligmann and the assiduous decorating firm French and Company, vied with one another for Savonarola chairs and Dante chairs, terra-cotta sculptures, and majolica pitchers. Peripheral antique buyers contented themselves with fifteenth-century meat choppers, the soundless trumpets of medieval heralds, sixteenth-century laundering irons, and Umbrian tablecloths five hundred years the worse for wear.

The Davanzati Palace sale was called a classic among auctions. It was, at all events, a trailblazer. A year later, Professor Volpi was back with another pageant of Italian art, and by the following year, the perils of German submarines notwithstanding, he had persuaded his venerable compatriot Stefano Bardini to cross the ocean with a half-million-dollar auction from his treasure house in Florence. Incited by the rising prices, Vitall (the Pasha) Benguiat bought in the sales with one hand, and with the other, suffused the AAA with shimmering silks and velvet stuffs and Renaissance embroideries. G. T. Kirby, sensing a bonanza to be exploited, employed agents to scout sales in Italy, empowering them to pay cash advances to scavengers of Renaissance and Gothic objects. Horace Townsend wrote eloquent, if indulgent, catalogues from descriptions and proveniences furnished by the antiquarian-consignors. Titians and Tiepolos abounded, if the attributions could be trusted. Paduan bronzes and della Robbias came over by the carload, acres of sgabello chairs, forests of lugubrious cassoni.

Palaces, churches, villas, sent their heritages westward via professorial Italian dealers. But of all the Renaissance and Gothic artifacts that went under Kirby's hammer, no consignment from abroad shed such radiance in the galleries, or caused such consternation in the bidding, as the fifty lots of stained glass that had belonged to the New York stockbroker-connoisseur Henry C. Lawrence, who lived in the sublimity of bygone ages at 166 West 88th Street and died in 1919.

In a darkened farther room of the AAA, visitors gasped when confronted by those exquisite fragments of stained and painted glass, arranged in shadow boxes with floods of light behind them—opaque mosaic panels of intense, pure color that had somehow survived the lost churches of the thirteenth, fourteenth, and fifteenth centuries. "A house would wear them as a woman wears jewels," the *Times* reporter wrote.

Competition was fierce for the late Mr. Lawrence's windowpanes. Joseph Widener, having decided to buy most of them, commissioned Duveen to bid for him. Hearst naturally wanted them too, and so did many other habitual prize winners in Kirby's stable. But this time the favorites ran second. In the audience, on that January afternoon in 1921, a stranger appeared who refused to be outbid. He was a tall young man, in his middle thirties, and his lean face betrayed nothing but a kind of boyish frankness. As piece after piece fell to the nonchalant newcomer, underbidders shook their heads skeptically and a worried note crept into Kirby's incantations.

At length a panel came up that Duveen was determined to secure for Widener. It was a thirteenth-century piece, about 31 inches square, portraying a half figure of Christ, with a purple face, a yellow crown, a white and purple robe, and a yellow mantle. In the background was a portion of a Jesse tree, with scrolled acanthus leaves of white, green, purple, and red on a field of blue. Duveen offered $5,000 to start, but when the stranger had calmly run the bid up to $70,000, Widener's emissary shook his head disgustedly. As Kirby banged his gavel, the tension in the audience exploded in volleys of applause; but the young man kept his eyes fixed on the stage and pretended not to notice.

"Is he a fake?" Duveen demanded of G. T. Kirby in a rasping whisper.

"I don't know." G. T. shrugged.

Kirby beckoned to his son from the rostrum and handed him a note: "Find out quick who this guy is—if he's got any money."

The young man had diffidently scrawled his name on a card handed him by a porter: "Raymond Pitcairn, Philadelphia." It was a name unknown in collecting circles. G. T. rushed to a telephone and called a banker in Philadelphia. A few minutes later Kirby smiled benignly as he glanced at the slip of paper his son put before him and went on selling without a pause. "Pittsburgh Plate Glass—worth 20 million," the scribbled message read.

Eighteen of the thirteenth-century panels fell to Raymond Pitcairn. His bill was $153,850. Art dealers with business cards in hand swarmed around the "new one" when the sale was over, but he told them his name was A. P. Raymond and hurried away. It was not until nearly two months later that the *Times* reporter Asa Steele, in a piece called "Romance of Glass," disclosed the bidder's real identity, and also, the motive behind his casual invasion of the AAA.

At Bryn Athyn, Pennsylvania—a name that means "hill of cohesiveness" in the Welsh language—Raymond Pitcairn was building the Cathedral of the New Jerusalem. It was an undertaking that had been started in the nineteenth century by his father, John Pitcairn, a lean, bearded Scotsman whose two zealous preoccupations were the plate-glass industry and the revelations of the Scriptures according to the Swedenborgian doctrines of the New Jerusalem Church.

At first a firm of architects had been employed to build the Bryn Athyn church on a hilltop of Pitcairn's 700-acre estate near Philadelphia. They worked for years and turned out something vaguely suitable for an English parish—a far cry indeed from the spiritual and symbolic tenets of the New Church. Meanwhile Pitcairn's son, Raymond, had grown up in the Swedenborgian faith, and also, with a fanatical absorption in the history of art and architecture. He became more and more obsessed with the quest for beauty in stone, metal, and glass. The building of the church became the passion of his youth, and in 1913 his father put the project wholly in his hands.

Raymond Pitcairn outlined a fifty-year building program that began with the pulling down of most of what the uninspired architects had accomplished. It was his dream to go back in time some seven hundred years and revive the methods that had produced the great cathedrals of the Age of Faith. He did not wish to copy, he said, but "to establish in this twentieth century an organization which will produce work as beautiful as that done in the thirteenth century."

Connected with the Bryn Athyn church there was already a Swedenborgian settlement and an academy for the education of the New Jerusalemites from kindergarten through theological school. Now, Raymond Pitcairn established a system of neomedieval workshops for architects, builders, and artists. Granite quarries were opened within a half mile of the site where the white shrine of Bryn Athyn was to rise—or rather, evolve, for no less than four times was the main tower rebuilt as Pitcairn and his architects altered their conception of spontaneity and grace in mass, line, and shadow. Great white oak trees were felled in the Bryn Athyn forest and hewn into roof timbers or left to await the inspiration of wood carvers who, in the next half century, were to fashion them into church furniture and decorations. A foundry in a neighboring ravine supplied the metal for milled screens and panels; men were sent to Europe to study the windows of the great cathedrals; and in two studios on the Pitcairn estate artisans strove to create again the old-time glories of stained glass.

By 1921 a tentative model had been set up of the cathedral as it would perhaps appear when completed. The plan included a bishops' council hall, cloisters, towers with curious gables and connecting structures—the whole creating, as Asa Steele described it, "an impression of a fortified monastery of the early Middle Ages." The part of the church called the sanctuary was partially completed. It contained an altar symbolizing the "Throne of the Apocalypse," flooded with blue light from adjacent windows. On the altar was a great book covered with gold and flanked by three great tapers on either side.

The floor was ultimately to be composed of gold mosaic, representing the "Sea of Glass." The walls, still blank, were to picture apocalyptic angels, also in mosaic. Elsewhere in the church, monumental windows were to tell the Old Testament stories in the long-lost colors of the stained glass Raymond Pitcairn acquired at the AAA.

Inaccurate reporters said that the panels were to be installed in the Bryn Athyn church, but this was not so. Most of the subjects derived from the New Testament in the thirteenth century were foreign to the precepts of the Bryn Athyn theology. The faith of the General Church of the New Jerusalem centered on "The Word" as set down in the Book of Revelations, and on its internal meaning as revealed by Emanuel Swedenborg. Pitcairn wanted the fragmentary windows merely "as a source of inspiration" for his artists.

Now that the windows of that astonishing cathedral have been completed, the visitor to Bryn Athyn cannot fail to admire them— though possibly the old secrets of making colored glass remain as dark as ever. And as he leaves that strangely impassioned attempt to recapture the lofty religious and artistic experience of another age, many a cynical tourist, in common with the *Times* reporter who was sent to interview Raymond Pitcairn in 1921, "finds his eye wandering back again and again and again to the holy place on the hilltop, to its nave and sanctuary of glistening white, linked to a noble tower which soars upward in fascinating, though somewhat puzzling, beauty—a structure as complex as a human personality."

European castles and their contents, often of dubious artistic merit, kept Kirby's hammer clicking. But there were castles on the home front to be emptied too. On the rocky heights of Garret Mountain, overlooking Paterson, New Jersey, lived an octogenarian silk manu-facturer, improbably named Catholina Lambert, in Belle Vista Castle, a turreted stone fastness of English fourteenth-century aspect. Catholina Lambert was a short, stout, simplehearted old man. He liked to recall that from the age of ten, when he had been put to work in the infamous textile mills of Yorkshire, he had often said, "If I had money, I would buy a castle and fill it with wonderful paintings and sculpture." At seventeen he had obtained a one-way ticket for the land of the gold-paved streets, and in due time, he had his castle— rocks, battlements, paintings, sculpture, and all, to say nothing of such wonders as that 12-foot hall clock that kept A. T. Stewart informed of the time and so many other matters as well. But by 1916, when the castellan of Belle Vista was eighty-two, his silk mills had fallen on bad times. His four hundred paintings, pledged to a mortgagee, were consigned to the AAA for sale—as the doting old collector said, to pay his honest debts.

If it broke Catholina Lambert's heart to part with his paintings, no one would have known it. He was on hand every hour of the exhibition to bid them Godspeed. Like a lecturer conducting a band of trippers on an art-appreciation tour, he would pass from picture to picture, reliving the moment of excitement when he had bought this one or that one, offering his opinion on authenticity and quality, though readily admitting that his judgment might be fallible.

Perhaps his *Portrait of a Rabbi* was not a Rembrandt (though a man in Boston had said it was); no doubt his El Greco was a copy; and probably there was something wrong with his Titian, his Tiepolo, his Tintoretto. Ah, well, were they not beautiful at any rate?

"But see here . . ." The garrulous old man would pass on to another room. The Monticellis! Ah, forty years or more ago he had known Adolphe Monticelli well. Poor, tragic Monticelli, often he had sold his pictures for a crust of bread and a glass of absinthe in the cafés of Marseilles. These panels (canvas, alas, had been too expensive), were they not poetic? This lady with a fan, this one in a yellow dress, those cavaliers on white horses, those *fêtes champêtres,* these children bearing flowers. They were not his best work, perhaps. But these three large canvases Lambert had bought directly from the artist. Were they not dazzling? Those merrymakers in a punt, that group of ladies in the forest, that mystic autumn with the château in the background. There were twenty-nine Monticellis in all. Belle Vista Castle was indeed a bleak and empty place without them.

And here was Ralph Albert Blakelock, an American no less benighted in his fashion, driven by poverty and neglect into the insane asylum, where, it was said, he painted $1-million bank notes to support his delusion of immeasurable riches. Eleven of Blakelock's visions of the old West were hanging among the Courbets and Delacroixs, the Constables and Lawrences.

There were other living artists represented—four good paintings by Renoir, six by Monet. They would be very valuable in time.

As anyone could see, the moods of Belle Vista Castle had ranged far and wide. There, beyond the Luini altarpiece and the Van Dyck with a question mark, were seven Pissarros, eight Sisleys, three Boudins. Was it not a magic world—that shifting panorama of French fishing ports and vessels, of glassy seas and cows at pasture, tile-roofed houses and poplar-lined roadways, animated towns and winter land-scapes, of canals and villages and old church towers, the Seine alive with tugs and people, the ever-changing blue-gray skies of Normandy?

It was an auction of strange bedfellows and even stranger contrasts in the prices. The Luini altarpiece, *The Madonna Enthroned* (Sir William Agnew had called it one of the three greatest Madonnas in the world), went to the Brooklyn Institute of Fine Arts for $33,500; but the *Saint Francis* of El Greco could do no better than $600. The *Holy Family* of Andrea del Sarto made $27,000, but the *Holy Family* of Tiepolo went for $1,250. *The Meeting of Saint Germain and Sainte Geneviève* by Puvis de Chavannes, wonderful to say, made $18,000, a Botticelli *Madonna and Child* brought $22,000; but the Rembrandt the old man had thought so beautiful went for $3,200.

To have determined what was really what and by whom would have taken a corps of experts. Some who bought the real found themselves with the false, and in other cases, possibly the situation was reversed. To this day there are men with magnifying glasses poring over old masters from Belle Vista Castle. As recently as 1954 a *Madonna and Child*, ascribed to Andrea Salai in the Lambert cata-logue and sold to Mrs. Spencer Kellogg for $1,950, was pronounced "a true Leonardo" by "an internationally noted art authority" in Chicago. Leonardo or not, Catholina Lambert would have said, it was beautiful in any case.

But it was not the unlikely possibility of undiscovered Leonardos, nor yet the tidy sums bid for unexceptional Holy Families, that put the crescendo of excitement into Kirby's patter as the Catholina Lambert sale wore on into the fourth night. It was the moment when Blakelock's *Brook by Moonlight* fell to the Toledo Museum of Art at $20,000. Blakelock had been one of those home-grown artists the AAA had set out to encourage and promote at that grand reopening back in 1885. Now, the graybeard auctioneer saw it as a vindication of that august institution's early prescience that under his hammer a Blakelock landscape should bring the highest price that had ever been paid for an American painting at auction.

Nor was Blakelock the only native artist whose works could now command fancy prices. In 1918 he was nosed out as high man in the American category when a sunlit brook by Alexander H. Wyant soared to $21,500. The 1917 sale of Dr. Alexander C. Humphreys' American paintings produced a George Fuller, *Girl and Turkeys*, worth $15,600, a tribute the bidders failed to shower in any considerable part on some very good pictures in the Humphreys collection. Thomas Eakins' *Professionals at Rehearsal* brought $650. A small Albert Ryder that would be a gem in any modern art collection sold for $600. Three years later, at the Mrs. Roland C. Lincoln sale, Winslow Homer's *Wild Geese in Flight* evoked a winning bid of $28,000. But by 1920 even that was not a new record for an American painting. At the George A. Hearn auction of 1918, George Inness, twenty-four years after his death, had at last proved himself the sweepstakes winner Kirby had been selling tickets on since 1883. *The Wood Gatherers*, for which Hearn had paid $5,600 in the Thomas B. Clarke sale of 1899, fell for $30,800, a height never again to be achieved by the American brown tree.

No less exalting to Kirby's ego, in view of the ridicule that had greeted their works at the AAA in 1886, was the growing appreciation of "The Impressionists of Paris." At the Hugo Reisinger sale in 1916 a Pissarro, *Femme à la Chèvre*, sold for $5,100—though, to be sure, the seven Pissarros in Catholina Lambert's auction a month later brought an average price of only $1,010. In 1917, when Kirby sold some of the Monets collected by his onetime partner, the late James F. Sutton, *Vue de Bordighera* brought $15,900, a price not to be surpassed by a Monet at auction until 1957. Renoirs from Belle Vista Castle that a blind man could now appraise in six figures went for $1,225 and $3,600; nevertheless, Catholina Lambert's *Girl Knitting* made a Renoir record of $16,200. After Renoir's death in 1919 his stock took a sharp upward turn. At a sale in 1920 *Dans la Prairie* brought $28,000 and the now-famous *Canotiers à Charenton* fell at $27,000. In the same auction a Manet, *Devant la Psyché*, brought $12,400. Sisley, too, appeared to be on the fringe of the Very Valuable. The best any of Catholina Lambert's eight Sisleys could do in 1916 was $2,050, but by 1920 a Sisley, *Inondations à Moret*, brought $6,300.

In 1921 the Paris art dealer Jacques Seligmann consigned to the AAA seventy oils and pastels from the large number of works unleashed by Degas' death in 1917. The high price was $17,000, for a seated figure of a woman called *Portrait in White;* pastels could be had for as little as $650, though a number of ballet scenes and racetrack studies passed the $10,000 mark. Together, the seventy paintings and one drawing brought $226,000, about what one of the better pictures would be worth today, but a total Kirby could boast as a long-delayed triumph for Degas in America.

It had taken the Madison Square sports three decades to adjust their vision to Degas and Renoir; and now the term "modern" had come to include a quite different kind of painting. In January 1922 it fell to Kirby to conduct the first market test in America of such great contemporaries of the impressionists as Cézanne, van Gogh, and Toulouse-Lautrec, along with works by painters whose pictures, in their turn, were regarded as beneath the dignity of a barbershop.

At the time of the historic Armory Show in 1913 the old guard had railed against postimpressionist art with a barrage of nonappreciation unprecedented in the annals of choleric criticism. Contemporary art as exemplified in that gigantic display was "a part of the general movement discernible all over the world," said a *Times* editorial, "to disgust and degrade, if not to destroy, not only art but literature and society too." The cubists and futurists were arrant humbugs, nay anarchists, "trying to block the wheels of progress in every direction."

"The thing is pathological!" wrote Mr. Kenyon Cox, a Man Who Knew certified by the *Times* as a sound artist and a rational human being. "With Matisse, with the later works of Rodin . . . it is no longer a matter of sincere fanaticism. These men have seized upon the modern engine of publicity and are making insanity pay."

Insanity, whether it paid or not, had long had the support of Dirkan (Khan) Kelekian, a dealer and collector acknowledged in this country and abroad as the foremost authority on Oriental textiles and Near Eastern antiquities. An Armenian born in Turkey, who sometimes called himself a native of Persia (whence came the title Khan, bestowed upon him in recognition of his services as that country's honorary consul general), Kelekian had been seer and counselor to a generation of art-hungry millionaires. Through such princely patrons as B. Altman and J. P. Morgan, Henry Walters, John D. Rockefeller, and Isaac D. Fletcher, the Khan Kelekian had endowed the museums and private collections of the United States with a galaxy of dethroned splendor. Among his more conspicuous transplantations were the Winged Bull and Winged Lion that once guarded the palace of Ashurnasirpal II in Nimrud in Assyria, and some twenty-seven centuries later, began to stand vigil in the Metropolitan Museum.

"Papa" Kelekian was a gifted, wise, and greatly revered man, white-haired and white-bearded in his later years, of whom Frank Crowninshield wrote:

> He is a creature so curiously compounded that under his grim and sometimes awesome visage, he combines, in one person, the qualities of a Persian satrap and a properly accredited archangel; of Genghis Khan and the Chevalier Bayard; of Thor, the God of Thunder, and St. Francis of Assisi.
>
> . . . Certainly no man is more favored or more loved. Our affection derives not alone from his manifold benevolences and fixed determination to help those in distress, but from the comfort of his companionship, the great simplicity of his manners and the almost supernatural serenity of his soul.

His reputation as spademan of ancient cultures aside, this marvelously concorporate being was an impassioned admirer of race horses and modern art. Despite "that solemn and stately mien of his," Frank Crowninshield attested, he "befriended any and every discouraged artist who came to him for solace, encouragement or aid." In the course of his benefactions and out of his wide acquaintance with the vibrant world of French painting, the Khan Kelekian had assembled a gallery that the critic Seymour di Ricci called the most significant and instructive gathering of masterpieces by artists of the last hundred years that had been brought to the attention of this country. It was this collection that Kelekian was moved to sell at the AAA in 1922.

A glance at the Kelekian catalogue now—and at its prices—can be an unsettling experience for art lovers and hindsight speculators inured to the $800,000 Cézanne, the $324,000 Gauguin, the $1,300,-000 van Gogh.

Of the sixteen choice works in that auction-hall debut of Kelekian's close friend André Derain, the highest price was $1,300 for a large Fauvist landscape. Vases of flowers and Derain figure pieces, submitting to the halloas of an indulgent Thomas Kirby at $10 and $25 advances, brought from $130 to $525. Utrillo was rated no higher than $300, the price of both *Effet de Neige* and *La Rue*, two of his best white-period pictures. A third Utrillo, *Le Château*, fell at $160.

Bonnard's *Fillette à Table avec un Chien* brought $525. A portrait of Madame Hessèl by Vuillard made $350. Fauve river scenes by Vlaminck went for $250 and $350.

There were six paintings and two drawings by Matisse. Four of the paintings brought from $300 to $625; but Joseph Brummer—who, like Kelekian, was a sapient dealer in both ancient and modern art—paid $1,000 for *La Fenêtre sur le Jardin,* and the Detroit Institute of Arts bid $2,500 for a large 1916 Matisse interior called simply *La Fenêtre.*

The farseeing Detroit Institute also got a Raoul Dufy at $75 and its renowned van Gogh self-portrait at $4,200. To Brummer, at $4,400, went van Gogh's *La Cueillette des Olives,* now in the collection of Mrs. Enid Haupt and, in light of present-day sales, of inestimable value.

Gauguin's *Maternité (Tahiti)*, subsequently to become one of the glories of the Lewisohn collection, moved no one to bid more than $7,000, and $3,100 was the high bid for Toulouse-Lautrec's portrait of Cipa Godeski, later bought by Edward G. Robinson and now in the collection of Greek shipowner Stavros Niarchos. Of the remaining three Toulouse-Lautrec portraits, the Brooklyn Museum acquired two: *M. Sescaut* at $1,400 and *Portrait de Femme Assise* at $1,600. The fourth, a portrait of an anonymous misty-eyed woman, fell to John Quinn at $1,900.

No bidder was more active, or more richly rewarded, than John Quinn, the hardheaded Ohio-born bank lawyer who, before his untimely death in 1924, was a courageous and astute patron of arts and letters and one of the world's most sagacious collectors of modern paintings. Ten of the works that made the John Quinn collection famous came from the Khan Kelekian's auction. Among them were a major Cézanne, *Paysage de Provence,* at $9,500 and a 1919 landscape by Picasso at $2,000. A rare bargain—at $1,800—was Corot's *Italienne Assise a Terre, Accoudée sur Sa Cruche (Italian Woman Seated on the Ground, Leaning on Her Pitcher)*, one of the small figure pieces which even in 1922 were scorned by fashionables panting to pay $30,000 for a misty Corot dawn on the river. Rarer still—at $5,200—and perhaps John Quinn's greatest coup at that sale so redolent with hindsight ironies, was Georges Seurat's famous *Jeune Femme Se Poudrant,* now in the Courtauld Collection in London.

Another prudent bidder was Miss Lillie P. Bliss, a founder and benefactor, seven years later, of the Museum of Modern Art. Miss Bliss made off with a 1914 cubist Picasso, *Grande Nature Morte: Le Compotier*, at $575, a Cézanne portrait of Madame Cézanne at $9,800. It was thanks to her tenacity and to that of her competitor, Dr. Albert C. Barnes (plus, it was said, a little puffing from the Khan Kelekian's shills) that Cézanne emerged as far and away the stellar attraction. To Miss Bliss at $21,000—a record price considered unaccountable and even scandalous to 1922 commentators—fell the large Cézanne still life of apples, dishes, and draperies that is now a cornerstone of the Museum of Modern Art's collection.

Having divested himself of his modern masters, Kelekian lived on to beguile the art world with his colorful presence for thirty years. Then, in 1952, old and ill and partly blind, he rose one January morning from the bed in his suite at the Saint Moritz Hotel, placed his slippers side by side before a window facing east, and clad only in his long underwear, plunged to his death in the courtyard twenty-two stories below. He did not live quite long enough to see the modern-art imbroglio of the mid-fifties, when the 161 pictures Kirby had sold for $254,870 would have been worth inestimable millions. As it was, Kirby, who personally doubted that Picasso and Matisse were here to stay, called the prices phenomenal.

Withal, the Million-Dollar Voice, flowing on and on, was nothing if not impressive. Now the papers sometimes spoke of the little man with the white goatee as the George Washington of auctioneers. "There is only one Thomas E. Kirby in the world—he is the AAA . . . a milestone, an example," *Arts and Decorations* wrote at the time of his seventieth birthday. "Mr. Kirby is growing gray in honesty," *Art News* added. "His is a business as full of pathos as of romance, of great victories too, recorded in the dollars and cents that are so often the seamy side of art."

That there was only one of him Thomas Kirby was supremely aware. He had grown gray in honesty, but he had also grown more imperious, and more and more cantankerous. From the rostrum, he scolded the clients; behind the scenes, he scolded his lieutenants. He referred to Otto Bernet as "my first assistant auctioneer," but Otto sold only tarnished splendor. To the majority of the clients Bernet had become the most popular figure in the galleries, but he remained a corporal in the vainglorious camp of an old conqueror basking in the sun of those many dollar victories.

In 1918 the Parke Gallery ceased to function. For with the expanded sales at the AAA, the line between art and overflow had been lost, and the subsidiary house had threatened to assume the black character of a competitor. Major Parke was taken into the main establishment as chief of the bureau of appraisals. Parke had an uncanny flair for predicting art values, but his job was severely complicated by Kirby's habit of going over the appraisal sheets and revising the figures according to his own fancy.

One instance of the old man's whimsicality Parke always remembered. When, in the natural course of events, Captain De Lamar died, leaving the embellishments of his mansion to return to the auctions whence they came, Parke was sent as usual to make the appraisal. What were those sentimental pictures worth now, in 1919, Alma-Tadema's *Love's Missile,* Raimundo de Madrazo's *Sortie du Bal,* and all those ghostly marble statues, the coy *Greek Slave* with chained hands discreetly placed that had once stood in A. T. Stewart's lofty hall, the *Zenobia* that had endured the frozen oratory of *Demosthenes,* the Thomas Crawford *Flora* that had been the pale companion of Mrs. Stewart in her prowling midnight hours? How high would some bidder go for the Mad King's bed from the Yerkes palace, or for the Great Mosque Carpet of Ardebil?

Five hundred dollars each, Parke marked the marble girls. The *Greek Slave,* which had been so famous that miniature casts of it had stood in hundreds of Victorian parlors, might be worth three to four thousand still, Parke thought, and he was right. It sold for $3,550 to ex-Governor Franklin Murphy of New Jersey. As for *Zenobia* and *Flora,* Parke had called them almost on the nose. *Love's Missile* was still worth $3,100—but how Madrazo's charms had diminished! *Sortie du Bal,* which cost $16,500 in 1898, brought only $2,000 now. The Mad King's bed went for a like sum, which was (despite the fact that Rose Lorenz had published the information that the Mad King had never tossed a sleepless night therein) $600 more than the Captain had paid for it. But the rug of Ardebil . . . ah! that was quite another matter. De Lamar had paid $27,000 for it; Parke added $3,000, figuring that the Captain had got a bargain; and when the Great Mosque Carpet came to the block, it sold to Duveen for $57,000.

As always, when his prognostications fell beside the mark, Parke faced the terrors of the verbal whipping post. No sooner had the Ardebil carpet been sold than he was summoned to stand at attention on the carpet before the acidulous old auctioneer. "I'm shocked and ashamed of you," Kirby began. "For the length of time you have been in this business it is unforgivable to value a rug at ten thousand dollars that sells for fifty-seven!"

"Ten!" said Parke in astonishment. It was a familiar scene, but this time he rebelled. Turning to the original appraisal of the deceased Captain's assets, he said, "You know your own writing, don't you, Mr. Kirby?"

"Yes."

Parke then dared to show the forgetful old man where, with his own hand, he had drawn a red line through the original $30,000 and revised the estimate downward to $10,000. It was a tactical breach. The tongue-lashing the Major received for the impiety of "talking back" was far more violent than it would have been for any number of erroneous predictions.

When there was art property to be sold, Parke was seldom allowed in Kirby's rostrum. He was, however, permitted to preside over the routine book and print sales. Kirby did not have the lust for books he had for art, and Rose Lorenz despised them. Swann's efforts notwithstanding, the musty realm of printing remained in the afterglow of the galleries' effulgence. Parke, who was never a man to open a book unnecessarily, took no great pleasure in hawking literary relics. But, in common with Gus Kirby, he recognized their strategic importance in the rivalry with the Anderson. With Swann's collaboration, he managed to bring a measure of dignity and glamour to the AAA book auctions; and in those last years of the old regime, when both men would have been outcasts but for the protection of G. T. Kirby, Parke and Swann formed a coalition based on mutual respect that lasted to the end of their lives.

Autographs and first editions, which did not lend themselves to orgies of decoration, received short shrift from Rose Lorenz; for with the necessity to produce ten glamorous stage sets in the time formerly devoted to one, her majesty and temperament increased tenfold. Now her yardstick was almost always lost. Now, a formidable woman of Wagnerian stature, she ruled the new stenographers and all the other interlopers G. T. Kirby had employed—with her stick, as she had always ruled the cringing supporters of her protean star part. Her staginess was comical, but no one dared to laugh. Her stridency increased with the threat—unspoken, but nonetheless apparent—that Gus Kirby, if he should ever succeed his father, would take her kingdom from her. With the sense that time was running out, her demands in the name of her aging lord protector grew more tearful and grandiloquent. Only now it was not "Mr. Kirby" who threatened or forgave, but "Mr. Thomas E. Kirby," lest by some chance the name of the father should be taken for that of the son.

"My poor Mr. Thomas E. Kirby!" she would cry, spreading her arms in Brunhild fashion, if a spear carrier should be guilty of real or imagined fallacy. When Mr. Thomas E. Kirby breathed a simple order, all normal duties had to be suspended; and Rose, sweeping through the galleries, brandishing her stick (when it could be found), saw that this was so. For nowadays Mr. Thomas E. Kirby's nerves were almost always bad.

She was a ham, but as she grew older, she was also pathetically human. For the gala sales she would take her Benguiat pearls with some little ceremony from the vault. She would gown herself in velvet, with a touch of old lace or chinchilla. Her Prussian features had grown hard, and there were puffs and wrinkles impossible to conceal, but she still longed to compete with the lilies of the social field.

Her longing for attention would break through like a chink in the stanchest armor. In her two houses, she gave lavish parties for the gallery employees, out of loneliness perhaps; for there was a back-street quality about her life, for all its surface glitter. The parties were mostly failures. If the guests enjoyed themselves, she felt left out; if they did not, she was offended; and always jealousies arose to sour the champagne and spoil the charm of her largess.

An invitation to her country house was the equivalent of a royal summons; and the rooms were severely graded. The favored week-ender occupied the blue room, but from then on, the accommodations grew smaller and progressively more squalid. A staff member who slept in luxury one Saturday would know that he had incurred the Lorenz disfavor when on the next he was assigned to the magenta cubbyhole behind the kitchen. If by chance the weekend turned out to be pleasant, the volatile hostess would make amends for it on Monday by nagging more than ever. As one of her former underlings put it, she was like a cow that gives a pail of milk and then kicks it over.

It was the milk of human kindness that Rose now made a fetish of distributing. No minor subject would have dared approach her for a favor, or even for a raise in pay. And yet, when the inevitable vicissitudes of working people's lives reached her by the grapevine, Rose Lorenz was generous in her feudal way. Then would come the bountiful gesture: the baskets for the sick; the trips to the seashore for the children; the toys, the bicycles, the unexpected holidays. Weddings, divorces, and funerals were Kirby's province, but Rose would loosen the purse strings on lesser occasions—to an extent that was remarkable in the hard, commercial world of the time.

Her health, in common with Mr. Thomas Kirby's, was perpetually on the verge of collapse. James P. Canny, the late Parke-Bernet expert on literary Americana, once recalled a strangely moving little incident. In the latter days of the Lorenz regime, Canny was a book handler in the department that was dust beneath her feet. One day when she was making a tour of inspection, Canny looked up from his work and said, "Hi'ya, Miss Lorenz. How do you feel today?" It was no more than the casual greeting of an outgoing, irrepressibly sociable youth. But, though he did not know it, Miss Lorenz had been absent for a day or two suffering a partial "collapse."

She stopped and looked at him. "A little better, thank you," she said. "I think I feel a little better today." She swept her wan brow with the back of her hand and passed on.

Later in the day she summoned a very apprehensive James Canny to stand before her on the dread carpet he had never seen before. He was trembling as he entered the inner sanctum, but though in the presence of the Borgia, as it were, he had nothing to fear.

"I want you to know," she said, "how much I appreciate your inquiring after my health." No one of her girls, she went on bitterly, had thought to do as much, not Parke, Bernet, or Seaman, no one but little Jimmy, of all her seventy-five ungrateful subjects. "When is your vacation?" she inquired in a weary but expansively kind voice. Jimmy told her, and when the time came, there was an extra week's salary in his envelope, to say nothing of a raise in pay upon his return.

It was as if the old auctioneer and his consort were running a race with time and progress, a shrill-voiced marathon that could end in no rewards they had not already known. And inevitably, time caught up with them. For as the febrile twenties dawned, the witches' brew of progress was bubbling madly in the pot. It was a brave new day, when all that was old was expected to vanish. "On with the dance" was the cry on every front; "Make way for the new"—the new prosperity, new pleasures stimulated by bootleg whisky, the new buildings that were to rise almost like mushrooms overnight, the new extravagance that was to fill Park Avenue and Miami with old masters aged, like the whisky, overnight and Italian furniture old or new but worm nibbled in any case. White-haired Thomas Kirby would have devoutly wished to spend his last days on Madison Square with the memories that old men cherish, but his son, Gustavus, had other plans.

The rambling 23rd Street galleries that Charles A. Dana's *Sun* had once called the most beautiful in the world were outmoded. The red plush walls and dark-stained woodwork, the unpalatial staircase and the creaking floors, were no longer grand in the sense that they had been in 1883. The old skylights rattled in the wind and frightened the new stenographers when the rain beat hard against the glass. The new generation was perhaps more flighty than the old. When there were thunderstorms the female help turned pale and had to be sent home, and some of the most intrepid art lovers cringed when the elements were wild. Rats ran over the account books and chewed the papers in the files. Being rats, they even had the audacity to mingle with the patrons in an all too familiar way. One afternoon when Mrs. Arabella Huntington was in Gallery A, feeling some Oriental rugs, a big, bold rat came along and felt them with her. Tom Clarke, anticipating a total eclipse of the Huntington patronage, was frozen with horror. But all the lady said was, "Here, pussy, pussy"; for Mrs. Huntington, too, was growing old, and her eyesight was not what it once had been.

The skylights could have been repaired, a Pied Piper employed to decoy the rats; but Madison Square was no longer chic. Not only the Anderson Galleries but the entire fine arts trade had followed the northward movement of the city; and Gustavus Kirby, as part of his plan for perpetuating the AAA, had bought the plot of land where stood the Lester Studios at Madison Avenue and 57th Street. Now, he approached his father with the idea of leaving Madison Square. The conversation, though no doubt an awkward one, was probably not quite as stiffly oversimplified as the elder Kirby reported it:

"I think it is time we thought about building up on Madison Avenue," G. T. said.

"We?"

"Well, I have an offer for the property that will give me a great profit. In fact, it is so large I could accept it and retire for the rest of my life on the interest."

"You had better retire."

"Oh, no," G. T. protested, "I've got too much pride in the American Art Association. If I were offered a million or two million profit, I wouldn't accept it, because I am going to erect on that plot the American Art Galleries, such an American Art gallery that it will be a monument to you and the association."

Old man Kirby wanted no monument. He did not like the inexorable prospect that the word implied; nor would he have any active part in what was for him an eleventh-hour undertaking. Nevertheless, the great art gallery came into being, one of the truly beautiful structures that have risen in New York only to be subsequently destroyed.

Built on the foundations of the old Lester Studios, G. T. Kirby's auction palace covered the entire block front on the east side of Madison Avenue from 57th Street to 56th. Its long orange brick façade, designed by J. D. Leland and Company of Boston in the best and simplest tradition of the Italian Renaissance, was not intended to take the breath away, but to form a serene and dignified focal point for the city's new art world. Somehow it seemed to do precisely that. Even before its walls had weathered a season's storms, its unostentatious profile had settled into the landscape, not as an intrusion, but as a graceful punctuation mark to the rows of brownstone dwellings that still lined Madison Avenue in 1922.

Inside, the corridors had a cool white-plaster, time-washed sumptuousness, like some noble house left over from the Old World, before the rich interiors bogged down under baroque excesses of decoration. There was nothing ornate. Some of the walls were hung with velvet, to be sure, and the deep-pile wine-colored carpets (the color came to be known as American Art red) were certainly luxurious, but these details were offset by long vistas revealing a judicious correlation of arches and square, stately portals. There were low ceilings with light, incurving upper walls and wide, plain moldings; there were long halls and many well-proportioned chambers flowing together to make a harmonious procession of parts—many levels, many planes and passages, many little stairways leading through the nineteen tranquil rooms that were to hold the treasure waiting for the fateful hammer.

The grand staircase would not have done for Louis XIV or for Charles T. Yerkes, but it was beautiful in its broad, discreetly ornamented way. The proscenium of the main assembly room on the third floor was embellished with gold leaf; its rostrum would have enhanced the dignity of a bishop; but the only other decoration was the admirably wrought grillwork of the balcony surrounding the three sides not occupied by the stage.

Though the building was five stories high, it had no windows above the second floor. Irrespective of the position of the sun, the light of day fell on much of the 30,000 square feet of exhibition space through skylights ingeniously fitted with louvers. In the picture galleries artificial lighting was filtered through prismatic lenses to provide an even diffusion of light from floor to ceiling.

Never before in any city of the world had a building of such taste and magnificence been dedicated to the conduct of art and literary auctions. In all, Gustavus Kirby had spent $2,250,000, and though the new art center belonged exclusively to him (and to the insurance company that held the mortgage), it was the proudest moment of his life, he said, when he was able to turn it over to his father, then seventy-six years old and in the sixty-fifth year of his working life.

Thomas Kirby tried to appear grateful. "God bless my boy," he said. "I know I've got a real son, and I appreciate it." But when the time came to move, in November 1922, the old man was reluctant to go. On the last day, when the old galleries had been deserted, he stayed down there alone, pacing the whole day through among the dust and echoes. How often, in his profession so intimately related to times of trouble, had he seen the house dismantled, the bits and pieces of a proud life scattered, or handed on to a younger generation. Now it was his life that was being scattered. For Madison Square had been his life, his home, the scene of all he had so tyrannically built and so jealously defended. Now the AAA that was Thomas Kirby would be no longer personal, but a mere association, one step even from a corporation; for it was certain that in the uptown palace he would ever be a stranger. He sat in his old rostrum and tears rolled down his cheeks.

But Madison Square, too, was passing, or had passed. From the broad windows where he had stood with James F. Sutton forty years before, he could see but one or two of the old houses now. Through the dried leaves of the November trees, he could still glimpse the Saint-Gaudens *Diana* atop Stanford White's ill-fated Garden, her drawn bow poised gaily if a little foolishly, her arrow still unsped, her modest sash long since blown away, to the horror of the pursed-mouth citizenry. Though made of bronze, *Diana* too was temporary, for Madison Square Garden was now to be demolished. What fanfare there had been at its opening in 1890! What hats, what feathers, what flying colors! But the Moorish-French-Italian pleasure palace had been a jinx. Its prize fights had never made a cent of money, nor its grand ballets, its dog, fish, horse, or pigeon shows. Not even Buffalo Bill, Jenny Lind, or Yousouf (the Terrible Turk) had turned a profit, not the handsome assembly hall where Stanford White had wanted Kirby to conduct his auctions, not the swimming meets in the gigantic pool, nor the battle of Santiago reproduced as on a mimic ocean, nor the imitation Venice with the young blades paddling around in gondolas buying ice cream for their dolls. Like the prize ring and the roof garden, the tank had been a place of death, of drownings and the bodies floating to the surface, of foul play and dank, sinister implications. Now no one any longer wanted to support the place. An insurance company had grabbed the land, a Gorgon-headed sister to the one with the terrible bells that had usurped the ground where Catharine Lorillard Wolfe and S. L. M. Barlow had so grandly lived when a young Thomas E. Kirby had come to Madison Square.

Almost nothing remained that had been meaningful forty years before. Even the Chamber of Horrors had moved its wax statues to Coney Island. The Flatiron Building, which in 1902 had caused conservative folk to shake their heads at its twenty-one story audacity, was outmoded and a pygmy now. Delmonico's and all the old hotels were gone, the Brunswick, the Saint James, and Albemarle, the Hoffman House with its Bouguereau *Nymphs and Satyr* that Captain De Lamar had liked so well he had had an 8-foot copy made for his mansion. (It brought $260 in his sale.)

The hysteria of war—which in New York had centered in Madison

Square—had come and gone: the Liberty Loan drives, the dema-
gogues competing through amplifiers with the senescent patter of the
Million-Dollar Voice, the Altar of Liberty, the tremendous victory
arch studded with forty pieces of dreadful sculpture and hastily set up
to mark the spot where Rodman Wanamaker had greeted the first
returning troops.

These things had come and gone, but the old statues remained, a
seedy procession of forgotten men: Farragut flanked by Loyalty and
Courage, Roscoe Conkling, Chester A. Arthur, a monument 51 feet
high erected to the memory of a Major General Worth no one could
readily have identified. Seward's head sat on a superfluous cast of
Lincoln's body, an economy measure that few would be likely to
notice, least of all the barbarian horde of insurance workers the
subway disgorged each morning to shuffle papers in the ugly fifty-
story tower with the clock with hands that weighed a thousand
pounds. The white-collar masses rushing across the paths that Mary
Jane Morgan had trod with spendthrift heart and measured step were
doubtless even unaware of the existence of Thomas Kirby and the
AAA in those antiquated galleries to which no others on this continent
could compare—before progress and decay set in.

Perhaps it was for the rustle of old brocade that the old man wept,
for the horsecars, the carriages, the tall hats and ridiculous bustles,
perhaps for the decorous ways and fine houses that had passed and
left him standing there, a small man, frosty-white and ludicrously
severe, hawking some half-forgotten picture that had probably never
mattered as much as he supposed. What had been beautiful was in so
many instances now no longer beautiful. And yet the paint and canvas
had not changed. Could these things have been no more than the
shadowiest of symbols after all: the vases made of rarest, thinnest
porcelain, those heroic canvases that had won prizes in the Salons?
Could it have been only the money that had meaning, and not the
beauty, if beauty there had been? No, the money and the pride had
been part of it, but by no means all. There had been some other
motive stirring in the best and the worst of the tall, grand figures in
that passing show. It was, perhaps, a longing for the infinite, if that
could be a way of saying it, a search not only for the past but for a
sense of continuity they hoped to find in art and books and all that
had been created or cherished and preserved—a wish somehow to
cling to that which does not die.

There is no reason to suppose that these were Kirby's thoughts on that sentimental afternoon. But it was beyond a doubt the gnawing, all-pervading dread of leaving—not just of leaving Madison Square—that brought the tears into the sharp, trade-hardened eyes of the white-haired little man with the silver-rimmed glasses, the white goatee, and the handleless gavel he fondled now as the ensign of all he liked to think of as his greatness.

Up at the palace, they were waiting. In the new inner sanctum, Rose Lorenz was having an unprecedented case of nerves. "My poor Mr. Thomas E. Kirby! His pictures aren't even hung right!" she cried at the sight of the framed photos of his triumphant moments tacked up helter-skelter on the walls.

The brash insurance-company bells tolled for the last time in Kirby's ears—B flat, F, G, E flat. The November light began to fail. He turned his back on the empty building and left it to the rats and fate.

In the new assembly hall the Father of the Auctions was scheduled to make "a few remarks" before five hundred distinguished leaders of the art and book world who had been invited to an "informal reception" from four to six. But Kirby warned his audience at the outset that he could not cover his subject in a few remarks. His speech, as released to the press, covered seventy legal-size typewritten pages. The seventy-five employees of the AAA were seated on the stage behind closed curtains, waiting like a graduating class to appear at the proper moment for their diplomas. While they waited, and the distinguished leaders tried not to shuffle in their seats, Kirby, in his wing collar and swallow-tailed coat, launched into that unmercifully detailed summary of his forty years on Madison Square.

For the first hour or so, the speech was amusing. There were anecdotes to be told, and the old man knew how to tell them. But as the recital of those dollar victories went on and on, it seemed to lack human interest. The thousands and the tens of thousands flowed from Kirby's tongue with awful monotony as he relived his years in terms of cold statistics. The employees, trapped behind the curtains in their Sunday garments, could remember nothing later except that the dinner hour passed and they were very hungry.

At last the curtains parted. While the tired listeners applauded, the Father then acknowledged the faithful services of his wilted business family, down to the humblest porter. He summarized at length the matchless virtues of the great Lorenz, who took a queenly bow in her sables and her Benguiat pearls; he complimented Otto Bernet on having been a good apprentice, and even spoke of Parke's services as having been of some value; but mainly, in conclusion, he dwelt upon the glory of the Million-Dollar Voice.

Kirby's eulogy need not have been boring, if he had allowed someone else to make it. His pride and his asperity aside, his influence on the auction world had been incalculable. His innovations had set a truly revolutionary pattern: the catalogues, the exhibitions, the splendor that had brought the private buyers and kept the dealers' rings at bay. Moreover, his stubborn honesty and his undeniable talent had made the pattern work.

But beyond all that was the romance of the times he had known. Kirby had sold $60 million worth of art and allied objects—a mere fraction, to be sure, of the enormous accumulation of thought and artistic creation that had come to America since the Centennial Exposition of 1876, but a cross section, nonetheless, of the taste of two generations. In the span of his career all the great collections had been formed, or at least started. All the palatial mansions had been built. Nothing remained now but to tear them down and disperse their contents. All the great collecting fields had been explored: from ancient art to the primitives, to the crafts of colonial America, to Picasso and Matisse. Nothing remained now but to distribute and redistribute the things that had been gathered—with additions, of course, but with no new categories of any large importance.

This was the real significance of Thomas Kirby's adventure on uncharted waters. If, in his tradesman's vision, he somehow missed the woods for the trees, the fact remained that art in America, for better or for worse, was many times his debtor; for without him, there would have been no élite auctions.

The long speech with everyone starving was Kirby's swan song, whether he knew it at the time or not. Within six months he had been deposed. Parke and Bernet, weary of apprenticeship, had started an undercover revolt, with more than the tacit approval of Gustavus Kirby. The Major's hair was already gray—he was forty-nine—and Bernet, at forty, was growing bald. It was time, they thought, to seek their fortunes; and they connived to seek them jointly. Bernet was the leader of the insurrection (which was the thing that hurt the old man most, for Otto had been Kirby's favorite). Tentative negotiations were started with certain of the golden clients Bernet had come to know through the years. Hearst, among others, toyed with the idea of financing a colossal auction center in New York. Then, one day, Bernet was sent to Lenox, Massachusetts, to arrange a sale for Cortlandt Field Bishop, whose mother, Mrs. Florence V. Parsons, had recently died. The Bishop millions were legion in the auction and collecting world; and there, at Lenox, Bernet and Parke found their backer.

Thomas Kirby heard rumors of the negotiations with Mr. Bishop. Trembling with rage, he called the conspirators before him.

"There are traitors in our midst," he rasped, with a savage glance at Parke.

"Don't look at me," said Parke. He knew the old man was not unaware that his own son was at the root of the plot to force him to retire.

"Either you buy the business or get out!" Kirby shouted, the Million-Dollar Voice choked with sovereign wrath.

Mr. Bishop bought the business. At the end of March 1923 he paid the Kirbys $500,000 for the name and good will of the AAA and signed a lease with G. T. Kirby on the splendid new galleries. The Kirbys, father and son, agreed not to engage in anything resembling the auction business for a quarter of a century. Parke and Bernet signed ten-year contracts with Mr. Bishop at an annual salary of $15,000 each, plus a percentage of the profits.

Mitchell Kennerley, from his comparatively low-rent establishment three blocks away on Park Avenue, wrote to a business acquaintance: "It is a long story, but Mr. Kirby and his son were obliged to withdraw from the AAA. Mr. Bishop is a very rich man who was persuaded to back Bernet and Parke. The day the contract was signed he sailed for Africa for nine months. They are paying $100,000 a year rent and I give them less than 2 years to last."

Until the end of the 1922–3 season, Kirby's voice reverberated through the hollow monument his son had built, though now and then he would permit one of the traitors to conduct a sale. It fell to Parke to disperse the antiquities gathered (in large part at Kirby's auctions) by the late lamented Enrico Caruso, along with the great singer's personal effects, even down to his lace shirts and hats and boots. It was perhaps the only auction at the AAA that ever opened with an invocation.

The Major, looking very courtly and handsome in the new mahogany rostrum, was about to begin when a tall man in the audience got up and said, "Let us rise and stand for a few moments in silent prayer for the great Italian-American whose collections are about to be sold." Everyone in the room stood up, and remained standing, reverently and silently, for a decent interval. Then the congregation sat down and proceeded to haggle over plumes, daggers, capes, Greek coins and Byzantine amulets, Syrian bottles and Il Riccio bronzes, a sixteenth-century altar and the gold-embroidered train of the Queen of Naples, many wigs, the Pagliacci costume ($25 complete), many hundred specimens of glassware dating back as far as the year 2000 B.C.

In April 1923 came the first great sale held in the new building—the effects of the late international banker William Salomon. The Salomon mansion at 1020 Fifth Avenue was renowned for the costliness and authenticity of its embellishments; to Kirby, the supergala auction meant the chance to make his exit in a rain of millions. By even the most cursory appraisal, Salomon's treasure would have doubled, perhaps even tripled, the Yerkes record of 1910; for this time the mansion as well as its contents was to be sold by the AAA. But there were disappointments. Mrs. Salomon decided to reserve for her remaining years $750,000 worth of the household goods that had belonged to Renaissance princes and French court ladies. An even blacker disaster occurred when the ineluctable Sir Joseph Duveen, who had sold Salomon many of his choice items, persuaded the executors to withdraw fifteen paintings by the Italian masters and sell them to him privately for a price rumored to be more than $1 million. And lastly, though Kirby wept and pled, pointing out that the Tiepolo frescoes alone were valued at $500,000, no one would bid a nickle for the mansion. Imperial palaces on Fifth Avenue were already going out of fashion.

Nevertheless, bidding for the Salomon treasure intermittently ran wild.

Brokaws were there, and Huttons, Elisha Walker, Jesse Straus, and Russell Law, Hearst of course, and even Senator Clark in person, for the splendor of 30 East 57th Street had erased the last moral blemish from the auction hall.

There was new money, too, and vulgar money, perhaps stemming from the bootleg trade. In one of the duller stretches, Kirby was struggling along trying to sell an undistinguished console table for $200 or $300 with the privilege of another like it should the bidder fancy a pair. The price had gone to $250 when a woman's voice cut in with a shrill offer of $2,000. Kirby assumed that the lady had been sampling bathtub gin and continued to repeat the $250 offer, angling for a raise to $260. The voice cut in again: "Two thousand dollars!" This time Kirby did not stop to bicker. Down went his gavel, and the lady had her tables for $4,000 the pair. She could have had them for $520, but then she could not have glanced around at George Gray Barnard and Mrs. Charles E. Dillingham with such devil-may-care smugness.

Some of the prices made headlines. A Fragonard, *Portrait of Mlle. Colombe as "Venus,"* brought $41,000. A sixteenth-century bronze wine cooler sold for $17,500. The late Mr. Salomon's Louis XVI bed—described as the most sumptuous in America—brought $6,300. His sedan chair, formerly the bedizened vehicle of a King of Sicily, brought $4,000. (In the catalogue Rose Lorenz had aptly suggested that the local shortage of rickshaw boys could be got around by converting the thing into a telephone booth.)

"Thomas E. Kirby, at his best," the New York *Herald* reported, "seemed to be literally carried away by the enthusiasm of the event," particularly at such moments as the one when a garniture of three Urbino vases fell to Duveen for $101,000. But midway in the festivities the Million-Dollar Voice broke down. Rose Lorenz, bypassing the traitorous Bernet, with whom she was on bad terms, sent for Parke, and for the first time, the Major had the chance to cry a sale in thousands before an assembly cloaked in millions. At subsequent sessions, Kirby resumed his place in the rostrum, but with the failure to sell the mansion, his grand farewell trailed off with a thud rather than with a last resounding battle cry. When the Salomon total had been added, it came to $1,293,047.50, a substantial sum to be sure, but not even a full $100,000 more than Mary Jane Morgan's cache had brought, back at the beginning of that long grandisonant career.

Mr. Bishop took possession of the AAA June 1. Ironically, Kirby's last sale was a book sale, and not even a distinguished one. A few reporters came, and the Father of the Auctions made a cheery little speech. He was not decrepit, he said. Some of the papers had depicted him as a doddering old man in his eighties, and he resented it. He was only seventy-seven. Moreover, he was not going away because he was broken down. "I am going away," he said, "while I am capable of walking away, and I don't have to crawl or creep or be carried." He was retiring, he told the press, to write his memoirs—in collaboration with the equally unbroken Rose Lorenz.

It was a job he never finished. Eight months later he died—of eczema, the obituaries said.

EIGHT

ENTER MR. BISHOP

Doubtless O. B. and the Major (as Bernet and Parke came to be familiarly called) imagined that Cortlandt Field Bishop, world traveler and millionaire extraordinary of New York, Lenox, Massachusetts, and the Ritz Hotel in Paris, would be content to supply the capital and let them run the AAA as they saw fit. Instead, they found themselves transported with hurricane velocity to the fringes of Mr. Bishop's baroque, enchanted world—a world of ships and docks and long black motor cars, of breathless speed and conspicuous consumption, a world tingling with the exuberance of the Roaring Twenties, and its own peculiar climate of exorbitance.

"He was our angel," the Major would say in later years, with the bemused expression of a man recalling some improbable beneficence he no longer has. The word called up a flood of images. Mr. Bishop at the age of fifty-three, in the throes of his first tumultuous brush with trade. Mr. Bishop in a coonskin coat, a stubby, swart, short-legged man, overflowing with small talk on his favorite topics: speed, the weather, the time it took to go from here to there. Mr. Bishop roaring down from Lenox in one of his incredibly fast motorcars. His ebullient voice, his walking stick and Homburg hat, his raised eyebrow, the oblique cast of his sardonic eye, his baronial paunch and compound chin, his mustache—a thicket of November shrubbery in the dark garden of his inscrutable visage.

Mr. Bishop *in persona propria* (as he himself would define his material presence in the galleries), stomping through the halls with short, fast steps, withering hapless mortals with short, fast sentences studded with unanswerable barbs. Mr. Bishop *in absentia*, roaring up and down the Continent on the trail of negotiable antiquity. Mr. Bishop on a donkey in Beirut, on a camel in a cream-colored straw hat. Mr. Bishop playing leapfrog in the Paris Ritz. Mr. Bishop's letters, tapped out on a portable Corona and dated by the Church calendar. ("I, Cortlandt Bishop, Master of Arts, Bachelor of Laws, Doctor of Philosophy, Commendatore of the Corona d'Italia, Knight of the Legion of Honor, President of the American Art Association . . ." one written on the Vigil of the Blessed Epiphany began.) His cables.

("Send me two vice presidents at once," an early one from some-where in Europe read.) Mr. Bishop's wrath and Mr. Bishop's plea-sure: the dead bugs he sent to persons in disfavor, the ripe cheeses he mailed to those in his good graces. Mr. Bishop's whims and inexpli-cable conceits: the gold coins from empires long defunct which he carried in his pockets, the postage stamps he sometimes gave as tips. Mr. Bishop's mansions, rare books, and vaults of treasure; above all, Mr. Bishop's millions, which he so lavishly expended on the AAA.

It was old money that Mr. Bishop brought to the latter-day ecstatic of the auctioneers, money seasoned by many generations in the plutocratic sun, and with it, Mr. Bishop had inherited an epically unquiet soul. A preponderance of the Bishop fortune had descended, prophetically enough, from Catharine Lorillard Wolfe, the Lady Bountiful of Madison Square. In the spring of 1887, in her vast and silent mansion at 13 Madison Avenue, the richest unmarried woman in the United States had embarked on the black sea of eternity (to preserve the primrose flavor of her obsequies) to echoes of the Million-Dollar Voice crying up A. T. Stewart's terrestrial baggage across the way. Sole and regal heir to the wealth amassed by John David Wolfe, the shrewd Manhattan hardware merchant, and by old Peter Lorillard, the snuff and tobacco monger, upon whose death in 1843 the newspapers had coined the new word "millionaire," the Lady Bountiful had left behind a trail of charitable endeavor. She had endowed Grace Church and embellished it with stained-glass windows, for she was among the proud pewholders there. She had enriched the Museum of Natural History and left the Metropolitan Museum its first big cash windfall, along with the patchwork of Salon paintings on her walls. She had established schools for female Chris-tians in Denver and Topeka, a theological seminary in Ohio. She had endowed the Newsboys' Lodging House, homes for the sick and shelters for the homeless, missions to convert the heathen in foreign countries, missions on the waterfront for turning drunkards to the Lord.

But for all that, millions remained. From among her many cousins Catharine Lorillard Wolfe chose twenty as her heirs. She was, however, no egalitarian. She left her great house on Madison Square and a dynastic portion of her wealth to her favorite cousin, David Wolfe Bishop—millions in cash and many strategic parcels of Manhattan real estate that would one day become incredibly valuable. All of it, with time's increase and sundry other fortunes, was to descend to David Wolfe Bishop's elder son, Cortlandt.

Cortlandt was seventeen, his brother David Wolfe Bishop, Jr., four years younger, when the Bishop family moved into the dusky magnificence of the Wolfe mansion on the square, with its gray servitor at the door, its Nubian bronzes bearing dim gas jets in the shadowy halls, its perfumed air, Etruscan cists, and temple jades, its small, bereft aristocratic dog, its twelve maids ceaselessly patrolling its parlors, where the sun intruded but in slender shafts.

When they were not on horseback or the high seas, the perpetuators of the dynasty adopted the Lady Bountiful's domestic arrangements, if not her social piety. They were Old Guard and tolerably highbrow, but perhaps a little slapdash too. The terrible-tongued *Town Topics*, which kept a sharp eye on all the rich (except when blinded by a financial consideration), always harbored an editorial notion that David Wolfe Bishop had donned sheep's clothing to deceive his spinster cousin and once reported in its columns that the new lord of her manor was said to be given to "harmless attentions to the genus domesticus known as parlor maids." The Bishop boys were wild, the less aristocratic neighbors said. Cortlandt, at seventeen, was a cub-size grandee with golden spurs and too much pocket money. Parvenu beldames with marriageable daughters despaired at his ennui with regard to ballroom politics. The grand tour, which other scions of the banker-and-broker set could look forward to as the cultural bonbon of their education, held no broadening prospects for him. He had already been to Europe sixteen times.

But whatever the pagan excesses of the Bishop upbringing, the Almighty, in his Protestant Episcopal manifestations, retained a foothold in the dynasty. The Grace Church Sunday school counted young Cortlandt, if not his brother, among its *summa cum laude* scholars. Many years later, when the sulphidic Mr. Bishop was in his mid-fifties, a cross-examining lawyer, probing at some old skeletons in the family closet, demanded of him if he had known a certain clergyman once rampant in Madison Square.

"Yes, he taught me the word of God," Mr. Bishop thundered, implying that no accidence of it had since escaped him.

The Bishops loved their money, but the patterned formal pageantry of the pseudo-aristocracy appealed to them no more than its primer of childish conformities. At Newport the Lady Bountiful had built Vinland on Ochre Point fourteen years before Cornelius Vanderbilt glorified the land adjoining with The Breakers. The Breakers has been called the most stupendous house ever built in America, but Vinland was no shanty. On her wind-swept, stylish promontory the Lady Bountiful had transplanted full-grown elms to shade her pale, patrician figure. God had surely made the trees, though not in that locality. In her dining room she had Longfellow's "Skeleton in Armor" depicted stanza by stanza around the walls. The Bishops, however, showed no disposition to frolic with the witless Mrs. Astor and her rachitic new Four Hundred. On the distaff side, Cortlandt and David could boast in their pedigree Van Cortlandts and De Peysters. John Bishop had ogled the sea nymphs in the August moonlight on Bailey's Beach in 1630. He had been a member of a colonial legislature a hundred and seven years before the first John Jacob Astor landed in Baltimore with his seven flutes. The tribe sprung from that remote progenitor had known too long the appanages of wealth and leisure to bore themselves with Newport's ritual pomposities.

Between ocean crossings, the Bishops preferred the rustic tranquillity of the Massachusetts countryside. David Wolfe Bishop had bought land at Lenox in the early seventies, and by annexing nearby farms, had developed one of the most beautiful estates in the Berkshires, with a stable of the finest horses. Young Cortlandt, already showing symptoms of his lifelong craving for perpetual motion, would ride forty or fifty miles a day in search of excitement—fires, floods, train wrecks. He had a passion for disaster.

Then came the bicycle. He was a scorcher on the highways, the old-fashioned opponents of the hot run and nickel-plated donkey said. Awheel, in skullcap and knee breeches, his head sunk jockeylike between curved handlebars, on dirt roads that were rough and rock strewn, muddy, rutted, and uphill a good part of the way, he could cover the 150 miles from New York to Lenox in a day and a half.

Such maniacal feats were vehemently decried by the long-time social arbiter of Lenox, Mr. Richard Goodman, whose land and pre-Revolutionary cottage, Yokun, bordered the Bishop estate. Partly through Goodman's starchy efforts, life's major pestilences—the railway, the *nouveaux riches*, and the big American hotel—had been kept away from Lenox. But the new insidious cult of self-propulsion, the social arbiter prophesied, must surely spell the doom of "America's one quiet but fashionable country resort."

Back in the middle of the century, Lenox had attracted the pastoral-minded literati. Longfellow and Oliver Wendell Holmes had stayed there; Hawthorne had written a book there. In 1838 Fanny Kemble, the great English actress, had written from the crossroads hotel, "We laugh, we sing, we talk, we play, we discuss, we dance, we ride, drive, walk, scramble, saunter, and amuse ourselves extremely. . . . The village hostelry . . . is having a blossoming time, with sweet young faces shining about it in every direction."

Some years later, high in a maple grove on what was to become part of Cortlandt Field Bishop's lordly manor, Fanny Kemble bought a quaint old cottage, which she called The Perch. But rustic innocence was already doomed. The pastoral life became more and more confused with Istrian marble and replicas of the Petit Trianon. Ironically, Lenox came to boast a hill bedizened with a granite castle—Anson Phelps Stokes's Shadowbrook—which Cleveland Amory, the preeminent authority on such matters, rates second only to Newport's The Breakers.

David Wolfe Bishop's architectural sentiments were offbeat for his time, but exuberant nonetheless. With the Lady Bountiful's fortune he built Interlaken, a neo-pre-Revolutionary mansion combining the eighteenth-century Lenox jail and scaffold and remnants of the old town tavern with such contemporary foibles as a ceremonial staircase flooded by the opalescent rays of an outsize Tiffany-glass window. His sister, Mrs. Matilda Bishop White acquired the five hundred acres to the east and adorned the site of Fanny Kemble's Perch with her sumptuous villa, called The Maples. Mrs. White, *Town Topics* wrote in 1887, "has for some years been in a retreat, as her mind is affected, while her son follows a rather wild life abroad." Whether retreat or queenly battlement, The Maples towered above the green hills like a beacon and had the finest view in all the Berkshires.

Across the road Mrs. William D. (Emily Vanderbilt) Sloane built Elm Court. All around, the Valhallas of the social gods and goddesses bloomed, while Goodman, who was a lawyer, mourned the passing of the Berkshires' "legal and literary life" and shuddered for the contamination of "those clear, quiet, refined, active brains" destined—he supposed—to inherit, if not the earth, at least that portion of it known as Lenox. Bitterly he flayed the ostentatious and called for the restoration of the simple life "before our fashionable friends from the city" polluted Lenox with their "coachmen and footmen and butlers and maids, their formal livery and their jangling chains."

But to no avail. Deplorable as all this was, it was as nothing to the day in 1897 when Cortlandt Bishop appeared on the Lenox roads in a motor-driven tricycle imported from France. There were said to be ninety of the godless contraptions at large in the world, and it was considered a major calamity that Lenox should be plagued with one of them. The whir of the motor could be heard for a quarter of a mile. It coughed, spat fire, and gave off noxious gases. It frightened the horses, drove the women scurrying for cover, and portended—the gentlemen of clear, quiet brains foresaw—the total destruction of peace and decorum in the Berkshires.

The horse-drawn citizenry rose in anti-Bishop fury. Richard Goodman, Sr., had passed on, the year before, to an orbit of even greater tranquillity, but he had left Yokun in charge of two daughters and a son—a trio of such heliotrope refinement that all three remained permanently unmated. Out driving one afternoon with his handsome bay gelding, Richard Goodman, Jr., had the misfortune to encounter the motorized Mr. Bishop on the highway. The gelding shied; the buggy lurched into the ditch. The pristine Mr. Goodman fled in unmanly terror, leaving the horse to fend for itself.

There were precedents for dealing with such indignities. In Newport, Frank K. Sturgis had horsewhipped young Hermann Oelrichs for scaring him with his infernal machine on Bellevue Avenue. Goodman chose to take parliamentary action. At his bidding, the selectmen of Lenox met and solemnly decreed that no vehicles other than those drawn by horse, mule, man, dog, oxen, or goats should henceforth be driven at more than six miles an hour or manipulated without having one wheel in the gutter of the road at all times.

Even if these restrictions had been observed (and they were not), the three-wheeled terror would have remained a belching menace. Volunteers for the civil defense were inspired to post warnings on a pillar of the Curtis Hotel for the guidance of the horse-drawn populace. When Bishop's horseless carriage was known to be at large, Goodman could approach the village crossroads tentatively and read: "SEEN AT 8 THIS MORNING HEADED FOR STOCKBRIDGE." Whereupon he would bow to the better part of wisdom and turn his bay gelding in the opposite direction.

Things went from bad to worse. By 1899 Cortlandt and his brother David had each imported a four-wheeled contraption called the *pétrolette*. A year later the wild boys of Lenox both had new French motorcars. Cortlandt's was a so-called Red Devil; David's a White Ghost. Anti-Bishop legislation notwithstanding, the aboriginal hot-rodders were said to have whizzed through the elm-lined streets at the excessive speed of fifteen miles an hour. Goodman and his bay gelding were beside themselves.

"Why don't you confer with Mr. Bishop in a friendly way?" a conciliatory townsman suggested. "Won't he listen to reason? Doesn't he know anything? Can't he be made to see that this machine will drive people away from our beautiful town?"

"Know anything!" the choleric Mr. Goodman exclaimed. "He knows too much. He gets the best of them all on the argument. That's just the trouble. He even predicts there will be lots of them on the road in a few years, and I tell you we must stop them now!"

But there was no stopping them. David, the younger of the Bishop squirelets, surrendered wholly to the homicidal new sport of the rich. He became a racer and joined in the early perilous endurance runs from New York to Buffalo. He would rampage through the Lenox streets with the supercharger roaring, scattering the ladies with white parasols, profanely drowning out the pastor's Sunday morning orisons. What education he received was from tinkerers and private tutors. Cortlandt was no less noisy, but—as even Mr. Goodman had to admit—he was no fool. At Columbia University he had taken honors few men born to the rigors of self-indulgence bother to acquire. Between trips to Europe he tossed off his bachelor of arts degree and his master's. Within another year he had his Ph.D. By the time he was twenty-four he had sailed through Columbia Law School and passed the bar examinations; but it was as a litigant, not as a practitioner, that Mr. Bishop consorted with the law courts for the ensuing forty years.

In his own good time, Cortlandt Field Bishop took a wife. Oddly enough—for he was no partisan of organized snobbery—he chose his true love from among the ranking princesses of the Four Hundred.

Amy Bend, the handicappers all agreed, was unsurpassed in delicate blonde loveliness by any graduate of the charm schools of the eighteen-eighties. Society's tipsheet, *Town Topics*, rated her at the

top of the list of "the handsomest and best placed girls in America
. . . who trip at the sight of the McAllister wand and are as charmed
by the voluptuous nonsense of their social routine as are canaries by
figs and loaf sugar." She had inherited the beauty of her mother, a
purebred belle of the Townsend family. Her father was a famed
cotillion leader. "No one today can lead as George Bend did,"
Delineator wrote in 1904, "and as *The Blue Danube,* so redolent with
memories of the past, creeps with sighing cadences about the heart-
strings, dames who no longer love their mirrors smile at that never
forgotten turn with the Brummel of a happy springtime."

The Bends's fortune was a memory of that happy springtime too,
but they could hardly count themselves poor with two such gossamer
daughters in the marriage market as Amy and her younger sister,
Beatrice.

The value of a Meissonier was locked up in Amy's ball gowns, and
she was launched among the blades of 1889. What she wore and
where she wore it consumed a tide of printer's ink: "Amy Bend
enchanting in that delicate shade of pink," "Amy Bend in purest
white," "Amy Bend at Mrs. Astor's ball, exquisite in pink and
white." Her points were weighed and charted and shamelessly assessed in print—her vivacity and corporeal dimensions, her lovely
voice, her golden hair, her spritelike grace and nimble wit.

Presently there were nibbles. *Town Topics* reported that Jack
Astor, "fluttering about among the tempting clusters of women like a
bee in a garden," had singled out Miss Amy Bend. This Astor—John
Jacob III—was a jolly fellow. He liked to push crew members of his
yacht overboard and once strung up a cook he found sleeping on deck.
Town Topics felt that his nature must necessarily be uplifted by "a
maid with such a sunny smile and eloquent eyes." But this never came
to pass. (He married Ava Willing of Philadelphia, and later went
down on the *Titanic.*) The bees continued to flutter: Lanfear Norrie,
Willie K. Vanderbilt, recently divorced from Alva (the Titaness) and
old enough to be Amy's father. "Miss Bend has been engaged so
many times . . ." *Town Topics* grumbled, "the speculation as to her
matrimonial future has become rather wearing."

Time went on; the ball gowns and the watering places ran up an
awful debt. *Town Topics* remained gallant but noted "clouds suffus-
ing Miss Bend's countenance" at one of Mrs. Cornelius Vanderbilt's
Newport luncheons. ("Not that the face was unlovely in its somber

state . . . ") Oh, well, her press champion asserted, "Miss Bend can command a thousand scions of a thousand noble houses, and by losing one, nine hundred and ninety-nine remain."

The nine hundred and ninety-nine notwithstanding, the lovely Amy Bend almost withered on the vine. The *Sun* reported that there had been "mashing" once at Newport when the fleet was in. *Town Topics* said the *Sun* was bold and flippant. Intelligence came from the Whitney stables at Aiken that the demoiselles of Bend were "spirited": Miss Beatrice, it seems, rode astride. (And she remained single, too, until the age of forty-three, when she married Henry P. Fletcher, diplomat and sometime chairman of the Republican National Committee.)

As for Amy, *Town Topics* had to admit that she had a mind of her own. Trip though she did to McAllister's wand, the fragile lady—who by the vagaries of fortune would one day control the fate of the auction halls—was no featherbrained Newport troll.

She was pushing thirty when she encountered her Prince Charming on a godless motorcar. In the summer of 1899 she had visited the William Douglas Sloanes at Elm Court, across from Interlaken at Lenox. It was love at first sight, the charm reporters wrote. "Of course," said *Town Topics*, attempting to shrug off its Lenox correspondent's tardiness in picking up the scent, "being just across the road, Mr. Bishop was able to carry on his wooing in comparative privacy."

The Bends had a rustic cottage across the Hudson River, high up in the Catskills at Onteora Park. From Elm Court, Amy Bend betook herself there. Cortlandt followed on his *pétrolette*. Whether for love or sport, it was no mean feat to motor up the wooded mountain road, which in places rose almost perpendicularly to the sky. The road was not greatly changed from the days when Rip Van Winkle's jolly dwarfs played ninepins there and rolled their beer kegs down the slope; there was a cable car for less adventurous travelers, but Mr. Bishop chose to risk life and limb chugging up the steep incline. Often he would make the last ten miles on foot, but sometimes he would arrive triumphant at the cottage door in a trail of smoke and with a thunderous salvo of explosions.

Amy Bend was enchanted with her slim, tempestuous dark suitor. And why not? In the snapshots she saved from that romantic summer he bore a smoldering resemblance to the causeless rebels who were to be the sultry godkins of moviegoers of a later day. He offered her adventure and security, a grand tour that would never end. He could give her wealth and many mansions. He offered her himself, his agile brain, with all its quixotry and curiosity. He gave into her keeping his restless heart, with all its childlike yearnings, its baroque intoxications, and the strange dark places that somehow belonged to another age— one of troubadours and saints and jugglers, of crowns and coronets, and Lucifer's darkling angels.

In October 1899 they were married. Seven months later David Wolfe Bishop, Sr., died, leaving his fortune in three parts to his widow and two sons.

Now the giddy life began in earnest. Everyone sailed away to Europe. David Wolfe Bishop, Jr., bought a Paris house, a great estate at Joncery-sur-Vesle, chartered a yacht each winter, and skylarked around the Continent with such sinister members of the international set as Harry K. Thaw. After an interval of mourning barely acceptable to *Town Topics*, Mrs. Bishop married John B. Parsons, the millionaire sugar-trust attorney. The Lady Bountiful's house on Madison Square was sold, and soon afterward, demolished. The Bishops joined the northward march of New York fashion. Cortlandt and Amy bought a town house at 15 East 67th Street. But their New York house was never more than a transient shelter. Paris was the axis of their pleasure round, Lenox the home port of their ceaseless travels.

They were inseparable companions. With one wheel in the ditch, the lovely Amy Bishop roared past the Lenox villas in a cloud of dust and social disapproval. With four wheels on the road, the newly married Bishops whizzed by the crossroads in the newest Panhard racing car. The ladies on the long veranda of the Curtis pointed the finger of abomination. The Bishops in their brazen chariot disturbed the afternoon's repose. Blue blood or not, the delicate blonde beauty was more carnival queen than matron in her turbans and her gay silk dusters, with her many-colored floating veils. The prevalence of devil-wagons imperiled the lives of innocent and guilty. The roads were no longer safe for man or beast. Teamsters resorted to profanity; dogs, mules, and children were said to have been poisoned by the fumes.

Europe was no less hostile to the pioneering motorists. Italian peasants called Mrs. Bishop "the masked one" in her veils and cried out that they had seen the devil. In a tunnel outside Naples two men set upon the fiery chariot and beat its occupants with cudgels. Battle-scarred but dauntless, the plucky motorists continued on their tour, dispatches from Salsomaggiore said, chugging north through Italy, back to the Place Vendôme in Paris, back once more to Lenox with a bolder, louder-belching motorcar.

They plowed through streets of mud in Pittsfield. Leather-jacketed and goggled, they ventured into uncharted territory. Daring feats were accomplished: the conquest of Molasses Hill, the scaling of Jacob's Ladder. Their misadventures filled the local papers. Mr. Bishop hit a pig in Cadenabbia; heavy damages were paid. A bull attacked his car near Stockbridge—with justice, the antimotoring forces said.

Now and then there was a pause. Mr. Bishop fell ill with meningitis—due to the effects of automobiling, his horse-and-buggy doctors said. Mrs. Bishop had a baby, a daughter born on Transfiguration day 1902, according to her father's method of reckoning dates. Mr. Bishop considered the event twice blest. They named her Beatrice ("the delight of my soul"), after Amy's sister, and called her "Beatricia" out of poetic sentiment for Dante's guide through Earthly Paradise.

By the time she was four months old, Beatricia was suspended in a wicker cradle in the rear of an automobile. "Depravity!" the women of the Berkshires cried. Several villages passed ordinances against subjecting innocent babes to the rigors of automobiling. For a time, health officers would flag down the Bishop devil-wagons to see if any children were concealed inside.

But the health officers soon relaxed their vigil. Miss Beatrice was left to coo at Interlaken, while on and on the Bishop safari went. New and better cars were imported, sometimes two at a time, at a cost of $10,000 each. Now long-distance driving was the thing. Mr. Bishop failed to get from New York to Lenox in one day; he arrived two hours behind schedule, the press reported with a snicker, "the automobile being driven the last twenty-five miles on the rims of two wheels." The madcap Bishops set out for Boston—and made it, the blue-blooded Mrs. Bishop alighting at the Common in her pale blue dusty veils, laughing and none the worse for wear. They sailed off to the Pacific, taking a small car with them on the boat. They ventured into the Sahara with a Panhard twenty horsepower motor, taking all parts in duplicate, escorted by a caravan of camels stacked with tires, food, water, and tanks of gasoline. They consorted with snake charmers and sheiks, scared the daylights out of everyone, and covered 2,500 miles in six weeks. "The machine may prove a traveling oasis and supplant the camel," Mr. Bishop predicted to *The New York Times*. "It may be trite, but it is true that this is a very small world."

Then came the balloons, the flying machine, the zeppelin. "Bishop Up in a Balloon" headlines read in 1906, while Mr. Bishop hovered over Paris in a perilous contraption inflated with illuminating gas. He came down forty miles outside the city and announced that automobiling as compared with ballooning was a prosaic sport. He financed Glenn Curtis in the building of his first airplane. He put money in the zeppelin. It would soon supplant the steamship, he told the press, and everyone could float across the ocean once or twice a week. But for all his talk about defying gravity, Mr. Bishop secretly abhorred high places.

"He never liked to go up in anything," Mrs. Bishop revealed a half century later. More often, it was she who would represent the family aloft. "I was the first woman to ride in an airplane, in California." She smiled and shuddered at the recollection. "There was nothing but a board under your feet, and the thing made such a racket!"

The grave ladies of the Curtis could view the dissolute Amy Bishop hanging in a basket above the English Channel. Her pictures were printed in the Sunday supplements: Mrs. Bishop on a camel, her veils floating in the desert winds; Mrs. Bishop in a flying machine at Le Mans; Mrs. Bishop stranded on an Alpine pass with a faulty carburetor.

"I loved the traveling!" the still vivacious Amy Bishop would say with fervor in the twilight of her middle eighties. "I loved Java. You could reach up and pick the orchids." In the gold October sunlight, on the terrace of The Winter Palace at Lenox, restlessly knitting, restlessly glancing now and then at the blue hills stretching off into the distance, she would recall those old motor routes, the landscapes and the colors, the people and the places. Her voice was like a bell forged long ago of finest tempered metal; her oblique, impressionistic comments were unbefogged by the vagaries of senescence. Her blue-gray eyes would dart and change with the kaleidoscope of memory, and in the midst of some multiradiant summer, abruptly she would turn and say, "I had a lovely life."

The four steel knitting needles clicked; the sun sank behind the blue Taconics. A Berkshire wind came up across the terrace. With the Palace lighted, the mists of time would settle like an evening fog. Inside, through the mauve-toned windows, the stone dogs guarding the terrace turned into grimacing shadows; and there, among the ghosts of feasts and revels, the talk turned to darker chapters in the labyrinthine past.

In December 1911 David Wolfe Bishop, Jr., committed suicide in Paris. Dangerously though he had lived, he had not died gloriously on the speedway with the supercharger roaring, but in the Rue de Siam with a bullet through his head. He left his millions, many gold snuffboxes, a collection of old watches. (Time was always of the essence on the Bishop pleasure bark.) He left a letter to his mother, a letter to a faded actress enclosing (it was said) a check for $250,000. For all his yachts and motorcars and beautiful estate at Joncery-sur-Vesle, in his thirty-seven years the younger of the Bishop lords had found no tolerable way of life. Rather, he had demonstrated with a bleak excess of drama that happiness is perhaps not best achieved by pursuing it at breakneck speed. It was a sobering thought for the Yuletide season 1911. But movement was the antidote to melancholy. The Bishops traveled on.

They made a marathon journey from Lapland to Spain, toured France with the King of Greece. They lingered on the Mount of Olives, introduced the Sultan of Morocco to the euphoria of speed. War came, and they toured the great Northwest. They brought the smell of gasoline to the Canadian Rockies and the Hawaiian Islands.

The horsepower and the entourage increased. In the great Hispano-Suiza, the nonpareil of Mr. Bishop's motorcars, they circled the Mediterranean time and time again. With Alphonse, the French chauffeur who hardly ever got to drive, they covered fifty thousand kilometers a year, sometimes accompanied by a chief of state, sometimes with Beatricia, spartan and ungainly in the middy blouse she chose to wear in defiance of her mother's inimitable radiance.

By the time the automobile, in its humbler manifestations, had filtered down to the masses, the gallivanting Bishops had toured the Western world as it had not been toured before. Abroad, Mr. Bishop was known as "the millionaire globe-trotter and promoter of good highways." He had contributed money for the betterment of roads in France; he had put up road signs all over Europe, with footnotes reading "Presented by Cortlandt Field Bishop of New York." He had dined with the King of Italy, the President of France, with Warren G. Harding in the White House; he had talked motorcars for half an hour with the Pope. In his fifty-two years he had made fifty-one annual trips abroad, and by his own account, he had spent more than half the hours of his life driving an automobile.

But while the footloose Bishops wandered far, they always wandered home. David Bishop's share in Interlaken—and his third of the estate—had reverted to Cortlandt and his mother. In addition, when Mrs. Matilda Bishop White died, in 1907, her son having succumbed to the wild life abroad, the Bishops inherited her fortune, and with it The Maples and its five hundred acres. The lands combined stretched far and wide. One day they would all belong to Cortlandt, and in his way, perhaps Mr. Bishop loved his Berkshire acres almost as much as his fast motorcars.

On woodland trails, through swamps, and over rolling meadows, on horseback, often with the daughter he adored beside him on her mount, he would survey the length and breadth of his terrain. Around the lakes and through the valleys, he would traverse his private scenic roadway like Jupiter enraptured, accompanied by Husky and Lasky, a pair of colossally unfriendly Alaskan Malamutes. With his short legs—which bulged as he grew older—laced into puttees that always seemed about to burst the seams, he would tramp the hills and forests at a breathless pace, planning projects for a hundred years of growth, pine forests to replace the blighted chestnuts, clearings for flock and herd, dwellings for the tenant farmers who, he envisioned, would cultivate the lands in pastoral contentment for generation after generation.

Hustling, bustling Mr. Bishop, the Albany *Times-Union* called him. "He never set foot in Lenox without the reverberations being heard for miles around." His canine retinue was a menace to the public safety. Husky and Lasky were said to be more wolf than dog; and Mrs. Bishop's German shepherd, Lupo, guarded her ethereal person with a ruthlessness beyond all call of duty. If a Bishop dog broke loose, the citizens would flee to barricades. The pastor's bulldog, a nearby resident, lived in mortal terror. At intervals the pastor would appear in police court on his behalf, seething with un-Christian vengeance. Mr. Bishop paid his fines with pleasure and prized the news items as *verba sapienti* to thieves, kidnapers, Bolshevists, and poachers.

His pets were pampered, but Mr. Bishop's zoological beneficence did not extend to the beasts of the field. If a wildcat was said to be at large, he would organize an exterminating party and offer the killer a reward. Should a rattlesnake trespass in his Eden, he would call the men to arms, roll out the barrel, and lead the charge himself. The local braves came running, for Lenox was a temperance town, and as a Pittsfield paper put it, Mr. Bishop's exterminating parties were in reality "a generous wetting of parched throats."

The fence-viewers would tremble at his coming. They could be certain that they would be called out. Victims of an antiquated law, their pay was twenty cents an hour for a ten-hour day. But Mr. Bishop was a specialist in old laws. Setting the pace himself, he would require the hapless petty officeholders to trudge the length and breadth of Rattlesnake Mountain, goading them to meticulous, if unwilling, scrutiny of his frontiers.

He was prone to quarrel over boundaries. When Dan R. Hanna built a boathouse on a common lake, precipitating an overflow on Mr. Bishop's private scenic highway, scores of lawyers were locked in internecine combat. Both millionaires were obstinate, but Mr. Bishop was obdurate. He had not only truth but beauty on his side. Had not his scenic roadway been given a paragraph in the Baedeker? Had not he himself, *in persona propria*, laid out that idyllic lakeside path for his perambulations with unfriendly Malamutes?

But while he led the Lenox cottagers a merry chase, in less exalted circles the reverberations of Mr. Bishop's presence were frequently benign. He gave his father's collection of Americana to the Berkshire Museum, erected a memorial to Hawthorne, gave money to buy October Mountain from the Whitneys and preserve its fourteen thousand acres as a state forest. In moods of noblesse oblige he sent food and firewood to the needy, provided for the local orphans, pensioned native farmers who had come on evil days. He was kind to ne'er-do-wells and dreamers. He went around on holidays with baskets for the poor.

He would make the rounds in his Rolls or his Isotta, a man with many gold-filled purses to give out. On the way, he would encounter suppliants: men with visionary schemes (who always seemed to be waiting in the streets); the civic-minded with a project that could do with his support. He would pause and listen, with the motor running. The petitioners must needs be brief. He had a thousand missions to accomplish, and time was always running out. But he would usually oblige.

Tradesmen for miles around adored him. For Mr. Bishop loved to go to market. Hustling, bustling, sonorously commanding, he would stomp imperiously through their stalls. His gruffness could make the skinflint merchant cringe, but the quality storekeepers looked upon his visits as milestones of prosperity. They would bring out the things that they had saved for him. This one had a ham cured by an old New England process; that one, a cheese, a wine only the lord of the manor could intelligently savor. One would have a machine; another, a farm implement, a gadget that Mr. Bishop had not seen before.

The post office was his most urgent stop. His day depended on the mail. He required, above all other things, that its couriers be by nothing stayed. On Christmas if the stagedriver of Lenox lay about in sloth, Mr. Bishop himself would take over his appointed rounds. "The Millionaire Mail Carrier of Lenox," the *Berkshire Evening Eagle* called him, and told how he had hauled the Christmas parcels in his "seven-thousand-dollar automobile."

He would brave the wind-piled drifts, the blizzard's fury. For it was winter that Mr. Bishop loved above all other seasons in the Berkshires—perhaps because for him it had more drama, perhaps because locked in his unquiet bosom there was some lost ideal of outdoor peace and simple piety in communion with the wide New England skies. Against a sheltered slope below The Maples, he built The Winter Palace, a long white house ironically mistitled, for it was the least palatial of all the Bishop dwellings. With its luxury concealed by farmhouse elements, its provincial hearth and vaulted ceiling made of ax-hewn beams, it remained through all his later years Mr. Bishop's Arcadian snug harbor; and there, between his ceaseless travels, he would pause to revel in the delights of winter, its vigor and its bluster, its hazards and its grandeur.

It was the snow he loved, deep, inexorable, pure and silent. With it, came that tingling sense of well-being that would penetrate as if by magic the childlike places in his secret heart. He would make the rounds on snowshoes, over buried meadows, through white-silent woods, across ice-covered ponds, to the far reaches of his glistening domain. He would ponder on the world with all its scars concealed, the deep white sleep that would purify the land, the miracle of regeneration. He would watch the blue-black pines against the sky, observe the ways of small furred animals. He would listen to the awesome quiet, the crackling of the forest, the call of winter birds, the footfall of a deer. He would reflect upon the delights of solitude, savor the cold that gave meaning to his nighttime fire.

But the snow, too, the white peace he loved, was something to be challenged and defied. He imported a metal-belt tractor, the first of its kind that had been seen in this country, a duplicate of one a French explorer had used to cross the Sahara. Gleefully, astride his snow-defying monster, Mr. Bishop plunged through twelve-foot drifts and vaulted old stone walls. Lordly and elate, he caroused through Lenox streets, spurting snow clouds like Proteus abreast a foam-piled sea. He invited everyone to ride with him, thrill to the monster's power and share the intoxication of his new gigantic toy. When the deep snow came, he plowed the roads and fetched the mail from distant places, even when the trains were stalled.

Lordly was the word for Mr. Bishop, but there were still lordlier days to come. In 1922, when his mother died, the whole Bishop fortune came into his hands. He bought the AAA. He bought the Paris *Times* because he did not like the Paris *Herald*. He bought the Paris Ritz because once the management deigned to tell him the suites were all filled. He financed a chain of hotels in the Sahara desert. As time went on, he bought $1 million worth of rare books. There was money to be lavished on the land. Not Interlaken, nor The Maples, nor The Winter Palace would do for the Lenox house of Bishop that was to stand forever and pass down through Beatricia to an illimitable posterity. Interlaken and The Maples were torn down, and on the site of The Maples, Mr. Bishop built Ananda—a name meaning, in the lexicon of yoga, the abode of bliss and happiness.

It took a hundred men two years to build Ananda Hall, its tall Ionic columns, its travertine stone chimneys and terraces of red quarry tile. Surrounded by five hundred feet of wall, screened by trees that had survived the Revolution, shaded Fanny Kemble, and sheltered the "affected" Mrs. White, it stood serene and splendid in the great park said to resemble the gardens at Versailles. The finest view in all the Berkshires was turned into the superfinest. From a tower rising from the copper-shingled roof that looked like burnished gold, the

Cortlandt Field Bishop: astride his favorite mount in the Libyan desert in 1930 (BERKSHIRE EAGLE); and at the wheel of his snow tractor, which he often used to transport mail between the railroad station and the post office in Lenox, Massachusetts (BERKSHIRE EAGLE).

Lord of Lenox could see not only all his lands but distant Graylock as well.

Inside, seventy rooms were devoted to the cause of bliss. When the mansion was completed, in 1924, reporters came from magazines

Cortlandt Field Bishop of Lenox, New York, and Paris (SHAPIRO STUDIO).

Bishop and his wife, Amy Bend Bishop, at Ananda Hall in Lenox (BERKSHIRE EAGLE).

inclined toward "taste." They gurgled over the white telephones, the seven mantels from old English houses, the architecture some thought colonial others thought Italian. They took pictures of the bathrooms and a chair that Washington had slept in one night when beds were scarce. The 15-foot kitchen sink of German silver, a lady writer felt, "represented self-expression at high tide." There were larger houses, the bedazzled lady wrote, "but none in which there is such an extraordinary mingling of quaint and curious . . . convenient and comfortable . . . the rich and the unusual."

Mr. Bishop's houses, relatively speaking, were not ornate, but the pastoral life at Ananda was a long way from simple. Liveried servants gave the place less an atmosphere of bliss than of life in one of the new movie theaters. Detectives roamed the parks by day; Holmes men prowled the balconies at night. Thirty-five farmers raked Mr. Bishop's hay and, in winter, grew his carrots and tomatoes under glass. Miss Beatrice's retiring lodge had a marble swimming pool the like of which Hollywood had not yet contrived. Mr. Bishop's pets had their own utopias, his trained tortoise and his Madagascar cats, his Pernambuco monkey with the table manners of an educated child. Husky and Lasky had marble bathtubs 4 feet high. Their retiring lodges had lounging couches and pillows stuffed with down. Prince Chin Chin, an imperial monkey who crossed the ocean seven times on Mrs. Bishop's head, took up residence in the greenhouse with the roses and carnations. But for the inveterate traveler Chin Chin, eternal summer had no balm. He grew paunched and dour. Two more monkeys and a sociable parrot were acquired to keep him company. But to no avail. He bit a Japanese servant and was banished to the Springfield zoo. There he bit the hand that fed him and came to the proverbial tyrant's end.

To reduce the cost of maintenance, Mr. Bishop organized his abode of bliss and happiness as the Berkshire Estates, Incorporated. He would assume the role of plain New England farmer, he said, and engage in agriculture, lumbering, reforestation. The newspapers were skeptical. "It is unlikely," one remarked, "that he will personally plant many potatoes and pitch much hay. Europe has more attractions."

The prediction was supremely accurate. For all the beauties of Ananda and the vigor of its plans and projects, Mr. Bishop seldom tarried long in the Berkshires. The snows of Lenox had their counterpart in the sands of the Sahara, the abode of bliss and happiness its prototype in Suite 18 of the Paris Ritz. "We were never here in summer," Mrs. Bishop said, recalling the well-worn old itineraries. "Only in winter, sometimes from November to February. Then Paris, Egypt—the Second Cataract—and Jerusalem by the end of April."

En route, and mainly by remote control, Mr. Bishop ruled his auction halls, the Paris *Times,* his farms, apartment houses, office buildings, and hotels. From Morgat, Tripoli, or Aix-les-Bains, he kept a telescopic eye on his financial nexus in New York, a coupon-cutters' garrison occupying the entire thirty-second floor of a down-town banking house.

By autumn 1923 the galleries on 57th Street had been intricately bound up with the global splendor of Mr. Bishop's semiprivate life. The Kirbys' old-fashioned partnership was turned into a lawyers' palindrome of interlocking corporations, with Mr. Bishop himself president of them all. O. B. and the Major were permitted to call themselves vice presidents and to cling, fascinated and bewildered, to his flying coattails. In bristly notes tapped out on his Corona he boosted them into a vertigo of action. For in his new-found zest for trade, the AAA was Mr. Bishop's most intoxicating divertissement.

America was waking up to art, he told the press; and with the impoverishment of Europe—sad as it was to contemplate—he would make the galleries on 57th Street the greatest auction market in the world, greater than Christie's and Sotheby's in London, greater than Charpentier's and the Hôtel Drouot in Paris.

NINE

IN THE WING GLOW OF
THE ANGEL

AMERICA WAS WAKING UP TO ART—the pronouncement was as banal as ever, but one that now seemed destined for fulfillment, at least in the field of furniture and the decorative arts.

Collecting in its higher echelons had resolved itself into the search for the masterpiece, a search conducted by its more serious contestants under the guidance of such oracles as Duveen or Knoedler. But with the spreading out of wealth, the Renaissance and Gothic spirit that had hovered over the palatial mansions since the days of Stanford White had produced, if not a great awakening, a phenomenal excrescence of dark walnut, polychrome, and crimson damask.

Gothic crypts and penthouse cloisters topped Manhattan's new steel towers. Credenzas and cassoni were as prevalent as Cadillacs and Buicks. Tall red chairs and refectory tables flanked by forged-iron torchères stood on wobbly floors artfully dilapidated by synthetic termites and scattered with Turkish prayer rugs from Italian chapels. Grim sacristy doors creaked on sixteenth-century hinges. Water—or prohibition champagne at a hundred dollars a bottle—trickled from dolphins' heads surrounded by mosaic panels. Light emanated from Venetian chandeliers or filtered through medieval Spanish lanterns. Madonnas in wood, paint, majolica, or terra cotta smiled benignly on the revels born of speed, material progress, and the alcoholic daze. Vamps in slinky costumes lurked in the glow of cloudy mirrors said to have reflected the charms of Florentine signoras. Cocktail-party cosmopolites lolled in choir stalls and gulped uncivilized concoctions. Jazz-age wives, liberated from their corset stays and girded for the war against frustration, returned from the couches of the new psychoanalysts to brood on their neuroses amid a labyrinth of chapel screens, predellas, lavaboes, and lecterns.

Taste-writers flourished, and most of them advised Italian-Spanish. Country houses built in what the art-of-living magazines called "the carefree Mediterranean style" expressed the "romantic yearnings" of the new suburbia. Stucco, tile, and wrought iron abounded, scrolled gates leading nowhere, arched doorways, and windows fitted with archaic grilles. ("Behind just such a grille," a rhapsodic writer from

Arts and Decorations trilled, "in an old house in Seville or Madrid, has a Spanish señorita often listened with beating heart to the tinkle of a serenading guitar.") Victorian mansions were hastily remodeled to resemble corners of a doge's palace. Saints replaced the painted cattle that had cost papa so much money. Villas and haciendas blazoned the success of Hollywood's new deities. Lairs the Visconti might have called their own proclaimed the lawless victories of Great Gatsbys on Long Island and the bold conquistadors of Chicago.

Down in Florida the land bonanza precipitated a resounding boom in gold water faucets and archaic pomposities. Vizcaya, James Deering's winter fun house at Miami (now the Dade County Art Museum), contained—in the exclamatory opinion of *Architectural Review*—"more actual examples of old woodwork, furnishings, and detail than could be found in Italy in a six months' study of its works!" It had required what the *Review* called an instinct vigilant in aesthetic darkness—to say nothing of seventeen International Harvester millions—to summon from the noble ordonnance of the past an ensemble of terraces and fountains, parterres and perspectives, of such pomp and prodigality and ostentation. Farther north, café society architects—in particular Addison Mizner, aided in the more fraudulent aspects of the business by his miscreant brother Wilson—were copying rooms from the Davanzati Palace for the locust population of Palm Beach and its environs. As the price of watery lots zoomed, Renaissance Florida fairly teemed with motorized gondolas and Miznerized perspectives. New-rich grandees and paper-profit Borgias became connoisseurs overnight of churchly lore and the gadgetry of princes, of copes and tiles and cassapancas, Urbino plates and Bolognese late-sixteenth-century bread chests.

According to Treasury Department figures, the annual declared value of antique works of art imported into the United States rose from $478,000 in 1909, the year the import duty was lifted, to over $21,500,000 in 1919. It would seem that there was nothing left in all Italy and Spain. An examiner in the United States Appraiser's Stores publicly declared that 75 per cent of the "antiques" imported during the postwar years were fakes. Moreover, works of genuine significance were prohibited from export under the laws of most European countries. These sobering facts aside, in the years since Elia Volpi's trailblazing Davanzati Palace sale of 1916, subsidized imports had regularly augmented the natural flow of possessions at the AAA.

Now, through a parent company Mr. Bishop called the Art Sales Corporation, capital was provided for a momentous displacement of things Renaissance and Gothic.

Foreign dealers who could assemble auctionable collections were paid advances in six figures in return for chattel mortgages on their shipments. Rustlers, scouts, promoters, were employed on a scale unheard of in the Kirby era. Envoys were sent abroad to ferret out consignors. Alliances were formed with agents familiar with the terrain. Intermediaries were paid 2 per cent for fruitful introductions. With these and other lines of communication, O. B. and the Major set out—in summer when there were no sales—on the crowded highways of the last great European treasure hunt. Mrs. Parke went along; Mrs. Bernet went too, the better all to broaden their horizons. And with his galvanized vice presidents, sometimes leading, sometimes following, went Mr. Bishop himself, lordly and ebullient in his Hispano-Suiza, wanton and peremptory in the distribution of his largess.

Paris was the rallying point, Suite 18 of the Ritz the command post from which Mr. Bishop, when in residence, badgered his diverting auctioneers. There, as Parke would later recollect, their not consistently angelic angel was even more demanding than on his whirlwind visits to the galleries. His itinerant vice presidents were made to feel like dancing bears. The telephone at Parke's lodgings in the Hotel Edouard VII would ring night and day. "Meet me at the bank when the clock strikes nine. . . . Come to the Place Vendôme. Be there in eleven minutes."

Parke despaired of describing the pace: "It was always go here, go there; or no, I've changed my mind, we'll go somewhere else." It seemed that Mr. Bishop never slept, and he could not bear to be alone. He would rout the drowsy Major out at six in the morning for a brisk uphill walk to the Butte Montmartre, capped off by a five-mile hike through the Louvre. Or, when real or imagined auction fodder beckoned, whichever vice president was in attendance might be required to be in Pisa or Florence or Madrid in less time than it took to make the trip.

Sometimes these safaris would be undertaken in the Hispano, with Parke a reluctant passenger with Mrs. Bishop, Alphonse the chauffeur, and sundry members of the entourage. "Alphonse was wonderful," in Parke's recollection. "Alphonse knew everything." But the chauffeur's skills were sparingly employed. After a few minutes at the wheel, Alphonse would feel a poke in the ribs, coupled with the command to stop. "Get over there," Mr. Bishop would order grimly. "I'll do the driving." The speed was hair raising for a man of Parke's moderate disposition. Happily, though, the peril would be of short duration. Before much ground had been covered, Mr. Bishop would tire of his vice president's company and put him off at a railway station to proceed to their common destination on his own.

The nightmare quality of the grand tour notwithstanding, Parke managed to woo a procession of consignors abroad. Baffled by the languages of which he had no knowledge, on guard against the wiliness of antiquaries hungry for American dollars, he annexed as interpreter and conegotiator the Neapolitan dealer-expert Ercole Canessa, who for some years had purveyed "great finds" from the late B. Altman's former private gallery on Fifth Avenue. Canessa—though his name became anathema to Mr. Bishop—was on many counts a dominant factor in the Italian-Spanish invasion. But of all the Major's allies no envoy, scout, consignor, or advisor played so proliferating a role as Vitall (the Pasha) Benguiat, the graybeard rug peddler who for so many years had dispensed his wares through Kirby on Madison Square. No other dealer was allowed to dip so deeply into Mr. Bishop's coffers, no trader bound his fate so intimately to the wheel of fortune at the AAA.

For the Pasha, now in his middle sixties, saw himself as on the threshold of his golden age. With the Art Sales Corporation his backer, he had only to sign a promissory note to obtain a hundred thousand dollars, or two, or three, to support his ever more expansive buying tours. With Mr. Bishop's capital, he bought collections outright and consigned them to the AAA. He formed a coalition with Ercole Canessa to scout foreign sales (and inevitably sued Canessa over the division of the spoils). With age and borrowed affluence, the grandiosity of his person burgeoned. His gray-glistening beard, the Homburg hat, the prewar cut of his Bond Street-tailored suit still underlined his likeness to the late King Edward. In his buttonhole he wore an orchid. His wide mustaches curled humorously at the ends; his prophetic dark eyes gleamed with a satanic *joie de vivre;* his enormous stomach loomed—a stomach that he said had cost $1 million to put on.

On the great ships of the French Line he would rent a suite, one room for himself, another for his luggage, containing a pope's ransom in rugs and Renaissance textiles. On 57th Street he stalked the galleries with a proprietary air. AAA employees were required to make obeisance as to a satrap reviewing the minions of his realm. The uniformed attendants stood at attention when he passed. But, like Old King Cole, he practiced a roistering noblesse oblige. If the Negro staff gave a holiday dance at a jazz casino in Harlem, the Pasha would be there in a box, with two cases of prohibition whiskey—one for the crowd, he would say merrily, the other for himself.

He no longer quarreled with his brothers, or with such lesser Benguiats as the thieving nephew Mordecai. Though, to be sure, the Pasha was no stranger to the law courts. Only recently he had hauled Cartier, the jeweler, into court in the matter of the Pearl Necklace.

It was no ordinary necklace Vitall had picked up on his travels— from a roving Bolshevist, it was said—and consigned to Cartier for sale on a profit-sharing basis. The legend still persists that its 389 faultless pearls once belonged to Catherine of Russia. Back in the early twenties, café society publicists were writing breathlessly about the Empress Catherine's "famous $1,500,000 pearl necklace," then encircling the neck of Mrs. James H. R. Cromwell, whose father, the motor magnate Horace Dodge, had bought it from Cartier. These advertisements of the cost of Mrs. Cromwell's entry in the Phila-delphia–Palm Beach jewel competition threw Vitall into an under-standable passion. Cartier had paid him a mere $616,375, as against the $996,450 that would have been his cut on a $1,500,000 sale. The lawsuit made page one. Mr. Cartier's lawyers were constrained to bring some sort of proof that Mr. Dodge had really paid only $825,000 for the necklace. Everyone was mortally embarrassed. The pearls lost caste; the Pasha lost his case; and in view of the devalua-tion, cynics were even found to doubt that Mrs. Cromwell's trinket had ever caressed the royal purple of the Empress Catherine's bosom.

But this and all the other contretemps of a parlous occupation were, as the Pasha said, like bubbles in his champagne. He had prospered through the years, but his profits, whether from pearls or rugs or sumptuous textiles, had gone into the Magic Carpets (as Mr. Bishop called them) of his "private collection"—into these and the grandiose settings for his ubiquitous affairs.

In Paris, where the firm of V. & L. Benguiat maintained home quarters on the Champs Elysées, the gay old Pasha would stroll the

Grands Boulevards in company with his nephew Salvatore, son of Leopold, now slated to become a "second Vitall," and already, the Pasha graciously acknowledged, his successor as "the handsomest man in the world." In season, the clan would repair to the villa Benguiat in Nice, an imperial extravagance on the Promenade des Anglais, composed of forty sea-swept chambers, some of them lined with green sixteenth-century cut velvet and lighted by $10,000 chandeliers. There the wondrous Pasha could be found, between shopping tours, seated in the grand ballroom where no balls were ever held, munching the dates and dried shad roe he said accounted for his silken skin and zest for frolic, or chewing on a large salami, teetering the while a *fille de joie* on each of his gouty knees.

Or, accompanied by his brother Leopold (who, though "utterly useless" to him in the business, was taller and bore an even more striking resemblance to the late King Edward), Vitall would make his stately progress down the Promenade, keeping a sharp eye out for the "chippies" and the traders lurking in the boulevard cafés. Though he deplored mechanical contrivances, as he deplored the modern age, the Pasha, in company with Leo, would sometimes go motoring in a pure white open car. *In toto* the firm of V. & L. Benguiat—ensconced in the rear seat, with Salvatore at the wheel—would essay the Grande Corniche, a pair of archaic outsize dignitaries resembling for all the world two jaunty Eastern monarchs on a respite from the cares of state, their gray beards glinting in the Riviera sun, Vitall's arms gesticulating in appreciation of the scenery. Until, one day, deprived of oil and water by the dream-beguiled Benguiats, the white car caught fire, as the Pasha had always known it would.

In Tangier there was another Benguiat palace. But in New York, a place the Pasha privately thought fit for pigs, he lived a relatively spartan life. A white-topped table in the Childs' restaurant then at Fifth Avenue and 57th Street was his office and his club. There he met his cronies and the men involved in his recondite business deals. His sleeping quarters were in a modest 57th Street hotel. He dined with his Levantine collector-protégé, young Leon Schinasi, or—more often—in Major Parke's apartment.

"Could he eat!" the Major would exclaim in remembered amazement. He would consume the lion's share of a three-rib roast, push back his chair, draw his murderous-looking pocketknife, and while stalking up and down the salon, peel and eat a dozen oranges. His gourmanderie appeased, he would rearrange the furniture, for he was restless, and didactic in his notions of décor. As he moved the chairs and tables, he would talk—of visionary schemes that, backed by Mr. Bishop's millions, would make the AAA an ever-flowing fountain of the timeworn and the priceless.

At Parke's vacation camp on Brandt Lake in the Adirondacks the Pasha would commune with God and nature, and revel in the therapeutic mountain air. His health was poor; he always traveled with his shroud. (It was plain white, unadorned and unembroidered, for he was a religous man, with no delusions about barging into the hereafter in a blaze of priestly gauds.) Surrounded by the pines and tamaracks, peace and the harmony he called *adahert* would come over him. For he loved the great outdoors. He would wax poetic and quote the Prophets, freely translated, with Benguiat variants on their themes. He would install his great bulk in a rowboat and spend the day alone on the water, meditating on the brevity of life with a jar of caviar and concomitant provisions to sustain the mortal flesh. His hirsute countenance would glow against the deep blue water as the tiny overladen boat drifted in transcendent calm, a sight at once bizarre and beautiful, all out of keeping with his Brobdingnagian, trade-hardened ways.

In a room above the galleries—a room no one was allowed to enter save in his presence—the Pasha kept his trunks and boxes. "These are my babies," he would say, when one of his cases had been opened, its contents poured in lambent heaps upon the floor. Here, still, was the Animal Rug from the Marquand sale of 1903. Here were the great rugs called Isfahan, with their coruscating, inimitable rose-crimson ground. Here was a millefleur carpet of South Persia composed in its entirety of a blaze of tiny gemlike flowers; a Kuba rug with four black tulips recurring in a cruciform figure of who could tell what dim and misty origins; a Mongolian carpet depicting the tree of life against a silk ground woven in the colors of the sea, with running stags and crimson pomegranates picked out in sky blue and golden yellow. Here was a so-called Damascus carpet, with Moorish tile designs in red and green, woven at Constantinople, perhaps as early as the fifteenth century; an Indian rug with Greek crosses and stacks of henna surrounded by borders of olive brown containing the eight Buddhist symbols (the wheel of the law, the canopy, the knot of eternity, the umbrella, the lotus, the vase, the conch shell, the twin fishes). Here were Turkish rugs woven in abstract geometrical figures

under the Sunni Mohammedan dogma that forbade the representation of living things; the rugs called Polonaise, their silk pile enriched with gold and silver, their design a baffling intricacy of
amorphous clouds and gleaming branches, bats, cinquefoils, palmettes,
Herat leaves and pinnacles, their flowers—carnations, violets, peonies,
primroses, lotuses, jasmines—an everblooming garden of paradisian
profusion.

The Pasha's men, meticulously trained to lift the carpets in a
certain manner by the corners, would billow them and lay them so
that the light, falling at an angle on the pile, would dramatize the
fluctuating values of the colors. A corresponding light would come
into the Old World trader's eyes, his million-dollar stomach would
expand with epicurean pride, and with hands upraised in a gesture
both ludicrous and ecstatic, he would discourse in rich Turkic accents
on beauty and its probable rewards.

It almost seemed that Benguiat had outdone himself, one commentator wrote. For now, with Major Parke the lyric crier of his
wares, the Pasha's trunks poured forth their bounty in a series of
great sales. Under the hammer came the annals of the human spirit
told on many looms, in glistening, iridescent, and wonderfully intricate Renaissance textiles with colors time had sometimes enhanced but
never been able to dim, in rugs that all but sang the onetime might of
the Safawid dynasty and yet, somehow, reflected the tranquil sweetness of a hedonistic age, the longing so peculiar to the East for things
unearthly, mysterious, and perfectly harmonious.

It was common for the Isfahans to soar to $60,000. But Vitall
never saw the money. It went to pay back Mr. Bishop and pave the
way for more loans, against the proceeds of the next haul. Spurred by
the drumbeat of Parke's hammer, the Pasha bought as he had never
bought before. In Portugal he bought the state carpets from the royal
house of Braganza, carpets he had been angling for for the past
eighteen years. ("Nothing is ever lost," he used to say, "but only
delayed somewhere.") In Florence—with a quarter of a million
dollars advanced by Mr. Bishop against the auction of its contents—
he bought the Davanzati Palace, lock, stock, and barrel.

No matter if the fourteenth-sixteenth-century palace so enthusiastically scraped down and restored by Professor Elia Volpi was a notorious white elephant. (It had been emptied of its chattels more than
once since the Volpi sale of 1916, but it had a way of filling up again.)

No matter if the walls were damp, the upkeep high, the neighborhood run down. Now, for a season or two, in the very street inhabited
in bygone centuries by the rich silk merchants of Florence, the Pasha
grandly kept house. Now briefly, before the packing boxes broke the
spell, he could strut beneath the fresco depicting Saint Christopher
with the Child Jesus (a work much copied in the fun houses of
Florida) or stalk among the pictured walls inspired by the long love
song of some nameless Tuscan troubadour. When Mr. Bishop, breez-
ing through in his Hispano-Suiza, deigned to pay an early morning
call, the Pasha greeted him in a retrospective silk lounging robe and
curtly said that visitors were not welcome before noon. For now, at
night, when the mundane modern commerce of the old Via di Porta
Rossa was stilled, the rummager in vanished centuries could roll back
the mists of time and play the grand seignior in company with imaginary clowns and jugglers, with blazing torches on the staircase and
phantom cinquecento horses pawing in the courtyard, while contemporary signorinas lolled with twentieth-century abandon among
the soft goods earmarked for the heated contest in New York.

It was a contest that, apart from the exploits of the Pasha, drew
much of its excitement from antiquary Florence. The glorious old city
swarmed with Bishop-endowed traders ferreting out the last vestiges
of Umbrian and Tuscan chattels. Professor Elia Volpi, while Benguiat
presided in his former palace, was at his Villa Vitelli, stocking up for
another AAA triumph. Professor Luigi Grassi was assembling a rival
collection at his Montagliari Palace. Chevalier Carlo M. Girard
obtained trappings from a score of villas, including those once inhabited by Boccaccio and Robert Browning. Chevalier Raoul Tolentino and the rampageous Signora Tolentino, who annually brought at
least one mammoth auction to 57th Street, were latching onto countless bas-reliefs said to be by Donatello and the della Robbias—along
with such items as the skull of "a warrior beatified," the gates of
Brunati's villa, an onyx bathroom with four breast-high walls, tub,
and bronze faucets in the form of mascarons. Similar activities were
going on in Siena and Venice, Genoa, Naples, Bologna. In Rome
Professor Paolo Paolini conjured up Botticellis no one else would
have supposed existed. In Spain the Ruiz brothers, Luis and Raimundo, boldly ripped off church doors, scooped up the medieval
nails, snatched the priestly velvet, and made off with the iron, the
tiles, the very worm-gnawed boards from the floors. But it was in

Milan that the auction-hall strike loomed that set Mr. Bishop agog—and in the end proved to be his juggernaut.

Word of the Chiesa collection had come to Parke via Benguiat and Canessa in the summer of 1924. What it contained no one really knew, except that there were pictures by the great masters, and it was huge. The Major, then in Paris, passed on what information he had to Mr. Bishop, a mistake everyone lived to regret. But, Parke recalled acridly, "Bishop had to know everything. He always wanted to butt in. He never knew the fundamentals of when to speak and when to keep his mouth shut."

The collection Achillito Chiesa, son and heir of a rich Milanese coffee importer, had traded his birthright for turned out to be as bewildering a mess of pottage as ever confounded an auctioneer. Originally Achille Chiesa, the father, had started buying art with some idea of leaving the city of Milan a memorial to his name and Midas touch. Achille had died, and his son Achillito had taken over. Achillito was no world-beater at the coffee trade, but it was, to quote the Chiesa publicity, "impossible for him to resist the lure of fine works of art." He had run up his investment in old masters, Gothic ivories, monks' chairs, and the like to an estimated equivalent of $7 million, largely on credit, before bankruptcy set in. Now the irresistible lay heavy on the hands of a waspish council of Milanese creditors known as the Ars Committee, whose job it was to turn the follies of Chiesa back into cash.

Confronted by the Chiesa grab bag, Parke was wary. There was an indeterminate number of pictures, some with illustrious names attached. There were pictures on the walls, in stacks and bins, in warehouses, pictures out on loan in other cities, other countries; for Achillito had been generous as well as prodigal. An accurate appraisal would have taken time and a corps of experts, but Parke's instinct for values told him to be conservative. With Canessa as interpreter, he spent a week at the bargaining table. The Ars Committee demanded cash advances, reserve prices, even guaranteed returns from the auction. All this Parke refused. He set his terms high and gradually lowered them to the point where it was clear that he would go no further. The papers were yet to be signed, but when the Major left Milan, it was understood that he had booked the Chiesa collection on a straight commission basis.

Scarcely had he departed, however, when Mr. Bishop breezed up in his Hispano-Suiza. He spoke Italian and made friends with Achillito and his circle. (Italians, if they were attractive, were a weakness of Mr. Bishop's.) The Ars Committee sensed a lamb to be shorn. For his part, a glance was enough to convince Mr. Bishop that the spoils of Chiesa would make the great sale of the century. The Ars Committee persuaded him that they were hounded by buyers. Speed seemed to be of the essence, and speed was Mr. Bishop's forte. With a flourish of his angel's pen, he signed a contract guaranteeing a minimum return of $1 million from the auction.

Exuberant over his bold stroke, Mr. Bishop exhorted his vice presidents in notes tapped out on his Corona: "You have the Chiesa now; it is up to you to make an event out of it, and then we can get anything and everything in Europe." In a press release from Paris, which made page one of *The New York Times*, Mr. Bishop called the "$7,000,000 collection" the greatest thing that had happened to the AAA since Yerkes. Interviewed by reporters at the galleries, Parke was laconic. Asked if the auction would bring $7 million, he resorted to the *non sequitur*. New York was a great art center, he said.

An outpost of the AAA was established in Milan. Experts were called in from Germany and elsewhere to write certificates of authenticity. Cataloguers were set to poring over the jungle of pictures and art objects. An ingratiating young Italian named Luigi Albrighi was hired by Mr. Bishop as overseer and liaison with the Ars Committee. Albrighi, who had dashed about the Continent with Achillito on his buying sprees, was said to have an intimate acquaintance with the Chiesa collection. Whatever else he had, he had charm. As curator, traveling companion, and court favorite, he made his way into the Bishop entourage, dashed about in the Hispano, commuted at the AAA's expense from Milan to the Paris Ritz to the Plaza in New York, and in season lent his handsome presence to the abode of bliss and happiness in Lenox. "He was only on the payroll a few years," said Parke.

What with one thing and another, it would take a while to bring the Chiesa pictures to the block. (It took, in fact, two years to catalogue, transport, and sell the batch Mr. Bishop called "the jewels of the first water.") Meanwhile, the scavengers abroad were not idle.

The AAA became a seething cosmorama of the many-splendored centuries, its walls a blaze of gold galloon and Holy Families, its halls an ever-flowing stream of choir stalls and cassoni.

Week on week the galleries would brood with Christian personages, the saints refulgent on Urbino plaques, the Resurrection in Limoges enamels, the Virgin in paint and bronze and terra cotta, the Sacred Heart on a table runner, Our Lady on a Valencian water pitcher. The rooms would glow with sentiments, all befogged by time's passing—with the wondrous prodigality of Venice, its lacquered and gilded baroque forms, its chandeliers and glass flowers, its doges' chairs and tables carved with chimerical mocking lions, its cloth of gold and cloth of silver, its fringed prie-dieus and cloudy mirrors. The halls would glower with the mercantile exuberances of Florence, its Tuscan carved-walnut cassapancas, its massive furnishings sculptured and gadrooned by a race of master carvers, its great ladies— their rouge boxes and ivory fans, their amethyst- and crimson-colored velvet robes—depicted in the ruby-toned gold luster of majolica. Then the marble ghosts of pagan Rome—its virile busts, its reclining gods and allegorical figures with arms and other parts of their anatomies missing—would have their day. The rooms would be filmy with old laces or fierce with arms and armor. The noble houses of dead and vanished courtiers would appear; their chairs and tables would be set out, their blazoned shields and banners, weapons, emblems and devices, but the knights and lords were all absent, their once impassioned causes all fought and finished. When their day in the galleries had passed, the somber Gothic world would take their place; its crucifixes and sobrieties would appear—the piety of monks, the solemn bigotry of Church dogma, the wood-carved saints and stone-carved bishops, the grandeur and the trivia (a Gothic chastity belt with the key missing, a silver crown said to have been worn by a Spanish saint), the furniture pickled by time, or some other means.

The avalanche was indescribable; the shipping agents grew rich and richer. No old hand at the Parke-Bernet now has forgotten those frantic hours between Friday's dark and Saturday's dawn which each week saw the mounting of chamber after ghost-filled chamber out of the fragments and pomposities of the inexhaustible palazzi.

With their trappings came the beetle-browed and dollar-hungry antiquarians, professori commendatori all of them, belaureled by the crown of Italy, beribboned for their sagacity and prowess, knights of the Order of St. Maurice and St. Lazarus, connoisseurs forced reluctantly to part with the fruits of years of sacrifice and study. They came with credentials attesting to their reputations in historic cities and artfully hinted that the bounty they had taken so much trouble to tote across the ocean consisted of personal possessions. They were the choice pieces they had hoped, alas, to live and die among, or at worst, they were wrung from royalty and nobility buffeted by the cruel and changing times. Cataloguing was done according to mendacious fancy. For whatever it was worth, each and every object—the foreword often stated—had been personally authenticated by its purveyor, a cultural ambassador who, though he may have descended to activities redolent of trade, was a traveler not without honor even in his own country.

The bidders came. Hearst came, imperial Hearst, with his wild ardor for all things Renaissance and Gothic. La Cuesta Encantada, his vaguely Hispano-Moresque castle at San Simeon, begun in 1919, yawned for treasure and more treasure. For castles yet unbuilt he stuffed warehouses with miserere seats and Renaissance portals. His newspapers, his unimaginable business empire, he directed in minute detail from his prodigious mind and memory; the projects he personally supervised would have given nervous breakdowns to a cordon of industrial giants; and yet, now, when he was in his fourth decade of collecting, no sales catalogue was too dull for his perusal, no pursuit more gratifying than to dally for an afternoon before the rostrum.

"He was a great man to have in an auction sale," Parke said nostalgically in later years. It was the understatement of all Parke's understatements. Hearst's bids, whether in person or by proxy, were the indispensable condition for the Italian-Spanish sales.

Opposing him were the decorators and the dealers, set designers to the strivers—in particular French and Company, colossus of decorating firms, whose operatives could concoct a fully equipped palazzo (and endow a parvenu with what its declamatory proprietor Mitchell Samuels called "the taste of connoisseurs") in less time than it took to say Lorenzo de' Medici. Hearst, or his agent, and one of the Samuels brothers who comprised French and Company would contest the choice pieces, often with the latter victorious. But Hearst the underbidder was not necessarily Hearst the loser, for Mitchell Samuels claimed to have sold him "seven or eight million dollars' worth of stuff," no small part of which Hearst's bids had already boosted in the auctions.

Less constant, but no less flamboyant, were some of the transient buyers. Opera fans could read that the great Jeritza had joined the auction chorus and spent $8,950 at one of the Tolentino sales. Votaries of desert love thrilled to the intelligence that Rudolph Valentino had driven up in his snakeskin roadster and carried off to his Falcon's Lair (for $475) a Gothic pointed-arch chest with a façade of cathedral windows and other tendencies to spurious gaudery. Clarence Mackay, who spent an estimated $25 million on shelter and appurtenances at Roslyn, Long Island, would come to scrutinize the gleanings of the professori with a roll of $10 bills in one breast pocket, a wad of fives in the other. If he liked what he saw, he would pass out tens to the gallery attendants; if not, he would captiously fling them fives. Apart from its immediate rewards, a visit from Mackay could be used as a forecast for the sale. A $10 day boded high prices; a $5 exhibit could portend failure.

Albeit much that was dredged up by the professori was on the side of mediocrity, Madison Avenue and 57th Street, for victims of what was called "the Renaissance complex," became more and more the crossroads of desire. Inside the long, low, labyrinthine building, time would seem to have been turned back three hundred years. Outside, before the neoclassic portal, John Seville, the Zouave-like, gold-trimmed doorman, had the swagger of the "Era of Wonderful Nonsense" and also something of the robustiousness of the age of condottieri.

A lusty, burly, never wholly sober Negro, Big Jack had arrived at his niche through many salty areas of endeavor. He had been a sailor, a circus roustabout in charge of elephants, a piano player in a bawdy-house. He had braved the wind and rain in front of Kirby's door downtown. Now, on 57th Street, policemen tipped their hats to him. The traffic rules were his to make or break. Only art lovers could park in his demesne. In mufti he was a power in the ward politics of Harlem, a philanthropist to his people, a thirty-second-degree Mason, a raconteur of unparalleled ribaldry. But he was no snob. In uniform he was an imperator beloved of auction regulars. With a pint of whisky tucked inside his coat against the cold, he would welcome the art-intoxicated sporting set with unabashed familiarity. "Hi there,

Bill," and "Ho there, Marion," he would greet Hearst with Marion Davies lilting on his arm. If refugee prince or Tammany potentate paid a visit, Big Jack might usher him upstairs in person. Sweeping his gold-braid cap to the floor he would announce the dignitary's presence with a bethralled roar to the startled browsers among the household sediment of the knightly years.

Now and then the local scene produced a spectacle. In January 1926 the greatest crush the 57th Street galleries had yet seen turned out for the C. K. G. Billings "Famous Masterpieces of the French, Dutch and English Schools." Sheep and cattle, pool and forest, had become ludicrous examples of an older generation's taste in painting. But thanks to such bidders as Uncle Eli Springs (*in absentia*) and Colonel James Elverson, Jr., publisher of the Philadelphia *Inquirer*, the Barbizons once more evoked tribute in five figures. A watery Corot (*Les Baigneuses des Iles Baromées*) soared to $50,500. Millet's *The Haystacks*, with countless sheep in the foreground, was still worth $26,000. Billings, from his California retreat, complained that such pastoral idyls as a Troyon ox-drawn hay wagon ($16,500) did not bring what he had paid for them; but the old horse trader should have been satisfied. Three months later, at the auction of the legendary Mrs. Astor's gallery, a Troyon flock of twenty sheep full-face, with a splendid dog to guard them, could be had for $1,350.

Eighteen years had passed since two thousand people whose destinies had never crossed *the* Mrs. Astor's rose-strewn path had gathered before her citadel at 840 Fifth Avenue to see her small, expensive coffin carried out. Time had wrought great changes; war and its aftermath had put a brusque end to *La Belle Epoque;* Hollywood had spawned new deities with a mystique far more potent than Mrs. Astor's had ever been; and yet the Mrs. Astor myth, part ridicule, part sentiment, lived on in song and story. Two thousand people, and more—admitted by card only—daily crammed the weeklong exhibition on the premises to see her tarnished lares and cross the threshold of her Francis château, soon to be demolished, its ground reconsecrated to the uses of a synagogue.

Gray, sparrowlike women traveled from distant places to bask for an hour in the penumbra of the society queen who had personified their girlhood dreams of glory. Two Midwestern housewives, on the only trip they had ever made to New York, came and sat by a window the whole day through in two spurious Louis XVI fauteuils. They wanted to see Fifth Avenue from Mrs. Astor's drawing room, they said. (They could have bought it, its panels, doors, and mirrors, and all its gilt rococo ornament, for $1,000 under the hammer.) One afternoon at closing time a little old woman in black crepe, with holes cut in her shoes for bunions, rattled at the "superb wrought-bronze inner gateway." Please, sir, could she come in, she entreated timidly. "I just want to sit in an Astor chair." The guard let her tiptoe into the great hall. Her old eyes glittered as she glanced in wonder at the sportive cherubim and winged sphinxes, the 9-foot candelabra, the sculptured Caen stone fireplace. As the April twilight filtered softly through the rose-tinted glass dome overhead, she poised her tiny figure for a moment on the edge of a gilt brocade state chair, smiled happily, and crept away.

But these shrine-revering pilgrims were no prospective bidders. "Is that it!" a female victim of the new sophistication exclaimed in derision at the ballroom that had been the Valhalla of the Four Hundred. "Now, I ask you, who would want it?"

The crowd that trailed O. B. and the Major from room to room for two eight-hour days was moved to no exorbitance. *Le Repos*, a mural-size vision of exhausted picnickers by Kirby's mascot painter Jules Breton went to $3,800. But a 6-foot battle scene by Detaille, a veritable massacre, painted no doubt from those lifelike dummies strewn about the dude painter's garden, brought only $425. Gilded chairs whereon debutantes and dowagers had dined in vacuous solemnity went for $15. The "superb wrought-bronze inner gateway," for all its redolence of exclusiveness and snobbery, was worth no more than $500.

Far more lucrative, and in its way more gala, was the clearing out of "Clark's folly," twelve blocks farther up Fifth Avenue.

In 1925 Senator William A. Clark had died at the age of eighty-six. Thirty thrush-voiced choirboys trilled his $77-million soul to rest. His funeral, like his life, was a superspectacle. From the bowels of the 121-room mansion that was to outdo all other mansions the colossal organ wailed and sang and whined. Its sixty-five stops all lent their sirupy voices to the wild-haired, brazen Copper King's send-off. The great organ bawled and brayed; the choir organ swelled and sobbed and twittered, its tremolo stop full out; the echo organ magnified the caterwaulings; the thirty-one combinations united all the pipes in one last earthly blast; the twenty-three couplers brought the manuals together in a peal of lamentation that may well have given God-fearing residents of Fifth Avenue the impression that the Day of Judgment was at hand.

The Senator had held court for only thirteen years in the house that took thirteen years to build. "Should its rooms come to be recognized as better than its company, it will be correspondingly costly to demolish," *Architectural Record* had said. Now, in *The New Republic*, spoilsport eulogist Robert Littell wrote:

The Clark house on Fifth Avenue is coming down. In a few days the Senator's palace will begin to chip and crumble away and be pried off with crowbars into dismembering trucks. Its fat corduroy ribs will sink down nearer and nearer to the sidewalk, with a click of bricks and puffs of plaster dust, until at last its $7,000,000 worth of minerals has become nothing but a hole in the ground, a hole full of rubble and loose earth and water. . . . From the hole in the ground —by this time worth a great deal more than when the house stood upon it—steel girders will rise, and by the end of the year a respectable flat packing-box of an apartment house will have removed all trace of scandal.

But before the wreckers could undertake their Herculean task, there was the disposition of Clark's art collection to be settled. In a last bold cultural onslaught, he had bequeathed the cream of what he considered the "best and sanest in art" to the Metropolitan Museum —with the condition that the museum provide and maintain in perpetuity "a well-lighted gallery, or galleries, for the exclusive occupancy of the W. A. Clark collection." Time, he knew, would erase the stench of greed and scandal, time and twenty-two Corots, twenty-two Monticellis, eighteen Cazins, six Boutet de Monvels. These and much, much more the dying Copper King had to give—a portrait of himself "by Bernard of Paris," 125 additional pictures of the museum's choice, Vitall Benguiat's smothering array of Isfahans, Fortuny's hard-won *The Choice of a Model*, a luscious sampling of the cut-rate wonders Rose Lorenz had so amiably purveyed.

The Metropolitan refused the bequest on the ground that it was not a necropolis. This contingency the testator had foreseen. His second choice was the Corcoran Gallery in Washington. The Corcoran trustees, too, were reluctant to accept, until Clark's widow and daughters offered to pay for a wing to entomb the spoils. The Corcoran then consented to preserve the "best and sanest" for posterity; and when all was ready, President Coolidge formally opened the

W. A. Clark shrine, almost within the shadow of the Senate chamber wherein the Copper King's fleeting presence had been called "a shameful thing for the whole nation."

In their pique at the Metropolitan, the Clark heirs had bestowed upon the Corcoran Gallery a far more munificent portion than the will required. But even after subtracting the shrine's allotment (which Frank Jewett Mather described as giving one a feeling "as of being pickled in malmsey or shampooed in honey") enough pictures and art property remained for a half-million-dollar auction sale.

Who but Rose Lorenz should have been in charge of this phase of the Clark obsequies? Who had a more intimate acquaintance with the booty that still crammed the Fifth Avenue bastion? She had put it there; it was the will of the Clark heirs that she should direct its conversion back into cash, under the aegis of the American Art Association.

Out of storage came her yardstick; out of retirement came the gray-haired sometime power behind the rostrum. Once more, for a fortnight, the decorative genius of Miss Rose H. Lorenz prevailed. In the partially stripped mansion she prepared her last imperial exhibit, all as the departed Mr. Thomas E. Kirby would have liked to have seen it done. Her nerves had never been more frayed. Day and night her reassembled minions perched on ladders. No upstart functionary of the new regime was permitted in her presence. With the zest of bygone days, she draped and redraped the yards of Benguiat velvet, hung and rehung the leftover carpets, the 103 paintings the Corcoran had not chosen. She prepared the Copper King's Circassian walnut banquet table for a phantom last supper, spread it with the cloth that boasted fourteen paintings from the Louvre reproduced in *point de Venise* lace, set it with the royal blue Sèvres porcelain and the solid silver of Renaissance design. She decked the palace halls with flowers, and when the exhibition opened, played her hostess role once more to a card-invited public that strained the capacity of the 121 rooms.

The furbishings were to be sold *in situ*, but the picture sale was held in the grand ballroom of the Hotel Plaza. Nothing was too good for an event so fervently stage-managed. O. B. was banished from the rostrum. Only the Major's golden voice was permitted to cry up the once priceless milkmaids and cows at pasture, the Arabs halted and the spirited white horses, the thatched-roof cottages, the peasant laborers and village fetes, the shadows at the close of summer day.

Lovers of newer art tended to sneer; two or three hundred dollars bought old masters, flocks and herds, and Painted Ladies that had been shown with pride on the Senator's afternoons. But the older generation, caught up in the spirit of the occasion (and egged on by Rose in her furs and satin, acting as proxy bidder for the Clark family) now and then bid up to $10,000 or $15,000 for a Daubigny or a Jules Breton, or a pretty girl by Sir William Beechey.

Back at the mansion, for three long afternoons the crowd swooped down upon the residual splendor: the Gothic-style pool tables, the *point de France* lace flounces, the extraordinary 9-foot bird cages, the many silver chancel lamps Vitall Benguiat had sold the Senator back in 1906. Rugs rejected by the Corcoran brought $16,000. Biblical sofa pillows, depicting the vicissitudes of Joseph, brought $7,200.

The house stripped of its grandeur became, in Robert Littell's words, "a peerless piece of ludicrous solemnity." But its public funeral was not quite over. For some weeks, visitors were allowed in at fifty cents a head—a final insult, Littell thought: "Admission should have been free or ten dollars. There is no heat in the place, and shivering couples look at tattered walls where once hung Corot, Whistler, Troyon, Gainsborough. . . . Gone, all gone. Red baize hangs on the gallery's walls, spiked with gigantic nails, and which nail was for Corot, which for Troyon, who can tell?"

The Clark sale was a footnote to an era; for Rose Lorenz, a grand farewell performance. She did not return again. Restless, ill, embittered, she lived eight more years in dowager seclusion on the proceeds of her sceptered sway, augmented by the $50,000 Thomas Kirby affectionately left her in his will. In 1934 she died, in a Park Avenue hotel, leaving to distant and presumably unloved relatives her money and her Benguiat pearls, her mink and outmoded chinchilla, a purple umbrella, many decks of playing cards well-thumbed from games of solitaire. Her obituaries bristled with names of exalted patrons who had predeceased her. But even at the time of the Clark finale, her day as priestess of the auctions had fully passed.

Her many functions had been taken over by young adjuvants of the new regime. The exhibitions that had furnished her with prolonged creative revels were now set up in a single night's labor. The catalogues, which were to achieve a pinnacle of excellence under Miss Mary Vandegrift, were already being metamorphosed by modern design and typography. Their contents, under the scholarly hand of

Leslie A. Hyam, showed traces of a Cambridge education and a prose style that by the time of the Stillman painting sale of February 1927 had permeated the literature of the AAA.

"This assemblage of world-famous works of the great masters," the prolegomenon to the Stillman catalogue began, "undoubtedly marks the apogee of important events in the history of art distribution in the Western world." Tribute was paid to the "brilliance and imagination" of the deceased collectors, James and Charles Chauncey Stillman, dynastic rulers of the National City Bank; and a graceful disquisition followed on Rembrandt and the vagaries of fortune, the imaginative Stillmans having seized upon two Rembrandt portraits—one of his son Titus, another called *The Evangelist*—from the master's last, tragic years at Leyden.

To be sure, auction-goers of the Gomorrhean twenties might have been even more diverted by some mention of vagaries in the con-nubial relations of Stillmans about to relinquish hold on the pictures: James A. and his piquant wife "Fifi-of-the-tabloids." Brilliantly and not without imagination the Stillmans had hugged the divorce-court spotlight for six years of the lurid decade Frederick Lewis Allen said (in *Only Yesterday*) the tabloids presented as a "three-ring circus of sport, crime, and sex." The Stillmans' carnal antics, and in particular, the bizarre determination of the president of the National City Bank to prove himself a cuckold, had so enthralled newspaper readers that, as Allen said, "workmen forgot to be class-conscious." During those six years, fourteen of the Stillman pictures had been on loan to the Metropolitan Museum, but the immortal names they bore—Giovanni Bellini, Pontormo, Murillo, Lorenzo di Credi, Rembrandt, Moroni, Tiepolo, Il Francia—formed a lackaday roster compared to the lustful names of Fred Beauvais, Fifi's alleged Indian paramour, and Florence Leeds, the showgirl world famous for concubinage with the head of the bank said to have amassed the first billion.

Inevitably the auction-room debate over the Stillman pictures ran second in sensation to the courtroom debate over the paternity of little Guy Stillman. Nevertheless, the thirty-seven paintings brought 716,950 good, hard Coolidge dollars, 270,000 of them for the por-trait of Titus—a price that held the world's auction record for a Rembrandt until *Aristotle Contemplating the Bust of Homer* set off the $2,300,000 explosion at the Parke-Bernet thirty-four years later. Duveen was the buyer (prior to the sale he had offered $75,000 for the picture over the counter), and from Duveen *Titus in an Armchair* went to Dr. Henry B. Jacobs of Baltimore, who subsequently gave it to the Baltimore Museum.

Apogee or not, the Stillman sale marked Parke's apotheosis as the First Gentleman of the Rostrum. There was never anyone like him, people said. Kirby's Million-Dollar Voice passed out of memory, or his cant in retrospect seemed tawdry compared to Parke's subtle, more powerful mystique, his gentleman-of-the-old-school charm. His gray hair had receded to the advantage of his broad, high forehead. His trim mustache, the sensuous depression beneath his lower lip, his strong chin and full soft-white cheeks and jowls, the dark-rimmed glasses that framed his penetrating steel-blue eyes, all combined somehow to form a strikingly handsome countenance. With a Rembrandt on the boards, his magisterial presence, framed by the dark canopy of the Church-of-England pulpit, took on a glow commensurate with the business at hand. Lesser works acquired an aura they may or may not have had. The wholeness of his concentration, the dynamic self-persuasion his admirers called "conviction," could hold the bemillioned crowd in thrall. His very tone and gaze exerted an incantatory spell. His melodious numerical crescendo could sweep an audience into a free-spending trance. As the tide of bidding mounted, he would lean forward in the rostrum, his eyes ablaze, the fateful hammer in his hand outstretched. The spectators would lean forward in their chairs; underbidders whose budgets never needed balancing would go a little higher; aficionados of the artistic sporting life would boost the price impulsively, panicked by the threat of the impending gavel-click.

It was his marvelous voice, they said, that accounted for his conjurer's aplomb—a voice full, rich, and compelling, now strident and metallic, now low, attenuated, goading. But behind the voice there was the inner energy of a superb performer. By a kind of self-hypnosis, he believed, for the moment, in what he was doing; and, as in the presence of a "truthful" actor, the crowd believed too. The empty mouthings of the huckster, the routine jargon of the witless crier, never spoiled the show. Reticence and understatement were the essence of Parke's style. "This is a good painting," he would say quietly of a canvas another auctioneer would cry up as the greatest little painting ever sold.

But on those rare occasions when a masterwork was the subject, the

First Gentleman would turn and contemplate it as if a hallowed thing had descended on the stage. Turning back, he would envelop the multitude with the same flattering respect. "There is nothing *I* need to say to *you* about this picture," he would begin, with real or feigned humility. The vibrance of his tone would produce a reverent hush. A word or two more and the mob would be united by this contagious high opinion—of itself, no less than of the object on the block. The hounds would feel like connoisseurs; bidders keyed up for the contest would congratulate themselves on their taste; dealers would consider stretching their maximum appraisals; and quickly, while the house was with him, Parke would call an opening bid.

The bid that set the pace might be a palpable offer or it might be a sum picked on impulse out of thin air. He dared to start things high. His boldness made old hands around the auctions gasp. As a long-time observer put it, Parke could *smell* money in an audience. When the time was right, he dared to bluff. And so certain was his instinct for the disposition of the players that his hand was almost never called.

Once the opener had been topped, Parke's mounting mercenary paean, contraposed with the callers' blasts, might sweep the bidding without lapse to climax and catharsis. Or, if midway the customers grew laggard, he would pause to inject an exhortatory note. But it was not with any lush garrulity of trade opinion he needled his audience. Rather, he would read a pertinent quote dug up for the occasion from the lexicon of art scholarship. Slowly then, deliberately, the nagging would recommence, rising to a quick staccato as a warning to the tricky, last-minute entrant. His timing was magnificent. He could spot a predatory gleam in the last row of the balcony, an endurance bidder in the most tenebrous of dark horses. An unerring sense of drama told him when to shout and when to murmur, when to sell and when to coax a little longer. The procedure, like the audience, was infinitely varied, the performance never twice the same. The result—according to widespread, if unprovable, conjecture—was that, given a collection of inherent value, Parke could get at least 25 per cent more for it than any other auctioneer.

There were those who, in assessing the Major's virtues, were moved to panegyric. "He is a historical precedent," a follower of the great sales here and in Europe wrote:

IN THE WING GLOW OF THE ANGEL

Few people understand the exquisite artistry of Hiram Parke's performance, the grace, breeding and hidden force which molds a pack of rapacious wolves into a pliable audience. And it is all done in such a charming way. With his judicial eye fixed upon them, those cold-faced harpies who want to steal back down, ashamed of the prices they have come prepared to pay. For how can you steal right in front of the lord chief justice, especially when he has such a good opinion of you? . . . Parke knows how to handle these hounds and I believe there are very few others who can do it as subtly. If he were in England he would be knighted.

The writer of that unpublished letter, a veteran collector-speculator, had come to his hard view of auction-goers as a consignor of objects of questionable inherent value. Bargain hunters and dealer combines, it was true, abounded at the sales. Parke could flail the freebooters with a lofty scorn and scold a temporizing audience until the rapacious wolves looked down at their catalogues in shame. But the votaries of the thronelike rostrum did not all come to steal. There were those who did not want a thing if it was cheap. Collecting sports of the devil-may-care twenties took pride in telling how the First Gentleman had mesmerized them into paying twice what they had intended for their auction trophies. It was on such giddy clients that he exercised his masterful technique.

It was less a technique than a sense of vocation, as Parke himself defined it. "I believe one is born with a natural flair for selling," he would parry when asked about his success formula. But flair, he admitted, was not enough. "I knew what I was selling," he would boast in later years. "I had a good memory. I studied, sometimes for weeks before a sale." Homework must certainly have been a factor. His education was meager, his aesthetic responses minimal, his affinity for art based wholly on its value. And yet the French and Italian words, the technical terms and historical references, the artists' names, the foreign-language titles rolled off his tongue in an amazing facsimile of knowledge.

The Major was laconic about his wizardry, but in reminiscing on the photographs representing his great moments in the rostrum, he professed to a kind of extrasensory perception. "I always knew who was going to buy it," he confided while reviewing object after high-priced object. "I don't know how I knew, but I could tell—a look, a kind of tension, a sort of vibration, a brain wave maybe, something that was a dead giveaway. I knew, but"—he was quick to defend his integrity—"I never took advantage."

Away from the throne-chair, a similar, perhaps psychic, intuition guided him in the delicate negotiations when momentous sales hung in the balance. Face to face with the lawyers and bankers who held the power of disposal over most dead millionaires' possessions, his preternatural diplomacy was as ingenerate as his flair for extracting the last dollar in the heat of battle. In the wrangle over terms, he knew, whether or not by previsionary flashes, when to bluff and when to bargain, when to concede, when to go on talking. Men liked to do business with him. They responded to his candor, his sagacity and fairness, his gracious manner and the hard core of worldliness behind it. Heirs bewildered by pathless wastes of accumulation turned to him for counsel, drawn by his professional composure, the ministerial aura with which he imbued his office. If the situation called for it, and there was valuable enough property to sell, he would assume a paternal, if reserved and courtly, role in all sorts of matters. To some he became a refuge from the depredations of art dealers, mediator in family quarrels, mentor and protector in the tergiversating world of the rich and heavy-laden. Testators on their deathbeds were known to warn inheritors of their collections not to make a move without consulting Hiram Parke.

Men liked to do business with him, but there were few, if any, among his close associates who could penetrate the surface of his cool reserve. He maintained a wall against intimacy, it seemed. If he used the word "friend," he meant a contact well-disposed to him in the politics of art selling. Even Benguiat, who ate all those Gargantuan meals at his table, was in Parke's book merely "a good customer." In the exhibition halls, as host to the ranking clients—and to the hounds, for whom he had the glamour of a matinee idol—he bowed and smiled and turned on his professional charm. Outside the public view, he was aloof, unbending, bloodless, even cruel in his ambition to dominate the AAA.

The fire was all expended in the rostrum, the warmth reserved for the exigencies of trade. His mind worked on a single track; he had one end in view—the raising of an edifice that would tower with his stature, not only as a crier (the auctioneer was still in a sense shady) but as man of business unchallenged in his field. To that end, he sweated under Mr. Bishop's tyranny and held his peace. ("Bishop was crazy," he would say wryly, when Mr. Bishop's day had long since passed. But Mr. Bishop was also rich, and riches, above all else, elicited the Major's forbearance.) "I was always fair to him," the Major would say pointedly in any discussion of the AAA's inscrutable (but not demented) angel. In truth Parke was, even in his heartlessness, a paradigm of fairness—politic, dispassionate, and judicious to the point of dullness.

His private life was a model of propriety, thanks to the day-in-day-out devotion of the vivacious, if subjugated, second Mrs. Parke (whose acquaintance he had in fact made—oh, the pleasance of obscurity!—in an Atlantic City movie theater). The bulwark of his office was his special—and indispensable—assistant, Mary Vandegrift; but even when Miss Vandegrift had become a key collaborator in the auction spectacle, Parke's most fervent acknowledgment of her indispensability was to call her "a fine girl."

Beneath this emotionless façade there was, to be sure, a dynamo of temperament held in reserve. There was even a stream of sentiment and bulldog loyalty that would show itself in time of crisis. But in the striving twenties no one would have supposed the Major possessed these frailties. So effectively were they concealed that those who knew him best and most admired his abilities could say of the magnificent persuader that he was "a cold fish."

Not so Bernet. Outside the rostrum it was O. B. who had the human touch. His countenance was a mirror of the solid virtues. His bankerly paunch, his portrait-by-Bachrach look were commonplace enough. His stance in the galleries, thumbs thrust sagaciously in his vest pockets, was the alpha and omega of propriety and trust. But O. B., too, had his façade. Middle age had turned Kirby's rotund second lieutenant into a folksy, expansive, jolly man, somehow unrelated to the $50,000 picture, vase, or rug. To O. B. the folkways of the rich were an endless source of Pickwickian adventure. Like Mr. Pickwick he was gullible and gregarious, curious and perpetually astonished, almost a caricature of the man of consequence he saw himself to be. There was something of the clown in him. In moods of spontaneous buffoonery, as for instance when he was inspired to mimic Leslie Hyam's lord-high-chief-justice posture or the Pasha's Turkish ecstasies, he could be genuinely funny. In the rostrum, alas, he made stale jokes, which invariably fell flat.

At the peripheral sales unworthy of Parke's talents O. B. waged an endless losing battle with syntactical refinements. "Fitted for electric," he would declare enthusiastically of a jug made into a lamp. He would season his pedestrian patter with shopworn badinage. "Not too large for your apartment. . . . Go out and try and duplicate it at twice the price!" All geese were swans to Otto. "A great little picture," he would exhort the lukewarm bidders anent a vagrant saint or Holy Family. He wheedled and he barked, but he had no real rapport with the audience or with the objects on the block. In his spiel, he never knew how much to put in or what to leave out. O. B. could not bluff. He disliked—or never understood—the prevarications and borderline deceptions basic to the auctioneer's mystique. Perhaps he was too much of the salt of the earth ever to have become involved in the flamboyant profession of his choice.

But Bernet was an incurable optimist. The vicissitudes of life—his first, unhappy marriage to a niece of Rose Lorenz, other tribulations of a family nature—had in no way corroded his self-esteem or dampened his enthusiasms. In suburban New Jersey, where he lived with his second wife and son and daughter, he made himself a minor pillar of society. There he was a raconteur, a club member, an after-dinner speaker, a lecturer on art and antiquities, the distinguished vice president of New York's auction citadel. The denizens of suburbia applauded him; the employees of the AAA adored him.

In his vice presidential capacity, O. B. worried about a thousand things: the mechanics of the galleries, the staff, and the electric bill, the tact required in treating with the public he thought of as "the swells," the dilemma that arose if Mrs. Hearst was present and Hearst swept in with Marion Davies. (He solved the problem once, when Mrs. Hearst was down front with her eyes glued on the Major, by shunting Hearst to the balcony. The Hearsts spent the afternoon bidding against each other for a mess of Spanish tiles, the irony being that win, lose, or draw, Hearst still got the bill.) O. B. would drape the nude statues in the interest of decorum. He searched the crannies of old furniture for cash or jewels stashed away and forgotten. (More than once he found a cache and returned it jubilantly to the consignor.) He was always on the move and delightfully inefficient. For all his corpulence, he was like a dancer on his feet. He bustled through the offices with obfuscating messages and orders. He would fling open doors, stick in his head, and blurt out a fragmentary comment (subject and predicate never quite jibed in his sentences) with scarcely a break in his light-footed progress. Somehow he always seemed to be out of breath. He suffered from a variety of nonspecific maladies, but even the recital of his symptoms had a melancholy buoyancy; and boundless was his concern for his fellow man. When Mr. Bishop made his cyclonic appearances *in persona propria* O. B. would set off the whispered alert, "Bishop's coming . . . Bishop's coming," lest some unwary employee be caught napping and peremptorily receive the ax. In the touch-and-go business of making the expanded galleries pay, O. B. was a booster of morale. It was Bernet who always knew that next season would be a banner one, while Parke, when there were no Rembrandts on the horizon, was prone to look on the dark side of things.

All this good-natured fumbling was anathema to the Major. Bernet embarrassed him. His barking from the throne-chair, his guileless ways, his tradesmanlike sincerity, marred the institutional veneer. In public the mismatched partners were egregiously polite to each other, like a pair of vaudeville comics in a rhapsody of mutual esteem. In private they were beset with an almost total disparity of vision. Nothing O. B. did or said could win approval from the Major; and Bernet, in turn, was irked and hurt by Parke's withering superiority. They were obsessed with one objective, but O. B.'s eyes were on the trees, the Major's on the forest. Parke abhorred details; Bernet loved them. Bernet liked to talk around a subject; Parke was close mouthed, taciturn, explicit. Parke was bold and extravagant with Mr. Bishop's money; Bernet was cautious, a penny watcher. O. B., with his Kirby-Lorenz training, was a stickler for long-established precepts; to the Major, Kirby was a crude ringmaster who could not have functioned in the changing times. The irreconcilable vice presidents bickered over petty matters, wrangled over points of policy; but mainly they sulked in a hollow truce of noncollaboration and addressed each other with ludicrous formality. Parke might sometimes use the familiar "Otto," in the starchy tone he used to call a menial. O. B. never deigned to say "Hiram." It was "Mr. Parke," or in conciliatory moments, "Major." Parke's hauteur was deliberately intimidating. "He could fix you with a fishlike stare, say nothing—and you would cringe," a member of the staff recalled. Bernet made a vocation of not cringing.

The rostrum was of course the main point of contention. Parke, without so much as a by-your-leave, abrogated all the big moments to himself. Bernet, out of deference to the star's brilliance, patiently hawked the second-rate. But Parke also, in contempt for O. B.'s artlessness, contrived to exclude him from sale-booking maneuvers requiring shrewdness and finesse. Bernet he thought unfit for high-level diplomacy. His foggy grammar would grate on the ears of the second-generation titans, many of whom had even been to college. His garrulity and *Gemütlichkeit* muddied up the élite image. The times, like Kirby's mantle, had in Parke's view passed poor Otto by. But in the jockeying for position, O. B. had one inestimable advantage. He was, nominally at least, the Major's superior. For by Mr. Bishop's decree, Bernet was general manager of the galleries.

It was Bernet Mr. Bishop had chiefly trusted with his capital, Bernet he favored by reason of long acquaintance, but also for his very lack of guile and polish. Urbanity was Mr. Bishop's birthright and prerogative; wherefore in his entourage he had a preference—it could even be said a penchant—for the garden variety of people.

Unquestionably the master hand was Parke's, but in a practical sense, O. B.'s contribution was substantial. Like Parke, he had the unlettered expert's sense for values; unlike Parke, he had a tolerance for mediocrity that made him entrepreneur of the steady flow of bread-and-butter sales that kept the galleries running week on week. High prices were what stuck in the public mind, but the gala auctions were few and far between. It was Bernet who enthusiastically chased consignments large and small, who pondered the obituary pages for news of seasonable disaster and traveled to Peoria or Chicago or Montreal to get in on the ground floor. It was Bernet who made the AAA a rendezvous for private buyers whose walls would never know a Renoir's glow, Bernet who conducted the charity auctions Parke disdained, who fussed over the amenities and nurtured the good will for which Mr. Bishop had paid a half a million dollars.

In the rostrum, too, O. B. had his following. Often consignors would ask to have it written in the contract that Parke would conduct the auction, but there were those who preferred the bailiff to the judge. Some thought O. B.'s jovial, down-to-earth muddling more effective than Parke's high sentence when the stakes were of less-than-masterwork caliber. There were consignors who asked to have Bernet cry their sales and many absentee buyers who, out of an abiding faith

Hiram Parke and Otto Bernet at Lenox—"Mr. Bishop's three dogs."

in his honest-tradesman mores, would commission him, and only him, to bid for them in the sales. Thus, in spite of the magnificent persuader, O. B. had a wedge in the prestige.

Nor was Mr. Bishop above promoting the rivalry between his

vaudeville-team vice presidents. He exulted in their seriocomic disharmony, delighted in thwarting Parke's dispostion to make Bernet the fall guy in the act. In Paris O. B. and Mrs. Bernet, who erstwhile had been his stenographer, were permitted to bask in the splendor of the Ritz. Parke and the stylish Mrs. Parke were relegated to the less proprietary Edouard VII. Sometimes, in mockery of the First Gentleman's manner, dispatches from the ever-tapping Corona would commence "Sir VP," or "My Lord Hiram." No one would have called O. B. Sir anything, but now and then Mr. Bishop would favor him with a conspiratorial "Dear Otto."

Both VPs cast themselves as heroes in the Bishop-endowed drama. Both played the queasy role of courtier; both tramped Mr. Bishop's Lenox acres, rode on his snow-defying tractor, charted the élite auctions' course in the great hall of Ananda with the ominous sentries pacing off the hours on the balcony overhead. Together they had their picture taken in their derby hats in company with the fierce survivor of Ananda's canine guard. ("Bishop had three dogs," Parke used to say wryly, "me, Bernet, and Husky.") Both jumped to Mr. Bishop's call in Europe. Each made his separate report in weekly letters to far places. ("Put in a few mistakes," Bernet would tell his amanuensis, "so he'll think I wrote it myself.") Both sent flowers to the boat, paid homage to Mrs. Bishop and the entourage; and for a long time O. B.'s roses smelled a little sweeter.

There was rivalry within and rivalry without, for three blocks away on Park Avenue the Anderson Galleries loomed, an implacable competitor. On the book front, Arthur Swann had rejoiced at the advent of Mr. Bishop, who was himself—to use Swann's phrase—an "advanced collector" of rare books and prints. Freed from the restraints of Kirby and Lorenz, the AAA's militant book chief redoubled his efforts to lure the big sales from Mitchell Kennerley and the Anderson and make himself major-domo of the literary auctions.

Now Swann's forte, the long-time theme of his bombilating sales talk, became the fuller-explanation catalogue, replete with long descriptions, bibliographical notes, and fascinating minutiae, illustrated with photographs of rare bindings and facsimile pages. Book collectors, Swann had always argued, read catalogues more avidly than books; and, he reiterated, logically enough, the more lavish the prospectus the greater the stimulation to possess. To be sure, the glossy catalogue cost more money, but from the standpoint of the consignor, Swann developed a potent argument in its favor. A collector who had stocked his shelves from Rosenbach, James Drake, or Gabriel Wells might find that after liquidating his investment at the AAA he had a record of literary discernment that was somehow more impressive than the actual volumes had been on his shelves. Heirs feeling guilty about disposing of morocco-bound evidence of paternal bookishness could, on the one hand, reap the cash, and on the other, retain a comforting "monument"—as Swann called a really elaborate catalogue—to the "collectorship" of the departed.

But while the publications of the AAA had an exhilarating air of requiem or triumph, as the case might be, the Anderson remained the favored consortium of the book-bidding cabal. Mitchell Kennerley's catalogues were crisp and reticent in the English tradition, their manila covers trademarked with the woodcut of the Gutenberg-Faustus print shop that had adorned the famous Hoe catalogues, their descriptions written less as bait for the amateur than as texts for the dealers who guided their munificent disciples through the labyrinth of bibliophily.

Munificent many of them certainly were, and clamorous with excess profits, for nothing in the Roaring Twenties did stancher service as a badge of cultural arrival than a display of literary baubles. Most exemplary and avid were such giant monument builders as Owen D. Young and J. K. Lilly, the Indianapolis drug manufacturer, but the book bandwagon rolled on through the varied roads of fortune, from Jerome Kern, the songwriter—an obsessed, not to say "advanced," collector—to unlettered politicians like W. W. Cohen, who bustled into the Anderson and said to Anthony Bade, "Just buy me what you think I ought to have."

Cohen, a Tammany bigwig and Wall Street speculator, who liked to drive the wrong way through one-way streets while the cops saluted his magic license number, was bucking for the House of Representatives. Bade chose Americana as an appropriate specialty, bought him $50,000 worth of books, and then found himself summoned with irksome frequency to Cohen dinner parties to explain to boorish constituents the status value of a $3,450 first edition of *Leaves of Grass* and such other items as he had judged a well-appointed Congressman should have.

After serving his one and only term as a lawmaker, Cohen sold his books, ironically at the AAA, where he got twice what Bade had bid for them at the Anderson (not to mention a monument in the archives). Then, in the way of speculators, he began collecting all over again.

Such breezy customers were not uncommon. Even poor men bought first editions—as they bought "growth stocks," in the hope of cashing in on the rising market. The big-league dealers, it was estimated, listed some fifteen thousand clients in various localities and stages of advancement. But relatively few were auction addicts. Arthur Swann's hue and cry notwithstanding, almost all the bidding was done by the cabal. Normally no more than about 150 of what were called the "privates" would assemble at either gallery to watch the show.

With Tony Bade in the rostrum, the show at the Anderson was the superior attraction. The tall, lean young man, with the delicately chiseled, clerical-looking face, who as a boy had stood agape in Robert Hoe's book-crammed brownstone, had taken out his auctioneer's license in 1923. An Anderson auctioneer had died, and as a candidate for the vacancy, Bade was given an endurance test before gallery personnel simulating an unruly crowd. "They heckled me and tried to throw me off," Bade related years later, when he had sold many million dollars' worth of mainly literary chattels, "but I kept my head—and got the job." His real-life debut was before a female audience in fervid conflict over a mess of linens from the bedchambers of William Rockefeller. But within a very short time, Bade was acknowledged as the country's most capable and ingratiating "book spellbinder."

"I had lived with books," Bade said modestly. He could have boasted that he knew what he was selling. The items might all have come from his own library, so articulate was his presentation, so fault-less his pronunciation, so facile his allusions to their history and content. But behind the sensitive, almost ascetic appearance of the young man on the high stool at the Anderson was a fiber that was stern and even tough. He knew his audience—the sportive antics of the cabal, the baser instincts of the bargain hunters, their age-old devices to confound the crier—as well as he knew his books. His mobile features and expressive voice were kept in superb restraint, but he could be masterful even before such lordly bibliopoles as Gabriel Wells and Dr. Rosenbach. His pace and timing gave the sales an urgency that relieved the monotony of volume after volume on the block. The worn old jokes and clichés he avoided, but he could look down over his glasses and utter an impromptu aside that was pertinent and witty; and when the lot was worth it, his melodious baritone could make the rafters rumble.

Bade's histrionic talents gave spirit to the seances of the cabal, and Fred Chapman still presided with equanimity over most of the art sales, but at the Anderson the role of auctioneer was secondary to that of Mitchell Kennerley.

Now in his late forties, Kennerley was a man of vaunted reputation. His "unrivaled showmanship" was legend, his sagacity and bonhomie, and qualities variously referred to as "spirit of enterprise," "vivid imagination," and "wise diplomacy." A man of letters said of "M. K.'s carefully guarded sanctum at the Anderson Galleries" that it was "the most interesting chamber in New York, where one hears the best and shrewdest talk about books that I know anywhere." A modern typeface named Kennerley brought international acclaim to Frederic William Goudy as the greatest type designer since Caslon; and, as M. K. quipped, rendered his own name immortal. When the sculptor Jo Davidson made a series of portrait busts of "men who knew more or achieved more than their contemporaries," three of the subjects were John D. Rockefeller, Otto H. Kahn, and Mitchell Kennerley. *International Studio* found the Kennerley bust to be "imbued with an Olympic repose which suggests the familiar portrait busts of Goethe." Those who failed to note in Kennerley the Olympian repose of Goethe simply called him a "charming fellow." He was still esteemed as publisher of the artistically printed books he occasionally brought out in limited editions. As head of the Anderson he was extolled by the *Antiquarian Bookman* as "the most accomplished, the most brilliant" impresario.

Dissenters from this encomiastic chorus were apt to be soured associates who found M. K. even shrewder about money than in talk about books. Or they were castoff acquaintances who had run afoul of his fierce conceit and overbearing urge to be cock of the walk. "He was a great actor," the man who wrote so extravagantly of the Davidson bust said years later, "sometimes very pleasant . . . a saint or a rat, a genius or a scoundrel, depending on your viewpoint." But dissenters were not particularly vocal in that heyday of Kennerley popularity. He was a gasconading figure in the smart set—a man's man on the one hand, and on the other, devastatingly attractive to women. Long estranged from his wife, an absentee father to his three sons, he lived beyond his means at the Hotel Plaza, strode the decks of ocean liners with his silver-headed walking stick, swaggered through the mansions of Long Island's leisure classes with the gay-dog vigor of the Roaring Twenties, and when not otherwise engaged, illumined the Anderson with the incandescence of his Olympian person.

The AAA's book department exuded no such vibrant worldliness. Swann, puritan and pedestrian by nature, was no man to star among the champagne set, or even—except for an adventitious sodality with the dour, lone-wolf Gabriel Wells—to find much favor with the bibulous, keen-witted cabal. Moreover, he was the victim of an antipathy on the part of Mitchell Kennerley far transcending mere commercial rivalry. "I don't know why he hated me so much," Swann said ingenuously in looking back. "I never spoke ten words to him in my life."

It was, more accurately, scorn rather than hate. To Kennerley, who preened himself among the rich and clever, Swann was an unctuous gadfly who made a fetish of pseudosincerity, a windy bore with little on his mind but the price of books and a tradesman's acquaintance with their title pages. By fair means or foul, Kennerley meant to rout so busybody an antagonist from the auction scene. His churlishness went so far that he even blackballed poor Swann from a coveted membership in the Grolier Club, the supreme sanctum of bibliophiles.

The malevolence was, of course, two sided. Garrulous with anti-Anderson propaganda, and relentless in pursuit of consignors, Swann did a yeoman's job of discrediting Kennerley, and kept the book-sale totals at the AAA—about $1 million yearly—neck and neck with those at the establishment of his formidable rival; for this feat, Mr. Bishop rewarded him, albeit temporarily, with the title of vice president. But despite all Swann's zeal, the more newsworthy events took place under Kennerley's banner. The AAA struck no such Golconda of publicity as the sale at the Anderson Galleries on the night of February 15, 1926, of the perfect Melk copy of the Guten-berg Bible.

The traffic in Gutenberg Bibles had been sparse since the great Hoe sale of 1911. There had in fact been a certain slackness in the bidding for the one copy to appear at public sale, in London in 1923, the copy that had once been in Cardinal Mazarin's library. It had fallen to Dr. R. at $43,500, and Rosenbach had sold it to the New York stockbroker Carl H. Pforzheimer for about $60,000. Now the Melk copy had come to light, the ninth to cross the Atlantic, and in all likelihood, the last destined for the auction block.

Almost from the time it left the press at Mainz this two-volume paper copy of the Bible—fresh, clean, every leaf sound and genuine—had reposed in the Benedictine monastery at Melk in Austria. Then, in June 1925, the good monks of Melk, being long on Bibles and short on cash, had been prevailed upon to sell their Book of Books to Edward Goldston, a London dealer, for £12,000. Goldston attempted to dispose of his find in England for the equivalent of $65,000, and having no success, turned it over to Mitchell Kennerley for public sale in New York.

While Swann looked on with unabashed envy, the unrivaled book was exploited with all the furbelows of unrivaled showmanship. Scarcely anyone within reach of press or radio failed to hear something about the birth of printing, the Anderson Galleries, and the enterprise of Mitchell Kennerley. For eight days of presale festivities Anthony Bade stood sentry over the 472-year-old volumes while multitudes filed past. The bidding would most certainly be between Dr. R. and one or two of his rivals. But the people had a right to look.

As it turned out, one unanticipated contender did show up. W. Evarts Benjamin, whose deceased wife had inherited a portion of the H. H. Rogers Standard Oil fortune, cast a beneficent eye on the Bible and inquired of Bade if it would not make a nice gift to the Cathedral of St. John the Divine, as a memorial to the late Mrs. Benjamin. Conceivably the Protestant Episcopalians then charged with completing the third largest meetinghouse in Christendom, which for more than thirty years had been under construction in a blighted region of Manhattan, might have been more gratified with the wherewithal to raise a Gothic spire than with a book to cloister in its vaults. But the Bible would make a nice present, Bade wholeheartedly agreed.

By the night of the sale, sufficient excitement had been worked up to cram the Anderson with spectators and bring a rubbernecking crowd to the corner of Park Avenue and 59th Street. During the preliminary bout, a sale of English books belonging to Robert B.

Adam of Buffalo, the bibliophilistic élite ate and drank. The Morgan Library's Belle da Costa Greene gave a banquet. A. Edward Newton, whose *The Greatest Book in the World and Other Papers* was then on the stands, wined and dined his coterie at another. By ten-thirty, tribute having been paid to the primordial press at Mainz, the impecunious monks of Melk, and the literary bull market of the Roaring Twenties, Belle Greene in festive garb trooped into the little red theater, with the book lords in her wake. The crowd made way and closed in behind. Before the curtains concealing the Book stood Tony Bade, like a grave young priest poised to begin an awesome symbolic rite.

The curtains parted. Bade called for order with three raps of the gavel and asked for an opening bid. Belle of the Books rose on cue and made it: $50,000, an honorary gesture, to be sure, for the Morgan Library was well-supplied with Gutenberg Bibles. The congregation indulged in a sonorous ovation, either for the fascinating Miss Greene, or for the two leather-bound volumes in the spotlight, or from awareness of the neatly arranged coincidence that $50,000 had been the final, not the opening, bid for Robert Hoe's vellum copy of the Bible fifteen years before, when the great book boom was launched.

Bade's exordium topped the interrupting clatter. Gabriel Wells signaled $55,000. A measured rise got under way, first at $1,000, then at $500, with many of the bids coming from predestined also-rans with an urge to contribute to the festivities, or at any rate, to see their names in the papers as underbidders.

Before long the minor contestants dropped out. The field narrowed to Gabriel Wells and Dr. R. At $83,000 Wells gave up. Bade, his weather eye fixed on W. Evarts Benjamin, began the count: "Once . . . twice . . ." With the fall of the gavel but a second off, Benjamin made his dark-horse move. Rosenbach responded. The race took on new life. Thousand by thousand, the cathedral's well-wisher egged on the bland, imperturbable Napoleon of Books. At $100,000 the gleeful claque applauded. Bade disdained to pause. His arioso baritone swelled on until, at $106,000, Mr. Benjamin turned parsimonious. The hammer dropped to the familiar refrain: "Sold—to Dr. R.!"

The third largest meetinghouse in Christendom, its Gothic spires even today a figment of Episcopal imagination, has had to draw its inspiration from less sublime editions of the Word. Rosenbach's client was Standard Oil-rich Mrs. Edward S. Harkness, and through her beneficence, the Melk copy of the Gutenberg Bible is now enshrined at Yale.

However paltry it may sound now, $106,000 had a thriftless lilt in the headlines of 1926. (It remained the world's record price for a printed book until 1947, when the Bay Psalm Book superseded it at 151,000 much-inflated dollars.) But if modest folk were shocked that anyone would pay $106,000 for a book, they were presently to be stunned by the tribute exacted at the Anderson Galleries for a mere name written on a sheet of paper, and a name of not much consequence at that.

A breed of collector thrived in the twenties inspired by no loftier motive than to have *all* of something—all the works of an author in their first editions, all the prints of Currier and Ives, the autographs of all fifty-six signers of the Declaration of Independence. The goal of the signers was the more attractive for its obstacles. Jefferson and Franklin, who had kept the inkpots flowing, were as weeds in a garden patch, but there were elusive revolutionaries who had signed the prime historic document and very little else. Among them, Button Gwinnett was the edelweiss, the almost unobtainable.

The known facts of Button Gwinnett's short life are meager. He was one of the five delegates from Georgia to the Continental Congress. Having signed the Declaration, he returned home, held office as president of Georgia for two months, and got into a quarrel with General Lachlan McIntosh, one of Washington's military aides. McIntosh denounced Gwinnett in the assembly as a scoundrel and a lying rascal. The two men fought a duel. Gwinnett was mortally wounded, and died May 19, 1777. His eulogy in the *Lives of the Signers* reads: "His sun rose suddenly. Its course to the zenith was rapid and brilliant; its descent was hurried and ominous of evil, and it sat in blood."

Gwinnett had been a slave trader and an unprosperous plantation owner. He died insolvent, but 149 years later his financial sun rose posthumously to a dazzling zenith at the Anderson Galleries.

The ascent began in January 1926, at a sale of the collection of Colonel James H. Manning of Albany, New York. Colonel Manning had acquired (in 1912, for $4,000) one of the nineteen Button Gwinnett autographs then known to exist, a signature on a will Gwinnett had witnessed in 1770. It fell to Dr. R. for $22,500. Subsequently the attorney general of Georgia brought suit to recover the document, on the ground that it must at some time have been purloined from the state archives. The claim was not sustained by the courts, and Rosenbach resold the autograph to the Reverend Dr. Roderick Terry, socialite clergyman of Newport.

Newspaper coverage of these events set off a chain reaction among rummagers in old storage places. A Mrs. Arthur W. Swann (no relation to the AAA's Arthur Swann) found a Gwinnett signature among a cache of documents handed down from her grandfather, Theodore Sedgwick of Stockbridge, Massachusetts. She bustled it off to the Anderson, where it brought $28,500—also from Dr. R.

Shortly after that, John Cecil Clay of Mamaroneck, New York, came up with his Gwinnett pot of gold. Clay, a sometime commercial artist, had been an invalid confined to a wheelchair for many years. Ill, despondent, and sorely in need of money, he was leafing through a magazine one day when the story of Mrs. Swann's windfall caught his eye. The name Gwinnett somehow rang a bell. A descendant of the Ashmead family of Philadelphia, Clay recalled that there were some old family papers stored in an outbuilding on his mortgaged property and that his ancestor John Ashmead had had correspondence with members of the Continental Congress. Among relics of his great-great-grandfather he found a letter dated July 12, 1776, signed by six members of the Marine Committee of Congress. One of the six was Button Gwinnett. "I just lay back in my chair and relaxed," Clay said. "I relaxed for the first time in nearly twenty-five years."

The Anderson men were summoned, and made off with the letter. The following day, as an improbable sequel to an improbable good-luck story, the barn in which the Ashmead papers had been stored burned to the ground.

It developed that the Marine Committee letter was the only known document, other than the Declaration of Independence, that linked the enigmatic Button Gwinnet to national affairs. The bidding, on the night of March 17, 1927, was furious and dogged between Rosenbach and Gabriel Wells. Dr. R.'s winning bid was $51,000.

Concurrent with these book-and-autograph high jinks Mitchell Kennerley pulled off a grand coup in the field of art sales. The Anderson, having no angel, had perforce kept aloof from the Italian-Spanish traffic, but in the summer of 1925 a Kennerley scout named

Carl Freund got wind of an immense treasure-trove in England. Viscount Leverhulme, progenitor of the Lever Brothers soap empire, had died, leaving his country seat The Hill, in Hampstead, rife with the consequences of a prolonged orgy of artistic shopping.

The Leverhulme estate, in need of the equivalent of around $1 million to pay death duties, had already consigned the contents of The Hill to the London firm Knight, Frank and Rutley for a fifteen-day auction in the fall. Carl Freund learned, however, that the executors had grown apprehensive about the English market's capacity to absorb the many tons of artistic flotsam the late Soap King had stored. Freund wired Mitchell Kennerley, and Kennerley took the next boat from New York.

Subjected to Kennerley's wise diplomacy, Knight, Frank and Rutley and the Leverhulme estate agreed to transfer the auction to New York, provided the Anderson would guarantee $1 million return. The combined prestige of Mitchell Kennerley and the late Viscount Leverhulme obtained a loan from a bank, which Kennerley posted as security, and by October 1925 the press here and abroad was carrying portents of the colossal auction the Anderson Galleries had copped.

A ripple of vexation passed through the House of Lords. The Earl of Mayo applied to the British courts for an order restraining the export of the "famous Leverhulme collection." The courts declined to act, but the international publicity his lordship's peeve set off fostered the impression that all that gallimaufry of objects would look fine in the British Museum.

The Earl of Mayo's rancor was as nothing compared to that of Mr. Bishop over "what our rivals have done to stab us." In Paris he banged out letters to his vice presidents. "We need publicity, we cannot get enough of it, but Kennerley has stolen a march on us." His spirits rose, however, when he bustled over to London. Kennerley had fallen for "a lot of junk," he reported gleefully. "It appears that the executors did not dare put it on the market in London, believing that Americans were ignorant enough to pay high prices for that bad stuff."

For all that, the Viscount Leverhulme's effects were transported to New York in forty-four lift vans—of such sturdy and elaborate construction that they are functioning to this day as garages somewhere in suburbia. Kennerley did everything wrong, according to his critics at the AAA. Well-known British "authorities" were employed to turn out a stack of befuddling catalogues in the English idiom of *caveat emptor*. The 2,336 lots ranged from English furniture through rugs, bronzes, books, tapestries, and porcelains, to 296 paintings that ran the gamut from a serviceable Goya portrait to giddy travesties on the talents of the English big six barefacedly presented with whatever attributions the purveyors to Lord Leverhulme had given them. But nothing seemed to matter. Art magazines purred with superlatives, overwhelmed by the quantity and variety of the collection, and above all, by its origin. The sudsy fame of Lever Brothers had glamour, the rags-to-riches story of its founder, born plain William Lever, and through his contribution to world cleanliness, buried the first Viscount Leverhulme.

For a month beginning February 9, 1926, Americans ignorant enough to pay high prices stormed 489 Park Avenue, as did some who were not so ignorant. The Renaissance and Gothic vogue notwithstanding, fine pieces of Chippendale and Sheraton went as high as $15,000. In other cases the good carried the bad. An eagle-head armchair that made $4,250 turned out to be worth only $300 upon its reappearance at a less bewitching auction in 1933. But for that month the bidders had a high old time. Uncle Eli Springs reveled in the prints and porcelains. Governor A. T. Fuller of Massachusetts enriched his stately home of New England with many a lackluster notion from The Hill. He paid, wonderful to say, $31,000 for *Caller Herring* by the Pre-Raphaelite painter Sir John Everett Millais. A little lower on the scale, the Goya, catalogued as *Portrait of Pepe Illo*, brought $25,000, and lower still, purblind art lovers desiring a Correggio could have one for $350, or a Constable, or an appalling choice of Painted Ladies at about the same price. The Leverhulme collection may have been predominantly "junk," but no one, not even the exasperated Mr. Bishop, could disparage Mitchell Kennerley's showmanship, or the grand total—$1,248,503—his bold venture racked up.

Double was the irony in that figure for the AAA. The $1 million Kennerley had gambled on the Leverhulme was an even match for the $1 million Mr. Bishop had guaranteed the Ars Committee against the sale of the Chiesa collection of Milan. But whereas Kennerley had gambled and won, the Chiesa affair was an unholy mess.

Achillito's "$7,000,000" grab bag—the irresistible ivories, enamels, velvets, and majolica platters—proved more resistible in New York than in Milan. The pictures—many of them—on second sight turned out to be brackish. The better ones had been inventoried as national treasures by the Italian government. Tenebrous methods used to get certain paintings out of the country put everyone in peril of the high-riding Fascisti. So chaotic had the politics become that it was difficult to know whom to bribe. The crew in Milan headed by Luigi Albrighi —who was, Mr. Bishop said, not only charming but invaluable—ran up expense accounts appalling to O. B. and the Major. With the tightening of restrictions on travel for Italian citizens, Albrighi himself became something of a national treasure. "You cannot imagine the trouble we had getting him on the boat," Mr. Bishop wrote after one of Albrighi's departures from Le Havre. A muddled saga followed—of withheld visas, manipulated permits, and vulpine emigration officers, of breakneck chases in the Hispano-Suiza and hairbreadth crises with one Albrighi foot on the boat, the other off it. The publicity, Mr. Bishop concluded gleefully, was wonderful in the French papers—where, of course, it did the AAA no good.

Somehow 345 Italian, Dutch, Spanish, French, and Flemish paintings did get to cross the ocean in installments, accompanied by Albrighi and supposititious catalogue descriptions. Sales were scheduled in parts, at five-month intervals. Hearst and Samuel H. Kress were active bidders (numerous Chiesa pictures are among the Kress gifts to the National Gallery), but most of the higher-echelon collectors were suspicious of Achillito's old masters. At the sessions held in the fall of 1925 and spring of 1926 Mr. Bishop, in a mulish attempt to bolster prices, had the paintings and art objects he termed "the jewels of the first water" bid in for his own account by Ercole Canessa. Many lots fell to Canessa, and thus, in view of the million-dollar guarantee, were in a sense bought twice by the AAA's intransigent angel.

Canessa, the ostensible purchaser, put the buy-ins on display for sale in his art gallery. Customers were slow to appear, and by the following November, Mr. Bishop, then in residence at Lenox, had come to regret his face-saving operation. Nagging directives issued from The Winter Palace: "I would like the Canessa/Chiesa holdings liquidated. . . . I am in no sense an antiquity dealer, and do not wish to become one." Still, not much liquidation took place, and Mr. Bishop, in wrath against Canessa, ordered the holdings repossessed by his vice presidents. O. B. and the Major, also with no wish to become antiquity dealers, were charged with disposing of the presumably already sold "jewels" by private treaty. With some persuasion, Hearst came to the rescue and took the two most valuable pictures at their knockdown prices—a fourteenth-century primitive by Agnolo Gaddi at $27,000, another, by Orcagna, at $45,000. This was, however, no immediate boon to Mr. Bishop's cash position, for Hearst was always imperious about accounts payable. Once the pictures were hung in his apartment, he proceeded to contemplate them on extended approval.

Mr. Bishop fumed and fretted. A flock of Chiesa duds remained, some of which Mr. Bishop had shipped back to Europe. Those, along with several hundred lusterless pictures that had never left Milan, Albrighi and various picture dealers attempted to unload on the Continent. More money was spent in restoring and framing pictures that could not be shown in their derelict condition. An auction was held in Milan. Not much was sold. Pictures were put out on option in Rome, Paris, Berlin, and other cities; pictures traveled back and forth in a continual transatlantic migration. At one point there were some three hundred minor works whose peregrinations no one at the AAA could trace.

The Chiesa juggernaut rolled on. The Ars Committee snarled and threatened lawsuits, the while exacting payments on their million-dollar guarantee. Chiesa sales were still being held in the thirties. Bernet (who always got the tedious assignments) spent a decade off and on with a succession of lawyers in acrimonious dispute with the bankers Mr. Bishop came to look upon as his Milanese Shylocks. A final accounting was perhaps never made, though a Chiesa total of $698,397 eventually appeared in the galleries' reports; but by the summer of 1926 it was already clear that, what with the buy-ins and expenses, the greater part of the million pledged to the Ars Committee would be lost. "One man can wreck us," Mr. Bishop wrote despondently from Biarritz, "as I myself have done with the most honest intent."

Wreck was too strong a word. Though the Chiesa fiasco consumed the profits, the AAA was a Niagara of action. Year by year the totals mounted—$4 million, $5 million, to more than $5,500,000 for the 1926–27 season. Money was nevertheless a continual preoccupation. Large sums were constantly tied up in subsidies to Benguiat and the professori. The tradesmen buyers, the decorators and the dealers who absorbed much of the Italian-Spanish influx, had to be given credit to keep them bidding freely in sale after sale. Their bills ran on from month to month, and even year to year. Hearst, as Parke said, was a great man to have in an auction, but his empyreal resources notwithstanding, he was unconscionably slow to pay. ("How did Hearst get to owe us $319,000?" Mr. Bishop would bluster at his Corona.) Parke would be obliged to hound the great man like a common bill collector. If cornered, Hearst might make a partial payment in promissory notes; if pushed too far, he would threaten to return the Chiesa paintings, which Parke in no event wished to have back on his hands.

Mr. Bishop's love affair with the auctions blew hot and cold. Where was the interest on his money? he would inquire of his vice presidents darkly. What in fact had the deployment of so much capital accomplished toward the creation of the greatest art salesroom in the world? The halls had teemed with mediocrities. "The Paolini and Tolentino sales have destroyed much of our prestige abroad," the letters dinned with refrainlike constancy. (The latter reference was to a lurid Tolentino auction at which fifty-two old masters had sold for an average price of $99.80 per old master.) He would rather have the galleries closed, Mr. Bishop carped, than sell some of the things raked up by the professori. "Anderson can take care of them." Moreover, the dealers and their machinations were giving the place a bad name. On that subject, the notes from Europe took on a commanding vehemence: "It seems to be the general impression over here, and elsewhere, that the AAA is absolutely controlled by two dealers in particular. This impression must be obliterated at all cost."

Benguiat and Canessa were the two conspirators on whom Mr. Bishop's displeasure focused. Canessa (whom Parke called, in the final analysis, "an honest antiquarian," implying that the quality was rare, if not unique, in his experience) had fallen out of favor during the Chiesa maneuvers. The Pasha, to be sure, was working hand in glove with Parke.

"I was making rug prices," the Major said in later years, looking back nostalgically to the battle of the Isfahans on those tense December afternoons of 1925 and 1926. But Parke's prestidigitatory feats notwithstanding, the great Benguiat sales had as much façade as substance. The Pasha, pacing the rear of the auditorium, rhythmically striking the back of one hand against the palm of the other, pausing now and then to take a bite of sausage, or if the opportunity should present itself, surreptitiously to rub a hunchback for good luck, captained an inexorable boosters' claque. When a Persian carpet soared to a resounding figure, it might be on its way to the home of a golden client; but then again, it might not. If a rug fell to a dealer on terms with the Pasha, it might mean that the lot was permanently sold; or it could mean that the Pasha, by prearrangement, had merely let one of his pets out on a leash.

So it was when the Animal Rug at long last made its reappearance on the auction block. How checkered had been the fortunes of that 6-by-12-foot strip of carpet—which John Kimberly Mumford had called "probably as near perfection as the woolen carpet of the East has come, or will ever come"—in the years since an upstart Vitall had bought it for $38,000 in the Marquand sale of 1903. Ephraim had borrowed it for his ludicrous museum in Saint Louis; Vitall had rescued it from a predatory sheriff; Mrs. Hearst had all but seized it in the dark days of the Knickerbocker loft; Mordecai had stolen it and dragged it through the law courts in the long case of Benguiat versus Benguiat; its beauty, its value, its state of preservation, had been disputed by witnesses and lawyers, restorers and malevolent employees. By rights it should have been threadbare with so much wrangling. But here it was, with all its symbols and near-perfections intact—its dark green, almost black background, its orange stems and moss-green creepers putting forth leaves, tendrils, and incredibly delicate flower shapes to form an otherworldly utopia inhabited by deer, gazelles, sheep, and goats, in flight from invading lions and leopards; its central medallion of Isfahan rose-crimson surmounted by a branchlike arabesque in silver thread and four hawklike birds of prey; its border of rich golden-yellow, interlacing branches, and rose-crimson plaquettes with couplets from the poetry of Saadi in silver-woven calligraphy. "Oh, Saki," one of the couplets read in translation:

. . . the zephyr of the spring is blowing now; The rose has become fresh and luxuriant.

The bidding started off in high key that 1926 December afternoon. The callers' blasts ricocheted off the velvet walls; the Pasha's fist struck his open palm in tempo with Parke's importuning cries. The initial volley over, two main contestants emerged: the blue-nose dealer Parish-Watson and Benguiat's friend young Leon Schinasi, connoisseur. At the strategic moment, Schinasi, the veteran under-bidder, dropped out, and Parke knocked down the Animal Rug to Parish-Watson at a neat $100,000—by far the highest price a strip of carpet had ever brought at public sale.

With the tumult and the bravos the rumor was permitted to leak out that Parish-Watson had been representing Joseph Widener. Headlines appeared in the newspapers—"J. E. Widener pays $100,-000 for 15th-Century Persian Rug"—followed by the supposition that the rug of rugs would enter Widener's "world-famous art collection at Elkins Park, near Philadelphia." The story was not quite contrived of whole cloth. Widener had in truth come to the galleries with Parish-Watson to see the Animal Rug. He had even, it was said, challenged Parish-Watson and Benguiat to find a place for it in his Elkins Park museum. No unfilled cranny had been found, and Parish-Watson, bearded in his posh emporium, had to admit that the naming of Widener as the buyer was premature, an exaggeration. He would like to sell the rug, of course—to Mr. Widener if he cared to buy it. But Widener did not buy the Pasha's much-buffeted carpet, nor had Parish-Watson bought it in the headline-making sale. After all the hue and cry, the Animal Rug returned like a homing pigeon to the Benguiat room above the auction hall.

Perhaps the old rug peddler did not really want to sell his carpets, unless for sums commensurate with his fanatical pietas for the remnants of old cultures he dug up. He had fought for them through half a century of cunning and connivance. They were his self-esteem, his "babies," the affirmation of his omniscience and travail. In his way, perhaps he loved them; perhaps he merely had a deluded notion of their value. Trade was the elixir of his life, trade and the feel of the exquisite in the hands that were said to have eyes. He wanted money, but he wanted things much more. He was obsessed with all the buried icons to be discovered and displaced, a victim of his own insatiable quest. "No matter what he sold or how much it brought," Parke said, in a tone of compassion for an affliction that could in no way be cured, "he would go out and buy something that cost twice as much." He was greedy, but he did not want to pile up wealth. Many times he could have put a fortune by. He was a wayfarer, an adventurer; and an adventurer disdains to count his cash. The Benguiat auctions totaled in the millions, but the room upstairs still glittered like a sultan's palace. The money, Mr. Bishop's money, would, the Pasha supposed, go on forever—the money and the caviar, the chippies and the booze. Promissory notes were slips of paper, "a writing," for which the Pasha had small use. All his property was mortgaged—the Magic Carpets and his Renaissance textiles, the palaces in Nice and Florence. His debt perpetually hovered around a half-million dollars. But the Pasha was magnificently unperturbed. He loved to hold a brilliant auction, with the luster of Parke's talents avouching the luster of his wares. The lesser items would be sold; if the Magic Carpets rose to the marks he had set for them, he would let them go; if not, he could wait until the Americans he secretly disparaged should be better educated as to their worth.

He could wait, though his Edwardian beard was turning white, but Mr. Bishop and the AAA could not. From Santander, Mr. Bishop dispatched an epic memorandum on the subject of Benguiat: "He must liquidate every cent he owes us, and as soon as the sale is over he must be evicted from our premises, bag & baggage, vi et armis, we retaining enough of his property to repay anything he may still owe. This is final. In the words of one W. Shakespere, 'I stand not on the order of his going. He must go.' "

The Benguiat liquidation sale was scheduled—and postponed, for by the first weeks of 1927, the fever for Persian carpets and Renaissance textiles showed alarming symptoms of abatement. The rich crimson that Genoa and Venice loved had begun to pall. Now, suddenly, no one fancied a Borgia throne, or a rug to put under it at twenty, forty, to sixty thousand dollars. There had been rumblings in the stock market; Renaissance Florida had blown away—a substantial part of it, at any rate—in the September hurricanes. The betempled crackerboxes of New York's élite had come to look profoundly foolish in the age of speed and social revolution. Polychrome had filtered down to Sears, Roebuck and the masses. Machine-carved walnut was the rage in department stores. A funereal calm hung over the Italian-Spanish auctions. Long-faced and pontifical, the professori stood vigil over their choice pieces and bought many of them in. "I'm ruined, ruined!" Signora Tolentino cried in an outburst of Italian histrionics before the dwindling congregation at the annual big Tolentino sale.

There were, all the same, rich Italian and Spanish cargoes en route to the AAA. When, in midwinter 1927, the Conde de las Almenas' antiquities arrived from Madrid, the galleries were transformed into a veritable museum of old Spain.

It had taken many months to negotiate the great Almenas auction and there had been many fingers in the pie: Benguiat and Canessa, O. B. and the Major, many lawyers, Mr. Bishop and sundry members of the entourage. The old Conde de las Almenas was of a mind to cast off the vanities of this world and go into a monastery, as he said, to make his soul; but he did not propose to cast them to swine. He was understandably on guard against auctioneers and dealers. He had held out for outrageous terms and impossible guarantees, until the day Parke arrived in Madrid. Like many another cautious consignor, His Excellentissimo had been captivated by the First Gentleman's grace and Old World charm. Though Parke spoke no Spanish and the Conde no English (*"Dólares* for the Count" was the one phrase that needed no interpreter), formal, reasonable—and gentlemanly—contracts were at length drawn up for what promised to be the all-time high in Spanish sales.

Once Parke and the Conde had come to terms, operations in Madrid were put in charge of Arthur Byne and Mildred Stapley Byne, a scholarly husband-and-wife team with a practical knowledge of Spain's artifacts and the means of exporting them. It had been the Bynes who had engineered for Hearst what was perhaps the supreme Hispanomanic folly—the transmigration in its entirety of a twelfth-century Cistercian monastery from the remote village of Sacramentia to a warehouse in the Bronx. The job had been a mite of trouble. Some 250 tons of moldered cloister had to be dismantled stone by stone, each stone numbered and charted for reassembling, the whole packed in straw in 10,500 cases. Irate villagers opposed to the plunder banded together and attacked the workmen. Forty kilometers of road had been built at Hearst's expense in order to transport the timeless and immovable to the nearest railway. When at last a fleet of freighters brought the monastery into New York harbor, customs inspectors refused to let the straw into the country. The giant puzzle had to be uncrated, the straw thrown overboard, the stones put back into their 10,500 cases—where they remained, still unpacked, when Hearst himself had been moldering for some time.

The Bynes were used to trouble, but from their interim reports to Parke the deployment of the Almenas treasure appears to have been scarcely a less nerve-racking chore than that presented by Hearst's cloister. Spain's political situation changed almost daily. The Conde de las Almenas had royal permission to export his collection, but he was no pet of the ruling military party. A scandal blew up over false declarations made to the watchdog Art Commission by a dealer (one of the Ruiz brothers), Spain's busiest marauder and veteran consignor to the AAA. A new law, with dreadful penalties, was passed, a complex of regulations which, but for the Bynes's agility in circumventing them, would have immobilized most of the Almenas collection as national treasure. The old Count hovered between the vision of *dólares* and the vision of his noble person meditating in a dungeon rather than a monastery. Every time he saw a packing case, he wanted to call the whole venture off. The Bynes, who stood to collect a fine commission, had constantly to allay his fears and rekindle his faith in the golden hammer. Torrential rains, an epidemic of typhoid fever, and numerous other calamities prolonged the work and multiplied the cost. But at length, the Count's collection, minus a few rarities left behind to assuage the Art Commission, did get on a steamer at Valencia. The final embarkation was nothing short of a triumph, Arthur Byne wrote Parke in a state of mental and physical exhaustion. "This you must impress on the public."

A public but recently given to ecstasy over the most trivial of Spanish relics certainly should have been impressed with those brooding halls of carved-wood gilt and painted figures; of medieval saints and polychromed pine prophets; the Mater Dolorosa in all pertinent situations; Queen Isabella at her devotions; martyrs and inquisitors; lions, griffins, angels; Hispano-Moresque pottery; trestle stands and plateresque cabinets; varguenos, Gothic chests and coffrets. The 324-page catalogue, written by Mildred Stapley Byne out of a profundity of learning, was nothing less than a Baedeker to Spanish antiquities, illuminating the history and provenience not only of significant art works but of such esoteric items as healing stones and almoners' purses, the portals and pilasters of obscure provincial palaces, the seventy-eight panels of a fourteenth-century Mudejar painted wood ceiling, down to and including the Conde's ancestral lace nightcaps. Visitors were privileged, too, to view the old Count himself, looking very handsome and aristocratic among his displaced lares. For at the last moment he had decided to come along, though he had taken a vow never to cross the ocean.

But the connoisseurs were spiritless and not too numerous at that week-long exhibition in January 1927. The Conde saw the handwriting on the wall. So lukewarm was the reception for his precious lares that he wanted to cancel the auction and accept an offer a dealer made to buy the collection en bloc for 1,500,000 pesetas. "No. *Dólares* for the Count," Parke reiterated firmly, and in the face of the Spanish-Italian deflation, the sale went on.

At moments in the long three-day auction, the fiery bidders put the bargain hunters to rout. Sixty dollars was the limit anyone would go for a seventeenth-century lace nightcap, but a folding metal camp table said to have been used by the Emperor Charles V, a unique specimen that looked like a beat-up object from the scrap heap, brought $12,500. An eleventh-century Mozarabic chess piece, the companions of which could be seen only in the Louvre, moved Mrs. Templeton Crocker to bid $5,600. Thanks to Hearst and the Papal Duchess (and multi-bemillioned) Mrs. Nicholas F. Brady, a gratifying levitation was occasionally provoked by bishops' thrones and pious figures. But a fine community of saints and martyrs could be had for prices in the hundreds. An exquisite life-size Catalan early fourteenth-century carved-wood St. Peter cost the Metropolitan Museum a mere $1,100.

The total for the sale—artistically one of the greatest in the galleries' history—was $318,792.50, not all of which, however, was for the Conde de las Almenas treasure; for the Bynes had cunningly filled in the gaps in the collection with rare finds of their own, and Canessa had added some Italian pieces illustrating the relation between Spanish and Italian craftsmanship. The *dólares* the Count received, though adequate to keep body and soul together in a cloister, were—when the Bynes had been paid and the AAA's commission and other expenses deducted—a mere fraction of what he had been led to expect. He recrossed the Atlantic an embittered man muttering curses on the pharisaical Americans. For a time, he stayed in Paris, not daring to return to Spain for fear of the Art Commission's vengeance in the matter of export irregularities. (The $5,600 chess piece, for instance, had come over in the Count's overcoat pocket. It was so small—3¼ inches high—it had not seemed worthwhile to ask the Art Commission for a permit.) In French, he wrote laments to Parke about the great loss he had sustained in his sale and begged Parke, as one gentleman to another, to make affidavits to the effect that the chess piece and other items had not really been

Almenas property—a deception the Major refused to join. When last heard of, the old Count was in his monastery, but whether meditating on his soul or the mirage of American dollars the annals do not record.

Post facto lamentations were now the order of the day. On the very Saturday that saw the last of the Almenas treasure scattered, the halls were sumptuously refurbished with the long-awaited, much-heralded Grassi collection, the grand prize of all those junkets to Florence. Most venerable, and temperamental, of all the professori, Luigi Grassi, the grand old man of antiquary Florence, had come with almost princely fanfare with the "private collection" from his home, the Palace Montagliari: his Tuscan hat racks and Venetian cradles, his Ligurian cupboards and Umbrian sgabellos, his statues, bas-reliefs, majolicas, and damasks, his fifteenth-century forks and knives, his Gothic crimson velvet dalmatic, his collection of Renaissance jewels, his collection of fifteenth- to seventeenth-century bedroom slippers, his helmets, swords, and battle-axes, his fourteen richly-carved cassoni, his abundance of nursing chairs, banquettes, and tables. Alas! he had come too late. All this—a total of 580 lots—brought, to the professor's ire and sorrow, a mere $265,415.

Despite Parke's warnings that things were going poorly for the gentlemen from Florence, in the spring Professor Elia Volpi arrived with "the very rarest works of art and furniture" he had been able to gather since his storied Davanzati Palace sale of 1916. He was an old man now, in poor health, and terrified of being cheated. But he was confident, he said, of being received by the art lovers of America with that good will and deference formerly accorded him. Who could have forgotten that classic among auctions a decade earlier? Who was there so ignorant as to be unaware of that sometime fountainhead of Italian treasure, the palace in the old Via di Porta Rossa so magnificently restored by Professore Commendatore Volpi (and now—though the publicity was careful not to mention it—the stamping ground of the Pasha Benguiat)? Not, certainly, the art journals and the newspapers. No more respectful welcome could have been accorded Professor Volpi's return voyage—the last, he said regretfully, that he would ever make to this country.

The press was deferential, but in the market place there were forebodings of disaster. Not only were auction-goers surfeited with vestigial art works and heavy grandeur, a miasma of intrigue had settled over the Italian traffic. Cutthroat tactics, always rife among the professori, now took the form of what seemed to Volpi sabotage. The Grassi sale had been a disappointment; and Grassi, the chief antiquary to pass on what plunder should leave Italy, had been in no mood to favor his distinguished competitor. Many had been the aggravations in getting export permits for Volpi's "rarest items." Some had perforce been left behind, and some that did get out, the Professor's rivals whispered, were perhaps no great loss to the country.

For all that, Volpi was determined to have his valedictory at auction. "The campaign displeases me which is unjustly moved against me," he had written Parke from Florence. "However, I assure you that I shall know personally how to put those slanderous gentlemen in their places." After all, his things were of superior artistic value. Had Professor Grassi, or any of the others, brought works by Michelangelo, Donatello, Leonardo—to say nothing of a small picture that Volpi, if no one else, attributed to Raphael? Moreover, when the Professor disembarked, he had in tow the materiel for a "unique event" at auction—an entire Venetian cinquecento room of state to be set up in the galleries, complete with "frescoed walls by Bernardo Parentino, frieze adorned with sculptured busts by Rizzo, and superbly painted ceilings."

Crusty as his bravado sounded, as the time of the auction approached, what with the slanderous gentlemen and the apathy of collectors, Volpi's confidence wavered. The works ascribed to the immortals were withdrawn from the bidding and exhibited in a room apart, for private sale. No one seemed to want the unobtainable: a Raphael, the "Volpi *David*" by Michelangelo, a coat of arms by Donatello, the small wax horse by Leonardo da Vinci. To avoid slaughter in the auction hall, reserve prices were placed on other items the Professor particularly valued. None of them was sold. For three days O. B. and the Major faced a few stragglers in the salesroom. No one wanted a credenza for $10,000, or a room of state *in toto*. The total came to less than the $150,000 the AAA had advanced to Volpi against the 521 lots in his sale.

The defeated old antiquary landed in a hospital bed. But though gravely ill, he was eager, at whatever sacrifice, to settle his accounts. After some bargaining, Parke sold the Donatello crest to Edsel B. Ford, cut-rate, for $75,000. With that, the advance and the AAA's commission were paid off. There was little else that anyone would buy. The Venetian room of state stood around all summer in the darkened galleries, a ghostly encumbrance to O. B. and the Major, until Hearst came along and took it off their hands.

Thus, ironically, it was Volpi, the first to pioneer in what he called a far-away country, who rounded out the Italian-Spanish era. "Suddenly it was all over," Parke said, in baffled recollection of a decorative frenzy that had lasted—so far as the AAA was concerned—almost precisely ten years.

The weather was beautiful that spring, Parke wrote Mr. Bishop, who was sojourning in Cairo; no one could recall its ever having been finer for the time of year. The weather was beautiful, but everyone was in a bad humor. Foreign sales had fallen short of advances made before the Italian-Spanish debacle. Lawsuits were brewing both by and against the disgruntled professori. There were notes outstanding from big-buying dealers overstocked with riggings for palazzi. The Benguiat showdown was still pending. Hearst still owed a few hundred thousand on cumulative purchases. The affair Chiesa was a bubbling caldron of threats and recriminations. Once more, the season's gross would surpass all previous totals, but there were uncertain portents for the future.

Everyone was in a bad humor, especially Mr. Bishop. His notes, uncommonly terse, sometimes tapped out on picture post cards to save postage, reflected a black mood stemming only partly from disaffection with the auctions. For in the sphere of familial and financial matters storms had blown up to buffet the sovereign course of the eternal pleasure bark.

Long had the Bishop fortune been a subject of recurrent litigation. The old will of David Wolfe Bishop, Sr., who died in 1900, had had its share of ambiguities. The wills and codicils of tributary testators had provoked a chronic embroilment with the law courts which added zest to Mr. Bishop's days and ways. Long and stubbornly—almost, it could be said, nobly—in his scorn for the insolence of office, the seneschal of the house of Bishop had fought off the tax collector, the meddling of surrogate and appraiser, the claims of rebuffed charities and barratrous pretenders. Mr. Bishop's two coheirs—his mother and his brother while they lived—had cared little for the intricacies of law and finance. Grandly, sometimes under threat of arrest for contempt of court, the more willing horse of the team (to use Mr. Bishop's phrase) had arrogated to himself the guardianship of that sprawling complex of lands and trust funds, old legacies, and tributary fortunes. With the death of Mrs. Bishop Parsons in 1922, all the family wealth had devolved to him; but by chance, and only by chance, in the course of the proceedings set off by that event, an obscure clause had come to light in the original testament of David Wolfe Bishop—a proviso that in the event of the death of one of the brothers, his function as joint trustee should be taken over by the Bank of New York and Trust Company. This eventuality had occurred with the suicide of David Wolfe Bishop, Jr., in 1911; and now the bank, ignorant for years of its right to coprotect the dynasty, proposed to assume its share of the burden.

The notion of a bank as his financial buddy, retroactive to 1911, was abhorrent enough to Mr. Bishop. But even more maddening prospects were brought to light by those delvers in old papers. One was the contention that Mr. Bishop had not inherited outright the two one-third shares of the fortune accruing from his mother and brother, but was entitled only to a life interest in them. A scrutiny of the old will's vagaries gave rise to the opinion that those two parts of the estate—impervious to appraisal, but in the twenties presumed to be well in excess of $20 million—should have been held in trust for David Wolfe Bishop's descendants of the succeeding generation. This was the gist of the matter that, once plunged into the legal jungle, produced such an excrescence of juridical involvement that a lifetime, it seems, could be consumed in a mere reading of its recorded documents.

It was Mr. Bishop's contention that the David Wolfe Bishop trust had expired, that the fortune was his outright, that the bank was therefore a meddling impostor. On the surface, the Bishop will case, in its tortuous course up through the highest courts, was an expensive caprice, its goal the *ignis fatuus* of an inordinately stubborn plaintiff. Whichever way the decision went, Mr. Bishop stood to lose nothing tangible compared to the cost of the legal lights he employed, among them Charles Evans Hughes before his appointment as chief justice of the Supreme Court. Whatever the outcome, Mr. Bishop had undisputed possession of one third of the fortune; the use of the remainder was his for life; and upon his death, the two thirds in litigation would automatically go to his daughter Beatrice, the sole descendant of the Bishop clan.

But therein lay the grim motive behind the law court struggle. For Beatricia, the sometime delight of Mr. Bishop's soul, the scion reared in his own image to perpetuate the dynasty, had defected from the parental roof. Lacking testamentary rights in two thirds of the fortune, there was no way Mr. Bishop could effectively disinherit his renegade progeny.

The father-mother-daughter feud (irrelevant in its detail, but in its repercussions, of long-range significance to the auction saga) was classic in its intensity—a real-life correlate, it was said at tea tables in and around Lenox, of the Eugene O'Neill dramas that so disturbingly probed the New England conscience. Mr. Bishop had brought his daughter cheeses at Vassar, but something had gone wrong. He had taken her on the grand tour, and she had thrown her arms around her parents in the Hispano and cried, "Oh, mummy, oh, daddy, I love you so much!" She had found life real and earnest and styled herself an "intellectual." She had used the galleries to do personal work, dressed in middy blouse and flat heels. She had gone to the Sorbonne and Columbia and had a Phi Beta Kappa key. She had concerned herself with the human condition and dabbled in the works of Sigmund Freud. But something had gone sour.

The culmination came with a colossally unfilial, never-to-be-forgiven act directed against Mrs. Bishop—an act that cast a tragic blight forever on the abode of bliss and happiness. It was an affront the fragile Amy Bend Bishop at first felt as her death knell. Nor would Mr. Bishop, after the final rupture, ever be the same again. His moodiness increased, his lordly eccentricities, his restlessness, his love of speed.

In the recollection of his friend Miss Edith Nixon—a chief protagonist from that time forward in both the Bishop drama and the auction story—he would stand morosely staring at the desert sands, the seas, the rolling hills of Ananda, a man melancholy and bereft. But the travelers rolled on. And grief, whatever its searing properties, in no way deterred the Lord of Lenox from relentless battle with his persecutors, real or imagined.

Now the entourage, as permanently constituted, was a close-knit threesome: the Bishops and the Irish-born-and-bred Edith Nixon. She had come—this handsome and capable Miss Nixon, destined to become duenna of the crippled Bishop ménage—into the baroque ambiance of the Ritz in 1923, originally as a lady's maid, her detractors liked to say, but in reality as a companion to Mrs. Bishop, now aging but still beautiful enough to be called an enchantress, if at times unworldly and befuddled in the role of wife, mother, and great lady. Whatever her condition of entree, Miss Nixon was not one to remain a menial for long. She brought with her, efficiency, warmth, and mother wit, a kind of native, earthborn intelligence. Her sparkling eye, her lilting speech, her comeliness and high spirits were from the first a tonic. Her sway increased in proportion to the affection she generated. She brought her thrifty sister Anna from Ireland to be housekeeper at Ananda; she hired and fired, and put a hundred things to order. To Mr. Bishop she was a rare spirit to be cultivated. He undertook her education. He gave her books to read and tested her achievements from behind the wheel of the Hispano. He taught her to revel in the appanages of wealth and leisure. The grand hotels, the watering places, the great hall at Ananda, were transformed by her vitality. She tramped the scenic roadway with Mr. Bishop; in the splendor of the Ritz they played leapfrog while Mrs. Bishop smiled and knitted.

Of all the companions of Mr. Bishop's years there were but two who remained permanently loved and trusted: the blond, aristocratic Amy Bend Bishop and the blue-eyed, dark-haired Irish girl he referred to simply and eloquently as "my friend." Nor was there any jealousy in that tripartite household. To Mrs. Bishop young Edith Nixon became a rod and staff of comfort. After the crushing affair with Beatrice, she would speak of her protector as Christlike in her mercy and goodness. It was through Miss Nixon that she found a new lease on life, one that turned out to be of remarkably long duration. "I could not have gone on living without her," a vivacious octogenarian Mrs. Bishop said thirty years later.

Miss Nixon's allegedly Christlike qualities might have provoked a snide guffaw from such onlookers as O. B. and the Major, who viewed with puritan askance that unconventional ménage. But it could not escape them that as Mr. Bishop's friend and confidante the Hibernian lady had no uncertain power. In the bear dance for their angel's favor they sent flowers to both distaff members of the trinity and paid the dual obeisance Mr. Bishop required. These compliments Miss Nixon did not enthusiastically return. The auctions were not her favorite among Mr. Bishop's diverse interests. Her eyebrows raised at the sight of the Major's expense account. Sternly practical and unbeguiled by the whimsicalities that beset her liege, she did not look benignly upon an enterprise that paid dividends in romance instead of cash.

And in fact, by the troubled spring of 1927, Mr. Bishop himself had come to share that negative outlook. With a battery of lawyers drawing fees in the will case, with the Chiesa juggernaut a blow to his purse and pride, what with one thing and another, he had come to think of the auctions as a luxury he could no longer afford. In a note to O. B. from Venice ("This is for you and you alone . . . to be shown to no one and its contents not to be divulged to HP") he wrote lugubriously of abandoning the plush galleries on 57th Street.

It was in vain for Bernet to predict, with his customary optimism, that next season would be "a dandy," for Parke to note that death, the auctions' time-honored ally, had laid hand on H. E. Huntington, on Mrs. William Salomon, and others of the art-laden citizenry. Mr. Bishop, brooding on life's injustices in the shadow of the Sphinx or astride a donkey on the sands of Morocco, refused to be cajoled. Nor was Parke as confident as his letters and his cables sounded. Without the Italian and Spanish imports, which could not longer incite the bidders to exorbitance, a spate of sales from local sources would be needed to keep the galleries bustling. Hope might spring from fortuitous mortality, but though a veritable plague were to stalk up Fifth Avenue, there was the niggling Anderson to share the bounty.

To be sure, the Anderson had fallen behind in the 1926–7 season. Its sales had amounted to only about half the $5,612,716 total recorded by the AAA. But the competition had taken on a mutually destructive aspect. Commission cutting had reduced the profits, sometimes to the point of no return. Each side cast aspersions on the other's ethics and ability to get the most for a consignor. Pejorative references were made to connivance with the traders, the dealers' rings, the cabal, the art-world speculators. Evidence there was, certainly, behind some of the crosscurrents of gossip. Who could have denied that Mr. Bishop had financed the Italian-Spanish influx in consort with the professori, that Parke had drunk hob and nob with Vitall (the Pasha) Benguiat, that the Anderson had held sham sales for dealer combines that merely wished to boost the price of mediocrities, or that Kennerley had gone to England and bought collections outright, in violation of the cardinal principles of unbiased auctions?

But at the root of the conflict was the need to obtain enough art and literary property to support two glamour galleries. The truth was that there was simply not enough for both of them.

The possibility of a merger had come up more than once in the deliberations of Mr. Bishop's board of directors. A monopoly was, it seemed, obviously indicated for the future of the elegant auctioneers. It was therefore music to the ears of O. B. and the Major when, in mid-May 1927, Mitchell Kennerley allowed the rumor to go forth that he might be receptive to the idea of selling the Anderson to the rich old gentleman—as he cynically referred to Mr. Bishop—already so deeply committed to financing the world's great auction center.

By now the Anderson Galleries, Inc., was Mitchell Kennerley's to sell. Originally there had been stockholders. In 1919, of the corporation's 3,500 shares, Kennerley had owned 120. The galleries had prospered off and on, but "owing to the need to build up working capital," it had not been considered prudent to pay dividends. Investors had been relieved to sell their non-income-bearing stock to Kennerley, so that by 1927 the Anderson was substantially his, and like the AAA, a pawn in the haphazard adventures of its quixotic owner's life.

The suggestion that Kennerley might capitulate to the AAA was made by indirection through Vitall (the Pasha) Benguiat, who could, of course, be depended upon to relay it in confidence to his friend Major Parke. It was coupled with such plausible vagaries as that Kennerley, weary of the auction struggle, had other plans for his meteoric talents, one of which was to go into the publishing business in England. Having put out this provocative feeler, Kennerley, the very next day, embarked on the S.S. *Majestic* for Europe.

Parke, whether by coincidence or swift decision, took passage on the *Olympic* and six days later checked in at the Savoy Hotel in London. Kennerley, having arrived the night before, was already ensconced at the Carleton. Each man ignored the other's presence. Kennerley had made it clear that he wished to be sought and not do the seeking, and Parke was well aware that he faced a cunning adversary, to whom a direct approach would give a tactical advantage. For a week they played a game of cat-and-mouse diplomacy, while rumor spread through art-trading circles in New York and London that a merger of the two galleries was pending. Their only contact was through a Johnny-on-the-spot lawyer who, having heard the merger rumor by the grapevine, attempted to act as intermediary (and later sued Parke, unsuccessfully, for a go-between's commission of $125,000). Through that voluble intruder, Parke learned that Kennerley proposed to reveal his terms only in direct negotiation with Mr. Bishop, who was then motoring incommunicado on the Continent. From the same source, Kennerley found out that Parke had already exchanged cables with the elusive Mr. Bishop, and that Mr. Bishop was willing to talk, presumably with checkbook in pocket.

Kennerley crossed over to Paris and put up at Mr. Bishop's Ritz. (It was, he said, for Mr. Bishop to look *him* up, not vice versa.) Mr. Bishop was not in Paris, but Parke was, presently—at the Hotel Edouard VII. The cat-and-mouse game continued; the suspense mounted; and in the end, the Major's staying power proved the stronger. The night before Kennerley's scheduled departure from Paris, he sent Parke a note asking him to dine "informally." Parke declined on the ground of a previous engagement, but consented to see Kennerley later that evening.

The leery rivals met with a grace that was memorable as their first and last endeavor to outcharm each other. Parke agreed to make an appointment for Kennerley to see Mr. Bishop at the first respite from his travels. A meeting was arranged, a few days later, for some time in July. Kennerley, having returned to London, wrote: "Dear Mr. Parke . . . I hope you will be present and that we may return to America together. I feel that together we can do marvels!" Clearly, this affable Kennerley had dropped his bluff about quitting the auction arena. Parke, however, had no intention of doing marvels with the irreconcilable opponent whose mores he viewed as deriving more from the rat and scoundrel than the genius and the saint.

But the Major was not present when the inscrutable Mr. Bishop first supped with the enemy that summer in London. The price Kennerley asked for the name and good will of the Anderson Galleries was $500,000. Mr. Bishop, lugubrious with his own frustrations, and in no mood to throw good money after bad, would certainly have sent the bodacious Mr. Kennerley packing—but for a twist in the proceedings whereby each contrived to see in the other the means to a devious advantage. Contracts were drawn. Parke, called in for the formalities of the purchase, expressed shock at the value Kennerley put on his foundering business. (He settled for $417,500.) Bernet, apprised of this latest caprice of their headstrong angel, wrote bluntly from New York:

> . . . I feel, Mr. Bishop, that you should know this . . . an art man . . . told me that the Anderson business was for sale, and said that it could be purchased by you for about $200,000 or even less. Mr. Parke can corroborate this, as, when he was in London he was informed by another man (who even went further) and said he would guarantee to close the sale for $200,000, if Parke would authorize him to do so. These two stories coming from two entirely different sources must contain some truth, and I cannot help but feel that we are dealing with a man who, perhaps, cannot be relied upon fully.

It was a letter Mr. Bishop did not answer, for in that summer of distrust and rancor, he confided in no one save the distaff members of his entourage, Mrs. Bishop and the omnipresent Miss Nixon. Moreover, the new rapport with Kennerley had O. B. and the Major as its unwitting victims. Mr. Bishop devoutly wished to be free of the auctions, but not without his capital. Kennerley, on the other hand, wished to be kingpin of the combined galleries. In the game they undertook to play together, the $417,500 which so concerned Bernet seemed almost as good as back in Mr. Bishop's pocket, plus his investment in the AAA, his interest, and the Chiesa losses. For, given a little time, Kennerley expected to annex an angel of his own in the person of Mrs. Margery Durant Daniel, the twice-married daughter of William C. Durant, organizer of General Motors.

Mrs. Daniel, who had a touch of the prescriptive ennui of heiresses, was a collector of books and sundry rarities—a rich patron of the art galleries, as the tabloids chose to describe her. What she called her "artistic association" with the Anderson had developed into a romantic association with its proprietor. It was openly acknowledged that they proposed to marry. The engagement had a dashing air of unconventionality about it, in view of the fact that both parties would be in need of a divorce. But it had the stanch approval of the motor heiress' benign father. Papa Durant called Kennerley a charming fellow, an intimate friend who would be more than *persona grata* as son-in-law number three. There were, however, intermediate steps in that excursion into heiress hunting. Kennerley, whose financial position would not have borne much investigation, needed capital to tide him over. Expenses of the high life being what they were, he had decided to sacrifice temporarily—in Mr. Bishop's safekeeping—his one negotiable asset, the name and good will of the Anderson Galleries. With cash in hand to expend lavishly, he would proceed to the business of the divorce court, his wooing, and his nuptials. Once the very rich Mrs. Daniel had become Mrs. Kennerley, according to that tenuous gentlemen's agreement, he would buy back from Mr. Bishop the auction hall monopoly, both the AAA and the Anderson, for $1,500,000.

For obvious reasons, neither O. B. nor the Major was privy then, or for a long time in the future, to the plot conceived with so cavalier a disregard for their proprietary status in the red-plush halls that had become Mr. Bishop's puppet theater.

PONDER ON THESE THINGS

A GRIM PUPPETEER WITH TANGLED STRINGS, a moody and more than commonly inscrutable Mr. Bishop now undertook to run the show from such far-flung places as the ice fields of Norway, Marienbad, and the shores of Lake Lucerne. Baffled indeed were Parke and Bernet by his reluctance to eliminate the costly and irksome competition with Mitchell Kennerley. In reply to inquiries from clients and reporters, O. B. and the Major were enjoined to deny what everyone knew— that Mr. Bishop had bought the Anderson Galleries. But even while the straight-faced denials were issuing from 57th Street, Mr. Bishop made liars of the AAA's ostensible proprietors by ebulliently proclaiming through the Paris *Times* his acquisition of the auction hall monopoly.

Out of the new rapport with Mitchell Kennerley had come a wave of thinly veiled hostility to the AAA's vice presidents. The Bishop notes to Parke were ominous and ambiguous. "Dear VP," a typically cryptic one read, "I have learned many things since I bid you farewell in Piccadilly Circus, and I propose to make good use of my knowledge." Taunted by such mysterious, never explained portents, O. B. and the Major were made to feel like sometime favorites victimized by an encircling conspiracy.

Overseers from Mr. Bishop's downtown coterie—a lawyer, a banker, a treasurer—were made directors of the holding company that now controlled both the AAA and the Anderson. Meetings were called, for the purpose—Parke and Bernet expected—of discussing and settling the merger of the two houses. But no merger took place. Instead, it was announced that the two galleries would be run separately, and Mitchell Kennerley, far from retiring from the auction arena, issued glib press releases about his forthcoming season. The Anderson's activities would be greatly expanded, he said, even to the point of opening a branch in London to book more great collections like the Leverhulme.

Protesting their undying loyalty, O. B. and the Major begged to be "made conversant with whatever movements" were being made. But in vain. Mr. Bishop, *in absentia*, issued swift and arbitrary dicta.

Among the first, coming like a bombshell, was the edict of expulsion for Arthur Swann. Parke and Bernet were for once united, in anger and defiance. The Major unequivocally refused to collaborate in the dismissal of his long-time colleague, now in his fifties, in mid-career, and so recently rewarded with the title of vice president for luring sales away from the Anderson. Never before had he run counter to Mr. Bishop's judgment, Parke wrote coldly, but the hand of Mitchell Kennerley was blatantly apparent in this. He was convinced, the Major later said frankly, that Kennerley wanted, more than anything else, "someone from his concern running our book department—his main object was not so much to sell his business, but simply to have Mr. Swann out of the way."

O. B. implored the lord of all the auctions to reconsider. There were important book sales, contracts Swann had long been negotiating, that would certainly be lost. "Please, Mr. Bishop," Bernet's letters began, with cajoling humility, and went on to predict the wanton destruction of the book department Swann had so laboriously built up. Where, Bernet asked, was the confidence Mr. Bishop had always expressed in him and Parke? Should not they know the inside workings, and not be kept in the dark? Plaintively, O. B. wrote, "All Mr. Parke and I have in mind is the good name of the AAA and its great future success, which we know will ultimately come."

The protests fell on deaf ears. Swann was summarily banished by a Bishop deputy, for no reason more specific than implied disloyalty to the auctions' tergiversating angel. Separated from the auction melee, where for twenty-five years he had been a bouncing, irrepressible leader, Swann went into the rare book business to sulk and ride out the storm. A young and inexperienced man was sent over from the Anderson Galleries to act as book chief in his place. The most that could be said for him, Parke reported to Mr. Bishop, was that he displayed "a willingness to do when shown."

In reply, Mr. Bishop gloated tersely: "It will not be long before Mr. Swann will be forgotten."

The fall season opened, with the rivalry between the two galleries more virulent than ever. Efforts to cooperate with Mitchell Kennerley and his manager Milton Mitchill, Parke found, led to nothing. The race for sales went on, the commission cutting, the maneuvers for prestige and priority—a pointless conflict that Mr. Bishop seemed gleefully to encourage, to the detriment of his own purse. His letters accused O. B. and the Major of failings—at times great, and at other times, trivial. The mail was a relentless preoccupation. Catalogues failed to reach him in Copenhagen, Oslo, Spain. The man who shipped them was incompetent, a jackass. A cablegram complained that too much postage had been put on a letter and demanded that the culprit be summarily fired.

Money was the theme of every jeremiad. All debts were to be forthwith collected. Hearst was to be forced to pay up, his addiction to the easy payment plan once and for all curbed. Buyers and sellers who still owed money were to be dragged into court or otherwise beleaguered. Though Parke reiterated almost daily that sales had been arranged to clear up the remaining indebtedness of the subsidized consignors, over and over Mr. Bishop dwelt on past errors. The Italian-Spanish epoch had been disastrous, the association with the professori and other slippery traders a Parke-inspired folly. A petulantly unrealistic manifesto ended: "I wish all dealers eliminated and things brought back to where they were in Mr. Kirby's time."

Vitall (the Pasha) Benguiat, who still owed the AAA a fortune, was of course the knave among the proscribed traders. The V. & L. Benguiat clearance sale, postponed because of the spring doldrums, was scheduled for the first three days of December. Once more the halls were turned into a galaxy of time-worn colors, of velvet prayer cloths and gold-and-silver-woven fabrics, of masterpieces of needlepoint and Renaissance laces. The walls were hung with tapestries from the Davanzati Palace. Down from the room above the galleries came the Magic Carpets.

The crowd assembled as before—the Pasha's claque, the speculators and the traders, a few rug fanciers, die-hard collectors not yet surfeited with prayer cloths, orphreys, chasubles, and altar frontals. The Major put his best foot forward. The fiery bidding once more ostensibly prevailed. But if the Pasha's things were, for the most part, no longer stylish, the Benguiat tactics had in no way altered. The recorded total for the sale was more than a quarter of a million dollars, but when the smoke had cleared, a preponderance of the lots the Pasha called his "babies" returned, as usual, to the cloistered room upstairs. A third of what was sold was, more accurately, leased—to a furnisher of Renaissance palaces, with no immediate prospects for payment. And when the cash was stacked against the credit, Benguiat still owed the AAA $140,000.

Mr. Bishop was by then in residence at Lenox, to revel in the Berkshire snows. In the dread formality of quasi-legal jargon, he admonished Parke from The Winter Palace, "You will please see that no merchandise belonging to V & L Benguiat and pledged to the American Art Assn. Inc. as security for their notes or the notes of either of them, be removed from custody of the Am Art Assn Inc without written authorization from us to that effect."

Parke had no choice but to carry out the sentence against his friend the incorrigible Pasha. The room upstairs was locked, the old rug peddler banished from the market place that for three decades had been the life line of his prodigal career.

The *Dies Irae* cast of the note exiling Benguiat, and of other choleric dispatches issuing from Ananda, was no doubt intensified by events not directly connected with the auctions. It was perhaps not wholly chance that the impounding of the Magic Carpets coincided with the wedding day of Mr. Bishop's apostate daughter, Beatrice.

No grand reception rocked the great hall of Ananda. The ceremony—this, at least, in the family tradition—took place in Grace Church on Broadway, so long a citadel of Lorillard-Wolfe-Bishop patronage and piety. Mr. and Mrs. Bishop did not attend. The bridegroom was Adolf A. Berle, Jr., sometime infant prodigy of Harvard Law School, later to be known in Washington as The Brain, and in years ahead, to apply his cosmic cerebrations to national and world problems with a messianic selflessness made practicable through relief—as *Current Biography* put it—"of his financial cares by his marriage in 1927 to Beatrice Bend Bishop of New York." Now, at thirty-two, Berle was a whiz-bang corporation lawyer, political economist, and Thinker, trenchantly described as the "cocky little devil of the sharp mind and sharp pen." Financial relief on a multi-million-dollar scale was not an immediate emolument of the Grace Church wedding, but the future held promise. Mr. Bishop had just lost a round in the ambiguous lawsuit known by the short title of Bishop versus Bishop, his daughter being the most prominent litigant. As things now stood, Bishop would be compelled to share the administration of the estate with the bank, and upon his death two thirds of the fortune would descend to Beatrice. There would be appeals, long and voluminous and costly, but Mr. Bishop's hope of final victory could not have been much bolstered by the circumstance that in the brainy spouse she called Playmate, his daughter had annexed some very high-blown legal talent.

With Mr. Bishop *in persona propria,* with the abode of bliss and happiness a seeming mockery, its lord embittered and embattled, and the auctions increasingly the butt of his erratic humors, the 1927–8 winter was, to say the least, a stormy one for O. B. and the Major. In The Winter Palace, with Mrs. Bishop and the comforting Miss Nixon, or occasionally in the town house at 15 East 67th Street, Mr. Bishop stalked and brooded. Speeding down from Lenox, he would make sudden, unpredictable forays on the galleries. Stomping through the Renaissance passages, the grim-faced angel would find nothing to his pleasure. Hired hands cringed at the sight of his cane, his Homburg hat, his coonskin coat. Questions answered or unanswered, queries withering and patently rhetorical, voiced paranoid suspicions of incompetence and treachery, of imagined plots to nibble at the AAA's finances and the dynastic Bishop fortune.

The Anderson, too, had its share of visitations. But for all the caprice behind the scenes, in both Mr. Bishop's houses the harried auction impresarios strutted with success and pride and revitalized self-confidence. For now, suddenly, the days of the great sales were upon them.

Once more the bulls were rampant in the financial arena. The race for bona fide culture kept pace. Fortune smiled benignly on the AAA; Parke's voice soared to the singing obbligato of the Wall Street ticker. Gone from the posh halls were the subsidized traders, Benguiat, and the wily professori. In their place, the catalogues blazoned the names of distinguished local consignors. The palace furnishings the late Mrs. Salomon had held out, or bought in, at the time of the William Salomon sale of 1923 brought $666,761. French and Company paid $1,500 for a festooned and gilded state bed, said to be the most sumptuous of its kind in America, and $28,000 for a marble bust of Madame de Wailly by Augustin Pajou (which had been bought in at $45,000 in 1923 and was destined to sell again, for a mere $5,000, in 1941). Elisha Walker, who had learned the knack of banking from old William Salomon, paid $44,000 for a Beauvais tapestry suite made for Marie Antoinette and took home, as well, a courtly portion of eighteenth-century fans and candelabra, commodes, and jardinieres.

Included in the 1928 Salomon auction were architectural exuberances—Renaissance doorways, columns and pilasters, chimney pieces replete with winged cherubim—from the imperial Salomon mansion at 1020 Fifth Avenue, which had recently been razed. ("A sensitive mind," wrote Henry McBride in the *Sun*, "could be forgiven for brooding for a while upon the impermanence of the edifices man erects for himself.") Impermanent may have been the new fortunes and the edifices rising in the great roar of the Wall Street twenties, but the ticker-tape watchers, all unaware of the coming debacle, clogged 57th Street to vie merrily over the residual trappings of such inveterate builders as Mrs. O. H. P. Belmont, who back in the eighties had bestirred society as Alva (the Titaness) Vanderbilt. Auctions in six figures followed one upon another. Week by week, the easy, almost tax-free money flowed through the AAA to the beat of the ever-clicking hammer.

In March the scene shifted to the Anderson Galleries and the seventy-seven paintings that had adorned the Madison Avenue edifices of Charles H. Senff, a sugar magnate related by marriage to the sagacious Mrs. H. O. Havemeyer. Under her influence, the collection had been made in the last decade of the nineteenth century. It was then left to gather dust until 1928, when the death of Mrs. Senff threw it on the market, and Mitchell Kennerley's audacious commission-cutting tactics secured it for the Anderson.

Kennerley valued the seventy-seven pictures at $1,500,000—a gross miscalculation, it turned out. Two respectable Frans Hals portraits were knocked down at what Parke, gibing Mr. Bishop for the Anderson's ineptitude, called bargain-basement prices. One, of a Dutch lady, went to Knoedler at $55,000; the other, of a Dutch burgher, fell to the now legendary Dr. Albert C. Barnes of Merion, Pennsylvania, at $47,500. A "celebrated" Velásquez, *Portrait of General Marchese Spinola,* sold for $53,000. *Woman Reading,* an admirable Corot figure piece (which had cost $4,000 in 1895) brought $31,000 from Mrs. Louise Senff Cameron, a niece of Senff, who gave it to the Metropolitan Museum.

These were good pictures. The collection distinguished the Anderson with the best painting sale it had ever had. Prices, said the press, were indicative of the bullish art market. But the total—$580,375— was far below the $1,500,000 anticipated. The auction was very badly

Judge Elbert H. Gary, an important figure at auctions and one of the most colorful men in the world of finance (BETTMANN ARCHIVE).

managed, Parke wrote Mr. Bishop, who by then had fled Ananda for the Ritz in Paris. It would have brought at least $200,000 more, he asserted in an overt stab at his rival, if it had been held at the American Art Association.

A month later the Major had the occasion to blazon his and the AAA's supremacy in something more concrete than words.

No event of the Bishop-Parke-Bernet era had so stirred Parke to action as the death, in August 1927, of Judge Elbert H. Gary and the tip-off through private informers that his art collection would be sold.

Gary, the shrewd and sanctimonious, self-righteous, some said "priggish," judge turned financial hero, who, with J. P. Morgan, formed the United States Steel Corporation, had lived with aristocratic hauteur in a museumlike house at Fifth Avenue and 67th Street, amid his portion of the costly equipage then fashionable for America's mighty. It was said that he did not pose as a connoisseur, but pose he did, in enormous pride of possession, his steel company manipulations having made him many, many millions. With them, in all arrogance, he may have planned to live forever. A few months before he succumbed, at the age of eighty, he had moved north on Fifth Avenue to an even more empyreal mansion at 94th Street. There he reinstalled pictures by the English big six, his fine French eighteenth-century furniture, his Hals, his Rembrandt, and his peach-bloom bottles, his palace carpets and the rugs that had once belonged to Charles T. Yerkes, and his $1 million worth of Sèvres china, from which such high personages as Queen Marie of Rumania had assuaged their royal appetites at his quasi-royal banquets.

Connoisseur or not, the short, foppish, pompously respectable "czar of the steel trust" had come far in matters of artistic perception since his novice days back in the nineties, when he would make a foray into Kirby's salesroom and come off with a "Sir Thomas Lawrence" Painted Lady at $130 or something called *Hello!* by one Louis Moeller at $160. In his last years, he was known as a Sir Joseph Duveen pupil, though in actuality Duveen had supplied but a fraction of his purchases. The collection he left behind, nevertheless, like the Judge himself, had all the schoolbook virtues. And it had a very high market value. What with the aureate name of the deceased, plus the quality-dealer label, a hullabaloo would be certain if the Gary art was to come up at auction.

To Parke it was imperative that this should happen—and at the AAA. Hardly had the eulogies been printed when the Major (Bernet having been banished to the side lines) plunged into a vigorous campaign to persuade the lawyers and bankers who controlled the Gary fortune. By mid-September Parke's otherwise dreary report to Mr. Bishop contained an ambiguous note of cheer. "One of the matters we are working on," Parke confided, "should be closed within the next ten days, the most important sale that has been held in this country since Yerkes, and we are all sworn to secrecy until the matter is finally consummated."

From Biarritz, Mr. Bishop replied acidly that he was "not pleased to learn that there are things which are too secret to be told to the President of the AAA." All the same, Parke, remembering the Chiesa fiasco, kept his hand concealed, for in the politic game he was playing, the cards were delicately stacked.

The joker in the pack was the high-powered Sir Joseph Duveen, in his capacity as friend and advisor to Judge Gary's widow. At the outset Duveen offered $1,500,000 for the collection intact. Nonsense,

Parke retorted, and declared unequivocally to the executors that an auction would bring at least $2 million. Based more on hunch than demonstrable precedent, it was a bold prognostication, and it was even bolder for Parke to deny the adequacy of Duveen's extremely fair offer and to risk his pontifical displeasure. Moreover, the prices the Major envisioned would indeed be hard to get without the support in the salesroom of the irascible Sir Joseph and the financial peers of Gary, most of whom were in the Duveen stable. Duveen, on the other hand, could scarcely afford to sabotage an auction of works or types of works that he himself was touting at ever-soaring prices. This was Parke's trump card. The details of the subsequent maneuvers were always conveniently befogged in the Major's recollection, but presumably Duveen, who, in any case, had a high respect for Parke's ability, was made to see the advantage of a public affirmation of Duveen-made values. The executors were persuaded to gamble on an auction, and by the end of October, Parke was able to reveal to Mr. Bishop the name of Gary and report that plans for the sale were in the making "although not in such shape as to be given to the public."

Throughout the winter, plans were made and remade, with Duveen, by virtue of his avuncular relation to Mrs. Gary, as chief meddler. At his behest, the sale date was changed from January to April; at his demand, the paintings were cleaned by Duveen Brothers experts, the descriptions written and rewritten. But at long last, the handsome de luxe catalogues were printed. The grand ballroom of the Plaza Hotel was engaged for the picture auction, the Gary sale publicized as the greatest of the century.

Far beyond even the Major's expectations were the caterwaulings of art lovers on the long-to-be-remembered night of April 20, 1928. So great was the crush of ticket holders that descended on the Plaza, the Fifth Avenue Association had to be called upon to cope with the limousines. Into the grand ballroom, the seating capacity of which was 1,600, trooped 3,600 people, men in tailcoats, women in the vivid plumage of the era. Seats were not reserved, so young men from the Y.M.C.A., in rented tuxedos, were recruited to hold places for latecoming titans, some of whom tipped their sit-ins as much as $50. Duveen's man was there. (Duveen himself rarely attended an auction.) It took Parke twenty minutes to plow his way through the mob and minutes more to subdue the applause that hailed him as First Gentleman of the Rostrum. The business at hand got under way. The sporting crowd, anticipating the knockout rounds, was tense but restrained during the preliminaries: the disposal of Gary's Barbizons and a few nineteenth-century genre paintings, mostly decreed out of fashion now, in this Duveen-taught generation. But even some of these, under the momentum of the occasion, went at far more than their appraised value: a watery Daubigny at $23,000, a feathery Corot at $32,000, an Anton Mauve farm wagon at $3,000. A Fragonard self-portrait went to $52,000. Then came the British ancestral portraits and, Parke was gratified to note, a flurry of boosting on the part of Duveen's man. A Sir Henry Raeburn, *John Lamont of Lamont,* valued by the appraisers at $9,000, brought $44,000. Sir Thomas Lawrence's *Mrs. John Allnutt* brought $45,000. Then the frustrated bidders must have said to themselves, Enough of this—because, suddenly, caution seemed to vanish. The next lot up was John Hoppner's portrait of Lady Dashwood-King (a small picture, 30 by 25 inches). It soared, as the wondering crowd gaped, to $90,000.

Now the mood was set for the night. As Gainsborough's *The Harvest Waggon* was ceremoniously revealed, the whole room burst into spontaneous applause. For minutes the carnival spirit prevailed. The painting was one of the few authenticated Gainsborough landscapes, and of those, one of the best. The Major, in his glory now, fixed his reverent gaze upon the glistening 4-by-5-foot canvas and waited for the boisterous tribute to subside. Portentously, then, he announced, "For this picture, ladies and gentlemen, I have an opening bid of two hundred thousand dollars."

The gasps from the enraptured spectators went unheard. Without pause, the Major intoned the signaled bids. Within seconds, the price was $300,000. A minute later, Duveen's man had bought *The Harvest Waggon* at $360,000.

The tumult eventually died down, but not the murmured comment. Informed persons knew that *The Harvest Waggon* had cost Gary, a few years earlier, less than half the sum it had just brought. The gloating executors must certainly have breathed hosannas to Parke, for in the official inventory of Gary's estate *The Harvest Waggon* had been appraised at a mere $60,000. Just once before had a higher price been paid for a picture at auction—that, too, for an English painting, Sir Thomas Lawrence's portrait of Miss Mary M. Barrett, nicknamed *Pinkie,* also bought by Duveen, in London in 1926, for about $19,000 more. So enthralled had the American citizenry been with the price that crowds of people had paid a dollar each to see *Pinkie* on display before Duveen deposited her for eternity, and a modest profit, in old Henry Huntington's library at San Marino. Now Gainsborough's rollicking landscape filled with peasants would surely share Miss Barrett's pecuniary fame, and the AAA the publicity of the indomitable Duveen. (In time Duveen would sell *The Harvest Waggon* to Frank P. Wood of Toronto for $450,000. Wood, in turn, left it to the Art Gallery of Toronto, where it now hangs, despite a 1959 attempt to steal it by knife-wielding thieves who gave it a good slashing.)

The climax was over, but the festivities in the Plaza were by no means ended. There was still a Reynolds to be sold, for $55,000, a Romney, for $50,000, another Raeburn, for $46,000, a Gainsborough portrait, for $56,000. The Frans Hals, *A Young Cavalier,* brought $85,000; the Rembrandt called *A Warrior Putting on His Armor,* $86,000. It was indeed the greatest sale since Yerkes', by far the most riotous evening's entertainment at an auction that the Roaring Twenties had seen.

And still there were more sensations to come. Back in the galleries on 57th Street, in three afternoon sessions, the steel czar's numerous other lares went under Parke's hammer. At the last of these sessions, Duveen himself made a rare personal appearance. Sitting close to Parke, up under the thronelike rostrum, the great Sir Joseph did a fair day's shopping. To him fell the Judge's royal Isfahan palace carpet, at $106,000 (a price the banished Vitall Benguiat could never achieve, and one that surely sent him into one of his apoplectic rages). Much of the eighteenth-century French furniture went to Duveen: a Beauvais tapestry suite made for Louis XIV, at $60,000; a pair of boudoir tables made for Madame Pompadour, at the staggering price of $99,000.

It was, however, an unpretentious piece of French sculpture that set the hall on end that final afternoon. Among the loveliest of Gary's possessions was a marble bust, 17½ inches high, by Jean Antoine Houdon, modeled in 1788 after his infant daughter, Sabine. Duveen had bought the bust at a Paris auction in 1912 for about $100,000 and subsequently sold it to Gary. Houdon was, in fact, one of the supersalesman's specialties. With a contagious frenzy of appreciation, Duveen had promoted the eighteenth-century sculptor's work for years, snatching up all available examples and passing them on to his chosen clients at ever-mounting prices. Now, with the particularly exquisite *Sabine* on the block, Sir Joseph, in the front row, was obviously prepared to vanquish all niggling contestants. But, as the Major used to delight in saying, anything can happen in an auction. To his scarcely concealed delight, five bidders stayed in the field up to $175,000. At that price, already inflated (*Sabine* had been appraised at $75,000), the bust could surely have been expected to fall to Sir Joseph. But well to the rear of the apparent victor, a self-composed young woman continued nodding. Up and up the melody of numbers floated, until—at $245,000—Duveen hesitated and grimly shook his head. Parke leaned over to him. "Are you all through, Sir Joseph?" he asked, as if incredulous at such a show of penny-pinching.

Sir Joseph remained grim and immobile. Parke knocked down *Sabine* to the lady in the rear. Then, pointing his gavel at Duveen, he said graciously, but with just a trace of covert irony, "Sir Joseph, this is the first time I have ever known you to be outbid on an item of this rare caliber."

Duveen got up and stalked out.

The heroine of the *Sabine* contest was Miss Catherine Swann, an employee of Knoedler's, Duveen's chief rival. She was, of course, bidding for a client. The client turned out to be Mrs. Edward S. Harkness. Thanks to her beneficence, *Sabine* now sheds her luster in the Metropolitan Museum.

Resounding and never to be forgotten, or surpassed, was the Gary triumph for Hiram Parke and the AAA. When all was counted, the total came to $2,293,693—more than the landmark Yerkes record, more than three quarters of a million above Duveen's fair offer, and almost $300,000 more than Parke's prediction to the executors. "People were dazed," *Art News* wrote, summing up a barrage of press superlatives.

From Seville, Mr. Bishop sent a cable of one word: "Delighted."

Anno mirabile, the AAA's chroniclers dubbed its 1927–8 season, with its unprecedented gross of nearly six and a quarter million dollars. But by January 1929 the tumult was at the Anderson. This time the action was set off by ink and paper—the library of Jerome Kern, the songwriter.

Among bibliophiles and bibliopoles Jerome Kern, "the father of American operetta," was celebrated not so much for the endearing melodies of *Show Boat* and a mint of other songs and Broadway musicals as for what he himself used jovially to refer to as his "weakness." He could not pass a bookstore. A small, amicable, quiet man, with tremendous stores of nervous energy, Kern wore horn-rimmed glasses, smoked constantly, poured forth hundreds of facile tunes with the radio blaring in his ears, and modestly called himself a dull fellow with a little talent and lots of luck. In a chronic state of collectomania, he amassed in his Bronxville, New York, house a superlative library of rare first editions, manuscripts, and autograph letters. Most, though by no means all, were in the field of English literature. He was a prudent buyer. An insomniac with a prodigious memory, the Melody King, though not much of a reader, nightly pored over old volumes and acquired an impressive knowledge of collecting points and technicalities. His first editions were among the finest extant, many of them unique in that they contained notes or autographed sentiments by the authors. He depended on no book-seller for instruction. Nor was he, for all the immensity of his earnings, an easy mark for the price-gouging dealer. "What, three hundred dollars for a book!" he would exclaim affably. "That's a lot of money to me." At the same time, he did not balk at paying $2,000 for one missing page to complete his original-parts edition of the *Pickwick Papers*, with all the quaint notices and nineteenth-century advertisements issued with its serial installments.

It was perhaps the chase that intrigued Kern most. For once in possession of his enviable cache, he decided to sell. His books were a source of worry, he said. But he also may have had a premonition. Luck had dogged him all his life. He had hit the jackpot with almost everything he wrote; he had missed embarking on the *Lusitania*, and probable death on her ill-fated voyage, because an alarm clock unaccountably stopped and failed to wake him up. Now, in the closing months of 1928, when Wall Street still portended sky-high profits, some instinct told him to cash in not only his books but also his stocks at their inflated value. With no apparent regret or sentiment, Kern consigned to his friend Mitchell Kennerley the 1,482 choice literary items he had so intensively sought out.

Rare books were booming like watered stocks, and the Kern collection, Kennerley knew, would be manna to the bibliopolistic cabal and its far-flung coterie of clients. The covetous of two continents were alerted, and Kennerley, who, to be sure, could fumble a painting sale, prepared with all his showman's acumen for, to use his words, "another romance in the pages of book collecting."

Departing from his tradition of cryptic listings, he drew upon his publisher's flair for fine bookmaking and designed an illustrious two-volume hardbound quarto catalogue glorifying the books to go on the block in glossy photographs and documented descriptions. As the banished Arthur Swann had long maintained, the dealers had but to show such glamorous volumes to their clients and their pangs of desire would be marvelously sharpened.

No contingency was unforeseen. In his thoroughgoing preparations, Kennerley assessed the bidding potential of the dozen or so most active bookmen. Of these, he counted essential to the anticipated high jinks in the salesroom the two most jealously combative: Dr. Rosenbach and Gabriel Wells. On them, without their knowledge, Kennerley took out an insurance policy with Lloyd's of London for $250,000, against the hazard that death or incapacity should preclude their presence in the flesh at the ten sessions of the auction.

The celebrated consignor himself ignored the promotional strategy and went on writing music. But on the January night before the first session, Kern, who declined to attend the auction, came to the back room of the Anderson for a farewell look at his books, stacked there ready for the hammer. He had spent something over a half million dollars for the 1,482 items in Mitchell Kennerley's lush memorial catalogue. Jokingly, Kennerley said, "Jerry, what would you take right now for the whole lot?"

Kern smiled and sucked thoughtfully on his pipe. "Oh," he said, "I'd take six hundred fifty or seven hundred thousand."

Kern was a man who loved to send telegrams. The following night he sent a terse one from Bronxville. It read "My God what's going on?"

What was going on was that the astonished auctioneer, young Tony Bade, perched on his high stool before the velvet curtain, was asking for, and getting, opening bids at the maximum prices Kern's rarities had been estimated to sell for. Happily, both Gabriel Wells and Dr. R. had survived without calamity. They were grimly present, with the fire of battle in their veins, and so were two relative newcomers to the rare-book scene—Barnet J. Beyer and Alwin J. Scheuer, both hell-bent to spend themselves into the big league. The entire cabal was there, and the fringes of the cabal; and in the teeming hall were such welcome bibliomanic faces as Richard Gimbel, Owen D. Young, and an agent for J. K. Lilly of Indianapolis.

When all the chips were down, and the tenth session ended, the dogged players had heaped into the pot $1,729,462 for Kern's half-million dollars' worth of books.

Most staggering of all the knockdown bids—made by Gabriel Wells, after a thumb-wagging, head-nodding skirmish with Dr. R.— was $68,000 for Shelley's own copy of his *Queen Mab*, with manuscript revisions. But there were many other runaway items, among them:

Charles Dickens' *Pickwick Papers*, in the original parts	$28,000
Henry Fielding's *Tom Jones*, uncut, in the original binding	29,000
Thomas Hardy's manuscript of a portion of *A Pair of Blue Eyes*	34,000
The manuscript of Charles Lamb's contributions to Hone's *Table Book*	48,000
One page of the manuscript of Dr. Johnson's *Dictionary*	11,000
A four-page letter by Poe quoting Mrs. Browning's opinion of "The Raven"	19,500
Pope's manuscript of the first three books of the *Essay on Man*	29,000
A large-paper copy of the first issue of *Gulliver's Travels*	17,000
The first edition of Fitzgerald's *The Rubaiyat of Omar Khayyam* (which, as Kennerley noted in the catalogue, was at one time sold for twopence)	8,000

Ah, gone were the days, the commentators muttered, when a Gutenberg Bible could be had for less than someone would now pay for a volume of Shelley. The great Hoe sale, with its seventy-nine sessions (and only a couple of hundred thousand more in the till) could be forgotten. Rare books as speculative investments had proved a far better gamble than most mundane commodities. Prices were marked up. International cables flashed the roll of the bibliomaniacal drums. Scarcely an exclamatory adjective was omitted in the prolix reports of the bookmen at the Anderson wallowing in the prosperity of the bizarre twenties.

Jerome Kern paused in the composition of his newest operetta to send Mitchell Kennerley and his staff a gracious telegram of congratulation and appreciation for their "wonderful conduct of the auction." The next day he went out and bought a book, the first of a new collection that would be sold for his estate by the Parke-Bernet, though for no such astounding figure, far off in 1962.

While Kennerley and the Anderson were exulting in the Kern triumph, the AAA was the scene of another epochal event: the discovery of America by rich collectors. To be sure, the pursuers of bed warmers and cobbler's benches, pine cupboards and butterfly tables, had long been rampant. Ever larger had grown the tribe of antique hunters, and ever greater their zeal, stemming in part from the chauvinistic aftermath of World War I. But it took the explosive Howard Reifsnyder sale of April 1929 to broadcast the fact that a highboy made in colonial Philadelphia could be worth as much as a *secrétaire à abattant* made for Marie Antoinette.

Though Howard Reifsnyder was a solid man of affairs, *Antiques* magazine said, inclination had led him into "exploring life's pleasantest byways." He was certainly one of the pleasantest of collectors. Reifsnyder was a wool merchant in Philadelphia, an eminent and public-spirited citizen, and to quote *Antiques* again, "a vital and endearing personality" whose acquisitive journey through untrammeled antique territory, motivated by a deep historical awareness, earned him ungrudging veneration as a connoisseur of colonial artifacts.

Well in advance of the scavenging dealers, Reifsnyder had roamed the Pennsylvania countryside, buying up at modest prices the household embellishments of early German settlers: their painted marriage chests, cradles, pots, the plain beds and chairs and tables fashioned out of maple, pine, and hickory in the years of hard and thrifty living. From a far different colonial heritage, he acquired mahogany and walnut furniture epitomizing the age of Chippendale in and around Philadelphia, where eighteenth-century cabinetwork achieved its highest expression in beauty of carving and design. Attending auctions, invading ancestral parlors, he assembled and restored an authoritative material record of the early culture of Pennsylvania and of other eastern regions as well. The sumptuous was represented in signed pieces by master craftsmen reflecting the growth of colonial wealth; the utilitarian, in homey things of everyday life—lamps and rugs and curtain knobs and coverlids, clocks, mirrors, pewter, silver, glass.

Reifsnyder loved to display his things and his knowledge of their social origins. Superb pieces were in everyday use in his old house on Walnut Street. His library contained a wealth of source material on American craft products and, experts on the subject said, the most complete collection on this side of the Atlantic of original publications issued by English eighteenth-century cabinetmakers. A business caller could, seeing the fiddleback chairs and gate-leg tables in the Reifsnyder offices on South Front Street, well imagine that he had stepped back in time to Ben Franklin's Philadelphia. On extended loan to museums were unique and exceedingly rare items. With unfailing willingness, the generous antiquary contributed to historical exhibits wherever they were held. Curators and students were provided with photographs and given the freedom of his house and library. Articles were published in antiquarian journals. Thus by the time the Howard Reifsnyder collection came up at auction, it was one of the most noted in the country.

In the intramural rivalry between O. B. and the Major, it was O. B. who scored this time. As early as 1924 Reifsnyder had deemed his journey through the byways complete, their impedimenta too great a burden to maintain. He proposed to sell his large house and simplify his life. Toying with the idea of an auction, he called in Bernet, with whom he had an amiable association dating back to the Kirby era. O. B. was impressed with the importance of the collection and estimated that it would bring $150,000. But in the pinch, the dissemination of his things was too hard for Reifsnyder to contemplate. He kept his house, and the 1924 sale fell through. In 1927 negotiations were resumed, with O. B. altruistically extolling the joys of the unfettered life. Apartment living was all the vogue now, he counseled in voluble sales letters, and "many of our best and wealthiest families" were opting for that mode of living. Again the auction was put off. The following year Reifsnyder almost came to the point of decision, but he was spared the wrench of parting. In January 1929, with the packers all but at the door, he died—at the untimely age of sixty. Whereupon O. B. took over, in derby hat, with bereaved countenance, and scheduled the sale for the month of April.

Reifsnyder's indecision turned a handsome profit for his sons and widow—and for the AAA. Year by year, month by month even, the interest in vintage American craftsmanship had been growing. Now, in April 1929, the collection Bernet had formerly assessed at

$150,000 brought $605,449. But the cumulative total was of slight significance compared to the radiance of the occasion and the largess provoked by the more coveted lots.

Never in all the French and Italian cavalcade had the halls been more vibrant with the luster of old wood and millionaires. *International Studio*'s reporter found "an air of drama everywhere." The evocation of colonial life and times impressed that sober journal's emissary as "far more thrilling from the theatrical—nay, the dramatic—point of view, than the show-shops of Broadway, grinding out their monotonous and conventional little shocks." Before the rostrum, the same commentator was agog at the assembly of "connoisseurs of practically unlimited means or agents with unlimited reserves. . . . This battle of collectors" he ventured in rash prophecy, "will probably never be duplicated in an American salesroom."

Battle there was, four days long, with many a lull and spurt, many a spontaneous burst of applause. Amateurs who never saw a million rubbed elbows with the opulent, often without knowing it, for some of those of unlimited means appeared incognito and cunningly bought under assumed monikers. A militant lady in a tweed suit could make off with a pair of hurricane glass shades at $720—but only if they were hurricane shades that had not taken the fancy of William R. Hearst. It seemed that Hearst (having paid his arrears, or some of them, and promised Parke to do better in the future) was bidding as if to glut a wing of San Simeon with bridal chests and slant-top writing desks, Sheraton canopy bedsteads and old New England wagon seats. His opponents were formidable and determined, notably Francis P. Garvan, long one of the most indomitable buyers in the American field.

Garvan deprived Hearst of much of the silver and pewter, and even of a William and Mary lowboy (circa 1700)—at $4,800. It seemed an easy victory later, as the contest heightened over the fine furniture of the Philadelphia school. Mrs. George P. Bissell paid $18,100 for three Queen Anne side chairs. Thomas Curran, bidding for the Pennsylvania Museum, was driven up to $26,000 for a mahogany chest-on-chest and to $33,000 for a Benjamin Randall "sample" Chippendale armchair with a carved head, said to be of Benjamin Franklin. Most hard-fought of all was the duel over the "very important" rococo Chippendale mahogany highboy made about 1770 for the Van Pelt family of Philadelphia. Hearst and an all-too-familiar adversary, a pseudonymous Mr. H. F. Winthrop (in reality Henry F. Du Pont) were the die-hard bidders, with Hearst the loser—at the staggering price of $44,000.

In the giddy antique market of that spring the Reifsnyder doings were a revelation, the repercussions wide and long-lasting. Native works of skilled craftsmen gained immeasurable prestige, and to this day, the auction is considered historic in the chronicles of collecting events. (The illustrated catalogue, now a rare book, is worth from $50 to $100.) Forthwith, in the 1929 spender's gambol, colonial highboys became the quarry of the house-proud and the stylish. Authentic pieces were called priceless, their value multiplied; and the AAA was credited, if not with the discovery of America, at least with its tumultuous exploitation.

But now again, to the dismay of O. B. and the Major, the spotlight shifted to the Anderson. There, eleven days after the last Reifsnyder session, were sold Carl W. Hamilton's two illustrious old masters: the Fra Filippo Lippi *Madonna and Child* and the very rare Piero della Francesca *Crucifixion*. The show and the showman, Kennerley, were widely publicized. The ten-minute auction was the first to be broadcast live on the radio in this country, and the presumably enthralled public was privileged to hear Duveen Brothers' bid of $375,000 for the Piero *Crucifixion*, a new record, eclipsing the AAA's price for *The Harvest Waggon* by $15,000. Reactions behind the scenes were nevertheless distinctly churlish. The proceeds for the two pictures had fallen ridiculously below the $1,450,000 the Kennerley propaganda had said they were worth. Carl Hamilton was displeased with the Anderson. Major Parke said that Kennerley's auctioneer, Fred Chapman, had bungled the sale. Moreover, it was Parke's contention, in an acrid report to Mr. Bishop, that the AAA had been robbed.

For Carl Hamilton had first wanted to consign his pictures to the American Art Association. He had proposed to pay a commission of $10,000, plus expenses, and in addition, 5 per cent of whatever sum the auction might bring above $600,000. This had seemed fair enough to Parke, in view of the publicity the sale would bring and the minimal labor involved. But the contract could not be made, because Mr. Bishop, through the watchdog directors charged with putting the AAA on a paying basis, had put into effect a formal resolution prohibiting O. B. and the Major from accepting any sale for less than a 10 per cent net commission. Over at the other branch of the auction-hall monopoly, however, the flamboyant Mitchell Kennerley was operating under no such restrictions. The AAA directors would not make an exception without Mr. Bishop's consent. At the time, Mr. Bishop was brooding incommunicado in some far place, and Hamilton, though he would have preferred to hold the auction under Parke's baton, had only to walk up the street to get the Anderson to agree to his terms.

Already embittered by the inconsistencies and arbitrary dicta of their absent liege, O. B. and the Major were moved to the point of rebellion by the Hamilton affair. The First Gentleman of the Rostrum was exasperated by the loss of prestige involved in his having been deprived of the sale of the picture that topped in value his golden *Harvest Waggon*. The maddening thing was that the Anderson, though no less Mr. Bishop's property than the AAA, was free to act as an ever-more-virulent rival. What, Parke demanded in an aggrieved letter to Mr. Bishop, was the sense of maintaining a house divided against itself?

But this, and other appeals by the AAA's vice presidents, went unanswered. For on the crest of the roaring 1929 prosperity, Mr. Bishop combined the American Art Association and the Anderson Galleries.

The plot hatched in London—for Mitchell Kennerley to use the future Mrs. Kennerley's capital to relieve Mr. Bishop of his investment in the two houses—had not come off. Whimsicality had always affected the history of the two galleries. Now the course of untrue love immeasurably altered that of the élite auction business.

What with the capers of the sporting life and the estranged Mrs. Kennerley's procrastination in going to the divorce court, Kennerley's unconventional engagement to the twice-married motor heiress Mrs. Margery Durant Daniel had been a stormy one. Gossips in and out of the press had freely purveyed unverifiable sidelights on the vigorous and money-tainted courtship, a two-year series of disenchantments having to do with fiscal trickery, infidelity, and the well-known swagger of Mrs. Daniel's gascon suitor. Then, somewhat belatedly, but in advance of the other yellow journals, the *Mirror* reported in a headline, "Kennerley Jilted by Rich Patron."

As Arthur James Pegler retailed the final chapter in the *Mirror*, the bare facts were that, after getting her divorce in Reno in the fall of 1928, the affianced heiress had "ignored her obligation" to Kennerley, "declined to receive her distinguished admirer," and gone to Florida, where she met "a younger and handsomer man" named John Hampton Cooper. The Pegler version went on to tell how, "when Kennerley became aware he was no longer persona grata to the woman he had hoped to wed, he sought interviews with her on several occasions." Rebuffed, and doubtless maddened by the recalcitrance of the golden calf, he had sought the intercession of the lady's financier father, William C. Durant, who called Kennerley an intimate friend and regarded him with affection as a prospective son-in-law. To no avail: "The latter, while sympathetic, was powerless to afford aid."

Despite the vigorous opposition of Papa Durant, Mrs. Durant Daniel married the young and handsomer Cooper in early May 1929. Interviewed on the subject of the "jilting in high life," the newlywed Mrs. Cooper spoke of her artistic association with Kennerley but declined comment on his conduct as a fiancé. Privately, she was quoted as saying that she had married a "nice man" instead.

Mr. Bishop, on the subject of Kennerley, was more blunt. "He was a bluff throughout and will ever be," the auction lord said flatly.

For two years, while Mr. Bishop alternately hoped and fumed, Kennerley had schemed to gain control of the auction-hall monopoly, either through the spoils of matrimony or by some other means. Not only had he failed to promote the million and a half dollars Mr. Bishop wanted, but through the vagaries of the Bishop-Kennerley financial arrangements, he wound up owing Mr. Bishop close to $100,000.

While Kennerley bluffed and stalled, Mr. Bishop had sought other buyers. Parke and Bernet, who had vital interests to protect, attempted to find a new angel, or group of angels. Prospects were not wanting, but given the dense entanglement of Mr. Bishop's personal accounts with those of the galleries, the lawyers and accountants were hard pressed to arrive at a valid financial statement. Mr. Bishop insisted on impracticable conditions, at the same time reiterating his determination to wash his hands of the irksome business that paid him (by his method of figuring) no return on his investment. As late as

June 1929, despondent over another adverse decision in the long-drawn case of Bishop versus Bishop, he had written O. B. a melancholy, almost affectionate letter from Venice. ("This is for you and you alone . . . its contents not to be divulged to HP"), saying that O. B. need not blame himself, but his ownership of the two galleries had been of no avail and he saw no other way than to take his price and get out.

Then, with characteristic abruptness, Mr. Bishop changed his mind. Business was better than it had ever been. The dream of colossality returned. With a sweep of his hand, he closed the Anderson establishment on Park Avenue and merged the two companies in the 57th Street building.

The romance was over. The auctions would be made to pay. In the realization that his fitful meddling—as in the matter of Chiesa—had done the AAA no good, Mr. Bishop divested himself of authority and appointed Kennerley's long-time secretary and treasurer, R. Milton Mitchill, Jr., president and treasurer of the consolidated galleries. The move was made in part to avoid a choice between O. B. and the Major, but there was reason in it also. Milton Mitchill was a shrewd, down-to-earth businessman who cared not a jot for books or art but was credited with having turned, in spite of Kennerley's sumptuary rashness, a high ratio of profit on the Anderson's sales volume.

Parke and Bernet swallowed with what grace they could their resentment at being made subordinate to a second-string functionary of the enemy. They could at least console themselves that Kennerley himself was excluded from the reorganized galleries. (He grandly announced his retirement from the auction scene and went to Europe, with the intention, he said, of living there for the rest of his life.) In tactful letters to Mr. Bishop at his haunts abroad, O. B. and the Major pledged they would cooperate with the new regime. "I trust," Parke wrote, with a touch of irony, "that the many changes being effected will rebound to the benefit of the business."

Extensive alterations were made in the 57th Street galleries to accommodate the expected increase in traffic. New bookrooms were furnished, and exhibition halls were added. The handsome orange-brick building was spruced up, and by autumn the lettering on its façade read "AMERICAN ART ASSOCIATION–ANDERSON GALLERIES,

INC." At the end of September the merger was formally announced and given wide publicity.

On October 29 the stock market crashed.

The effects of the debacle in Wall Street were not immediately reflected in the auctions. Under Milton Mitchill's freehanded management, the merged galleries had enjoyed a fair 1929–30 season, with now and then some respectably high prices. In the wake of the epic Reifsnyder sale of the previous April, consignments of American antiques were numerous and hopeful. Colonial American chairs, tables, silver mugs, and Hepplewhite secretaries—comprising the 514-lot estate of Philip Flayderman of Boston—went to four and five figures. Albeit many of the higher priced heirlooms were bid up and bought in by the Flayderman interests, it was at this sale that the estimable lawyer and philanthropist Francis P. Garvan (whose wife's name is commemorated by the Mabel Brady Garvan collections at Yale University) was driven to pay $9,700 for an iron spoon anvil used by Paul Revere. The gloom downtown notwithstanding, the silver-mad Mr. Garvan bid $5,500 for a strainer that had once helped to purify the punch of one Jabez Bowen, who had had something to do with the history of Rhode Island.

The death of Mrs. H. O. Havemeyer, whose bequest of fine works by Degas, Monet, Manet, and many others so enriched the Metropolitan Museum, also provided an abundance of residual treasures to be sold at auction. They were not, certainly, the astute lady's topnotch treasurers; but the canny Chester Dale, future benefactor of three great museums, acquired a Jacques Louis David, *Portrait of a Young Girl in White*, at $26,000. An early Cézanne, *L'Enlèvement*, was sold to Knoedler & Company for $24,000. Oscar B. Cintas, the Cuban sugar baron, bought a *St. Peter* generally thought to be by El Greco for $15,000. Circus man John Ringling got *La Maîtresse de Goya*, said to be the most important Goya ever offered at auction in America, for $21,000.

Estate sales were rare, but since Mr. Bishop had abrogated his authority to Milton Mitchill, the dealers, who had always worked hand in glove with Mitchill at the Anderson, moved in to fill the gaps. With the golden, unreal twenties past, there was an overstock of unstylish Spanish furniture, Persian antiquities, Chinese art objects, lackluster eighteenth- and nineteenth-century paintings. The exile of Vitall (the Pasha) Benguiat had lasted two years. By special dispensation of Mr. Bishop, he had returned in the spring of 1929, with an array of fabrics. Now, though the Magic Carpets remained locked in the room upstairs as security for his unpaid debt, the handsome face and preposterous figure of the Pasha again stalked the galleries at intervals, amid tapestries, Italian furniture, and priestly vestments for which Major Parke could still occasionally entice an acceptable bidder. Inspired by the Bishop capital, Mitchill dispatched scouts abroad (especially to France) with power to make advances; and shipments of more-or-less eighteenth-century furniture came over to tempt bargain hunters. All in all, with the help of a few good book and print sales, the AAA–AG's first season achieved a sales total of about $4,500,000.

Mr. Bishop declared himself satisfied and said the merger of the two galleries were fulfilling his expectations. Whereupon, with Mrs. Bishop, Miss Nixon, and the entourage, he took off for the Sahara desert (and those motels he had financed in the oases). The cars were heavy laden, portions of the trek not without peril. For protection against marauders, the French government obligingly provided a battalion of the Foreign Legion, several batteries of artillery, four airplanes, and two thousand Moorish cavalrymen stationed along the way.

After nine months and thirty thousand miles of motoring in Africa, Europe, and the British Isles, the Lord of Lenox returned to Ananda, voluble as ever on such subjects as the mail service in Timimoun and highway conditions on the route presumed to have been taken by the Children of Israel for the Exodus. One of his jolliest divulgations was that in the Valley of the Kings speed cops were mounted on camels, and thus powerless to overtake offending motorists. As for conditions on the Continent, he was pessimistic, except for a degree of approbation for the power and prestige of Mussolini and the nice new roads he was building.

Back in Lenox, Mr. Bishop said the financial panic might lead to serious consequences. But to celebrate his sixtieth birthday, he expanded the already ducal Abode of Happy Living by buying Yokun, the estate of the long-deceased Richard Goodman, onetime Berkshires social arbiter, whose bay gelding had run wild in the nineties at the sight of the Bishop striplings in their devil wagons. Long had Mr.

Bishop coveted the Goodman land, parts of which bordered Ananda on three sides, but it could not be bought for any price so long as any of the unwed Goodmans survived. Now, with the passing of the last spinster, the clan had died out. Jubilantly Mr. Bishop razed the time-honored house, built in 1780, and added sixty rolling acres to the dynastic manor no Bishop generations were to inherit.

Prosperity was just around the corner, or so the slogan went, but all was far from well at the galleries on 57th Street. "Next season will be a dandy!" Parke had predicted to Mr. Bishop in the spring of 1930. O. B. had concurred, saying that it would be "so big that it will completely eliminate your obligation and make us all as happy as we were in the beginning of our enterprise." The glowing prospects, however, turned out to be mostly mirages.

The death of Thomas B. Clarke, the collector-dealer who from the very beginning of the Kirby era had been a bulwark of the élite auctions, released for sale the most important collection of American historical portraits ever made. Since Clarke's will had provided for their disposal, it was assumed that they would be sold at the AAA–AG, with an appraised value of more than $1 million. To that end, the gallery cataloguers, aided by the most qualified experts, studied the collection of some 175 portraits and assembled a mass of relevant scholarly documents. The executors, however, under pressure from several institutions, decided to sell the collection en bloc. A kind of auction took place in a conference room of the City Bank–Farmers Trust Company. No paintings were in evidence, and the assemblage consisted of a few bank presidents and museum representatives, none of whom lifted an eyebrow when Major Parke, who presided, announced on behalf of the estate that a minimum bid of $1,250,000 would be required. Later, the collection was sold to Knoedler & Company for a price said to be around $1 million, and it became part of the Mellon collection in the National Gallery in Washington. But the AAA–AG lost out on what would have been the greatest of its Depression sales.

Another disappointment was Vizcaya, the grandiose palazzo of the late James Deering in Miami, Florida. Milton Mitchill, exulting over the prospect of a mammoth sale, called the contents of Vizcaya "the finest collection in America today" and predicted that it would bring between one and a half and two million dollars. O. B. and a staff were sent to Miami to catalogue the almost uncountable items.

But in an atmosphere of apple sellers, suicidal stockbrokers, and general apathy for the Italian taste, the Vizcaya sale was withdrawn.

The emissaries Mitchill dispatched to Europe sent back big expense accounts and turned up sales that came to be known as "Mitchill's lemons." The case of the Marchesa Piero Ricci was a particularly sour example. The lady, reported Carl Freund, who had in the past been a Mitchill scout at the Anderson, was a personage of some distinction (with a number of titles to choose from) in Italy and Saint John's Wood in London, where she deigned to sponsor an antique shop under a cloak of anonymity. She possessed a good many pictures with impressive Italian attributions, numerous large pieces of furniture, and other miscellanea. Freund, impressed with the lady, her titles, and her possessions, induced Mitchill to advance her a considerable sum, and her trappings duly appeared on the auction block at the AAA–AG. The Marchesa's things turned out to be heavily mortgaged; her character, not quite in keeping with the nobility of her titles; her objects, all but worthless. Some of her best pictures went as high as $25; cassoni, choir stalls, and credenzas sold for $30—when they could elicit any bid at all. The Marchesa wound up owing the AAA–AG $19,000, a debt never to be collected, for though she nominally owned a fine park and villa near Venice, her property was all mortgaged. She was said, Mitchill's investigator reported, to lead a dissolute life and to have very bad habits; his last dispatches indicated her to be conducting a "boardinghouse" in London.

The Countess de la Béraudière was more genuine, and so were most of her objects. The Countess could trace her pedigree—or at least that of her deceased husband—from the Third Crusade up to the late nineteenth-century Paris auctions of the multitudinous Béraudière possessions. Of these, she still had many on hand, some of which Carl Freund persuaded her to trade for American dollars. The sum her auction grossed—$277,455—was considerable for the times but far below what the Countess, who accompanied her collection to New York, had been led to expect. Though her famous marble bust of the Comtesse de Sabran by Houdon fell for $80,000, the price was less than a third of what the galvanic Major Parke had got for Houdon's *Sabine* two and a half years earlier. The Countess was mightily displeased. When her Lancret portrait of Madame Pompadour fell for $400, her language gave way to deplorable inelegance. "I spit on you!" she cried out at the agent Freund. "I spit on Parke! I spit on all of America!"

Leaving his new president and treasurer to his own devices, Mr. Bishop turned his back on the nation's panic and found surcease in travel. He went to Crete and Cairo. He went to Jerusalem to stand on Calvary on Good Friday. But back at the Ritz in Paris, in the spring of 1931, he wrote O. B. and the Major: "Dear VPs . . . The collapse of our business . . . has been a blow. . . . 30 E. 57th is living in a rainbow or sleeping in a bed of down or chicken feathers. . . . I think the AAA–AG is like the valley of dry bones; read the Bible and work your skulls or at least their contents. . . . I have 3 cars; the last will do 90m an hour; so with a bit of gas can worry along but I hate to see the AAA sink lower day by day in every way."

As the Great Depression deepened, Milton Mitchill took to drink. He kept secrets from O. B. and the Major. In fair weather, Mitchill, who was a bookkeeper at heart, might have made a competent president and treasurer of the AAA–AG; now, in foul times, he brooded in his office, behind locked doors, with the records of his financial manipulations. O. B. was meanwhile, as he said, "traveling around like a lunatic trying to dig up sales." Parke put on as eloquent a show as ever in the rostrum. People were still buying, though the bargain hunters inevitably predominated. Consignors were reluctant to consign. Sale after sale fell below the most conservative estimates. With one sixth of the population applying for relief, it was no secret to the staff of the AAA–AG that the fate of a business trafficking solely in the inutile was uncertain. And yet there was a constructive side too. For it was in those bleak years that the younger generation—Mary Vandegrift, Louis Marion, and Leslie Hyam—developed much of the skill and ingenuity they were to put to good use in presiding over the élite auctions in the not too distant future.

Dedication was the word for O. B. and the Major, their three disciples, and some other survivors of the R. Milton Mitchill, Jr., regime. But for all their efforts, by February 1933, when Mr. Bishop returned from abroad with Mrs. Bishop and Miss Nixon to enjoy the Berkshire snows and the pleasures of Ananda, he returned to find the AAA–AG at the nadir of its fortunes. Parke and Bernet, who saw themselves as Mitchill's victims, went in their derby hats to meet their sometime angel at the dock, with their own—for once consensual—report of the follies of mismanagement. Mitchill had, however, stolen the march on them. He had taken a boat and met the ship at quarantine to mollify the auction lord and explain the situation. Unfortunately, as Miss Nixon recalled later, he was drunk.

In Mitchill's own vernacular, "The jig was up." The treasury was empty. There were unpaid obligations of at least $200,000. Despite some ostensibly successful auctions, operating losses had mounted through the Depression years. The deficit for the previous season alone had been $152,000. Sales in the first half of the 1932–3 season had brought niggardly bidding. Mitchill had given credit right and left. Advances had been made to impoverished European sellers that exceeded the worth of their consignments in an ever-falling market. To bolster prices and keep dealers in the sales, deferred payment had been urged upon them. Some were bankrupt now; most could not pay. Milton Mitchill's clandestine deals with the art-and-book-world denizens had failed. He himself turned out to owe the galleries $73,827.90 when, a few months later, he declared himself a voluntary bankrupt. "Mitchill lied about everything," Mr. Bishop said sadly. "It is a relief to know that he did not steal, but his lavish credit was nearly as bad."

Parke and Bernet were called to a conference in The Winter Palace at Lenox. More in sorrow than in anger, Mr. Bishop spoke of the ten years he had backed a glamorous but profitless enterprise. It was not their fault, he knew, that his dreams and hopes had come to naught.

Mr. Bishop had mellowed with the times. He was no less ebullient, but his health was not particularly good; his moods were grim and glib by turns, and to O. B. and the Major, enigmatic. It was as if he no longer trusted his lordly impulses, his cavalier imperatives. He gave the flinty, fiercely loyal Miss Edith Nixon power of attorney over his funds and a strong voice in their disposition. He gave Miss Nixon The Winter Palace and made her, in effect, his heir apparent. He had adoption papers drawn up, but they were never legally executed.

His disenchantments had been many. The costly and convoluted lawsuits had gone against him. There had been no reconciliation with his daughter, Beatrice. Perhaps it was concern for the winter birds of

Lenox, the baskets he carried to the hungry, the firewood he sent to the poor, that led him to see himself now, half seriously, as a latter-day St. Francis. (He had always had a romantic affinity for the Church's lore and dramatis personae.) It was a conceit for a multi-millionaire, but he had been generous, if not self-effacing; he had made many pilgrimages, albeit in high-powered motorcars; he had been free with his fortune; he had given much, and in return, had received a modicum of balm and—what irked him most in the case of the AAA–AG—no interest on his money.

But Mr. Bishop had not taken leave of his senses, nor had he really lost his fondness for the auctions. It had even, perhaps, increased, in the way of a parent's attachment for a stricken child. Seated at the dining table in The Winter Palace, attended by the watchful Edith Nixon and the patrician Mrs. Bishop, he allowed O. B. and the Major to plead their case. He was not easy on them, though he conceded that they were the only ones left he could trust. The chips were down, as Miss Nixon put it later; the talk was straight from the shoulder. Long had Mr. Bishop been aware of the rivalry between Bernet and Parke; long had he, Mr. Bishop, favored the former. But Parke was the more commanding figure, the First Gentleman of the Rostrum. The vice presidents' ten-year contracts, dating from 1923, were over. Now, if—together—they thought they could save the ship from sinking, Mr. Bishop would give them five years, with limited financial backing, and let them try it. Parke, however, would be president; Bernet vice president and general manager. O. B. had no choice but to take second place.

R. Milton Mitchill, Jr., was given $10,000 to resign from the AAA–AG and nullify the agreement that made him president and treasurer. On February 23, 1933, Mr. Bishop's board of directors elected Hiram H. Parke president and re-elected Otto Bernet vice president. For working capital, Mr. Bishop arranged for bank loans of $162,000, with the stipulation that the interest was to be paid out of the galleries' earnings.

Mr. Bishop then took off for Alexandria and Port Said. En route at a stopover in Italy, he wrote to Parke, under the dateline "Cernobbio, Lago di Como, Corpus Domini anno xi" ("xi" standing for the eleventh year of his involvement with the auctions), to remind him that "every $ counts these days" and to complain that fifteen cents postage had been wasted on a catalogue mailed to him in Paris. The Pope seemed well and happy, he added, and the Italians joyous, it being *anno santo*.

Neither the well-being of the Pope nor the plight of the lair of art buyers on 57th Street could have been considered of wide significance in those grim, panicky days during which the new President, Franklin D. Roosevelt, declared his historic ten-day bank holiday. But to O. B. and the Major the resuscitation of the ailing galleries was a life-or-death challenge. Parke set about to collect long overdue old accounts inherited from Mitchill, most of them uncollectable. Hearst, once more, was importuned to pay some thousands.

Stringent economies were instituted. O. B. assiduously turned out lights and endeavored to restrict the number of telephone calls. The staff was cut to the bone. Veterans of the Anderson who had enjoyed Milton Mitchill's protection were the first to feel the ax. Fortunately, the rent on the beautiful Renaissance building could be lowered. Landlord Gustavus Kirby—who could once have sold the property for $5 million—had fallen victim to the Depression. The mortgagor, an insurance company, had taken over, and a new lease was negotiated at $60,000 a year instead of the former $100,000. But in the halls, the plush façade was kept, the atmosphere of elegance that Parke, above all others, conceived to be the hallmark of the pageant.

The housecleaning task was, to say the least, harrowing. The book department, where Mitchill's machinations had been most insidious, had fallen to a state of very low repute. His book chief, W. H. Smith, Jr., was found to have duped consignors with false promises and damaging misrepresentations. Underhand conspiracies had been made with unsavory traders to boost prices and buy in books that were never paid for. Parke now had to face the repercussions, and with what diplomacy he could muster, make compromises and settlements with Smith's disgruntled victims. The Major bombarded Mr. Bishop with demands that the exiled Arthur Swann be reinstated as book chief. Mr. Bishop, with a not uncharacteristic about-face, began to see the sometime villainous Swann as the mastermind of bookdom. As soon as Mitchill's man could be ousted, Swann was reinstated, with Mr. Bishop's blessing and the title of second vice president.

Despite his titular inferiority to Parke, Bernet was bouncing with the optimism that typified his role. The old galleries, he declared, were brimming with renewed youth and added vigor. For the past ten years he and Mr. Parke had been saddled with someone who interfered with their plans. Now they had a free hand, to run the business as they saw fit. Although they were taking over a "hornets' nest" of bungling, at "the most terrible time," Mr. Bishop had put his faith in them. The mistakes had to be corrected, and O. B. was sure he and the Major could "do the trick." "If only," he wrote a correspondent in England, "we can get some sales."

A scouring of prospects did turn up a full program of sales. Low-value consignments Mitchill had refused to take were crowded into open dates. None of these spring 1933 auctions was noteworthy, and some of them were decided failures. But money was dribbling into the till, and prospects for the coming season were relatively good. By summer a benign, if somewhat melancholy, Mr. Bishop wrote from the Ritz in Paris, "I linger in hopes that I may see the AAA out of the red before I go hence and am no more seen."

The hornets' nest, however, was not easy to clear out. Epitomizing the many tribulations that confronted the new management was the well-nigh senseless altercation with a highly combative gentleman named Shirley Falcke.

Shirley Falcke was a trim, wiry Englishman, a career captain in the Blues, the Royal Horse Guards, famed for their pageantry in the changing-of-the-guard ceremony at Whitehall. His compatriot Leslie Hyam later described him as "a Georgian nobleman with a long feudal past and more human charm than any other man alive."

Nobility notwithstanding, Captain Falcke was subject to the ignominy of seeking gainful occupation. He had come to the United States in 1925, when he was thirty-six and no longer actively a gentleman-at-arms. Having a dilettante's familiarity with art, he associated himself with the AAA as a free-lance expert. By 1927 he was a salaried employee, working along with Hyam on the catalogues. But Falcke's real allure for the galleries was his ability to mingle on terms of equality with people in England who might have something to sell. In the spring of 1930 Milton Mitchill sent him to London, haring for consignments. Falcke, his wife, and his Yorkshire terrier spent a luxurious summer at the London Ritz (which Mitchill remonstrated was outrageously expensive), hobnobbing with the better classes and hinting that their pictures and other impedimenta should be turned into cash.

Hyam was not alone in appreciating Falcke's urbanity. Officials at the AAA–AG—save for the discreet Major Park—coddled him as a prime asset. Mitchill voiced the dream that with such a man abroad, the London auction houses might soon look to their laurels. Bernet referred to him as "our good friend Falcke" and arranged for him to pay a call on Mr. Bishop when the auction lord was at Claridge's in London. "You cater to him and be as nice as you can," O. B. counseled. Falcke did as he was bid. He arrived at the hotel with the gift of a brace of grouse. So overwhelmed was Mr. Bishop by the dead birds (no one, he said, ever gave him presents) and the intelligence that the good Captain could drink tea with Lady Astor that he made Falcke a part-time member of the entourage.

The "rich old gentleman," Falcke said later, used him to gain entree to British society. It was true that Mr. Bishop and Mrs. Bishop and Miss Nixon were taken by Falcke to call at a number of fine houses, but it was the rich old gentleman's indulgence that in time established the Captain himself in fine style in Mayfair. As the Bishop hegira moved on, they exchanged amiable quasi-business telegrams between London and such way stations as Jerusalem and Alexandria; and although Mr. Bishop complained to New York that "Lord Falcke" expressed himself at full rather than deferred rates ("Ask him to read in the Saturday Evening Post what he might have done with Listerine toothpaste purchased with the savings"), he came to look upon the British charmer as a fresh hope for the torpescent galleries.

Falcke ran up an expense-account bill of $4,500 at the Ritz and returned in the fall of 1930 with a contract for one good sale. Mrs. Ambrose Monell, widow of the former president of the International Nickel Company, had—as Falcke put it—a few masterpieces stuck away in storage. He persuaded her to sell them. There was a Rembrandt, *Portrait of a Rabbi,* from the Yerkes sale (wherein it brought $51,400) that went to Oscar B. Cintas, the Cuban sugar baron, for $75,000. A Turner, *Venice: The Giudecca,* also a Yerkes veteran, was knocked down at $85,000, but it was bought in by Falcke, acting as Mrs. Monell's agent. (Falcke, in a later sale, has a dispute with the galleries about his acting as an agent for consignors to protect them from bargain hunters.) The "masterpieces" retrieved from storage included some heavy Gothic and Renaissance furniture, which appealed to Hearst, and some beautiful stained-glass panels—sixty-four

lots in all, bringing $355,465. Falcke received from the AAA–AG a
2 per cent commission on the gross, and a boost in his prestige.

That winter he was sent to England again, this time in pursuit of
one particularly luminous prospect. The luminary concerned was the
newly titled eleventh Marquess of Lothian (Philip Kerr before he
succeeded to the title), lecturer, writer, and diplomat, then a member
of the London Round-Table Conference on India, and later to be
British ambassador to Washington. The forty-nine-year-old Marquess
was obliged to raise some £200,000 to pay death duties on the
ancestral properties he had inherited upon his elevation to the peer-
age. Blickling Hall in Norfolk and Newbattle Abbey in Scotland
contained fine paintings of the Italian and English masters and a great
library, the foundations of which had been laid by a Lothian ancestor
in the time of Charles I. Despite the ebbing market, at least some of
the Lothian birthright would have to be put up for auction. Captain
Falcke's mission was, if possible, to deploy the sale across the ocean to
New York.

His Lordship, Falcke said, was no easy mark, being "somewhat
difficult, and advised by everyone in England." Luckily, the well-
connected Captain had a means of approach through an acquaintance
with one of Lothian's sisters, Lady Minna Butler-Thwing, and her
husband, Francis, a comrade at arms, also with the rank of captain.
The previous summer Lady Minna had taken Falcke to Newbattle
Abbey for a look at some of the treasure. From there, Falcke had
telegraphed Bernet, who was then on the Continent, to join him in
estimating values. O. B. had confirmed, after a mere glimpse, that the
Lothian heirlooms would make a great sale in America. A few days
later, Lady Minna had led Falcke on a tour of Blickling Hall, after
which he had declared himself blinded by the auctionable chattels in
the houses and bank vaults of Lothian.

Though the Marquess himself had remained difficult and invisible,
the influential Lady Minna, distressed though she may have been
about all this "soulless finance"—as Falcke called it—was inspired to
lend a helping hand by the promise, confirmed in writing by Bernet,
of a 2 per cent commission on the proceeds should an auction for her
brother materialize at the AAA–AG.

In time, Lady Minna, concealing the greed in her noble eye, had
arranged a first meeting with Lord Lothian. Falcke and the Marquess
had had breakfast together, and the charm must have been laid on

thick, for before the kidneys and bacon had digested, Falcke had written New York that His Lordship's attitude "leads me to believe that he will entrust me with the management of his affairs."

It was not all charm, of course. The arguments for selling in New York made sense. The pound, then at $3.47, stood at a disadvantage over the dollar. The financial situation in the United Kingdom had never been worse. The great London auction houses were selling little, with few native bidders able or inclined to meet the customary reserve prices. To be sure, London was the acknowledged auction center of the world, the American Art Association–Anderson Galleries virtually a nonentity to Lord Lothian. But on the other hand, there was Shirley Falcke, the gentleman, to vouch for its character, acumen, and ethics.

The subtle process of persuasion (and Falcke's expenses at the Ritz) went on for months, with the Marquess vacillating and Lady Minna valiantly bucking for her 2 per cent. Falcke could report only a ripening camaraderie with His Lordship—breakfasts, luncheons, trips to the ancestral mansions, visits to the Lothian-owned coal mines, which Falcke had to view *ad nauseam,* as he said, along with the books and paintings. In New York O. B., who was Falcke's coadjutor in the project, fretted that it was "a nervous sort of business," this waiting from day to day. Falcke replied that one must understand the English temperament; to try to hurry the matter would look suspicious.

At length, over a June breakfast, Lord Lothian peremptorily said to Falcke, "You have sold me an idea." He had decided, the Marquess said, to retain the paintings for the present and consign to the AAA–AG a portion of his bibliographical treasure. O. B. and W. H. Smith, Jr., Mitchill's book department vice president, hastened to England to make selections from among the twelve thousand items in the Lothian mansions and the vaults of Barclays Bank, no one of which had changed hands for a hundred years or more.

A sale was made up of 168 titles, ranging in date from the eighth to the nineteenth century: illuminated manuscripts with exquisite old bindings, early American documents, and a manuscript in the Anglo-Saxon tongue called *The Blickling Homilies,* consisting of 149 sheep-skin leaves of sermons and exhortations to piety inscribed by monks in A.D. 971, a treasure honored in histories of English literature for as long as it had been known.

Meanwhile Falcke, on a weekend visit to Milton, the ancestral seat of George C. W. Fitzwilliam near Peterborough, had booked an extraordinary document of American origin to be sold as an addendum to the Lothian collection. It was a paper known as the "Olive Branch" Petition, adopted by the Continental Congress on July 8, 1775, signed by forty-six members, and dispatched to King George III in duplicate by two emissaries on two different ships, to insure against loss at sea. Rated by some bibliographers as second in interest only to the subsequent Declaration of Independence, the seven carefully penned pages represented the last official effort of the thirteen colonies to avert a full-scale revolution—as John Adams wrote, "to keep open the door of reconciliation; to hold the sword in one hand and the olive branch in the other." The petition, which His stubborn Majesty declined to receive upon the throne, had recently been discovered at Milton among the papers Edmund Burke left to the second Earl Fitzwilliam. George Fitzwilliam had already offered his find, without success, to several American dealers, thus presumably diminishing its good will at auction. Nevertheless, in view of its primacy in the field of Americana and the fact that the other signed copy was interred in the Records Office in London, Fitzwilliam authorized Falcke to put the "Olive Branch" on the block at the AAA–AG.

When it became known in England that the Marquess of Lothian had sent his heritage of "national gems" to America for disposal, there was a storm of indignation. The British Museum was "very much upset." Peers, patriots, booksellers, and a society known as Friends of the National Libraries were incensed that so valuable a collection should have been lost to the nation without warning. Sotheby & Company, London's foremost book auctioneers for generations, in a long sour-grapes statement, called the decision disastrous. Why had a British luminary so rudely snubbed London? the press angrily demanded. Admittedly, Britain's resources were limited, but such action had never before been taken by the owner of a great English library. To all of which, Lord Lothian replied, "One has to get the best market for the things one is obliged to sell." His implication that prices were higher in New York was, antiquarian bookmen declared, unfounded. Exceptional prices paid in the past in America were not for material of this caliber. The sale of such relics abroad could result in nothing but fiasco. What was more, there ought to be laws, as in Italy and France, to prevent objects of national importance from leaving the country.

Such were the maledictions in Great Britain; and in New York there was fear that the books and manuscripts would indeed draw niggardly Depression prices. The auction was scheduled for January 29 and 30, 1932. Since the date had been set, Wall Street stocks had fallen three quarters in value. Happily, there was an angel to come to the rescue. Mr. Bishop was in residence at Lenox that winter. And it was Mr. Bishop *in persona propria* who essayed the heroic role in putting the Lothian sale over.

For despite his constant plaints financial, the auction lord was still a buyer of antique literature. Albeit there would be no book-enchanted heir to browse in the future among the treasures he amassed, a strongroom of the Bankers Trust Company in Paris held a Bishop library that book sleuths thought might have cost $2 million. Other rare volumes were stashed in the almost always vacant New York house at 15 East 67th Street, and at Ananda Mr. Bishop was building an impregnable vault to protect the books and prints he kept there. Among the rarities Lord Lothian had put up for sale, there were some that the Lord of Lenox coveted.

Whether at his own galleries or at auctions abroad, Mr. Bishop bought his books and prints incognito, using a stand-in bidder. (Sometimes he would absent-mindedly have two secret agents bidding on the same lot, one against the other.) In the plans laid for the Lothian, he appointed as his agent Barnet J. Beyer, a bookdealer—or perhaps the better word was "operator"—who had first come into prominence as a free spender at the Jerome Kern sale. For a 5 per cent commission, Beyer was to bid up to specified limits on the Lothian lots Mr. Bishop wanted. But there was a further, *sub rosa* arrangement with Barnet J. Beyer, of which Milton Mitchill's book chief was the architect. Mr. Bishop was induced to set up a Fund (spelled in the top-secret papers with a capital F) to permit Beyer to bid extravagantly on whatever lots threatened to command low prices. Thus the dealers, in particular the affluent Dr. Rosenbach and Gabriel Wells— the two champions sure to be the main factors in any such sale—would be driven to "pay through the nose for whatever they might buy." Lots boosted too far and knocked down to the Fund were to be kept by Beyer in his stock, for eventual resale. Until the books were disposed of, Mr. Bishop was to receive 6 per cent interest on his investment. The profits, if any, when the books were sold were to be divided fifty-fifty between him and Barnet Beyer.

With the Lothian sale thus fortified against the market doldrums, a magnificent de luxe catalogue, expressing the lordliness of the consignor, was printed. The exhibition drew large crowds and was termed "glorious." Shirley Falcke nervously awaited the outcome in London; the Marquess himself was en route to Bombay to treat with the intractable Mahatma Gandhi; but the watchdog Lady Minna and Captain Butler-Thwing were in attendance at all hours to lend a noble aura and talk up the merchandise.

When the two mid-Depression winter nights came, the old glamour once more returned to the salesroom. Admittance was by invitation, with reserved seats for the solvent. Once more the bookmen and collectors—and close to a thousand onlookers—assembled, some in evening clothes, as for a gala. In the rostrum, Anthony Bade gave one of his inspired performances. The doings, though calm, and as befitted the troubled times, uninterrupted by applause, made the front pages of the newspapers.

Star billing among the Lothian manuscripts went to the Tikytt Psalter, dated around the beginning of the fourteenth century, penned in Latin, and illuminated by John Tikytt (or Tikyll, or Tykitt), prior of the Augustinian monastery of Wyrkesopp. Brother Tikytt had spent many years on those indescribably beautiful miniature paintings—human figures, escutcheons, Bible scenes, embellished in pure gold, in splendrous blues and reds, pink tones, transparent green—and had died before the Psalter was completed. His life work fell, for $61,000, at a flick of the little gold pencil of Dr. A. S. W. Rosenbach. The underbidder was Barnet J. Beyer.

When George Fitzwilliam's much-publicized "Olive Branch" Petition came up, it was Gabriel Wells who triumphed at $53,000, about six times the sum Fitzwilliam had been offered at private sale. "This will go directly into my safe," said Wells; and so it did, for he had bought the 1775 futile plea of the revolutionary Congress jointly with his good client Lucius Wilmerding, the distinguished New York financier, bibliophile, and philanthropist. Sixteen years later, six months before his death in 1949, Wilmerding gave the historic document to the New York Public Library.

Egged on and abetted by the Fund-endowed Beyer, Dr. R. and the doughty Gabriel Wells were as grimly competitive as ever, carrying off between them books of England's first printer, William Caxton, illuminated Books of Hours, royal bindings, royal manuscript Bibles, and—on a $23,000 bid by Dr. R.—the hoariest of the Lothian treasures, an eighth-century Latin psalter.

But it was Barnet J. Beyer who won the distinction of spending the most money at the sale. As Mr. Bishop's agent, Beyer bought about 80,000 worth of books. Among them, at $31,500, was the manuscript of a 1410 French translation of St. Augustine's *City of God*. Another purchase destined for the Ananda vault was the Lothian perfect copy of the first dated Bible of 1462—the price $19,000. Bidding for his own account, on long-term credit extended by the indulgent Milton Mitchill, Beyer also bought, at $45,000, the only known copy of a 1476 illustrated French-language Boccaccio, *De la Ruine des Nobles Hommes et Femmes*.

Although his boosting underbids totaled about $150,000, Beyer's only major purchase for the Fund was *The Blickling Homilies*, at $55,000. In view of the claim that it was the sole important Anglo-Saxon manuscript not owned by a public institution, plus the belief that no American library owned a single page of Anglo-Saxon and the rumor that Yale University coveted the *Homilies* but could not raise the money at the time, it seemed that the Fund had made a reasonable investment. Mr. Bishop's $55,000 paid the bill, and thereby the seed was planted for a lamentable future battle between Barnet J. Beyer and the AAA–AG.

Due in large part to Mr. Bishop's underground support, the Marquess of Lothian's total came to $410,545 (£117,000 at the current rate of exchange), considerably more than His Lordship had been led to expect. With the addition of the $53,000 for George Fitzwilliam's "Olive Branch" Petition, the two-night auction was considered a prodigious victory over the odds of financial panic. The crystal balls of England, it seemed, had been befogged by wishful thinking. Even the London *Times Literary Supplement* called the brilliant total achieved "not only amazing but unprecedented."

Everyone was very happy—Shirley Falcke and O. B., Milton Mitchill and his book chief, who had prevailed on Mr. Bishop to gamble on the Fund, the Marquess of Lothian in far off Bombay. Lady Minna Butler-Thwing received her cut—$8,210.90—and declared herself well pleased. "We are on the map again," Mr. Bishop said. Falcke had pulled off a great piece of business. Though the net profit had been only about $10,000, with the Lothian as precedent and the British upper classes so conveniently hard-pressed, the AAA–AG might yet find prosperity in the form of consignments from abroad.

The booking of the Lothian sale had inspired the notion of Shirley Falcke's opening a London office. An impressive location had been found: a luxurious house at 77 Brook Street, Grosvenor Square. The AAA–AG signed a long lease, with a proviso that it could be terminated upon ninety days' notice at the end of the third year. Falcke was employed to represent the galleries in London for three years from December 1, 1931. His contract was also subject to termination upon ninety days' notice. The four-story house was to serve as office and living quarters, the expenses to be paid by the AAA–AG. Falcke, his wife, his dog, and six servants moved into the sumptuous establishment and proceeded to entertain on a lavish scale. This arrangement could almost have been called an economy measure, for the Captain's expenses at the Ritz while angling for the Lothian sale had been over $9,750.

However many prospects may have been attracted by the tone and elegance of 77 Brook Street, a paucity of consignors materialized during the next three years. A few distinguished personages—among them the Marchioness Curzon of Kedleston, Lady Lovat, and Lord Bute—entrusted Falcke with the sale of pictures and art objects. Some of the paintings were, or were said to be, by great artists, ranging from Velásquez to Boucher to Van Dyck and the English portrait painters. Many of them were, as Falcke ruefully admitted, slaughtered in the market. One consignment of forty-three "masterpieces" from Arthur Nicholson, characterized by Falcke as a "private dealer in poor health and unable to carry on any more," was an outright failure. Nicholson's pictures were so shopworn, his reputation on both sides of the water such, that almost no one would bid on what Falcke had termed his beautiful and very fine Titian, Nattier, Rubens, Van Dyck, or Lawrence.

The AAA–AG's London manager continued to gad about with Lady Minna and Captain Butler-Thwing, lunching with the scions of old English families, and trying—as it turned out, futilely—to nab the great Lothian paintings. The results were negligible, and disenchantment with the commission-hungry Lady Minna and her husband set in. Butler-Thwing demanded a salary, apparently for little more than eating on behalf of the AAA–AG. He was a fraud and a tippler, Falcke eventually reported, who kept him running over half the country to see things not worth the boat fare to America, who arrived for interviews swaying drunk and speechless, who burned a hole with his cigar in a couch in Brook Street, and who embarrassed Falcke to death by his behavior. To be sure the brother-in-law of Lord Lothian took Falcke to lunch at Sir Charles Gunning's. The sale of five pictures resulted, but the lunch as a lunch was a "mortifying experience." Said Falcke of Butler-Thwing, "He acted like a fool and dropped his food about all over the place, and the Gunnings thought him quite mad."

For all that, temporarily at least, "things went merry as a marriage bell," Falcke recollected later. If there were no great profits coming out of Brook Street, there were at least prospects. There were, in particular, the Duchess of Mecklenburg's bones.

The great find was not all bones, though that was Mr. Bishop's word for it when his approbation turned to scorn; nor were the bones the Duchess' own personal tibiae and fibulae, but rather the contents of some thirteen hundred prehistoric graves excavated under the direction of her late mother, H. H. the Duchess Friedrich Paul of Mecklenburg, in and around the former Austrian province of Carniola (now mostly a part of Yugoslavia).

Archaeologists by the score could be found to confirm the significance of the treasures of Carniola in the evolution of European civilization, but what was Her impoverished Highness, the present Duchess Marie Antoinette of Mecklenburg, to do with a warehouse in Zurich full of bones and glass, pots and bits of armor? Shirley Falcke's solution was to send the twenty-thousand-odd artifacts to the AAA–AG for auction. The whole scientific world would come flocking. "I feel sure," he wrote Mr. Bishop, "this sale is going to be a sensation."

In all fairness, it must be said that everyone concerned more or less agreed—Parke, Bernet, and Mr. Bishop himself, who after a visit to Zurich, ordered a scholarly catalogue and a lengthy exhibition with a competent lecturer to educate the ignorant and idle who would be drawn to 30 East 57th Street, if not to buy, to look.

The Duchess, of course, did not have the money to finance the export of her unique consignment. Fifteen thousand dollars was appropriated by the AAA–AG for cataloguing, packing, and shipping. In addition, Falcke prevailed upon the galleries to spare a few hundred dollars a month (for about six months) "to keep the Duchess from actual penury pending the sale."

Identification of the objects from the Carniolan necropoli was entrusted to Dr. Adolf Mahr, identified as the greatest living authority on the Hallstatt civilization. In collaboration with numerous celebrated professors, Dr. Mahr produced, in Zurich, a catalogue inscrutable to all but the most specialized savants. The sale was scheduled for January 1934.

At the exhibition, apathy prevailed. The ignorant and idle failed to come flocking, and so did most of the learned. Museum archaeologists who had expressed enthusiasm had no authority to buy. Institutions were hard up. Competitive bidding would, it appeared, be almost nonexistent. Foreseeing an auction to empty chairs, Parke canceled the sale. Agreement was made with the Duchess of Mecklenburg for the galleries to offer treasures over the counter. The Peabody Museum of Harvard University bought a batch of them for $6,300. The rest were trucked upstairs to molder, as they had been doing for two or three thousand years, until, in the course of events, they were sold—or it might be said, thrown—to desultory bone fanciers at a bankruptcy receiver's sale.

Some months before the Carniola overstock chalked up its losses, Parke had protested the expense of Falcke's merry life in England. Repeatedly in the summer of 1933 the Major wrote Mr. Bishop, who was then lingering, for reasons of economy, in the British Isles (where, he reported gleefully, "the dollar goes upward day by day in every way"), that the cost of keeping the ménage at 77 Brook Street was out of all proportion to the return. The bills kept pouring in— large bills for advertising, weekending with the upper classes, and sundry frivolities. Moreover, though Falcke's own bookkeeping was maddeningly vague, it appeared that he owed the galleries thousands of dollars on loans and personal advances from the Mitchill era.

Mr. Bishop promised to treat with the gadabout Captain, but Falcke was clearly making the most of the presence of the "rich old gentleman" on home ground. The Bishop entourage had been with Falcke to Newbattle and Blickling. (Lord Lothian, Mr. Bishop observed, had used the *Homilies* money to put cast-iron radiators in

Blickling.) As for the London office, said Mr. Bishop, "I am convinced that Falcke will make good; I have seen of myself what he is after; it will take time." Great Britain was full of good things Americans alone seemed able to buy. "My Lords," Mr. Bishop wrote O. B. and the Major in a mood of farcical mendacity, "I have wined and dined with the best quality of the Realm & His Majesty has summoned me by Royal Command to His Presence."

Once the guided tour was over, however, the Falcke charm palled. Open hostilities broke out in November. Falcke had booked a sale of twenty paintings, eleven of which were eighteenth-century English portraits belonging to Sir Albert James Bennett of Kirklington Hall, Nottinghamshire. The names of the English big six were still glorious. A gala auction was anticipated, and Falcke crossed the ocean to attend, as did Sir Albert himself. As it turned out, the night of November 16, 1933, appeared to be, if not a gala, a notable evening for bread-line times. The total was $125,000. Sir Albert's eleven portraits brought $58,300. Mr. Bishop, Mrs. Bishop, and Edith Nixon also attended the auction, and when it was over, Mr. Bishop congratulated Sir Albert on having had a good sale. Not so at all, Sir Albert replied gloomily. Shirley Falcke had bought in most of his pictures, in accordance with prearranged reserves.

A few minutes later, when Falcke joined Mr. Bishop and the ladies, he was greeted with the ardor reserved for thieves and traitors. Morally, if not legally, he was guilty of playing both sides of the fence. The more weighty were the words of scorn in that the attack was opened by the usually gracious Mrs. Bishop. (Had she not, after all, known many men of duplicity and charm in her society-belle era?) Her remarks are not recorded, but when Amy Bend Bishop chose, she could, for all the beauty of her intonation, put a knave succinctly in his place.

Falcke was bitterly offended. His honor had been impugned, and he was nothing if not honorable, being an officer in the King's own guard. His indignation was compounded the following morning, at a conference with Major Parke that Miss Nixon attended. The subject was sham sales and secret reserve prices. To be sure, Sir Albert, or any other consignor, had the right to bid in his pictures (and pay the full commission) or have someone else do the bidding for him. But Falcke, as an employee of the galleries, could not ethically contract to protect an owner's property himself. By such tactics, he had made a mockery of this and other sales he had procured on false representations. Miss Nixon, virulent protector of the Bishop interests, accused him of skulduggery with an Irish rancor considerably less ladylike than Mrs. Bishop's ire.

Sir Albert and the other consignors Falcke had saved from the bargain hunters paid the commission on the prices called from the rostrum, picked up their change and the pictures purchased from themselves, and went home to England. But there was further business to be taken up with Falcke.

Though the charming Captain's accounts were, to say the least, untidy, Parke's bookkeepers estimated that in two years the London venture had cost about $50,000, while returning commissions of $28,-637.41. Nor was the outlook good for the future. Even if Falcke was to ingratiate himself with a spate of art-rich, money-poor Englishmen, there was no longer an advantage in selling for dollars, for the value of the pound had risen from $3.47 to $5.15. It was resolved by the board of directors to close the British outpost. Falcke vigorously protested. He was offered a free-lance agency to book sales on a commission basis. This he refused. After a month of wrangling and threats of reprisal, he sailed for England, his vaunted charm turned to venom, to seek advice, he said, on how to treat with his American oppressors. The same steamer bore a formal notice of dismissal terminating his employment at the end of the ninety days (from January 27, 1934) stipulated in his contract.

In perspective, what followed might appear a small tempest in an English teapot, but at the time, it seemed like a tornado.

Faced with the loss of his plush resort in Mayfair, Falcke unleashed a torrent of vituperation. With his wife, and dog, and servants, he remained a squatter in the Brook Street house, the lease on it not being terminable for almost a year. On the premise that the AAA–AG was still liable for expenses at the London office, he ran up bills for everything he could contrive, but particularly for transatlantic telephone calls and hundred-word cables—to Parke (who had "framed and tricked" him), to Bernet ("I have sent Parke my ultimatum and will give him no further grace"), to Mr. Bishop, to Mrs. Bishop and Miss Nixon, who would be hauled into court for defamation of character, to Mayor La Guardia of New York, whom he advised to look into vaguely defined malpractices of élite auctioneers.

From Lenox, Mr. Bishop, in one of his more orotund memos to Parke, issued his own ultimatum:

To Our Trusty & Well Beloved Sir Hiram Parke, Lord President, AAA/AG ltd: HEAR THOU: KCB, VC, PC, KC, DSO, SOB, NG, CWA, CCCCCC, NIRA; Greetings; Know thou: Silence is golden. Be drawn into no controversies nor verbal conflicts with one Shirley Falcke, of London, late of His Britannic Majesty's Body Guards. Reply not to his insinuations nor insults; keep ever silence.

As regards the defunct London office, pay all our lawful obligations but nothing more. Pay not through him but rather direct. Above all pay him nothing upon account of salary etc. until such time as he shall fully & satisfactorily account for all overdrafts or sums to him advanced according to his contract or in contravention thereof or other wise.

Herein fail not at thy Peril.

In Witness hereof I have set my hand this 29th day of Jany in the year of Independence the one hundred and sixtyeighth.

God save the Commonwealth of Massachusetts.

For all its syntactical frivolity, Mr. Bishop's dispatch underscored the line of defense the association was to follow.

Falcke retained a firm of London lawyers. Gullible indeed must they have been to pursue a case on some of the fantasies of their aggrieved client. Though no paper existed entitling him to commissions, he now demanded 2 per cent of the gross on all the sales he had procured as a salaried employee. Other sums he claimed were owed him—bringing the total to over $15,000—were either for his own personal expenditures or offset by some $20,000 advanced to him, mainly during the slipshod Mitchill era, and unaccounted for in his records. Plainly, it was Falcke who was in debt to the AAA–AG. But it was less the spurious claim for money that Falcke and his solicitors counted on to procure a settlement than the outraged Captain's posture as victim of "a racketeering and illegally operated auctioneering business." He was, he said, in possession of facts that would be extremely embarrassing if made public, facts obtained from his personal knowledge of the operations of the association and from discharged employees (meaning the former president, Milton Mitchill, and his book chief, W. H. Smith, Jr.). The association had better compromise and pay Falcke off, his solicitors hinted darkly, or his revelations would make ruinous publicity in both London and New York.

The association hired lawyers too, on both sides of the Atlantic.

Their fees and expenses would come to more than the pay-off Falcke sought, but Parke and Mr. Bishop were agreed that not one cent should be paid for tribute. Falcke's fury mounted; his "personal activity," as his solicitors called it, could not be restrained, even by them. Having failed to rouse Mr. Bishop while he was still in Lenox, he bombarded him with telegraphed insults at the Paris Ritz, until the manager declined to accept any more threatening communications, on the grounds that he would not be a party to blackmail. Among the cabled maledictions to Parke, the archenemy, one contained the gratuitous information that Falcke had given the "Chief Magistrate of New York" the full details of his case. If his just claims were not settled immediately (*e.g.*, "within six hours"), he would communicate widely with the New York press and other interested parties; he would, moreover, "solicit the aid of the auctioneers licensing board in New York, of the Law Society, and the Governor of the State."

His jeremiads having evoked only the response that the AAA–AG would pay its just debts and nothing more, Falcke issued, in mid-April 1934, a writ against the association and commenced proceedings in the London courts. Mr. Bishop was advised by counsel to stay out of Great Britain to avoid being served with papers. Mrs. Bishop and Miss Nixon too, should the process servers be able to trap them, ran the risk of being dragged into tedious court proceedings for alleged slander. One way or another, the vengeful Captain was determined to have some of the "rich old gentleman's" money.

Further to harass his former employers, Falcke sought as his allies his sometime English consignors. He advised those whose pictures had been bought in that the advertisement of "unrestricted sale" in the catalogue was illegal, since the buying in had been done (by him) with the knowledge of the management. Clients whose accounts had long since been settled were induced to sue, or threaten to sue, for rebate of commissions paid on lots bought back, the trumped-up complaint being that pictures bid in by their owners were technically "withdrawn" and so not subject to the cost of sale. Sir Albert Bennett's solicitors put in a claim for $4,150. Others followed this example, on the flimsiest of pretexts. The association would pay, Falcke assured his coconspirators, to avoid damage to its reputation.

Claims and threats of legal action evolved from just about everything Falcke had touched. Dr. Adolf Mahr, who had concocted the useless catalogue for the Mecklenburg bones, turned up with a bill and a lawyer to collect the fee that had been sent to Falcke to pay him. So, Mr. Bishop commented bitterly, the soldier was a thief in addition to other things. The theft of mere money, however, seemed to concern Mr. Bishop less than the purloining of his maps and guidebooks. For in the summer before Falcke's fall from grace, Mr. Bishop had left his encyclopedic motoring data for the never-ending safari in Falcke's care. Now the spiteful Guardsman, who held his ground like a besieged defender at 77 Brook Street, refused to deliver so much as a tattered road map to any Bishop deputy. It was perhaps this more than the direct blows at the AAA–AG that moved Mr. Bishop to insist that Captain Shirred Eggs (one of his epithets for the soldier) be at all costs "interred in a bankrupt's cemetery," without an ill-gotten dollar to pay "for the grave or the casket of gold."

The gadfly Captain was not the only enemy on a litigious rampage against the AAA–AG that spring. On the home ground, out of the connivance in the Milton Mitchill era with the bookdealer Barnet J. Beyer, grew a legal wrangle as exacerbating as the siege abroad.

Underlying the hostilities with Beyer was the matter of *The Blickling Homilies*, the Anglo-Saxon manuscript Beyer had bought with Mr. Bishop's $55,000 in the Marquess of Lothian sale of 1932. The joint venture, whereby Beyer was to liquidate the investment and split the profit with Mr. Bishop, had been a fizzle. Time had passed, and Beyer had found no purchaser. Mr. Bishop, having lost faith in Beyer, wanted the *Homilies* in his possession. Beyer had refused to give up the manuscript, citing a sloppily written letter of agreement authorizing him to keep it until a sale could be effected. A battle of words followed, and, Beyer testified later, Mr. Bishop accused him of "illegally withholding his property."

Aside from the feud over the *Homilies*, Barnet J. Beyer was in deep trouble with the galleries. Milton Mitchill, during his ill-starred regime as president, had encouraged his crony Beyer to bid on credit in the book sales. Beyer had given promissory notes for purchases made in 1930 and 1931 and had pledged as security a number of literary properties, along with a life insurance policy for $50,000. At the time Parke took over the presidency, there were still two outstanding Beyer notes, listed as frozen assets, which Mitchill had been renewing for some three years. The smaller of the notes was for

$3,187.70. In his anxiety to wrest *The Blickling Homilies* from Beyer, Mr. Bishop, in the spring of 1933, agreed to cancel that note, charging the loss to his own account, and further, to pay accumulated interest and insurance costs that brought the total *Homilies* ransom to $4,257.87. For this bounty, Beyer delivered the thousand-year-old manuscript to Mr. Bishop and voided the contract privileging him to peddle it indefinitely.

There remained among the dubious assets of the Parke-managed AAA–AG the second, and much larger, Barnet J. Beyer note, for $23,000 plus periodically accruing interest. With the rare-book trade dormant, Beyer's collateral—which he fondly valued at around $100,000—had attracted no affluent customers. Rather than sacrifice the security in the Depression market, Parke had extended the note to January 1, 1934. Two months before the note was again to fall due, Parke proposed to Beyer that some of the pledged books be included in an important auction Arthur Swann was planning for the early part of January. Since the note was not yet due, Beyer did not have to consent, but he did so, he said later, because of Swann's assurances that he knew of private buyers honing to acquire some of the fourteen selected lots—in particular, the three Shakespeare folios (the second, third, and fourth) that were the most valuable items of Beyer's collateral.

In all this, Parke acted as wary diplomat, for relations were tenebrous between Beyer and the AAA–AG. Though Beyer had been the winner in the *Homilies* altercation, there remained a residuum of ill will. Beyer, in fact, hated his sometime partner Mr. Bishop. Moreover, Beyer and Arthur Swann were at the time engaged in a legal wrangle over who owed the other money on a fuzzy deal they had made during Swann's exile from the galleries. But Parke had brought Beyer and Swann together in a peace conference and—so Beyer's story ran later—induced them to cooperate. The inclusion of the Shakespeare folios, Swann and Parke were supposed to have said, would lend "tone and standing" to the sale. Beyer was reluctant, in view of the uncertain times, to put up the folios he valued at $23,500, but Swann, he said, had convinced him that when the auction was over, he would not only owe the galleries nothing but would have a good sum to his credit. The fourteen Beyer items were catalogued for, as Parke emphasized in the contract letter, "free and unrestricted sale."

The three-session auction Swann had assembled from numerous

consignors was intended, in his windy prognostication, to revitalize the supine book business. Many of the 497 lots were justly described as "of outstanding importance," the most outstanding being the earliest extant manuscript of "The Star-Spangled Banner."

On January 4 and 5, 1934, the bookmen duly assembled, but the auction was not an unqualified success. The yellowed sheet of paper on which, in 1814, Francis Scott Key copied out the verses that became the national anthem brought a $24,000 bid from Dr. Rosenbach on behalf of the Walters Art Gallery of Baltimore, where the historic holograph is now preserved. But Barnet J. Beyer's mortgaged properties did not fare as well. At the first two sessions, bidding on the Beyer lots was perfunctory, the prices nowhere near Beyer's estimates of the lots' worth. Before the last night's auction, when the three Shakespeare folios were to go on the block, Beyer demanded of Parke that he be permitted to protect them by bidding himself. Parke refused and instructed Anthony Bade, the auctioneer, not to accept any bids from Beyer.

At the sale that night Beyer nevertheless did attempt to bid, and Bade ignored his signals. Only $7,800 was obtained for all three Shakespeare folios. The total for Beyer's fourteen items came to $9,995, which meant that he still owed over $16,000 principal and interest on the note. He had been double-crossed, charged Beyer. His property had been sacrificed designedly and maliciously at an unpropitious time. He took refuge in the law.

Specifically, Beyer asked for an injunction against the sale of the remainder of his security, on the grounds that he had been the victim of fraud. The "Statement of Facts" his attorneys produced reviewed in its lengthy ramblings the quarrel over *The Blickling Homilies* and alleged, among other things, that Mr. Bishop had sought to "wreak vengeance" upon Beyer by ordering that his protective bids on the Shakespeare folios be ignored. Beyer's strained relations with Arthur Swann were cited as background for the alleged lies and treachery that lured the folios to their doom. For Swann's wealthy buyers had not appeared, and no one but dealers had raised a hand on behalf of Shakespeare that night.

Half truths and pure fiction occupied much space in the Beyer sob story, but the gist of the case was contained in the words "unrestricted public sale." As it had always appeared in the catalogues, "unrestricted" was intended to mean that there were no reserve prices,

secret or otherwise. In this instance, Parke had made a point of including the phrase in the Beyer agreement, to insure that the collateral
would legitimately be sold. But Beyer and his lawyers, in a variation
on one of Falcke's themes, interpreted "unrestricted" to mean that
anyone, including the consignor, was entitled to bid. Beyer had been
denied this right. To support his charge of discrimination, he detailed
numerous instances wherein the auctioneers were alleged to have
knowingly permitted consignors to bid up and buy in their property.
High on the list of tradesmen indubitably in connivance with the
galleries was Vitall (the Pasha) Benguiat.

Money was the burden of Mr. Bishop's notes and cables—money,
and exhortations to fight the predators to a finish: "I hope Beyer will
be crucified soon. . . . CONCEDE NOTHING GUARDSMAN, STIFFEN
ONSLAUGHT. . . . I will stand for no further holdup whether in
London or New York. . . . It would seem that we are considered
fair game for any armed blackmailer who saunters along. . . . Many
people everywhere live on blackmail. Do you recall Albrighi?"

The sometime charmer Luigi Albrighi, now a "crook," like other
exiles from the entourage, had perforce not been forgotten. In Italy
three separate lawsuits with him were still pending, a residue of the
nine-year-old Chiesa bungle.

The tone of the Bishop letters was sometimes ominous: "I would
rather close up the Galleries than pay any more than our just
debts. . . . I shall be sorry but that is what will happen if we stand
for paying blackmail."

How, in any case, was the association to pay even its just debts?
The accounts receivable were unreceivable. The dry bones of Mecklenburg moldered in the attic. The Beyer pledges were frozen in the
law court's clutches. The fees of "our learned counsel" were forever
mounting, though their services availed nothing. The Benguiat carpets remained in pawn; the Pasha still owed $115,000. "Ponder on
these things" was the recurrent theme of the almost daily letters.

It was a blackmail scheme and nothing more, Parke asserted in a
report to Mr. Bishop. Nevertheless, Beyer motions in pretrial proceedings were made throughout the spring and summer of 1934,
prolix motions, which Parke and the lawyers had to counter with
adroitly worded answers. Worst of all was the demand by Beyer's

attorneys for an omnibus order to permit examination of all the records of the association. This motion was denied. But Beyer had his spies within the gates. With a sheaf of names and dates and figures, he enlisted the services of the press. Two long articles were featured in *The New York Times*. The headlines of the first one read "FAKE ART AUCTIONS CHARGED BY DEALER—Anderson Galleries Denies It Bids Against Public, as Alleged by Beyer—QUARREL OVER Ms. CITED—Anglo-Saxon Rarity Led to Ill Feeling and Discrimination at Sale, Says Suit."

"Beyer is worse than the daemon," Mr. Bishop commented from abroad. The court had ordered that five officers and directors of the AAA–AG, among them Mr. Bishop himself, must submit to oral examination. He was advised to stay out of the country. With Falcke on the east and Barney B. on the west, he wrote resignedly from Lago di Como, "soon I can go nowhere but to h**l."

The AAA–AG manifestly was the butt of a conspiracy of discharged employees and ingrate debtors. Disclosures in support of Beyer's muckraking divarications could only have come from ousted president Milton Mitchill, Jr., and his vindictive book chief, W. H. Smith, Jr. Falcke was known to be in league with the disgruntled crew Parke had succeeded. And doubtless lurking in the background as agitator, if not coconspirator, was the deflated cock of the walk Mitchell Kennerley, who still owed Mr. Bishop money, and still hoped, by hook or crook, to control the auction-hall monopoly.

Ponder on these things, Mr. Bishop counseled O. B. and the Major, and do not waste money on postage (". . . a double letter is 8¢ not 10¢ to Europe"). Now the Great Depression was becoming a reality, even to the Lord of Lenox. He was poor, almost too poor to bid at the Beraldi book sale, forthcoming in Paris, "the last of its kind in history." The loans he had guaranteed to keep the AAA–AG running would have to be repaid; the bank had his collateral and had him "in its pocket." The New Deal taxes were ruinous. Franklin Roosevelt's idea was to disperse all fortunes, large or small. "Ponder these things in your hearts. Vide Gospel Secundam Lucan . . . and the Lord have mercy upon your soul." (Had it not been, according to St. Luke, the tax collector who had driven the Virgin Mary into a stable to bear the Holy Infant?) It was imperative to save money. Parke should tell his people to use digits in radios and get an expert to show them how to send cables cheaply. "A little care will save many $ for Shirley et al."

Falcke and Beyer must be driven to the wall and shot dead and their bodies left for the vultures to devour. Debts must be collected, the loans paid off. Parke, Mr. Bishop trusted, could get him out of the bank's stranglehold.

"Sell the Magic Carpets," almost every letter said. Sell the Magic Carpets, " or else insure them and lose them." But no one would buy Benguiat's much auctioned rugs, now held by the bank as part of the collateral. Sell *The Blickling Homilies*! The $59,257.87 tied up in the old manuscript would be a help. But neither Yale nor any other institution could afford it, even at cut rate. His homily was his own funeral, Mr. Bishop sadly quipped.

In the letters for O. B. and the Major to ponder there were social notes from divers places. Mr. Bishop had seen John D. Rockefeller daily in Taormina. ("He drinks but water and uses another name at times.") But the oil king, in his mid-nineties, was of no mind to buy rugs or homilies or any other trinkets. At the Grand Hotel National, Lucerne, Herbert Lehman had been a guest twice. "Hearst, his 3 sons etc., Marion and her 3 Hearst children were here in 17 cars; the Astor jilted bride is here now." In Venice Mr. Bishop slept in the bed Hitler had slept in, and slept well.

"A noi, a noi," many of the epistles ended. To us, to us; for Hiram Parke, Otto Bernet, and the once exiled Arthur Swann were the only honest ones left, Mr. Bishop had decided. The notes tapped out on the traveling Corona were warm, even at times mellow. It pleased Mr. Bishop to invest his helmsmen with respectful titles. From Turkey he greeted all three in turn as "Effendi." Habitually, the salutations read "My Lord Hiram," "Sir Otto," "Sir Arthur." From Monte Carlo a post card sent to "Sir Arthur Swann, Knight Commander of the British Empire" queried rhetorically, "Why don't we embalm Beyer?" The Italian "a noi" would be supplanted on German soil by "auf Wiedersehen, Mahlzeit, Heil Hitler, Hochachtungsvoll." Often the churchly blessing *pax vobiscum* would end an almost brotherly text. Envelopes were embellished with purple sealing wax in the form of a cross. A memorandum sent to Parke on the vigil of the Blessed Epiphany had a note of secular encomium: "You and O. B. have done marvels." Even Miss Nixon, guardian angel to

Thomas Fortune Ryan, wizard of finance and art collector, who bought at auctions without the assistance of dealers or experts (BETTMANN ARCHIVE).

the auction angel, was moved to write an encouraging note from Naples. The global news was depressing, she said; the only bright spot was the American Art. "The dark clouds of Shirley Falcke and the other man will pass." From Wadi Halfa a benign Mr. Bishop wrote, "Dear Mr. Parke Pasha. . . . If the loan can all be paid off, we shall be able to run the place in peace and comfort." Alas, in the mood of the times, he concluded: "But peace is far away and the world is retrograding. A noi, CFB."

For the retrograding times, O. B. and the Major had a lucky season. A flurry of good sales made the 1933–4 accounts show a profit, the first since 1929–30. But the chief clients of the auctions, the free-spending industrial tycoons, were almost gone. Many were dead or had lost their fortunes in the 1929 crash. O. B. and the Major recognized this but were not unduly worried about it during the 1933–4 season, when they were, for one thing, busy trying to extricate the AAA–AG from the Beyer and Falcke messes, and for another, concerned with the dispersal of several important collections, including that of the fabulous Thomas Fortune Ryan.

O. B. and the Major knew they were about to bid farewell to an age of splendor, and seemed to conduct each sale as if they were managing the goodbye performance of an aging coloratura and would, when the ivory hammer was lowered for the day's last lot—a chrys-elephantine champlevé enamel perhaps, or an Empire harpsichord— sound the final cadence of the aesthetic endeavors of an era.

By evoking an air of reverence in the presence of the art they peddled, they instinctively fell in with the mood of the younger generation. Leslie Hyam, in the catalogues he wrote, exuded respect for what he called "apotheosized art." He was full of the idea that art has a mystical essence and is basic to emotional and spiritual fulfill-ment. His descriptions of each revered object detailed not only its history and significance but also its signs of wear and tear, in which Hyam almost invariably found evidence of a timed yet timeless progress through the finite realm. His introduction to the Thomas Fortune Ryan catalogue begins with a quotation from Tolstoy: "We cannot fail to observe that art is one means of intercourse between man and mind." Art, Hyam goes on to say, is "one of the essential conditions of human life. . . . A great collection [such as that of Thomas Fortune Ryan] "is therefore a complex chord of varied conditions of human life. . . . A great collection" [such as that of the history of human feeling."

The three-day Ryan sale began on November 23, 1933, exactly five years after the day on which Thomas Fortune Ryan died at age seventy-seven. Interest in the synthesized history of human feeling may perhaps have impelled one or two people to attend, but most of those in the crowded hall were probably a great deal more interested in the personal history of T. F. Ryan, wizard of finance and legend in his time.

Born in Lovingston, Virginia, 1851, and christened with what later seemed a prophetic middle name, which may have been his mother's maiden, or middle, name—no one seems to know for sure—Thomas Fortune Ryan was a penniless orphan waif at fourteen, and at seventeen, a gangling six-foot youth walking the streets of Baltimore, Maryland, in search of a job. His first recorded employment was as an errand boy for John S. Barry, a Baltimore dry-goods merchant. He rose to the position of underwear clerk, apparently found favor with the boss's daughter, and then, in 1872, took off for New York, where his first Wall Street job was as a messenger boy, or pad-shover, in a brokerage house. The next year he married Ida Barry of Baltimore, and helped by his new father-in-law, ex-boss, he was soon a partner in his own Wall Street house. By 1874 he had a seat on the exchange and was on his way to becoming very, very rich.

However by 1894 Ryan had lost his first fortune on Wall Street and vowed never to venture into finance again. In response, his wife declared, "Either you go back to the street where you belong, or the children and I will return to Baltimore and the protection of my father." Fearing domestic turmoil more than the struggles of high finance, Ryan returned to Wall Street and eventually proved himself, according to William C. Whitney, with whom he expanded the streetcar lines of New York City, then founded the American Tobacco Company, "the most adroit, suave and noiseless man American finance has ever known." By 1906 Ryan was worth approximately $50 million.

Soon Ryan was in control not only of the American Tobacco Company but of the Equitable Life Assurance Society, the Morton Trust Company, and the large and powerful National Bank of Commerce. When King Leopold of Belgium invited him to head a syndicate to evaluate and exploit the resources of the Congo, Ryan accepted with alacrity. In December 1911 he said for publication, "I am interested not only in the industrial development of the Congo but also in its social and moral conditions." Perhaps. But one observer later complained that "just what he did to improve these conditions has never been reported."

Profits made by exporting Congolese diamonds, gold, and copper did much to improve Ryan's own condition. By 1912, with assets of $300 million—and, it was said, a $10-million cash balance at the Guaranty Trust Company—he was at the peak of his power, and ready to direct more of his attention to his personal life. He retreated intermittently from the world of high finance to a four-thousand-acre farm in Lovingston, Virginia. There, in the town where he was born, he would rise at cock crow, dress in a Chinese silk robe, a large, floppy straw hat, and bedroom slippers, and meet with his field managers over coffee and creamed bananas to discuss his cattle and crops. After having reveled in country life, he would return to business affairs and to the Fifth Avenue mansion he had constructed in 1908 and then immediately remodeled to suit his wife's taste.

The only elegance Ida esteemed was that found in church interiors. She turned each room in the newly remodeled house into a private chapel, stuffing it with Renaissance choir stalls and reliquaries. Ryan objected that the house was oppressive, not spiritually elevating. He told Ida that if she wanted a church, he would build her one. Of course Ida wanted a church, and in 1913, at the cost of $1 million, T. F. built St. Jean Baptiste on the corner of Lexington Avenue and 76th Street. But Ida would not stand for any of the Florentine furniture in the Fifth Avenue house being removed to furnish the church. Ryan accepted her intransigence, but he insisted that she thenceforth direct all her decorative efforts toward beautifying the church, and only the church: if she bought any more Renaissance cathedral pieces, they must be installed there and not at 858 Fifth Avenue. Ida agreed, but she did more than furnish St. Jean Baptiste: she contributed over $20 million of her husband's money to religious causes.

To escape the claustrophobic atmosphere of his Fifth Avenue house, Ryan bought the adjacent northside property, which had previously belonged to Charles Yerkes. He had the house razed, but he kept, and interspersed throughout the garden he had made on the cleared land, the thirty-two white marble columns that had once heralded Charles and Mara Yerkes' aspirations to elegance. Ryan's cloistered garden, rhapsodically effusive with roses, lilies, birch trees, jungle vines, and Italian statues, covered over a third of a city block; into it he would come in Chinese silk robe and bedroom slippers to breakfast either in the ornate teahouse or in the circular stone and wrought-iron pavilion. While breakfasting, he would read, not the day's financial news, but Greek and Roman historians.

Ryan's garden gave him a place to breathe, and to walk without stumbling over furniture, although entanglements with the foliage were certainly a possible hazard. In the house, he also took measures to free some space. Though Ida was adamant about maintaining her obstacle course of antiques, Ryan managed to clear the fourth-floor ballroom, in which previously no one could possibly have danced without injuring a crucifix and suffering the consequent anathema. Here Ryan built a gallery in which to assemble his collections of Gothic and Renaissance sculpture and paintings, of tapestries and Oriental rugs, of Limoges enamels, Italian majolica, and Chinese cloisonné, and of Oriental bronzes and bronzes by Rodin. He bought without the assistance of dealers or experts, but what he acquired proved that he needed no help in judging aesthetic value. Like his wife, he accumulated a great deal—even such things as Renaissance choir stalls. Eventually his gallery became so cramped that almost all the sculpture had to be removed to the garden.

Pleasant as it was, Ryan's Fifth Avenue oasis offered him only temporary respite from the business world. In the middle of a line from Plutarch, he would suddenly become restless. An idea about some business matter had come to him. He would drop the book immediately and begin to pace the garden, pulling leaves from the bushes and crushing them in his hand while he concentrated on a plan. Then, when he had decided upon a course of action, he would stop pacing. A self-confident, if not serene, smile would light his face. He would pick a flower, fondle it, then toss it aside or stick it into a cup half filled with tea, and go quickly to his rooms to dress.

He would choose a severely cut business suit, and assume in the interim of donning it, an expression of supreme deviousness and hauteur. He would then go to meet with his business rivals, or they would come to him. In the latter case, they usually came trembling. Ryan on his own territory could be either masterfully evasive or so formidable he commanded immediate obedience. Usually he was both.

He might say to associates that he did not feel up to discussing business and would rather show them his art collection. When the tour was finished, they were usually easier to manipulate, and Ryan would then conduct his business with coercive force. Even his wife and sons—he had five, three of whom survived him—feared Ryan in his "business moods." They dared not disturb or distract him, for his wrath could be draconian. Allan A. managed to repress his antagonism to his father in these times only with great effort.

Ridicule of the elder Ryan in the press pleased son Allan very much—so much that he sometimes read critical editorials aloud to guests, or passed around cartoon caricatures for them to see, much to his father's embarrassment. After a few such incidents, Ryan tried to underplay his son's public manifestations of hostility by seeming to enjoy them. He obtained some of the offending clippings, had them framed, then hung them in his private study. Now Allan would not have the satisfaction of being the only member of the family to label T. F. Ryan a moneyed monster.

But while T. F. laughed contentedly, or in apparent contentment, at his supposed meanness, Allan A. protested with all the seriousness he could muster. A final schism came in 1917, when Ida Barry Ryan died on October 17, and on October 29—just twelve days afterward—a twice-wed widow named Mary Townsend Lord Cuyler became the new Mrs. T. F. Ryan. Allan fumed that his father's action was disrespectful, disgraceful, indecent, disgusting. The other sons, John Barry and Clendenin J., appeared to be indifferent. Ryan ordered Allan A. out of his presence; Allan left, and never returned.

Five years later, after an unsuccessful venture with automobile stocks, Allan was a declared bankrupt, with the $16 he had in his pockets constituting his total cash assets. When T. F. heard about it he first feigned surprise, and a moment later, smiled vindictively and said, "Let him sweat." The two remained irreconcilable, even to Ryan's death.

T. F. did not leave Allan a penny of his millions, although his will did provide for the recalcitrant son to receive his father's pearl shirt studs and to have an equal opportunity with his brothers to buy at appraised value any of Ryan's art objects before they were auctioned. Allan ignored this inheritance, but did accept his father's money through his brothers John Barry and Clendenin, each of whom agreed to give him $25,000 a year for the rest of his life for not contesting the will. John Barry and Clendenin could easily afford the allowance, for Ryan had left them $29 million each. But the money seemed, somehow, malign. Once in possession of his fortune John Barry bought demonically, as if attempting to fling it from his hands. In a period of a few months, he bought over 330 items—including twenty umbrellas—from Tiffany's. Yet he neglected the bills for his purchases until Tiffany and Company at last sued him for the $75,000. John Barry also neglected paying his share of Allan's yearly allowance, for which Allan sued him without success.

Clendenin Ryan apparently could not live with his inheritance either. Putting his head on a pillow of Rembrandt etchings in a gas fireplace, he killed himself on August 2, 1939. This, however, was not the end of T. F. Ryan's tragic legacy. One of Ryan's grandsons pursued distraction frenetically. He bought Mont Tremblant, a ski resort in Quebec, and became its operator, but he could stay there only for short periods. During one of his absences, restlessness, or something—perhaps the curse of his grandfather's wealth—got the better of him; and on September 12, 1950, he supposedly jumped—it was unlikely that he fell—from the Warwick Hotel in New York City. Clendenin's son Clendenin Jr. was an active political reformer who suffered from severe manic depression, caused, some said, by complications that resulted from the malaria he contracted in the South Pacific during the Second World War. On September 12, 1957, he shot himself with an army automatic in the same house in which his father had killed himself.

In November 1933 these tragedies had not occurred. The people gathered at the AAA–AG for the auction of T. F. Ryan's art collection could not possibly have thought of it as reflecting any malign legacy. Yet they were fascinated by Ryan's works, which were of such excellence as to make Ryan's untutored acquisition of them seem an awesome accomplishment indeed. Hyam's catalogue had more than adequate reason for superlatives, especially with respect to Ryan's Limoges enamels. Two from the earliest group, produced by the Monvaerni atelier, an *Adoration of the Infant Christ* and a beautiful *Crucifixion,* fetched $1,800 and $3,250 respectively. From the next group, by the Nardon Penicaud atelier, a superb *Entry into Jerusalem* brought $6,750, and a *Triptych* notable for its "wealth of candescent blues, purples, and greens" went for $4,000. Also from the Nardon Penicaud atelier was a set of twelve plaques that had once belonged to the King of Portugal and was now sold, for $12,000, to T. F. Ryan's son Clendenin, who had overlooked it at the private sale held for the family before the auction. In the last group of Limoges enamels were the works of the Limosin family, including a *Portrait of the Connetable de Bourbon* by Léonard Limosin *c.* 1525 and an oval *Stag Hunt* by Jean Limosin, a descendant of Léonard. Léonard's portrait was sold for $4,600, while Jean's oval plate brought a more generous $6,200.

Other outstanding items in Ryan's collection were a sumptuous woven Pieta, which brought $11,000, and an Isfahan carpet, $13,000. Among the many fine pieces of sculpture by Rodin were two studies of *Deux Enfants Jouant,* which brought over $1,000 each, a marvelous life-size muscular nude figure of St. John the Baptist, had for a bargain $1,500, and a strangely brooding *Napoléon Enveloppé dans Son Rêve,* which brought $1,000. The least valuable paintings, those by Sorolla y Bastida, whom Ryan had known personally, were purchased mainly by J. P. Getty. The highest price of the sale was the stunning $102,500 Duveen paid for a Francesco Laurana marble bust dated 1475 and believed to represent Princess Beatrice of Aragon; the companion male head brought considerably less, $16,000. The total for the Ryan sale was $394,937. Hardly had it ended before another magnificent private collection—that of Edith Rockefeller McCormick of Chicago—was scheduled for dispersal by the AAA–AG.

The second oldest daughter of John D. Rockefeller was the undisputed queen of Midwestern society, and her possessions, previously those of European royalty, were considered worthy of her. She died in August 1932, and late in 1933 the trustees of her estate consigned most of her belongings to the AAA–AG. Early in December O. B. hurried to Chicago to choose the items—918 of them, including laces and silver, jewelry and furs, rugs, tapestries, and French furniture, and the Great Lady of Chicago's one Corot—that he felt would sell better in New York than in the Windy City.

The Major, busy trying to untangle the AAA–AG's legal affairs, agreed to conduct the New York sale, but he willingly surrendered the rostrum for the subsequent Chicago auction to O. B., whose lack of sophistication would not, the Major felt, be conspicuous in the Midwest.

The four-day New York sale, which brought a total of $330,617, began on January 2, 1934, and the Chicago sale, which brought considerably less, followed it.

Times were changing, and a new type of collector with different tastes was emerging. The few industrial tycoons who had had the foresight to extricate themselves from the market and survive with fortunes intact would go on buying, but the most important purchasers would be new collectors—younger ones, most of whom were not tycoons, but members of the professional class and some well-to-do businessmen, and many of whom, unlike their predecessors, developed a yen for contemporary art.

It was not, at first, a strong yen. Nor did it, at first, have anything at all to do with the works of contemporary American artists. Initially American artists, especially those who scorned the borrowed Beaux Arts tradition of the French, were ostracized, or more often, simply ignored.

The works of the painters of the so-called ashcan school—the name was one of derision, which stuck—founded around the turn of the century by Robert Henri, a Philadelphian transplanted to New York's Greenwich Village, were glaringly realistic and sometimes downright seamy. Many people called them barbarous. The artists—first Henri, William Glackens, John Sloan, George Luks, and Everett Shinn, then Arthur Davies, Ernest Lawson, and Maurice Prendergast, who joined the original five painters in a group called the Eight—were sensitive to the social injustices of the times. Their canvases depicted the dehumanizing effects of industrialization, and public acclaim for them was not forthcoming. Social criticism in art did not interest the upper classes. Tycoons preferred diaphanously draped maidens to crones clothed in rags, noble battle scenes to views of rotting tenements, sylphs to syphilitics.

The painters of the ashcan school persevered, as did the impressionists and postimpressionists, but unlike their French contemporaries, who attempted to extend the boundaries of their medium, the Americans preached social reform. Few collectors heeded the call of the revolutionaries, or even bothered to notice them until February 1913, when their works were exhibited alongside those of modern European painters at the historic Armory Show—more properly, the International Exhibition of Modern Art—in the 69th Regiment Armory in New York. Even then, most of the American public's attention—and shocked curiosity, and derision—was focused not on the works of the ashcan artists or those of another well-represented native group, the 291, formed by photographer Alfred Stieglitz and painters Alfred Maurer, Charles Demuth, Max Weber, John Marin, Arthur Dove, Joseph Stella, and Marsden Hartley, but on the French works, especially those of the cubists and futurists, who were all but unknown in the United States before the Armory Show opened.

Only the most courageous of the younger generation of collectors, among them Lillie P. Bliss, John Quinn, W. C. Arensberg, and Mrs. Cornelius J. Sullivan, came and bought. But these collectors, including Miss Bliss, who had been known to sing hosannas to the Stateside radicals, seemed to prefer the European contributions. The American artists had to bow to the supremacy of their French contemporaries—then, and for decades after.

While modern French painting slowly gained public favor, American painting failed to stir the imaginations of collectors. Robert Henri's ashcan group was never fully recognized; some of the Stieglitz group won acceptance in the fifties, but this was mostly because their works were rather vigorously touted by dealers. They did not cause any auction-room commotions until very recently. Nor, for that matter, did the modern French painters—until the fifties, when prices for their works suddenly skyrocketed.

When this occurred many observers were baffled by the comparatively enormous sums of money paid for contemporary French works. Some interpreted the phenomenon to be the result of inflation; some insisted that collectors, after years of absorbing innovations, were finally willing to shell out for modern art. Others were quick to note that while contemporary French paintings brought extraordinarily high prices, old masters were selling for just as much, and more. Tax accountants, these observers said, knew why.

The reason was disturbing, if not disillusioning, to many art lovers: rich collectors who donated paintings (or other works) to public museums were allowed to deduct from their taxable income the appraised, and sometimes collusively overappraised, value of the works at the time they parted with them. For collectors in the uppermost tax brackets, many of whom have been lauded—and rightfully so—for their aesthetic enlightenment, giving away paintings turned out to be quite profitable. It was, in particular, more profitable than selling the paintings, then paying the government's capital gains tax on the amount they had appreciated.

Some great gift collections were already assembled before the tax laws enacted after the Depression made wealthy folk deduction hungry. Mrs. H. O. Havemeyer began buying impressionist paintings even before Kirby's first American sale of them in 1886. She bequeathed some of her choice Monets to the Metropolitan Museum of Art. Both she and Mrs. Potter Palmer of Chicago, who were among the first Americans to collect impressionist works, gave their collections to the public. These two ladies were exceptionally enlightened members of the late nineteenth-century generation of collectors. Some of the younger generation, notably Mrs. John D. Rockefeller, Conger Goodyear, Chester Dale, and Lillie P. Bliss, also formed great portions of their gift collections before the Depression. Many of these collections were composed of modern paintings bought at bargain prices, primarily during the twenties, when a slew of younger collectors committed themselves to modern art, but not to the point of paying more than mere pennies for the works they bought.

American expatriates, among them Gertrude and Leo Stein, began collecting impressionists and post-impressionists while living in Paris. Many of these Americans were artists themselves, and thus particularly interested in acquiring fellow artists' works. A few American collectors who remained at home were also attracted to these ultra-modern works. Such collectors, and undoubtedly many of the art accumulators who followed in their wake, were not motivated by the thought of tax benefits. The enlightened objective for a private collection, whether composed of moderns or of old masters, was, many younger collectors agreed, having it evolve into a public institution. Thus Andrew Mellon, who in 1931 paid $8 million to the Soviet Union (through Knoedler) for twenty-three paintings, among them Raphael's *Alba Madonna* (priced at $1,166,400) and who later gave the U.S. government this hoard, plus other paintings, plus sculpture, and money for a building to house the lot—hence the National Gallery of Art in Washington, D.C.—became something of a hero. Yet Dr. Albert C. Barnes of Philadelphia—another great collector—definitely did not.

The "terrible-tempered" Dr. Barnes had not been conspicuously choleric in his younger days, when after working his way through medical school, he had made a quick fortune by manufacturing a drugstore product, an antiseptic called Argyrol. He was not a robber baron. Nor was he an abuser of the Philadelphia ideal of brotherly love; rather, he seemed—initially anyhow—a leading exponent of the ideal in action. In 1924, after having collected art intensively for twelve years, Barnes decided his collection was ready for public presentation, and on March 19 he formally dedicated it and the building that housed it to the people of Philadelphia and Merion, the Philadelphia suburb where he and the collection resided. Leopold Stokowski and John Dewey were among those at the dedication. Barnes seemed barely able to restrain his pleasure at the people having found his ceremony and collection memorable; he applauded the speakers and the audience alike.

The public did, indeed, recognize Barnes's gift—which eventually consisted of, among other works, more than two hundred Renoirs, nearly one hundred Cézannes, over sixty Matisses, and almost thirty Picassos—to be magnificent. However, the affair between Barnes and the public was short-lived, for Barnes grew to feel that visitors to his foundation did not really appreciate the treasures on display, and so decreed that fewer and fewer people would be privileged to view them. Access to the galleries became difficult, then almost impossible. On one occasion Barnes reportedly refused admittance to a supplicant female art lover by abruptly informing her that the last woman he had allowed in had left him with, as he phrased it, "the clap." The public seethed, and finally after Barnes's death in 1951, began a nine-year lawsuit. The plaintiffs contended that since the foundation had been set up as a tax-free corporation, it must be opened and kept open. The court agreed.

Barnes had bought often at the AAA–AG, and he and Major Parke knew each other well enough to lunch together a number of times. On these occasions the Major, watching Barnes's dramatic gestures and trying to follow his rambling diatribes, nervously nibbled at his meal, and returned to the galleries exasperated. As a precaution, he always made certain that luncheons with Barnes were scheduled for days on which there was not an afternoon sale to conduct. Then he could spend what was left of the day in quiet recuperation. Parke found Barnes interesting, but he became increasingly reluctant to meet him socially; he never visited Barnes's foundation in Merion, though the invitations were numerous and insistent.

Though Barnes bought at auction, he bought mainly from Durand-Ruel, who in 1942 sold him Renoir's *Mussel Fishers at Berneval*—for $185,000, at the time the highest price ever paid for an impressionist painting. When Barnes died, his collection was said to be worth between $50 and $100 million. Barnes might have shrugged at this appraisal; more probably, the misanthrope of Merion would have asserted, loudly and with gestures, that the value of art cannot be expressed in terms of money.

Unlike Barnes, most younger collectors trusted the public taste. Most intended to turn their collections over to the public sooner or later, and formed them accordingly, a few buying exclusively at auctions, and others, needing advice and instruction, relying on dealers—either such established luminaries as Knoedler, Duveen, and Durand-Ruel or the younger Pierre Matisse, Sidney Janis, and Edith Halpert. The buying habits of the new generation of collectors would have no great effect on the auction market, but their selling—or rather, nonselling—habits would, for the élite auctioneers depended on private collections as their primary source of marketable art. If these collections were given away instead of redistributed at auction, the supply of auctionable art would be seriously depleted.

During the early thirties there were auction sales of modern art, but none that were successful. It was not long after the McCormick sales that the managers of the Chester H. Johnson Galleries called on the AAA–AG, for what would perhaps be the greatest bargain sale in the AAA–AG's history. In the store rooms of the Johnson Galleries of Chicago, which the courts of Cook County, Illinois, had ordered to liquidate, was an extraordinary and abundant assortment of modern art, auctioned by the AAA–AG on November 14, 1934. A Juan Gris painting, *Head of a Man* went for $17.50; a Braque still life, *Lemons and Tea Cup*, was taken by a vigilant young collector, W. P. Chrysler, Jr., for just $185. A Redon, *Le Violoncelle,* depicting a centaur with a cello before a dark mountainous background, went to Bernard J. Reis for $90. The three Matisses in the sale fared well above the average: *A Woman Reclining in a Chair* went to Mrs. Ben Hecht for $500; Walter P. Chrysler, Jr., paid $375 for *Femme Assie dans un Fauteuil;* and *Near Colliouve* brought $675. The paintings suffering the worst were those by Fernand Léger, with the top price for one being $60 (given by Bernard Davis for *Composition with Pipe*). Léger's *Composition in Red and Yellow* sold for $10 less, and his extraordinary *Composition with a Key* went for $10 less than that—to the bargain gleaner of the day, W. P. Chrysler, Jr. Not one, but three Léger pencil drawings were purchased by Georges Wilmet for $20.

Works by Degas and Picasso were by this time much sought after, yet Degas' *Femme Mettant Son Corset* and *Femme Assise* brought only $550 and $1,125 respectively, and Picasso's *Supper Party* would not bring a penny more than the $400 for which Norman K. Winston bought it. Strangely, two Redon pastels brought comparatively high prices: $600 and $1,500. Francis Picabia's *Index,* painted in 1929, fell to Elmer Rice for $140, while Giorgio de Chirico's *Les Jeux Terribles,* with two human figures, brought $100 from Bernard J. Reis. (Another version of *Les Jeux Terribles,* with a seated woman holding a mass of architectural toys and looking out to a blue sea, was bought by W. P. Chrysler, Jr., for $210.)

The sale total was an insignificant $25,347, undoubtedly because modern painting had, at that time, so few admirers. W. P. Chrysler, Jr., Mrs. Ben Hecht, Elmer Rice, Norman K. Winston, Bernard J. Reis, Durand-Ruel (who bought Renoir's plaster *The Head of a Girl* for $650), George Gershwin (who paid $700 for Modigliani's *Dr. Devaraigne*), and Pierre Matisse ($420 for Dunoyer de Segonzac's *Old Church*) formed a group of buyers well aware of the artistic value of the works that went under the hammer in November 1934, but their artistic insight was not shared by most of the art collectors in the United States, where the era of high prices for modern art lay far in the future. This period brought with it the winds of change. But prices for paintings did not reflect a greater interest in modern art until many years later, when some of the same paintings sold in the Johnson sale for insignificant amounts were later to bring considerably higher prices. One such example was *A Woman Reclining in a Chair,* by Matisse, which was sold by Mrs. Hecht in 1965 for $23,000.

Never would the AAA–AG hold a sale of modern paintings that prospered, for long before the market for such works flourished, the AAA–AG would collapse.

ELEVEN

DRIFTING TOWARD ETERNITY

THOUGH THE 1933–4 SEASON WAS A SUCCESS, bringing in a total of $3,442,434.24 and pleasing Mr. Bishop greatly—"You have made history and fully retrieved position organization," he wired O. B. and the Major from Florence—the AAA–AG was not in good health. The ceaseless assaults of conniving litigants put O. B. and the Major, who had long sensed the impending demise of the association, perpetually on the defensive, making it difficult for them to attend properly to day-to-day affairs, and making Mr. Bishop's congratulations seem decidedly premature. True, the AAA–AG had made a profit, but it was certainly not prosperous: some of the bank loans had been paid off, but there were other loans, and there were mounting fees to lawyers; and with little hope of selling the Benguiat rugs at public sale, the future looked grim.

Throughout the summer of 1934 the Barnet J. Beyer case boiled in and out of court. A war of words, Parke had called it—aptly, it proved, for it was chiefly on a semantic nicety that the court was to rule against the AAA–AG. The long-used phrase "unrestricted public sale" had appeared in the advertising for the Beyer auction; therefore, the judge declared that the AAA–AG had deprived Beyer of his rights by not permitting him to make protective bids. In mid-October the decision was upheld by an appellate court, which ruled that Beyer's indebtedness to the galleries be considered fully paid and ordered the return of his remaining collateral. The sum of $20,258, plus several thousand dollars in legal fees, was charged off as a loss on the association's books, and though few auction-goers would notice, from that time forward, the baneful word "unrestricted" never again appeared in advertisements for public sales.

The Beyer decision roused Mr. Bishop from his euphoria. He railed against the lawyers who milked his pockets. "Do you realize," he wrote Bernet from Aix-les-Bains, "that every penny you make goes not to stockholders, but to lawyers and blackmailers?" "It is too bad you work and lawyers get your sweat," he wrote Parke from Paris. "You are good men and true, but you are not always wise, like myself."

For what relief it may have been, the lawsuits pending in Florence by and against Luigi Albrighi as an offshoot of the old Chiesa muddle, one of Mr. Bishop's own blunders, were settled that fall—by an Italian AAA–AG lawyer who perhaps had simply grown weary of court proceedings that were, he said, "dragging along indefinitely." Still at large were some carloads of Chiesa furniture, art objects, and paintings of dubious authenticity. A stack of pictures consigned by Albrighi to an itinerant Italian dealer had disappeared. The dealer had turned out to be a common thief, but time had passed, and an amnesty decreed in 1932 relieved him from the fear of prosecution under Italian criminal law. Albrighi himself was said to be living with "some girl," who claimed that all the Chiesa furniture and art in their establishment was hers. Since he owed several thousand dollars on notes held by the AAA–AG, and could not account for the numberless Chiesa white elephants entrusted to his care, Albrighi, who was seriously incommoded by the absence of his lawyer (this gentleman had gotten himself jailed), readily agreed to a settlement whereby no one got anything. O. B., in particular, breathed a sigh of relief, for now he would no longer be required to make wearisome summer trips abroad looking for stray cassoni and Italian culprits. With the payment of the final legal fees, the net losses of the nine-year Chiesa bugbear could be written off the association's books.

In the summer of 1934 Mr. Bishop had written of his hopes to return to the United States in the fall, "to bide a wee" at Ananda. No one was to be told of his arrival. Thieves and blackmailers were everywhere, it seemed, waiting to pounce on him *in persona propria*. "You have got to get me out of New York State secretly from the pier," he instructed Parke and Bernet. "I want no papers served on me." He would not pause at the galleries; he would not open his 67th Street house. He could not afford to live there any more.

O. B. and the Major, alerted by earlier communications from abroad, feared for Mr. Bishop's health. "I am drifting toward eternity," he had solemnly cabled before writing from Egypt on February 29, 1934. "It is the coldest winter Egypt has known since Moses was conceived in sin. I long for peace and comfort. Misery, my friends, is the same in the Sudan as anywhere—Paris, Rome, or Seattle. Goodbye is the best word I can give." From Paris he wrote to

"Dear Lord Hiram": "I send from the Ritz on this Holy Thursday following a Vigil on Palm Sunday which brought nothing but blood-shot eyes, a gloomy greeting. No analogous resurrection for me this year. Nor for Paris either. The scandals are beyond belief, and every day the situation gets worse. Anything may happen. It's death that everyone wants. I suppose that's the reason for the extraordinary quiet of Paris. One would think the war was on. A feeling of depression and worry and hatred permeates everyone and everything."

Two weeks later, in another letter to Parke, Mr. Bishop was spluttering not quite coherently on the subject of Captain Shirley Falcke: "When I stood yesterday on the hills of Verdun, I was determined to be free of Captain Shirred Eggs. Obviously, we've both thought of murdering each other." In a subsequent note Bishop advised Parke that he felt Leslie Hyam was conniving with Falcke: "I am more and more convinced that Ham and Eggs are pulling the wool over the eyes of you and Otto. Hyam is in close league with S. F. and is double-crossing you day by day in every way and laughing in his undies."

There was no reason for Bishop to doubt Hyam's loyalty. Hyam had little to do with Falcke other than to occasionally say hello to him. In a detached way, he admired Falcke's charm and elegance, but he had also said that Falcke "superimposes charm upon charm to the extent that one senses him to be inscrutably devious, a bemusing renegade." Parke and Bernet knew that there was no conspiracy between Hyam and Falcke, but they also knew that it was futile to explain this to Mr. Bishop, who might begin, if they did not allow the injustice to Hyam to ride, to suspect them too. Had not Bishop already indicated to Parke that he found a hint of betrayal even in the few, perfectly ordinary administrative blunders O. B. made?

"O. B. requires an efficiency expert to look after his correspon-dence," Mr. Bishop wrote from Italy on October 16, 1934, shortly before he returned to the States. "I could say more than he did in his last radio in less than half the words and at less than half the cost. Get him a handbook. I don't want to save for Shirley Falcke and his accomplices, but propriety and succinctness are inexpensive and neces-sary for the equilibrium of any business firm. But, of course, you and Otto are doing your best."

* * *

It was a wan and subdued Mr. Bishop that O. B. and the Major, in their derby hats, met one chilly November morning at the dock and led away, with Mrs. Bishop and Miss Nixon, to a motorcar waiting to speed them off to Massachusetts. Despondent Mr. Bishop surely was, and not primarily over the tribulations of the AAA–AG, or even over family difficulties, although the great Bishop will case, involving his sovereignty over much of his fortune, had dragged on for ten years, and it had appeared that his distinguished counsel wanted it to drag on for ten years more. Bishop had just "choked off" that distinguished counsel and hired another, but the law's delay and his dream of peace and justice preyed endlessly on his mind.

Moreover, it was evident that Mr. Bishop was ill—how gravely, he, and perhaps his doctors, could not have known. Precipitating the immediate trouble was an infection resulting from a bout with a French dentist who had pulled an ulcerated tooth. The infection had spread, and at the Abode of Happy Living, Mr. Bishop intermittently lay weak and feverish, brooding on the ups and downs of his widespread interests. Later in November he suffered the first in a series of debilitating heart attacks.

That fall and winter there were no sorties to the lakes and hills of Ananda. The servants and the sentries trod softly; the motorcars dozed in their garages. The Berkshire snows had to be viewed from the windows; the winds braved only as howls coming inside through the gardens patterned after those at Versailles. There were no frenetic daily trips to the post office, no roaring descents upon the 57th Street galleries. But there was still the mail, with auction catalogues to be studied, for if Mr. Bishop had little strength to rummage through his multifarious collections, he was still impelled to add to them. During the 1934–5 season, he placed bids on the Wheatley mezzotints in the Eli B. Springs auction, on prints and lamps in the sale of the possessions of the late Judge Gary's widow.

The auction lord wished to be informed of everything, but now the faithful Corona clacked out no quixotic or imperious memos. It was seldom that he even spoke on the telephone. Now Miss Nixon was his surrogate in the many-faceted world of lawyers, agents, hirelings— among them O. B. and the Major. It was she who asked ominous questions that seemed to contain veiled threats, she who called for particulars, facts, rumor, prognostications, and advisements on varied aspects of the association's travail. Not the least avidly perused were bulletins on the activities of the archenemy, Captain Shirley Falcke of London.

Bishop would not die in peace until he saw Falcke lying in a pauper's grave. "Fox flesh!" he would utter contemptuously, gritting his teeth and digging his fist into his bed. "Skinned! I want him skinned and put to the buzzards!" he managed to scrawl to Major Parke with a poorly functioning fountain pen that blotted the page in a way suggestive of a diagram for a massacre.

Perhaps Falcke had good reasons to feel persecuted. Surely Bishop's desire for vengeance was somewhat unwarranted. But Falcke was living evidence of Bishop's own failings, his whimsical behavior, his flamboyant egocentricity, and Bishop, as he neared the end of his life, had grown to despise himself. By condemning Falcke, he seemed desperately attempting to ameliorate his own guilt.

Falcke, however, had no intention of being Bishop's scapegoat. He howled that he was not going to be sacrificed to insure Bishop's emotional equanimity. He would not die to make Bishop's dying easier. He followed a cable sent to Mayor La Guardia of New York City, in which he denounced the AAA–AG, with a letter to the president of the Board of Aldermen, in which he did more than simply complain. He compiled an entire treatise against the association, accusing it of illegal policies. He stated that the settlement offered him when the London office was closed had been canceled by Mr. Bishop for reasons of personal hostility. "I did not come up to his expectations as far as social introductions for him in England were concerned," Falcke wrote; he also suggested that Bishop was attempting "to conceal the misdemeanors of the management," and in effect, he solicited the recipient of the letter to start a thorough inquiry into "the flagrant violation of the statutes of your State made by the AAA–AG," in which practices, Falcke contended, he had been made "an unwitting cat's-paw." Falcke sent copies of this letter to various newspapers and to *Art News,* which forwarded its copy to Major Parke—who sent excerpts to Mr. Bishop.

When Edith Nixon read the excerpts aloud to him, Mr. Bishop fumed again from his bed that the blackmailer must be stopped, killed. His fulminations had a debilitating effect, and in the winter of 1935, his heart condition worsened.

Miss Nixon wrote to Major Parke that she could no longer tell Mr. Bishop the news of Falcke's doings without undermining his strength. Therefore Parke was to respond to Falcke's threats with indifference. Parke passed this instruction on to the New York and London lawyers of the AAA–AG. W. W. Miller of Hornblower, Miller, Miller and Bostin of New York sent to R. S. Taylor of Taylor and Humbert of London all the information he would need to answer any of Falcke's accusations and guaranteed that either Major Parke or O. B. would testify if a case against the AAA–AG came to trial in London.

On February 11, 1935, Falcke delivered the particulars of his litigation against the AAA–AG to the London courts. As soon as she knew, Miss Nixon telephoned Parke, and rescinding her previous order to be indifferent—indifference might strike Falcke as a mask for fright, or weakness—insisted that Mr. Bishop's stand be upheld no matter what the consequences. The AAA–AG might suffer because of unfavorable publicity, but it must stand the gaff. It would not be coerced or intimidated into paying Captain Falcke one cent more than he was fairly and justly entitled to. As the phone conversation progressed, Miss Nixon found it increasingly difficult to restrain her Irish temper. The AAA–AG would, she exclaimed, "fight to the death!" Later, and under very different circumstances, she might smile at her antagonism to Falcke. But not now. And not until long after June 1935, when the Falcke case came to trial.

Before June 1935, the state of affairs at Ananda was to be greatly altered. Miss Nixon and Mrs. Bishop had thought that by humoring the Lord of Lenox, and assuring him that his business matters would be effectively taken care of, they could encourage him to live. They bought him another roadster, but to no avail. The automobile joined the others in the garages; Mr. Bishop would never drive again. On the morning of Saturday, March 30, 1935, his doctor gave him only twenty-four hours to live.

Although neither Miss Nixon nor Mrs. Bishop informed the estranged daughter, Beatrice Bishop Berle, that her father was dying, Beatrice knew, probably from a newspaper reporter. That afternoon she appeared at Ananda, escorted by her husband, Adolf A. Berle. There were Holmes guards on the grounds, and when Beatrice and her husband arrived, they had to push themselves into the entrance hall. Beatrice did not give her name; she demanded to see Miss

Nixon and then said that she and her husband would wait in the library.

A guard went upstairs, summoned Miss Nixon and Mrs. Bishop from Mr. Bishop's bedside, and told them what had happened. Miss Nixon knew immediately that the two people were Beatrice and her husband. So did Mrs. Bishop, who was extremely agitated, still feeling hurt by Beatrice's efforts, before breaking away from the family completely, to have her declared insane. Mrs. Bishop went to her room without a word, leaving a reluctant Miss Nixon to rouse Mr. Bishop.

Asked if he would like to see Beatrice, Mr. Bishop shook his head, no. Told that Beatrice and her husband were downstairs and waiting to see him, he said in almost a whisper that he would see them if Beatrice would come up with her mother.

Miss Nixon said she would tell Beatrice, whom she then gently urged to comply with her father's condition. All Beatrice had to do was say, "I'm sorry, Mother."

Beatrice's husband interrupted Miss Nixon: "Come on, let's go."

Miss Nixon saw Beatrice kick him to be quiet. She continued pleading with Beatrice, speaking of the gravity of Mr. Bishop's condition, and saying that though he had at first indicated he did not wish to see Beatrice, when he was told of her presence, he made the condition that he would see her if she apologized to her mother.

Suddenly Miss Nixon stopped speaking. Mrs. Bishop had appeared, looking frightened and tearful, in the library doorway. She seemed to be waiting for her daughter to come to her.

But Beatrice did no such thing. Looking at Miss Nixon, she said, "I came only to see my father." Then she and her husband silently swept past her mother and out the front door.

Beatrice did not see her father, and thenceforth, if she and her mother by chance came into each other's presence, Mrs. Bishop would turn away, or close her eyes. Eventually her bitterness deepened to such a degree that she would not allow Beatrice's name to be mentioned in her hearing.

After the Berles' exit, Miss Nixon and Mrs. Bishop returned to their vigil beside Mr. Bishop's bed. He died at 7:50 that evening, his last words being, "I never thought I would die so young—sixty four. . . . Count to sixty-four and I am dead."

Miss Nixon would allow no one but his wife to see Mr. Bishop in his casket. What funeral there was took place in the hall that led to the library at Ananda. An excerpt from the twenty-first chapter of Revelation was read—"I will give unto him that is athirst of the fountain of the water of life freely"; then Mr. Bishop's remains were taken for burial to a cemetery in Brooklyn. The papers reported that Beatrice came to the funeral at Ananda Hall, but their stories were incorrect. However, at the graveside ceremony, Beatrice did appear, but she hid behind a tree. Miss Nixon noted, when she returned to the grave the following morning, that the flowers she and Mrs. Bishop had put on the grave were taken off and a bunch of flowers Beatrice had bought had been substituted in their place. Miss Nixon was of course glad the daughter had visited her father's grave, but did not, could not, speak of it to Mrs. Bishop.

O. B. and the Major pledged that they would win the Falcke case as a final act of respect to their deceased angel. When the case came to trial, O. B. was chosen by the AAA–AG's directors to testify on behalf of the firm in London—much to O. B.'s distress, for he was acutely self-conscious about his lack of polish and did not want to face the English aristocracy in court. In America his grammar was acceptable, but in front of a high court, facing a judge in a powdered wig, would he be able adequately to explain the intricacies of the AAA–AG's case? And if the AAA–AG lost the case, would he not be blamed by the directors, and perhaps even by Major Parke, who would have reason for attempting to remove what they considered to be another of the association's burdens?

O. B. felt it was he who was on trial. He was also upset about testifying against Falcke because he had personally encouraged Falcke to make a success of the London office. He had hoped to join him there if the business grew enough for Falcke to need his help. He had written Falcke of this hope, and now he feared that his letters might be cited in court, and misinterpreted there, damaging the AAA–AG's case.

To make things worse, the directors of the AAA–AG were freighting O. B. with a cargo for his English trip—the Benguiat rugs, pledged by the Pasha to the galleries, and by the galleries to the bank. Upon arriving in London, O. B. was to deliver the Magic

Carpets to Barclays Limited, a firm with suitable facilities for exhibiting and selling them. Benguiat was not to be allowed to meddle in any way, but he nonetheless followed O. B. to London, after sending the Major a note saying that he was going only to attempt to facilitate possible sales of his "beloveds."

Major Parke immediately cabled O. B. to beware of any encounter with the Pasha. "There is no telling what he might do to ransom his kidnapped babies." O. B. took the Major's warning to heart, and when his ship docked in England, he left it reluctantly, keeping a constant lookout for the Pasha and, at the same time, struggling with the burdensome valise that held the Pasha's precious rugs.

Fortunately O. B. did not encounter the Pasha. The rugs were safely entrusted to Barclays' Piccadilly offices, and there Benguiat soon appeared. When temporarily reunited with his family, he wept unceasing "strands and threads," as one Barclays' employee reported.

Realizing that he would have to part with his carpets, the Pasha cried, "My grief swallows me." He put his hands to his head in a melodramatic gesture, then declared, "Only the grave remains." As his words reverberated, his rotund body trembled, and he verged on collapse. Pride saved him: he could not allow himself to succumb to public grief. After a long final perusal of his glorious collection, he drew himself up and silently stalked from Barclays. Two years later on March 17, 1937, Vitall Benguiat would die in his seventy-eighth year.

Before going into the courtroom, O. B. had written out his testimony and documented Shirley Falcke's entire association with the AAA–AG. Falcke was wrong—O. B. said—in alleging that as an implied term of his employment, he was to be paid a commission on sales of collections the owners of which he had introduced to AAA–AG officers; no employee of the AAA–AG had ever been paid such a commission. The salary paid to the employee represented his total remuneration. The introductions claimed by Falcke were the object of his employment, and all were obtained during the course of it. The only sale the association agreed to pay Falcke a commission on was the Monell sale, and this was only because in this exceptional case, Falcke was acting as the consignor's personal agent. Before Lord Lothian's collection was auctioned, the AAA–AG agreed to pay Lady Minna

Butler-Thwing 2 per cent of the gross proceeds, but there was no similar agreement with Falcke—for that sale, for the sale of George Fitzwilliam's "Olive Branch" Petition, or for any subsequent sale.

In the last two hours of his day-long testimony, O. B. explained the circumstances of the closing of the London office and made it clear that Falcke's expense claims arose as a result of the Captain's poor bookkeeping, not the AAA–AG's underhandedly and abruptly cutting off his supply of management funds. When O. B. stepped down, the mood of the court seemed to have shifted in the favor of the AAA–AG. In a later session of the trial, Lord Lothian testified on behalf of the brooding, increasingly inarticulate plaintiff, but even an English peer could not make Falcke's fabricated claims seem just. On the day Lord Lothian testified, Falcke himself was questioned, about his expenses while managing the London office.

On Falcke's expense account was a very peculiar item—"Supper for a dog . . . 7s 6d"—to which the AAA–AG's lawyer called the court's attention. Falcke was asked, "Is that what it costs for a dog to have supper at the Ritz?"

The Captain assumed an arrogant pose. He started to answer, then stopped. To keep himself from stammering—a habit he had recently acquired, much to the amusement of many of the spectators of the trial—he took a deep breath, then exhaled slowly in a manner indicative of fatigue and boredom. At last he replied: "I cannot say."

Raucous laughter ensued in the courtroom; then silence.

The examining lawyer paused to look serious for a long moment. Then he continued: "Evidently the dog was off his feed a bit on a later date—when the charge was only five shillings. Am I not correct?"

Falcke lifted an eyebrow and shrugged. His expression indicated that he relished being guilty of so amply appeasing the appetite of a dog—doing so was irresponsible perhaps, but it was also admirable in an aristocratic sort of way.

Still, after the shrug, Falcke said, "I am not going to charge the company for my dog."

The official referee immediately spoke out: "Well, somebody has charged for it."

Falcke did not respond. The referee seemed momentarily taken aback; then he asked, "Was it a large dog?"

"No," Falcke answered, "a Yorkshire terrier."

Again laughter was heard in the courtroom.

When an air of something like gravity was reestablished, the examining lawyer asserted, "The dog cost practically two pounds a week."

Falcke responded immediately, as if anxious to end the tedious inquiry without further ado: "I am not going to charge for those things, and if the accounts have gone in badly"—he paused for a moment, dropped his head slightly, and assumed a self-consciously humble expression—"then I apologize."

A few days later, the official referee announced his decision: Falcke's claim for commissions on sales secured by him for the AAA–AG was disallowed, as was his claim for $3,000 for extra expenses in February and October 1934, as was his claim for $230 for his journey to New York for Sir Albert Bennett's sale; he was, however, entitled to approximately $1,000 for two month's salary because of premature termination of the contract under which he was employed.

Falcke settled with the AAA–AG for $15,000 to cover court costs (the AAA–AG's expenses had totaled almost five times this amount).

At the beginning of September 1935, the AAA–AG's London counselor reported that Falcke, after all his "volcanic whimpering," had settled down and miraculously opened an attractive little art shop in Duke Street, Saint James. "No doubt, the shop is taken in his wife's name, and he is only an employee, but it is certainly extraordinary that he has been able to get together some sort of business."

But Falcke's ambitions did not lie in managing an attractive little art shop. He would repose there only for a short while.

When O. B. returned to New York, covered with glory for his conduct during the Falcke trial, he was still not at ease; he had begun to develop the ulcers that tormented him for ten years and eventually proved fatal.

Earlier he had been worried about Cortlandt Field Bishop's will. Following Bishop's death he and the Major anxiously awaited the announcement of the will's provisions. O. B. constantly fretted, yet ineffectually hoped that, in the end, everything would work out for the best. The Major, however, sensed that Mr. Bishop may have been as impulsive in the writing of his will as he had been in the conduct of his life and regretted that he had not had the courage to force the auction angel to face his ineptitude for commerce: had he been more forceful, Mr. Bishop would have given him definitive power over the galleries while alive, and would not have left the business in such a muddle at his death. Now, waiting for the will to be filed, the Major felt a strong impulse to leave the association without a further word, for Edith Nixon and Mrs. Bishop had not answered his queries about their plans for the future, and he sensed that something was wrong.

Both O. B. and the Major knew that a draft of Bishop's will, which they had seen in 1933, specified that the AAA–AG was to be continued and developed under their management; the draft also confirmed stock options Mr. Bishop had given them much earlier, in 1925, providing that if Mr. Bishop's executors or trustees ever decided to sell any of their shares in the association, Otto Bernet and Hiram H. Parke, if then still in the association's employ, were to have "a preference . . . in equal shares" for the purchase of the stock on terms acceptable to the executors or trustees and "equal to such bona fide offer as may be made by another or others."

On April 8, 1935, the will was filed—and O. B. and the Major found their worst fears realized: the option provisions had been stricken, and Edith Nixon and Mrs. Bishop were in complete control of the galleries.

Parke and O. B. were outraged. Would it be possible for them to follow the edicts of two ladies even more removed from reality than Mr. Bishop had been? Soon they learned that Edith Nixon and Mrs. Bishop were about to leave for Europe. Once again there would be cabled instructions, which O. B. and the Major would somehow have to incorporate into the business policies of the AAA–AG. Parke startled O. B. by saying, "This time I'm running away to Never-Never Land and sending out my own cables, directing world politics." As he looked at the Major, O. B. saw that he was completely serious—at least about leaving the AAA–AG. He tried to discourage Parke agreed, but all the while he protested that by staying he was he go?

O. B. persistently pleaded with the Major to remain, and at last Parke agreed, but all the while he protested that by staying he was compromising his personal integrity.

Mr. Bishop's will caused other repercussions. New Englanders were agape at learning that Beatrice, Bishop's only child, had been cut off without a cent. Editorials expressed disapproval; some of the more inflammatory ones called their readers' attention to "the disgraceful conduct" of Bishop's life, implying that he was of licentious character since he had thrown his daughter out of the house, and remained indifferent to her. Mrs. Bishop and Edith Nixon were not disturbed, and even Beatrice kept silent.

Edith Nixon and Amy Bend Bishop of course had no cause to complain about the provisions of Bishop's will, which gave each of them an immediate $20,000 bequest and half of the rest of the estate in trust for life. Mrs. Bishop and Edith Nixon would, the testator hoped, occupy one of the houses on his Lenox property. It was his wish that they live in one residence, and not separately; however, if they did not want to stay together, he made adequate provisions for them to be able to choose and maintain separate dwellings.

Miss Nixon and Mrs. Bishop chose The Winter Palace as their home, for they knew that Ananda would be too expensive to maintain. Eventually Ananda was torn down to save the high annual tax bill it incurred.

At Bishop's death his estate was appraised to be worth close to $3 million. But the estate was heavily indebted, mainly to lawyers. Unpaid bills amounting to tens of thousands and four to five years overdue were suddenly brought to the attention of a bewildered Mrs. Bishop and a stunned Miss Nixon, on whom the responsibility of settling the debts fell.

The only bill Miss Nixon paid in full was that of the AAA–AG's solicitors in the Shirley Falcke case, and this she did only out of respect to Mr. Bishop. Although Miss Nixon proved to be a strong-willed businesswoman, she was fighting a lost cause in trying to straighten out the tottering Bishop estate. In 1943 she finally became Mrs. Bishop's adopted daughter in order to establish a more definitive legal position in relation to the estate. She had, prior to this, neglected to sign the adoption papers Mr. Bishop had drawn up a few years earlier.

When Beatrice reappeared in May 1938 to contest her father's will, Miss Nixon did not interfere. Beatrice and her mother would never be reconciled, and Edith Nixon feared that any involvement on her part would only fire the hostility they already had for each other. She did help Mrs. Bishop when called upon, but this was not often, for Mrs. Bishop appreciated her reluctance to take part in the family quarrel and asked her to help only with the most perfunctory legal tasks. Beatrice by this time had already secured the remainder of her grandfather David Wolfe Bishop's estate, some $8 million, which her father had rigorously but unsuccessfully battled to control. Beatrice's suit against her father's estate in 1938 for $875,000 arose from what she considered the mismanagement of the principal of another estate she inherited through him from a great aunt, Matilda White. When Cortlandt Field Bishop died, Matilda White's estate went to Beatrice, but it was worth only a small fraction of its previous value. Beatrice calculated that the depletion brought about by her father's faulty management was $875,000; the courts awarded her a $515,000 settlement.

Mrs. Bishop fumed as she relinquished the money; her own daughter was driving her to the poorhouse. Bishop had left a gross estate of $2,847,201, which netted $490,392 after debts and expenses, one of which was the settlement with Beatrice. "What would I do if I were poor?" Mrs. Bishop desperately asked Miss Nixon.

"It will never happen—never, never," Edith Nixon said, calming her, and distracting her from her troubled thoughts by encouraging her to knit—the result, an endless smothering scarf.

"I never learned how to do anything," Amy Bishop recalled later, her knitting needles clicking as she spoke. "I was taught only to dress, arrange flowers, nibble at my food, make beautiful gestures, and make a good marriage. I was taught to be a personified luxury. It makes me think I was merely an expensive item in an exclusive store. I loved my husband—adored him—but he never expected me to do anything. Once, in New York, I went to teach the poor Italians to sew. I could speak their language and I felt sorry for them. Oh, I knew they didn't want to learn fine sewing . . . but sewing was the only thing I knew well enough to teach them.

"One woman I remember—with eight children and expecting a ninth. She hated her husband, didn't want the child, and asked me what one does to abort a child. I told her what to do. I didn't even know I knew what to do—but, evidently, I did, for I learned later that the child had been successfully aborted. That was the only time I ever did anything, ever worked—teaching the Italians fine sewing. But I was so upset by the experience with the pregnant woman that I told Cortlandt about it, and he was enraged. He wouldn't let me return."

Having seen poverty, Mrs. Bishop feared it the more. But surely poverty could not befall her.

She depended entirely upon Edith Nixon, and yet as circumstances became worse, there were times she regretted sharing her husband's estate with her. Then she would become very silent, very jittery. Sometimes she would tremble. Yet she knew Miss Nixon would sacrifice everything for her. Everything. She must take Edith to her heart, consider her as she would herself . . . as part of herself. They would fight for survival together. And win.

At the height of her economic fears, in September 1943, Mrs. Bishop brought legal action against her daughter, alleging that Beatrice had obtained her father's estate by taking fraudulent advantage of her, since she was not then represented by counsel. Mrs. Bishop's affidavit related the entire family feud in minute detail, replete with nostalgia and mild hysteria. It was, according to one newspaper, "encyclopedic" in scope.

Beatrice's husband, Adolf A. Berle, who handled the case for her through his law firm, replied by recalling that Mrs. Bishop had been represented by counsel throughout Beatrice's suit, and citing evidence to prove it. Mrs. Bishop lost her case, and never again would acknowledge her daughter's existence. Miss Nixon had to caution everyone who came to visit not to mention Beatrice's name.

Between 1935 and 1937 the two women were, despite their money problems, hopping around the world. They hopped with less resilience than before, but nonetheless they hopped, for had they not been taught that wandering the world, either as a bird or as a pilgrim, was the only worthwhile occupation?

Wherever they alighted, Miss Nixon, acting as business manager for herself and Mrs. Bishop, felt impelled to correspond daily with Major Parke. In doing so, she completely neglected Otto Bernet. But then, she had no faith in O. B.'s business capabilities, and distrusted him as well.

Early in June 1937 Miss Nixon wrote the Major of Mrs. Bishop's wish to sell her husband's library: Mrs. Bishop had been very pleased with the series of sales of her husband's engravings, etchings, furniture, and Chinese porcelains, which had brought $276,145 in the fall of 1935, and was eager to have his infinitely more valuable collection of books turned into cash. The Major replied by suggesting the best possible way in which to go about selling the books, and the earliest possible time—the spring of 1938. But Mrs. Bishop wanted the sale sooner—say, in the fall of 1937. Since it was then almost summer, the Major had Arthur Swann send a letter confirming the impossibility of a fall 1937 sale. After seemingly endless quibbling, in letter after letter, Miss Nixon agreed that perhaps the Major was right, and she accepted April 1938 as the time for the sale, and with Mrs. Bishop left the Paris Ritz for the fiords of Norway.

The Major found Edith Nixon's correspondence tiresome and annoying. He now was planning not only an effective way in which to work around the two women but also a way in which to extricate himself and what he considered his business from their hands. Caution and patience, however, at this point were mandatory. Meanwhile the letters started coming from London, where the women settled for a short while. It was here that Edith Nixon received a letter from Captain Falcke, which she read and reread, quite unexpectedly, with an open mind. She said nothing of the letter to Mrs. Bishop. Strangely she found herself swayed by Falcke's rhetoric. The charm she had been warned of and was now experiencing for herself—she found it tasteful, she said later, and above all, interesting—was inherent in the letter, the tone of which was actually abject and apologetic. It seemed that Shirley Falcke longed for forgiveness. Perhaps Miss Nixon and Mrs. Bishop would find it in their hearts to forgive him. If he still proved a scoundrel, they could claim that at least they had practiced Christian ethics. A few days later, and still without a word to Mrs. Bishop, Edith Nixon sent a note by messenger to Falcke's office at his wife's Duke Street art shop. The messenger was received by a rather harried woman, the former Mrs. Falcke, who first told him that the Captain was no longer associated with her or her business, then directed him to another address. He rushed there with the note and gave it to Shirley Falcke, who told him to wait for his answer.

Miss Nixon's note suggested that the two of them have tea and a conversation somewhere either that afternoon or sometime the following day.

Falcke's rather daring reply was: "How about a ride in a horse-drawn carriage, which will arrive at your doorstep 4:30 sharp?"

Miss Nixon was intrigued by it, and by the news that Shirley Falcke was divorced from his wife. Her first impulse was to say no. She was afraid of Mrs. Bishop's reaction if she saw her with Falcke. Yet she could not bring herself to send another messenger. Falcke's note was certainly indelicate, but it was difficult to resist. She wanted to hear his side of the story. Perhaps, if she managed not to arouse Mrs. Bishop's curiosity . . . perhaps by going out a little early for some fabricated reason, then meeting the carriage, so Falcke's arrival would not disturb Mrs. Bishop . . .

The time for Falcke's arrival grew nearer and nearer, and Edith Nixon had still not decided on a suitable excuse for going out. Maybe Mrs. Bishop would simply not ask. To Miss Nixon's amazement, she didn't.

Saying only that she was leaving and would be back soon, Miss Nixon hurried to meet the carriage. A clock had already chimed 4:30; it was almost 4:35. Could Falcke—the scoundrel—be late?

But as she looked out onto the street, she saw that a carriage was waiting and that a slim, elegant man was coming from it toward her. Nervously she stepped outside.

An instant later Shirley Falcke swept her into the carriage . . . and, as she regained her breath, they began to talk animatedly. Captain Falcke encouraged Miss Nixon to tell him of nearly forgotten childhood impressions, and she, in turn, found it increasingly difficult to be reserved in his presence.

They met a second time, also secretly. This time, however, they went only for a walk in the park. Miss Nixon had decided in the interim that she had been much too friendly with Falcke. In the future she must be more withdrawn. Detachment was a necessity.

At the second meeting, Falcke seemed to sense her uneasiness. He spoke of something unexpected that had come up, to which he must attend immediately, apologized for inconveniencing her, and then, after she had said that she would see herself home, and he had promised to get in touch with her again soon, he hurried off. After this encounter, Edith Nixon was pensive, and walked home slowly.

Shirley Falcke's brief interlude with Miss Nixon was followed by a package he sent to her containing the letters sent to him, during his management of the London office, by Otto Bernet. He was certain these letters would supply the evidence that would clear him of any undermining tactics against Mr. Bishop's beloved association.

Upon first reading the letters, Miss Nixon was deeply troubled. Bernet had, it seemed, encouraged Falcke to expect the commissions Falcke later claimed were his due. One letter alluded to a possible Falcke-Bernet partnership, were the London office ever to break with the association.

Perhaps Bernet had meant no harm to the association, and had made this proposal only to further a business relationship with someone he liked and had had a great deal of respect for. But perhaps not. Edith Nixon had never trusted O. B. Perhaps for good reason.

As damaging as anything else in the letters—maybe more damaging than anything else—were the harsh opinions of Mr. Bishop. "He thinks of me as fat and stupid," one letter said, "and excuses his own overweight as a result of omniscience." As soon as she could control her fury, Edith Nixon sent a letter to Falcke, promising she would do all she could to see that justice was given him.

He answered that he did not want his exposure of the letters to cause her or Mrs. Bishop any trouble. He had given them to her only to establish his moral character.

No, she answered to that; he had been wronged, and she must give him justice. Bernet would have to be dismissed. In fact, the entire AAA–AG would have to be reorganized. Please, would he give her the honor of his advice?

He answered coyly: "Perhaps."

She insisted and finally commanded him to come to her in order to discuss the matter further.

He came, and together they told Mrs. Bishop the entire story. As soon as Mrs. Bishop's tears had subsided, Edith Nixon announced that the three of them must return posthaste to the States.

Falcke said it was impossible for him to go. Edith and Mrs. Bishop pleaded, but he remained steadfast. Surely they understood his position? He could not risk the possibility of another public humiliation. He had merely wished to point out to the ladies that he was not so irresponsible and mercenary a person as the London trial had made him seem. He then politely excused himself from their presence.

The next day, the two ladies booked passage for their return to the States. They were to leave within the week, the last week of September 1937.

Once back in New York City, Edith Nixon called several of Falcke's acquaintances, whom he had recommended to her for possible guidance in reorganizing the association. Milton Mitchill and Mitchell Kennerley were summoned. Each seemed to be expecting the summons, and were ready to act immediately. So was the Major, who had decided to make a formal proposal to buy the AAA–AG. Of course, he couldn't do it alone, since he did not have enough money. He convinced a trembling O. B. to assist him; also, Arthur Swann, their chief bookman, and Edward W. Keyes, who at that time was the association's comptroller.

On October 5, 1937, they offered Mrs. Bishop and Miss Nixon $150,000 for their stock in the association and requested the executrices of Mr. Bishop's estate to accept or reject this offer in writing on or before October 15, 1937.

Before the ten days were up Edith Nixon told the Major about O. B.'s letters to Falcke. She firmly stated to Parke that she and Mrs. Bishop would have nothing more to do with him so long as he continued in association with Bernet. Parke refused to betray his vice president, and that was that.

Soon after, the Major heard a rumor, a true one, that Milton Mitchill, a voluntary bankrupt in May 1933, had somehow rebounded into affluence and made a sizable offer to the ladies for controlling shares in the association. Obviously he still coveted the presidency (he had lost it in February 1933) of Mr. Bishop's merged companies.

The ladies refused Mitchill's offer too. They were delighted with his interest in the association, even offered him a job as an advisor on the board of directors, but they did not "feel right" about selling so much of Mr. Bishop's precious stock at that moment. Mitchill took this rejection rather badly. Not only his business activities but also his personal life seemed to take a tragic turn. Shortly after his offer was rejected, his wife died. This blow caused him unassuageable grief. Alone and unoccupied, he allowed himself again to drift into financial straits. Two years later, on November 28, 1939, he shot and killed himself in the bathroom of his apartment at the Peter Cooper Hotel.

Mrs. Bishop and Miss Nixon, during their first few meetings with Mitchell Kennerley, had taken a great liking to him. He had, they felt, the pioneering spirit that was, then as in the past, typical of and

Mitchell Kennerley, littérateur, head of The Anderson Galleries and of the AAA–AG.

essential to a successful American businessman. Also, he was undoubtedly intelligent, and thus clearly capable of quickly refining the
wilderness of the association's business affairs into a rationally ordered
topiary garden. And—perhaps most important—he was charming, in a
way that reminded Mrs. Bishop of her husband.

When the Major heard of the plan to reorganize the AAA–AG and
make Mitchell Kennerley president, he and O. B. sent through their
lawyers a rather subtle and distinctly long-winded ultimatum: either
they accept and respect Parke as president and desist in the nonsense
of reorganizing the association or he and O. B. would find themselves
other jobs.

"We have been given to understand by our clients that an effort
may be made to induce you to vote the majority stock of the company
for the purpose of adding to the Board Mr. Mitchell Kennerley, and
possibly certain other persons friendly to him," the letter began.

We are advised by our clients [it went on] that Mr. Kennerley at the present time owes the American Art Association–Anderson Galleries, Incorporated, a sum in the neighborhood of $70,000; that a suit was brought against him for the recovery of the amount of the indebtedness and that Mr. Kennerley is at the present time in default under that suit, having interposed no defense thereto. . . .

We suggest from the information given to us by our clients and detailed above, this would not be the time to jeopardize the business by any action which would restore to power in the corporation a management which, to say the least, produced disastrous results in the past, or to inaugurate any change in policy or executive control.

We must advise you that rumors of impending change have been circulating and the business of the Company is threatened with injury because of them. We do believe that in the interest of the corporation, these rumors should be settled and that if you agreed with the position taken by our clients, prompt information should be given to the employees and other persons interested in the corporation, that no change is contemplated, otherwise there is danger of important sales being lost.

The ladies were indifferent to the evidence. Nothing could sway their faith in Mitchell Kennerley, who happened to be the dear friend of their dearest friend in London. Edith Nixon abruptly called a meeting of the directors of the AAA–AG on Friday, November 12, 1937.

Major Parke realized that he had become the women's foe. He came into the conference room with Otto Bernet hiding in his shadow. He had decided that he would not compromise his position. His opportunity to extricate himself had come. He would not share the management or give up his presidency to Mitchell Kennerley.

After hearing the ladies' proposals, which were as odious to him as ever, he said in a contemptuous tone, "I will leave. And if I do, I will take your business with me."

The ladies, sitting in tight-lipped conclave with their advisors and counteradvisors, were adamant. By the end of the afternoon, on a day Parke later wryly called his personal Black Friday, the illustrious auctioneer had quit his job. Bowing with the lofty elegance that had served him so long and well in the rostrum, he left his erstwhile employers to their own headstrong devices.

He tarried only long enough to collect Otto Bernet—"You're a stone around my neck, but you're coming"—and to gather around him some forty key employees who, rallying to him in the crisis, chose for better or for worse to desert the ladies too. Then, with hardly a sentimental nod to the world-famous galleries that under his banner had housed the most renowned events in the history of American auctions, Major Parke stalked out into the cold November streets.

It was perhaps the most dramatic act of Major Parke's career, for he was, outwardly at least, a mild-mannered man, gracious and untemperamental, given to any kind of compromise that would not injure his position. The seemingly mystical intuition that in the rostrum told him just how far to go, and when the limit had been reached, served him as well in coming to terms with hundreds of art traders, hard-boiled moguls, and poker-faced bankers. Backed by the Bishop millions, he had gone on treasure-hunting expeditions in England, France, and Italy, and through all the great cities of America; usually he had come back laden with spoils. But Parke had no money of his own, and now, suddenly he was responsible not only for his own fate but for O. B.'s and for the livelihood of some forty workers.

"He was like Moses leading us through the wilderness," Leslie Hyam said years later. Parke was then sixty-four, and with his white hair, looked aristocratic, if not precisely patriarchal. If he did not literally stride along 57th Street with a motley crew of art experts and bid callers at the coattails of his immaculate Chesterfield, he did at least move moderately briskly, leading a group inspired to follow in sheer blind faith. For Parke had no promised land to head for, no shelter, even for the night. What he did have was the respect of about ten thousand bankers, dealers, and collectors throughout the country. This, plus an incomparable talent for conducting auction sales.

The children of the auctions did not wander long however. Mitchell Samuels, proprietor of French and Company, who had in the past bought carloads of rugs and tapestries in sales conducted by the Major, offered him neighborly shelter in French and Company's annex a few blocks down the street. There, among the gilded cornices and the mascarons, Parke and his band stopped to catch their breath and pool resources. Many of the forty displaced employees cooled their heels in throne chairs while, on Renaissance credenzas, secretaries sorted the papers they had grabbed in flight, and typists perched on sacristy benches pecked away at borrowed machines on Tuscan writing tables. From a Sienese sarcophagus Mary Vandegrift issued an evasive story for the press. And before the night was over, Parke's reputation, it was discovered, had not been built for nothing. A few emergency telephone calls made by him and the staff who huddled with him in Mitchell Samuels' smoke-filled office, and the art-selling world rallied magnificently to the rebels' support. Overnight enough money was borrowed to form a corporation. Duveen chipped in magnanimously, without tangible security, and so did jeweler Harry Winston; Otto Bernet and others on the staff contributed life savings, mortgaged insurance policies, borrowed from wives, mistresses, and brothers-in-law. By the next day, Saturday, November 13, 1937, the Parke-Bernet Galleries came into existence, homeless and meagerly endowed, but with due formality and a strong outlook for success.

Less than two months later the new galleries were able to announce their first sale, for while vice presidents and cataloguers were sitting among the lecterns and prie-dieus, wondering how long their salaries could be paid, Jay F. Carlisle, a prominent Wall Street millionaire, had had the grace to die, and his executors had been persuaded to launch the new firm with the sale of the multitudinous Carlisle possessions. Nothing could have been more felicitous, for in the eccentric world of élite auctions the provenience of the objects to be sold is fully as important as the intrinsic value of the things themselves. A rose to wealthy auction-goers is not a simple rose. Whose rose was it? is the question. In this case, the answer was ideal.

Jay F. Carlisle had had many friends, belonged to many clubs. He was a horse man, a dog man, president of the Labrador Retriever Club, and president of the Palm Beach Golf Club too. His pallbearers included Walter P. Chrysler, Jr., and other notables. His genial life had been spent accepting ribbons and trophies and loving cups. His wife, who had died the March before, was Mary Pinkerton, daughter of the famous sleuth. And best of all, Rosemary, the Carlisle mansion at East Islip, Long Island, had been visited by hundreds of potential clients of the auction sales. The furnishings at Rosemary—the snuffboxes and ivory miniatures, the sporting prints and tinkling wineglasses—had an aura all their own, which enhanced their cold commercial value. It was clear that Providence had dispatched the Carlisles for Parke's convenience, and just in the nick of time.

"We were called upon to do something extraordinary," Leslie Hyam said afterward. And something extraordinary they did. Hyam went out to Islip with three teams of cataloguers. Stenographers worked in double shifts, driven by the exigencies of the cause. Photographers took pictures by day and developed them by night, for the house was jammed with small objects—rare Staffordshire, the bronze cowboys of Frederic Remington, a singing bird fashioned out of silver. The mere numbering and sorting were prodigious labors, for there were, when all was counted, four thousand items. And yet, somehow, the entire catalogue was turned out in a week, and without an error.

Meanwhile Parke had acquired almost as a gift, through old business associates, a temporary lease on four floors of a vacant building on the northeast corner of 57th Street at Fifth Avenue, an elegant retail store built for the Dobbs Hat Company and vacated by them in the dark days of 1932.

In his foreword to the Carlisle catalogue, the first of thousands Parke-Bernet has since issued, Leslie Hyam wrote, in an understandably romantic mood, "The pleasant house at Islip and the Carlisle collections are set before you in this book . . . where we greet you as old friends. . . . We can make the porcelain tulips grow for you again, as they were growing in the Queen Anne secretary . . . but you must visualize for yourself the rest."

Nine thousand people came to visualize, and many returned to buy. At the first day's sale society shoppers mingled with reporters, veteran auction hounds, and art-world notables, drawn by the sense of participating in a daring adventure. The four hundred seats were filled in an hour in advance, and hundreds of curious observers stood up. There were flowers and applause, and there was a speech by Gustavus Kirby, son of the AAA's founder. Major Parke, as he approached the rostrum, received an ovation appropriate to a conquering hero. After modestly acknowledging the tribute, he got down to what he said was "the real business of the day"—the sale of Mr. Carlisle's effects.

Gustavus Kirby and Mrs. Leon Schinasi disputed for the honor of buying four nondescript highball glasses worth perhaps $25. Kirby paid $225, and thereupon made another little speech, about the sentiment motivating his extravagance. The launching of a battleship could not have been more gala. The Carlisle heirs profited splendidly from the brilliance of the occasion, and it was amply clear to everyone that Parke-Bernet was in business to stay.

Hiram Parke, in his later days, at the rostrum. To Parke's extreme right is Anthony Bade, an auctioneer. To his immediate left is Louis J. Marion, who later became chief auctioneer.

Riding high on the tide of the Carlisle sale, Parke and Bernet booked sales for a formidable list of consignors. By the next winter barely the crumbs of the feast were left for their former employers.

After Parke's exodus, Mitchell Kennerley became president of the AAA–AG, which, under his direction, began to impress the art world as being an outdated, even reactionary institution. To make things worse, some of Kennerley's oldest friends deserted him, charging him with being incorrigibly dishonest. He tried to defend himself. Hadn't he shaped the literary taste of America by publishing so many new and important young writers? Yes, but hadn't he also given them slim royalties and kept them in poverty? He argued that they had all been poor, and that he had remained poor throughout his publishing career: "I've gained neither riches nor widespread fame." His friends, however, remained disdainful. And Kennerley was strangely sensitive to their disdain.

He began his precarious term as the AAA–AG's president by offering the library of the late Parke E. Simmons of Evanston, Illinois, on November 18 and 19. Romantic and Victorian editions interested a group of buyers of such temperate predilections that the evenings were completely uneventful. Prices were low. However, the total realized from the 608 items, $20,017, was not insignificant and convinced the stockholders that the AAA–AG was on the road to rehabilitation.

Kennerley's second sale, held on November 27, was of prints from a number of rather unimportant collections. It brought in $26,205, a sum that pleased the ladies immensely. "We want no great vacillations," Edith Nixon said, "only steady increases."

Kennerley shrugged, knowing the totals at Parke-Bernet sales would be infinitely greater, and would increase steadily. To compete, the AAA–AG needed sales ringing up the hundreds of thousands. Thus Kennerley hurried to begin the Bishop library sales, which would not, however much Kennerley wanted it, be rushed.

Preparations for the sales would not have been completed until 1939 had not Kennerley threatened physical violence to his sluggish employees. When he wasn't railing at anyone, however, he was gloomy and acutely self-deprecatory. As soon as the "Bishop ghosts"—his phrase for the manuscripts and books—ceased to inhabit the AAA–AG, he planned to excuse himself from the presidency and leave.

Though the arrangements, particularly the impressive flower displays, for the sessions of the sale were spectacular, Kennerley would not give himself credit as production designer. Rather, he said, he was "mortician and chief mourner." As the crowds gathered on the afternoon of April 15, 1938, he hid. Miss Nixon and Mrs. Bishop asked the ushers where he was, and getting no answer, wandered around the galleries in search of him.

Finally he appeared, disheveled, and wearing an old shirt open at the neck and a pair of trousers that was much too large. The ladies were perplexed. He suggested they be seated, but they insisted that he sit with them. He refused, but said that perhaps he would join them later. He had so many little matters to attend to, and of course, he must dress.

They finally, and reluctantly, took seats. The noise in the hall ceased immediately. A few moments later Kennerley heard Anthony Bade's voice eulogizing Mr. Bishop and his collection.

Kennerley motioned for an attendant, whom he asked if Gabriel Wells and Dr. Rosenbach were safe. The guard looked puzzled, but answered that they were in the hall and seemed to be in good health and temperament. Kennerley relaxed momentarily. He had had Gabriel Wells and Dr. Rosenbach insured by Lloyd's of London for $100,000 each for the duration of the first two parts of the sale. Now that they were there and healthy, he only hoped their purchases would equal the amount of the insurance.

He went to his office for a moment to renew his strength, unable at the time to face either the success or failure of the sale. No matter what the outcome, he felt that the demise of the association was inevitable.

Upstairs the fight was on for the acquisition of one of Bishop's most prized possessions, *The Blickling Homilies*. It was a brief fight, ending with Dr. Rosenbach's purchase of the Anglo-Saxon manuscript for $38,000, or $17,000 less than Bishop had paid for it in 1932. The audience was disappointed, and when Kennerley entered the hall, no one noticed him.

The prices did not improve. The firm of Charles Sessler of Philadelphia paid $20,250 for an important illuminated manuscript, St. Augustine's *City of God*, that had cost Mr. Bishop $31,500 in 1932. The loss was considerable, enough to make Kennerley slouch in his chair, while Mrs. Bishop, who had been fidgeting with a pearl brooch, stuck herself with the pin and squealed in audible consternation. When Dr. R. later paid just $12,000 for a Bible published in Mainz in 1462, he then turned toward her and smiled. She smiled back, weakly, and Miss Nixon nodded. Kennerley slouched even lower in his chair.

For Kennerley it seemed that the romance of book collecting had come to an end. He no longer metaphorically referred to dust particles that collected on books as golden motes of knowledge and history. There was no thrill in the auction hall for him. Books were bought simply to supply the missing editions in collections that were destined for the shelves of bureaucratic institutions. Two great collectors were at the Bishop sale. Yes, but old and tired. A great many dealers were there also, but very subdued and reserved.

Kennerley did not lift an eyebrow when a copy of William Blake's *Songs of Innocence and Experience,* printed and illuminated by Blake himself, went for a mere $5,400. As the afternoon session of the sale ended, he rose to leave without speaking to the Bishop ladies, who seemed to have grown more anxious about his health, and more puzzled by his bad humor, as the sale had progressed.

When they returned for the evening sale, they found him completely changed. He was lively, and conversing convivially with early arrivals. He wore a gardenia in the lapel of his tuxedo. When he saw them, he excused himself from the group surrounding him, came to greet them, and escorted them to their seats. But he did not sit with them. Instead, he remained standing, close to the entrance of the salesroom.

The bidding was no more animated than it had been in the afternoon. Yet Kennerley seemed intensely pleased, even when the sale ended and he was told that $139,135 was the total for the day.

Three hundred thousand a day was the least he was willing to accept, but he smiled—and under his breath, cursed the numbers. Everyone else, including Bade, the Bishop ladies, even the press, thought the day a tremendous success. Kennerley laughed bitterly.

On the second day, bidding was as restrained as on the first. Dr. R. paid only $3,400 for a 1786 copy of Robert Burns's *Poems,* then bowed to Gabriel Wells as a sign that he would allow his esteemed fellow dealer and collector to purchase without further competition from him. Rosenbach had already spent over $75,000; his friend, less than $30,000. Wells immediately bought four more volumes, all at bargain prices. After the sale, Kennerley headed for Bade, to tell him that if he didn't push the bids higher, he would soon be selling magazine subscriptions.

Bade answered deferentially, saying that he was tired and would be willing to discuss the development of the sale in the morning.

"Ten o'clock in my office!" Kennerley barked.

Bade nodded.

The next morning, however, he did not appear at ten or at eleven, by which time Kennerley was beside himself. After frantically phoning everyone he knew to be even remotely acquainted with his chief auctioneer, he left his office and started through the galleries, screaming, "Bade! Bade! Where is that——" Employees and visitors—one of whom Kennerley knocked into, treated to a sarcastic bow, then left—were agape.

Finally, Bade rushed in at the main entrance, and somewhat out of breath, told Kennerley, "I breakfasted with Dr. Rosenbach . . . and he went on and on about . . . Bishop's magnificent library."

Kennerley started to accuse him of double-crossing him, of being in cahoots with Rosenbach and letting the books fall to him for minimal bids, but as Kennerley started to speak, he choked. There were tears in his eyes. Bade jumped to compassion. "What's wrong?" "You're not . . . you're not deceiving me, are you?" Kennerley cried.

"I don't understand. Deceiving you about what? Please tell me." Anthony Bade took his employer's trembling arm and led him to his office, all the while telling him in a consoling and reassuring tone about his meeting with Dr. R.

In the office, Kennerley revealed his fears and his desire to leave the association—"before it collapses"—to a sympathetic Bade, who said he understood Kennerley's worries but thought they were a bit exaggerated. Kennerley grew calmer.

A few hours later, as if nothing had occurred, when Kennerley entered the auction hall, he seemed indifferent. As the sale progressed, nothing perturbed him. When the first illustrated edition of Dante's *Divine Comedy*, with nineteen plates attributed to Sandro Botticelli, came to the block, he remained impassive. Bidding began at $3,000; there were $1,000 advances, then long pauses. Twice Bade slowly said, "Last call"—once at $9,250, and again at $11,250. He looked to Kennerley for strength, but Kennerley was staring at his hands.

Finally, after Dr. R.'s $13,500 bid, and an extensive silence in which the audience sat motionless, Bade angrily slammed the hammer to announce, "Sold!" and then, startlingly, closed the session.

That evening Dr. R. paid $500 more for an important French illuminated manuscript on vellum, Jean Froissart's *Chronicles, 1326 to 1385*. At the sale's end, Kennerley left without a word to anyone. When he did not return to the galleries for a week, Bade was alarmed. He had phoned Kennerley after his first two days' absence, but there was no answer. On the third day, he had reached him and told him that the total for the sale was a happy $325,932. Kennerley had replied, "I'm sleepy."

Kennerley reappeared the following week, seemingly well, and seemingly eager to begin the second part of the Bishop library sale. Again he called for flowers; again his humor and charm abounded. But Bade looked deeper; he saw that Kennerley was troubled.

When the Pembroke *Hours* brought only $14,250 (from Gabriel Wells), Kennerley seemed gleeful. And when the results for the second part of the sale—a mere $209,287—were announced, he seemed unable to contain his delight. There were reasons for his joy: relief that the sale was over, and that in the period between its first and second parts an offer had been made by Milton B. Logan, then secretary-treasurer of the association, to take the burden of the business off Kennerley and the ladies by buying it. At his first bid of $185,000 for controlling stock in the AAA–AG, Kennerley accepted for both himself and the two women, not realizing that Logan lacked both the finances and the ability necessary to assume control of the galleries. But for the time being, Logan's proposal seemed reasonable and reassuring to Kennerley, in light of his own determination to leave the association and, hopefully, to leave it in good hands. Though Kennerley rejoiced at the close of the sale and at the possibility of leaving his position, Bade did not trust this emotional show. Evident in Kennerley's desperate attempt to make everyone happy and to put his affairs in proper order were traces of misery.

After one last auction, of Mr. Bishop's stamp collection early in May, Kennerley resigned, and Bade, who stayed with the AAA–AG until its 1939 demise and then, two years later, joined the newly formed galleries of Herbert A. Kende (another ex-employee of the AAA–AG) at Gimbel's department store, lost touch with him. He often asked mutual friends about him, but got no answers. No one knew exactly where Kennerley was; everyone seemed mystified by his erratic behavior.

Miss Nixon and Mrs. Bishop returned to London in June 1938. They were to visit with Shirley Falcke, then to continue to Paris and fetch the rest of Bishop's books to New York. The ladies had no idea what they would do with the library then—perhaps sell it at the AAA–AG.

When they met Falcke he suggested they let him sell the books. He said that Kennerley had told him the association could not survive under any management; therefore it was senseless to risk losing money on the French library. "But," said Mrs. Bishop, "there are two more parts to sell of the American library. Do you think we should cancel the sales?" Falcke said no; she need not worry, since Mr. Bishop's books would bring high prices anywhere.

Her worries immediately multiplied. She had just paid out a great deal of money, $515,000, to Beatrice and was afraid for every remaining penny. "I've never had to think in terms of three little zeroes. It is horrible to be forced to such extremes."

Miss Nixon, however, was not so frightened. She had great faith in Falcke and helped him strengthen the tearful Mrs. Bishop, who finally agreed to take his advice and finish the American library sales at the AAA–AG, then sell the Paris books under his auspices.

The trio left for Paris together, Falcke and Edith reassuring Mrs. Bishop at every turn of their passage. Falcke was no longer worried about his reputation, and since he and his wife were divorced, he was completely free to leave London. Edith and Shirley Falcke drew closer together. "My children," Mrs. Bishop said softly, "I have had to search in order to find my children."

They promised always to care for her, never to leave her. And by the time they returned to New York with the Paris library, Edith Nixon had married Shirley Falcke.

The marriage caused some scandal, and a great deal of amusement, especially among the staff of Parke-Bernet. Yet, it appeared that the couple—or rather, threesome—was idyllically happy.

They got to New York just before the auctioning of the final part of the American library in January 1939. The ladies were alarmed that the third part of the sale, conducted in their absence, had brought only $81,377, and when the fourth part brought a total of only $10,874, they were panic stricken. Falcke did not know what to say to them, and in the end, decided it was best to say nothing except that— he swore it most eloquently—the Paris library sale would soon put Mrs. Bishop in golden slippers again.

Mrs. Bishop laughed. "You treat me as if I were a fairy princess," she said. "It's adorable of you, but I know what 'in the red' means."

Falcke argued that her idea of poverty was absurd, then hurried to organize a sale for the Paris library. But it was almost ten years before the sale took place. He excused himself indefinitely with, "Bishop's

American Library flooded the market with too many rarities. We must wait until there is a really good demand." Meanwhile he was using his wife's cash to tempt Herbert A. Kende out of Gimbel's department store into a partnership with him. In 1948 he succeeded, and became president of the Kende Galleries, which relocated at 119 West 57th Street.

By this time Kende had lost Anthony Bade, his chief auctioneer. Without Bade's dynamic force in the rostrum, the sale of Bishop's French library, on December 7, 1948, brought such prices as $24,000 for a 1501 copy of Aesop's *Fables* and $20,250 for a 1734 copy of Molière's works with five Boucher drawings. Seymour di Ricci, a widely known French bibliophile, had said that the library was worth in the neighborhood of $1 million. The sale realized only $325,900.

Falcke excused himself from blame for this total by telling Mrs. Bishop of his futile attempts to get Bade, who had left Kende to take the rostrum at Parke-Bernet, to auction the library.

Falcke had tried to lure Bade back to Kende's by using Mitchell Kennerley as bait. A search was made for the fallen Kennerley. When found, he was offered a job.

"I only take presidencies," he said, "and not even those . . . now."

Nonetheless, Kende told Bade that Kennerley was in his employ. Bade seemed momentarily interested and agreed to Kende's invitation to "Come on down and look at the books."

When he arrived, Kende ushered him straight into the back office. There sat Mr. and Mrs. Falcke, who tried to convince him that since he had already auctioned the American library, it was his duty to auction the Paris library too. Bade said that it was no great defeat for him not to auction all of Bishop's books. "I'm immensely attracted to the books . . . but I do not find them so attractive that I can disregard the moral character of—"

Here Falcke interrupted saying Bade was rude, and Bade, who could not abide Shirley Falcke, stood to leave, saying first that he would conduct the sale for $1,000 a day.

Falcke motioned to Kende.

"All right," Kende said, "we'll pay you that."

"Not at any price," Bade said conclusively as he walked toward the door. But before leaving he asked to see Mitchell Kennerley.

"He's left the galleries," Falcke said apathetically.

"Might I infer, before you hired him?'"

Their eyes met, and Falcke rose in complete calm. He almost laughed as he said, "Thank you, Mr. Bade, for coming. I hope to see you at the sale."

Bade did not return.

On the afternoon of February 22, 1950, Mitchell Kennerley's body was found in his apartment, where he had hanged himself.

That afternoon Bade learned from his answering service that Kennerley had called him the evening before. Later he learned from friends that Kennerley had also called Shirley Falcke, to whom he had reported the news that he had inherited $50,000, from someone in the South. Wasn't it wonderful? All his problems were solved!

After this announcement there was a long, painful pause. All he needed—there was another long pause—all he needed was $500 to claim the inheritance and to tide him over. Falcke answered that he was short of cash, but any bank would lend Kennerley the money if only he showed the will. Kennerley said he hadn't thought of that. How simple! Hurriedly he said goodbye.

After Kennerley killed himself, Falcke—to the chagrin of Bade, who was terribly upset by the death—said in a public statement that the suicide was simply the culmination of an institutional tragedy. Yet perhaps, despite Bade's protestations to the contrary, Falcke was right. If so, then the lead in the tragedy's penultimate act was played by Milton B. Logan, formerly of Brooklyn, to whom the AAA–AG had been sold in 1938.

Born in 1891, Milton Logan was undersized and owlish-looking, prey to his childhood fellows' pranks. After graduating from high school, he ventured for the first time to Manhattan, where he took a job as night clerk in a hotel. Soon he left this job and returned to Brooklyn to manage a lunch wagon. Later he worked in one of the cafeterias owned by the New York Telephone Company. And soon he managed them all. Possibly because of ensuing corpulence, and a realization that the mixing bowl could not alchemize flour to gold, he left restaurant management to tackle real estate, taking a job with the firm that handled Mr. Bishop's vast account. Bishop was at the time investing in all sorts of absurd plots of land. When he and Logan met, Logan was superintendent of the 57th Street building that housed the AAA–AG. Bishop found him amusing, and in a matter of weeks, made him his private secretary.

Due to Logan's awe of his benefactor, whose endless monologues were, he thought, far more fascinating than the tales of Marco Polo, he worked tremendously hard to please him. He took almost adequate care of Bishop's accounts, and shortly before Bishop died, was made estate manager and also secretary-treasurer of the AAA–AG. After Mr. Bishop's death Miss Nixon could not bear to part with Logan, and Mrs. Bishop concurred, saying he was their only tried and tested friend. In addition to managing the estate, he was given the task of spying for the ladies on the activities of O. B. and the Major. As a manager, he was middling competent; as an informant, vague. He had never particularly disliked either Parke or Bernet, but he fostered the ladies' antagonism to them and did nothing to allay their fears of being betrayed. Mrs. Bishop and Miss Nixon were grateful, and Logan was sufficiently sure of their esteem that after Parke and his followers left the AAA–AG he slipped unobtrusively into O. B.'s vacant office, and despite Kennerley's hostility to him—"You and I conversing? Never!"—set up shop as a vice president.

When he learned that Kennerley was leaving, and that the ladies might sell out, Logan panicked. He was certain to lose his job if the ladies sold. The only way to stay was to buy the galleries and become president himself. He had never dreamed of such a feat; nor did he have the money to accomplish it. Nevertheless, he made the ladies an offer of $185,000, a sum that had suddenly struck him as acceptable. Somewhat to Logan's surprise, it was. And all he needed was $10,000 for a down payment.

Logan did not have $10,000, but an old friend, John T. Geery, with whom he had gone to school—Sunday school too—in Brooklyn, surely did. Geery had his own successful insurance office and wrote policies on works of art for many of the AAA–AG's clients. Logan invited him to lunch, and without any trouble, got him to agree to lend him the down payment.

Soon Logan asked Geery to pay the remaining installments as well. Their partnership led to a fatal case of the blind leading the blind. Supposedly, Geery withdrew his partnership in the Brooklyn Dodgers in order to raise the capital to become a half-owner in the galleries. Together, Logan and Geery formed the Amaranga Company for the purpose of assuming ownership of the galleries; but, in the end, it would be Geery alone who owned the galleries, with Logan as president, left alone to manage them, doing approximately nothing. What little stock in the company Logan did buy he paid for with the two ladies' own money, appropriating it—cleverly, he thought—from the galleries' working capital before the final sales transaction.

Logan was elated, yet faintly fatigued, merely by walking through the deserted galleries. There were layers of dust on the rostrum, and a musty smell, like that in a mausoleum, rose from the velvet. There were few sales. Now and then some etchings would come to the block, and there was a Polish émigré's imported furniture—dark, heavy, completely sedate pieces—sold on two rainy days. On these days, if a buyer feared he was hearing things, perhaps the faint stirrings of Chopin, it was only because Logan had hired a pianist to play "ever so" softly on lot No. 220, a cumbersome ebony piano inlaid with mother-of-pearl, dated 1845, so as to encourage, but not to disturb, the economic meditations of the guests. The only sale that caused any excitement was on April 20, 1939, when Logan brought to the block *The Madonna of the Pinks*, the first Raphael of unquestioned provenience ever offered at public sale in the United States. The master's Madonna was said to be one of his finest works, but it brought only $65,000 from a bidder the press referred to as a "lady in a blue hat." Her name was Mrs. Drury Cooper, and she was remembered not so much for the blue hat as for the brown paper bag in which she stashed her newly procured Raphael.

The painting had been consigned by Baron Felix Lachovski of Paris, who considered the action a careless one when he heard the sale price. He did not receive full payment for his painting, but at first, uncertain about whether or not he was being shortchanged, he kept quiet. Logan was quiet too, leading Geery to think everything was in order at the galleries.

Later that spring, however, Geery began to worry a little—for one thing, he had yet to receive a single dividend on his AAA–AG stock. He decided to have the books examined, and when the auditors' report described Logan's bookkeeping as a "senseless show of figures scattered upon ledgers," he was incredulous, then furious. How could Logan have been so incompetent? Geery examined the report, again and again, and the more he read, the more disheartened he became. Finally he threw the papers aside. He began talking to himself, and writing the notes to himself that the newspapers later referred to as "suicide installments." The first said, "I have been sucked in."

Still finding it hard to believe that the business was so close to collapse, he went to the galleries and examined the books firsthand. "Sick, incurably sick," he then wrote in his journal.

In the files, however, he had noticed the life insurance policies Mitchell Kennerley had taken out on Dr. Rosenbach and Gabriel Wells for the duration of the first two parts of the Bishop American library sale. These gave him an idea—with which he toyed for several days before he called Logan to tell him about a "great plan."

Geery's story was that a friend of his named Gerold Echelmann, who was once a German U-boat captain, later became a code expert for General Chiang Kai-shek, and now and then smuggled a few art treasures out of the mainland of China, had agreed to arrange to ship to the AAA–AG a collection of porcelains worth between $7 and $10 million. Logan was delighted with the thought. Geery told him the shipment would arrive at the end of June or the beginning of July. Logan spoke eagerly of a November sale, and Geery, nodding, suggested that it might be wise to insure Logan's life for the sale's duration. Logan agreed.

On June 19 Geery took out a $100,000 policy on his friend's life with Lloyd's of London. He paid the first premium, for three months—during which nothing fatal happened. July arrived, and passed; there were no porcelains on the way, but for the time being, anyway, Logan was not suspicious. Eventually Geery would have to renew the insurance policy again and again, and would spend more than $4,225 on premiums.

But first, on August 10, 1939, the AAA–AG's licence to auction was suspended because of the complaints of four creditors who charged that their claims against the galleries could not be settled because of the management's irresponsibility. More, the AAA–AG could not pay its rent on the building at 30 East 57th Street and was suddenly without a home. Geery filed a petition for reorganization; however, while it was pending, there was another disaster: on November 4, 1939, Logan was indicted for defrauding more than sixty of the AAA–AG's clients of some $65,000. Among those wronged was Baron Felix Lachovski of Paris, who had received only $20,000 for his Raphael Madonna. He wailed that he had been swindled out of $34,000, since he was supposed to have received $54,000 after the

AAA–AG's commissions. Logan was arrested and two days later Geery was arrested too, as an accomplice to Logan in defrauding the AAA–AG's clients. Their case was to come to trial in March 1940, and bail was set at $5,000 each. Both immediately supplied bond.

Geery had no idea that Logan's misappropriations equaled grand larceny. He feared that his petition to reorganize the association before the spring of 1940 would be rejected. It was. After this there was nothing left for him to do except file a bankruptcy petition, since he could not come up with the missing money and he knew that Logan couldn't either.

During Logan's term as president of the AAA–AG there had been no financial statements. There were no inventory records. The file cabinets had become storage drawers and filled up with rubbish. What little bookkeeping Logan had done indicated he had wrongfully withdrawn $2,847 from the corporation's accounts. In December 1939 the AAA–AG was defunct, and Geery was more than ever determined to take revenge on Logan. "I will not die alone with the AAA–AG," he wrote.

Outside the building that housed Geery's insurance office was a newsstand run by John Poggi, a man of dubious character. Though Geery found the man contemptible, he had confided in him a number of times, and had learned that Poggi had once been arrested for robbery (the case was dismissed in court), and that Poggi's brother, known as "Killer," a notorious East Side gangster in the days of Prohibition, was serving a life sentence in Sing Sing. Geery became more and more intimate with Poggi, who listened more intently when money was offered him. He agreed to help Geery in any way he could.

Soon Geery phoned Logan and told him that he had news of interest to him. Logan was apprehensive—Geery had been acting strangely, he thought—but he agreed to meet Geery at a midtown hotel. When he arrived, exactly on time, Geery told him he had been trying to get him a job, to help him pay his lawyer and court costs for the forthcoming trial. Logan was puzzled. Then Geery said he had already set up an interview with a prospective employer—for that evening—and that a man named Wilson was waiting to drive him to the meeting. Without giving Logan a chance to say anything, Geery then took his arm, propelled him outside and into a car parked at the curb, and left him.

The man behind the wheel was Poggi, who drove for a few minutes, then stopped in front of a drugstore, got out of the car, and said, "Wait. I'll be back."

Logan did not wait, and was walking rapidly away when Poggi returned, caught up with him, and announcing that the interview had been indefinitely postponed, offered to drive him home. Logan refused the offer and took the subway home.

The next morning, Geery phoned Logan and apologized for the inconvenience he had caused him. The mystery surrounding the venture to the proposed interview frightened Logan, but not enough to make him stop seeing Geery, whom he met soon afterward for a legal conference in Geery's office. When it was over, Geery started to walk Logan to the subway, then turned back, saying that he'd left his watch in his office and was going to get it. As he approached the building, he paused near the newsstand and signaled to Poggi. Logan was at the head of the subway steps—he had not looked back.

Poggi rushed quietly at him and gave him a violent shove as he was starting down the iron-edged steps.

Logan screamed as he fell headfirst down the steps. Miraculously he escaped serious injury. He got up quickly, felt for blood on his head but found only bruises, then looked around and up at the subway entrance. There was no one to be seen. Poggi had vanished. Logan picked up his hat and hastened to catch his train.

For the next few days there were no other attacks on Logan, who met Geery several times, in peculiar places—chosen, Geery said, in order that they might elude possible assailants that would be harmful to both of them. Once, when they were in Geery's car, Geery said he'd promised to get a license plate for a friend. Logan shrugged and waited outside a municipal building, but when Geery returned to the car with the plate, he made a note of the number.

On Monday, February 19, 1940, Logan and Geery again met in Geery's office, where they decided they would attempt to get a postponement of their trial. After hours of conferring, they could decide nothing more, and Geery offered Logan a lift home. Logan accepted. Then Geery said that first—it would only take a minute—he wanted to examine a building he was interested in buying. Logan said that was all right; he was in no rush.

When they got outside, Poggi was waiting near the newsstand and immediately started toward them. Logan recognized him. He was apprehensive, but he said nothing.

After introductions, Geery asked Poggi to come along to look at the building. He could use another opinion. Poggi nodded and said, why not go in his car, which was parked right around the corner? Good idea, Geery said, taking Logan's arm.

As they neared the car, Logan noticed the license plate—the same one Geery had picked up a few days before. He said nothing and got into the back seat of the car with Geery. Poggi drove, and when they arrived at the building, braked the car sharply, causing Logan to fall forward.

Geery opened his door; Poggi, his. They got out in unison. Logan returned to a rigidly upright position. They asked him to join them. He said that he would wait in the car. Geery and Poggi slammed their doors without replying and entered the dark building.

Logan waited, growing more and more frightened. Suddenly he saw Geery coming toward the car and supporting a seemingly lifeless figure. Logan sprang from the car and rushed toward Geery, who did not answer his dazed queries. Instead, Geery opened the back door of the car, and with a giant thrust, shoved Poggi in. Poggi fell in an irregular heap. Logan saw that Poggi was still alive. He immediately arranged Poggi in a more comfortable position, then got into the front seat with Geery, who said nothing as he drove the car, staring at the road.

Soon, to Logan's amazement, Geery began to laugh softly. He said, as his laughter gained volume, that Poggi was the one who had been trying to kill them. Logan turned to look at Poggi in consternation. Suddenly Poggi opened his eyes and grinned. Logan gasped, almost shrieked.

Poggi, leaning forward, had pulled an iron pipe from under his coat. Logan cried to Geery to stop the car and defend himself. But the bludgeon was aimed in Logan's direction—at his head.

Poggi hit again and again as the car continued moving at a moderate, well-controlled pace. When the attack was over, Geery dropped the supposedly dead Logan on the highway, then drove back to his own car. He and Poggi parted without speaking.

But Logan was not dead, and though his skull had been fractured, he was not quite unconscious. With great effort, he managed to get to his feet and stagger to the curb. A passing patrol car rushed to him as he fell into the gutter.

Unaware that Logan was still alive and on his way to the hospital, Geery drove to the Waldorf-Astoria, where he was to meet his wife and son to celebrate his twenty-first wedding anniversary with a lavish dinner. As he had planned, he entered the hotel lobby blood smeared and seemingly dazed, and incoherently—but not too incoherently— cried that he and Logan had been atacked.

As a crowd gathered around him, he lurched, with his bewildered wife and son tagging along beside, to a telephone booth. Leaving the door open, he repeated his muddled tale first to his lawyer, Herbert Plaut, then to the police, who advised him to report to the nearest station, which he did not do. Instead, he asked his son to get the car and drive him and his mother home. The boy, Donald, did as he was told.

When the family got home, Geery despondently commented that the house was cold and that he was going to the basement to stoke the furnace. First, however, he went to his room.

His wife and son were silent. Moments later, they heard a shot.

Geery had gone to the basement, put a revolver in his mouth, and pulled the trigger. Beside his body were the "suicide installments," the last of which read: "This is the limit. I have lived in hell since May through someone else's deception. Plaut knows all. Let him take care of yours affairs."

By the next morning Logan had regained consciousness in the hospital. He was hazy about just what had happened, but not about the license plate he had seen on the car. The police traced the number and found that the plate was registered in the name of John Poggi.

Poggi was eventually tried, and sentenced, in October 1940, to ten to twenty years in Sing Sing, the same prison in which his brother was incarcerated.

Logan was tried too, and was convicted, in March 1941, on three counts of first-degree and six counts of second-degree grand larceny— the charges for which he and Geery had been scheduled to stand trial. He escaped the maximum (thirty-year) sentence for his crimes and was placed on probation for ten years. The presiding judge commented, "The jury recommended mercy in this case. Undoubtedly what they had in mind was the fact that this defendant suffered very severe punishment before he came to trial."

Recalling the whole AAA–AG story, Shirley Falcke later suggested that Mitchell Kennerley's suicide might be considered simply a redundant death spasm of the ill-fated organization. The AAA–AG had been so long in dying—in fact, so persistent in dying—that Falcke jokingly pondered, "I wonder who'll be next. Perhaps me."

But Falcke survived. In the early 1950's he resigned from the presidency of Kende Galleries, which was going out of business, and moved with his wife, Edith, and Mrs. Bishop to Lenox, to dwell within the confines of The Winter Palace. Here they hoped finally to retire to a peaceful existence, though even here, they were pestered by perennial litigants pressing claims against the Bishop estate. After years of practice, however, they had found a means of eluding these mercenary menaces—absolute indifference.

For the first time, Mrs. Bishop could chant her memories endlessly and without interruption. "I loved Java. You could reach up and pick the orchids. Wasn't that so, Edith?"

Her memories were confirmed and more important, shared. For Edith always agreed, whether Amy fantasized or recalled accurately. "There were times when we couldn't see our feet for the clouds," Edith said.

Here in the concentrated luxury of The Winter Palace, Falcke contemplated his life and the nobility of his purpose in protecting his archenemy's two heiresses, one of whom was now his wife. He laughed that it was perhaps not such a lofty purpose, since it was definitely tinctured with revenge, not only against Bishop but also against the world in which Bishop had failed, the strange and dirty world of art trading. But perhaps, from this viewpoint, there was no scandal in Falcke's marrying Edith Nixon and watching out for Mrs. Bishop; certainly there was no venality. He actually acquired a degree of moral stature in doing so. If there were those who thought a little less of him than he thought of himself, he did not see them. He said that he had forgotten the bitterness of the past. He took to making repairs on some of the cars that had for so long remained dormant in the garages.

Mrs. Bishop was, again, driven through the countryside at breakneck speed. She would hold her hand out the window to feel the air rushing against it, and say in girlish glee, "Life, life, it's so wonderful."

After some years of peace and comfort in the confines of The Winter Palace, Amy Bend Bishop died on July 20, 1957. A few weeks later, on August 15, 1957, Shirley Falcke, the charming moral enigma of the auction world, followed her in death. Mrs. Falcke was left alone at The Winter Palace among the priceless rugs from the Benguiat collection, some of which had mysteriously reappeared from London, the Italian primitives, a Donatello, and some anonymous bronzes. Perhaps she would travel again, perhaps she would not, but come what may, she retained her memories and her fascination in the rising star of the Parke-Bernet Galleries.

TWELVE

THE VENUS ON
MADISON AVENUE

THE DEMISE OF THE AAA–AG allowed Major Parke to gain a virtual monopoly in the art and rare book auction market in the United States, but not without trouble, and not until near the end of the fickle, quirky nineteen-forties. Throughout, the Major maintained an air of gentlemanly serenity, reassuring to consignors, collectors, and his staff, and perhaps more than a little irritating to would-be competitors, the last of which had bowed to Parke-Bernet's supremacy by 1950, when the Major, having made Parke-Bernet America's one outstanding institution for the auctioning of art, stepped down from the rostrum and went into retirement.

The twenty-two months after November 1937, when the Major and his flock departed the old AAA–AG, were the worst, with the summer of 1939 one of particular gloom and despair. At issue was the raising of what Mary Vandegrift later called "a paltry seventy-five thousand dollars," needed to move Parke-Bernet from its cramped, inadequate four floors at 57th Street and Fifth Avenue into Kirby's spacious Renaissance building at 30 East 57th, just one short block away. The building had been vacated by the AAA–AG and was being offered to Parke-Bernet for lease starting in October, but where was the money to come from? Good friends had all been tapped; insurance policies were already in hock; and the founders' savings accounts had been drawn on to the limit. Then, at the eleventh hour, someone had an idea: since fine illustrated catalogues were an integral part of the auction business as Parke-Bernet conducted it, why not ask the printers, designers, and other graphic arts people who would profit by the galleries' success?

Asked they were. The needed funds were borrowed, and Major Parke, O. B., and the errant faithful were back at the old stand on the corner of 57th Street and Madison Avenue for the fall season in 1939. A few months later, under more prosperous circumstances, the Major paid $12,500 to a referee in bankruptcy and got in return the defunct AAA–AG's name and so-called good will. Since it was debatable how much real good will was left after Logan's and Geery's machinations were exposed in the press and courts, many of the

Hiram H. Parke, in a typical pose (ROY STEVENS PHOTO). From left to right (*below*) are Louis J. Marion, Arthur Swann, Parke, and Leslie A. Hyam (ROY STEVENS PHOTO).

Major's colleagues thought little of his buy. The Major, however, said it was "protection," and he wanted all he could get.

Among his problems were strained relations with O. B., for though the Major especially liked the marriage of his and O. B.'s names—Parke-Bernet—with its succinct connotations of elegance, he did not especially like, and often openly disdained, O. B. himself. "The people's auctioneer," he called him—meaning that he was hopelessly plebeian.

Yet the Major was never one to keep the "people," those human beings without traceable legacy or fortune, from attending sales or visiting exhibitions. A dollar from each, he had to agree, could implement—or even, he whisperingly conceded, "found"—a fortune. Thus, O. B. directed a major portion of Parke-Bernet's advertising campaign toward the middle class. However, though he was almost solely responsible for attracting the people of modest means into the galleries—and hence responsible for a good three fifths of the galleries' profits—he was never given due credit.

Regular press releases prepared by O. B. and Mary Vandegrift tempted buyers of moderate means into the galleries by listing the bargains had during the last season and implying similar bargains would be available in the next. The first of these releases, issued in 1938, proclaimed that "hundreds of articles of relative rarity and genuine aesthetic merit were had for prices ranging from $25 to $100," then went on to cite specific items in specific 1938 sales and to conclude that at Parke-Bernet auctions "held once or twice each month from January to June" the masses might reasonably expect to pick up at least some of the secondhand property of old-guard millionaires for next to nothing.

The masses responded from January to June of 1939, and the next year and the next . . . until 1943, when O. B.'s singular bargain pushing came to an end. Ridden both by ulcers and by the Major, he had decided to appease the first by having less truck with the second. It didn't work. The ulcers got worse; complications ensued; and two years later, on October 13, 1945, Otto Bernet died.

Occasionally during the two years of semiretirement between 1943 and his death, O. B., feeling "up to par," would return to the galleries to conduct afternoon sales of unimportant merchandise—"barnyard rallies," he called them—attended by flocks of middle-class folk who secretively nibbled sandwiches in lunch hours rescheduled to coincide with the time of the sale. After O. B.'s death, these sales were fewer and less exciting, and Parke-Bernet lost the common touch. O. B.'s huffing and puffing was gone, and with it, the easy familiarity that had obtained between officials and staff at 30 East 57th Street. There were no more polished red apples brought to lovely secretaries, no more earthy anecdotes that took a day to dramatize and tell. Suddenly the atmosphere at Parke-Bernet took on a kind of chilled impeccability, and if the middle-class public came at all, it came primarily out of curiosity, or self-consciously, for purposes of "cultivation"—but not to buy.

A month after O. B.'s death, the great book collectors began to go. Jerome Kern, who died November 11, 1945, was first; then Gabriel Wells (November 6, 1946) and Belle da Costa Greene (May 10, 1950). Dr. Rosenbach, perhaps the greatest bookman of them all, died on July 1, 1952.

The Major, never known as an auctioneer of books, responded rather apathetically. He disliked the dust, and the study of calligraphy, illumination techniques, and bindings fatigued him. Never did he have faith that his experts could absorb all this knowledge well enough to classify with any accuracy a book of dubious origins. And the Major demanded absolute accuracy—it was part of his "honesty vow."

Arthur Swann, the galleries' book expert, was growing old and would retire in the 1950's. True, the wayward Anthony Bade had joined Parke-Bernet in November 1944, but Bade could not fill Swann's place as book cataloguer and auction the books too. When he tried, he said he was "drowning in the alphabet." The only way for him to manage was to keep everything to a minimum, which is just what he did, though he regretted having to do it, until he himself retired in 1962. Long before that, in 1947, he did conduct one great literary sale, and obtain at Parke-Bernet the highest price ever paid for an American edition.

The Whole Booke of Psalmes Faithfully Translated into English Metre, otherwise called the Bay Psalm Book, is revered as the first book printed in the Anglo-American colonies, but not as a thing of beauty. It is small, sloppy in its typography, and replete with errors, which the printer quaintly suggests "you may amende as you finde them obvious"; its text, the combined poetic effort of an indeterminate number of Puritan divines, though conceivably faithful to the sentiments of King David, could scarcely be recommended for displaying metrical skill or lyric charm. Nonetheless, the psalter is the oldest printed relic of America's cultural baby steps, and as such, a choice morsel to collectors of literary Americana.

Seventeen hundred copies of the Psalms "newly turned into Metre"—enough presumably to supply those of the Bay Colony's faithful who had thirty-five cents to spare—were printed by Stephen Daye and his son, Matthew, at Cambridge in 1640. By the time the Puritans had left off singing the execrably rendered verses and the bibliophiles had taken over, eleven known copies were left. The one called the Crowninshield-Stevens-Brinley-Vanderbilt-Whitney copy found its way to the Parke-Bernet 307 years after its printing—and was cause for wonder and rejoicing in the otherwise moribund bibliophilic world.

According to the research of Zoltán Haraszti, keeper of rare books at the Boston Public Library, the first owner listed in this old book's hyphenated pedigree, Edward A. Crowninshield, a mid-nineteenth-century Bostonian respected for his scholarship, sagacity, and other laudable attributes, came by his rarest of literary bibelots in a very shady manner. In fact, he all but stole it.

In the early eighteenth century, the Reverend Thomas Prince, pastor of Boston's Old South Church and a book collector of no mean prescience, thoughtfully stashed away in the library of the parsonage five copies of the Bay Psalm Book. The pastor died in 1758, leaving his now priceless collection of early American literature to the church, with the stern admonition that it be forever kept intact. Ninety-two years later, in 1850, while the Prince collection, or part of it, was still gathering dust in the parsonage (it is now snugly entombed in the Boston Public Library), the unequivocal terms of the old pastor's will weighed lightly, if at all, on the conscience of Samuel T. Armstrong, a deacon of the church who was persuaded—no one knows how—by Edward Crowninshield, to relinquish one copy of the Bay Psalm Book in return for a new binding for one of the other four copies. Robert Wallace, who told in *Life* magazine (November 11, 1954) the details of this and two other slick transactions whereby the Prince library was swindled out of three fifths of its eternal cache of historic psalters, estimated that the cost of the Crowninshield binding—it was imitation leather—could not have been more than $1.

Crowninshield died nine years after his clever transaction with the deacon, and his "Valuable Private Library" was sold intact to Henry Stevens, a London bookdealer, for $10,000. Stevens took the Bay Psalm Book to London, and failing to dispose of it there, had it rebound in dark brown crushed Levant morocco and sold it, in 1868, to George Brinley of Hartford, Connecticut, for about $750. In 1879 it was bought at auction for Cornelius Vanderbilt, for $1,200. It then knocked about Vanderbilt premises for the next sixty-eight years.

Cornelius Vanderbilt's daughter Gertrude, Mrs. Harry Payne Whitney, inherited the book, and when she died, in 1942, it became an asset of a charitable and educational trust set up under her will. In 1946 the trustees, Mrs. Whitney's two daughters and her son, Cornelius Vanderbilt Whitney, pledged $94,200 from the trust for a new obstetrical unit at the Community Hospital of Glen Cove, Long Island. They put the Bay Psalm Book up for auction with the announcement to the public that the proceeds would be given to the hospital as part of the grant.

Part indeed! The shabby little psalter had in it the power to provide golden forceps and swansdown couches for the prospective mothers of Glen Cove.

No copy of the Bay Psalm Book had come into the public market since 1879, when Cornelius Vanderbilt had acquired this one. Speculation ran high as to what it would bring in 1947. Chief among the contestants was the great Dr. A. S. W. Rosenbach, the legend of whose invincibility in the auction hall was world-wide: how familiar, for three decades, on two continents—and how disconcerting to his rivals—had been the refrain, accompanied by a brisk click of the ivory hammer, "Sold—to Dr. R.!" To be sure, the Napoleon of Books, alias the Terror of the Auction Rooms, or Rosy, or Dr. R., already owned one of the eleven extant copies of the Bay Psalm Book. (The best of the three from the Reverend Prince's hoard was in the John Carter Brown Library, Providence, Rhode Island; one—with a number of leaves missing—belonged to Mr. Adrian Van Sinderin of Brooklyn; the Prince collection still had two of its original five; Harvard had one; one belonged to the American Antiquarian Society; and the New York Public Library, the Huntington Library of San Marino, California, and the Bodleian Library at Oxford each had one.) But this, the last complete copy from the Prince collection of the Bay Psalm Book ever likely to be put up for sale, was too seductive for the seventy-one-year-old bibliophile to ignore. He had a niche picked out for it. Harvard had one, why not Yale? Prior to the sale he convinced some of the university's high-tax-bracket graduates that their alma mater could but languish among the poor in spirit without a copy of the quaint psalter. A collection was taken up, and by the night of the auction, the friends of Yale had authorized Dr. R. to bid up to about $86,000. (The exact sum the Yale boys were prepared to pay was, of course, known only to Dr. R.)

When it was rumored that not only Dr. R. but also his opposition would be well heeled, a winner-take-all pool was formed by Parke-Bernet experts and some rare-book dealers, who gazed into their crystal balls and placed token bets on what the book would bring. The lowest prediction was $50,000; the highest was $101,000, which even the more sanguine augurs thought a wild shot in the dark.

Two hundred people showed up for the sale on a cold night in January 1947. Sightseers and bibliophiles came in evening dress to pay homage to the most coveted literary treasure to be auctioned in twenty-one years. Not since the night in February 1926 when a Gutenberg Bible had fallen—to Dr. R.—at $106,000 had there been such a glamorous event in rare-book circles.

Dr. R. did not appear in person, but he sent his right-hand man, John Fleming, who sat hunched in the front row and looked, if anything, barely interested in the proceedings about to commence.

Cornelius Vanderbilt Whitney—known to the press as Sonny—and his two sisters and cotrustees, Flora W. Miller and Barbara W. Henry, were accompanied by Major Parke, to whom Sonny Whitney had just revealed his intention of competing for the book himself. He had asked the Major to sit with him and signal his bids to the rostrum. The Major didn't know why Whitney wanted the book. Was he moved by twinges of latent sentiment at the thought of parting with so venerable an heirloom? Or, aware that Dr. R. intended Yale to have the book, did Whitney, a Yale man himself, wish to deprive his alma mater of its prize? Or was it that the famed horsebreeder-capitalist's sporting blood was aroused? Perhaps he merely wished to boost the price and give the Terror of the Auction Rooms a run for his money. In any case, should the historic psalter fall to him, Whitney said, he would first lend it for exhibition to educational and religious institutions and then give it to one of them.

With the forces thus arrayed, "the hot prayer book" as *Life* later called it was placed in halo lights before the congregation. In the rostrum, Anthony Bade looked like a trim, sensitive-featured curate about to read an inspiring passage. In a deep baritone made deeper by the import of the occasion, he opened the bidding at $30,000.

The more impressionable onlookers gasped at the boldness of the start, and above their whispers and murmured comment, the sale got under way. Except for some gratuitous offers by the thin-pursed, the initial contest turned out to be a duel between Dr. R.'s man, Fleming, and David A. Randall of Scribner's. Randall, it subsequently turned out, had been commissioned to "angle" for the book on behalf of J. K. Lilly, the Indianapolis drug manufacturer, for the magnificent library he later gave to Indiana University.

In measured pace, $1,000 at a time, the price advanced to $55,000. Then, suddenly, the spectators stiffened to attention. From the rear of the hall, where Sonny Whitney sat, came a $5,000 jump.

Fleming and Randall proceeded with their $1,000 raises, unperturbed. A strategic bold advance will sometimes drive the timid or parsimonious to cover, but these bidders remained nonchalant. The crowd, however, sat now in almost breathless expectation of another salvo from the rear.

It came at $90,000—with a full measure of shock value. For Whitney, summarily dispensing with the Major's services as intermediary, and flouting the convention of the signaled bid, shouted out in a loud, ebullient voice, "Ninety-five thousand dollars!" The effect could not have been more startling if a heckler had spoken out in church.

Randall now retreated, having reached the $90,000 limit set by J. K. Lilly. Fleming, to be sure, had already gone above the sum reputedly in Yale's collection basket. But Dr. R. had mentioned no limit to Fleming; he had told him his instructions were simply to buy the book. Fleming signaled a $1,000 raise.

"Ninety-six thousand dollars," Bade called from the rostrum.

"One hundred thousand!" Whitney shouted from the rear.

Spectators rose to their feet the better to get a look at a multi-multi-millionaire in action. There was a spattering of applause—cut off by Fleming's nod and Bade's concordant chant, "One hundred and one thousand dollars . . ."

"A hundred five!" Whitney shouted.

Fleming nodded.

"One hundred six thousand dollars," Bade announced, almost with a tremor, for this was a historic figure—the price paid for the Gutenberg Bible knocked down to Dr. R. by Bade himself in 1926. Veteran observers, aware that an all-time record was about to be surpassed, responded with cheers. Bade, anxious not to break the spell, hurried on above the noise: "One hundred six thousand dollars! . . . Do I hear the seven?"

He did . . . and the eight . . . the nine, the ten . . .

At Whitney's bid of $140,000 there was a momentary lull. Fleming, still outwardly impassive, withheld his hitherto prompt nod, possibly feeling a tremor at the heights to which he was being driven. The heads of the spectators twisted from Whitney to the tiny book in the spotlight, then inquiringly to Fleming, and back again to Whitney, the apparent winner.

Bade, with his instinct for timing, did not fill the gap with urging. It was a pause he deliberately allowed, an interval wherein both bidders could foretaste the thrill of victory, the ignominy of defeat.

Fleming, who perhaps was only savoring the drama's climax, let the suspense go on just long enough, then nonchalantly signaled his bid.

"One hundred forty-one thousand dollars!" Bade triumphantly announced. Even he thought the game was over.

"Two!" . . . "Three!" . . . "Four!" . . . "Five!"

At Fleming's bid of $145,000, Whitney stood, and like a man exasperated by a tiresome argument, shouted, "One hundred and fifty thousand dollars!" He sat down with the air of having put an end to a foolish wrangle.

Slowly, calmly, Fleming nodded. Bade, with no pause now, called, "One hundred fifty-one thousand dollars!"

There was silence in the hall. In the words of the New York *Herald-Tribune* reporter, "The place was so quiet one could have heard a thousand-dollar bill drop."

Bade's exhortation continued, but without response. "I have a hundred and fifty-one thousand dollars. Do I hear a hundred fifty-two? A hundred fifty-one thousand . . . a hundred fifty-one . . ." Politely now, as if offering another sandwich from a heaping plate, "May I say a hundred fifty-two?" Then, as if he might be a little hard of hearing, "Do I hear a bid of a hundred and fifty-two thousand dollars?" He did not. Sharply the hammer clicked. "To Rosenbach." The whole gallery stood and cheered.

"Imagine," an abashed lady spectator remarked, "the price of thirty Cadillacs!"

In the role of victor, Dr. R., seraphic in expression, was later photographed looking through his pince-nez at the open psalter, his lips parted as though in scriptural utterance. The publicity was global and unstinting. The price was, the Napoleon of Books said blandly, "very reasonable." He did not comment on how much the proof of his invincibility had flattened his wallet, but it was said that Yale benefactors contributed another $35,000 or $40,000, and the deficit was made up by Dr. R.

The rare-book tyrant had pulled off one of his last and grandest auction-hall coups. As a climax to his long and abundantly profitable life in trade, he could afford a prodigal night's sport.

During his twelve years as supreme ruler of the galleries, the Major—except perhaps on the night of the Bay Psalm sale—remained indifferent toward books, focusing his extraordinary abilities on the auctioning of art, and of furniture, jewelry, and other items less dusty and more attractive to him than printed matter. Among these were the exorbitant spoils from the exorbitant Park and Fifth Avenue residences dismantled as the wrecking crews of the forties proceeded, in accord with the strange American predilection for destroying what has only just been made, including that built to last "forever," to tear down one after another of the dynasts' replicas of Old World castles to make way for new, taller, and uglier buildings. Many of the castles were no more than a quarter of a century old. No matter. One by one they were razed, and with the Major presiding, their treasures were redistributed at auction.

The Dean of American Auctioneers, as the Major came to be called, was assisted in his endeavors by three protégés—Mary Vandegrift, Louis Marion, and Leslie Hyam—who came to preside over the galleries when he retired in 1950. All three were young and dynamic and had been brought by chance, or near chance, to join Mr. Bishop's association soon after he purchased it. None was signally predisposed to dedicate a lifetime to its frenetic operations. Particularly not petite, blond Mary Vandegrift, the first of the three to

Dr. A. S. W. Rosenbach studying a copy of the Bay Psalm Book purchased for him by his agent at the Parke-Bernet Galleries for $151,000 (PRESS ASSOCIATION, INC.).

stumble—with a slip from an employment agency in hand—into the building at 30 East 57th Street and thence to the Major's office.

Her name, in truth, was Mrs. Mary Kingsbury, but she and the agency neglected to state it legally and precisely, for she was a young girl, just out of school, and there was still, in the early summer of 1923, a prejudice against married women in business. She had barely heard of the élite auctions, but as the bride of an army officer, she had come to New York from Philadelphia, and having time on her hands, decided to find something to do for the summer. As she recalled later, the harried Major, about to take off on some urgent mission, barely glanced at her over his shoulder, then told her to sit down and go to work. This she did—with some misgivings, for the place, only recently acquired by Mr. Bishop, was bedlam, and what she was to go to work at was anything but clear.

It was a crucial moment, which was to help determine both the pattern of her life and the future of the association. For there, in Parke's office, with him, she continued to sit for the ensuing years of his turbulent career. And there, though Parke has gone, she remains to this day, as executive vice president and a director of the Parke-Bernet.

"Miss Vandegrift looked so beautiful that day she came in to get the job with Mr. Parke," said Marion Caming, an assistant cataloguer who happened to be present at the time. "She wore a blue dress." Years later the cut of the dress and the peculiar aura of vitality that entered with its wearer were still vivid in Miss Caming's mind. The image of a bluebird suddenly at large in that somber antiquary atmosphere which so long persisted in Miss Caming's mind was perhaps symbolic of the new regime. In earlier days Rose Lorenz would instantly have banished little Miss Vandegrift to some less dignified employment suitable for a creature apt to be preternaturally inflammatory to male workers.

But while it may have helped her over the rough places, it was not feminine charm that the extraordinary Miss Vandegrift contributed to the élite auctions. It was, at first, perhaps no more than a female knack of making order out of chaos. Her business experience was negligible and it would have taken a clairvoyant eye indeed to detect within her tiny person the latent skills that could not have been readily duplicated in any dozen persons from the employment mills. But everyone was fumbling and bewildered by the intricacies of a business—or romance—so long subjected to the whims of its dictators. And gradually Mary Vandegrift, who (with the Major's blessings) was off half the day taking courses at Columbia, New York University, the Art Students League, and the Metropolitan Museum—then up half the night, cramming and writing interminable reports—made her desk in Parke's office the storm center of Mr. Bishop's gusty enterprise.

"There was work to be done, and I did it," she says vaguely, trying to remember how it all came about. Her job was at first untitled, undefined, for in that maelstrom of activity the same problem seldom arose twice. In 1937 she was formally identified as the publicity director of the new Parke-Bernet Galleries, but the title did not describe her job, which was simply to steer the ship—by instinct if necessary—when there was no one else to take the wheel.

For a long time the bluebird, if not of happiness, at least of comfort and good cheer, looked upon her job as temporary, a stopgap. She had no real thought of carving herself a lifelong career. She was a married woman, with other fish to fry. After a while, there was a baby. But pushing a perambulator was uninspiring compared to the perpetual excitement of the AAA, and she knew that Parke, a hero to her, needed her on the job.

"I really wasn't very efficient at first," she said later. But one incident, an early one, made clear to her how important to the galleries she had come to be.

An exhibition opened, for one of the big but not otherwise noteworthy sales of the 1924–5 season. The crowd was pouring in the doors, but there were no catalogues. The Major came from the galleries to her desk. "Where are the catalogues?" he demanded.

"I don't know, Major," she said. Catalogue problems had never been in her province. "The printer hasn't sent them."

The Major looked her straight in the eye. He never lost his temper, but as all old hands recall, his gaze—the cold, hard stare he sometimes used in the rostrum—could be hypnotic.

"What can *I* do about it?" Miss Vandegrift asked.

The Major's answer came in that still, tense voice the public knew so well when the art of persuasion was running high: "Do you know what I'd do? I'd go down to the presses and get them."

After that, the catalogues were never late again.

Such menial errands, however, were peripheral to Mary Vandegrift's indefinable position. More than anything perhaps, she became a kind of gentle arbitratrix of the AAA's jealousies and rivalries, its frequent disputes, and the vast differences of opinion as to just how Mr. Bishop's enterprise was to become the greatest art market in the world.

As general manager of the galleries, O. B. in theory had superior authority, but Parke's was the master hand. He was the showman, and whether or not his business acumen surpassed O. B.'s, more often than not he played the leading role. The Major hated anything unpleasant. He avoided conferences, disliked contact with the staff. Mary Vandegrift was his tactful bearer of bad tidings, the liaison between him and O. B. when the weather was stormy. The timbre of her voice, its warmth and underlying humor, made it impossible to take offense. She was an ideal go-between, and with her sixth sense for

diplomacy, sometimes even succeeded in getting Parke and Bernet—
"two gentlemen," she called them—to agree.

With its stepped-up activities the AAA became a frantically busy
publishing house. Because, as she said later, "There was no one else to
do it," the job of editor somehow fell to Mary Vandegrift. The
Major, when he thought about this, raised his hands in bafflement and
said, "I don't know how she does the work she does." For it was all
done quietly, good-naturedly, with an unobtrusive distaff efficiency,
somewhat as a woman in less glamorous circumstances might have set
the meals on the table, kept the house in running order without
troubling its other occupants with news about where she got the bread
and how the servants had behaved.

But the auctions had little in common with family dinners. They
were, and are, a form of theater—and without realizing it, Mary
Vandegrift allowed herself to become stagestruck. There were no
hours any more, as Mr. Bishop's juggernaut clanged and zoomed
onward. Midnight was perforce the same as five o'clock. And soon
Mary Vandegrift realized that the auctions had taken over her life.
Her husband wanted her to go to Europe. Parke said no; someone
else would have her job when she came back, he said. She did not go.

Inevitably her marriage went on the rocks and a divorce followed.
She met the man who was later to become her second husband—the
son of A. Edward Newton, a writer and book collector—at the galleries in 1940, when he was there to arrange the sale of his father's
book collection. Thus Miss Vandegrift's true loves seemed only to
arise within the realm of the ivory hammer's muted snap and the bid
callers' impassioned cries. Her job absorbed her waking hours; at
night she dreamed of it. Twice she left, in protest against backstage
policies she would have no part in. Moral problems resulted from the
maintenance of a half-white, half-black staff; she objected to how
Negroes were dealt with, for in what was for many years a citadel of
Bourbon snobbery, Mary Vandegrift managed to maintain a fierce and
even militant sense of social justice. But she could not stay away long;
Parke, his desperation transcending the stiff pride few people ever
saw humbled, came to fetch her and capitulated to her point, in principle if not in practice.

Oddly, in a world focusing on two of the traditionally shady
professions, art-selling and auctioneering, the three people who survived the turbulence that was to beset the AAA, and who came to

preside over Parke-Bernet during the fifties and the first half of the sixties, had, though totally disparate in all other traits, one rare quality in common—an ingenuous, indomitable, almost naïve honesty that transcended every eccentricity, every vanity, every flaw.

Honesty plus firm determination to succeed were Louis J. Marion's only discernible qualifications when Mary Vandegrift hired the red-haired boy—in knee pants, she used to say—as a helper in the mail-room. Perhaps the pants were not literally knee length, but their wearer had the breathless energy of a boy dashing in from a sand-lot. He had not bothered to go to high school, for he was in a hurry to get on with life. He was of Italian parentage—a fact no one would have discerned if he had not proclaimed it, for he was the image of the all-American boy. He was not ashamed that his parents were working people, members of a minority group, but he dreamed of two cars in a two- or perhaps a three-car garage, and he realized—as did others—that if he had not been an Italian, he might not have been in such a hurry. The simplicity of his outlook was somehow very winning. And the American dream worked for him.

Louis Marion had a genius for turning casual acquaintances into devoted friends. The first step in self-revelation was usually the offhand statement, "I'm just a fellow with a night school education, and there was never much time for that." Spoken heartily, with a broad grin and no trace of pretension, it was a beginning few people could resist.

The mail sacks, the tons of catalogues, had never before been sent forth with such eagerness, such muscular dispatch as that displayed by Louis Marion when he started work at the AAA. He was wide-eyed at the nature of the business. "You mean they pay ten thousand bucks for a broken-down old bench?" He wanted to be in the office, where he could find out what this was all about.

The mailroom chief liked him as did everyone. He gave him some fatherly advice. "Look," he said, "you're making eighteen bucks a week; me, I'm getting twenty-seven. Fellows like you want too much. Stick to your job, and some day you'll be getting as much as me. Pretty soon you'll be running the Addressograph machine; it isn't hard." The mailroom chief remained the mailroom chief as Louis Marion ascended.

Louis cornered Edward Keyes, whom Mr. Bishop had installed to count the millions rolling in and out. Keyes liked him and put him on a stool in the accounting department, posting figures in the books. "I hated to leave the mail department," said Louis. "They were all so nice to me there."

They were nice to him in the accounting department too. His curly red pompadour, his animal spirits, raised the lady bookkeepers' morale. But what had this to do with $10,000 benches imported from the country his parents had fled to escape starvation?

He hated the back office. He encountered O. B. and told him so. The front office was where he wanted to work, and if Mr. Bernet could not find a place for him there, he would resign and peddle his talents to some other organization.

O. B. had his mind on more imperial matters. He recalled his own long years of apprenticeship, and told Keyes to make out a final paycheck for the impatient seventeen-year-old. But while the check was in the making, the image of the ebullient young apprentice persisted in O. B.'s mind: was not this eager youngster perhaps a second Otto—a son of immigrants, determined to get ahead?

When Louis came to get his check, O. B. tore it up and made him a relief record clerk in the salesroom. Marion was on his way.

The record clerk can learn to be an auctioneer. He sits at the elbow of the crier, learns values, sees the endless stream of objects, the faces and the signals of the clients. There was a long road ahead before the well-liked boy became the well-liked man, but success, Louis never doubted, was written in gilt on his far-off star.

Major Parke already had a stand-in, a protégé named Henry Russell, who could double for him in the rostrum. Russell, in his twenties, was a charmer, a fast, if superficial, learner who would, few people doubted, one day fill the Major's shoes. He was dashing and sophisticated, a dream boy to the ladies who came to the matinee sales. In him the Major saw a reflection of his own youth and sensibility, which, with adjustments—mainly a more effectively imposed self-discipline—might enable him to cope with greater responsibilities at the galleries.

An accountant by trade, Russell had been sent to apply for a job, got the wrong address, and ended up at the AAA. In years to come, he was often to get the wrong address, usually because of his on-the-job detours through saloons, sometimes with the jewels for the next week's auction in his pocket.

Parke trained him from the ground up, and the time came incredibly soon when, standing outside the salesroom, one could not tell their voices apart. Harry Russell, now dead, would have inherited Parke's mantle but for the weaknesses of the flesh—weaknesses the red-haired, well-liked Louis Marion could avoid. While Russell nursed his hangovers, Marion was out playing baseball or pitching horseshoes, attending a mass or amusing himself in the harmless pleasure dens of the Holy Name Society. In contrast to Russell, he was steady, serious, dependable—a man's man, with a firm, honest handshake. He was also, when occasion arose, the darling of older and richer ladies than those to whom Russell appealed.

His favorite friends were firemen. As his horizons broadened, his friends included fire commissioners too—and mayors, and bankers, and bishops—but his values never altered. He remained ebullient, but ingenuous. And in the course of time, he took the Major's place in the rostrum.

The 1924 arrival of Leslie A. Hyam as a member of the AAA's cataloguing staff was an event that no one saw as unduly propitious for the association. O. B., in particular, was somewhat appalled, or perhaps intimidated, by young Hyam's scholarly British air. What had the Cambridge manner to do with the auction carnival? Competent, even doggedly meticulous though Hyam might be at the tedious job of cataloguing, he was by any standards a rare bird to stray into the world of art redistribution. Never did it occur to O. B.—or anyone else in 1924—that the tall young man beguiled by the pursuit of knowledge would one day preside over the galleries' complex destiny.

"The direction of cataloguing then," as Hyam said later, "was to present the object with a description corresponding to the most optimistic expectations of the owner." The tradition of the unlettered expert prevailed. O. B. and the Major and the men who grew up under their tutelage were "experts in values"—a term no one of them could have precisely defined—and were supposedly able to recognize "quality" in various works of art. The Major, whose instinct for appraisal was uncanny, could detect this "quality"—a combination, said Hyam, of aesthetic merit and salability—to an astonishing degree, but when it came to the technicalities, he was, like most other "experts in values," wholly inarticulate, and thus unable to make the AAA's catalogues, elaborately illustrated though they might be, a satisfactory source of information for increasingly sophisticated collectors.

Most of the routine cataloguing was done by Frank H. G. Keeble, a brilliant man, with approximately equal predilections for art and the bottle. Keeble would disappear with the catalogue copy, dead drunk, and a manhunt through the speakeasies would have to be organized to get the copy to the printer on time. But even had he been a sober, solid citizen, he could never have kept up with the flood of objects coming through Mr. Bishop's AAA. Keeble had one assistant; he could have used twenty. Since the AAA's doors were not exactly being beaten down by erudite cataloguers, the Major decided to search abroad for a new assistant.

Hyam heard of Parke's intention through George H. McCall, the research scholar who supplied the great Duveen with his omniscience (and was shamelessly underpaid for it). McCall had met Hyam during the two weeks Hyam had been a minion of Charles of London, a brother of Sir Joseph Duveen who, while receiving $20,000 a year for not using the Duveen name, conducted a flourishing, if incognito, art and antique business in New York. Charles of London had the Duveen arrogance, if not Sir Joseph's Midas touch. "He had an evil temper," Hyam said, "which he took out on the help in front of the customers." This sort of thing Hyam, then a floundering young man of twenty-three, could not—and did not—abide.

A Cantabrigian with a prodigious capacity for scholarship and a degree in physics, Hyam was English by persuasion no less than by birth and education. He spoke like an Englishman—in clipped accents, barbed phrases, lofty tones—and this plus his abiding scorn for mediocrity sometimes made him seem a snob. He was not, he said. What's more, he had bourgeois origins to cite—as he often did—in support of his disclaimer: when he was a child his father's chain of clothing stores had failed, and the elder Hyam, then forty-eight, had begun life all over again as an $18-a-week factory worker.

Hyam's father immigrated to New York. Young Leslie stayed in England, got a thorough British schoolboy education, and won a competitive open scholarship to Cambridge, from which he emerged with second-class honors in physics, only to find that the urgent wartime need for physicists had subsided, and the best jobs graduates could hope for were in teaching. Fired with the conviction that he was destined to undertake some major portion of the world's endeavor, Hyam escaped the limbo of the schoolroom and went to Germany, where, abandoning physics for finance, he proposed to a group of bankers a grandiose plan to solve Germany's reparations problem by refinancing its railroads. Nothing came of the scheme, and Hyam, after a year on the Continent, and a chaotic love affair with a woman ten years his senior, joined his father in New York.

Hyam spent his first ten months in the United States sitting in the public library and writing a novel, which he threw away. After his disillusioning two weeks with Charles of London, he thought of himself as a man without a profession. He was tall, tolerably good-looking, impeccably tailored—and practically penniless. Yet when McCall offered to introduce him to Major Parke as a potential cataloguing genius, he protested against the perpetration of any such fraud.

"Nonsense," said McCall. "Go over and tell him you're a Cambridge graduate. Look as English as you can."

Hyam wore a double-breasted coat, spats, a Homburg hat. "I sat down after George introduced us," he recalled, "and listened to him launch into a lengthy eulogy."

Parke offered him $40 a week. In the course of the conversation, it came out that the assistant cataloguer with whom Hyam would be working was only getting $35. Hyam had a twinge of conscience. "Why don't you take me on at thirty-five a week?" he said. "Let me start at that."

The Major raised his eyebrows and agreed. Whereupon Hyam, who did not want to plunge precipitously into cataloguing a maelstrom of disparate objects, said, "I can't start for six weeks. I have certain matters of a personal nature to settle."

He went to the Metropolitan Museum and crammed. In six weeks of intense study, he attempted to fill his mind with images of all the principle decorative and artistic works of man. It was a fantastic project, on the surface so naïve that it was many years before Hyam revealed to anyone the source of his practical education in the arts.

He bought three loose-leaf notebooks, carefully measured to slip neatly into his pockets. In them, in tiny pictures and almost microscopic printing, he compiled a guide to the creative vision of man— three minuscule encyclopedias. Their pages are now foxed and brittle, but the signs and symbols, the names, statistics, dates, are still clear. From *A* for Arabic symbols, and *B* (Bronzes) to *V* (Virgin) and *W* (Weaving), they present a galaxy of aids to recognition nowhere else to be found. Under *F* are the ages of great furniture—of oak, of walnut, of satinwood and mahogany, of English and American master cabinetmakers and of France's *maîtres ébénistes;* names are indexed with their dates and identifying symbols; motifs are neatly drawn and dated, moldings sketched, dovetailing in drawers, details of locks and hinges, interiors and linings. *C* is for Chinese art—the bells and kettles, the miniature animal figures used as weights on the dress of corpses, the porcelain and its marks and motifs, the embroidery, the products of the various dynasties; *C* is also for the Church, with thirty pages revealing how to identify the saints and twenty-five depicting religious symbols—the iconography of candlesticks, the hierarchy of crosses, the habits of monastic orders. Subindexed under *C* (Church) are the forms of martyrdom from *A*, "Anvil, limbs broken on," through *W*, "Windlass, entrails wound upon."

Every page of the notebooks is thick with information. There is a Russian transliteration key; the shapes of vases are drawn and labeled, the riggings of ships, the stitches of lacemakers, the stems of glasses, the forms of lacquer boxes, the hallmarks of old silver; there are tiny complex maps of Asia Minor, old Persia, and the provinces of Italy; the arms of the great families are drawn in colors. On and on the hastily compiled pages go—dizzying, overwhelming, bewildering—through the congeries of time, the inexhaustible fertility of the human mind. They are a revelation of the prodigious scope of the mind of their compiler. A lesser intellect might have bogged down before completing such a project, but then, the notebooks were intended merely to supplement visual images stored in memory during those incredible weeks at the museum. (Memory was always one of Hyam's strong points.) From his early youth whatever he retained fell into orderly visual patterns, which he was capable of evoking at will. Historical facts, for instance, were recalled on an imaginary clock, falling into logical positions on the numbered dial. Surprisingly, for much of his life Hyam supposed everyone had the same kind of mind.

Armed with his notebooks, Hyam discarded Cambridge clothes for a smock and went to work with Keeble and his assistant at the AAA.

Many years later, surrounded by the flotsam of the ages in the barn-like cataloguing room above Parke-Bernet, he shuddered at how green he was. "A curious thing about this whole business," he said reflectively, "is that then nobody had the slightest idea of the amount of knowledge required!"

Keeble, Hyam soon discovered, was paid on a piecework basis—so much per lot—and with the cost of Prohibition liquor being what it was, he was loath to turn over any major task to his salaried assistants. Hyam was supposed to help Keeble write the catalogue for a huge sale of reproductions of French furniture from a Chicago importing house. There were so many lots that every floor of the galleries was used to display them; hundreds of chairs stood in rows, and hundreds more hung on the walls. But Hyam wrote not a word. On a piecework basis, Keeble made over $5,000 for that one singularly monotonous catalogue. And Hyam began to regret that he had naïvely taken $35 a week when he could have had $40.

Soon, however, Keeble's other assistant left the hurly-burly of 57th Street for the relative tranquility of a Westchester antique store, and not long after that, the day came when Keeble's catalogue copy could not be found in any speakeasy, police station, or other resort of the intemperate. It was never found, but poor Keeble was found—dead—on the floor of his apartment, a victim of bad Prohibition booze. The next morning Hyam—"No one thought it peculiar," he later said wryly—was given full charge of cataloguing.

Almost from the outset there was trouble with Benguiat over the cataloguing of his rugs. The Pasha, as Hyam was well aware, knew a very great deal about rugs and textiles. He had eyes in his fingers, as the men around the galleries used to say. His instincts were infallible, but his notions of history were based on hearsay. Hyam was eager to learn rugs. He tried to get close to the Pasha in his room upstairs; he even went to night school to study weaving and fathom the mysteries of the Ghiordes and Senna knots, the intricacies of warp and weft and pile. Scholarly books that had recently become available—books the Pasha could not read—convinced Hyam that dealers, once the public's sole source of information about rugs, had perpetuated many myths. A glance at the history of Persia's Safawid dynasty proved that many rugs could not be as old as the dealers claimed they were; the place names from which rugs took their titles were frequently misleading:

the great rugs called Isfahan had never rested on their looms in the shadow of the mosques of Shah Abbas, for few, if any, rugs were made at Isfahan; Polonaise rugs were not made in Poland; Hispano-Moresque rugs were not made in Spain.

When the great Benguiat rug sale of 1927 came up, a huge folio catalogue was designed, with color plates and elegant typography—one of the most beautiful art books of the era. The old rug catalogues had been written by Dana Carroll under the Pasha's thumb. What Benguiat said, Carroll wrote; and the Pasha was of the belief that anything he said thrice over was true.

It fell to Hyam to edit the copy for the Pasha's great sale. "Listings ranged from the nearly possible to sheer nonsense," Hyam said later. "All Isfahan rugs—according to the Pasha—were sixteenth century; the gold and silk Polonaise rugs were sixteenth century too, though no silk rugs had existed in the sixteenth century." Hyam went through the catalogue fixing dates, adding long paragraphs of his own composition, and here and there, changing an impossible origin. When the Pasha got a copy, he stormed into Major Parke's office, dark lightning flashing from his eyes, his arms upraised, his fists doubled as if clenching thunderbolts.

What was this? His babies turned by a mere writing into upstart bastards! His Isfahans not made at Isfahan! The sweetest flowers of his life's endeavor turned by some brazen English boy into mere modern seventeenth-century pieces!

In vain the Major tried to play the diplomat. What matter if the Isfahans had been made at Herat? A rose by any other name or century would smell as sweet and bring as high a price.

"A writing!" roared the Pasha. On that subject he flailed the Major as he had flailed his nephew many years before. "I tell you, dear, a writing has never done anything but harm!" He pounded at the paragraphs of scholarly description with his fists, ran his finger up and down the pages of documentation, opinion, erudition, fact. "I tell you, dear, you people think it is understood that all your earnings go for paper and ink as they did for the ancient orators," he shouted. "I have told you the day you do not see any more paper and ink, that is the day your eyes will be opened. I have told you to throw into the sea all the books and all the announcements. I tell you, dear, all this is peanuts!"

The Major, aware that Mr. Bishop's corporations currently held the Pasha's notes for upward of $1 million, abandoned wisdom as the lesser part of valor. He knew that Hyam had taken pride in the catalogue. Who would tell him that his masterpiece was not going to be printed as he wrote it?

Mary Vandegrift still remembers vividly the sense of impending crisis as, alone with Hyam in the office (for the Major made a cowardly exit), she fortified her voice, tried to seem nonchalant, and said, "Mr. Hyam, Mr. Parke and Mr. Benguiat feel that these descriptions are much too lengthy. . . . They want some changes. They have marked corrections for you to make."

Hyam didn't say a word, she remembers. "He laughed. Then he went over to the window and stood there, looking out. After a moment, he turned and came back to the desk, picked up the catalogue—and walked out."

Mary Vandegrift expected that he would quit his job—he was so manifestly out of his element in trade. He did not quit. Instead, he seemed to shrug and accept the impossibility of fighting city hall.

Miss Vandegrift now thinks that, whether he knew it or not, Leslie Hyam's fierce determination that someday knowledge, precision, the search for truth, would dominate the auction enterprise dated from that episode.

The Pasha's victory was not unalloyed. The distinguished rug scholar Arthur Upham Pope, writing in *Art News*, reviewed at length the beauty and importance of some of Vitall's carpets, and at the same time, pointed out some of the errors in the beautifully printed catalogue. In the salesroom, rumors of the great Benguiat's mendacity undermined his reputation for omniscience to the point where the Major, from the rostrum, had to make a humiliating speech, acknowledging that a discussion had arisen over two of Mr. Benguiat's undeniably great rugs, alleged to have been woven in the sixteenth century. The Pasha was ill at the time, but from his bed of pain, he had reaffirmed his "unshakable confidence in the great age of these rugs." Perhaps "unshakable" was a mite too strong a word, for the Pasha, doubtless weakened by fever, had made just a shadow of concession to doubt; he was, he said—and the Major duly reported from the rostrum—willing to guarantee the two disputed rugs "in the final instance, as having been woven no later than the seventeenth century."

Though subsequent Benguiat catalogues compiled by Dana Carroll endowed the Pasha with such offhand attributes as "a certain scholarship," many collectors were not entirely convinced. The era of declaration without definitive proof was on the wane.

If at first Mary Vandegrift, Louis Marion, and Leslie Hyam were a perhaps timorous triumvirate, by the time the Parke-Bernet came into being, they were anything but. From the outset, their consolidated efforts to implement the Major's commands—and thereby make a way for themselves—were crucial to his and the galleries' success. Hyam catalogued and planned; Miss Vandegrift converted his plans to action and coordinated them; Marion sold. And, yet, at times many of their duties were interchangeable. Parke's stunning successes in the rostrum during the forties were in each instance preceded by indefatigable preparations on the part of this trio. Because of their remarkable ability to intertwine and, at the same time, maintain their independence, as early as the 1940–1 season, their consolidated efforts for the sale of Mrs. Henry Walters' possessions created a great furor among auction aficionados.

The primacy of women was reasserted in Hyam's catalogues for her sale—they were imposing volumes with the feel of great books.

Long ago, as Mrs. Pembroke Jones, a Southern belle with a rich stockbroker husband, a niche in high society, and a Carolina drawl, the lady who was to be called "one of the most enthusiastic collectors the world of art has known" had joined a treasure hunt with the immensely wealthy Henry Walters. On long safaris in his ocean-going yacht, *Narada,* by treaty with many princely houses, as well as at auctions in the United States and abroad, Walters amassed some twenty thousand works of all countries and all epochs for the Walters Art Gallery of Baltimore. For the last nine of his eighty-three years, he took the widowed Mrs. Jones as his first and only wife. When he died, his elderly widow found herself presiding over a cavalcade of beauty and technical brilliance unrivaled by that of the other great ladies.

The French rooms of her mansions in New York, Newport, and her native Wilmington, North Carolina were illumined by the porcelain subtleties of rose de Pompadour and rose du Barry, and unearthly Sèvres blues. Sculptures by Houdon, Clodion, and Falconet mingled with a galaxy of signed pieces by the greatest *ébénistes* the world has ever known—such sovereign relics as a commode fashioned for Marie Antoinette, another (by Lelu) purchased by King George III of England at auction on the public square at Versailles after the French Revolution.

France was her first love, but the enthusiasms of Mrs. Walters did not stop there. She also had a taste for Greco-Roman antiquities, Gothic choir stalls, and carved ivories, the arts of Persia, China, and Japan; her syllabus of personal adornment included a collection of Renaissance jewels that Catherine de' Medici might have worn with pride.

Parting from all this was not easy, but there would be no post-mortem scramble, Mrs. Walters decreed, for her lustrous objects. In 1941, at the age of eighty-one, she undertook her own valedictory, consigning the cream of her collection to the Parke-Bernet.

Reluctantly, for with her reverence for eighteenth-century France went the unregenerate snobbery of the Faubourg Saint Germain, she permitted the unworthy populace, imposing catalogues in hand, to examine what the catalogue's foreword called "this dead-and-gone world of exquisite beings—out of all of which peers the marble mocking face of Voltaire [by Houdon], who was to bring about its overthrow." France in 1941 was under a yoke more barbaric than any Voltaire could have thought possible, and it was a public grimly concerned for its future that came to bid on the Walters' collection. Prices were not high. No matter. Mrs. Walters had no need of money. Within two years, death had caught up with her. But through her great auction, she achieved a niche in the gallery of connoisseurs. Few are the collections of French art, private or in museums, that are not in her debt. Again and again her treasures have reappeared at auction, often to be knocked down at ten or twenty times the amount paid for them in 1941. When the final lot of her enormous collection was sold, Parke-Bernet accounted a total of $613,072.

Though the trio's successes, guided by Major Parke, accrued steadily during the forties, they were nevertheless distraught by the war and O. B.'s departure from the galleries. They managed to withstand the horrors of the war, but O. B.'s departure caused them—and Major Parke himself—particular grief. Though Marion inherited O. B.'s position in the rostrum for the afternoon sales, he feared that these sales would not fare as well under his direction. He committed fewer and fewer bargains to Mary Vandegrift's annually published bargain list—not because he lacked O. B.'s flair, but because there was less bulk and more quality merchandise auctioned at the galleries. The galleries, even before the end of the war, were becoming an increasingly expensive market place. The first outstanding sale conducted by Major Parke and his three protégés without assistance from O. B. began the season after his semiretirement, when Mrs. J. Amory Haskell's collection of Americana came to the block.

Margaret Riker, as the magpie Mrs. Haskell was born in 1864—in Newtown, Long Island, on land occupied by the Riker family since the seventeenth century—was said to have shown alarming symptoms of collectomania by the age of twelve. Later she developed a virulent case of ancestor worship involving a life preoccupation with the legend of the Riker family, whose lands in and around New York once included Riker's Island, and a compulsion to acquire artifacts inspired by the American heritage. Her home in New York and the farm near Red Bank, New Jersey, to which she moved her birthplace, lock, stock, and barrel, reputedly harbored the most extensive collection of Americana ever brought together by one person.

Extensive to the point of gluttony were the hoards of glassware, silver, and furniture. Miles of prints exemplified a young country's artistic tastes—or at least, its culturemongers' glossy version of them. In a stultifying redundance of the banalities of Currier and Ives and other lithographers the idylls of country life were depicted, the delights of sport and nature, urban improvements, and mechanical devices. A cerulean iconography of the United States in the nineteenth century radiated from a stupefying overabundance of crockery ware, with cities on bowls, Mount Vernon on pitchers, tombs on coffeepots. There were blue beaches, blue parks, rivers, lakes, waterfalls; blue banks and colleges, railroads and churches; blue factories, mills, and ironworks; many blue insane asylums. The physiognomies of famous people dazzled forth from blue platters and tureens; the arms of the states were emblazoned—in blue—on dinner plates; the blue Constitution decorated soup plates. Events in history, naval victories especially, glimmered in apochryphal blueness on cups and saucers. And no scene was depicted but once, for in her ardor, Mrs. Haskell bought two or six or more of everything.

The famous physiognomies showed up again on whisky bottles and chintz panels. National scenes and sentiments were reiterated on transfer-decorated pottery; the landscapes, arms, and eagles, on Lowestoft porcelain. Repetition was never a deterrent to Mrs. Haskell in the exercise of her retrospective passion.

Her galleries bulged with candlesticks and kneading bowls and Bible boxes, curtain knobs and tavern signs and weather vanes, ship's bells and gazing balls, homespun coverlets and old copper milk cans, bandboxes and salt boxes, herb cabinets and commode-shaped crocus pots, courting mirrors, powder horns, tea caddies, stoneware crocks, and pietistic samplers. Not satisfied with the full-blown objects, she also collected everything possible in miniature, compounding the redundance with cabinetmakers' models and children's furniture.

Merely to count her spoons and chairs, her washstands, sugar bowls, and miniatures of colonial great-great-grandfathers, would have been a task of unthinkable tedium. Her collection overflowed into museums. Eager to share her obsession with the world at large, she would loan a barnful of tea services, lowboys, flip glasses, and fox-hunting punch bowls, with no appreciable dent in the total.

In time these thousands upon thousands of relics large and small, rare and commonplace, descended upon the Parke-Bernet. What it had taken sixty-some years and a fortune to assemble, it took the galleries ten months of intermittent sessions, from April 1944 to February 1945, to recirculate among the lesser Mrs. Haskells and an army of "Ye Shoppe Keepers," for $602,428.

The Major did not attempt to circumscribe the bulk sales after 1943. He wanted them to continue even in O. B.'s absence. But there were fewer patrons willing to entrust their collections of plaster casts to the galleries, for consignors of art property of moderate value preferred dealing with O. B. Not only this but the decreasing number of notable private collections made available for auction as more and more collectors gave away their treasures instead of selling them led the Major to devise another kind of sale—the group category sale—which was extensively tested in the 1946–7 season. That season the galleries grossed an impressive $6,019,153, but the Major was worried by a drop in attendance at exhibitions, and also a drop in the average prices paid for what he called "the general run of property offered." He decided that though, unlike O. B., he might never be loved by masses of people, he could, with Leslie Hyam's help, make himself interesting to the select few—who would then come and buy and find it enchanting.

In the "stately adagios" that (according to one of his friends) typified his catalogue prose, Hyam propagated a stately image of the Major, who indifferently coexisted with it. Once he suggested to Hyam that a few irregularities might perhaps be in order. "You know," he said, "I'm quite anonymous."

"Admit to being an institution," Hyam answered. "It's that simple. And there's a certain beauty to being a block of limestone that's made good."

The Major thanked Hyam for his opinion, then agreed. "It's true," he said. "I've become—and I think quite consciously—a smoothed and not really very pretentious boulder of the establishment. I suppose I'll remain so."

He did—at least until the nineteen-fifties.

The big sale of the 1948–9 season was that of the magnificent Joseph Brummer collection of early Christian and Byzantine material (Joseph Brummer was a dealer in antiquities), which realized $739,510 and saw the Major, and Marion, his eager and capable successor to the rostrum, bowing respectfully to the purchasing bids of museum curators and Hyam discussing with them the artistic and historical significance of the works. In a few instances Hyam, the accuracy of whose catalogue astounded most of the experts, was given the exquisite pleasure of conceding an error. He would listen intently to the correction, hanging on each word of enlightenment; then, shaking his head rapidly, he would take the knowledgeable one's arm and earnestly solicit—almost plead for—further information.

The 1948–9 season marked the end of Major Parke's reign over the galleries. In 1950 he left the responsibility for their management to Hyam and retreated into semiretirement. He kept the chairmanship of the board of directors—then and until 1957—but devoted himself more and more to his home and to caring for his wife. He kept the presidency until 1953, when Hyam succeeded him. "I give you to each other," the Major told Hyam, Mary Vandegrift, and Louis Marion. "And it's all yours."

Part of the triumvirate's heritage was the present home of Parke-Bernet, a then spanking new building at 980 Madison Avenue. It opened on November 10, 1950, with a private preview for two thousand art-world notables, who guzzled champagne by the gallon as they listened to speeches by Hyam, the Major, and Robert Dowling, the art-conscious real estate magnate whose company began putting up the galleries' new home when the old edifice at 30 East 57th Street was scheduled to be wrecked and replaced with an office building.

At first there was some uneasiness about whether art and auction hounds would forgather as far uptown as 980 Madison Avenue, on the block between 76th Street and 77th. There needn't have been. Business, including the group—or "and others"—sales flourished in the new building. Starting in 1946, the Major had constructed these sales in such a way that they did not seem to differ significantly from those of private collections. The advertising for them emphasized not the category—English garden furniture of a certain period, for example—but the name or names of the most prominent of the consignors.

The Major knew all too well that the name of the owner of a work was often as valuable as the work itself, especially if the work was one of cabinetry. Time and again, buyers overpaid for furnishings they believed to evoke the wealth and glory of former owners. Hyam called such buyers "voyeurs," and scorned them. To him art was timeless, unownable; and the Major merely recited the social register as a poem, selling the timeless and unownable, along with some works Hyam thought remarkably bland, to well-heeled but poorly educated, quite unworthy pleasure seekers. Hyam catalogued the items of the "and others" sales as carefully as he had the magnificent Limoges enamels belonging to Thomas Fortune Ryan, but sometimes when he handled them and pondered their probable fate, he would speak aloud to them, consolingly, and with love.

He was never aware that he was overheard.

During the fifties, sales of important paintings produced phenomenal results. For a time tastes had been changing, and no one was certain of just what direction they would take. The interested public seemed thoroughly confused: were the Barbizons really as lugubrious and sentimental as critics said? were the landscapes Corot painted for opportunistic reasons masterworks nonetheless? was it possible for one to relate, in the twentieth century, to medieval Italian art? and what about the old masters?—was Rembrandt the greatest painter who had ever lived? or was Frans Hals?

Probably the hardest question raised was that of whether or not modern art was really art. It had been a troublesome question as far back as 1886, when Thomas Kirby showed "The Impressionists of Paris" at the old AAA. It was still a troublesome question during the forties, but by then the prices paid for modern art—modern European art, that is—were on the way up . . . and up. Never again would contemporary imported paintings be had for such pitiable prices as those paid at the Chester H. Johnson sale in 1934; never again would Norman K. Winston or W. P. Chrysler, Jr., take home a Renoir or a Matisse for little over $100. In the forties these gentlemen could, and did, procure similar items for a few thousand; in the fifties both would sit and smile in the auction hall at the hundreds of thousands bid by their friends for paintings similar to those they had earlier bought for almost nothing.

In December 1939, when the collection of moderns belonging to the late Mrs. Cornelius T. Sullivan, one of the founders of the Museum of Modern Art, was auctioned, a Cézanne portrait of Madame Cézanne brought an astounding $27,500—the highest price of the season for a single item. A portrait by van Gogh climbed to $19,000, a sum that would have dazed the impoverished artist had he lived to know of it; and a Derain still life, *The Window on the Park*, brought $3,500 (from the Museum of Modern Art, which put it on immediate exhibition in memoriam to Mrs. Sullivan).

In 1943 Frank Crowninshield's collection of modern paintings was auctioned, with another Cézanne portrait of his wife bringing $16,500, van Gogh's *Nature Morte: Glaïeuls*, $11,000 and a Monet called *A Portrait of a Child*, $19,000. Three years later still another Cézanne portrait of his wife brought $24,500 at an auction of paintings from the collection of the late Sir William Van Horne, K.C.M.G. Toulouse-Lautrec's *Gueule de Bois* brought $30,000 and his *Femme Rousse Assise dans le Jardin de M. Forest* $27,500 at the same sale. After this, prices for modern art remained about the same until the fifties, then suddenly skyrocketed, as did all art prices.

In the 1944–5 season genre and Barbizon paintings from the collections of William H. and Cornelius Vanderbilt were auctioned, and appraisers fearful that the sale would be a fiasco sat dumbfounded as the total paid for the flocks of sheep and herds of cows, rustics, and the cottages depicted in somber umbers climbed to an impressive $323,195, much of it due to Millet. According to the nonscornful critics, something sincerely gentle and mystic, an indecipherable quality hovering within Millet's paintings, made *The Water Carrier* bring $30,000 and *The Sower* $26,000. Of course the Vanderbilts had paid much more for the paintings, but these prices were significant for a period when the whole painting market was in a muddle, and when, from the host of works offered to the public, those of a few artists were being selected—more accurately at Parke-Bernet, it turned out, than in any art historian's speculations—for economic apotheosis in the next decade.

Among the chosen were the works of Rembrandt, Hals, Rubens, and Van Dyck, of Constable and Turner, Watteau, Fragonard, and Chardin, of Velásquez and Goya, David, Ingres, and Delacroix, and of the French impressionists and post-impressionists. In the sixties, after the exhaustive exploitation of nearly every private collection available in the United States, even minor pictures by these painters brought staggering prices. Said Mary Vandegrift in the spring of 1969, the only member of the triumvirate then still associated with the galleries, "It's almost frightening that the supply of works of quality is now so limited. The public mustn't starve, and at present, though tastes for art are appeased, I'm not certain that the art is particularly nourishing. The limited supply isn't a threat to us—not at all. If anything, it's to our advantage. But it hurts the general public, because prices have become so outrageous. Because of the competition, I expect a new set of world records every season."

Upon occasion—four particular occasions during the nineteen-fifties—the reconciling of men's acquisitive passions reached epic proportions for the Parke-Bernet triumvirate, which was besieged with success to such a degree that Mary Vandegrift cried at the close of more than one season, "It's fleeing time most definitely!"

Four times on the tide of the fifties' convulsed economy the competition of the rich drove the take for an auction of an exceptional private collection above a million and a half dollars; on three, the $2-million mark was passed. In January 1957 the patricians and the plebeians alike were set agog by the dispersal of the multitudinous possessions of the late Mrs. Sarah Mae Cadwell Manwaring Plant

Hayward Rovensky, whose succession of husbands had financed her progress from humble origins to aureate dowager status. In the democratic melee at the Parke-Bernet the bids totaled $2,438,980 for her jewels, including the pearls for which she had traded her first Fifth Avenue mansion to Cartier back in 1916, and the contents of her dwelling—her Beauvais tapestries, Savonnerie rugs, her Adam and Hepplewhite commodes.

There were gasps in the salesroom when a Chelsea soup tureen in the form of a rabbit brought $12,000, and when a gilded silver toilet service was knocked down at $50,000. And there was an uproar among the spectators, and later in the press, when a 213-carat diamond necklace soared to $385,000, then the highest price ever paid for a single lot at auction in the United States.

The next November the passions of possession were embroiled in even greater hoopla—in artistic circles at any rate—when the historic Georges Lurcy sale racked up a total of $2,221,355 for sixty-five modern French paintings and the eighteenth-century French furniture and *objets d'art* that accompanied them.

For Lurcy, opulent surroundings were a necessity, conducive to the peace that permeated his life, but not affording him inspiration. Money could easily buy works of art. It was simple indeed to give a thousand here and a few there for a painting, but if this was the extent of the exchange between the collector and the artist, then Lurcy would rather, he said, spend equivalent sums of money on vegetables to confound his palate. "I don't want change for the bills, money buying money. I want the money reaping paradise—in a fashion as mysterious as the artist's simple oils producing it. That's the inspired use of money, conceiving it as a formidable creative medium."

He bought quietly, unobtrusively. The money for a work was given with a whisper of gratitude before, with quickened heartbeat, the adored painting was carried home for contemplation. Lurcy was known to hold his paintings in his arms, to wonder over brushstrokes, to say, "The priceless temptation of art gives one everything—delectable stings, a hint of pepper and sun, the effortless crush of the teeth into a morsel of cantaloupe."

He began collecting in Paris, where he lived for more than half his life. When he moved to the United States, at the outset of World War Two, his collection, already formed, did not attract any particular attention. Not until after his death did he gain glory as a col-

Georges Lurcy amid some of his treasures: a $200,000 Renoir, a $29,000 soupière, a $14,000 commode, a $2,500 chair (PARKE-BERNET GALLERIES).

lector; in his lifetime he was known only as a genius of banking and finance, and for much of that lifetime, he was known not as Georges Lurcy, but as Georges Levy, born in Paris in February 1891, the son of a modest Jewish family originally from Alsace.

The Levy family had always shown a marked potential for scholarship. Georges excelled from the cradle to the day he died. He graduated from the School of Commerce on the Avenue Trudaine with twenty-two prizes and a job offer from a large brokerage firm—at 60 francs a month, a sum that was accepted, Georges promptly informed the man who was to be his superior, only because he was eager to prove just how vast an injustice, how great an insult it was. But as he roamed about the city delivering stocks for clients, he began to question what he wanted for his life. Money and luxury? Yes. But then, he felt the inevitability of being wealthy. He could not avoid it. He wanted more than wealth—but what that was he did not know.

He never did find a completely satisfying answer. But possessing and studying works of art helped him feel calmer, cease questioning for a while. The emptiness was somewhat mitigated, particularly in the presence of impressionistic paintings. "One day," he said late in his life, "an airborne seed pod of happiness somewhere in those mists and fogs seemed to catch hold. I've yet to discover where on my person, but the growth spread rapidly to the heart, and I've grown into a shimmering equilibrium."

He began to buy even before he was twenty—drawings and the canvases he could afford. By the time he was twenty-two he was an executive at the Banque Rothschild and could afford even expensive paintings.

On the side he made a few wise investments in stocks with a little money from his weekly savings, and quickly became a rich young man, able to install his mother and brother in quarters on the best avenue in Paris. The millions came with World War One. Unable to participate as a soldier, for though strong in mind and heart, he was physically weak, he determined nonetheless to help defend France—to make it, somehow, invincible. The answer to how? came, he said later, as he watched the ducks in the Jardin du Luxembourg. Hydroplanes.

Until then, these machines had functioned badly. Georges set engineers to finding out why, and soon they had a design and an engine they were certain would work. Gambling on their assurances, Georges invested all his capital in a factory at Argenteuil.

Soon the hydroplanes made there were skimming efficiently over the water. Soon the factory expanded. After the war Georges sold it and returned to the Paris Bourse. "To have continued constructing those contraptions would have ruined my love of nature," he explained. "I would have nothing else to do with war—nothing. I had a desire to bury my money and see if it would grow, resurrect in some other form . . . and I felt that such a delicate transient substance as happiness needed insuring."

He paused, smiled, then said, "Perhaps, since in fact we relished every mood, even sadness, I should correct myself and say that after the war, I actually felt only the need to insure life—my life and the lives of my friends."

Georges was never prey to exploitation, perhaps because he wanted to be generous, and his generosity humiliated the mercenary. "How much do you need?" he would ask; then after hearing the answer, "Are you sure that's enough?" Often he would add, "Come to supper, and . . . uh, join in the presence of a beautiful woman."

His guests were from every walk of life, with a special abundance of painters, ballerinas, actresses, and writers, one of whom gushed after a visit to Georges' Paris apartment, "The nudes of Matisse surrounded by the celestial wreaths of Renoir, Pissarro, and Monet gave one chills, weakened one's knees, and one fell into a comfortable chaise, to drink cognac, elixir, nectar—whatever . . . or perhaps to take draws from a pipe of hashish and later eat great portions of roast chicken with a dressing as mysteriously spiced as China in the Middle Ages."

Georges' apartment was always open. "I played forever," he once said. "What better attitude in the wake of philosophic unanswerables? But I have, nonetheless, enjoyed myself as lucidly as possible."

He studied just one painting a year, for many years. But his walls were covered with pictures. He needed to be surrounded by pictures, he said, for "especially in impressionism, the periphery is as important as the focal point. If you have ever seen Monet's wall of water lilies, then you know what I mean. What you see is gorgeous eternity—an immortality so lovely . . . so lovely." Once, pointing to a section of blue, gold, and rose in a Bonnard, he said, "We must die there . . . we must! And we must take this heaven with us."

In the summer he entertained at a villa in Deauville called La Terrasse, or more often, at his Louis XVI château in the village of Meslay le Vidame. There he played, but never frivolously. "People were sacred to him," one of his friends said. "An arm of an actress would be blessed many times in an evening; the hands of a young man praised endlessly; the color of eyes studied. Often he would stop a meal to announce, without embarrassment, that his guests were beautiful and that he prayed for their well-being."

In 1937 he married an American girl, Alice Snow Barbee of High Point, North Carolina—primarily, he said, because "I'd never seen such thin delicacy compounded with such ample fecundity. She was exquisitely feminine and slightly poor, as I hear all young Southern ladies are. Still, they supposedly live in such fine houses, attended by hosts of fly-swatting servants—but enough. Why tease you unbearably with the multitude of her charms? I warn you she is the only luxury of my life I do not share."

"Share willingly," he might have said, for when Georges seemed to frolic a bit too blithesomely among the demimondaines, Alice would take revenge by fainting in the arms of a valiant, if frightened, young pianist, who patted her comfortingly . . . then caressingly. Scenes with Georges often followed. Then protestations of undying fidelity, thereafter—for each. Then what Georges called "sky-blue ecstasy."

In time Alice and Georges, who was also the mayor of Meslay le Vidame (population 200), fled to the United States to escape the anti-Semitic wrath of Hitler. Shortly before they left, they attended a hunt given by Comte Waldner de Freundstein on his Allier estate. There, according to the writer of a biographical sketch in *Paris Match*, Georges was struck by "the magnificent domain of Lurcy-Lévy"—particularly, by its name.

Soon he had decided that of Levys there were too many; thenceforth he would call himself Lurcy. He was not afraid of being a Jew, but why not protect himself and his wife? It was a practical thing to do, and simple.

Before departing for the States, he deeded his château at Meslay le Vidame to a newly elected mayor, specifying that it was to be made into a sanitarium. When he arrived in America he had with him only Alice, their personal things, and his paintings. Feeling he needed a calm period of adjustment, he settled in Chapel Hill, and to the amazement of students and faculty alike, enrolled at the University of North Carolina as a candidate for a master's degree in political economy.

Professors put off answering the fifty-year-old financial genius's questions in order to ask him their own. His answers took over whole class periods, for he knew the peculiarities not only of the European markets but of the American ones too, and he drew extraordinary comparisons. In 1943 he was given his degree with honors, and like other ambitious graduates, he migrated to New York City, where he functioned as an advisor to many American businessmen.

By 1945 he had installed Alice, himself, and the art collection in a newly purchased house at 813 Fifth Avenue. That it was an avenue other millionaires were leaving perturbed him not at all. "Compared to Paris," he said, "Manhattan is diseased, and Fifth Avenue from the fifties to the sixties is the only habitable area. It is a city where aviaries and caged trees are an absolute necessity." The horrors of the city impelled him to buy a large Long Island estate, to which he retreated intermittently for hunting and entertaining.

In 1950 he allowed himself to be coaxed into joining a firm of New York investment bankers. But his life was nearing its end. He had cancer, which he knew could not be cured. His pallor increased, yet his smile broadened, and still he gathered pictures, adding a last few touches to his collection, as a dying man of another era might have added an urn or two to his tomb.

He died in September 1953. Before then, he spoke prophetically of the lovely people, "the throngs," awaiting the dispersal of his property and desirous of his paintings. "What a beautiful auction they will make," he said. An unprecedented auction they made indeed.

Never in the history of American auctions was such a stir created. The executors of his estate did as his will bade them—consigned the paintings, along with his furniture and *objets d'art,* to Parke-Bernet, for a sale scheduled for November 1954. Mrs. Lurcy, however, objected to so quick a sale. It was well known, she claimed, that the galleries were in cahoots with dealers. Hyam, ruffled, protested. But Mrs. Lurcy, determined to stop the sale, sent lawyers to court to ask that she be permitted to remain in the Fifth Avenue residence—with its art and furnishings. The court ruled in her favor, and for four years—until Lurcy's executors decided to fight his widow and submitted to the court the bills for the upkeep of the house and its furnishings—the public was kept waiting for the release of the priceless works. Convinced Mrs. Lurcy's extravagance was eating into the estate, the court ruled that the collection should be sold. In June 1957 Mary Vandegrift informed the public that the sale would be held the next November.

The news created unprecedented excitement, with heavy pressure on the ruling trio of the galleries. The technicalities involved in staging an auction of such magnitude were not so great a concern as was conducting the sale in a way that would have pleased Mr. Lurcy. Hyam assured the executors that although it would be difficult to do with crowds of rich pushing and shoving like hungry cattle for admittance to the galleries, a halcyon atmosphere would be maintained throughout the sale.

Hyam and Mary Vandegrift set to work on a catalogue they were determined to make a masterpiece—despite the obstacles posed by Mrs. Lurcy, who would not allow them into the Fifth Avenue house to do the cataloguing. They succeeded well enough for Dr. Alfred M. Frankfurter of *Art News* to say (in the introduction) that it was the finest catalogue of an art collection ever compiled.

Mrs. Lurcy broke down a number of times before Parke-Bernet officials. She wept vehemently, because she loved the paintings as she had loved her husband. But, though Hyam pleaded with her, she would not allow a public exhibition within the house.

After the paintings and furniture were carefully removed, she remained in the empty palace, clenching her fists in anger. The staff of Parke-Bernet did not hear a word from her. Hyam and others tried to reach her, but her doorbell remained unanswered—the phone and letters too. She did not attend the exhibition or the sale at the galleries.

So successful was the exhibition that, said Mary Vandegrift, "It became abundantly clear that as commodious as the great salesroom of Parke-Bernet was, it was not going to be large enough." Hundreds of requests for tickets were pouring in daily, and on such short notice, no place—no theater, no hotel ballroom, no armory—large enough and grand enough to house the sale could be found.

Closed-circuit television—never used at an auction in the United States—was suggested. The triumvirate was doubtful about it; nevertheless, it was finally decided that closed-circuit television would be used to relay the works of art to the two largest exhibition galleries, A and D, which were adjacent to the salesroom. Even so, the audience had to be restricted to seventeen hundred people—seven hundred in the main salesroom and a thousand in the adjacent galleries. Among the seventeen hundred admitted to the Parke-Bernet on the historic evening of Thursday, November 7, 1957, were some of the most consequential people in the world. Those who sat in the sales-room had white tickets; the others, with pink tickets and fewer millions—most of them—sat watching the 6-by-8-foot television screens in galleries A and D. Pinks and whites alike had begged to be allowed to come and spend their money.

In the main salesroom Eleanor Roosevelt sat beside Helena Rubenstein—Miss Rubenstein dressed as the richest gypsy in the world, Mrs. Roosevelt as the most stolid librarian. There were choice examples of Rockefellers, Fords, and Vanderbilts. The entire crowd —except for James Rorimer, the director of the Metropolitan Mu-seum, who arrived on the nose of eight—was seated by seven o'clock, an hour before the sale was scheduled to begin.

Mr. Rorimer was granted a spot on the floor beneath the rostrum in which to crouch. Among those in the chairs were Mr. and Mrs. Alexander N. Goulandris, Mr. and Mrs. Winthrop Aldrich, C. Douglas Dillon, Mr. and Mrs. Chester Dale, Madame Jacques Balsan, Mrs. Alfred Lasker, Mr. and Mrs. Robert Lehman, Baron Eric von Goldschmidt-Rothschild, and Charles Durand-Ruel of Paris. Mrs. Stavros P. Niarchos had to sit in a wing off the stage. As the evening progressed, gossip had her wearing wings, which were whis-pered to be shedding gold dust every time she moved. Later, a fashion commentator, confronted by a photograph of her dressed quite simply—no wings—said, "She obviously removed the cumber-some things in order to sit more comfortably."

Louis Marion, facing the greatest assemblage of wealth an auction-eer had ever faced, fanned the fire of bidding subtly, with a minimum of eloquence. Rarely did he raise his voice, and then, only to return, minutes later, to a gentler tone. And all the while, the bids thundered from the callers stationed on every side. Singing cry topped singing cry: "Ten thousand." . . . "Twenty!" . . . "Thirty!" . . . "Forty —in the rear!"

From the adjoining galleries the microphones distorted the calls, amplifying them to frenzied shrieks. "Forty-five in Gallery A!" . . . "Fifty thousand—Gallery D!"

Intermittently the crowd applauded, as picture after picture soared beyond all previous economic tributes to its artist: Vuillard's *Aux Tuileries*—$70,000; Monet's *Femme dans un Jardin*—$92,500; $95,000 for Toulouse-Lautrec's *Aux Ambassadeurs, Gens Chics*.

The television rooms provided several surprises—from the dark horses in Gallery A and the dark, dark horses in Gallery D. Though the handicappers who assigned the tickets may have figured them as also-rans, no second-class art lovers they!

When Renoir's *Mme. Le Brun et la Fille* was knocked down, for $22,000, to a buyer in Gallery A, angry hoots were heard from D. D's auxiliary auctioneer calmed the storm, and a moment later appealed to Marion to reopen the bidding—because he had failed to notice and relay a bid in time.

Marion said, in essence, too bad; can't do it.

Hisses and boos were heard. The microphone, unable to handle the volume of noise, squealed, screamed. Marion stared ferociously at the audience, then placed the ivory hammer in the center of the rostrum and leaned forward with both hands pressed against the sides, waiting for the audience to be quiet.

"Thirty-three years I've been in this business in some way or another," Marion finally said, "and when a bid's late, I will not reopen. However"—he paused, and some people thought they saw a slightly mischievous smile—"when a bid is relayed by all these electronic gadgets, and a caller is a bit slow to boot, there might be some reason for doing so. Now"—he paused again—"though I don't think this is a particularly democratic audience"—another pause, while the spectators won over by Marion laughed—"I'm going to put it up to you. How about it? Shall I reopen? All in favor—come on. Gallery D witnesses, here's your chance."

From Gallery D old ladies who had perhaps never before raised their voices in their lives shouted, "Yea!" At least one of their husbands joined with a long-forgotten varsity "Rah!" But an almost equal amount of noise was heard from Gallery A.

"Well," said Marion, "I'm going to reopen it anyway, and I don't want to hear any more—except bids—do you understand?"

Gallery D cheered its victory, but nonetheless, lost again to Gallery A, for $500 more.

Marion enunciated an indignant, "Really, Gallery D," and proceeded to the next item.

Team spirit erupted again in Gallery A when Mrs. H. H. Jonas bid up to $175,000 for Gauguin's *Mau Taporo*. The dark horses urged her upward and cried out, "No, no," and "That's not fair!" when Marion knocked the picture down at $180,000, to Alexander Goulandris, who was in the main salesroom. Until the uproar subsided, Marion listened to it as if to a Shelley ode; then he shrugged. The audience in the main room laughed heartily. Mrs. Jonas hushed her supporters. She had evidently not heard the "hundred" that had preceded the "and seventy-five thousand dollars," and she was aghast that she had almost gone over her head, although she was certainly wealthy enough to finance her drowning.

Gallery A had to console itself with lesser winners. A 7-by-10½-inch Gauguin went to S. P. Mugar of the Star Market in Newtonville, Massachusetts, for $24,000. A Mrs. David Klau, hitherto unsung in collecting circles, annexed a greeting-card-size Renoir for $22,500 after a bold encounter with the shadow horses of Gallery D.

Moving in swiftly on the stretch, Gallery D had its revenge and captured two Derains, a Boudin, three Dufys, a Vuillard, a Sisley, and two Renoirs for a total of $109,250.

At the climax of the sale, Mrs. Jonas of Gallery A once more sailed into the fray, and once more her supporters rallied to her cause. Before them loomed Lurcy's favorite Renoir, *La Serre*, depicting a woman standing in front of a greenhouse overflowing with blooms. Lurcy had cradled this painting in his arms, rocking, and saying, "It is a dream. We must not wake it, and yet . . . I wonder how one sings a lullaby to the sun."

For this poem of the civilized jungle, which had cost Lurcy $24,000 in 1940, Mrs. Jonas—alert now to the "hundred"—bid up to $180,000. Her opponent, sitting in the main salesroom, was Henry Ford II, looking mildly perplexed, like a sport fan watching a chancy play. He pursed his lips, furrowed his brow, and watched his agent (in a nearby seat) take the painting at $200,000. Mrs. Ford, looking hypersensitive in pearls and black, sighed nervously and said to her husband, "Thank you, darling."

Ford watched his agent carefully as he also bought Bonnard's *Femme Nue*, for $50,000. He bent forward thoughtfully a number of times, letting his arms rest on his knees. Alexander Goulandris bought the next Bonnard, *Still Life with a Cat*, for $70,000. An agent for Paul Mellon (the son of Andrew Mellon) bought the $95,000 Lautrec, *Aux Ambassadeurs, Gens Chic*, which depicts a young couple sitting together in a café, eyeing each other appreciatively, but with a certain sniffy, humorous arrogance; Douglas Dillon purchased the $92,500 Monet, *Femme dans un Jardin*, for loan to the Metropolitan. Lurcy's other Lautrec, the very spectacular and flamboyant *Aristide*

Bruant, was bought by Peter Nathan, a Zurich dealer, supposedly for Stavros Niarchos, the husband of the wife in the wing—and wings.

A New York dealer, E. J. Rousuck, paid $57,000 for Pissarro's *Le Pont-Neuf, Paris,* for William C. Wright of Philadelphia. Degas' *Danseuses* brought $50,000, Renoir's *Roses* and Sisley's *Les Loing à Moret,* $37,500 each. Seventeen of the twenty-four painters represented made new world records, and Lurcy's sixty-five paintings earned $1,708,500, then the highest total ever recorded for an auction of fine paintings.

There were no restrictions on attendance for the sales' two subsequent sessions, at which Lurcy's furniture and *objets d'art* were sold. The curious—sightseers and impecunious addicts as well as captains of finance—came in droves; and while the rich manipulated prices to heights worthy of their concern ($20,000 for a Louis XV writing table, for example), people in more modest circumstances did carry off such prizes as a nice Chinese rug for $45, a very good Louis XV carved and painted cabinet (catalogued as repainted and restored) for $175, twenty-three Wedgwood dinner plates for $40, a seventeenth-century Italian table (then out of fashion) for $300, a carved walnut Louis XV-style table for $20, and a K'ang Hsi baluster jar for $60. As in every estate sale, there was somthing for everyone—though most was for the rich. Mr. Robert Lehman, who paid $29,000 for Lot No. 335, a Sèvres soup tureen dated 1757 that had cost Lurcy $3,000 at the Walters sale in 1941, did not complain of disappointment.

At the close of the sessions, the press paid tribute the world over to the sublimity of French impressionists and soup tureens. But more was written of the staggering $2,221,355 total realized for Lurcy's 414 lots.

Lurcy's oddly mercenary requiem passed into its special niche in the history of golden auctions, but within a year the record total for his sixty-five paintings had been exceeded by almost half a million dollars in a twenty-one-minute sale, of only seven pictures—three Manets, two Cézannes, a Renoir, and a van Gogh—at Sotheby's in London. The pictures had belonged to the late German banker Jakob Goldschmidt. They brought the astounding sum of $2,186,800. The $616,000 paid for Cézanne's *Garçon en Gilet Rouge* was about

$320,000 more than the highest previous price a picture had ever brought at auction. The buyer was a New York dealer, acting as a proxy for Paul Mellon.

It was at this point that Sotheby's, by taking American collections and selling them abroad, became a major threat to Parke-Bernet. Just a few years earlier, in July 1954, another important collection, that of Wilhelm Weinberg's modern paintings, had slipped from the galleries and been sold by Sotheby's, bringing a total of $914,256. Though the threat was quite evident, it did not frighten the triumvirate noticeably until the sixties. The fifties promised money and collections enough to appease all major auction houses in the world. The Parke-Bernet Galleries had more lots than they could handle, and expanded their facilities instead of retreating from the fear of London competitors.

Almost a year to the day following the Lurcy sale, the bemillioned, beminked, and besabled crowd had once more assembled at the galleries. Again closed-circuit television operated in the adjacent galleries. The lure was twenty-nine modern French paintings, recently acquired by Arnold Kirkeby, a force in the hotel business, and they fell from the auction block with their price tags fairly dangling. Six of the Lurcy records for individual painters were surpassed, and five other painters—Modigliani, Berthe Morisot, Rouault, Segonzac, and Utrillo—whose works were not included in Lurcy's collection, topped their previous world records. A Picasso, *Mother and Child,* brought $152,000, by far the highest price ever paid at auction for the work of a living painter. The twenty-nine paintings brought $1,548,500. Millions for the moderns was becoming somewhat run of the mill. A social commentator feared ennui.

But the Goldschmidt and Kirkeby sales, the sublimity of their finances notwithstanding, could not recapture the romance of the Lurcy auction. Somehow they evoked the banality of a superspectacle repeated with brasher music and more dancing girls. The name of Germany's financial titan and the list of paintings he had snatched from under Dr. Goebbels' Aryan nose conjured up no hedonistic world of rose de Pompadour and grace, no lost Ananda, no pulsebeat of the heart's desire. No one waxed sentimental over the ninety-seven corporations Goldschmidt had controlled or his Berlin palace besieged by storm troopers. The redistribution of the salvaged paintings became simply a matter of cold cash. At the Kirkeby sale the wealth assembled was also colossal, but a public increasingly benumbed by figures showed a tendency to take it for granted. Inflation was becoming more and more a way of life. Newspapers had almost ceased to shudder editorially at the price of Cézannes. The London *Observer* suggested that the radio stock exchange report, after finishing the usual quotations for industrials, might proclaim, "Renoir, steady; Vlaminck and Manet, mixed."

Officials of the auctions who had been enchanted by the halcyon world of Lurcy doubted that Kirkeby, during his brief and fickle flirtation with modern art, had spent much time in contemplating either Modigliani or Rouault. Though the pictures were magnificent, the one indispensable condition for a glamour auction was lacking—a deceased consignor who had lived magnificently and collected in accord. Manet, Monet, Matisse, Rouault, took their turns upon the stage like actors who had bored their patron and were seeking a new engagement at a higher wage. For some absurd reason, the wage was tripled or quadrupled, but there were no cheers from the farther rooms. Mr. Kirkeby grumbled a little that his profits were not considerably greater, then left for the nearest airport without obliging the photographers.

Nor was London's historic total hailed as a collectors' triumph. Goldschmidt's son and heir, an insurance agent, had his picture taken beside the $616,000 *Boy in a Red Vest*. He looked as gleeful over his thumping capital gain as Cézanne's boy seemed resigned to the tragic loneliness of his creator.

To be sure, golden rain had fallen on the modern masters in these sales, but in neither case would anyone have summed up the new exorbitance in the phrase used by one of the Lurcy executors: "We had such a glowing sale!" What was missing was that aura of intangibles that surrounds a collection that has been lived with, loved, and left behind. At the Lurcy sale there was that peculiar magic that sometimes prevails in the auction hall—the excitement of stumbling on a footnote, a work of art that documents the nuances of a life. Another of Lurcy's executors said simply, "Georges would have been pleased."

During the fifties just one other sale earned in excess of $2 million and caused something of a furor. This, the sale of Thelma Chrysler Foy's collection, came in May 1959, a month after Hiram H. Parke's death. The sale was an appropriate farewell to a man who had propagated an air of grandeur in the auction hall.

The Major died on April 1, 1959. He was eighty-five years old, retired, but not until the very end had he stopped making his frequent visits to the galleries, where his presence was always greeted with respectful applause. There, as elsewhere, he was recognized as a man who had formed one of America's most revered institutions, and in doing so, had risen above meretricious salesmanship to evoke some of the magic of the things he sold.

Sometimes he would unexpectedly appear in his beloved galleries in the afternoon—an almost powdery white ghost with a beautifully soft voice. He would stand beside a Sheraton commode perhaps, and watch the people viewing one of the transient exhibitions. Somehow recorded in his astonishingly expressive face, his faded blue eyes, were the half-forgotten memories of the dry-goods wagon, the many sales, the many summers spent trailing Mr. Bishop through hallowed lands. The old gentleman could still flash a gracious welcome to a princess or to the Dowager Mrs. Hearst, though he might have forgotten her name. The Duchess of what, the Princess of where, he could not always remember, however noble the lady. He of the never-failing memory for faces, pictures, chairs, dynastic fortunes, would eventually leave the galleries and perhaps read the obituaries with a little interest, but not with the former relish.

The old gentleman faded gently into the past. And the month after his obituaries appeared, the élite populace, seemingly never more eager to part with its money, flocked to the galleries that bore his name to compete for the possessions of the late motorcar heiress Thelma Chrysler Foy.

At the time of her death in 1957 Mrs. Foy was eulogized as "the woman of the greatest taste in current life in New York"—a tribute based both on her wearing apparel and on the appanages of eighteenth-century French court life that had formed the setting for her progress through twentieth-century café society. In her houses and in her New York apartment she had made herself an ultraroyalist domain of gilt and porcelain, marquetry and bronze *doré*. On her walls were no fewer than seven Renoirs, plus some well-chosen pictures by such blue-chip artists as Degas, Vuillard, and Toulouse-Lautrec. Her chambers were a galaxy of things that other people had desired: adornments from the House of Morgan and the House of Rothschild, sculptures made for Catherine the Great of Russia, a toilet table at which the Empress Josephine had sat. Her salons were a joyous harmony of lustrous forms and silken weavings, a testament to the master craftsman, the porcelain factory's glory, and the giddy, hedonistic world of Malmaison and Versailles. Dark-haired and pretty, she had moved with mannequinlike grace over carpets woven with golden threads through groves of kingwood and palisander metamorphosed into the most eloquent expressions of the French cabinetmaker's soul.

It was a perfectionist collection; no note of counterfeit intruded. Relentless in her quest, the curator of that concinnate display would ceaselessly add new triumphs of acquisition, combing the world's great galleries to replace the almost perfect piece with one a hair-breadth nearer to perfection. She had a penchant for white, and for things in pairs. Her imperial white bedroom was glacially chaste; the full-length portrait of her that hung there presented a virtuoso study of a diaphanous white dress. Her pairs of eighteenth-century fauteuils glistened in off-white taffetas and velvets, accented by satins and brocades in the most delicate pastels. Commodes and cabinets presumed to be inimitable stood about in couples, as if to underline twice over the lady's aesthetic prowess and largess. It was as if two centuries of time had not touched anything. The cleaner and upholsterer were in perpetual attendance. A sofa or *bergère* demeaned by any considerable human contact was forthwith dispatched to be restored to its immaculate condition. Should either of Mrs. Foy's two highly privileged Yorkshire terriers, Baby Pie and Cupie Doll, be guilty of an indiscretion against the elegance of its milieu, the damage was straightaway repaired.

The sister of Walter P. Chrysler, Jr., and heiress of many millions, she had essayed the world of *ton* and quintessential snobbery equipped with a pedigree she had had traced to a king of the Ostrogoths said to have died in the year 230, to the Kyburg counts of Thurgau, and to other medieval worthies. Costumed by Jacques Fath and Christian Dior, she had made the scene on two continents, in company with her financial peers and social strategist Elsa Maxwell. She had the approval of the New York Dress Institute, the friendship of the Duchess of Windsor.

Her jewels were a legend at El Morocco. Her movements and

Thelma Chrysler Foy next to her Regency commode (LARRY GORDON PHOTO).

possessions were recorded in the gossip columns. With a built-in smile of noblesse oblige, she had been photographed for the glossiest of magazines, sometimes in a corner of "the finest house in New York," sometimes with her children—and later, though looking scarcely a year older, with her grandchildren.

She was determined to be regal, but she had her homey side as well. Sunday nights she liked to stay in and be cozy, with her porcelains and her husband. Forsaking the gold-and-white dining room,

593

they would have a simple meal before the fire, perhaps on the Louis XV tulipwood card table that was to bring $26,000 in the sale. After the servants had withdrawn, Mr. Foy would get out the X-ray machine that was otherwise used medically—to stall the developing leukemia from which Mrs. Foy suffered—and they would spend the evening X-raying the porcelains to make sure the butler had not broken one and had it surreptitiously mended.

Vain and purse-proud she was, and possibly obsessed. But the achievement of Thelma Chrysler Foy was not to be disparaged. With her fathomless resources, she had ventured into the knavish world of artmongers and put together, piece on piece, an edifice that was—to quote the Parke-Bernet's succinct encomium—"the wonder of all of us who are concerned with such matters, on two continents." Living in the shadow of an incurable disease, she had candidly pursued the ultimate in self-aggrandizement, until—in her middle fifties—her smile grew wan, then disappeared. The fragmentation of her setting called into service the skill and talent, the lifelong experience, of more than a hundred Parke-Bernet employees. Items from the dismantled *mise en scène* were painstakingly classified, appraised, and processed, their wonders submitted to the scrutiny of experts. Tidings of the great sale were bruited throughout the world of wealthy connoisseurs. Under the direction of President Hyam and Vice President Mary Vandegrift, a monumental two-volume catalogue was published, bound—significantly—in white cloth and lettered in gold. A veritable compendium of the glory that was France, its 375 pages described 772 lots, interpreting their intricacies of form and workmanship and chronicling their origins and past migrations. Many of the pedigrees read like excerpts from the Almanach de Gotha.

Reassembled in the eleven rose-taupe galleries for the presale exhibition—in two parts, for even that broad three acres was inadequate to show everything at once—the tendrils of aristocracy that had been Mrs. Foy's were a dazzling evocation of a way of life long perished. Aphrodite, life size in marble, by Giovanni da Bologna, stood serene and lucent just inside the doors, betokening the radiance to be seen upstairs; bronze and silver, gold and ebony, exuded their inimitable rays. Artfully lighted, grouped as for a palace ball, the cabinets and tables, the brocade chairs and satin sofas, the Renoir portraits and Degas dancers, the terra-cotta groups and marble figures, the porcelains of Vincennes, Sèvres, and Saint Cloud, transformed the rooms into a maze of wondrous contrasts and shifting vistas.

The immaculate collection could hardly have been more eloquently displayed. Its crystals were all polished; its rare woods rubbed to their accustomed luster. Its receptacles were filled daily with the pale-hued flowers the sometime mistress of those dulcet household goods had favored.

There were previews for the press, previews for the art-buying Maecenases. After that the public came—the covetous and the merely curious, the lovers of beauty and the well-heeled Philistines, the hawk-eyed dealers with their coteries, the curators of museums with the free-spending donors of tax-deductible munificence on whose support they depended. They came twenty thousand strong—the studious and the speculators, hounds and addicts, the quality collectors and the greenhorn Medici, the women who would rather go to an auction than a matinee. They paid $8.50 for the white-and-gold catalogue and plucked the rosebuds from the crystal vases for their buttonholes. Four thousand streamed into the galleries in a single afternoon—titans with the twang of Texas in their speech, Spanish-speaking bankers, Egyptian businessmen, and glamour girls from Hollywood. The hierarchy of the successful came, and the hierarchy of the unconscionably wealthy.

Appreciation welled in a variety of languages, and in at least one instance, manifested itself in costume: a waggish young woman appeared in a purfled white hat precisely copied from the 1891 creation in one of Mrs. Foy's Renoirs. The news photographers obligingly took her picture.

Men with minds of vaunted practicality debated the attractions of objects utterly impractical. Informed collectors, oblivious to the persiflage around them, marveled at the technical perfection of *choufleur* finials and inlaid floral sprays of kingwood and amboyna. Tyros of the female sex twittered over bibelots fashioned for queens and courtesans. Decorators of indeterminate sex waxed voluble before their clients in erudition gleaned hastily from the catalogue. The giddy world of Mrs. Foy's acquaintance made declamatory entrances and said her lyre-back chairs had always been adorable. Austere persons said the money was all in the wrong places nowadays. Dealers claiming to have sold "the woman of the greatest taste" a preponderance of her collection lingered at strategic posts, hoping to catch a glint of unfulfilled desire from a Mellon, Ford, or Rockefeller. Hardy souls with no respect for purity stood before the snow-white bed with its eleven-foot gossamer canopy and made indelicate comments. Two high-school boys in shirt sleeves discovered a stain on the ivory silk of a Louis XV dog's bed and were triumphant.

For eleven days and three evenings the élite crowd milled among the superb creations of clay and kiln, the gold-mounted powder jars and jewel-studded boxes, the bronze-mounted cabinets and delicately blushed fabrics. There were things that had passed through the Parke-Bernet before, recalling the brevity of life, the poignancy of altered fortune: sculptures from the Walters sale in the dark hours of World War Two, enamels from the great Rovensky sale of 1957, perfume bottles from the J. P. Morgan sale of 1944 (part of a group of thirty-four minuscule Chelsea figures, averaging the length of a man's little finger, which in the fury of the bidding turned out to be worth $34,325).

The literati could browse among the handsome volumes of the Foy art library, acquired *in toto* at the 1943 auction of Frank Crowninshield, editor, savant and—as *The New York Times* once phrased it—"a flower in the buttonhole of a large segment of the society of New York." Many of the books had been unopened and uncut when the *arbiter elegantiarum* consigned them to Parke-Bernet for sale. Now, sixteen years later, they were back, and in the same pristine condition—still unopened, uncut.

The exhibition was a high-pitched whetting of desire. Some among the divers multitude lingered to reflect upon a temporary world in which there are no permanent possessions, in which hovers a melancholy aura: the persistent overtone of finality and sadness that is ever present at auctions. But overall a raucous note prevailed—a Midas zeal coloring glib, unsentimental voices, the gleam of acquisition shining on otherwise blasé faces.

The stakes for the opening session of the five-part Foy extravaganza consisted only of the seventeen pictures classified as modern. In accord with long-established custom when fine paintings are to be auctioned, the sale was scheduled for the evening—a warm May night, with the trees outside Parke-Bernet burgeoning new foliage, the pocketbooks of picture buyers bulging with inestimable thousands. To avoid bloodshed and protect the serious bidders from the spectacle-loving populace, attendance was limited to ticket holders—seven hundred in the main salesroom, tactfully chosen from seven times as many applicants, and a thousand more in adjacent galleries equipped with closed-circuit television screens.

Long before eight o'clock the votaries had assembled in the plush-hung auditorium. The chairs and crimson couches were all filled. Green-uniformed attendants rushed to bring seats for imperious late-comers.

Seldom had the halls contained a more auspicious congregation: wealth assembled from many far-flung places—from France and England, Switzerland, Germany, Venezuela—bejeweled ladies and men of awesome self-importance, movie lords and celebrated actors, a billionaire or two from Texas, the emissaries of Greek shipping magnates, chevaliers of industry and scions of old houses from the length and breadth of the United States, agents with bidding orders for no one knew what princely clients grown panicky at the dwindling supply of modern art. Spectators leaned from the balcony; standees lined the rear of the theater; dark-horse bidders craned before the television screens, waiting to see the fourteen paintings and three small drawings about to be disputed over.

Louis Marion made his way through the crowded aisles to the steps at the right of the stage and mounted to the canopied rostrum. At a lower level, his assistants, the bid callers and stand-by auctioneers, took their places; the record keeper bent over his table. A distance apart, Leslie Hyam—a tall figure with prematurely white hair and the august dignity of a member of the House of Lords—assumed his customary vantage point. Coming barely to his shoulders, Mary Vandegrift, beautiful in evening satin, surveyed the assembled buying power and concluded that it could doubtless foot a substantial portion of the national debt.

Marion rapped his gavel. The hum of voices dwindled. The bid callers, assigned like stalwart outfielders to each section of the hall, stiffened at their posts, alert to pick up the most furtively signaled bid and relay it in a caterwauling to the pulpit. In the television rooms the auxiliary auctioneers tested microphones and assured their congregations that all bids would be clearly transmitted.

Unawed by so many millions on the hoof, Marion swept the audience with an easy, we're-all-in-this-together smile. On the floodlit stage, a green-uniformed porter placed Lot No. 1, a framed sheet of paper boasting Renoir's signature beneath a brown crayon sketch of a nude model with an outsize derrière. And with a minimum of preamble, the sale was under way.

"I have five hundred dollars to start. . . . Six. . . . Seven . . . at seven hundred dollars now."

It was a scene as familiar to habitués as a religious observance to the devout, a ritual with overtones of theater, imbued with something of the gambling hall's seductive aura—the perfumed air, the hush, the display of cupidity, attenuated by a reverence, of a sort. As the bids were signaled, the mercenary incantation of the auctioneer was punctuated by the callers' stentorian cries. "A thousand!" . . . "Fifteen hundred!" . . . "Two thousand, in the rear!"

The Renoir sketch brought $4,000, perhaps twice as much as it would have brought had it not once been owned by Thelma Chrysler Foy. But the moneyed crowd had not come to play for such peripheral prizes. The minor lots disposed of, Vuillard's *Le Salon*, impermanently created out of pigments mixed with paste on board, went to $27,500. A little oval portrait of a Gay Nineties prostitute by Toulouse-Lautrec, which had decorated Mrs. Foy's piano, and before that, the salon of a Paris brothel, brought $16,000, somewhat more than the famous old *maison de tolérance* itself had been worth in its Paris heyday. Renoir's charmer in the purfled hat fell at $92,500; his portrait of a golden-haired seamstress, draped to Mrs. Foy's taste in a shimmery white bodice, made a neat $100,000. So avid were the bidders to obtain a Renoir painted by Renoir that his *Lady with Parasol in a Garden* outran both—at $140,000.

Before a half hour had passed, two new world records had been established: *Femme Russe dans un Jardin* by Toulouse-Lautrec had soared to $180,000, and a Degas ballerina had been bought (appropriately by dancing master Arthur Murray) at the same price—the highest ever bid at auction for a work by either of these artists.

Each time the hammer fell, the nonbidders and the vanquished marked the prices on the margins of their catalogues with a flourish of vicarious satisfaction. In the rostrum, Marion, unshakable in his composure, called the mounting numbers slowly, bluntly, without niggling or histrionics. The audience maintained an almost poker-faced decorum. But beneath the surface, a current of controlled excitement surged—erupting in a murmur of appreciation and a sense of approaching climax as the porters brought onstage the sixth of the seven Foy Renoirs, *Les Filles de Durand-Ruel,* a sun-flecked, time-mellowed portrait of two teen-agers of the eighteen eighties seated on a garden bench in their summer finery.

Like many another work that now provokes raptures of exorbitance in the market place, the luminous outdoor portrait Renoir had painted in 1882, using as models the spirited daughters of his friend Durand-Ruel, had its long story. In 1886 Durand-Ruel, then impressionism's sole commercial champion, had crossed the ocean with it, shown it in Kirby's historic "Impressionists of Paris" exhibit in the AAA's Madison Square galleries, and then—since no one wanted *Les Filles de Durand-Ruel* at any price—taken it back to France (with scores of other canvases by Renoir and his contemporaries which are now the esteemed masterpieces in many great museums). Time passed, and *Les Filles de Durand-Ruel* was sold in Paris to a man named Aude, who—his ardor kindled, it would be pleasant to think, by the winsome charm of Renoir's portrait—married the older of the two sisters. The picture remained in the Aude family until the mid-nineteen-forties. Then both subjects being dead, the children sold it—for $15,000—to a dealer, who in turn bestowed it upon Thelma Chrysler Foy.

Now, seated in the Parke-Bernet salesroom was a man of sentiment—not to say of unimpeachable taste and judgment—who longed to redeem the portrait for the Durand-Ruel family. The nephew of the two young girls Renoir had so lovingly painted had flown from France prepared to bid $200,000. But even Charles Durand-Ruel, scion of the venerable dealer who had kept Renoir from starving, and a leading authority on art values, had misjudged the devil-may-care monetary rhapsodies of a New York auction.

The contest opened with a veritable bombardment of signaled bids. The callers voices boomed from all parts of the salesroom; microphones blared, relaying counteroffers from the television watchers. Within a matter of seconds, M. Durand-Ruel leaned back in his chair, and his face clouded with frustration, bade his aunts a fond farewell.

The bidding cooled off at $224,000. Marion turned in the rostrum as if to say his own affectionate, if tentative, farewell to the daughters of Durand-Ruel. Turning back to the audience then, he swept it with a look of mock reproof, then said, "I hate to see a good picture like that go so cheaply."

The tense onlookers—many of them aware that the price of *Les Filles de Durand-Ruel* had already surpassed, by $19,000, the previous auction record for a Renoir—responded with a murmur of attenuated laughter. The curious rose in their seats and craned to get a look at Colonel Capton Michael Paul (of Wall Street and Park Avenue), whose balding gray head had nodded the $224,000 bid.

"Once. . . . Twice." Marion raised his right hand, cupping the gavel. "Are you all through?" He paused, and lo! in the instant before his arm descended, a stentorian voice bawled, "Two hundred twenty-five!"

Colonel Paul responded with a defiant nod.

"At two hundred 'n' twenty-six thousand dollars!" Marion chanted briskly, and leaned forward on the rostrum as the race began again.

"Seven!"

"Eight!"

"Nine!" It was a tense, slow duel now, as the rhythmic thrusts went back and forth between the ambushed Colonel and his eleventh-hour opponent, unseen by him, unidentified by the crowd.

Thousand by thousand the daughters' ransom mounted, until—with a dour expression that could have been one of asperity, or military pride in a well-fought battle lost—the Colonel finally ceased to nod.

"Once. . . . Twice." Marion began counting as before. There was dead silence in the hall. Not a finger moved, not a Midas eyebrow was raised. The ivory hammer clicked, and *Les Filles de Durand-Ruel* was sold—at $255,000.

It could hardly be said that the most coveted of the evening's prizes went to feast the eyes of a hitherto deprived Renoir fancier. The unseen buyer, privileged to occupy a secluded niche in the salesroom by virtue of his familial relation, turned out to be the late Mrs. Foy's brother, Walter P. Chrysler, Jr., long conspicuous among the busier art collectors for owning, along with numerous other paintings, a warehouse hoard of some three thousand pictures—about twice the number Louis XIV saw fit to acquire for the adornment of the most magnificent court in Europe. In the aftermath of discussion, an observer contemptuous of a system of collecting apparently based on mere numerical prodigiousness suggested that the virtuoso of the House of Chrysler may have been less moved to splurge over a quarter of a million dollars on a picture he could have had for a tenth of that much a decade or so earlier by the desire to possess another Renoir than by the perverse pleasure of keeping someone else from getting it. The motives of art buyers being a miasma of psychological complexity, and in any case, inscrutable, such waspish speculation can be put down to the rivalries and cumulative frustrations indigenous to the auction hall. At all events, the winsome daughters of Durand-Ruel, whether carried off capriciously or to satisfy an all-consuming passion, showed up that summer at the Chrysler Art Gallery in Provincetown, Massachusetts, looking a bit discomforted amid an agglomeration of Sandwich glass and a curious disharmony of freshly painted pictures by contemporary abstractionists.

Meanwhile the Thelma Chrysler Foy sale made auction history. In the thirty-six minutes it took, that first night, to sell three drawings and fourteen paintings, $1,166,400 changed hands. But the spectacle had only started. Four long afternoon sessions followed—for the furniture, sculptures, and eighteenth-century paintings, the library, the porcelains and other decorative objects.

With no tickets required, the populace forgathered with carnival exuberance. Parking space was nowhere to be had, and nowhere was battle waged more fiercely than in the halls of Parke-Bernet. Wild were the caterwaulings of the criers, syncopated with the patter of Marion and his lieutenant auctioneers, now monotonous, now rising in crescendo to a jubilant five-figure climax: $27,000 for a pair of ebony consoles, $30,000 for a Savonnerie rug 320 years the worse for wear. A big-league English dealer shrugged his shoulders and went home to London. The prices were too high, he said—$14,000 for a pair of Meissen blue jays, $28,000 for a pair of kingwood and tulipwood commodes, $24,000 for a Louis XVI occasional table, $26,000 for a Persian gold and silver rug.

No moments thrilled the multitude more than those when the porcelain buyers skirmished over a Sèvres dinner service that Mr. and Mrs. Foy and their X-ray machine had whiled away many Sunday evenings with. They were nice dishes, and what was more, they had a built-in pedigree, so to speak, in the form of the monogram of the Cardinal de Rohan, who lived a life of plenary extravagance from 1734 to 1803 and earned a niche of sorts in history by his notoriously foolish role in the revolution-making scandal of the diamond necklace of Marie Antoinette. In 1772 the prince was sent as ambassador extraordinary to the court of Vienna. With his portfolio, he took along a dinner service fashioned at the great porcelain factory at Sèvres; fired with a turquoise ground, it was painted with exotic birds, etched and gilded with garlands, acorns, oak leaves, and sundry other intricate motifs calculated to impress the Empress Maria Theresa (who hated de Rohan) with the matchless sublimity of French art. Originally there were 340 pieces in the set; during revelries of state, a certain breakage no doubt occurred, and what with the ravages of time, forty pieces had survived to find their way to the home of Thelma Chrysler Foy. In the democratic melee at the Parke-Bernet they were knocked down to a dealer said to be acting for a potentate of Greek shipping; the price was $60,000, or $1,500 per piece.

And so it went through four warm May afternoons. To the rise and fall of rude hammer, the lustrous household goods so painstakingly gathered by Mrs. Foy were scattered; her edifice dissolved under a torrent of inflated money. All that remained was the beautiful white catalogue—that and $2,625,880, a grand total unprecedented in the history of art auctions the world over.

With Mrs. Foy's sale finished, Parke-Bernet rushed into the sixties with another astounding sale, breaking the Foy record, and establishing a new world record with the sale of twenty-four old masters collected by the late Mr. and Mrs. Alfred W. Erickson. But the general public found itself emotionally incapable of withstanding another multimillion-dollar auction crisis. Harsh criticism, lampoons, caricatures, abounded in the press. Despite them, Hyam was determined to make this his greatest sale, and he succeeded. Yet even he, it seemed, had hardened to the thrills of the hall.

"Who needs to care," he said, "since the outcome is inevitably successful? As long as we can get collections, the prices are like space mileage. And yet I continue to care about the outcome of sales, though there is something faintly deadly about it—atrophying, like the numbing effect of continually listening to an air hammer pulverizing asphalt.

"At the beginning, the money aspect was a kind of pestilence one endured. Later, it became ossifying. But I suppose the sound of the air hammer is only an amplified heartbeat against the thuds of the hammer's supposedly delicate ivory . . . and the screams of the bid callers. To bear such anxiety indefinitely leaves one a cinder. But I've borne it well. And look at Mary—she'll be beautiful at a hundred and eighty. And Louis survives because he's not attenuated his energies by trying to learn French or behave like an aristocrat. He's greatly respected as a man of his own making, quite like a Vanderbilt or a Carnegie, and actually he's the pace setter, the maestro and percussionist, and gets us all panting after fire engines.

"But I am a bit tired, and I'm rather sad that I'm not known or appreciated for my real contribution, which has been to make it possible for these—in some cases, silly—American millionaires to buy real Rembrandts or Matisses or Monets at whatever price they're willing to pay. And more important, I've spoken about how wonderful it is. And heaven knows, not merely as an advertising gimmick. Despite the fact that the galleries sell art, owning art is wonderful, and I don't think people realize how unprejudiced I am in this belief."

Before the evening of November 15, 1961, Hyam was at his most intensively active, for on that fateful evening he was to bring to the block one of the greatest private collections ever likely to come on the market in America. And in the collection, which would be bid upon by the most powerful and affluent group of art buyers ever to be assembled in one place at one time, was a single painting, one of three Rembrandts, that was valued at considerably more than $1 million.

Aristotle Contemplating the Bust of Homer had been bought by Alfred W. Erickson, cofounder of the McCann-Erickson advertising agency, in the twenties, when Erickson had paid Sir Joseph Duveen $750,000 for it. After the 1929 crash, the huckster-connoisseur, in the throes of a temporary personal depression, sold the picture back to Duveen for $500,000, and in 1936, when things were looking up, Erickson again bought the Rembrandt from Duveen, this time for $590,000—bringing the total cost of his love affair with the famous picture to $840,000.

That same year, Erickson died. *Aristotle* and its companion pictures stayed with his widow in the Erickson house on East 35th Street until Mrs. Erickson's death, in February 1961.

The Rembrandt *Aristotle* was unquestionably the *pièce de résistance* of the Erickson collection, but only slightly less coveted by museums and big-league collectors—billionaires, many of them—were Erickson's two smaller Rembrandts, his Crivelli, his magnificent Perugino, *St. Augustine with Members of the Confraternity of Perugia*, and his portraits by Van Dyck, Hals, Holbein, Nattier,

Fragonard, Cranach, Romney, Raeburn, Gainsborough. All, or nearly all, were masterworks the like of which had not often been found on the world art market of the last quarter century.

In one tense hour of bidding at the Parke-Bernet $4,679,250 changed hands. The Rembrandt *Aristotle* went to the Metropolitan Museum of Art. The director, James Rorimer, who had sat on the floor beneath the rostrum in the Lurcy sale, winked his bid of $2,300,000 for the world's most expensive painting. There was applause in the galleries, but the press was aghast at the price. The hullabaloo was world wide; the criticism of unprecedented vehemence—often with particular stress on one or another way in which 2,300,000 American dollars could be used to relieve human suffering. One writer alluded to eighteenth-century Russian exorbitance, then exclaimed, "So many hundred souls for a darkened canvas measuring 56½ by 53¾ inches." Another, noting that the Metropolitan already had some thirty Rembrandts, accused Rorimer of the greatest gluttony since the days of Versailles. Rorimer said only that he considered it important to add the Erickson Rembrandt to the museum's already outstanding collection; the price would be met by donations from several trustees and private individuals.

The second highest price in the sale was the $875,000 paid for Fragonard's luscious *La Liseuse* by the National Gallery in Washington; next was the $220,000 for Crivelli's *Madonna and Child;* then $180,000 for Rembrandt's *Portrait of an Old Man.* Wildenstein of New York paid $175,000 for Nattier's *La Marquise de Baglion, as Flora,* and the Carnegie Institute bought Frans Hals's *Man with a Herring* for $145,000 and Perugino's *St. Augustine with Members of the Confraternity of Perugia* for $125,000. A painting by an unknown Dutch master, *Scenes from the Life of St. Augustine,* commanded another $110,000 of the Metropolitan Museum's money. The third Rembrandt, *Prince Frederick Henry of Orange, Governor of the Netherlands,* was bought by Knoedler & Company for $110,000. One other painting topped the $100,000 mark—Cranach's *Princess Sibylle of Cleves, Electress of Saxony,* which brought $105,000.

After the Erickson sale, Hyam had to contend, much to his exasperation, with the threat of Sotheby's and other European auction houses that sold American collections abroad. He had constantly to assure consignors that their property would bring as much in New

York as in London, which Sotheby's was publicizing—to Hyam's "pshaw's" and "pooh-pooh's"—as the "art-trading center of the world." Americans, Hyam asserted—loudly and often—were buying most of the great paintings that came up for public sale anywhere in the world, and thus setting prices on both sides of the Atlantic.

In 1954 monetary restrictions had been relaxed in Great Britain, permitting foreign sellers to be paid in their own currency. Sotheby's had immediately launched a campaign to contract American art property for sale in London. A United States representative was chosen, and a New York office was established. Much to Hyam's chagrin, Sotheby's then began to advertise that London was recognized everywhere, "by those who take an interest in such things," as the principal center of international connoisseurship, and that "Sotheby's of London, founded in 1744," was "the most widely experienced auction house in the world for the disposal of works of art." They boasted from 1956 to 1960 of seasonal totals between $8 and $11 million. Their propaganda was very favorably detailed in a memorandum to overseas prospective clients, released in 1957.

The functions of an auctioneer, as interpreted by Sotheby's, include inspection of properties and advice to their owners, whether in Britain or overseas. For the last twenty-five years Sotheby Directors have paid annual visits to the United States to keep in touch with collectors, museum directors and librarians, and to maintain the Firm's close contact with the trend of collecting taste. Sotheby's has recently emphasized its special interest in American properties by the appointment of an Associate, with long experience of the transatlantic market, to be at the disposal of owners, executors or trustees in the United States, and to assist prospective consignors with the administrative details involved, which are much simpler than is often supposed.

In this connection, Sotheby's beg leave to remind all overseas clients who wish to take advantage of the high and stable prices, the low commission rates and the expert presentation of fine material which have long characterized their sales, of the following facts:

There is NO import duty on antiques of any kind coming into Britain nor on pictures or books of any date.

There is NO government or any other tax (as in some Continental countries) on sales by auction.

There is NO export duty out of the United States.

Payment of the proceeds of sale in London can now be made, without formalities or delay, IN DOLLARS.

It is often supposed that because American buying is one of the strongest factors in the international market, auction prices will automatically be higher in New York than in London. Facts and figures prove that (except for material of exclusively American interest) this is not so. The London market is not only more stable than any other; its prices are not only more authoritative; they have also been, for the past decade or more, steadily higher. This is due to a combination of factors: not least among them the magnetic attraction of a great international entrepôt for collections of first-rate quality; the experienced connoisseurship of Sotheby's staff; and the wide circulation achieved by the Firm's catalogues, in the United States as well as throughout Europe. Other contributory factors are the pre-eminently efficient and sensitive mechanism of the London fine arts trades; the proximity of Continental as well as British purchasing power, in competition with the many American commissions regularly and smoothly handled by the London dealers; and, finally, the international prestige and traditional integrity of a great London auction house.

The terms for offering property for sale by auction at the 34 and 35 New Bond Street enterprise are set as follows:

1. Pictures, Modern Drawings and Etchings, and all other works of Art, including Armour and Bronzes: Ceramics and Glass: Objects of Vertu: Old Furniture: Silver and Miniatures: Tapestries, Rugs and other Textiles: Musical Instruments 10% for lots over £100 ($280); 12½% for others.
2. Coins and Medals 12½%.
3. Jewelry 10%.
4. Antiquities and Native Art: Autograph Ltrs: Books and MSS: Engravings and Old Drawings: Japanese Works of Art and Prints: Oriental Miniatures 15%.

The above charges include cataloguing, advertising and all normal expenses of the sale after the property is received, except insurance and illustrations in catalogue, should such be required. Specially valuable lots may, in conformity with British law, be protected by a reserve, by arrangement with the auctioneers. In the case of lots which are not sold, a reduced commission is charged on the amount actually bid at the sale.

Sotheby's will gladly assist consignors in arranging for packing, transport and insurance, and are always ready to consider making an advance against such costs to overseas clients.

With this policy Sotheby's acquired the Wilhelm Weinberg and Jakob Goldschmidt collections. By 1961 it had lured enough American art property across the Atlantic to jump its sales total about $5 million over that for the previous year. The London firm had competed mightily against Parke-Bernet for the Erickson sale, with the outcome of the battle a tossup for a long while. The Parke-Bernet victory was due, at least in part, to the romanticism of Erickson's executors, who decided Parke-Bernet's stately and luxurious décor and the restrained elegance of its staff made it a better place for the dispersal of the advertising man's old masters than was Sotheby's, which, though ancient, disregarded its past and tradition by sending forth bright, aggressive young warriors to plunder sales.

Parke-Bernet's advantages of demeanor and setting were almost outweighed by one of the galleries' past rules: the forbiddance of reserve prices, which Sotheby's allowed. The management of Parke-Bernet realized at the outset of the sixties that an alteration in their policies, permitting reserves, would be absolutely necessary if they were to remain in commercial competition. Even before the Erickson sale, Hyam had advertised that reserves were allowed. But it seemed to consignors that Sotheby's had invented them, and thus that only at Sotheby's were real, authentic reserves available.

The threat of Sotheby's continued to hound the galleries, and Hyam, until the fall of 1963.

On September 10, 1963, Leslie Hyam was found in his closed car, a victim of carbon monoxide poisoning, quite possibly not accidental. A close friend said he had died because he wished himself dead. Why? The friend did not know, or would not tell. The reason was, he said, indiscernible, a mystery. It remains so.

After Hyam's death Louis Marion, Mary Vandegrift, and the board of directors were approached by Sotheby's with a handsome offer for controlling stock in the galleries. They said no. There had been talks between Sotheby's and Parke-Bernet as early as 1949 and there were more serious negotiations in 1962, which eventually fell through. Together, Parke-Bernet and Sotheby's would be invincible, ever more magnificent, ever more prosperous.

After the offer of October 1963 was rejected, Peter Wilson, head of the London firm, made a new offer, which the board of directors finally voted to accept.

Louis Marion used the considerable sum he got for his stock to form his own company, an appraisal firm called Louis J. Marion Associates. John Marion, his son, had been working at Parke-Bernet as an assistant auctioneer and appraiser since 1959; and, with no encouragement from his father, he remained at the job. In June 1965 he became a partner in the London firm, and he is now Parke-Bernet's chief auctioneer.

Mary Vandegrift sold her stock, but she, too, stayed with the galleries, and is there today as executive vice president—a position that entails the same amount of work as ever. Even when she has the time to vacation, she cannot escape the grasp of the galleries, for wherever she goes, she is cornered by people who once consigned property to—or bought property from, or visited, or read about—the galleries, and who want to know, "Was it really true. . . ?" Polite, usually extensive, and often poetic answers follow from Miss Vandegrift.

In August 1964, when Sotheby's took over what its executives considered the previously "family run" Parke-Bernet Galleries, they elected the Eton and Oxford educated, thirty-three-year-old Peregrine Pollen the galleries' new president. During the second season of his reign, Pollen, whose family contains many collectors, saw the galleries' total sales increase by $10 million. Several new world records were established—in that season and in those that followed it.

The extraordinary combined total of Parke-Bernet and Sotheby's for the 1969 season was $96,833,618. "This," said Pollen, "was because collectors have become increasingly aware of auctions as a successful method of disposing of important works of art and have seen that high prices can be obtained in New York for works of art which are presented in specialized sales and catalogued in a scholarly manner."

When asked whether it was important to maintain an air of elegance in the auction hall these days, Pollen hesitated, then said, "Yes and no, but I am sure Mr. Hyam would have disagreed with me. From the point of view of appearance, Sotheby's, both externally and internally, has remained substantially the same since the business was moved to its present premises on Bond Street after the First World War. Parke-Bernet has larger and perhaps more 'elegant' exhibition galleries. We would not like Parke-Bernet to be a carbon copy of Sotheby's, and yet many of our clients buy regularly in both houses."

The saga of Parke-Bernet and its predecessors is filled with endless scenes and players, sometimes moving and nostalgic, sometimes sordid, comic, or grotesque—a tale revealing now a rare instinct for beauty, now vanity and the accumulator's lust. But whether time has put a palace on display, the relics of a parlor, or a tribe of wooden Indians from the cigar stores of another day, the play enacted has one theme: the relation of people to things. Pride is there, and loneliness, the rich man's folly and the despot's spoils.

The Parke-Bernet Galleries stand today, strangely reminiscent of the past, with the relief of Venus still hanging heavily above the entrance, and the décor of the exhibition rooms recalling an age of velvet upholstery. Yet, the policies of the galleries are contemporary, the management startlingly aggressive—they are experts in an international market in which the stakes are high. The means utilized to capture this market are almost futuristic. But who is to say that the collector will not one day look with nostalgia upon closed-circuit television and computers for the part these devices played in helping him satisfy his acquisitive passion.